Reconciling Opposites

Reconciling Opposites

Religious Freedom and Contractual Ethics in a Democratic Society

W. Royce Clark

LEXINGTON BOOKS/FORTRESS ACADEMIC
Lanham • Boulder • New York • London

Published by Lexington Books/Fortress Academic
Lexington Books is an imprint of The Rowman & Littlefield Publishing Group, Inc.
4501 Forbes Boulevard, Suite 200, Lanham, Maryland 20706
www.rowman.com

86-90 Paul Street, London EC2A 4NE, United Kingdom

British Library Cataloguing in Publication Information Available

Library of Congress Cataloging-in-Publication Data

Name: Clark, W. Royce, author.
Title: Reconciling opposites : religious freedom and contractual ethics in a democratic
    society / W. Royce Clark.
Description: Lanham : Lexington Books/Fortress Academic, [2022] | Includes
    bibliographical references and index. | Summary: "The American justice system was
    founded on the idea of 'majority-rule,' but in a democracy this is achievable only if
    the majority has the interests of the whole at heart. As a solution, W. Royce Clark
    formulates a non-majoritarian ethic that would represent not just the interests of white
    Christian men but all citizens"—Provided by publisher.
Identifiers: LCCN 2021033842 (print) | LCCN 2021033843 (ebook) |
    ISBN 9781978708679 (cloth) | ISBN 9781978708686 (epub)
Subjects: LCSH: Majorities—United States. | Freedom of religion—United States. |
    Democracy—United States—Moral and ethical aspects. | Church and state—United
    States. | Representative government and representation—United States. | United
    States—Politics and government.
Classification: LCC JF1051 .C558 2022 (print) | LCC JF1051 (ebook) |
    DDC 320.473—dc23/eng/20211001
LC record available at https://lccn.loc.gov/2021033842
LC ebook record available at https://lccn.loc.gov/2021033843

To all the future generations who devote their
lives to a truly democratic republic

Contents

Acknowledgments

My thanks to all those that have helped shape my thinking, encouraged me, or even differed with me. Once again, I must express my dependence especially upon my wife, Dessie Clark, and her wisdom and continual support and love. Nothing would have been possible without her patient understanding, her careful questions and suggestions, her deep commitment to our marriage and our family, her continual interest in the field of teaching and the credentialing of Pepperdine students as teachers, and her interest in national political issues. Her encouragement has been supplemented by the interest and encouragement of our daughter, Elaine Böel, our son, Michael Clark, and his wife, Joy Clark, all of whom have been devoted teachers and scholars in their respective fields. I am also thankful for three grandsons, former colleagues, friends, and many former students from whom I have learned so much and been challenged. I am grateful for my anonymous reviewers, and especially for the endorsements by Profs. Daniel Rodriquez and DeWayne Stallworth.

I must add my thanks to the late Robert P. Scharlemann, my major professor and director of my PhD dissertation years ago in the Department of Religious Studies at the University of Iowa, for creating my interest in theology and the philosophy of religion, but also for his brilliance, precision of expression, and tolerance of most of us students who were on a much lower level of understanding. He was quiet but patient, an ordained Lutheran pastor, and, as I gradually learned, one of the main leaders in the Paul Tillich Society in the United States, and of worldwide influence. There were also three other professors at the University of Iowa in the years I was there, 1967–1970, who helped me more than they could ever know: Prof. Ken Kuntz, a musician and biblical theologian from whom I learned so much about the history and content of the religion of ancient Israel, and who was a constant encouragement to me in the PhD program; the late Prof. Laird Addis, of the School of Philosophy, a multitalented, very compassionate, and inspiring musician and philosopher by whom I was introduced to "existentialism," and who also served on my dissertation committee; and the very famous Prof. Sidney E. Mead, from whom I heard about the "Genius of American Religious Institutions" in his casual lectures, and his love for a variety of thinkers including Alfred North Whitehead. Mead, Addis, Kuntz, and Scharlemann were all gentle souls, unpresumptuous and humble, but genuinely brilliant and tolerant of different ideas, which ranks them in my mind with other great people in the world.

Five Pepperdine Law School professors were also a great encouragement in my maturing and appreciation of law: Professors Mark Scarberry, Charles Nelson, Greg Ogden, Wayne Estes, and James McGoldrick.

Over the years, I also have been impressed by many, perhaps most, of our Supreme Court Justices, for a variety of reasons, but especially when it was obvious that they were courageously championing the cause of a liberal (i.e., tolerant and inclusive) democratic republic. My heroes here include especially Chief Justice Earl Warren, Justice William O. Douglas, Justice William J. Brennan, Justice David Souter, and the late Justice Ruth Bader Ginsburg. They were original minds, thorough scholars, and lovers of a tolerant democratic society of which John Rawls writes. I stand in awe of many legal scholars and professors, including certainly of Rawls's life and work, as well as the consistent, breathtaking scholarship of Prof. Laurence Tribe of Harvard University.

Of course, this project would not have been possible but for the willingness and helpfulness of my acquisition editor, Dr. Neil Elliott, and assistant editor, Gayla Freeman, as well as Kellie Hagan, production editor for Rowman & Littlefield, and Arun Rajakumar, the project manager at Deanta.

Finally, I want to acknowledge with gratefulness the organization of public domain materials by Philip B. Kurland and Ralph Lerner, eds. in *The Founders' Constitution,* 5 vols. (Chicago: University of Chicago Press, 1987).

Introduction

As James Madison, Thomas Jefferson, and the other Framers of the U.S. Constitution realized, the democratic republic they were establishing was novel in modern history, a genuine voluntary sharing of life and destiny with each other, a government of, by, and for the people as a collective whole. Legal philosopher of Harvard, John Rawls, nearly two centuries later, often observed, speaking of the same voluntary sharing of our fates and fortunes, that since we all, as a nation, have agreed to that, we stand or fall together. That did not mean that we all experience exactly the same talents, opportunities, accidents, or even all have identical ideas and ideals. But in order to agree to such a schema of mutual sharing of the elements we *can* share, everyone must conceive the Constitutional democracy as a structure of voluntary fairness, and "fairness" is not a difficult term but something which is evident even to young children.

That fairness or voluntary sharing works only if it is truly voluntary and constantly perceptible and publicized, not something hidden or mysterious, or an emotion that we resort to only when we are feeling the pain or loneliness of suffering more than others, but something we embrace steadfastly even when it is only others who are suffering. One can achieve this by great empathy, compassion, and kindness. But Rawls suggested it could even be found within our very basic ethical agreement with the principles central to our social contract. This would mean that when that sense of unity and sharing is not evident, that absence reveals not only that we lack empathy, but that we are violating the very social contract to which we agreed to live with our fellow citizens. It is a deadly serious matter. It is not simply a sense of unity we discover first when we face a significant world war or when we have a wretchedly destructive pandemic, but is a genuine unity we agree to as equal citizens, a unity or sharing that affects all of our relations with all

other citizens in every aspect of our lives. Few families cultivate a disintegrat-
ing attitude of each member trying to get an advantage over the other family
members. Rawls was convinced that the same sense of unity would be possible on the level of a government if all people could somehow agree not to
take advantage of others. That would be a basic fairness by which we might
achieve "E Pluribus Unum."

If that sense of basic unity of all citizens is considered vital in order for a
nation to survive, then Rawls was convinced that the unity had to be made
explicit in the grounding ethical principles of our social contract or our
Constitution. That priority of unity of the totality of different citizens means
therefore that those basic ethical principles must occupy a place of primacy
in our attitude, comportment, and actual laws. It is not common, however,
for people to spend much time analyzing the ethics underlying actual laws,
not even common for the Supreme Court to spend time on such. Instead,
many citizens have inherited or been attracted to other sources or authorities
for their ethics, and have seen these as having priority over their whole life,
even if the principles of such did not originate with a democratic structure
nor address mutual autonomy, equality of basic liberties or even a common
unity of all which is great enough to accept significant differences. This other
ethical authority was in many cases a religious affiliation which brooks no
competition or questioning, or might be any number of different possible
comprehensive ethical schemas attached to any number of different kinds of
associations, as Rawls saw it. But since none of these embrace all citizens
of the nation, and many religious groups are exclusive enough to refuse to
be governed by the ethical systems of any other religion, as the Dalai Lama
showed, an ethic for the "new millennium" cannot possibly be based on
any religion. Further, as Rawls noted, not only have we become aware of
that when the religious pluralism became more self-evident within our own
nation, but many of these ethical systems assert that they are based on a form
of nonpublic reason or faith which makes them superior and impervious to
any questions or challenges brought by common public reason. Some of these
are built on unverifiable myths or alleged supranatural events or beings in the
past, and ultimately most of them form an absolute or incomparable position
which trumps anyone's voice who is outside that exclusive realm. That precludes the ethic from being acceptable to all citizens. This was realized by
John Rawls, and drove him to try to formulate ethical principles which could
stand by themselves, as "freestanding," that is, independent of any alleged
authorities, and resting only upon their acceptance by the citizens.

On the other hand, many people never think of the actual Constitution and
subsequent laws based on it as having an ethical foundation since most legislation and most judicial decisions avoid any possible mention of ethics. This
avoidance means that in the minds of many people, government's laws have

no ethical foundation, so it becomes easy for a religious person to criticize them and assume that his or her religious ethics should dictate to those laws. But when that is sought, divisiveness occurs, as Madison, Jefferson, Rawls, and so many other thinkers were aware. Rather, the nation's laws must be based on "freestanding" ethical principles which would be and are voluntarily acceptable to all citizens. That *voluntary agreement* forms the unity and is actually the only real "authority" in the matter of conceiving a social contract.

This does not mean that a religious ethic which is meaningful to a person necessarily contradicts or is the opposite of any ethic grounding the social contract or basic agreement through our Constitution. While many ethical principles of the two institutions may be very similar, what is different is the constituency of the group involved, their view of whether the ethics are ever questionable or simply absolute, the public reason or nonpublic reason that is used, and the comportments involved within each. It may be useful to think of such independent sets of ethics as one would think of having more than one set of clothes, but the similarities and differences will become clearer as we develop this analysis, and apply it to the democratic society of the United States in its historical evolution. This study stands by itself, but of course is not definitive on every tangent of the inquiry, nor do I think it is the only way to approach the problem of an ethic that all people could embrace. Just as I, like all learners, stand on the shoulders of those who have gone before me, extremely grateful for their contributions to scholarship, what I am engaging in is not the last word but more like a mere nudging in a certain direction which seems to me to be fruitful for the inquiry.

This study asks about the degree to which in U.S. history such a "freestanding" ethic—based on principles which help define one's "authentic being," derived from the universal "will-to-live"—lies at the heart of our democratic society and the U.S. law in general in its structures of justice. Most religions have proposed to their adherents that where the government's laws and their religion's ethics differ, the religion should dictate to change the government's laws. This is a carryover of the belief in the former Absolute, sacrosanct to nearly all religions. But as Rawls reminds us, religious pluralism is therefore inherently divisive, so the differences within religions can be tolerated only by a liberal democratic structure in which the universal and its principles are truly "freestanding" to provide a consensus or unanimous agreement of all citizens. We will see the inadequacies of the ethics of our ancestors in their treatment of other peoples, and we will trace some of the factors responsible for changes in ethics and the "freedom of conscience" that came from the Enlightenment and were so vital in the Great Awakening in the middle half of the eighteenth century.

Some Christians, however, have been persuaded that this nation was always intended by some greater power to be a Christian nation. The religious pluralism problem is not new, nor is the "myth" of the nation's religious founding, as Steven Green has shown. The pluralism was addressed not only by Madison and Jefferson in the late eighteenth century, but especially by John Rawls during the last half of the twentieth century, as we will see. All three and many other of the "Framers" of the Constitution saw the answer only in a "separation" of government and religions, so that neither would impinge on the other or be dependent upon the other, but each could best accomplish its own unique work independently.

The ethical base which I found in combining Nietzsche, Schweitzer, and Rawls, an ethic independent of any religion, is utilized to see how it superseded the former theocratic attempts of colonial governments by the insights and determination of the Framers of the Constitution as well as the historical "moral arc of justice" which was articulated with great impact of the Enlightenment's valorizing not simply the freedom of conscience, but of human reason and mutual autonomy, which were *not* values of the predominant religions. The book pursues the question critically even in the recent history of the United States in its social struggle for justice for all its people and includes an in-depth analysis of the Supreme Court's decisions over the relation of government to religion to mid-2020.

If James Madison insisted that civil government simply has no cognizance of religion, Thomas Jefferson felt the same way, insisting that religion was only between each individual and his deity, so it made no difference to him, as he said, whether his neighbor has 20 gods or none. Instead, government was to stay out of the sphere of religion, and the proper or only time for it to intervene in any religious person's life would be only if and when such a person violated the generally applicable laws, but not anything of a religious nature. Religious freedom was not unlimited, but by the definitions of the Framers within their historical context, it consisted of a freedom to believe whatever they chose, and a freedom to worship however and with whomever they chose (or not worship at all), but otherwise their freedom was no different from that of every citizen. Since any citizens could elect to be religious, this means that all these freedoms are available to every person, for the person to decide how to respond. We will see that in the 1940s, when the First Amendment was "incorporated" into state law by the Court's decisions (1940, 1947), the Court said it almost in the same words and spoke of the necessity of a "wall of separation" between religion and government.

Rawls also noted the problem of our becoming aware of the potential hostility in a society in which religious pluralism exists, and his answer is that it can be remedied only by a liberal democratic republic which has a *sense of unity* in its principles of justice that enable it to allow differences, so long as all citizens comply with the general principles or rule of law. That is what Jefferson also meant. These scholars did not think that being religious or not being religious should either enhance or detract from people's status or benefits as equal citizens.

I must offer a short word on method, since I realize there are many ways of approaching this problem. This is simply a path that has become meaningful to me through these particular scholars. It will become more obvious to the reader why I used certain scholars rather than others, but obviously there are many different ways to approach this problem. Further, I have avoided as much as possible citing secondary sources on them or texts that are only in languages other than English. For those who want to read some of these great scholars, most local libraries and online sources can supply enough to read to fill a lifetime. Whereas, if some of the original sources are not available in every library—for example, the collections of Jefferson's and Madison's papers—many of the quotations from Madison and Jefferson I have cited can be located in the *Founder's Constitution*, and much more can be accessed in Founders Online (https://founders.archives.gov).

I have not listed all the law journals over the years with the myriad of articles related to each of the Supreme Court decisions I have cited. The reader can access the Supreme Court decisions easily online, and keep abreast with the actual oral arguments as well as decisions, then proceed into the secondary law journals, though one must remember that many of those journal articles are put together by law *students*, not professors. Hopefully, this will be sufficient to enable the reader to pursue further research in English fairly rapidly.

Regarding the Supreme Court decisions, since they comprised *the only federal law* pertaining to religion until Congress passed the Religious Freedom Restoration Act in 1993, since the large number of these cases over the past 80 years would make it difficult for the reader to recall details if I waited to the end to offer any critique or judgments about any decision, I have offered some analyses with some of the cases, while the details of the case are still fresh in the reader's mind. Otherwise, a final critique would come when most of the details of the Court's arguments had long been forgotten. Hopefully this will not seem offensive, since I am in awe of the *breadth* expected of Justices, given the nature of the cases they agree to hear, and of the tremendous close examination of huge amounts of materials so many cases require. I try only to single out the most glaring problems, but not from any agenda except the basic ethic I propose and my commitment as a citizen to the democratic republic of the United States.

Whether the problem can be answered in this way is at this point still hypothetical or a mere proposal, so each reader will have to judge the degree of validity of both the problem and suggested answers which I give in much more detail. I write this recognizing that we all stand at slightly different or perhaps even quite diverse perspectives or vantage points. My purpose is not to criticize but to describe and evaluate, but, as even Nietzsche observed, any reassessment of our values requires a certain abandonment, destruction, or moving beyond to make room to create a new understanding. Therefore, I intend only to illuminate some vital connections that might help evoke in each reader a greater dedication to accommodate differences, to be willing to voluntarily share our fate and fortunes, and to feel a deeper sense of *indivisible unity* of the "one nation" which we repeat when we Pledge our Allegiance to our flag.

Chapter 1

Definitions, Scope, and Tools for the Project

What would be required of an ethic for it to be acceptable to all citizens? How would we measure whether it really works? Let me suggest how I understand certain words so they are not ambiguous as I use them. By the word "ethics," I am signifying judgments all humans make about people's voluntary or autonomous actions toward others as being "right" or "wrong," "good" or "bad," "consonant" or "dissonant," "beneficial" or "detrimental." That implies that if an action is involuntary, coerced, or even obeyed simply because of some authority another person has over me, my actions to that degree are not "ethical" because they are not my independent choice. In common usage, "morals" can be interchangeable with "ethics," although "ethics" usually indicates a group of moral rules or a system of such principles, and "immorality" is still used predominately to describe sexual actions that violate the norm, a much narrower focus than "ethics." One who simply obeys another person is obedient, but neither moral nor ethical, since moral character is not derived from some result but from one's own will to act a certain way. One is held "responsible" to the degree the action was one's own autonomous choice.

By "religions" I mean those groups that "worship" some deity, person, event, power, source, or entity, so are usually classified that way, even by those professionals within the religious institutions and by scholars of "religion" in higher education. They are groups or institutions that have traditionally believed in supranatural or metaphysical or mythical elements if not in that which is invisible and undefinable upon which their whole system of symbols, dogma, ritual, identity, ethics, and worship is grounded, a grounding that they take as absolute. Because of the different religions' variety and specificity of their unique symbols, dogma, metaphysics, they are not interchangeable with other religions, even if a few of their ethical principles are similar. Usually, these few common ethical principles existed in ancient

1

times even prior to the creation of formal religions. But the religions often insist that their ethical commands are valid *only* because they are grounded on their unique mythical/historical claims. This makes them unacceptable to the nonreligious or people who embrace other religions.

However, the feature I see them all having in common is their belief that there is that which is absolute, and they have access to it by which it alone enables them to be certain it is absolute, beyond any question, discussion, or negotiation.[1] By "absolute," I indicate that which is presupposed as unquestionable, whether one understands it or not. The assumption is that it could be absolute and a human might easily recognize it as absolute *without* understanding it or being able to explain it or even defend it.[2] Religions thereby often speak of "faith" as unquestionable but completely certain, more so than any form of reason. As the "incomparable," though associated with unique particularities which even involve historical claims, it is not presented by the major *religious institutions* as negotiable or open to human reason, even if occasional scholars have claimed otherwise.

This faith in something "absolute," however, is not restricted to traditional religions. There are ideologies, whether political, economic, or other, which, in their extreme forms approximate this "absolute" character common to formal "religions," so to that degree, the most common element in formal religions does not itself make them unique, but only their grounding this absolute on their unique mythical/historical claims. The unquestionable loyalty these other groups propagate is not really different from that in formal religions, even if their veneration or mode of worship or structure is less organized or more subtle. John Rawls often simply used the word "comprehensive" doctrines or schemas,[3] whether philosophical, ideological, religious, or ethical, for what I refer to here as "absolute."

Because it is absolute and not subject to public reason, as Rawls notes, any reference to such can easily put an end to discussions or conversations since the one referring to it is not open to questioning, and perhaps not open at all even to public reason. Rawls says the nonpublic reason or faith held by such institutions or associations is not usually open to change, compromise, or even cooperation.[4] That is the "opposite" of which the title of this book speaks, an attitude which is "opposite" the egalitarian and democratic stance of acceptance of uniqueness and difference of every individual, an ethic built on an "overlapping" consensus through "public reason" to which all citizens in a democratic republic agree, a principled consensus which expects strict compliance from all, which means freedoms but also responsibilities which are equally shared, but are reciprocally limited by the other citizens' equal voice.

In his *After Auschwitz*, Rabbi Richard Rubenstein's focus on "social solidarity" led him to suggest that Judaism and Christianity cannot regard each other fairly until they can get beyond the myths in which each is buried. He saw a possible answer in a diverse society which involves some covenant, realized long ago in the group involved in the Exodus from Egypt, but is also approximated to a degree in the present by the tolerance of religious differences in the United States. He attributed the latter not merely to the First Amendment, but to the fact that religious identity has here been only one of the many possible identities, not completely exclusive since the religious roots of American civilization are often spoken of as "Judeo-Christian" rather than simply "Christian," and the greater the number of roles or forms of identity one has, the less does any single one become an obsession.[5] This is true, but as we shall later discover, white, male, Christian identity has been present since the founding of the nation, and at times has threatened to eclipse any semblance of social solidarity in its White Supremacy or Christian Nationalist forms of xenophobia.

It might be that to suggest that a religious person quit thinking of his absolute as absolute is offensive if it only spells blasphemy to the person. But one needs to see even religious leaders such as the Dalai Lama insisting that the ethics of the new millennium cannot be supplied by any religion because there would be no way of making everyone happy. There would be an unending argument over "which" religion.[6] This would be most obvious to those living in a democratic society as a religious person realizes that a nation, which provides equal voice to all its citizens and embodies a religious pluralism, needs for religious people to be able to accept a *second set of ethics* based on "freestanding" principles since they cannot expect that every citizen will embrace their particular religious/ethical view. That would require one's working out mentally the relationship between the two sets of ethics, which involve the five differences we will list shortly.

Either of these routes of realizing what religious pluralism requires of a society might seem to a religious person to be a relinquishing of some of her personal identity, and appear to the leaders of the religious institution to be an abandonment of the institution's claims, so is quite difficult. This is probably the reason Rawls insisted that the process of *how* one decides on the proper relationship between the freestanding principles to form the social contract and the specific principles of one's comprehensive schema has to be left up to *each person* to decide.[7] This accentuates the autonomy which is characteristically presupposed in a democratic republic, but either option is possible, depending upon one's attitude toward that which one has espoused as absolute and one's comfort level. Other than these options, the conflict described by Rawls remains, even when one finds comfort in belonging to the "majority" religion in a country that has significant religious pluralism.

Ethical considerations and agreements are as old as *Homo sapiens'* most basic understanding between two or more people. Whether the first ethical agreements came about over exchange of goods or services or were abstractly simply for sheer survival or mutual coexistence in general is really irrelevant. All of these reasons for continual agreements in the social world of humans are obvious today. The formulation of such basic understandings about the parties' behavior toward each other has been motivated from a plethora of circumstances and powers, often articulated by a king, as they were extended into law with sanctions for those he ruled to serve his own interests. Eventually, similar kinds of collections of rules or norms were expressed by priests or religious leaders in various religions, also containing ideas of rewards and sanctions even of an otherworldly sort to motivate compliance. Usually, whether it was king or priest, the one wielding the authority behind the law invariably had considerable vested self-interests.

Today a person's awareness of rules, norms, and principles of behavior or relating to others may come from any number of these sources such as a religion or a government or even a smaller group with special interests or just one's family. Few people, if any, live in a vacuum that has neither laws that presuppose an ethical base nor at least ethical rules that carry social approval and disapproval from a group. Unlike ancient days, when much of this thinking began about what was appropriate behavior in people's relations with one another, we now have a pluralism of *competing ethical answers* from a variety of very different and basically conflicting religions and from governments that are organized quite differently with different senses of priorities and values so consider others as their enemies.

Most people are born into a state which already possesses a specific type of government so that relation one has to the existing government and its ethical structures of justice is not something voluntarily chosen, but something one later, in one's maturity, simply consciously and formally confirms to embrace, or in rare cases, denounce and become an expatriate in another country. Similarly, in many or most cases, those who are religious people were born into the parents' religion, so it is also not something originally chosen by them, but something they later chose to confirm as their identity and allegiance as mature individuals, or in some cases, simply abandon.

It is possible in either case to carry the identity of one's religious commitment or national allegiance while changing the other. The not-so-obvious reason for this is because one's commitments to these two *different constituencies* differ considerably in many ways, with commitments to the group based upon (1) the particularities of the constituency; (2) the group's views on the world which includes even metaphysical and mythical ideas; (3) its understanding of the scope of authority of each; (4) its understanding of reason, ethical norms, principles, and even civil law; and (5) the specific comportment required of one within the group. This difference will become more apparent as we develop our analysis, but for now we might suggest it is like one's having more than one set of clothes, some for formal occasions, some for casual wear around other people, some to do filthy jobs such as yard work, and some even to sleep in. They do not necessarily contradict or make a person a hypocrite when he or she slips on the different clothes, but rather reveal these differences of constituencies, scope, intention, purpose, and/or expected comportment.[8] These become crucial in our present study.

There is nevertheless a problem that occurs since most religions admit of *no compromise*. They have their absolute, which usually includes supranatural claims that no one can verify or falsify by accepted scientific method or "public reason," and their ethical claims are based on these. Only in recent history has significant religious pluralism within a specific nation become an obvious fact and divisive factor, divisive because of the different metaphysics of the various religions, and divisive because of the religions' unwillingness to compromise with public reason. Democracies allegedly are built upon the people (Greek- "demos") as a whole and that would presuppose differences, even reasonable differences. But the absolute does not admit of challenges, differences, or compromise. Philosopher of law, John Rawls, thought this awareness of the tension between a government and religious pluralism within it in the West did not begin until the Reformation,[9] though I would date it even much later, with the Enlightenment and mass migrations to the West, but the point is the same. In his words, which show the reason for the title of this book about "reconciling opposites," he wrote:

> The Reformation turned this possibility inward upon itself. What is new about this clash is that it introduces into people's conceptions of their good a transcendent element not admitting of compromise. This element forces either mortal conflict moderated only by circumstance and exhaustion, or equal liberty of conscience and freedom of thought. Except on the basis of these last, firmly founded and publicly recognized, no reasonable political conception of justice is possible. Political liberalism starts by taking to heart the absolute depth of that irreconcilable latent conflict.[10]

The reason I said this awareness came primarily through the Enlightenment rather than the Reformation is the fact that prior to the Enlightenment, few if any religious people in the West embraced what Rawls called "equal liberty of conscience and freedom of thought." The Reformation, however, did begin a trend toward individualism which developed eventually among some religious people influenced by the Enlightenment such as John Locke to embrace the idea of freedom of conscience, of which Madison, Jefferson, and other Framers spoke. But the religious pluralism experienced in the sixteenth century was primarily within groups or sects of a single religion, as internecine strife, even though enough to cause terrible religious wars.

Not only have we become much more aware of many different religions in the world as well as radically different types of governments, the differences of either one can be discovered within a single entity of the other. The Christian church has included authoritarians, fascists, libertarians, democrats, socialists, Marxists, capitalists, and the United States now includes within its constitutional republic large minorities of dozens of the traditional religions, and in some cases hundreds of different sects of single religions. So the diversity or pluralism is a fact. If theocracy demands a uniformity more difficult to attain among diverse citizens, it is because the absoluteness requiring that uniformity is sensed by many as too stifling of human freedom. Where it does exist today, such as Iran, it is very coercive and oppressive, intolerant of any religious difference that is significant. From where we stand today, we have also become aware of the development and changes or even the thorough relativity appearing within *conceptions* of government as well as *conceptions* of religion and religions. The absolutizing through which the Christian church passed in the second half of the nineteenth century in the Catholic Church's Syllabus of Errors and the declaration of Papal Infallibility as well as the Protestant Church's declaration of the plenary inspiration and infallibility of the scriptures in its war against Darwinism is now recognized as a rather myopic defensive view which mistakenly discounted change, development, and relativism.

Many if not most particular religious institutions still propagate their deity, truths, events, sacred scriptures, or other things as absolute, even if the trend is toward a secularization and away from religions in most nations' populations. But we also live in the days of considerable desacralization that began at least by the late eighteenth century, in which the human sciences began to develop from empirical data as the subject matter rather than from some form of an analogy of being and/or representation that was based on a "metaphysics of infinity,"[11] as Michel Foucault showed, and this empirical approach became paramount in governments in general, leaving behind only a few states or nations that still professed some form of a theocracy or mythical or supranatural grounding of its structures of justice.

Since the ethics of these religions was built precisely upon the religions' conflated mythical/metaphysical claims rather than more verifiable empirical data, this requires us to *revaluate our values*. In a democratic society or society of the whole people, more specifically a democratic republic, the conception is diametrically opposed to any and all forms of autocracy, fascism, authoritarianism, and heteronomy. Further, a democratic society does not idealize or even prefer some aspired uniformity in which all must embrace a single sect of a single religion or single view of anything—with the *exception* that all citizens must agree to a few basic principles of a social contract from which their constitutional government can be built and sustained. But otherwise, beyond the universally applicable general principles to which all citizens must agree, each person is at liberty to have his or her own special personal goals and ideas so long as he or she complies with those basic ethical-legal principles of the nation. That such a priority must exist should seem obvious since to insist that any particular single view of only *some* of the citizens should govern the *whole* will not succeed without eclipsing people's autonomy by coercion, thereby diminishing the very character and value of autonomy that is so significant to humans and to the humanization of society as well as the principle of democracy.

"Autonomy" simply means "self-rule" or being a law to oneself. "Heteronomy" means the "law of the other," that is, that some other sets the rules for me. "Democratic," as Rawls pointed out, is the "rule of the people," implying all the people, whereas "theocracy" means the rule by a god. Autonomy in an extreme form would be complete arbitrariness or selfishness of the individual, whereas heteronomy in its extreme forms could imply authoritarianism by an other entity or person in which one's own voice is not valued.

We will see in later chapters that the "lively experiment" of the democratic republic for the United States was conceived as the government which had a structure of universal representation with "checks and balances" on all different levels. It could not be a pure democracy as Madison saw, since that would have to be a very small group of people to work. But if all the citizens could express their interests through voting and/or through their representative in the local, state, and federal governments, then it would be a democratic republic, hopefully avoiding any form of autocracy as well as having the vastly different interests adequately represented to avoid any trouble of "majoritarianism," that is, of a group accumulating enough power to eclipse the interests of the minorities, even though it did not have the interest of the whole people at heart.

Such a government values the whole people *because* its most basic values drive it back to its instinctual ethical value, the human "will-to-live" as Schweitzer later defined it, even the "will-to-live" of all living creatures, or even as Nietzsche's "will-to-power" which was built upon life affirmation. This means it values the *unique voices of all citizens*, a mutual autonomy, no matter how different, as a *continual conversation*, even a continual debate over how to improve or achieve a "more perfect union" by applying more consistently those agreed-on basic principles to various situations and needs. It is not conceived as an infallible form, a static or fixed entity in the sense of being *absolute*. It reaches basic agreements on the most universally acceptable basic principles from public reason and formulates norms and even a Constitution and subsequent written laws, but recognizes that the "whole people's" agreement is the *final* authority in national matters, *nothing else*, and therefore it is always based on *public reason* in the ongoing conversation. This does not mean that a democracy is simply legal chaos or can never sanction any behavior, because the whole people can be assumed as agreeing to the basic principles so long as they willingly remain citizens and participate in the government, no matter how many objections they may have to certain lesser or minor decisions or procedures utilized by either the legislative or judicial branches of government. It makes provisions for possible amendments since the Framers were aware that they were finite in their perspectives and history could bring considerable change. But for the time prior to any significant alterations, the rule of law, as Rawls emphasizes, is final and requires exact compliance.

It is *un*likely that any society would negate the basic principle of the highest value being that of life itself. Most cultures realize that humans must also value a mutual autonomy or freedom which is limited only by the equal freedom for all, or even a structure which requires a basic honesty. These seem fundamental to any process of humanization. But the government and its defined justice are never a closed system incapable of being improved. Its legitimacy does not rest on merely any specific people in the past or their insightful formulations and limited understandings, even if we utilize their insights, but upon *basic principles* to which *all present citizens agree*, which carries with it a mutual trust that all citizens will *strictly comply* with such a rule of law to which they agreed. The oversimplified argument of the Constitution being either a living document or some eternally fixed document is a nonsequitur. Language changes just as "history" does and there is no single perspective of any single text any more than a single perspective of the universe, which is uniform and universal. Instead, there are defined forms of adjudicating laws, of reexamining what is fixed as "final" for the time, and even amending the basic document of the Constitution. Such a conception of the authority resting upon the continuing reason and will of the *whole people* stands in opposition to a plutocracy, fascism, or certainly to an "autocracy" which is a rule by *one*, whether that one is a human such as a dictator, king, or even an alleged god, even though the latter may be spoken of as a "theocracy." The difference is vast between decisions made by the whole people (even if by representation) and decisions made by only one. Only the former is humanizing; the latter is dehumanizing.

If one can understand that the imposition of any single religious ethic upon a government structure of justice creates divisiveness in most present societies, then is it possible to find a more *universal source of ethics* to which *all would agree*, a source which would itself spawn freestanding principles for all? The works of two giant figures of the past, Nietzsche and Schweitzer, suggest ethical values are *instinctual*. If they are correct, that comprises the first step in trying to formulate an ethic which is uniting rather than divisive.

The second step would be to add to their insight the thesis of Rawls that the democratic society can tolerate difference, if all citizens can agree to giving *priority* in matters involving the structures of justice to the basic principles they *all agreed* to live by. Now that we have introduced these three insightful figures, we must show in detail how such merging of their concepts or schemas would actually work.

INSTINCTUAL ETHICS IN NIETZSCHE AND SCHWEITZER

Friedrich Nietzsche (1844–1900),[12] who called himself an "immoralist" because of his opposition especially to the Christian ethics of ressentiment, is remembered for his insistence of a "revaluation of values." He argued that all values are only human values.[13] The *source* of values that came out on top of his own revaluation was what he called "will-to-power" or a "discharging of one's strength." Unlike Christian ethics which fights against instinct, Nietzsche insisted that any morality is instinctual. "To have to fight the instincts—that is the formula of decadence; as long as life is ascending, happiness equals instinct."[14] He said every mistake in life derives from the degeneration of instinct.[15] He insisted that even though it is *instinctual*, people nevertheless need to *reflect* on it rather than have no control over it.[16]

Basically, when engaged in a historical-psychological analysis of the origin of morality, he was convinced that it came from those who were oppressed, who had been forced to "obey commands."[17] Even though they resented this, over time they internalized it, and finally when some of them came into a position of power, they used that as the morality they expected to see in their subjects. It even worked its way into revolutions in its ressentiment and ended up measuring what was good and bad, or what was right and wrong was to be determined by its effect on people, that is, by the comparison of the joy or pleasure and pain. Its sense of causality was skewed, its values were otherworldly, its posture was crab-like in facing backward rather than forward, and it, even as most religions, was driven by some uncanny and unjustified idea of the "essence" of everything, including humanity.

It was so deranged that in Christian hands it posited bodily mutilation to cure certain "temptations," and celibacy and virginity as the highest ideals.[18] It succeeded by making otherworldly promises and leveling down the value of subjectivity, exceptionalism, and genius while advocating an "improvement" of mankind by raising the lower classes to an equality with those above them.[19] This refusal to consider contingency, difference, and "noble souls" reduced everything these systems touched, degrading any change or growth, and thereby turning all live ideals into static mummies.[20] Instead of following this reason which was so misdirected, he insisted that the "will to power" is the primary power of life, which must govern any kind of behavior, which means it will utilize reason to say "Yes" to life rather than the strident "No" he heard from especially religious morality.

Everything is in a state of process or change; nothing is static or beyond a need to change;[21] therefore, no perspective is sacrosanct or comprehensive, and antilife values are not true values but rather a self-contradiction. Real morality or ethics requires a person fighting and conquering the great dragon, the last enemy, this *heteronomous morality* named "Thou shalt."[22] True morality is owning up to one's own will,[23] based on one's instinctual "will-to-power" rather than being swamped by a heteronomous "Thou shalt" which was still present in Kant's focus on "duty."

With autonomy thereby realized, one can also see that there is only *one's own* way, not any single or "THE way" as Zarathustra emphasized.[24] There is no "redemption" of just a few favorite souls from history or even any sorting of the pleasant from the unpleasant. To those who really love life, they must also, like Nietzsche, love one's particular "fate,"[25] rather than resent it. But to love life means loving the whole of it, just as any "redemption" involves the whole, since, in a way, there is nothing but the whole.[26] Thus, finding one's self, who one really is, requires an "overcoming" of one's cultural or heteronomous self or a "going under" and finding *one's own* values that do *not* lead to chaos in the world when one realizes that there is no Absolute, no God.[27] Rather, as in the story of Zarathustra, one awakens to each new day refreshed and simply continuing in one's work of trying to help others, a sort of Socratic dedication with a different voice, but never to expect them to understand fully or to emulate oneself. Each must realize one's own "will-to-power" to be able to say one's own "Yes" to life with the strongest possible voice. That is to regain oneself by moving beyond such an absolute as Idealism, the self which one might have lost[28] in the heteronomy and chimeric values. So Nietzsche, contrary to uninformed ideas about him, was not a "nihilist" except in the sense of being a "nihilist" of the nihilism he found in the prevailing ethics or ideals which were so "Christian."

At about the time of Nietzsche's death in 1900, Albert Schweitzer (1875–1965)[29] was busy writing on the eschatological ethics of Jesus, then later of the eschatological ethics of St. Paul's "Christ-mysticism." While Schweitzer distressed many biblical scholars with his discovery, few were able to refute it. The "imminent" aspect of the Kingdom in both Jesus and Paul which he discovered was an unfulfilled prediction,[30] in fact, impossible in its mythical character. The truth of it was simply its spiritual elements of one's feeling called by Jesus to minister to others, and the mystical unity one has by being "in-Christ."

The eschatological feature, although enigmatic on the surface in its literal sense, carried the truth of a negating of one's present world in one's valuation in the light of the imminence of the Kingdom, a negation which placed a *new value* on human relationships rather than one's possession, ownership, and accomplishments in this world, so in that sense was actually a new "life affirmation." The precise ethical instructions within both Jesus's teachings and Paul's writings, by their eschatological orientation, were only valid if such a Kingdom would have come as it was conceived. But it did not, and Schweitzer insisted it could not the way it was conceived. Even so, as late as Paul wrote, some 30 years after Jesus was gone and the Kingdom had not come, Paul still pushed its imminence, and Schweitzer called Jesus's ethic an "interim ethic" (valid only during the interim prior to the imminent Kingdom), and he saw Paul's ethics as "status-quo" ethic of remaining in whatever state one was in when "called."

To Schweitzer, the eschatology was destroyed by Jesus's determination to force in the Kingdom by being crucified, yet that remains his victory, his integrity of giving his life for what he thought was God's will.[31] Paul's Christ-mysticism superseded that with such a unity the believer had with Christ that one could now be ethical without feeling one was compelled to it by the Torah. But, when one views Schweitzer's lifetime, the Christian Church had continued, even dominated the world in an imperial sense through Christendom, but the church had shown no ability to adjust its teachings to that of either Jesus or Paul, while deifying Jesus and turning Paul into a saint. The church's inability to historically certify its claims made it ethics dubious, as even Nietzsche saw, and its antiquated ethics was overtaken by new ethical theories that came especially from the spirit of the Enlightenment which were based on a sense of reason, equality, and autonomy, elements that were *missing* from Christian ethics.

By default, Schweitzer felt because of its compatibility with the new capitalistic world, this secular utilitarianism became the dominant ethic. This, to Schweitzer, was inadequate because it extended the ethical ideal or criteria of a single person into a *uniform* pattern to place on all humanity, nullifying uniqueness, and in many cases, with its feature of looking for the greatest good for the greatest number, resorted to a blatant form of majoritarianism which he felt stretched reason past the breaking point. Not only were individuality, uniqueness, and difference devalued, but a cost-benefit analysis seemed to reduce it to externals that could simply be counted. But to Schweitzer, it was instinctual, forming one's attitude toward everything, not a mere egoistic and artificial valuation of contrasting pain and pleasure.

During his many years in Lambarene, Gabon (Africa), as a medical doctor, Schweitzer came to an awareness firsthand of what "difference" really is, how exclusive any religion, ethnic group, or even nation can be, and how rationalism misses the real answer. His German culture did not readily translate into the culture of those he was serving, so he began to think in the local terms, to blend the two cultures' values. He traced civilization carefully and studiously and wrote his condensed *Philosophy of Civilization*. Here he insisted that Descartes's *cogito ergo sum* is not really the first datum of life. Rather, one is, one is living. The basic fact and therefore also the primary element of the human consciousness is its "will-to-live."[32] But, he insisted, it was a consciousness possessed by *all forms* of living creatures, not really human centered. It is the consciousness of this instinctual awareness, he claims, that makes *un*necessary so much knowledge about the world.[33]

To be ethical does not require a familiarity with any particular philosophy, religion, or science; no expertise of epistemology or ontology; as well as no familiarity with mythology or even theology. For an educated theologian/ medical doctor/musician, this was quite a leap. He still considered himself Christian and could find meaning in his Christian roots, but the uniting ethic was that which he discovered through self-awareness and awareness of others who were different, in fact, even the "will-to-live" that motivated all the animals in his new world. The "will-to-live" is *instinctual* and ubiquitous. As instinctual, it necessarily takes priority, or should take priority in all our thoughts and actions, yet can use and *needs reason* to direct that instinct but not to deny it. He called this "Reverence for Life." He also referred to it a form of mysticism, a mystical unity with the being of each other, *not* a union with Being-itself (or God, as totality of being) since that is not available, but only the *specific* being or life force in every living creature we meet.[34] This sense of unity with others reshapes one's entire attitude toward others. As the late Richard Rorty said, one's sensitivity to others has enlarged one's own "we" to include the others rather than think so much in terms of "us versus them."

By Schweitzer's adept analytical mind, this most basic awareness had to have priority over all rationalistic attempts to ground ethics. As much as he admired certain systems, they all seemed to have huge gaps, as he saw even Kant's purely "formal" ethical definition, which he thought consisted of only one formal principle, from which it was not self-evident how it would be developed beyond that. But, again, it was the utilitarianism that he most opposed which had by default continued to sweep through the capitalistic world, measuring everything on a cost-benefit analysis, which was simply an offshoot of the pain-pleasure approach of Bentham, Mill, and later utilitarians.[35]

Similarly to Nietzsche, however, by assigning the "will-to-live" to instinct, and unwilling to think that altruism was instinctual, he found it a bit difficult to explain why one would sacrifice for others, even sacrifice one's own life, the most noble of moral actions. He was convinced that somehow the recognition of the "will-to-live" in the other must create this equilibrium or even self-denial. But if it is neither rational nor instinctual, what accounts for it?

He spent much of the last two-thirds of his life in Lambarene and/or working for the hospital in raising funds throughout the world. He received the Nobel Peace Prize in 1954, as he was devoting much time even speaking against nuclear armaments. I have discussed Nietzsche, Schweitzer, and Rawls in *An Ethic of Trust: Mutual Autonomy and the Common Will to Live*, so cannot duplicate it here. I simply need to give enough detail that the reader can understand the basic principles, values, and processes by which we elect to view and evaluate the historical material we will soon cover. If both Nietzsche and Schweitzer saw the basic moral power and value as "will-to-power" and "will-to-live," and Nietzsche defined "will-to-power" as being completely life affirming, they also saw the material dependence of mind upon matter, of ideas even upon one's metabolism and diet. They viewed the world as a whole with many different parts, and all were related or relative.

Living was the end in itself, a process, not some imaginary end when living is terminated, and any ethic that hinders or denies living defies instinct and dehumanizes. Values therefore come naturally even through our own observation of our instinct or by viewing the same instinctual "will-to-live" in other living beings. To reach this point requires honesty, serious reflection, and trust of what one has received, including relations as well as ideas involving others. Somehow one can reach the point of "going under" or self-denial even if it *seems* to negate one's narrow "will-to-live" and be able to respond to others with compassion, though not "pity" which is a condescending shaming. This instinctual approach means all the extreme ideas of causality, will, or even the value of being over becoming, which was so prized in theology, lose their importance or are reversed. One's life is a continual process toward self-perfection or reasonably extending and maximizing that instinctual primary value; knowledge of other things or processes in the world are of lesser import.

RAWLS'S ETHIC OF JUSTICE AS
VOLUNTARY INCLUSIVE AGREEMENT

Harvard Prof. John Rawls, in 1971 and subsequent years, especially 1993, asked us to *hypothesize* that "original position" of negotiating a social contract from behind a "veil of ignorance." It was imagining oneself in an original contracting position, but knowing nothing unique about ourselves other than our basic needs which form a conception of "general goods." He insisted it remains only hypothetical, not some historical description,[36] but thereby shows us what true justice would require in real situations. By "original position" he did *not* mean what I was when I was born, and then gradually became aware of belonging to a particular family, of having a particular sexuality, of being part of a particular ethnic or racial group, even of the family's economic status. These may all be "original," but I had no choice in them. I myself had nothing to do in determining those things, so in that sense they are nonrational or "absurd" and not "deserved." They are simply "givens" of my particularity, "destiny" in the broadest sense,[37] or what Rawls called "happenstance"[38] elements of my situation in life. These and all other "happenstance" elements of one's life cannot simply be presumed to be valid interests in the pursuit of justice for a nation as a whole, since if one negotiates from these vested accidental elements, one may be negotiating only from a position of *irrational advantage* over others, which could even be totally contradictory of the intentions of those who were originally responsible for the unique traits, opportunities, or assets. Moreover, to these are gradually added one's discovery of certain political and religious (or antipolitical or antireligious) allegiances the adults in the family have, and these are usually influential on the children as well. These are all *inherited* "givens" and have *nothing* to do with justice but only "destiny" in the broadest sense.[39]

No one desires to be *disadvantaged* in life from the outset, whether by other specific people or by some law. So, in actual life, if one discovers that being of a certain ethnic, racial, sexual, religious, or economic group means suffering from other people's advantages, including their biases and discrimination, one would hope *not* to be in the disadvantaged groups. Or one might discover that having less money with which to buy food, clothes, or shelter, and less possibilities to attain an education by which one could access more and better opportunities to provide for oneself, would make life very hard, so one would hope also *not* to be in these groups. If one had no idea of what race, gender, economic, educational, religious possibilities, and identities one would be born into, with that consciousness, anyone would opt for *equality instead*—if he or she had the chance.

That very opportunity of equality *is* the *hypothetical* "original position" that Rawls is suggesting. Behind such a hypothetical veil of ignorance, people would negotiate to *avoid possibly being disadvantaged.* They would "hedge their bets" and not vote to approve some *inequality* of such irrational or happenstance elements such as race, sexuality, and so forth. Rawls thought they would likely all vote for an equality of liberties to the greatest degree possible for all citizens, just in case they found themselves in some status that was *otherwise* going to be greatly disadvantaged. I have yet to hear people arguing against Rawls's argument on this basic point. I really cannot imagine any disagreement on this, and from this "original position" behind a "veil of ignorance," he formulates the fair process and basic principles with which all people would likely agree.

Of course, Rawls's critics were correct in pointing out that these people still are assumed to have had knowledge of what and where certain inequities might be, what comprised good arguments, and so on, so they were not behind a veil of total ignorance. Rawls insisted that he was not speaking of an actual *historical* social contracting or original position but rather only a hypothetical one in which there would be an obvious voluntary acceptance by all of a *basic equality of political liberty* as their *first principle*. He said their ignorance was basically limited to the areas by which one could have an *advantage* over others or be *disadvantaged* by others. Otherwise, they knew generally what life and bargaining entailed. He further suggested they would also very likely come up with an agreement of a *second principle*, which he called the "difference" principle, which would provide some means of compensation for those who in the *actual* or historical situation ended up quite unequal or disadvantaged because of other factors.

I shall provide these two principles later, but here simply emphasize the meaning of his *hypothetical* "original position." He means a state in which one *does not yet know* (or can imagine oneself not knowing yet) what one's status would be—what race, sexuality, religion, financial condition, and so forth, or even how intelligent or strong one would be. But he also spoke of it as a state in which a "representative" lawmaker, not knowing the diverse specifics of every person he *represents*, nevertheless, tries to work toward an equality of voice in the process so his constituents will not be disadvantaged. But it is still a *hypothetical* position, a way of representing possible postures, but the "ignorance" may be clearer when one thinks of the "representative." That is the crucial point.[40]

If one does *not know* what race, sexuality, and so forth one will be, or the unique traits and assets possessed by ones constituents that one represents, precisely what would one negotiate for in the social contract? That is the question that was central to Rawls's exploration. Of course one actually *never* grows up not knowing his or her race or sexuality, his or her family's financial status, and so forth. But Rawls is saying in order for a *contracting process to be a fair process* itself, it must *hypothesize* an equality or an ignorance of the "vested" interests or the "happenstance," absurd, or wholly accidental elements. One cannot take these as deserved, and then always negotiate only in such a way to retain *those advantages that he was irrationally born into*, which, for example, in the past centuries in the United States, has certainly been the status of the white, male, heterosexual Protestant Christian middle-class citizen. Behind the "veil of ignorance," what would be negotiated for would be the most general goods needed by *all* people.

This means that the question is whether I am really able to *transcend my particularity* and ask what basic principles, structures, and ethics would I vote for, what kinds of laws, if I might just as easily turn out to be black, male, heterosexual, Muslim, living on the poverty level as I might turn out to be a white, female, lesbian, Protestant Christian, middle-class citizen. Or the question may be as simple as "Do I feel *challenged or threatened* in any way when I realize that there are more women than men in the United States, or when I hear that the Hispanic population is growing much faster than the Caucasian, or when I see that immigrants from India and other countries seem to be occupying a much greater percentage of the top executive and professional positions in the United States than a century ago?" Or, on the other hand, do I feel *indignant* when I hear that women and racial minorities make significantly lower salaries than white men in the same or comparable positions? Or, am I *upset* about the racial inequity represented in our outlandish incarcerated population and their treatment even in a pandemic, or the voter suppression that one political party utilizes to vanquish the voting right of all nonwhites? These questions drive me out of my "happenstance" or accidental givens, and, only by everyone being willing to remove such "absurd" or "nonrational" elements from their lives, can a reasonable process of *fair contracting* occur. This means a hypothetical, voluntary divesting by each citizen as the first step in speaking of anything like "justice."

Any social contract or structure of justice must flow out of a *negotiating position* which would *voluntarily be selected by every person* once they place themselves in this hypothetical original position behind Rawls's "veil of ignorance." In *A Theory of Justice*, he was convinced that the "mutual disinterestedness" of all participants as well as the "veil of ignorance," when the two are combined, produced not only an equality of voice but thereby also a *sense of reciprocity* which would evoke similar results to benevolence or altruism. The reason is that when the opting to divest hypothetically is strictly voluntary, it eliminates the grounds for any "envy."[41] That is, being "disinterested" in the welfare of others does not mean being indifferent to others' plight or needs. It means only that the original position of the veil of ignorance places all on the *same footing*, interested primarily or only in the general goods, so the individual's decision ends up *exactly* the same as all the others, and each person is aware of this. Thus, "envy" is precluded, and his or her decision is a *decision for all* with*out* some artificial insertion of a benefit or right for all, or being commanded to be compassionate, and is not merely a special benevolence or altruism.[42]

Rawls later, in *Political Liberalism*, explained it in different terms that it would necessarily have to involve "freestanding" principles which could be argued in the sphere of public reason, from which citizens could reach an "overlapping consensus," of at least a couple of basic principles to which *all would voluntarily agree.* Either way, one still has to *hypothesize* in order to come up with a *fair process*, without which there can be no real sense of justice. Even though he retained the two ideas of "mutual disinterestedness" and "veil of ignorance," he attempted to answer the charge of it being "egoistic" by distinguishing between "rational" and "reasonable."[43] He defined "reasonable" as an approach in which one welcomes participation in formulating norms for a society. This necessitates an agreement of both fair terms and a fair process by which the parties reasonably mutually accept whatever results, so to that degree it involves a sense of reciprocity. He sees "reciprocity" as located between some ideals of mutual advantage of everyone and altruism, if one takes altruism as being motivated by the general or *primary good for everyone.* He insists that "reasonable persons" are actually moved more by a desire of a social world in which people, free and equal, voluntarily cooperate with others by principles that all can accept which therefore form an overlapping consensus and fair society.[44]

In contrast, "rational" points to a "single, unified agent seeking its own interests." Yet he refrains from saying the rational approach never includes any concern for others, because it can include others the person loves. But, Rawls insists rational agents, unlike reasonable agents, have no desire to cooperate fairly with others, perhaps because they lack a "moral sensibility" toward others, and he concludes that such rational rather than reasonable people border on being psychopathic if their interests are "solely in benefits to themselves."[45] He also contrasts even more graphically the "unreasonable" person as one who, though perhaps willing to "engage in cooperative schemes," is "unwilling to honor, or even to propose, except as a necessary public pretense, any general principles or standards for specifying fair terms of cooperation. They are ready to violate such terms as suits their interests when circumstances allow."[46]

Thus, he feels that the reasonable approach, combined by the mutual disinterestedness and veil of ignorance, can lead to a fair or symmetrical positioning of parties in the original position, in which no one has an advantage over the others, and by the reasonable agent being willing to enter into the fair terms of cooperation, the reasonable is not only reciprocal but very "public." I am unsure that such distinctions between "reasonable" and "rational" can be more than suggestion, and I am not persuaded of how this is a mere extension of Kant's formulation of the difference between "categorical" and "hypothetical" or of his linking it to Kant's discussion of the forms of consciousness of "humanity" and "animality." It does appear that people should be easily able to understand that they cannot expect others to enter a contract with them when those others will be *disadvantaged by its terms* or the very process itself. Contract law does not honor a contract that allows for one to have an advantage over the other.

In this way, he offers a definite solution to the hiatus reached by the strong positions of Schweitzer's "will-to-live" and Nietzsche's "will-to-power" which needed some form of empathy or altruism or at least reciprocity of benefits in order to avoid a monism by their instinctual placing of the primary power or "will-to-live" and "will-to-power."[47] The equilibrium and sense of unity can be built upon the voluntary consensus of all, and includes all, whereas compassion or empathy is often either more limited in scope or primarily emotional responses, so lack a stable consistency that the reasonable "overlapping consensus" offers.[48] When these are combined with Rawls's general method and reciprocal element in the *agreement*, it can provide a natural starting point which can build first on the "will-to-live" and then Rawls's two principles in their lexical order or order of priority in which one does not sacrifice from the first to enhance the second. The *two principles*, reformulated by Rawls several times in *A Theory of Justice*, seem fully complete in the first part of *Political Liberalism* as the following:

a. Each person has an equal claim to a fully adequate scheme of equal basic rights and liberties, which scheme is compatible with the same scheme for all, and in this scheme the equal political liberties, and only those liberties, are to be guaranteed their fair value.
b. Social and economic inequalities are to satisfy two conditions: first, they are to be attached to positions and offices open to all under conditions of fair equality of opportunity; and second, they are to be to the greatest benefit of the least advantaged members of society.[49]

These are placed in a lexical order, but two principles he derives which are so fundamental from this are as follows: (1) no one may expect an increase of his or her liberty if it diminishes the general liberty of others, so the only intolerance that can be acceptable is when it is needed to prevent people from limiting the general tolerance of all; and (2) the primary criterion on social and economic inequalities has to be whether a law benefits most the least advantaged or least benefited. He was persuaded that it would be illogical for anyone who was behind such a "veil of ignorance" to not accept these principles. The first principle obviously is central to our inquiry since he sees "freedom of conscience" even having priority over "freedom of opportunity" and is persuaded that religious people profit most when they give allegiance to these two principles of the "original position" by which their "freedom of conscience" is guaranteed.

Why, then, do some readers find Rawls's theory so difficult, once one honors not only his idea that the veil of ignorance is hypothetical and precludes only certain kinds of knowledge which would give one an *advantage* in the bargaining? No contract law allows for one party of a contract to *hold an advantage* in the very *process* of contracting, no matter the knowledge, assets, ethnicity, sexuality, or other specific attributes of the party. The process cannot involve any form of compulsion or deceit which would negate the voluntary aspect of the agreement. Instead, it must be based on public reason which goes through the "political" process of reasonable negotiation. Yet in our capitalistic culture, and culture of possessing the greatest military weapons on Earth, we often hear that the proper and only way to negotiate is from "strength," which means exercising vested interests and irrational advantages to gain a greater benefit or voice in the outcome of the agreement, to be able to coerce the others or to protect one's nation's vested interests.

That is clearly the *opposite* of the fairness Rawls proposes for life within a democracy, since he felt his system preserved mutual human autonomy while appealing to a *process* which *all would consider fair and voluntary*, which would give it stability, and he saw his system as basically an adaptation of the moral direction in which Immanuel Kant was headed.[50] His system was built not on inequality but rather equality of *political liberties*, which all would desire as their first choice. However, any social or economic inequalities that occurred due to other factors would have to be also addressed hypothetically behind the same "veil of ignorance" and would necessarily attach to positions and offices, requiring that they be open to all by equal opportunity, and would have to benefit the least advantaged. Even so, this "difference principle" never levels out the "playing field" since no one would *willingly* sacrifice an equality of political liberty for a little extra compensation of another type, and political liberty and equality is by far the most crucial to a democracy. When political inequality continues to exist, it can create vast inequities in the social and economic areas of life, even if such things as gerrymandering or public proclamations of an election being unfair, when there is no evidence of it, appear on the surface not to affect the social and economic spheres of public life. They actually have and do.[51]

Rawls explained the different approaches between his *A Theory of Justice* and his *Political Liberalism*, in which he felt he made a mistake in the earlier work of assuming that all would actually be able to agree to a single comprehensive ethic which would give the free citizens their needed institutions of stability, but later he realized that such uniformity is too unrealistic to expect that, but instead, the very idea of a "political liberalism" or democratic society *presupposes* the *normal continuation of conflicting reasonable comprehensive schemas*, but can still propose a stability as attainable in an "overlapping consensus" of "freestanding principles" in the public reason. So the two principles remained essentially the same as did the "original position" and "veil of ignorance."[52] He simply needed further to explore certain areas such as the status of persons themselves, and remind his readers that this process is geared primarily for the agreement about *basic structures of justice*, not questions of the details of specific laws or exceptions to be made or possible interference with the structures, and that he did not intend for the method he proposed in *A Theory of Justice* to be a "comprehensive" schema, even if some interpreted it that way.

I do not intend to give a critical analysis of every profound point made by Rawls, but I am using his insights basically only to resolve the major problem in the ethics of Nietzsche and Schweitzer which was grounded on an instinctual "will to live" and "will to power"—the problem of explaining any self-sacrifice, sharing of benefits, empathy, compassion, or altruism, in the light of the overpowering strength each assigned to the basic *instinct* of self-survival and self-expression. It is within Rawls's idea of the basic aware-ness of differences between people that must somehow be tolerated in order for them to *coexist*, which results in a negotiation of an *agreement or social contract*, formal or informal, to which *all* involved voluntarily and wholly agree.[53] But, again, that depends upon the *hypothesizing* process which shows the most consistent and logical response, but it is not a description of any actual historical fact or event.

I must clarify Rawls's idea of the difference between "public" and "nonpublic" reason, which further explains his system and gives guidance to the direction this inquiry must pursue. It relates to Kant's definition of Enlightenment which involved his own insight into the difference he saw between public and private reason, a difference he explained pertinently by using a religious pastor as an example. Kant's view was that in his private role, the pastor, who had elected to follow that profession, was obligated to represent adequately and fairly the view of the religious institution. This was "private reason," since being a pastor was not obligatory on all citizens, but something he voluntarily chose as an individual. On the other hand, as a citizen of a nation, as a member of a large group of people with very diverse commitments and interests of their own, he was also obligated always to be in search of truth, the good, or justice wherever it would lead him, and of sharing it with the general public for their collective benefit.

If the two areas clashed in any significant way, he could continue to rep-resent both so long as the ideas he propagated in his private role as pastor were still basically not contradictory to what he discovered in his public role. He finally said, those doctrines of the religion could still be embraced so long as it was possible that they contained some vital connection with the truth he was discovering in his public role. When one realizes that Kant saw the essence of religion being a morally regulative institution rather than an ontological or metaphysical repository of truth, it is easy to see that both roles could be espoused by the pastor so long as his public role, his inter-est and participation in humanity and society as a whole, had *priority* over his private role. If he preached at church what was considered publically as unethical, such as racial or sexual discrimination, that would be unacceptable, hopefully to both sets of ethics. But the degree to which his religion's moral instructions were simply stricter than the public reason's standards, for example, if the church opposed the drinking of any alcohol, he could inform others of that which was allowed by law as one's free choice, while at the same time upholding the church's ban on all alcohol. But he could *not* encourage both as opposites, nor incite his church to try to limit the freedoms of outsiders by changing the public law to the church's stricter ideas nor try to insist to his church that its position of abstinence is immoral. They are two sets of ethics which function in different situations and do not *necessarily* conflict. To that degree, one can see why Rawls considered his endeavors as an extension of Kant's insights. But we must see also the slight way Rawls tailored this by his distinction between "public" and "nonpublic" reason.

"Nonpublic"[54] reason is that which operates within associations or organizations which are *options* for individuals to *choose* to belong to as a part of their unique individual final ends, goals, or values. This includes such associations as religious groups. But one is born into a political structure, and lives one's whole life within it, and since it operates with the basic public agreement or consent as the expression of the people as a whole, one has no choice about whether to live under it or follow its requirements. It *rightfully* has sanctions coming from the people at large which even can be used against associations and organizations as well as individuals that violate its rules of law. But in a democracy, the political conception of justice operates with an acceptance of diversity of citizens' interests, even of their reasonable comprehensive schemas or allegiance to a variety of religions. To the degree that these are grounded on public reason and therefore *not* grounded on some exclusive antirational metaphysics, they are tolerated so long as their members follow the political conception of justice, or, specifically, the Constitution and its other basic laws that all citizens have agreed to as a part of being citizens and enjoying the rights and protections of the structures of the government.

Rawls says their commitment to a public conception of justice means the reason of its citizens, in their relation to the necessary structure of its institutions and their purposes and end they serve requires "public reason" in three senses: "As the reason of citizens as such, it is the reason of the public; its subject is the good of the public and matters of fundamental justice; and its nature and content is public, being given by the ideals and principles expressed by society's conception of political justice, and conducted open to view on that basis."[55]

This definition necessarily reveals that there are limits on public reason, primarily confining it to constitutional essentials or issues, although, he admits, there could be exceptions. Whereas "nonpublic" reason may operate within scientific organizations, religious institutions, philanthropic organizations, even corporations, and the like, since one is *not* simply born into any of these, but instead, sooner or later, elects to belong or not, the specific rules under which they each operate may be different, so long as all citizens observe the rule of law articulated by its political conception of justice expressed by the Constitution in its manifold extension, a unity which all have agreed to uphold in a democracy.[56]

If voting for officials to run the government was only an organizational (nonpublic) or individual (private) obligation, one could vote by the reason dictated by those entities. However, Rawls insists, one does not vote for private interests but for the people as a whole, their welfare, so it is "public reason" that must control in their political advocacy as well as actual voting. This, of course, raises the question of when could a citizen vote to "coerce" political power over other citizens. The answer is "only when it is exercised in accordance with a constitution the essentials of which all citizens may reasonably be expected to endorse in the light of principles and ideals acceptable to them as reasonable and rational."[57] But, in order to be a "legitimate" use of such power, one must be willing to meet the "moral" obligation (not legal obligation) to listen to others who differ, must show "fair-mindedness" in decisions of what differences need to be accommodated, and of being able to explain how one's vote embraces those political principles or values on which all have agreed, explaining them in such a way that other reasonable citizens would accept or endorse their vote as consistent with the public values and principles.[58] Although he notes that government allows churches and other nonpublic institutions to exercise authority over their members (even as was seen in Kant), since apostasy and heresy are not "legal offenses,"[59] and the person is not deprived of any benefits or freedoms he or she has under the political power of the state by being excluded from the religious group;[60] nevertheless, when it comes to the actual content of public reason, he is adamant that the nonpublic or even private interests and principles have no bearing:

> [I]n discussing constitutional essentials and matters of basic justice we are not to appeal to comprehensive religious and philosophical doctrines—to what we as individuals or members of associations see as the whole truth—not to elaborate economic theories of general equilibrium, say, if these are in dispute . . . [but to] the knowledge and ways of reasoning that ground our affirming the principles of justice and their application to constitutional essentials and basic justice . . . [which] rest on the plain truths now widely accepted, or available, to citizens generally. Otherwise, the political conception would not provide a public basis of justification.[61]

Thus, one must understand that it is the very First Principle Rawls elaborates which protects religion, gives its members a limited freedom, but it also presupposes that one of the freedoms the religious person does *not* have by that is to reduce the general freedom for all by enlarging his or her freedom, or bring a nonpublic or private reason into the affairs of the political conception of justice, which means basically the constitutional system. This understanding people would either accept as fair, or they would be insisting simply on having their own way, coercing others to conform or get out, which is an inhumane treatment of one's fellow human and certainly not what a democracy is. This distinction must be kept uppermost in the following analysis when we finally sketch the Supreme Court's decisions over the past century, since the "incorporation" of the First Amendment into state law by virtue of the Civil War Amendments, especially the Fourteenth which guaranteed equal protection and due process to *all* citizens. His discussion of "equal liberty of conscience" in *A Theory of Justice* is even more pointed:

> It may be said against the principle of equal liberty that religious sects, say, cannot acknowledge any principle at all for limiting their claims on one another. The duty to religion and divine law being *absolute*, no understanding among persons of different faith is permissible from a religious point of view. Certainly men have often acted as if they held this doctrine. It is unnecessary, however, to argue against it. It suffices that if any principle can be agreed to, it must be that of equal liberty. A person may indeed *think* that others ought to recognize the same beliefs and first principles that he does, and that by not doing so they are grievously in error and miss the way to their salvation. But an understanding of religious obligation and of philosophical and moral first principles shows that we cannot expect others to acquiesce in an *inferior* liberty. Much less can we ask them to recognize *us* as the proper interpreter of their religious duties or moral obligations.[62]

Throughout my search for an ethic that all people can embrace, I have continually emphasized religions' "absolutizing," upon which Rawls here also bases his understanding. This is what prevents any religion from qualifying to supply the ethical base within a society that in fact has a religious pluralism, and a democratic republic as Rawls suggests, taking difference as something it has to accommodate, is probably the only type of government which can provide both a sense of unity as well as protection for peoples' differences. There are two ways I want to supplement his system as a valid alternative to the otherwise mixtures of utilitarianism and moral intuitionism. He, Nietzsche, and Schweitzer all proposed an alternative ethic to utilitarianism which they saw as deficient because it is simply an *extension* of a *single voice* as if it represented the whole of the people rather than being the actual

different voices of all the people which can be united in generalities by their
agreement.

The first way I would supplement his insights is to raise the question of
whether what he describes is not in fact *much broader* than requirements
of political structures which are appropriate, particularly to democratic
regimes. I believe the whole of his description can easily be seen as the *ethical procedure behind all human relationships*, since all human relationships
involve a mutual voluntary agreement, mutual commitment, and mutual
trust. He attempted to restrain from looking at a broader scope, basically
because his thorough analysis demanded so much even for the narrow limit
of the "political" schema of justice.[63] But I believe no relationship between
humans succeeds without these elements of agreement, even his two primary
principles. Nevertheless, I realize that the reason, scope, constituency, and
comportments are still different in private relationships from public structures of justice.

My second suggestion for Rawls's system is to understand that *mutual
trust is presupposed* throughout, though he seldom explicitly mentions it.
Mutual trust is also presupposed in Nietzsche and Schweitzer but is seldom if
ever mentioned, much less analyzed, an element that is essential to any unity
between humans, and even any relationship between humans and animals.
The closest any of the three came to discussing it is when Rawls assures his
readers that the person working in hypothetical original position behind a veil
of ignorance selects the most obvious first and second principles as he knows
all others do as well, and that is sufficient motivation for all to live by that
which they have accepted as a group. They can be *assured* that the others will
honor such a voluntary and fair contract. Yet, he also describes the "unreasonable" person in his *Political Liberalism*, a person who may only pretend
that he or she is willing to agree with the basic principles, but never really
intends to, but only to defraud or take advantage of the others by violating the
principles when he desires.[64]

Further, even in *A Theory of Justice*, as he was analyzing the "rule of law"
under the topic of "equal liberty," he showed the problem of a lack of trust
or a betrayal of trust, though he never referred to it as "trust." For example,
he wrote: "To be confident in the possession and exercise of these freedoms,
the citizens of a well-ordered society will normally want the rule of law
maintained."[65] He seemed to be overly confident that the participant's "legitimate expectations" would be met by the other people, simply on the basis of
everyone allegedly agreeing on the law.[66] But those "legitimate expectations"
are what is meant by "trust." And then he cited the possibility of tyrants or
dictators who deviate from the rule of law,[67] and even admits that "it is hard
to imagine . . . a successful income tax scheme on a voluntary basis. Such an
arrangement is unstable."[68]

So a "coercive sovereign is presumably always necessary, even though in a well-ordered society sanctions are not severe and may never need to be imposed. Rather, the existence of effective penal machinery serves as men's security to one another."[69] This was obviously written before it became public knowledge that the prisons were filled with a disproportionate percentage of poor, minority people, and many at the turn of the century were under incredibly punitive sentences for misdemeanors under "Three Strikes" laws and then through racial profiling and indiscriminate "Terry" stop-and-frisks with no probable cause and poor legal representation in Court.[70]

Finally, Rawls did use the word "distrust" when he stated "[t]here may, however, be no procedures that can be relied upon once distrust and enmity pervade society" (TJ, 231). He also was very outspoken on the great defect of "the failure to insure the fair value of political liberty," by allowing elections to be determined by private contributions rather than public funds,[71] or the partisan diminishing of political participation by suppressing the vote or system of one person one vote of those in the opposing parties (TJ226, 231). "Trust," in any case, needs greater exploration, since nothing destroys the unity of a nation faster than distrust of justice or a general distrust of the leadership of the nation—just as nothing destroys a marriage like a loss of trust or trustworthiness. That is the truth about all human relationships. "Trust" and "trustworthiness" may themselves have instinctual beginnings that motivate the baby, and last through childhood, but very quickly they begin to be rationalized, based on empirical experiences and evaluations of their fairness as one measures it by the reasonable expectations one has. We learn who to trust and who not to trust, and *that* is one of the most powerful determinants of our behavior.

THE EMPIRICAL MEASURING OF BOTH ETHICS AND LAW

Some in the legal field believe ethics is too fuzzy or nonempirical to measure, as if it were all built on an otherworldly framework. Yet many legal practitioners think they can ascertain the exact "intention" of past lawmakers, including the Framers of the Constitution. In truth, to a degree one does not have to be a mind reader to engage in either project. They both utilize hard data, empirical or phenomenal elements such as words people used, visible actions they engaged in, and they both consider these within the temporal, physical, and "historical" context. Of course one cannot read minds of any other people. But morality and ethics have never been about that, but rather judging the positive and negative consequences of *people's actions, including words*, with each other. And law *does* deal with that—with human acts and language—so they overlap. Both law and ethics are able to view certain *empirically sensed elements as constructive or detrimental to human relations*, and need not speculate about what is in one's mind that is not made evident by one's explicit speech or actions.

There are certain kinds of actions that usually serve as *empirical* evidence of one's frame of mind, especially when they corroborate each other. So both from the standpoint of *ethics as well as law*, if it is stipulated that a homicide has occurred, and the externals such as the owner of the gun, the location of the suspect in the victim's apartment with the victim, all point to the suspect, the mens rea (guilty mind) that can change a plea of a sheer accident or even manslaughter into charges of first-degree murder if law enforcement also turns up letters from the suspect to the victim in which the suspect threatens to kill him, or multiple witnesses testify independently of having the suspect tell them that he intended to kill the victim, or the victim had written in a daily journal about all the threats against his life by the suspect. Those are very telling words. Of course, they would have to be examined for authenticity, and a chain of custody might need to be established to show that the records have remained in police custody without alteration since they were discovered. These may well be sufficient—not a mind reading, but a reading of *empirical evidence* which itself *reveals* a *state of mind* which removes the incident from being merely an accident or manslaughter or negligence.

However, reading the intent of *ancient* people who were writing a law in a completely different situation can be difficult at best. If there are very few pieces of evidence by which to establish what Jesus or Gautama Buddha taught, and those pieces come from *decades later* rather than from known eye-witnesses, that makes reading the "intention" of the subject of that preserved data or documents quite unreliable. On the other hand, if we have literally thousands of documents involving the planning and prospects of a possible Constitution, of the different views from so many people being expressed, from that point all the way through even the long ratification process, it is not too difficult to ascertain the "intent" of some writers, so long as the language is not ambiguous or indefinite or strange to our present way of speaking. Yes, thousands of recorded speeches, published articles, personal letters, and the like from dozens and dozens of different people, many of which were contesting the others' views. This is a long way from mind reading, but even so, one has to bridge a cultural, historical, linguistic, and scientific gap to think that in some way these are *relevant*—other than simply *assuming* they are because one was born into a country following that social contract. But the questions of contingency or change bear on the issue of authority and relevance, and a present reader must always ask what reasonable grounds lie behind his or her acceptance of those rights, privileges as well as obligations and restrictions, other than one's being born into its jurisdiction. Does a reader today carry any illusions about framing a normative picture of structures and basic institutions of justice for the world that is now two centuries in the future? Or about framing a normative ethic now for a culture still two millennia in the future?

Ethical discussion has moved far during the past two and a half centuries, as has science. It would seem that the real difference between ethics and laws is simply that law cannot articulate every possible thing that might be *thought* and not even every possible action that might be *enacted*, whereas morality or ethics attempts to probe the cause with the possibility of diverting or preempting the commission of an unethical or illegal act—a "nipping in the bud," so to speak. So ethics can rightfully address not only actions and words but also *attitudes*, as the Dalai Lama shows,[72] attitudes which are conducive to ethical behavior or on the other hand, attitudes which lead to self-centered thoughts that are detrimental or destructive in their affecting unethical actions. If one can understand the danger of hurting someone is intensified if one fosters hatred and anger toward the other, one might try eliminating such attitudes from his or her life.

Law, however, does not make suggestions about one's attitude. Although law is morally or ethically attuned to the "good" or "right" or "just," so is concerned with the most socially constructive as well as the most socially destructive elements, unlike ethics, it attaches motivation, incentives, and sanctions to encourage the former and discourage the latter. Citizens agree to elevating certain moral areas to a legal status because they are deemed too important to be left simply to individual people's initiative to obey. They establish the penalties as incentives toward obedience necessary to justice, and they establish political structures which administer justice in its various forms, without which structures there would be no civil order at all. But in a democratic society, these decisions about what is "socially constructive" or "good" for the people, or what is "just," as well as those that are the opposite, are themselves decisions not made simply through personal whim, subjective tastes, emotions, imagination, or some committee or single person, and certainly not merely some notion that evidently they worked before in some ancient culture, or even the same country a century prior. They value public reason, especially in the face of the contingency of all life, including human ideals. So the decisions about what is "good" or "right" or "appropriate" or "relevant" depend upon the public reason, and it involves a continual assurance of the *voluntary agreement* by all parties, an ethical agreement by the entire citizenry, pertaining to empirically perceptible actions and words.

That was the way the Framers described their task of formulating the U.S. Constitution as the basic contract of the New Nation—a government of the people, by the people, and for the people, establishing via public reason the necessary visible structures and processes of justice agreeable to all. The people's collective insight affected the outcome of elections and informed the shaping of the laws through the people's representatives as the deciding body, of representatives who would be continually changed by having elections every two years, which would assure the *people's voice* was being heard in all its *diverse* forms and interests and as concerns and needs *continually change* with time. Were that not so, the Constitution would have not needed the legal procedure of being amended, without which there would be no Civil War Amendments incorporating federal law into state law, no equal protection and due process provided for all citizens regardless of their race, no women's suffrage that took another half a century, and so forth. Conceptions of what is ethically right have *changed* and will continue to do so, meaning laws are always subject to review, revision, and deletion.

Thereby, the nation and its citizens do *not* become enslaved simply to what once worked in prior centuries, as if *stare decisis* locks in the nation for all future time, certainly not by the intended two-year *turnover* the Framers built into the House of Representatives. They conceived the Senate as giving stability to the nation but with the House providing up-to-date insights and concerns, changing with the people and issues at large. Senators were to serve six-year terms rather than two and could serve multiple terms to provide continuity and a sense of stability.

On the other hand, to subscribe to a law of precedents *without* realizing even the built-in limits or ethical "checks and balances" the Framers had in mind, or to always avoid any ethical analysis of law but simply hunt for the right precedent cases and exact legal words that can be "dispositive" is to be woodenly fixed, stagnant, and unrealistic to the real relation between law and ethics and the changing world. It simply pushes the cause, rationale, or justification further back. A system that only builds on precedent with only incremental changes may give the feeling of consistency, but when one quits looking at the basic map and pays attention only to the width of the road, one may find oneself taking an incorrect turn and thereby creating new precedents on the old one but headed in the wrong direction. After enough miles, it may be too difficult to turn back, so one begins to look for a shortcut that would eventually get back to the original highway further up, perhaps pretending that one intended to take the long route since it was more scenic.

But even there one cannot avoid the connection finally with ethics since both ethics and law deal primarily with *human relationships*. Fortunately, back in the 1980s, Prof. Ronald Dworkin pointed out that the best reading of a law *necessarily is* the "moral" reading and illustrated this by elucidating specific cases. This dovetailed to a degree with Prof. John Rawls's classic works which utilized Kant, focusing on principles rather than ends, even a hypothetical beginning from scratch, in the "original position" of a *fair processing* of a *social contract* upon which to build the actual governmental structures of justice. Rawls intentionally linked this to the moral systems of Kant and Hume.

Ronald Dworkin extended it not simply to the general structural areas which were Rawls's focus, but to the very narrow and specifically implicit moral elements within the *actual arguments* behind specific cases before the Court. While his critique of Rawls seemed to miss Rawls's main schema which was for people to realize that "justice" must *transcend irrational advantages* in order to reach any basic agreement, Dworkin did emphasize a "moral" reading of the Constitution, which was also Rawls's approach.[73]

Conceivably, this concern with ethics or the proper relationship between humans can be detected as one moves even into prescientific, even prepolitical if not prehistorical eras, and even preliterate times as one finally may arrive at the point of human ancestors who encountered each other *agreeing somehow about peacefully coexisting* with each other rather than both living in continual fear of the other. So they *voluntarily agreed* rather than continue to fight, which was an *ethical decision* turned into an agreement or a "law."

It is that simple, even as John Locke described it, moving from a perpetual and potential "state of war" into a "civil state."[74] Unfortunately, neither the ethics grounding a law nor the ethics of its application are as simply determined. Often, a certain visible element is so strong, even a happenstance element—for example of being born so poor as to not be able to own property—that the ethics of all citizens having a right to vote slips by *without being noticed*, as it did even within Locke's limiting voting to property owners, while he was ironically upholding a newly articulated and broad freedom of conscience. Was property ownership really so related to responsible citizenship that one so poor as to not own property should not be given the right to vote?[75] Rawls correctly saw this as an incongruity—of depriving certain people of what *should have been seen* as their ethical and legal right by sheer contingencies or accidents.[76] Rawls's organization does not require every citizen to become well versed in the complex variety of ethical systems articulated over the centuries throughout the world, nor did either Nietzsche's or Schweitzer's since they both saw the primary datum being *instinctual* as a "will-to-live" or will-to-power. It may be that all that is necessary is for a citizen to see a basic principle which was acceptable to all from which other ancillary principles are generated, from which the general structure began to take shape. That is the virtue of Rawls's approach to a system of justice as fairness. But he did think one needs to be able to explain and defend how any principle or law he proposes is justified as compatible with the basic principles to which all have agreed. One can assume he felt the same way of defending one's vote if one made one's vote publicly known.

In Rawls's insight that a liberal democracy will be expected to accommodate conflicting comprehensive ethical schemas as a *normal* element, he distinguished between reasonable comprehensive positions and unreasonable ones, and for this, one must understand the implications of "public reason."

"Freestanding" principles which he insisted on appear to eliminate all religious comprehensive schemas since the latter all presuppose and insist that their ethics are *grounded* on their ancient metaphysics and supranaturalism, and in many cases, they insist such supranatural revelation is *beyond all human reason*. This stands in contrast with his statement that a comprehensive system such as a religious position need *not* be regarded as unreasonable. Of course it should not, nor should any proposed ideas be judged as unreasonable without a knowledge of their content or the way that content is viewed, for example, as being open to negotiation or being absolute so thereby nulling all competing views.

But if the principles they embody cannot stand on their own, cannot be valid in the religious person's mind without being explicitly connected with the mythical or supranaturalism, they could *not* be freestanding with that attitude. To be "freestanding," a principle must be valued by each person as a principle that is valid on its own face, not something that is valid only by having a supposed divine origin or because some authority insisted that it is, but only because its content is agreed as valid by the contracting group itself. More than that, their ancient metaphysics cannot be accepted as any more "reasonable" than would other pre-Copernican arguments in the social contracting. The definition of nonpublic reason as being outside the contracting process because of not including all people but only as those who voluntarily elect to join is certainly part of the disqualification of its attempting to participate in the political process or to reshape the Constitution to fit its peculiar ideas, which we have already discussed, but the basic antiquity and insistence of never changing should disqualify it immediately since it gives preference to views of an ancient world over the modern scientific world, which involves very empirical judgments.

Rawls's work appears to make obvious that any democratic society would have to assume that its very democratic nature carries the inherent meaning of tolerating diversity to the point that no one should ever have considered even thinking that just a single religion or comprehensive schema is or could be or should be its ethical ground. In addition, the *history* of the development and ratification of the basic Constitution of the United States will reveal this very diversity and liberal tolerance of difference at work. The Constitution of the United States was, from all empirical indications, derived *not* from any religion but from the Enlightenment ideas of autonomy, tolerance, freedom of conscience, very implicit secular moral ideas and ethical ideals, and the most voluntarily agreed significant values of the Constitution's Framers which included people like Madison who were so familiar with ancient cultures and political systems that they determined the strengths and weaknesses of many of them, as we will see in later chapters.

In this more tolerant posture of a liberal democratic stance, the Constitution differed considerably from the positions of some of the early Colonies and their much earlier Constitutions. This does not mean that none of the Framers were religious or even involved Christians in their new states, but they saw several of the former Colonies headed in the direction of a religious exclusivity forming the law, thereby repeating the very divisive conditions in Europe and England from which so many had fled. Their answer in the secular Constitution and Bill of Rights made explicit the U.S. Constitution's humanly contracted ethic underlying its structure, an ethic politically informed, whose Framers had debated various aspects of possibilities over months and months, with the final draft of the Constitution itself containing *no profession* of being a metaphysically derived ethic, or divinely informed or inspired, and with no references to *any* religion's ideas or ethics. To the contrary, it insisted on religious freedom to such a degree that it prohibited making religion a test for public office. This corresponds to Rawls's own distinction of the ethic he proposes creating a political conception of justice as opposed to religions' ethics as promoting a metaphysical conception of justice.[77]

THE GREATEST FREEDOM: FREEDOM FROM EGOISTIC MORALITY

The unity that is idealized patriotically, which a democratic society can provide by its tolerance or liberalism, presents and requires the greatest and most difficult freedom: a freedom from egoistic motivation and vested interests. This describes (1) the problem in maturing in one's moral thinking, beyond the primary stages of being rewarded or punished, depending upon whether we obey someone else or not, and hopefully finally arriving at a stage of a wholly abstract and autonomous decision to do the right thing for *others and self* simply because it is right, and (2) the problem of actually being able to free ourselves from giving priority in our thoughts, speech, and action to our accidental advantages or privileges which cannot be any base for articulating a political concept of justice simply because those disadvantaged by our advantages or privileges would never agree to it. The first freedom releases us from simplistic and childish conceptions of morality; the second freedom releases us from narcissism and selfishness. That would be a great freedom to experience, but it is easier to talk about than to achieve.

If the "will-to-live" or "will-to-power" (which is primarily valuing life) is really instinctual, the awareness of the "other" which coexists with us must possess a reasonable nudge of its own, which then necessitates either an irrational showdown or an agreement to live in some harmony. Reason bridges the gap between the egoistic survival instinct and the brutal necessity of social cooperation and agreement. It intensifies the instinct of one's *will-to-live* with one's awareness of *social need* even if the latter is not especially instinctual or altruistic, and the actual confrontation of or presence of the other forms a *reciprocal blending* and empowerment to be social creatures but also to survive or live. Reason steps in at that point of the presence of the other to show the way through some form of negotiation and agreement, even if crudely simple. But this kind of reason, to obtain an equilibrium, needs clarification and independence since one might easily be able to *rationalize* against the social pull and simply focus on one's own living.

In Lawrence Kohlberg's studies, he found that most adults never move to this most autonomous rung of moral reasoning in which one follows a universal principle because it is his own independent selection or value, not merely because it might be a law or what others think should be followed. Perhaps this is because people have been deluded into thinking they can be happy even if others are not, that they can succeed even when others do not, that they can really "live" when others cannot. And if so, this delusion may have been created by growing up in a society that is based on buying, acquiring, possessing, or of always feeling no limit in one's needs and desires that must be met even if they are not basic needs directly related to survival, or of a mentality that prefers instant gratification and no competition or at least have advantage over the competition—all of which is no longer the "will-to-live" survival instinct but the rational, pleasant side of the *immature* stage of reflection, that is, being motivated primarily by reward/punishment by an other. This is rational but *not reasonable* in a social setting. Rawls pushed the moral conversation into a hypothetical agreement that is completely uncoerced. If the principles can be formulated in such a way that all parties will agree to them out of self-interest, then the basic laws of justice do not need to await everyone maturing into Kant's and Kohlberg's higher levels of moral thinking. That was what Rawls accomplished.

Even as "generous" as I may become, if the only reason I give to someone in need is to make myself feel better, that is still *egoistic* motivation in its one-sidedness, not really moral or ethical. It was Kant who pointed out that the only "good" is the "good will," and not only is it difficult at times to detect what another person's "will" is, but one can also deceive oneself or be dishonest with oneself about one's own will or motivation, a dishonesty with self which Nietzsche also detected and deplored. Within the sphere of one's figuring out how to respond to others in complex ethical cases, the social desire and personal survival may appear to be at irreconcilable odds with each other even when they are not opposites.

In such times, or in situations in which one has habitually given in to his or her survival instinct in an exaggerated or nonsocial form, completely suppressing the interests of the other, it may be that one cannot be brought back to an equilibrium or balanced reasoning between these basic needs or desires without a severe shock such as a life-threatening scenario or a situation in which the primary social relation in one's life has dissolved. Unfortunately, sometimes the shock must be extremely severe to awaken a person to his responsibility to the others' "will-to-live" and to the others' reasonable needs which are equal to his own. Examples of the latter could be a divorce or death of a spouse of other most significant family member or friend. Or it might be receiving news that one has a terminal illness, or the surprise that a raging fire is endangering one's life and one's family. Shocks of a worldwide consequence are often hard for such a self-centered person to grasp, the sinister fact of the global warming which is altering perhaps permanently the habitable conditions of Earth, or, as in 2019 and following, the presence of a pandemic. Some people are so entrenched in self that even if the overwhelming view of science corroborates these world threats, they will deny them, and perhaps blame others for being such alarmists. The inability to yield and accept the fact of the threat reveals an unbending neurosis, some absolutization the person has developed which is off-limits to reason, even what Heidegger described as one's denial of one's own possible death, with its assignment of death as always what just happens to *others*, a failure to become authentically human as Dasein.[78] But more directly, one circumvents the whole question of "interest in the other" by Rawls's ability to press people to bargain hypothetically behind a veil of ignorance, and when they do, the agreed principles themselves will have the interests of all the people, and when such universal principles are violated, all realize the personal hurt.

On the other hand, for those who can feel the shock and admit the facts and threat, such a shock often can reverse the course of one's thinking and the direction of one's life. It can be the encounter which Richard Rorty felt one could experience in reading great literature, that is, increasing one's sensitivity to the needs of others as well as possibly to the unrecognized or at least unadmitted "cruelty" of oneself, which he saw as a first step in realizing a human solidarity.[79] He defined the aversion toward cruelty as itself the mark of being "liberal." And he suggested that among the most cruel things people can do to others is to intentionally make them doubt their ability to reason, which some people today call "gaslighting." Hopefully, such shocks will reorient us, enabling us, in Rorty's words, to "redescribe" ourselves and others in a more united and humane sense, an enlarged sense of "we" or "us" and a diminished sense of "they" or "them" (the nameless), forming a greater solidarity.

But if it is tragic when such a shock does not change a person's attitude, it also would be extremely sad if one had spent years oblivious to the equal "will-to-live" all others have, to the needs of the others which are as important as one's own, being indifferent or even reluctant to change, but finally does change and become ethical *only* by such a severe shock. Why cannot humans realize that their social need is as valid as their instinct to survive, and that either may actually depend upon the other, that they are radically interdependent and need to agree to share this life? Or why cannot people, who live in democracies which presuppose an acceptance of difference, realize that they have themselves come to own the nation's laws and its ethical principles by living in that state, and that all are responsible for keeping that contract. This is not coercion but honest, reasonable, and responsible mutual autonomy, operating from trust in each other and in the universality of the laws of that "original position" to which all agreed.

As Rawls concluded in his distinction between "rational" and "reasonable" agents, that the "rational" agents "lack is the particular form of moral sensibility that underlies the desire to engage in fair [social] cooperation . . . [so they] approach being psychopathic when their interests are solely in benefits to themselves."[80] The Covid-19 pandemic revealed the broad spectrum of the human character, from the most generous who willingly put their own lives in danger to minister to the sick (and many gave their lives in such generous commitment to others' lives), to the few who minimized it, mocked it, and could not see beyond their own selfish interests, people Rawls labeled "psychopathic," not simply amoral or ignorant, but intentionally and rationally (not "reasonably") *insensitive* to others' "will-to-live," so also quite unresponsive or irresponsible. Some sought only personal reward, praise, and adulation for themselves, because the shock was not a shock for them since they had no personal connection with the dying. The more public figures on both extremes will be remembered in history as either moral examples or as example of inhumanity or being psychopathic. That accentuates how great and how direly needed is the *freedom* of *being rid of moral immaturity* based on reward and punishments as well as being rid of the narcissistic and selfish habit of always wanting to preserve one's advantage over other people, the first steps of freedom to being a responsible citizen within a democratic society.

Homo sapiens has experienced many geographical, environmental, and biological crises which have threatened to obliterate not the Earth but the human species. So far, the species has been lucky to survive. But the Covid-19 pandemic jolted humanity to realize that its own perpetuation as a species requires a great degree of international, social, and informed cooperation to make sure of meeting such deadly threats with the best science, the greatest possible resources, and an informed plan or pursuit to annihilate the threat. The same expertise might even have to plan how to enable even a handful of humans to "survive" and to preserve a section of the Earth beyond all contamination so survival could be real. In any case, pandemics, global warming, and a possible nuclear world war are relevant issues because of their ability to annihilate humanity and/or ruin Earth. They are not small crises that can be subdued or defused by any single nation, leader, culture, ideology, or party, but require the world population to work as a cooperative, systematic unit. Life affirmation is instinctual, but can be perverted when it remains only self-affirmation or self-survival. That is not a social contract that any large group of people would endorse.

Survival of life and a life-sustaining Earth and Universe(s) require a sense of world-belonging, a world citizenship, a greater awareness of the "other," and a *unity* that supersedes all nationalisms, corporate monopolies, political identities and agendas, and all exclusivistic religious Absolutes. But it cannot arise as a "unity" only in international crises; it must exist there constantly *prior to* such worldwide problems. There is no room for an "America First" policy any more than "Iran First" or "Brazil First," or any other nation. There can no longer be pockets of this Earth where there is inequality or xenophobia of ethnic groups or races, or sexes or a discrimination against those who have become part of the physically or mentally "challenged" because of their births or misfortunes that were not their choices. There is no longer room for a "Country First" or even a "Humanity First" policy since life exists in many species and mutations and is interdependent in the most obvious and extreme sense. Any anthropocentric worldview is as outdated in its *hubris* as the ancient idea of Earth being the center of the universe. Ours is a balanced living environment and life forms that we did not create but are quite capable of ruining by upsetting its equilibrium.

The growing awareness of the sheer fragility of all living species on Earth that accompanies a pandemic causes the acquisitive and possessive lifestyles of *Homo sapiens* to fade almost into oblivion.[81] It is surely no longer possible to measure our lives in terms of what we have, possess, use, or own—whether objects, treasures, status, fame, talent, beauty, heritage, or wealth—that culture beckons to us to value as the most significant. More than ever, we hear Albert Schweitzer reminding us of the basic fact of our awareness, the instinctual cognizance of our own "will-to-live." It is an instinct that he said was *prior to all thinking*, so had priority over the Cartesian "I think, therefore I am," and any form of ethics built upon such a statement. This *instinctual* awareness is accompanied by our unmistakable *perception* of the same instinct or "will-to-live" in *all living creatures* that we encounter.[82] Pain and pleasure presuppose life which can experience them. They mean nothing if life is extinguished. Life has the priority.

So the first principles concern the preservation of life, which, uniquely, was what William James saw as the primary goal of religious people—to somehow lay hold on "more life" quantitatively and qualitatively, a richer, more abundant life.[83] Nietzsche, though nonreligious, also saw life being the first order of business. He insisted that his key to life was *amor fati*—a love of his fate,[84] a love which was so intense that he could "will-to-live" it over and over again and again, even just as it was, not with merely its joys and happiness, but with all the disappointment, tragedies, and illness—and he knew well about debilitating illness for the last half of his life—to will it all over just exactly as it was, surprises and all, and that, for him, was the real test as to whether one really loves life.

Yet the "survival" of the human species may require more than we can give, especially if people approach the social problems with incompetence, indifference, or with selfish motives, since all three can defeat the primary "will-to-live." There cannot be any "holdouts," any "insider trading," any minimizing of crises, hoarding, dishonesty, inhumane treatment, taking advantage of scarcity by selling necessities for extravagant prices. There is neither room nor time left for such distasteful egocentricity and narcissism. Any feelings of being an exceptional or superior individual or race or nation are myopic, misinformed, stupid, and offensive, because they reinforce actions motivated to gain advantage over others, actions based on only narrow, personal, or nationalistic interests which cannot provide for the inclusiveness and cooperation required by all humans in our future which has already begun. There is no room for an "elite," or "privileged," or "more equal" status when humanity and its Earth are in jeopardy, and no room for absolute answers that are off-limits to reasonable challenges. Everything in our world is related, and that makes it is all relative, not absolute or beyond question or even "too big to fail." It is "all on the table" and "all at risk."

John Rawls extended his scope of his first two books which focused on a democratic society to the global community in a separate study, *A Law of Peoples*, investigating international relations and issues, which included having to study how liberal and nonliberal societies can relate to each other or carry some unity. While I have spoken of the need to find a new "global" ethic, it cannot be global until people have utilized its approach successfully in smaller circles, various states and nations. In this present study, I am attempting to analyze the ethic of a trusting, mutual autonomy based on a common "will-to-live" within the particular democratic society of the United States, using some of Rawls's guidelines he saw necessary for democratic or liberal institutions, and the intuitive life affirmation as the primary ethical value as Nietzsche and Schweitzer articulated, as an illustration and test of how well it works.

While I am concerned with the ethics which are effective in family relationships as well as under the social contract of any given government, here especially I am concerned with the relation between the basic freedom of religion to the government within a *democratic* society or republic. We must see not only whether and how the nation has fared in formulating laws that could be voluntarily accepted by *any* and *every* person, as our suggested ethical guidelines supply when they include Rawls's two basic principles, but what the evolution in First Amendment law has shown regarding the actual *legal role of religion* in such a historical situation, as well as the work that still needs to be clarified and completed in order to meet the challenges of the future. In the process, I hope to show how these elements, which may *seem to be opposites* in some people's minds, can be worked out in a democratic society if it incorporates a trusting equality with mutual autonomy, built upon a reasonable control of the instinctual "will to live"—so, rather than being opposites, they can be complementary.[85]

NOTES

1. Soren Kierkegaard illustrated in *Fear and Trembling* this idea of the "Absolute relating absolutely" to Abraham, which no one else could perceive, much less understand since they were operating on only the "ethical" level. This was an extreme reaction against Hegel's description of the Abraham story of one putting faith in the invisible ahead of one's love of one's own child. Kierkegaard, *Fear and Trembling* and *The Sickness Unto Death*, tr. Walter Lowrie (New York: Doubleday Anchor, 1954); and G. W. F. Hegel, "The Spirit of Christianity," in *On Christianity: Early Theological Writings*, tr. T. M. Knox (New York: Harper Torchbooks, 1961).

2. This was certainly Kierkegaard's view. See note 1.

3. This term is found primarily in Rawls's *Political Liberalism* (New York: Columbia Univ. Press, 1993), e.g. 41, 44, 58–65, rather than his earlier *A Theory of Justice*, because in *Political Liberalism*, he is trying to show how reasonable different comprehensive schemas can be viewed as a normal part of political life within a democracy. John Rawls, *A Theory of Justice* (New York: Columbia Univ. Press, 1971).

4. Rawls, *Political Liberalism*, lecture II, 47–88. He pushes his terminology further than I would, as he insists that "full autonomy" is only political, not ethical, but he makes distinction only because he equates the "ethical" only with individualism and the whole of life, such as is covered in the liberalism of Mills and Kant, 78.

5. Richard L. Rubenstein, *After Auschwitz: History, Theology, and Contemporary Judaism*, 2nd ed. (Baltimore: Johns Hopkins Press, 1992), 148.

6. The Dalai Lama, *Ethics for the New Millennium* (New York: Riverhead Books, 1999), 26–27.

7. Rawls, *Political Liberalism*, 38, 140.

8. I have Joseph Flay's insight to thank here, although his concern of these different constituencies, scopes, and comportments was in his critique of Hegel's system. Joseph Flay, *Hegel's Quest for Certainty* (Albany, NY: State Univ. of New York Press, 1984).

9. Of course, Christians had been aware of Jews for a millennium and a half by then, and for a millennium had also been aware of Islam. But they were both regarded as "enemies" or relegated to a pariah state. The Reformation simply split a single religion into many different sects, but even then it was hardly a tolerated religious

pluralism since these sects engaged in religious wars following the Reformation. Religious pluralism existed on a large scale only by the First Amendment of the U.S. Constitution, without which Amendment, the religious constituencies would have continued to fight against each other, which is Rawls's point, that religious pluralism can basically exist only within a democratic government.

10. Rawls, *Political Liberalism*, xxvi.

11. Michel Foucault, *The Order of Things: An Archeology of the Human Sciences* (New York: Vintage Books, 1994).

12. For more detail, see my *An Ethic of Trust: Mutual Autonomy and the Common Will to Live* (Lanham, MD: Rowman & Littlefield, 2021). My analysis of Nietzsche is based primarily upon his *Thus Spoke Zarathustra; Twilight of the Idols; The Antichrist;* all in Walter Kaufmann, tr. and ed., *The Portable Nietzsche*, tr. and ed. (New York: Viking Press, 1954), and *The Birth of Tragedy; Beyond Good and Evil; On the Genealogy of Morals*; and *Ecce Homo*, all found in the Walter Kaufmann, tr. and ed., *Basic Writings of Nietzsche* (New York: The Modern Library, 1966).

13. Nietzsche, *Thus Spoke Zarathustra*, 171.

14. Nietzsche, *Twilight of the Idols*, 479.

15. Nietzsche, *Twilight of the Idols*, 494.

16. Nietzsche, *Twilight of the Idols*, 545–546.

17. Nietzsche, *Beyond Good and Evil*, 300–301. Nietzsche thought the ancient people divided between the commanders and those commanded. The former end up with a bad conscience or self-deceit since they deny instinct; the latter replace the former, under the illusion that what was commanded were the primary human attributes ("public spirit, benevolence, consideration, industriousness, moderation, modesty, indulgence and pity"), but they still are susceptible to someone who will emerge who will command *unconditionally*. Therein they too lose themselves.

18. Nietzsche, *Twilight of the Idols*, 487.

19. Nietzsche, *Twilight of the Idols*, 478, 501–505.

20. Nietzsche, *Twilight of the Idols*, 479–480.

21. Nietzsche, *Twilight of the Idols*, 479–480.

22. Nietzsche, *Thus Spoke Zarathustra*, 138–139.

23. Nietzsche, *Thus Spoke Zarathustra*, 139.

24. Nietzsche, *Thus Spoke Zarathustra*, 307.

25. Nietzsche, *Ecce Homo*, 714. He defined "amor fati" in himself: "that wants nothing to be different, not forward, not backward, not in all eternity. Not merely bear what is necessary, still less conceal it—all idealism is mendaciousness in the face of what is necessary—but *love* it." See also his description on 760–764.

26. For redemption of the whole, even all that is past by saying that one willed it and shall will it, see Nietzsche, *Thus Spoke Zarathustra*, 310. The theme of redemption of the whole since there is nothing other than the whole, see Nietzsche, *Twilight of the Idols*, 501.

27. The "madman" who speaks of chaos of people finding out the "death of God" but the message being too early, see Nietzsche, *Joyful Wisdom*, tr. Thomas Common, Intro by Kurt F. Reinhardt (New York: Frederick Ungar, Pub. Co., 1960), 167–169, and the "death of God" being recognized by the ugliest man, see Nietzsche,

Thus Spoke Zarathustra, 375–379. The reason the tidings did not adversely affect Zarathustra was because he had already become self-reliant.

28. He concludes the final stage of the "Three Metamorphoses of Spirit": saying, "the spirit now wills its own will, and he who had been lost to the world now conquers his own world." But to create, one must first destroy, overcoming the old most sacred "Thou shalts," One now says the "sacred 'Yes'" of creating a new one's own world (from *Thus Spoke Zarathustra*, 139).

29. See also my analysis of his ethic in *An Ethic of Trust: Mutual Autonomy and the Common Will to Live*. The primary works are Albert Schweitzer's *The Quest of the Historical Jesus, A Critical Study of its Progress from Reimarus to Wrede*, tr. W. Montgomery (New York: The Macmillan Company, 1959); *The Mysticism of Paul the Apostle*, tr. William Montgomery (London: A. & C. Black, Ltd, 1931); and *The Philosophy of Civilization*, tr. C. T. Campion (New York: The Macmillan Company, 1960).

30. Schwietzer saw in Jesus's prediction of the imminent coming of the Son of Man what could only be an interim ethic, as in the so-called Sermon on the Mount, and the imminent eschatology that was pervasive in Paul's writings likewise produced an ethic only for a very brief period, hopefully less than Paul's lifetime, so Schweitzer called it a "status-quo ethic" because of the shortness of time as depicted, for example in I Cor. 7. While that eschatology has been denied by many because of its negative implications for Christology, people as radically different as the world-famous Wolfhart Pannenberg and John Dominic Crossan have both realized the unavoidability of admitting the eschatology element, though in different ways. See my *Will Human Survive Religion: Beyond Divisive Absolutes* (Lanham, MD: Lexington Press-Fortress Academic, 2020), esp. ch. 8 for Crossan and ch. 9 for Pannenberg.

31. Schweitzer, *The Quest of the Historical Jesus*. Three quotations encapsulate Schweitzer's unique eschatological understanding: (1) "The whole history of 'Christianity' down to the present day, that is to say, the real inner history of it, is based on the delay of the Parousia, the non-occurrence of the Parousia, the abandonment of eschatology, the progress and completion of the 'de-eschatologizing' of religion which has been connected therewith. It should be noted that the non-fulfillment of Matt. x.23 is the first postponement of the Parousia. We have therefore here the first significant date in the 'history of Christianity'; it gives to the work of Jesus a new direction, otherwise inexplicable" (360); (2) "There is silence all around. The Baptist appears, and cries: 'Repent, for the Kingdom of Heaven is at hand.' Soon after that comes Jesus, and in the knowledge that He is the coming Son of Man lays hold of the wheel of the world to set it moving on that last revolution which is to bring all ordinary history to a close. It refuses to turn, and He throws Himself upon it. Then it does turn; and crushes Him. Instead of bringing in the eschatological conditions, He has destroyed them. The wheel rolls onward, and the mangled body of the one immeasurably great Man, who was strong enough to think of Himself as the spiritual ruler of mankind and to bend history to His Purpose, is hanging upon it still. That is His victory and His reign" (370–371); and (3) "The Jesus of Nazareth who came forward publicly as the Messiah, who preached the ethic of the Kingdom of God, who founded

the Kingdom of Heaven upon earth, and died to give His work its final consecration, never had any existence. He is a figure designed by rationalism, endowed with life by liberalism, and clothed by modern theology in an historical garb" (398).

32. Schweitzer, *Philosophy of Civilization*, 309. He regarded Descartes's "cogito" as paltry, arbitrarily chosen and abstract, a dead end, whereas "will-to-live" leads to a "mysticism of ethical union" not with an abstract totality of being but with specific beings, providing the instinctual "will-to-live" with a social dimension in mutual interdependence.

33. Schweitzer, *Philosophy of Civilization*, 282–283.

34. Schweitzer, *Philosophy of Civilization*, 282.

35. I do not have the space to evaluate Schweitzer's analysis of every thinker he examined, whether they were critical rationalists such as Kant or whether it is his opposition to "utilitarianism." The validity of his insight about the "will-to-live," just as Nietzsche's insight about the "will-to-power," neither one depend upon one having to agree with or even discuss all the ways they utilized to get to that point.

36. The hypothetical original position of the social contracting, with its veil of ignorance, or lack of knowledge of our uniqueness or the uniqueness of others, means one's knowledge of one's needs and others' needs is based only on the awareness of "general goods." Rawls, *Political Liberalism*, 75, 307.

37. "Destiny" and "free will" are a polarity in Paul Tillich's theology, so "destiny" is not just pointing to what one has to be in the future, but rather to that which is beyond free will. Paul Tillich, *Systematic Theology*, 3 vols. in 1 (Chicago: Univ. of Chicago Press, 1967), I: 182–186.

38. Rawls insists that the "original position" moves people past the "happenstance" elements or accidents of history which cannot be a basis for justice since they compete for a position of advantage over others. This elimination of competition by the "original position" would be agreed to by all because of the "veil of ignorance." *Political Liberalism*, 23.

39. Prof. Weinreb wrote a useful exploration of the development of natural law in its interaction with justice. His critique of Rawls was basically that Rawls wanted to eliminate all "desert" as unmerited, not just one's possessions one inherits but one own genetic inheritance. Weinreb fails to honor Rawls's insistence that the hypothetical original position of a veil of ignorance (1) is only *hypothetical* to supply a picture of justice which cannot be derived from merely competing irrationally vested interests; and (2) exists only to eliminate parties from taking advantage over others by virtue of these irrationally, absurd, accidental, or happenstance elements. In real life, they will still exist, but behind the social contract to which all agree, no one will utilize such to take advantage of others. See *Lloyd L. Weinreb, Natural Law and Justice* (Cambridge, MS: Harvard Univ. Press, 1987), 239. Weinreb concludes that we still suffer the same dilemma of the old cosmologies, trying to find a "meaningful freedom within a morally indifferent universe." He answers that nature provides chaos, while humans dream of order, and that human aspiration, though never achieved, must not be given up" (265). It might be more instructive not to see Rawls as such an extremist and to not paint freedom and cause as exclusive opposites, but more as one of several ontological polarities, as Paul Tillich did *in Systematic Theology*, I:174–186.

40. Whether it is the person herself or her "representative," there must be at least hypothetical ignorance of elements which could otherwise be used to take advantage of other people.

41. Rawls, *Theory of Justice*, 530–541, for his discussion of the elimination of envy by mutual disinterestedness or the "veil of ignorance" as being able to think only of common goods.

42. Rawls, *Theory of Justice*, 139–149.

43. Rawls, *Political Liberalism*, 48–54.

44. Rawls, *Political Liberalism*, 50.

45. Rawls, *Political Liberalism*, 51.

46. Rawls, *Political Liberalism*, 50.

47. Walter Kaufmann elaborated this problem in *Nietzsche: Philosopher, Psychologist, Antichrist* (New York: Meridian Books, The World Publishing Co., 1956), 158–180.

48. Rawls's approach of reaching an "overlapping consensus" through "public reason," a consensus all would agree to, is more realistic than a system which requires people to cultivate great empathy or compassion to get along with others. He actually contrasts the human society which has to have *discussions* about justice, discussions which he admits would never exist "in an association of saints" in which, *if* it could exist, "each would work selflessly for one end as determined by their common religion, and reference to this end (assuming it to be clearly defined) would settle every question of right." Rawls, *A Theory of Justice*, 120–130. But no such complete agreement exists in real society, which is instead filled with competing interests and people feel entitled to press for their rights on each other. Yet Rawls's insight about how to attain a basic political agreement is so obvious to the interest of every person that it is almost like that reasonable agreement comes instinctually, just as much as the basic ethical impetus of the obvious "will-to-power" or "will-to-live" was instinctual, needing to be guided by reason. No life is devalued in the process, but an equilibrium is attained.

49. Rawls, *Political Liberalism*, 5–6.

50. Rawls explained the different approaches between his *Theory of Justice* and his *Political Liberalism*. He thought in *Theory of Justice* he gave the impression of the "political justice" as if it were a comprehensive schema and there would be no disagreements. In *Political Liberalism*, he notes a democratic society *expects* even conflicting comprehensive reasonable schemas, but gains stability from basic freestanding principles to which all can agree.

51. Another obvious example Rawls addressed was the adverse effect unlimited campaign funds work on a democracy, since it tends to limit the public discussion and the subsequent legislation agenda to topics that are of central concern only to the biggest donors and biggest corporations, thus eclipsing the dialogue of the needs of the nation at large (*A Theory of Justice*, 224–226).

52. Many scholars after reading Rawls earliest works felt he was inconsistent when it came to economic inequality. Some even mistakenly think he preferred "inequality." His examination of *actual issues* always involved *real historical* situations vis-à-vis the basic principles of justice which were based on the *hypothetical*

original position of a veil of ignorance. As he spelled out his second principle, he talked about the possibility that economic inequality might create the incentive to accomplish the maximum benefits for all. This was parallel to his statement that the income tax area would require sanctions to actually work, and his statement that when one votes, one does not vote for oneself but for the whole people. He is saying that under the veil of ignorance, one *lacks specific* information for anything even to *be an advantage, incentive, motivation, or sanction* other than general goods which is not the issue. But since the principles are embraced voluntarily by all, it transcends all "advantages" without even needing altruism. The end result hypothetically is still based on what he called "disinterest" (i.e., the ignorance of specifics), *not* "incentive" or "altruism" or "generosity." For a slightly different approach, see also Brian Barry "Appendix C: Economic Motivation in a Rawlsian Society," in *Theories of Justice* (Berkeley, CA: Univ. of California Press, 1989), 393–400.

53. This is why his theory seems more reasonable in *Political Liberalism*, in which he points out that it requires a democratic structure in which the sense of unity is strong enough to tolerate differences without reducing mutual autonomy.

54. Rawls, *Political Liberalism*, 220–227. The "nonpublic reason" is not "private" since it involves many people. But it differs from a democracy in that it is shaped and utilized by various associations and organizations which are not mandatory, and its reason is not open to challenge by public reason, whereas a democracy is a political structure based on an overlapping consensus of public reason by all.

55. Rawls, *Political Liberalism*, 213.

56. Rawls's basic understanding of religions as professing to be beyond human reason, as therefore absolutized by each group, as opposed to any challenge or compromise, therefore as purely heteronomous, corresponds to the exclusivistic picture of the dissenters who comprised many of the religious colonists who were interested only in religious freedom for themselves and no others. They certainly did not prepare the ground for religious freedom in the United States, but that came only through Enlightenment thought and from the extensive experiences of the Great Awakenings, as we will show. The "liberalism" Rawls speaks of is a democratic structure which presumes difference which will be tolerated so long as a prior or superior sense of unity of the citizens grounds it. In that sense, it does place priority of the coexistence of all on a unity of freestanding principles which has to have *priority* over all the different and conflicting absolute claims of the various religious. History and Rawls both show the shift that became apparent from a religiously exclusive orientation to a secular one, manifesting the attempt to find significant religious freedom in New England as pure mythologizing, as Steven Green has shown. "Free exercise" since 1990 reveals the abuse of the Court to allow anything one wants to single out in one's life as one's protected "free exercise of religion," which tends to discredit the very phrase, miles removed from the Framers' common sense idea of "religious freedom" as *only* freedom to "worship" as one elected. Compare with Michael W. McConnell, "Free Exercise as the Framers Understood it" in Eugene W. Hickok, Jr. ed., *The Bill of Rights: Original Meaning and Current Understanding* (Charlottesville: Univ. Press of Virginia, 1991), 54–69.

57. Rawls, *Political Liberalism*, 217.

58. Rawls, *Political Liberalism*, 217–218.

59. Rawls, *Political Liberalism*, 221.

60. While Rawls admits that "it is usually highly desirable to settle political questions by invoking the values of public reason," he says there are exceptions. For example, "much tax legislation and many laws regulating property; statutes protecting the environment and controlling pollution; establishing national parks and preserving wilderness areas and animal and plant species; and laying aside funds for museums and the arts." *Political Liberalism*, 214.

61. Rawls, *Political Liberalism*, 224–225.

62. Rawls, *A Theory of Justice*, 208, italics mine.

63. I understand why he referred to certain positions as "comprehensive" or "broader" ethics than the political concept of justice, but also can see how the terms could easily be reversed.

64. Rawls, *Political Liberalism*, 50.

65. Rawls, *A Theory of Justice*, 240.

66. Rawls, *A Theory of Justice*, 235–236.

67. Rawls, *A Theory of Justice*, 236, 238.

68. Rawls, *A Theory of Justice*, 240.

69. Rawls, *A Theory of Justice*, 240.

70. *Terry v. Ohio*, 392 U.S. 1 (1968). In *Terry*, Officer McFadden was justified by the Court's decision of stopping and frisking a man on a public street under a mere "reasonable suspicion" that he either had committed a felony or was armed. But no crime had been committed, and the suspect was walking away from the area where he and his friend had been. After that, however, "Terry frisks" became legal with*out* the officer having to obtain a *warrant on probable cause*. This practice later put thousands of young African American men in the New York area in prison.

71. Rawls, *A Theory of Justice*, 226. In his words, "Universal suffrage is an insufficient counterpoise; for when parties and elections are financed not by public funds but by private contributions, the political forum is so constrained by the wishes of the dominant interests that the basic measures needed to establish just constitutional rule are seldom properly presented."

72. His Holiness the Lama, *Ethics for the New Millennium.*

73. Much of Dworkin's criticism of Rawls was over the meaning of the "veil of ignorance" and the "hypothetical" schema which means it is not real. He felt that any agreement Rawls saw possible within such hypothetical ignorance was simply incredible since it could not be in anyone's interest once they learned their own unique situation. He thought to hold them to what they bargain for behind that veil of ignorance would be unfair once they learned the specific interests, talents, and so on they had. He even spoke of in terms of a game. But Rawls is simply saying, if we can use the "game" analogy, that the rules for the game must be agreed to *prior* to people playing to prevent people taking advantage of the others. Rawls emphasized the difference between what one could know and what one could not know behind the veil of ignorance, and although that can always be challenged in various ways, if a person never is able to ask himself what he would have wanted in the laws and structures of justice had he been born into a different race, economic status, sexuality, and so on

then one has never proceeded to first base in being able to tolerate differences from oneself. Rawls simply wanted to move beyond people taking advantage of others and calling it a fair contract or fair law. Nevertheless, Dworkin's emphasis on the moral interpretation of our basic laws is correct, as is Rawls's ethical emphasis. See Ronald Dworkin, *Taking Rights Seriously* (Cambridge, MA: Harvard Univ. Press, 1977), ch. 6 for his criticism of Rawls; *A Matter of Principle* (Cambridge, MA: Harvard Univ. Press, 1985; *Law's Empire* (Cambridge, MA: Harvard Univ. Press, 1986); *Freedom's Law: The Moral Reading of the American Constitution* (Cambridge, MA: Harvard Univ. Press, 1996); and *Religion Without God* (Cambridge, MA: Harvard Univ. Press, 2013), among others.

74. John Locke, *Second Treatise on Government* (Indianapolis: Hackett Pub. Co., 1980).

75. This incongruity in Locke's position is an ethical blindness that often escapes people, probably parallel to Dworkin's mention that those who opposed the decision of *Brown v. Board of Education* did not *but should have* seen the moral dimension of the decision which ultimately should protect from the immoral uses of majoritarianism (Dworkin, *The Moral Reading*, 16–17).

76. Rawls, *Political Liberalism*, 287–288.

77. Rawls's basic theme is to develop a "political conception of justice" vis-à-vis some "metaphysical conception of justice." *Political Liberalism*, 10, 97. This approach is built on, among other things, his view that Greek culture developed moral philosophy, "based on disciplined reason alone," not involving "religion, much less revelation." Rawls, *Political Liberalism*, xxii. This helps explain how he saw the disciplined reason or public reason, as it reached an overlapping consensus, produced a moral approach, but not a religious one or ethical one which would eliminate the "free and equal" citizens (as well as their reason) who reasoned out the political conception of justice.

78. Martin Heidegger, *Being and Time*, tr. John Macquarrie & Edward Robinson (New York: Harper & Row, Pub., 1962), 279–311.

79. Richard Rorty, *Contingency, Irony & Solidarity* (Cambridge: Univ. of Cambridge, 1989).

80. Rawls, *Political Liberalism*, 51.

81. Dorothee Soelle, *Choosing Life*, tr. Margaret Kohl (Philadelphia: Fortress Press, 1981).

82. Schweitzer, *Philosophy of Civilization*, ch. 26.

83. William James, *The Varieties of Religious Experience: A Study in Human Nature* (New York: University Books, 1963), 506–507.

84. Nietzsche, *Ecce Homo*, 714.

85. I cannot judge the Justices' competence in many fields, but am often amazed at the breadth of knowledge they are required to have. I hope only that my JD combined with a PhD in Religious Studies should offer some valuable angles from which to analyze the court's grasp of religion and its decisions regarding those two religion clauses of the First Amendment.

Chapter 2

Diverse Freedoms within Unity

Basic Real Problems

This inquiry is simply a concern for difference and unity, specifically to see if it is possible that human life can operate with similarity and difference in both beliefs and ethical actions. Of course it is possible. People constantly adjust to both in manifold ways. But more narrowly, this study is asking whether or not, in a democratic society, even if not a pure democracy but rather structured as a republic or representative government, it is possible for both individuals and institutions to attain a sense of unity as a whole, which nevertheless allows for both extensive individual freedoms or differences such as religious freedom, while providing societal, political structural stability for all. Of course, a unity is actually thought to be a collection of differences into a larger whole, which shows that "unity" and "difference" are *not* really "opposites." Only "uniformity" (or "sameness") and "difference" are opposites. Perhaps, then, religious freedom and a secular government are not really "opposites" either?

If our concern is basically how they define human relationships, that is, the field we call "morality" or "ethics," we may discover that the difference between them is basically a matter of such things as constituents, scope, intention, purpose, and comportment, and these are sufficient differences to justify the "separation" initiated by Jefferson, Madison, and others in the First Amendment, but they need *not* be viewed as opposites. I will show the differences that require separation or limitations of each. If separations and limitations of each, based on constituents, scope, intention, purpose, and comportment, can reduce the potential conflict, then it is more reasonable than having two conflicting roles one has to meet, since that might sound like one's being a hypocrite or having a terrible cognitive dissonance. Instead, having two "sets" of ethical principles in this way is more akin to the idea of one's having two or more different types or "sets" of clothes, but it could also

45

be tools, or books, or vehicles, or types of fishing rods. They do not necessarily conflict, but they are designed for different occasions, which determine not only the precise scope of their employment, but also their appropriateness and applicability, as well as the different unique comportments one may be required to manifest. If one wears formal dress clothes to a very formal occasion, but the next day wears only a ragged T-shirt and worn-out jeans and tennis shoes to mow the lawn, this is not hypocritical, any more than thinking one can simply use the kitchen flatware for doing work on the engine of one's car, or thinking one's prize ancient split-bamboo fly rod for catching small trout is appropriate for a tuna-fishing trip. Different situations and relationships require different instruments. We may examine this analogy considerably more at a later point.

Rawls acknowledged in his introduction to *Political Liberalism*, the challenge of having to be tolerant of other religious individuals or groups which only became apparent in Western culture in the seventeenth century, by sheer proximity of the differences. If at first such tolerance was thought to be a loss of one's faith or heresy,[1] it was finally seen as a choice people had to make between "either mortal conflict moderated only by circumstance and exhaustion, or equal liberty of conscience and freedom of thought."[2] But as novel as that tolerance was in the United States, it was still extremely narrowly applied, since the country at that time consisted only of competing splinter groups within the Christian religion and a few Jewish citizens.

Even by the end of the eighteenth century, the Framers of the Constitution still did not view either the Native Americans or the imported African slaves as fully human, so certainly their religion was given no consideration at all. It was not a tolerance of non-Christian religions or of atheism in any sense, even if Madison and Jefferson spoke in such broader terms of different religions beyond Christianity. But today, major world religions occupy significant places within most nations; religious diversity is no longer simply a question of Christian sects. The people living next door, in many democratic societies, may be not simply a different type of Christian or Jew, but carry the identity of a Muslim, Hindu, Jain, Sikh, Buddhist, or any number of other religions.

What Rawls did not mention was the fact that during these past three centuries, because of the radical change that took place in the human sciences,[3] it was now becoming possible for the first time to study what it was to be human. And what even Foucault did not note was that much Christian theology itself began to move far beyond its earlier form of the "metaphysics of infinity" and any traditional "theism." Even if ecumenism as a movement did not accomplish much in the mid-twentieth century, the Parliament of World Religions which had convened at the end of the nineteenth century met again at the end of the twentieth century to try to formulate a global ethic. Religious leaders such as His Holiness the Dalai Lama have even suggested that ethical living is more important than belonging to a particular religion.[4] The most profound Roman Catholic theologian of the twentieth century, Prof. Hans Küng, after being forbidden to teach Catholic theology any longer, has spent the past several decades of his life working to transcend the earlier exclusiveness and narrowness of religions in a group search for a "global ethic," and worked with this Parliament of World Religions[5] as did His Holiness the Dalai Lama, who also published his *Ethics for a New Millennium* (1999).

While the Dalai Lama moved further than Küng in suggesting that it is more important that one be a "good person" rather than that one belong to any particular religion, even his basic insights still carried much of the Tibetan Buddhist flavor as he himself was aware, and the Parliament of World Religions intentionally *emphasized* its inter-*religious* base and *antiquity* as giving it *authority* to speak of its principles as "irrevocable" or universal imperatives for *all* people. Yet it appears it is basically this heteronomous or authoritarian approach which assumes some otherworldly certainty that makes this *objectionable* to most nonreligious people. No single person or single body can speak for humanity. If principles must gain their authority only by being *voluntarily accepted* by *all people* involved, this means the beginning point will likely be only a few basic principles upon which further constitutional principles can be coherently built, and these basic ones will stand in an order of priority or, as Rawls called it, a "lexical" or "serial" order. The two basic principles he is confident everyone would accept are as follows: (1) equality of political liberties and (2) social and economic inequalities which would be tolerated only if offset by an equality of opportunity and primary benefit of new laws going to the "least advantaged," determined by the latter's own assessment. He calls this second principle the "difference" principle. We quoted one version of these in the introduction, and others can be found elsewhere in those two initial books of his.[6] The two principles are in order of priority, so one would not be willing to receive a greater economic benefit to compensate for being deprived of some aspect of one's political liberty. Political liberty, which means primarily an equality of voice, has priority over any economic and social states. Simply put, it is one thing if a nation's structures deprive people sometimes of proper food and shelter, but to be denied equal voice in a democracy means one is being dehumanized. This is why Rawls saw the universal right to vote as the most valued.

Yet, ironically, it is much easier for people to hypothesize the need for the first principle, of equal political liberties than it is for people to hypothesize the "second principle," of determining compensation for social and economic inequalities from the position of the "least advantaged." For one who has considerable privileges and irrationally vested advantages, it takes a great deal of courage to imagine the hypothetical contracting behind the "veil of ignorance" in which one would have no assurance of possessing those advantages, whether they are racial, sexual, economic, or other. One might welcome the right to help determine laws when things are unequal, but one probably would not welcome actually being among the "least advantaged." But that is Rawls's point about "justice as fairness." Even if one finds it fairly easy to talk of being the victims or being on the "short end" in distribution of goods, it is quite another thing when one imagines it in graphic detail as a real possibility. This is what the "veil of ignorance" facilitates, and Rawls insisted this is not merely not knowing one's race, sexuality, family wealth, educational level, but even one's abilities or talents and even the happenstance conditions of one's present generation and the present state of society in general—*all contingent factors*—and he referred to this as his "thick" (as opposed to a "thin") theory of a veil of ignorance.[7] But *without* neutralizing the happenstance and irrational advantages, any social contracts drawn up will likely be influenced by those who have the greatest advantage, and such irrational position has nothing to do with justice nor with a democratic republic, and would not gain a consensual agreement.

If it has to be an agreement by *all* involved parties, this means it will have to be people who *desire* such a unity that they would *tolerate diversity*, which means they are probably people who *want to be or are living* within a democratic society. This is therefore *not* a search to figure out how an autocracy, dictatorship, theocracy, or other form of government can be ethical, since these are forms in which the people have their voices or autonomy *stifled*, whether by other small groups such as oligarchies or multinational corporation boards, single leaders, or even alleged gods. To stifle the autonomy of a human is a form of dehumanization to which it is difficult to see anyone voluntarily agreeing.

It was this audience Rawls had in mind in writing his *Theory of Justice* and *Political Liberalism*, people who *desire* to form a unity to share life with each other, a unity which includes reasonable diversity, structures of justice as defined *by the people as a whole* through some form of representative or constitutional republic. He was able to address the international scene of nonliberal societies only in his later *The Law of Peoples*. Even within his examination of the structures of justice within a democratic society, he disclaimed addressing a general ethic or even a general autonomy. Because I see the principles of mutual trust, mutual autonomy and equality of voice and opportunity, basic honesty, and a noncontradictory base of the common "will-to-live" as imperative for any human relationship, as I earlier noted, I believe to this degree, the principles *do* apply to ethics in general, not merely to structures of justice. Surely "justice" and all the qualities I just listed are as appropriate in a marriage as in government processes. The sense of fairness, honesty, trust, and mutual sharing of responsibility wrapped up in "mutual autonomy" based on the common "will-to-live" is crucial in all human relationships, or else the relationships are less than humane. If it is basically unethical for women to get paid less than men for comparable work, it is just as unethical for the distribution of labor roles within a marriage to discriminate against women. One cannot simply say one type of work is of less importance because it corresponds more naturally to mere custom or to the abilities or strength of one sex or the other, but the *scope* of work may easily distinguish the value of different *types* of work. That scope, purpose, and constituency involved in breast-feeding the baby certainly makes it more important than mowing the lawn, no matter how much strength the latter requires.

If, in a marriage, Rawls's first principle is *not* followed, so that one party lacks the liberties the other one has, it is dehumanizing. If, in a corporation, the executives prove themselves untrustworthy, or they do not follow through on their promises, the business is dehumanizing. On Rawls's second principle, if in a corporation, the *board* can award bonuses and extravagant increases in salaries to executives who already receive 50–300 times what their average employee makes, while never providing any significant benefit for the least advantaged in the company, the corporation is dehumanizing. Rawls's "second principle" would require the decisions on such bonuses made by the *least privileged* in the company and to *their benefit* when such inequality exists. That would be a real eye-opener if it ever occurred. If "justice" to Rawls consists not in some outside or external standard or ideal but rather is *made* "justice" by the *voluntary agreement* of the parties involved, then "justice" would also even be a part of a marriage and even close friendships, even if they do not have formal structures of justice *per se*.

This volume therefore examines the actual application or nonapplication of that formulated ethic in the democratic, constitutional republic of the United States, not because the United States is the ideal, but because it is the oldest surviving democracy. Since our primary concern is to examine the relation of religious ethics to the ethics underlying the laws of the nation, many significant ethical areas cannot be considered. Nor can we cover the vastly varied forms of nondemocratic societies and/or the coercion or loss of personal freedom and mutual autonomy experienced therein, since, as I earlier suggested, I believe any system of government that has to suppress or destroy autonomy is dehumanizing. The degree to which a variety of states become successful in their present pursuit to suppress the vote primarily among nonwhite constituencies will itself determine to a large degree how far the United States has moved away from a genuine democracy.

PROBLEMS OF MAJORITARIANISM IN A DEMOCRACY

The criteria for an examination of a particular democratic society cannot be simply a formulation of ideals, but must focus on reasonable expectations which are based on the recognized basic principles of the social contract accepted and recognized by *all* citizens as *their will*. It is invariably a question of how difference is to be accommodated within any unity because all unities will be comprised of entities which have considerable differences. This largely focuses on the degree any person can embrace a relationship in which others are quite different, how one judges how much difference is reasonable so will not become incompatible and destroy the sense of unity. The line was been drawn by the Framers and as well by Rawls as the difference between interests that are *not* those of the nation as a whole and those that *are*. When less than national interests are promoted by smaller groups to the point of challenging or overpowering the interests of the citizens as a whole, that is, "majoritarianism," something *explicitly* feared by both Madison, Jefferson, and in the twentieth century by John Rawls. Of course, in many respects, laws do gain validity often by a simple majority vote or a supermajority vote. That does not make them "majoritarian"; the latter title is appropriate only when a group, whether majority, small minority, or a handful of individuals, gain sufficient power to *overpower* the interests of the nation as a whole.

It is in this sense that Justice Jackson listed several of the rights in the Bill of Rights and said they are not subject to a vote and cannot be discarded by a majority.[8] They are the principles which are assumed to be approved by the *nation as a whole*, not just a special interest group. This distinction must be remembered lest one misunderstand and think Madison, Jefferson, Rawls, and others were fighting against the majority. They were fighting against special interest groups, no matter their size, groups which do *not* have primarily the interest of the nation at heart, which means a suppression of the interests of many minorities, and hypothetically could even occur in setting an actual majority of citizens at a disadvantage.

Rawls included in the list of possible "majoritarian" groups any religion or "comprehensive schema" which consciously exerts a power to shape laws with its less than national interests. I have earlier said that "religion" nearly always carries with it the claim of being Absolute, therefore beyond any question, challenge, or modification. But it need not always carry the same traditional trappings of "religions" in history, including belief in supernatural beings or sacred rites or formulae or scripture. It could be anything that is above any comparison so is not subject to "public reason." Sometimes elements of one's own identity and community can take on this status, for example, one's race or even one's sexual identity. There is little doubt that "White Supremacy" has become an equivalent "religion." When people together work out a strategy for defeating the ideals of a nation, even if it is only the idea of "equality," it could be said to have that as their "religion." If it does not reach that "absolute" point, it still could be regarded as quite incontrovertible and incomparable, so antidemocratic as a "majoritarian" power. Kurt Anderson's recent *Evil Geniuses* has shown how a small group of rich and influential people have manipulated the laws of the United States, as early as the 1970s with its terrible negative affect of *increasing inequality*, thereby creating more division in the United States, even if it used equivocal language to persuade people to support it, and of course, never used the specific word "majoritarian."[9]

Much of one's capacity to tolerate difference is shaped by one's family and environment long before one comes to a consciousness of the crucial question which affects every relationship. There are many different types or levels of "unity" that can be important to people's identities, from rather marginal unities such as being a "vegan" or vegetarian, or being a loyal alumnus of a certain school and its athletic teams, or being a cancer victim, or one's social status (wealthy, middle class, marginalized, or in poverty), or one's sexual identification, one's racial or ethnic identification, one's religious identification, or one's being a citizen of a certain town, city, or state, or one's being a citizen of a certain nation, or one's being a citizen of the world, or one's being a human, or one's being a living creature. In each of our lives, the hundreds of different identities (or sensed unities) are ranked, consciously or unconsciously, and others can often detect *our actual priorities* and preferred identities by our actions more than from our words.

If the nation's interests should come before private interests, this process of prioritizing can be seen on even a larger level. My approach here is to give priority to the *most basic* or most universal identity and interests and sense of unity or the general, and work down from there. That means the most important identity I have is being a *living creature*, but then, even more specifically, of being a creature that is conscious of and driven by its "will-to-live" or "will-to-power" in its unique life-affirming purpose. This shows the beginning of the Western historical reorientation of the sciences, especially of the human disciplines in the late eighteenth century, with a new emphasis upon the *empirical entities*, as documented by Michel Foucault. This can be observed, for example, even in the abandonment or change in meaning of a single ancient word such as the Greek *psyche*.[10] That is, Schweitzer's father was a Lutheran pastor, and Albert Schweitzer (1875–1965) was himself a Lutheran professor of religion. In Luther's day (sixteenth century), a primary presupposition of the human "essence" was still that the human being has an eternal "soul" (*psyche*), based on the continuing Platonic influence via St. Augustine. By the close of the eighteenth century, the old language, with its dated analogies and its reifications, was losing credibility in new sciences. The Enlightenment saw such thinkers as Descartes attributing the uniqueness of humans to one's reason through his "I think, therefore I am." The great Idealist theologian/philosopher, Hegel, who, in the early nineteenth century insisted he would be Lutheran till he died, used the word *Geist* (translated "spirit," "mind," or "reason") prolifically in his *Phenomenology of Spirit*, but even he still could not identify this with the physical human brain. After the further development of biology and anthropology, the empirical aspect became more central, as Michel Foucault had predicted and documented.[11] Although Schweitzer still used the word "spiritual" in his *Philosophy of Civilization*, as a medical doctor, he saw ethics rooted in the *instinctual* which was tied to all *actual living bodies*, not just humans, as their animating "spirit" not some invisible, Platonic eternal "soul." In this way the ethic became an obvious universal power not confined merely to the ancient dogma of some religious community.[12]

For this reason, I insert Albert Schweitzer's "will-to-live" and his "Reverence for Life" as well as Friedrich Nietzsche's life-affirming "will-to-power" or "discharging one's strength" as the priority or all priorities, the "first datum" of our experience, since this "will" is created not by reason or great analytical ability or accumulated knowledge, but both saw it as *universally instinctual*. In humans, it involves the possibility of reflection which makes its possessor rather unique, a part of *Homo sapiens*, a self-conscious being. But it does not thereby form an anthropocentric ethic, but rather feels the obligation to protect and defend all living creatures who have the same "will-to-live," not just fellow humans. By reason, one also can perceive that all these living creatures enjoy a certain livable environment on Earth which cannot be minimized, but needs nurturing, especially those living entities which are codependent. One's identity moves from the consciousness of being a joint tenant of Earth to being a part of a nation or state, perhaps even a state having a democratic structure, that is, one that truly is a government "of the people, by the people and for the people." These identities are compatible and can embrace each other, so they qualify as the highest or ultimate concerns and need cultivating, protecting, and nurturing for the life instinct to continue.

The hundreds of lesser or more specifically determined concerns are not as important. The higher concerns operate off more general principles than the lesser concerns or more specific identities. I could still be a citizen of the nation and of the world even if I went to a different school or no school at all, if I eat meat or not, and regardless of my racial or sexual identity. This being the case, the principles forming the national identity or of being a member of a democratic society or constitutional republic are more general, *universal and inclusive* than the principles regulating a university alumni group, particular religious group, or special sexual or racial group. I do not thereby diminish the importance of these latter identities, but only observe that they all depend upon one's being alive on Earth, being a conscious human being, and finding oneself within governmental, economic, and social structures long before established, in which one lives a peaceful coexistence with other human beings and various other forms of life.

Within the sphere of political justice in one's national identity in a democratic society, those principles therefore have *priority* over principles of my university alumni group and even my religious association. They are not only more inclusive and thereby could gain an agreement by all, but they are more basic to life itself in the ladder we elaborated above. Further, as Rawls emphasizes, organizations and associations differ from nations in the sense of the associations' "nonpublic reason," that is, their unique forms of reason, ideals, and purposes that are more narrowly tailored and which they do not want to be subjected to the general public reason to determine. Their identity is more specialized and membership remains optional, so is less a shared identity than that of the citizen of the nation, and, in religious groups is not only quite exclusive but even absolutized in that sense.

Ironically, however, Rawls spoke of such associations as sometimes having "comprehensive" ethical, religious, or doctrinal schemas as opposed to the very narrow scope of political justice which the nation has. The terminology can be flipped either way, as the broader versus the narrower concerns or vice-versa, and it can make sense either way. The significant thing is to realize that all of us have more than one identity, and these different identities entail different scopes, authorities, purposes, constituents, and comportments, thus, to a degree, different sets of ethics. This does not imply that they are radically in conflict, but simply that what is allowed in the small particular "associations" to which one belongs may not be allowed in the broader scope of the interest of all citizens of the nation. That means that what would be appropriate within that smaller, special group may not be applicable or appropriate to the whole of the citizens of the nation, so could not be made into the ethic upon which the basic laws for all citizens are grounded. But it can work the other way as well, that what is *permissible* on the national level may not be permissible by the standards or rules of certain associations.

Rawls assumes most people are born into a certain nation not be their choice, within which they can later can *choose* to belong to any number of "associations" which may have different scopes, types of reasons, constituencies, and expected comportments. This reveals the "separation" of government ethics from the ethics of the less-inclusive associations. One may belong to an association that is totally opposed to all forms of birth control, but one cannot use the authority of that limited association to try to force the nation to overturn its laws which allow for birth control. One has to distinguish between *permitted* by law to do something as opposed to being *mandated* to do it or prohibited from doing it. Being permitted by state or national law does *not* mean one therefore has to do what is simply permitted, whether drink alcohol or use some form of birth control or drive 80 miles per hour on a state's freeway. To fail to see this difference often leads to quixotic conflicts. But this also means that one cannot argue one's associations' ethical rules as if all citizens agree to the particular mythological or supranatural grounds of that specific religion to justify the specific law.

On the other hand, there are laws that do not present permission but require strict compliance, as Rawls notes. One may belong to an association of people who are convinced that it is unethical to have to pay income tax, but one cannot, on the basis of the authority of that association's (whether it is completely secular or religious) attempt to eliminate the IRS or even refuse to personally pay one's taxes as a citizen. One may belong to a group of pacifists, but one cannot use the authority of such a special group to be sufficient to eliminate the various armed services, the Pentagon, and so forth. One may believe that "Q" wants one to assault the U.S. Capitol and even kill the leaders of the government in that building, but that does not give one authority to violate the U.S. laws and actually do it nor to encourage others to attempt it. This would be true even if one could convince the majority of the nation's citizens, since a mere majority does *not* displace the authority which was established by the Constitution which was based upon the agreement of the *whole* people of the *basic* principles of the social contract.[13] If people were at liberty to do any of these things, the nation would be destroyed, one way or another. For example, if all citizens were allowed to decide on their own whether or not to pay income tax, there would be neither government nor all the services of security, necessity, and convenience that it provides, and without such funding, it would, as James Madison emphasized, have no respect among the nations, no way to defend itself, so would probably have been taken over long ago by some foreign power which *did* have financial resources via taxation.

It appears that much of the negative attitude people have toward things that seem burdensome at times because they are mandated stems from a lack of realization that in a democracy, the experiment is to responsibly *share* the *total experience* of being a nation. When one has agreed on the *basic principles* of the nation, one does not escape strict compliance by merely objecting to some law, neither to gain a special advantage for oneself, nor just out of pure stubbornness or protecting one's autonomy. There are legal ways articulated to change law, including elections of different possible leaders. However, if the ethics grounding the social contract do *not* expect a uniformity that eclipses all possible freedoms of individuals, or if individuals do *not* demand freedom to the extent of expecting to be exempt from the general or universal laws of the social contract, there would seemingly be a way of working things out.

But religions still present a problem since most or all of them have their own specific Absolute. Books are still being written suggesting that the U.S. government is discriminating against religions unethically if not illegally, or arguments are based on the presupposition that a certain religious group has a valid claim on eternal truth, infinite wisdom, or Absolute deity, an authority above all authorities of humans.[14] But as Rawls pointed out, there is no way of resolving the conflicts between absolutes or religions which elevate their faith above public reason. One cannot simply say one's religion is truer than another or absolute.[15] The conflict can be resolved only by the basic principles of the "original position" behind the "veil of ignorance" to which all have agreed. On the other hand, many nonreligious citizens believe the country is financially and politically favoring a single religion and thereby making others feel they are less worthy and less equal citizens, as strangers in their own country, and using public taxes for that single religion.

That pinpoints the nature of the problem, one addressed by Rawls but even anticipated by James Madison long ago, the problem of some form of "majoritarianism." As Madison saw it, the democratic goal, in its republican or representative form, does not intend to dictate uniformity and eliminate dissent, but to learn how to accommodate genuine difference,[16] or, in Rawls's terms, to shape from public reason a form of a stable government of United States that manifests a "well-ordered society" based on a "reflective equilibrium."[17] Madison envisioned the diversity of interests in different areas of the nation, even between the rural and metropolitan cultures, as well as the "checks and balances" he and others established in the Constitution of the relationships of the various divisions of federal government, to deter any consolidation of power in a single interest that was not the interest of the *nation as a whole*—as having multiple layers from the local governments, to state governments, finally to the representational federal government with the division of powers. That is, each level had the interests of the *whole* of *that level*, so at a local level, the interests being decided by the county or city would have to be for that group as a whole, then it would increase and become more diverse and inclusive on the state level to include all citizens' basic interests of the state, and finally would have to be the basic interests of the nation as a whole on the federal level. Obviously, one might say this is a form of majority rule itself, but the basic principles Rawls says are needed for the *social contract* at every level would be those to which *all* the people at that level would *hypothetically agree*.

The difference between a hypothetical "original position" and a historical event of such is, of course, that many people are simply unable to divorce themselves from the irrationally vested interests and advantages they have over others, simply incapable of hypothesizing any state in which they would not have such advantages. That means in real life, there will always be that problem, but that hypothetically, the basic principles even if only two, as Rawls articulates, of the "original position" would be agreeable to all, to *all who wanted* to engage in fairness and equality of voice rather than being irrationally advantaged, to all who realized that the only way the experience would be theirs is by sharing it with others. Those who ignore this would not be responsible members of a democracy.

Behind the veil of ignorance, no one would have agreed to special benefits or advantages to be given only to the wealthy, if they realized that they might easily turn out to be born among the poor and homeless. No one would have voted to give special power only to people who are above or below a certain height, or above or below a certain weight, or whose noses have a particular shape, or who are bowlegged. Such would be irrational if one truly had placed oneself behind the "veil of ignorance" and was aware only of general goods or if the negotiation is being done by one's representative who knows very few specifics about the separate interests of each member of his constituency which he represents in Congress.

The nation simply could not have been formed if the majority of citizens had been incapable of hypothesizing, of divesting themselves imaginatively of their inherited or happenstance advantages over others, and designed and embraced a system of principles that would be to the benefit of all, as much as any equality can be attained. Fortunately, they were able to do it. This is where one stands in awe of such giants as Madison and Jefferson for whom a new, great democratic republic was an experiment worth all of their effort and openness to different others, even to the point of self-effacement. They were not perfect people and lived still within their own culture of late eighteenth century, but they were willing to look ahead and realize the frailty yet necessity of human relationships which must embrace diversity rather than simply perpetuate continual friction and conflict or become odious forms of tyranny.

The Framers did not devise the Fifth, Sixth, or Eighth Amendments out of personal interests to protect themselves, but to help others. They likely had never experienced a violation of the rights they articulated in the Third or Fourth Amendments, either, but they saw many who wanted these rights guaranteed. They did not think that if they eventually became a president of the United States, they might be impeached, but they formulated a process of impeachment for a president in case it was ever needed. The "checks and balances" in the structures of the three branches of government had been debated for months, even if few of the people debating had ever personally experienced one out of control, except that their immediate prior history was a war they fought because England abused them especially by its unrestrained monarchial or executive power. They lived with lots of pain, but they also studied the past and were willing to hypothesize themselves beyond their actual situations.

As Madison drew it up, majoritarianism was negative because it elevated a special interest over the interest of the *nation*, gathering support somehow of a majority, thereby forcing its special interest upon all the others which was not to their benefit at all.[18] Of the three majorities that came to the New World with the immigrants—white, male, and Christian—our study here addresses in detail only the *third* of these, the religious majoritarianism, but the first two are even *more conspicuous* even if not seen as Absolute as is the religious majoritarianism. Unique interests and special forms of reason or even specific forms of ethics is the mark of associations or organizations which do *not* in themselves have to be concerned with political justice.

But majoritarianism could involve groups whose "majority" is *not* in its numbers of people but in the total assets they own or control which enables them to lobby and move the entire agenda of the government away from the common interests of the nation as a whole to their private or special projects or issues, which has in our day become true through the lobbying of large multinational corporations and the buying of candidates for public office by paying for their campaigns. Kurt Andersen's *Evil Geniuses* shows how even merely four very wealthy men could decide in the 1970s to change the national economy in a long-range program and deceitful tactics, and basically accomplish that within two decades or less.[19] Rawls's objection to this was that as long as campaigns are not paid strictly from tax funds, the candidates' agendas will never be able to express the *diverse interests* of the nation but only select agendas of donors.[20] That has been true on many occasions, but the United States has ignored Rawls's insight in *Citizens United v. Federal Election Commission*, 558 U.S. 310 (2010).

Majoritarianism can often be a subconscious attitude stemming out of a life of privilege, that is, a life in which one habitually experienced the *advantages* of being a part of a group which, by its power, can exert enough pressure on the government to further those advantages for the small group without realizing that the advantages were not in the interest of the whole people *nor deserved* but sheer accidents of history or the contingencies of birth. As Rawls insists, unearned or irrational advantages serve no positive place in our definition of *justice*. This, as well as the difference between public and nonpublic reason, marks the difference in constituencies, scope, authority, purpose, and comportments, and which makes each association such as a religion *unqualified* to interfere to change the government's justice derived from an "overlapping consensus" of competing principles based on public reason.

On the partisan-political level, history shows us how easy it is for bare *majorities* to become used to getting their way to such an extent that any competition that shows up is taken as a threat to their existence rather than a welcome partner in adding a new and diverse voice to a democracy. Many seem to prefer the game of "monopoly" even if agreement is attained only by their control or manipulation of others. Since Rawls's first principle that he believes all would agree to behind the "veil of ignorance" in the hypothetical "original position" would be a maximizing of equal political liberty for all, "advantage" and coercion can have *no place* whatever in the basic "original position." There will be sufficient room to debate or argue over problems by general "public reason" once people realize that all of these are *subordinate* to the consensus and unity arrived at in the *basic principles* of the "original position."

The problem in various cultures has been that sheer customary ways of conceiving of relationships as well as actual ethical and legal structures enable people to simply uphold whatever is the status quo or power structures without questioning them. If it has been male dominated, it is simply assumed that this is the best way or right form of the relationships and structures. Custom may become so strong that it continues strictly from unreflective habit even when males are *not* the majority, but came into their power through sheer brute physical strength or irrational traditions of taking ownership of assets or other means. While a national census of the United States may reveal that men are not in the majority sexually, they still exercise a majoritarian control in the U.S. government, and *this* is the place in which a majoritarianism is very dangerous to the democracy, the House of Representatives, the Senate, and the Presidency. One has to ask when are the full equal rights of *all women* going to be legally recognized on a par with those of men and complied with by every governmental agency?

Majoritarianism can be unintentionally blind, but it can also be an *intentional* form of discrimination, exclusive and unfair, harassment, even hateful, in different varieties. The most obvious form of *sexual* majoritarianism is not only sexual discrimination in favor of males, but also a majoritarian sexual discrimination against all forms of nonheterosexual identity, behavior, and relationships. Recent polls and studies by universities and media companies show how deeply this affects the LGBTQ community nationwide, eliciting a feeling of being thought of as a less than full citizen, as a realistic object of discrimination, which has lasting effects upon people's sense of self-worth, creating depression and agitating even thoughts of self-harm or suicide.

Further, the majoritarianism of an ethnic or *racial* group and of a *religious* group is as sinister in effect on the unity of a nation, even if the right to vote in the United States came to freed black slaves before any women received it. These sexual, ethnic, or racial identities and religious identities become so taken for granted in people's self-consciousness that some never conceive of anything being unfair as regards to what they want or expect for themselves as part of a majority, benefits that they are not concerned about securing for those *outside their majority*.[21] Are they oblivious to the fact that the minorities do not have those benefits, or is it only a form of denial or even pure selfishness? These three forms of majoritarianism—*sexual, racial or ethnic, and religious*—have plagued the social cohesion of the United States from its very beginnings or discovery by European explorers in the fifteenth century. After many centuries, they still exist, sometimes in strident, militant form, xenophobic, or even fraudulent forms in which members of a *majority pose* to be the victims rather than the victimizer as they persecute the "others," or as they demonstrate with their torches in a march at night, singing "Jews will not replace us!"—to which the president claimed there were good people on both sides.

Or the "majoritarianism" is seen not in a sheer number of extremely wealthy people which is less than 5% of the citizens, but in the power of their *accumulated wealth* which is itself a "majority" that controls public policy. So we see people advocating in even seemingly serious compassionate roles for a minimum wage of $15 per hour ($30,000 a year) while others object that it would wreck our economy. Recently in late 2020, some politicians became so courageous as to suggest a very generous minimum salary of $60,000 per year for public school teachers, while they themselves receive $180,000 to multiple millions per year. Many fail to see how ludicrous and utterly condescending that kind of "generosity" seems, or else they simply have become accustomed to having the advantages of an irrational system's salaries, commissions, bonuses, calculated, defined, and legalized by those on top of the pile whose justification, similar to the subterfuges Niebuhr saw people giving to justify racism, is that they who presently receive greater benefits evidently *deserve* it because they are among the few in the nation able to do the work, smart enough to do the work, respected enough to do the work, moral enough to do the work, or have sufficient connections with other wealthy people to do the work,[22] which all comes down to pure subterfuges from those *never* willing to see themselves behind a hypothetical veil of ignorance from which to decide on the basic principles of *justice* for the nation. Compassion and empathy and philanthropy will never cure this tunnel vision of the irrationally privileged who cannot for a second see themselves behind Rawls's "veil of ignorance." Often the tunnel gets more restricted with more privileges until one cannot identify in any way with other people because one is so used to being the sole focus of one's concern. That is not E Pluribus Unum, not even a game of Monopoly, but simply a self-manipulated and self-deceitful game of Solitaire.

This is the difference between an ethic which has as its base a principle of profit and economic growth and one that has as its base the common "will-to-live," a difference which allows those privileged by happenstance to speak against "entitlements" as if it were simply "transfers" from *their* private coffers rather than government programs requiring future recipients to pay from *their own* salaries over a lifetime *in advance*. The same mentality opposes single-payer health care systems even if it means half the citizens have no health insurance. Or they hide their corporate profits or keep things "off-shore" to avoid having to pay their fair share of taxes, and they even lobby for special benefits for themselves under the guise of a "tax break" for the "middle class" which actually *never* "trickles down."

Citizens' universal *rights* in some other advanced countries include universal single-payer health care, university education, adequate housing, livable salaries, and fulfilling work,[23] nearly all of which are conducive to the interests/identities we listed, by the way in which they are necessary to human life in general. Yet they are viewed by many people in the United States as unrealistic or far beyond the scope or interest of the U.S. system or possibilities. Better that each person learn to pull oneself up by one's own bootstraps—but what if one has no boots? Opponents label it "transfer payments," "socialism," "Communism," from their ideological embrace of "capitalism," which Andersen correctly assesses, is itself in actual practice far from free, fair, or even honest.[24] To determine whether a proposed benefit is a national interest, something needed by all vis-à-vis only an interest of smaller groups or a few individuals requires *honest scrutiny*. "Social security" is a program of forced savings by all citizens so they would have their needs met when they retired, no more irrational than cities taxing everyone so they have fire and police protection. But derogatory words such as "transfer payments" or "entitlements" are used by some with regard to Social Security, yet never are applied to the fire protection. Is it only because the taxes for fire protection go to a city or county to use to secure its protection, but the Social Security payments go directly to the individuals since they know best how to divide their income to pay their bills for the necessities?

Is it possible that the objections to a paid university education, or a single-payer government health plan for all, adequate housing, livable salaries, and fulfilling work come from just a small number of citizens who have themselves benefited from all those things without realizing the racial, sexual, and economic factors in their backgrounds which presented opportunities to them that put these goals *in reach* through their hard work and without realizing that millions and millions of their fellow citizens *lacked* even these backgrounds or irrational or accidental factors, which meant the same goals remained forever *totally out of reach for them*?

The U.S. culture, since the nineteenth century, has perpetuated the myth of self-sufficiency, first through its self-help "Luke Larkin" novels, in which there is only a minimal reference to a bit of "luck" in his becoming so successful. In many if not most cases in real life, were there not happenstance occasions, accidents, or unanticipated circumstances that occurred which actually made possible the opportunities for many people to attain adequate education to find fulfilling work that paid a living wage and provided health care, salaries sufficient enough that one could have some decent choice in housing, and hopefully accumulate enough to enable their own children also to obtain the necessary education to pursue the "American dream"? But many of us fail to see the pure accidents, the incidental connections with people who later offer us a chance to improve our situation. We find it easy to take credit for most fortunate accidents, to feel we have earned it all.

So there is a negative effect of "majoritarianism" *both* in sheer wealth and in sheer body count, not to mention by the status of those federal legislators, whose separation and even isolation from the marginalized is exacerbated by campaign contributions and powerful corporate lobbies. Of course, federal legislators claim to know the plight of the masses of homeless, starving, impoverished, but likely not 10% of these legislators have any close friends or relatives in those circumstances. They simply learn how to talk to get elected. Has the nation not had enough of this, with all the fabricated promises that turned out to be mere lies? But now the Covid-19 has shown the white majoritarianism particularly in the disproportionate deaths of racial minorities whose susceptibility to the disease and its very serious effects are only recently in early 2021 being recognized, much of which goes back to the xenophobic treatment of racial minorities throughout our history, placing those nonwhites in greater jeopardy by *in*equalities of opportunity, education, and basic economic goods, even food and drinking water.

Just prior to the turn of the millennium, renowned cultural historian, Jacques Barzun, at the end of his massive work tracing this history of the West for the past 500 years, predicted a future, *looking back from the year 2300*. It revealed a return of Dark Ages, in which most people would be illiterate or uneducated since education was narrowly dictated by the corporations, confined only to the subjects thought necessary to the corporations, largely mathematical and cyber expertise with some scientific knowledge. Elections and governments were no longer necessary, as the corporations ran the world, and all knowledge of past cultures was forgotten. He was optimistic enough, however, to see that over *three centuries*, the boredom of each group might finally be broken through by the inquisitiveness of a few people who discover cultural artifacts from the past, and find them meaningful, an enthusiasm which finally spreads and creates a renascence, an interest in living again.[25] The prospects of such a dark period of only the primary interests of the corporate world are also a rather terrifying majoritarian prospect.

Fortunately, the real wealth of any nation is not its GDP or its stock market, but *its different people*, their loyalty and commitment to a democratic republic, and the totality of their blended cultures into one of united pride. In this terrible Covid-19 pandemic, the U.S. death count as of April 2021 is approaching 600,000 of our citizens. Despite this, we have even occasionally heard a few political servants speak of sizeable losses of life as acceptable, or they have lied to minimize the seriousness of it, as if that is necessary to get the economy going again, as if the efficiently working economy is the greatest interest or value of the nation, and human lives rank behind it. Yet the nation is beginning to understand its *real interests and deeper wealth*, its *people and their will-to-live*, and no amount of diversion by certain individual's narcissistic interests, or small group narrow interests can be allowed to eclipse or dictate to the interests of the people as a whole.

In Rawls's schema, the diversity of the people is important and acceptable so long as all discussions of policy utilize public reason and all citizens strictly comply with the basic principles of justice of the "original position." A democracy which is really of, by, and for the whole people will prevent its culture from turning into a warring tribalism and will expect its state and federal representatives to express the diverse interests of the whole, reasonably discuss the nation's goals, policies, problems, and proper methods of reaching those commonly desired goals without resorting to obstruction and noncooperation with each other. The partisan politics' present hold is one of the most disastrously lethal forms of majoritarianism, and if it is not transcended, Barzun's predicted return of some Dark Ages is inevitable. There can be no United States without a very deep mutual respect, honesty, and trust since we *profess* to tolerate and *embrace significant differences* within our unity. That's the *sharing* "democracy" implies.

But a "unity" is a uniting of differences, and when the differences are not adequately represented, both differences as well as a sense of unity are lost. The present Supreme Court is almost completely monolithic in its sexual, racial, and ethnic makeup, and even more so by the religious affiliation of its members. The *only way* beyond this becoming an objectionable majoritarianism is for *all citizens, including Justices* to move beyond their "vested" and often irrational and inherited advantages and backgrounds through a hypothesizing such as Rawls advocated. If Madison, Jefferson, and other Framers of the Constitution could do this, surely the Court today can realize the necessity of this kind of separation from the "happenstance" elements of the uniqueness of each member's life in order to engage truly in impartial justice.

Recent Majoritarian Reversals in Religious Adjudication

We will see that the three obvious majorities that arrived on our shores with the European immigrants were racial, sexual, and religion—white, male, and Christian. Over the years, gradually the equality mentioned in the Declaration of Independence and recited as the mainstay of the "lively experiment" of this democratic republic has become somewhat more of a reality. But just as Erika Lee noted that the xenophobia in the United States has been here since colonial days, shifting from group to group that the citizens feared, so is still with us,[26] so the majoritarianism has not disappeared from our laws and attitudes but seems to be reversing the gains the nation had made in past decades.

We shall see that even the nation's interest in a "separation" of religion and state which was envisioned by Jefferson, Madison, and so many others, even church leaders, such as Isaac Backus—a "separation" which began even prior to the Constitution as colonies began to disestablish their religions when their theocratic attempts began to produce too much religious hostility as they had in Europe from which their immigrant ancestors fled. We will see how "majoritarianism" crept back into the scene both by the conscious creation of a myth of the nation's religious founding in different stages and by the Court's reversal of its direction beginning in the last of the twentieth century. It changed its standard test for the "Free Exercise" clause in cases involving the Native Americans' religion in *Lyng* and *Smith*, but then Congress intervened, attempting to restore the earlier tests the Court had articulated in 1940 and observed up until *Lyng* and *Smith*, but after the Court overruled the Congress's formulation, Congress revised its tests. By the *Hobby Lobby* case a few years later, "Free Exercise" was opened up by the Court to include legal protection even for for-profit corporations' "religious belief," even though "Free Exercise" as originally conceived was only freedom to *worship* as one pleases, if at all. But what would be the purpose in expanding "religious worship" to include every aspect of selling crafts or wood products? It came at a terrible cost to the "least advantaged," that is, those very people whom Rawls said should make the assessment of a law in situations of inequality.

The "Establishment" clause went through a similar development from its "incorporation" into state law in 1947 in *Everson*. There, the Court exalted the Framer's idea of the "separation" of government and religion, but, as we will see, thought their majoritarian decision was not a violation of that principle of separation even though it provided public taxes only to Christian parochial schools but *not* to other private schools. Many different issues of government involvement in, aid to, and endorsement of religion arose in the following decades, and in 1971, the Court defined in *Lemon* a three-pronged test for constitutionality under the Establishment clause. By 1983, it defied the standard it had created in *Lemon*, temporarily substituting a "historical" longevity test of Christian prayer in legislature, which was a clear violation of *Lemon*, so created significant tension. The "historical" test was used ambiguously on different occasions thereafter with confusion of what exact history was at issue. In the 1990s and subsequently, the Establishment criteria remained split because the Court had decided on so many different types of aid to parochial schools and different forms of people attempting to get religion into the public schools. By *Aguilar v. Felton*, new criteria were established, and by *Mitchell v. Helms*, 530 U.S. 793 (2000), the Court was holding that the proper criteria were only private choice and neutrality, with the parochial schools' indoctrinating purposes and the divertibility of government funds neither one as any longer a relevant consideration. By 2020, the

Court had decided that individual's religious choice or religious institutions' interests should be able to trump government standards for employment or health protection, even during a pandemic. The biggest problem for the Court was its involvement in religious disputes. We shall see that the Framers conceived of civil government having no "cognizance" or jurisdiction of religion, so should be involved with religious people only on the same level as with all other people, only with the generally applicable or universal laws all citizens agreed to.

Recent Reversals in Laws by Racial or Sexual Majoritarianism

The majoritarianism that spawns religious discrimination has a certain parallel with majoritarianism that has prompted racial and sexual discrimination in the past four decades, stagnating and even reversing the advances made in civil rights during the 1960s and 1970s in a number of ways. These more recent Court decisions and statutory laws developed in many cases from a fear of the other, a form of xenophobia, just as it did on some religious decisions made by the Court. Much of this innate bias originated from a lack of accurate knowledge or personal acquaintance of that "other." The lack of familiarity with the other, and subsequently of an unrecognized fear of the other (which is what xenophobia is), was due to years and even centuries of a culture's ingraining its people with their superiority, whether it was a religious, racial or sexual superiority.

An unrecognized majoritarianism operated in the increasingly conservative approach to criminal procedure in the United States. Similar to the other areas we mentioned above, in the mid-twentieth century the sense of unity within the nation influenced the Warren Court (1953–1969) to make real the liberty that was embedded in the Sixth Amendment, assuring that those indicted had counsel, in *Gideon v. Wainwright*, 372 U.S. 335 (1963). This was shortly thereafter followed by a Court ruling that suspects being arrested were to be immediately apprised of their rights to an attorney and that anything they said could be held against them, in *Miranda v. Arizona*, 384 U.S. 436 (1966). But *Terry v. Ohio* (1968) dropped the "probable cause" required for the right to stop and frisk to a mere "reasonable suspicion" that the suspect was either armed or had committed a felony. The United States's "war on drugs" began a rollback of former protections of citizens after *Terry*.

The famous "exclusionary" rule in criminal procedure was created in *Weeks v. U.S.*, 232 U.S. 383 (1914), allowing the suppression of evidence against a suspect if police had themselves broken the law to obtain the evidence. After C.J. Burger succeeded C.J. Earl Warren, the drug trafficking alarmed authorities, and overexuberant police were violating all kinds of rights of the Fourth Amendment to try to arrest guilty people. Burger summed up the problem saying the "exclusionary rule" had too high a cost for the slim benefit, in many cases, by a slight oversight of the local magistrate, the "guilty" go free. But how were they legally guilty without being judged, and how were they judged without the evidence of a crime. So he set in motion to *dismantle* the exclusionary rule, seeing it a judicial remedy which was ill conceived and was only intended to deter, but failed to do that. The exclusionary rule has largely been nullified by more qualifications and by *disclosures* of the evidence even to the grand jury. But was C.J. Burger saying that he could tell the guilty by the evidence illegally taken by the police, so it should be allowed, no matter how it destroys the public's respect for the law?

Finally, by the end of the century, in March 1994, the infamous "Three Strikes Law" had been codified in federal law, 18 U.S.C. §3559(c) A life sentence was probable for a person guilty of a serious, violent felony if he or she had been convicted two or more previous times, at least one of which involved a serious violent felony. Six months later, on September 7, 1994, the Violent Crime Control and Law Enforcement Act, 42 U.S.C. ch. 136 was signed. The "Terry" stop had made reasonable suspicion the standard, but now the suspicion was not simply that the person had or was about to commit a felony but even merely a statutory *misdemeanor*. On these changes or other provisions, between 2003 and 2013, New York City police stopped more than 100,000 persons each year, 90% of whom were either African American or Latino, and a great majority were found *not guilty* of anything.

One's "reasonable suspicion" allowed not only the stop and questions but even frisking if the officer felt the person might have a weapon. But racial profiling became rampant in many states, utilized to the fullest by local sheriffs such as in AZ, and the Rodney King incident in LA revealed a new police brutality. For those who have seen news videos in 2020 of police stops and treatments, one can see the reasonableness of the fear of the person being stopped, especially if he or she is a racial minority. If the policy has finally been scrubbed, the majoritarian tactics of intimidating and inflicting unjustified violence on minority suspects has *not* abated.

This would have horrified John Rawls who was trying to base the nation's laws on an ethic that was *fair to all*, giving no one an advantage over others, unless it was agreed to by all in principle within the basic principles of justice of the "original position." No one behind Rawls's veil of ignorance would have agreed to these measures since he might find himself in the racial minority and the one arrested and mistreated by police, even murdered by the police.

A similar attempted reversal continues to focus on several areas of human sexuality. The opposition to the abortion rights made legal under *Roe v. Wade* in 1973 was born as a form of majoritarianism in evangelical Christians preaching, protests, and attempts to overturn *Roe* by placing antiabortion judges and Justices on the bench. In 1993, the movement was partially successful through *Planned Parenthood v. Casey*, under the Rehnquist Court in a 7/2 decision. Though it still allowed abortion, it eliminated its trimester criteria in favor of the viability test and *lessened* the standard of scrutiny required. No decision since 1973 has received such organized opposition as *Roe v. Wade*, especially from certain religious groups for which it became many of the believers' primary reason for belonging to the religion. Yet by far the majority of women in the nation have desired to keep *Roe v. Wade* in place, even into 2021.

That means the attempts to overrule *Roe* have been a "majoritarian" pursuit, not that of the actual majority, but of other lesser groups whose interests conflict with the interests of the real majority of the citizens, the nation as a whole. By preaching against abortion in these conservative Christian churches, and by organizing demonstrations, electing officials to office who oppose abortion, the issue has split the nation almost as much as the racial splits.

The issue has become so emotionally charged over the years that open discussion or analysis from public reason of the pros and cons of abortion, how it relates to the basic ethic of the "will-to-live" which includes mutual autonomy, honesty, trust, and transparency, has been virtually lacking. Mythical or supranatural sources are utilized by some to suppress any opposition, without even exploring other ways to prevent birth by preventing conception, but those mythical religious sources, as we will later show, are not addressing abortion at all. The same religious fight has been directed at "same-sex marriage,"[27] despite the fact that the Court did approve of this, though ancient traditions continue to spawn a feeling of certain religious peoples' holding on to the Absolute because they have immunized themselves against public reason by the value they have given to "faith."

Finally, it is not a coincidence that these "reversals" of equality that have occurred in the areas of racial, sexual, and religious spheres would be accompanied by a reversal of the sense of equality required of a democracy even in the economic realm of American life. Kurt Andersen's *Evil Geniuses*[28] documents how the past half-century has seen a conscious abandonment of the earlier democratic egalitarian goals. They were *consciously superseded* by an oversimplified picture of some ideal of the past, creating nostalgia, deregulation, and a wholesale paradigm shift in the economic structures and their laws or even the social contract, and leaving in their wake a country with a terrible gap between the poor and rich, more than ever before. In Andersen's discussion of "Greed," he mentions Rawls's "thought experiment" of his "veil of ignorance," which he calls the "best test of a morally legitimate social contract." He mentions one's "ignorance" of one's race, gender, education, wealth, and so on and poignantly asks "Would you agree to sign your country's social contract and take your chances for better or worse in the social and political and economic system it governs?"[29] Of course, Rawls was asking a slightly different question, a bit more optimistic, since he assumed that everyone born into the nation would desire that the nation continue, that its democratic republic thrive. If justice can be detected only from behind such a "veil of ignorance," the question Rawls said one would ask is, what basic ethical principles would you finally agree to with all the others in order to ground the nation's laws? While Andersen's analysis of the change which came in people's idea of what kind of social contract they had with each other is bitingly perceptive, the shift was obviously a form of what we have been discussing here, of a "majoritarianism" which would have greatly disturbed not only Rawls but Madison, Jefferson, and other Framers of the Constitution.[30] Andersen thought many people in the 80s were still carrying with them a simplistic vision of economic equality for the citizens in some way, whereas, by the paradigm shift that was occurring during those years, it was like someone in a casino still dreaming that he splits the winnings with the house when it has actually turned into a zero-sum game.[31] That is apropos to the unrealistic attitude of the few small religious groups that get the court to approve of some token aid to them, when, compared to the taxes approved for certain other Christian groups, really make it almost a zero-sum game as well.

Majoritarianism of Religion and Immigration in the World's Two Largest Democracies

In recent years, the majoritarian religion in the world's two largest democracies, the federal administrations of India and the United States, have become more outspoken against nonreligious elements in the society as well as religious groups that they view as being too different. The Hindutva movement in India, sponsored by various groups including the BJP, has emphasized the Hindu tradition as the *proper identity* of citizens of India, though allegedly it can include also those of other religions which *originated* in India such as the Jain, Sikh, and Buddhist religions, but not imported religions. It has become nationalistic, and in some critics' eyes, fascist, in its treatment of people it judges as outsiders. To a degree, of course, Hinduism, as a religion, always had an immigrant ethnic and geographic element intertwined with its cultic practices and its theoretical and practical reason, even within the very name which points to the Indus River and the northern region of India, which is pretty similar to the immigrants conquering "America."

What is interesting to the outside observer is the fact that the religion of one group of immigrants, the Aryans, who invaded India in the mid-second millennium BCE, and no other immigrants have been selectively preferred by this movement. It is *as if they* were always the local or *native* people in the country or as if all other immigrant or imported religions are simply illegitimate *per se*. It is said that when Jawaharlal Nehru was asked what had been his greatest difficulty since Independence, he first replied, "Creating a just state by just means," but then following it with "Perhaps, too, creating a secular State in a religious country."[32]

That arbitrary distinction of one immigrant group's religion being the accepted one, thereby promoting a negative attitude toward all other religions, was manifest also from the earlier colonial days of the new colonies which later came to be the United States. The people who were already in the land and had been for perhaps 10,000 years were simply not counted by these European immigrants. Nor were the hundreds of thousands of African slaves these immigrants brought or bought to do their farming. The measure of being human was a combination of skin color and particular culture, and the local Native Americans or "First People" and imported Africans simply did not qualify. This was "white supremacy," combined with a sense of European cultural supremacy, not merely a scouting around for cheap labor.

The same irrational division between different immigrants occurred in the United States over and over, moving from one group to another in a xenophobic manner, and eventually the white people opposing the immigrants even spoke of themselves as the "native" people, although even their forebears were immigrants from Europe. The same xenophobic attitude was explicitly articulated by a U.S. president when he attempted to ban all Muslims from entering the United States almost immediately after he took office in the early part of 2017. Many Western countries already had considerable populations of Muslims, but the twenty-first-century wars the United States began in the Middle East spawned an extremist group, the ISIS, which graphically terrorized innocent populations, creating problems in various countries around the world in which Muslims were already residents and citizens. This especially raised the fear of letting in some active ISIS members, so the ban was proposed to keep all Muslims out.

The attempted proposed ban was originally ruled illegal because of its obvious overbreadth and its religious purpose.[33] But the irrational majoritarianism continued as the president later turned a blind-eye on the Charlottesville march by the neo-Nazis and other White Supremacists, in which one young woman was killed by a driver of a car. Even from the beginning of the Trump administration, it tried to prevent any immigrants coming from Central America or Mexico, no matter the talents they were bringing with them, or their dire needs for shelter and food, or even their willingness to work. They were seeking asylum, but found only hostility, even a separation of small children from their parents as an inhumane disincentive, which was largely *racial* majoritarianism and xenophobia, although xenophobia in U.S. history also often combined with a religious prejudice to give it a superpotency.

In these two examples in India and the United States, both political leaders and their parties seemed intent to consolidate power, if not claim sole power in their state, and place bans against competing religious or ethnic groups. In neither case was the whole episode due to the leaders or political parties being devotedly religious or actively belonging to the majority religion, nor just to their desire for violence. But they were catering to the most fundamentalist sects of both majority religions in order to personally obtain their votes, votes to exclude others who differ significantly. That is the unacknowledged majoritarian superiority felt by many people in various countries, which kills their incentive for equality of liberty or equality of opportunity for others.

This reveals that there is a problem even in, if not especially in, *religiously pluralistic democracies*, because of their presupposition of *including* variety and significant difference. Has it become simply a grudging or resentful acceptance of a fact which the majority would still like to change if possible? The problem will persist unless people can accept the fact that the ethical grounding of civil law by *any religion* is itself *divisive* in a religiously pluralistic society so can*not* be the obvious ethical ground of the alleged "democratic" government, unless they intend to force those outside that religion to knuckle under and conform or get out of the country. In other words, the attitude becoming continually more explicit is *intolerance of religious difference*, but ironically within a state designating itself "democratic" or of a tolerant posture, which becomes an oxymoron and hypocrisy.

Justice Jackson: "Beyond the Reach of Majorities"

When a particular religious group dominates the Court, "political justice" is more susceptible to being ignored or dictated by that religious association whose interests are *not inclusive* as are the interests and responsibilities of the structures of political justice. The confidence the Framers of the Constitution had in the Supreme Court's neutrality which to them justified a lifetime appointment is found also in Rawls's estimate of the Court. But what needs to be considered is what avenues exist to shield the system of justice if positions on the bench become completely partisan politicized, which they presently have. Rawls insisted that the Court stands as the exemplar of public reason, though it has not always made decisions consistent with that posture.[34] On those occasions, the ultimate decisions regarding the nation's laws have no checks or balance since the positions are *not* subject to the *vote by the people as a whole*, and some groups and individuals seem to view that as the real battleground, the agenda they have to control, without realizing such is a violation of the basic rule of law which saw the democracy as *not* a uniformity by a special majority dictating to others, but controlled more directly by the *diverse people as a whole* and its basic principles and Constitution. The courts, especially, were never intended to become vehicles of partisan politics, never promoting a majoritarianism, but neutral, blind, and fair in their administering of justice.

In Rawls's theory of justice as fairness, and his opposition to majoritarianism, he insisted that in many cases it needed to be offset, for example, by requiring a "super-majority" to pass laws, or other methods of diluting the power of a bare majority.[35] The *basic principles* which he speculated would be beneficial to all people behind the "veil of ignorance" and therefore voluntarily agreed on would have to be general enough to elicit a *unanimous* approval, *not* simply a *majority*. This is the reason Justice Jackson could write for the Court in 1943 in *West Virginia v. Barnette*, the freedoms of the Constitution and Bill of Rights place those rights of life, liberty, property, free speech, free press, freedom of worship and assembly, and other rights "beyond the reach of majorities" and they may "not be submitted to vote; they depend on the outcome of no elections."[36] "Beyond the reach of majorities" describes not simply Rawls's insights but those of Madison. Justice Jackson insisted, "freedom to differ is not limited to things that do not matter much. That would be a mere shadow of freedom. The test of its substance is the right to differ as to things that touch the heart of the existing order."[37]

Those basics comprise some of the foundation for the unity all citizens agree to live by. But the question then remains of how extensive or what particular actions would these differences include to be protected, or at what point would the government have to step in to stop a certain behavior if these rights are not otherwise limited? To Rawls, every issue comes back to the "original position" and "veil of ignorance," to the basic principles of justice by which all agreed to live. The answer to that question was given in the same way with different words originally by Thomas Jefferson, when he wrote in his "Bill for Establishing Religious Freedom" (1779), "to suffer the civil Magistrate to intrude his powers into the field of opinion, to restrain the profession or propagation of principles on supposition of their ill tendency, is a dangerous fallacy, which at once destroys all religious liberty . . . it is time enough for the rightful purposes of civil government for its officers to interfere when principles break out into overt acts against peace and good order."[38] That generality of the obligation of all citizens to follow the basic principles agreed on itself is the only guarantee of the peace and good order of the nation, the only guarantee of the very freedoms to which people want to appeal, so those basic principles have *priority*.

The primary issue of "reconciling" what I have called "opposites" was the basic question Rawls framed in different ways over and over, for example, as the "problem of political liberalism": "How is it possible that there may exist over time a stable and just society of free and equal citizens profoundly divided by reasonable though incompatible religious, philosophical and moral doctrines?" Put another way: "How is it possible that deeply opposed though reasonable comprehensive doctrines may live together and all affirm the political conception of a constitutional regime?"[39] The answer may be that one's particular religion is only one of many elements in one's identity, so easily takes a "back seat" to other concerns unless certain issues bring it to the front, and, even then it occupies one's conscious concern only to the degree that the particular issue does, but otherwise is given little thought. This was what Richard L. Rubenstein suggested is part of the solution to competing religious and ethical views especially in the U.S. culture.[40] In the more comprehensive schema, it may be, as the Dalai Lama suggested, that only about one-sixth of the world population is actively involved in their particular religions.

More Than One Perspective and Ethic, But Only One Nation

The idea of Rubenstein's may explain much: that people in the United States have many different elements comprising their identities which tend to minimize the possibility of a person overruling all other interests except her religious identity. It is somewhat analogous to having more than one set of clothes or tools, different ones for different jobs. In ethics, it is different sets for different constituencies, scopes, and comportments, which we mentioned. The problem is not simply that the two sides of the picture are each dominated strictly by principles violating the other, for example, that when one's religious view prohibits murder, the political system does permit it, or where one's comprehensive ethical schema demands honesty, the principles of the political system do not. It is not even as simple as saying that one's religious or ethical comprehensive doctrine forbids equality, whereas the political sense of justice demands equality, though that may be getting closer to the problem of their differences. Many elements are similar in any comparison, but (1) the people's inclusion within each is quite different, one into which the person is born, the other as an option to join or not; (2) the willingness to cooperate in reaching a compatible compromise is missing in the comprehensive doctrine of associations, especially the more they emphasize their authority; and (3) the authority of the two are radically different since the political conception of justice assumes the overlapping consensus of "freestanding" principles built on "public reason" which provides an *agreement* which itself is the extent of the authority, whereas religious comprehensive schemas often insist on authority derived not only from antiquity but from a divine source, far beyond the existing world and not subject to human reason.

The problem for the most part boils down to the *willingness or unwillingness* of parties to recognize the different sets of ethical principles involved
in the two different spheres, their differences, as I suggested, in constituencies, scope, and comportment, or their insistence of wanting to dictate their
religion's or association's position to the nation as a whole, even when they
know their religion and its metaphysics is *not* embraced by *all* citizens.
The First Amendment to the U.S. Constitution has two clauses, as it reads,
"Congress shall make no law respecting an establishment of religion, or
prohibiting the free exercise thereof." In religious circles, this disposition of
wanting to shape public policy from one's narrow religious views is found
among those who belong only to the denominations and sects of the majority
religion, seldom among a minority unless their freedom of worship has been
terribly infringed by the government. The religious majority, although not a
majority of citizens of the nation, presses the government to overturn many of
its laws or make new laws built upon its specific religious convictions which
are not a part of public reason and not open to negotiation but presented as
absolute. Or it takes the form of religious people pressing the government to
officially recognize their religion as *the religion* of the country, to establish
monuments on public or government property that are religiously specific in
their favor, to fund their religious schools with public taxes to teach their religious doctrine, to place the prayers of the majority religion within the public
school classrooms, and to avoid teaching things such as evolution which they
feel contradict the Bible.

This was what Madison feared, even though he belonged to the Anglican
Church in Virginia, when he viewed how its members and the institution
itself persecuted the Baptists but especially the Quakers in Virginia,[41] and he
worried not about a majority in the branches of government overpowering
the minority, because these were cumulative to represent all the varied interests of the whole population, but he worried about more localized social and
cultural majorities within the population,[42] which, when addressing religion
pointed to the possibility that a religious majority which could be spawned
not only by sheer number of members, but even by the aggregation of financial resources over the years, that the religion accumulation of assets would
exert themselves as financial power to pressure to shape laws conducive only
to its narrow interests.[43] He was fully aware of the history of the Anglican
form of Christendom, in which the merging of government and religion was
as detrimental as the earlier Catholic system which the Anglican Church
superseded in its more limited, national sphere.

A "democracy" (Greek: demos = "people") does not presuppose a nation
of clones, but of a *diverse* people, and further, that the diverse people rule,
thereby implying tolerance of differences, a form of "liberalism" by which
significant reasonable differences among the ways the "people" reasonably

conceive of ideas and enjoy their freedoms are *accepted* as *normal* rather than aberrational because they have *all agreed* to a prior and *more general ethical base* for their legal system of justice, one that guarantees their unity while providing them great personal freedoms. The slogan on U.S. currency reads, "E Pluribus Unum," but does not mean that any single individual is what the many should be. The "Unum" is a unity of diversity, not a uniformity eliminating difference. There are many problems of *un*recognized majoritarianism, but a recognized majoritarianism is simply a blatant violation of the most basic law in a democracy. The many different forms of majoritarianism in the United States raise the question about whether the nation really can be called a democracy.

THE PROBLEM OF RELIGIONS' ABSOLUTE ETHICS IN A DEMOCRACY

Since our concern here is primarily with the relation of religions to government, the other element we must open up is the *absolutism* of one's religion. It is detrimental to the sense of unity within a nation that embodies a religious pluralism and is even a more relevant argument against any religion dictating the ethical ground for a democracy's laws and structures of justice. Religious absolutism destroys autonomy and critical thinking. It has a long history of defying scientific discoveries, with excommunication and even death for the scientists. As a part of this absolutism, religious people have been indoctrinated to believe that only the religion they belong to is true and all others are false, that religious truth has priority over *any* truths coming from human reason, and only people who have the same faith as they can even be considered moral or ethical people. They often cite passages indicating that no good deed can come from a bad person just as no good fruit can be found on a bad tree.

This defensive posture provides the religious with little or no interest in even familiarizing themselves with what these other religious groups profess to believe, even when religious pluralism exists next door to them. Finally, they often have been taught that the religion they embrace has *never* really changed, or, the alternative, that even if it has changed, the particular group to which *they* belong *reformed or restored* the original or true form so overcame that apostasy or mistaken change the religion once suffered. This is true of nearly all the major religions in their competitive claims between their various sects, even if it requires manipulating historical facts or simply passing over uncomfortable aspects. One can nearly always find that one's ancestors or predecessors were responsible for all the good in the world and for none of its evils, if one just looks hard enough at a select group of data. Most of us know very little of our ancestors, yet we are pretty sure there were no horse thieves in the bunch.

Over the years, different individuals and diverse religious groups such as the Parliament of World Religions have attempted, in the spirit of ecumenism rather than absolutism or majoritarianism, to find ethical principles that the various religions have in *common*, so to be able to suggest or even demand a common "global ethic."[44] As commendable as the work and intention is, in the process, they have realized their inability to be really inclusive and satisfy all the different religions' unique and central claims, most important issues and interests. Their pronouncements remain basically ineffective because they are known only among small groups and totally unknown by the majority of the world's population. The group's very claims to antiquity are appealed to as a major factor of what gives them *authority*[45] in suggesting a global ethic, even though that very antiquity and exclusiveness disqualifies much of the content from even being adaptable by or relevant to a general public today, especially to people unaffiliated with any religion or those who regard the undertaking as an unjustified compromise of their religion.

If one were dealing with an actual theocracy for a civil government, that might be quite different. Yet the world is not a unity espousing a single god, one specific religion, or even a unanimous ethic. Most nations now have a religious pluralism within their borders, like it or not, even if they make it illegal. Iran's theocracy is basically a coerced citizenry which does not have sufficient freedom or power to rid itself of the theocratic machinery. Even to use a word such as "theocracy" is language totally foreign to the scientific world in which we live, and "science" or "technology" is not to blame, since these areas of exploration seem as natural to the human psyche as the continual quest for values and meaning. Humans are inquisitive, valuing, and social creatures who thrive off both stability as well as change. Since the majoritarian religions of most countries are so tied to their contingent identities (thought of as eternal), there is no possibility of the pursuit of a voluntary global unity accomplishing anything until people explore the necessary changes and awareness that would be required for any *universal agreement*, notwithstanding their *professed* democratic form of tolerance of the different.

In fact, history suggests that there is reason to believe that if the world or even any nation *did or does* try to embrace a *single religion*, it will be inherently divisive since it is by nature *exclusive* in its claims and demands for *uniformity*, and would become an oppressive, authoritarian, or coercive power with a dehumanizing prospect by its heteronomy since it would be built totally on a religious Absolute which *eliminates human autonomy* for most of the citizens. Even the present rigidity and exclusiveness of many very conservative sects of various religious groups is so strident that it is still very common to hear their leaders insisting that one cannot be moral or ethical unless one belongs to that specific religious group. Some even push Christianity's *otherworldliness* or idea of justification so far as to say that ethics really does not even matter since one cannot "save" oneself by trying to be a "good" person. Nothing kills one's ethical impulse as much as such ungrounded loyalty to a single ancient tradition. And ISIS used an otherworldliness of the promise of Paradise to talk young teenagers into becoming self-annihilating bombs in markets, schools, hospitals, and the like, thinking they will be rewarded for defending Allah or God.[46] Fortunately, the Dalai Lama, in his *Ethics for a New Millennium*, said he no longer considers it very important that people belong to any religion, that what is more important is precisely that they be *good persons*.[47] He thought that was within human power.

Nothing discredits humanity or even a specific religion more than to utter such exclusivistic and amoral words that one cannot "save" oneself by trying to be a "good" person, even if the speaker thinks they are based on the truth of *simul justus et peccator*.[48] I have elsewhere analyzed the problems the absolutizing has posed to religions, not only in dogma that impugns one's basic decency and reason by segregating humanity between the "believers" and "infidels" or the "good" and the "bad," or by impugning human wisdom, but also by basing its ethical claims on conflated historical-mythical ideas which leading theologians of the last three centuries have for the most part either abandoned or tried to redefine into a more "corroborating" form of reason or ecstasy, but to no avail.[49] Religion remains still attached to its absolutes, its exclusive symbols, whether an empty circle, a cross, a star, or other, or a particular "historical" figure, as well as to the metaphysics supporting it, a metaphysics which has been left behind by the human sciences since the eighteenth century as Foucault and others have documented, which *dissolves the base* of the religion's ethics, leaving it hanging in space, ungrounded.

While most people see the rigidity and exclusiveness in religions other than their own, it takes more courage to admit that their own religious group is basically closed to questioning its central mythical, supranatural ethical ideas. As the Dalai Lama pointed out, the reason an ethic of any particular religion can*not* be the ethic for humanity or a global ethic is because of these basic differences and conflicting absolutes. Any attempt to decide on "which" religion's ethics should be the base for civil justice would simply *never be resolved*.[50]

So the answer for a global or even national unity cannot be a matter of forcing a single religion's ethics on everyone, nor can it be a mere agreement of only a handful of ethical ideas such as prohibiting stealing and murder, since even these, when a part of a religion's ethic or law code, are grounded on the unique mythical claims. Those well-meaning Christians who have insisted on erecting monuments of the Ten Commandments on government property in the United States[51] are a prime example of the futility of the latter since only

5 of the 10 are ethical demands, only four of which could be turned into law, and the rest root their validity in one particular ancient religion, one particular god, Yhwh,[52] and one specific "chosen" people of God, Ancient Israel, which evolved into various Judaisms.

At that time, they had not yet even evolved into a religion offering animal sacrifices to their God, but did so probably with their portable tabernacle system long before they actually had a constructed temple in Jerusalem. Then for centuries, the sacrificial system was paramount for them as it was throughout the religions of the world. Further, the few ethical ideas they later read back into their origins do not prove the ethics came from Yhwh since many if not most cultures of those times had specific laws forbidding killing and stealing, commands that had been part of ancient secular law codes for *centuries prior* to the origin of Israel's Ten Commandments, so these basic ethical norms were recognized with*out* any deity demanding them.[53]

Such an example points to yet other issues besides majoritarianism and absolutism in thinking that a single religion and its ethic could establish the civil and criminal law or the structures of justice for a democracy. They are as follows: (1) most large religions (and comprehensive doctrines or schemas) come from ancient times and therefore have their own unique ancient historical-mythical groundings of their ethics, grounding with which people who are not religious or belong to other religions do not and would not be willing to identify with, whether they are absolutized or not; (2) most lay people of any given religion actually are familiar at most with only a few general ethical ideas of their own religion, while they have not seen the full historical-contextual scope of them, nor their contingency and specificity which never aimed at being a global ethic confronting any religious and ethical pluralism; (3) religions tend to distrust each other and the *non*-religious distrust most religions when it comes to allowing them to determine the nation's ethics and therefore law; and (4) a democratic society professes to be based on the people rather than any single entity, ideal, event, person, or even god, so the utilization of a single religion's ethic would never be agreed to by the diverse population but rather only those who belonged to that particular group of people.

THE LEGAL DISINTEREST IN ETHICS

When I suggest the answer to the basic question of this inquiry itself requires determining what the relationship *should be* between the ethics of "religions" and the ethics that underlie a social contract, this may sound very arrogant since it is immediately complicated if a democratic society is actually comprised of a religious *pluralism* as well as many citizens who are not affiliated with any formal religion. We have seen the very nature and claims of religions present one set of problems. Yet another type of problem further complicates the situation, the legal profession's minimizing if not disavowing the need to open up a moral questioning of the legal provisions and subsequent structures of society. The legal opposition to admitting that laws or the social contract of a democratic society need ethical grounding at all is more problematic than the religious myopic view since legal practitioners tend to assume the reach of law is all-encompassing without needing outside justification, somewhat similarly to the way religious people view their religion.[54] It is often referred to as a form of "positivism."

In reality, ethics is more universal than any religion or any nation's laws since ethics concerns *all* human relationships. Interestingly, the Supreme Court has insisted that it will never adjudicate on what is "central" to a religion, but simply leave it up to the religion to define. But, in fact, it often has, though without using that exact word. For example, we will see in later chapters that it accepted the centrality of the colportage work of the Jehovah's Witnesses as their preaching or worship,[55] while denying the parallel claim of the centrality of the "sankirtan" of the Hare Krishna groups.[56] It accepted the centrality of the Amish's philosophy of education of its children,[57] yet denied the Native Americans' of the centrality of its sacred ground or use of peyote in its worship,[58] and on and on. It is precisely the determination of what is "central" to a religion which should *not* be any business of any Court, as Madison said, the government "has no cognizance of religion."

But ethics is not necessarily tied to religion. It is much broader, although some of the Justices have not been cognizant even of that as one can see in the oral argument of *Van Orden v. Perry*. Ethics *should* be the business of all jurists and legislators. Most of them know this if they examine the *presuppositions* of their arguments over law, but the Court especially tries to avoid any semblance of deciding a case from a religious or ethical presupposition, and they want to go only by the actual words of the written laws, yet they are fully aware that most arguing over the law presupposes ethical principles without ever mentioning them as such. Even "textualists" can recognize the ethical dimensions behind a word such as "equality" without a dictionary.

This creates a hiatus, in which any number of *ungrounded presuppositions* seem to be able to run free and lodge undetected in the walls of the crevasse of legal method. These responses range from supposing there is really only one true religion, so all options should be ignored, and the social contract and all of its subsequent laws must simply take their cue from that religion's ethics and specific laws—to insisting that law stands totally by itself, and should not be informed by *any* ethic, though legislators may consider practical effects in economic or other terms. Or a jurist holds to the ethical nature of the goals or ends sought (teleology), while others minimize the goal and focus on whether the principles (deontology) are the correct ethical formula-tion. The law is an accumulation from centuries past so continues to legalize or make illegal ancient practices which are no longer relevant or have actually reversed in the public reason, for example, the view toward slavery, toward exclusive male suffrage by property owners, toward nonheterosexual identi-ties and lifestyle, toward even the ethical percentage of interest on loans, and so forth. How were these made without any ethical consideration? Was is not a specific ethic that determined *Roe v. Wade* and *Brown v. Board of Education* and *Miranda v. Arizona*?

The fact is that most ethics and laws do concern *human relations*, so *should* be coordinated and complementary rather than divisive or contrary. Civil and criminal laws also obviously address how people *treat each other*, which is what ethics addresses in general. But so does all other law, whether one thinks of constitutional law, Corporate law, Tax law, Torts, Evidence, or all the other areas. It is still *always persons* involved, whether parties to a con-tract, shareholders of a corporation or one who is bringing legal action against a business or agency for negligence, or even bankruptcies or mergers of large corporations, or, in some cases it is directing humans in their behavior toward other living creatures. Once again, we see the importance of Schweitzer's inclusive "Reverence for Life" which protected all forms of life.

Courts and law schools prefer to give the impression that it is all a giant building block of Legos in which each part snaps in exactly by virtue of earlier pieces supplying analogous facts as precedent. So the Court does not often speak of the validity of alternative interpretations except by its limited dissenting opinions which are usually following the same truncated method of finding precedent cases that can be "dispositive" by their analogous fea-tures, while learning how to distinguish facts of cases that oppose them, and/or referring to the dictionary definitions, as if word meanings are totally unequivocal and unchanging. What is relevant is *not* simply the written law, authorities cited, and legal dictionary meanings, but the *presuppositions* behind the arguments which are moral or ethical presuppositions seldom explicitly acknowledged.

When standards are changed by the legislature or by the Court, seldom are the ethical reasons made plain. For example, the "exclusionary rule" in criminal procedure which was originally created from a deontological ethi-cal reasoning was changed by the Burger Court to a teleological purpose by which the rule is no longer self-justifying, so only hanging on as a bare relic, judged only on a "cost/benefit" analysis by CJ Burger.[59] In a famous Iowa case in the 1970s, that went to the Supreme Court twice, all ethical analysis of the interrogation of defendant without his attorney was finally *ignored* and the appellate Court decided on using the evidence of the body based on a new doctrine of "inevitable discovery" by speculation of where searchers might have gone without the boy's manipulated confession and what the temperature was, so it was *inevitable* that the body would be found, and the Supreme Court bought it.[60]

What is the ethical rationale for not forcing a suspect to testify against himself, or the ethical principle that would ground the idea of allowing people to plead the "Fifth Amendment"? What moral reasoning stands behind the prohibition of "cruel and unusual punishment," and how does one figure out what that means today? Are students ever asked to analyze the moral argument or ethical rationale of treating a corporation with the "legal fiction" of a "person," or is the only consideration strictly geared to the monetary aspects and everyone invested in or working for the corporation being sheltered from personal liability, without asking morally whether that is fair to other people?

To think that most laws were actually framed with*out* the *legislators* having extensive discussions related to the moral or ethical dimensions of the laws at issue, is incredible and frightening. But if there were ethical discussions behind the legal decisions as well as laws, should not *the general populace hear them* in order to be able to understand *why* the laws and legal decisions say the specific things they do? Or were the legislators' arguments nearly always built on their particular vested interests or what they conceived the vested interests were of those they represented or those who lobbied most effectively?

Of course, all cases going before the Court are *only* of "vested" interests. If this is taken for granted as grounding the argument, does anyone bother to ask how a *contest between vested advantages* can serve as a *uniting* factor for a nation? There could be a compromise between the two sides, but as long as the advantages of irrational positions or sheer "happenstance" elements dictate, as Rawls points out, no real unity of significance will be experienced unless people can be convinced of the basic ethical principles underlying the laws that became dispositive. There will be winners and losers, but seldom a decision to which all happily agree, so *no real unity*. It is usually only a "zero-sum" game. If the feeling of unity is dislodged or exacerbated by a lack of trust in the *application* of the law, there is little possibility of restoring it without starting over from scratch at least hypothetically. But that seldom if ever happens in a country's history.

If Kant said to be ethical one had to realize that one was a vital part of the law-making body of a society, that was just as important as his saying one cannot treat rational beings as means to an end but only as ends in themselves or saying that our maxims we decide on must be ones we would all agree to live by as universal principles. But to feel one is an actual part of a legal system which was created centuries *prior* to one's existence and continues to be shaped by legislators *far removed* from one's perspective, makes one's identity as a vital part of the law-making *very fragile and hardly visible*.

Citizens of a democratic republic can and must play a more vital and direct role, *not* just an occasional vote every two years—to be responsible citizens. To accept the huge body of fixed law, and to accept the representative system of democracy of the United States requires not only understanding but a hefty amount of *trust* and *participation* in order to be committed to it when people are "born" into it for their lifetimes.

In statutory law, it is *not* sufficient to find an earlier statute which somehow is general enough to enable or make legitimate room to absorb the newly proposed narrower law that can be squeezed into its rib cage. And within common law practice, *stare decisis* and the analogous hunt resolves little. One can find analogies between any two sentences, but that does not mean that they are in agreement or the first sentence justifies everything the second one states. One must *specify* all the particular ways in which the law or set of facts in question is truly and relevantly analogous to the earlier, but *also explain* the degree to which the *differences* that do exist between the two cases do *not themselves prevent* the analogy from being valid. That element is often completely overlooked. If justification of every new law comes only from preceding laws, we are driven inevitably backward to the "first cause," the original law. But there is no presupposition that justifies that any original law from centuries back is as valid as a new law might be by its present universal agreement and updated concerns. So the "original law" or "original position" of the contracting gains validity *only* as a *hypothetical* exercise rather than as a historical ascertainment. This takes us precisely to the erudite work of John Rawls's "hypothetical" original position behind the veil of ignorance, which is the *only* way of reaching *unanimous agreement.*

But to understand his significance for this specific inquiry, we must remember the ethics which preceded him in both Nietzsche's and Schweitzer's ideas of the basic thrust, power, and value of life being life-affirming, as instinctual, and formulated as "will-to-power" or "will-to-live." While all three, Nietzsche, Schweitzer, and Rawls, fought against the predominant utilitarianism with its reduction of the uniqueness of individuals and even possible minimization of individual lives in its mathematical calculation of the "greatest good" and the "many," Rawls supplied the idea of a mutual agreement between either possible complementary parties or even possibly conflicting parties, a social contract, based on principles that *all would agree to*, not from some mysterious altruistic motive but even from "disinterest" or lack of knowledge of any specific self, including one's own self or those one represents in the negotiations.[61]

This was an interest only in the common goods, in the principles that all would agree to if they all were behind the veil of ignorance of any specific vested happenstance attributes or assets they had which, without that veil of ignorance, would be unfairly advantageous for them, an advantage based on nonrational factors which has nothing to do with "justice." In this "original position" the connection between an ethic and a system of justice can *become visible*, one which can be appropriate to a democratic society, in which mutual autonomy, equality, and trust are central and people receive maximum equal liberties. We carry these ethical themes and the instinctual base of the common "will-to-live" with us now in examining the history, especially of religion to the government in the democratic republic of the United States. As a prerequisite to making sense of religion in the United States, we must first show the evolution of Christianity from its relative beginnings to its absolutization and now to its possible relativization once again.

NOTES

1. Rawls, *Political Liberalism*, xxiv.
2. Rawls, *Political Liberalism*, xxvi.
3. Foucault, *The Order of Things*, ch. 7.
4. Lama, *Ethics*, 19–22.
5. Küng, see notes 44 and 45.
6. Rawls, *Political Liberalism*, 291; *A Theory of Justice*, 60–61; 302; §26.
7. Rawls, *Political Liberalism*, 273.
8. *West Virginia State Bd of Education v. Barnett*, 319 U.S. 624 (1943), at 638.
9. Kurt Andersen, *Evil Geniuses: The Unmaking of America, a Recent History* (New York: Random House, 2020).
10. The renowned late Christian theologian, Wolfhart Pannenberg, emphasized this difference, suggesting that the present anthropological understandings stress one's identity in one's bodily existence rather than just being some "soul." He used this to say the idea of a "resurrection" is therefore more meaningful in the present than the idea of "soul," and this became the central proof he used for his Christology. This can be seen from his first famous work, Jesus—*God and Man*, tr. Lewis L. Wilkins and Duane A. Priebe (Philadelphia: The Westminster Press, 1968), to his work on anthropology *Anthropology from a Theological Perspective*, tr. Matthew J. O'Connell (Philadelphia: The Westminster Press, 1985), to his final work, his three-volume *Systematic Theology*, 3 vols, tr. Geoffrey W. Bromiley (Grand Rapids: William B. Eerdmans Pub. Co., 1991, 1994, 1998). See my analysis of his idea in *Will Humanity Survive Religion? Beyond Divisive Absolutes*, ch. 9.
11. Foucault, *The Order of Things*, see esp. chs. 7 and 8.
12. His Christ-mysticism which was present in his *The Mysticism of Paul the Apostle* was a substitute for a God-mysticism, yet its focus was a single being. That single being was intensified in his *Philosophical Civilization* when he insisted that the awareness of the "will-to-live" creates a mystical unity, but only between oneself and *other specific beings*, never with Being as a whole or the Absolute, which distinguishes him considerably from Paul Tillich's mysticism.

13. In addition to Framers such as Madison being opposed to majoritarianism, John Rawls is not alone among modern philosophers who oppose it. See the comments made by Mark Tushnet, in ch. 5, note 20. Seeing the Christian "God" as generic does not alleviate the problem.

14. Steve Monsma, *Healing for a Broken World: Christian Perspectives on Public Policy* (Wheaton, IL: Crossway Books, 2008). Monsma sees many relevant problems and single-issue foci of different religious groups, but seems unaware of where Christian theology has evolved during the past three centuries. There is a need for a change of attitude, as even the Dalai Lama said, but it cannot require all citizens converting to any particular religion to make a democracy work. Rawls's answer is more logical.

15. Rawls, *A Theory of Justice*, 216–221.

16. James Madison, "Federalist LI," in James Madison, Alexander Hamilton and John Jay (eds.), *The Federalist Papers* (New York: Penguin Books, 1987), 318–322.

17. Rawls, *A Theory of Justice*, 20, 48–51, 119–120, 456; *Political Liberalism*, 8, 28, 45. "Reflective equilibrium" shapes a different form of political constructivism than does rational intuitionism (*Political Liberalism*, 90–99).

18. Ronald Dworkin extends "majoritarianism's" negatives not simply to being a more narrow interest than the whole of the people, but states that its idea of fairness is offended any time the majority does not get its way. That distinguishes majoritarianism's idea of a "democracy" from Dworkin's ideal of a moral reading of the Constitution and of "democracy," that the former is based strictly on a statistical or individualistic approach whereas the "moral" reading is based on a "communal" involvement. See ch. 1 in his *Freedom's Law: The Moral Reading*, 15–20.

19. Andersen, *Evil Geniuses*, esp. Parts Two and Three (33–242). The primary four who are named by Andersen, who formed a group and utilized the insights and strategy of Justice Powell (appointed to the Supreme Court along with Rehnquist by President Richard Nixon) whose famous document spelled out a long-term strategy to save both the Republican Party but also big business and the wealthiest citizens by establishing a network that combined nostalgia and simplicity with deceitful slogans about helping the middle class, while its policies were in direct opposition to that. It even involved cultivating the top law students from prestigious universities and persuading them to belong to the growing group of activists in the newly created Federalist societies. One of the group's primary objectives was and remains for Republicans and big business to take over the federal judiciary. Rawls would shudder at such a goal which cannot be in the national interest, but is very majoritarian.

20. Rawls, *A Theory of Justice*, 226.

21. How else could we explain the grossly disproportionate amount of African American males incarcerated in the United States? The staggering incarceration numbers are certainly *not* evidence of how well a system of justice with its appropriate ethical base actually works.

22. Reinhold Niebuhr, *Moral Man and Immoral Society: A Study in Ethics and Politics* (New York: Charles Scribner's Sons, 1960). I have added a few subterfuges but rely on his insight.

23. Derek L. Phillips, *Toward a Just Social Order* (Princeton, NJ: Princeton University Press, 1986), esp. 379–408.

24. Had Andersen felt the movement he traces was fair, he would not have given his book the title of *Evil Geniuses*. Most readers will not only see it as unfair but terribly shocking.

25. Jacques Barzun, *From Dawn to Decadence, 1500 to the Present: 500 Years of Western Cultural Life* (New York: HarperCollins, 2000), 798–802.

26. Erika Lee, *America for Americans: A History of Xenophobia in the United States* (New York: Basic Books, 2019).

27. Robert P. Jones, *The End of White Christian America* (Simon and Schuster, 2016). He documents that these evangelical groups have been built around a single issue of abortion since they lost on the legalization of same-sex marriage. That is a very narrow interest, not the interest of the nation, so it is majoritarian.

28. Andersen, *Evil Geniuses*, 153. In the author's discussion of how to remedy the problem in the second to last chapter, he refers to the "veil of ignorance" of Rawls in showing how, when people were shown pie charts of the distribution of resources in two hypothetical countries, and asked which they would prefer to join and thereby be randomly assigned by it to any particular category the nation chose, 92% selected the country that had the least inequality, so would have been regarded as the most socialist, and he notes that this anonymous country was Sweden, and the other was the United States. This was part of his argument that our citizens are turning more left than they realize because it has less inequality (351).

29. Andersen, *Evil Geniuses*, 153.

30. University of Baltimore law professor, Garrett Epps, in his *American Justice, 2014: Nine Clashing Visions on the Supreme Court* (Philadelphia: Univ. of Pennsylvania Press, 2014), in noting how the "originalist" or most conservative title begins to shift from J. Scalia to J. Roberts and J. Alito by 2014, he describes how J. Alito seemed to be mentally slipping in his professional preparation and presentations, offered a rather striking note on two other members of the Court which may be confirmed to the reader by the end of the cases we cover in this book: "Scalia's philosophy of 'originalism' was showing its age too. Justice Alito, in particular, seemed to take pleasure in openly mocking it. Neither Alito nor Roberts cared much for precedent, and neither showed a burning curiosity about what the framers of the Constitution thought about anything. Alito and Roberts were young, and their jurisprudence looked ahead" (57). Alito's role in changing the standards of the Establishment Clause by 2020 suggests Epps was probably correct at least with regard to J. Alito.

31. Andersen, *Evil Geniuses*, 152.

32. Although in the colonial 1830s, India had an English-influenced common criminal code drawn up for the nation, England allowed civil law to be governed by various religions and sects as was the custom. When Independence came, with the Hindutva philosophy already strongly politically represented with the RSS as early as the 1930s, with the final geographical and religious split between Hinduism and Islam, Nehru and his law minister, Dr. B. R. Ambedkar, pursued a common or secular civil code. While many were quite willing, the opposition was very vocal, insisting

that its civil laws were given by God, centuries before, even in the Vedas, and could not be tampered with. Historian R. Guha lists six basic suggested changes, which riled up the religious, which included awarding widows and daughters inheritance equal to what the sons received of their deceased father's intestate estate, granting maintenance to a wife who chose to live separate from her cruel, immoral, or diseased husband, allowed both husbands and wives to divorce under those same circumstances. It put an end to the *prohibition* of sacramental benefits and legal status given to lower castes in a marriage, prohibited polygamy, and allowed adoption of children of castes different from the caste of the adopting parents. This was being contested in the 1940s, with many Hindus saying they were being discriminated against even though they were the majority. Guha concludes, showing all the complex problems, and development in India from Gandhi to 2007, by asserting how fortunate it was that the secular democracy survived, without giving in to the majority for a single religion, language, or culture. See Ramachandra Guha, *India after Gandhi: The History of the World's Largest Democracy* (New York: HarperCollins Publishers, 2007), 233–248; 733–759.

33. "Religious purpose" may sound like a good reason for a law, but the Supreme Court, in trying to follow the First Amendment, in *Lemon v. Kurtzman*, 403 U.S. 602 (1971) defined a three-part test to avoid an illegal "establishment" of religion. The first prong of the test was that the law in question had to have a *secular* purpose, and for a time long that was taken to mean that if a "religious" purpose seemed more obvious in the law, it was illegal.

34. Rawls, *Political Liberalism*, 231–240.

35. Rawls, *A Theory of Justice*, 228–229. As important as the majority is to a democracy, Rawls opined that justice requires that the equality of freedom politically be protected for minorities, and this sometimes requires making various rights off limits, such as the one person, one vote, ideal, but also devices such as a supermajority in certain types of legislation, and others, in order to prevent majoritarianism.

36. *West Virginia State Board of Education et al. v. Barnette et al.*, 319 U.S. 624 (1943).

37. Barnette, at 642.

38. Thomas Jefferson, "A Bill for Establishing Religious Freedom," 12 June 1779, *Papers 2:facing 305*, in Philip B. Kurland and Ralph Lerner (eds.), *The Founders' Constitution* (Chicago: The University of Chicago Press, 1987), V: 37.

39. Rawls, *Political Liberalism*, xviii.

40. Rubenstein, *After Auschwitz*, 25.

41. "James Madison to William Bradford," 24 January 1774, *Papers* 1:106, in Kurland and Lerner (eds.), *Founders' Constitution*. I:60.

42. Carol Berkin, *The Bill of Rights: The Fight to Secure America's Liberties* (New York: Simon & Schuster, 2015), 42.

43. James Madison, "Detached Memoranda," ca. 1817, W. & M. W., 3d ser.; 3:554–60 (1946) in Kurland and Lerner (eds.), *Founders' Constitution*, I:103.

44. Hans Küng and Karl-Josef Kuschel, eds., *Global Ethic: The Declaration of the Parliament of the World's Religions* (London: SCM Press; New York: Continuum, 1993).

45. Hans Küng and Helmut Schmidt, *A Global Ethic and Global Responsibilities: Two Declarations* (London: SCM Press, Ltd., 1998).

46. When hopeless and desperate teenage boys were promised they would go down in Islamic history as heroes, and soon enjoy Paradise's well-endowed virgins administering to their every need, they were not merely being promised more "raisons." No one is quite that dumb.

47. The Lama, *Ethics*, 19: "I have come to the conclusion that whether or not a person is a religious believer does not matter much. Far more important is that they be a good human being."

48. The expression, originating with Luther perhaps, means one is *always both saint and sinner*, and it was probably the primary key to the theology and ethics of Paul Tillich. But what evidence is there that such a phrase is really true unless all it means is just that people are not perfect?

49. See my *Will Humanity Survive Religion: Beyond Divisive Absolutes*, and *Ethics and Future of Religion: Redefining the Absolute*, both published by Lexington Books-Fortress.

50. The Lama, *Ethics*, 26–27.

51. *Van Orden v. Perry*, 545 U.S. 677 (2005).

52. The sacred tetragrammaton (YHWH) to Judaism.

53. One can study the ancient code of Lipit Ishtar or the Hammurabi Code, or even the Ten Precepts of Buddhism, which was long before Buddha was thought to be deity.

54. If this sounds like an exaggeration of the legal profession's opposition to opening up the discussion to moral or ethical principles, see Ronald Dworkin, *Freedom's Law*, ch. 1.

55. In *Cantwell v. Connecticut*, 310 U.S. 296 (1940), the solicitation door to door by Jehovah's Witnesses was seen as equivalent of "preaching" or Free Exercise of religion and freedom of speech.

56. Hare Krishna groups lost two out of three times before the Court in 1981 and 1992, once on fairgrounds in MN and once in a NY airport, whereas the "Jews for Jesus" won in 1987 by an airport regulation in LA the Court saw as "overbroad." All were the same kind of activity that had been approved for the Jehovah's Witnesses but were busier scenarios.

57. *Wisconsin v. Yoder*, 406 U.S. 205 (1972).

58. *Lyng v. N.W. Indian Cemetery Protective Association*, 485 U.S. 439 (1988) and *Employment Division v. Smith*, 485 U.S. 660 (1988) and 494 U.S. 872 (1990).

59. In *Weeks* (1914), the principle was established that no police officer can break the law to try to find evidence that a citizen has broken the law. *Weeks v. United States*, 232 U.S. 383 (1914).

60. *Brewer v. Williams*, 430 U.S. 3887 (1977); *Nix v. Williams*, 467 U.S. 431 (1984). Different majorities first dismissed the evidence for violation of defendant's Sixth Amendment right which he had not knowingly waived, but the second time, a different majority convicted him of first degree murder, without his confession but based on the victim's body as an "inevitable discovery."

61. Even the more sympathetic interpreters of Rawls, for example, Brian Barry, in his *Theories of Justice*, in chs. 6 and 9, early on expressed consternation regarding

his position of how much "ignorance" of oneself was involved. Rawls made this perhaps clearer in *Political Liberalism* as he described the "original position" as one in which one's interests were *represented* politically by a person who was ignorant of all the different citizens' specific traits, assets, and so forth. But he also insisted over and over that the ignorance and disinterest always meant the same, an ability to *hypothesize* transcending the special, accidental interests of both self and others, as one's vote finally is, as he said even in *A Theory of Justice*, voting not for special self-interests but for the interests of the nation as a whole. This is not altruism but a simple ignorance of one's special traits and interests, and it is combined with an insight of how an agreement might make that more possible than people simply fighting it out. This means "justice" is not equated with any given virtues or any static formulation or outside party, but is rather "just" just because the involved parties *agree* to it.

Chapter 3

The History of Christianity
in the United States

Aspiration and Mythologization, or
Desacralization and Freedom of Conscience

It is easy to regard one's understandings as if they correspond exactly with reality. Unfortunately, or perhaps, fortunately, they often do not. Inasmuch as people inherit ideas and values from their families at very early ages which implant themselves deeply in their psyches, these often color reality by sheer chance, but also by *aspiration* or desire, and even subconsciously. This is what subjectivity, individual uniqueness, and imagination are all about. But they are often far removed from objective reality. Perceptions are usually reality in some sense, of course, but conceptions are one's mental tools, general names which one tries to match with what one perceives or even what one imagines. They may or may not have any necessary connection to the objects actually perceived. Could that occur with peoples' religious identities?

Religious identities often involve teachings that utilize *myths*, and Christianity is no exception. Although some of these are "pure" myths having no reference to anything historical but only to some environment of divine beings, many if not most have supranatural beings interacting with humans and/or nature *within history*.[1] In some cases, one can detect fairly easily that such a historical reference is only a dimension added later to an existing myth, for example, in the plethora of "flood" narratives and their heroes, but in other cases the mythical framework is later attached to some historical event which provides the event with normative status. Quite often, the end result does not correspond to any empirical reality so cannot be verified or falsified by historical method. On the other hand, some significant philosophers of religion such as Mircea Eliade have insisted that the truth conveyed by religious myths is (or perhaps even was) not meant to provide some historical truth but rather to supply a much deeper *existential* truth. This may be more apparent in some religions than others. For example, in the ancient Cherokee myth of the Big Buzzard creating the mountains and valleys of the Earth by his wings scraping the ground while it was still mud, one can say this truth is that the Cherokees lived in what they considered hilly or mountainous country. To go one step further, it is said that those people who schooled themselves in the two great epics of Hinduism, the *Ramayana* and the *Mahabharata*, used to be expected to add some details in their recitation of it, to make it more relevant and existential, if not more up to date. That may have included adding aspirations. Many religious people, however, take the historical allusions in their myths as very literal references to actual history and would be offended if someone told them that it was simply an "existential" or even an aspirational truth, or the person added some new details to the myth. We shall elaborate on myths later as we analyze desacralization and demythologization.

If *aspirations* can operate on even a subconscious level, so can "existential" symbols or stories or myths, but both can also be very intentionally created, used, and owned. Each person sooner or later probably has to decide on just what kinds of religious stories, symbols, rituals, and the like may have been intended as actual reality or at least profess to be reality, and what are only aspirations of someone or are existential truths rather than empirical history. But even then, since the intentions of an unknown ancient author are not inherently normative for all time to come, one still has to decide if one accepts any as meaningful and/or normative in any way.

The predominance of the Christian religion in the United States has given many Christians the impression that for some reason, "God" actually intended Christianity to be the religion of the nation. Those who are serious about this find the idea of antiestablishment principle in the First Amendment to the U.S. Constitution abominable. There have been many thrusts to such a simplistic identification. First, there is the insistence that history of the United States actually proves that intentional preference. Second, many are certain that the Christian ethics are unique, a part of God's final revelation, so they can be found only in the Christian scriptures or manifest by Christianity's history, and are superior to any other ethic. Third, the conclusion of these two claims is that only a Christian ethic should shape U.S. law since that was what God intended. For those who believe this, the religious pluralism in the United States is itself the problem, and if it were eliminated, they believe the nation would be Christian, a theocracy, with a united ethic and law.

THE "ASPIRATIONAL" INTENTIONAL CHRISTIAN MYTH ABOUT THE UNITED STATES

Is it possible that one's *aspirational claims* about one's religion might not end simply with rewriting or redescribing the religion's origins or history and significance, but might even influence one's view of one's *nation's history*, even if one's nation is a *democracy* rather than a theocracy? Even if the entire picture given was not aspirational, but some small parts of it were historical to which supernatural elements were added to form the aspirational claims which give it such powerful appeal to those open to the supernatural, it would still remain mythical if we understand "myth" as an idea by which one imagines some commerce between a supranatural world and the historical world in which we live. In this sense, either an aspirational element or a mythical element removes the story or claim or symbol from being verifiable by historical method. The acceptance of either the aspirational or mythical dimensions of one's own religion might resolve the problem by seeing the religious pluralism as an aberration or mistake. The mythical or aspirational dimensions provide one's religion with a superior claim, but when the claim itself is not verifiable, it will not convince those who do not already belong to the group.

The Muslim clergy which forms the central part of the Iranian state certainly has an aspirational view of the nation of Iran, thinking that all citizens *should be* faithful adherents of Islam, governed by Islamic civil and criminal law or Shari'ah. This may be a bit of an overreach, unrealistic for citizens who are informed of other possibilities or had non-Islamic upbringing. So it may not reflect the aspirations of all the citizens, or even be a historically true picture. But if the mythical elements are strong enough, and *not* taken to be merely existential truth, the political/religious leaders of the country might easily be convinced that their own picture of Islam and their state is not merely aspirational but the truth of actual historical facts. Does this mean that what *should* be is *what is*, thus the myth or aspiration are what necessarily is?

It nevertheless seems a bit of an irony, when such *aspirational exclusive* attempts to *rewrite a national history* occur within the two largest *democracies* I already mentioned, India and the United States, as some of the most conservative sects profess that their particular religion should be the *only one*, the *true identity, for all citizens*, because it simply was that way *prior* to all the immigration: in India, Hinduism; in the United States, Christianity. That's as specious as the white immigrants to the United States opposing other nonwhite or somewhat-white immigrants coming later, and referring to themselves as "natives" of this land, which Erika Lee documents.[2] The religious argument might make sense or be justified if (1) the nations were actually professing to be theocratic *rather than democratic*, and if (2) the religion being proposed as the true one is the *only one* that was *never imported*. But both nations profess to be thoroughly *democratic* governments, not theocratic. How then can the theocratic argument have any weight? Further, it was the Aryan immigration to India in the mid-second millennium BCE which brought Vedism which evolved into Hinduism. Similarly, it was the

European immigration to the shores of the "New World" from the fifteenth through nineteenth centuries which brought Christianity to what evolved as the United States.

These religions were both "imported" through immigrants. But there were *already* local residents who had been in both countries for *thousands of years*, and these local people had their own religions. Hinduism was not the natural or original religion of India nor was Christianity the natural or original religion of the United States. In both cases, the claim to be the "original" religion is *not* an accidental misreading of history, but an *intentional alternative history* or philosophy of culture at work. It was a conscious suppression of any value of the culture and religion of those who were conquered. Lee's analysis of this form of manipulating history in order to keep new immigrants from coming to one's country is simply a typical historical form of xenophobia in the United States. Xenophobia involves not merely fear of the other or stranger, but likely utilizes people's desires or aspirations as well as myths which can enhance one's particular xenophobic understanding of history and different cultures. But we must explain further the U.S. process of the origin of its myth of the religious founding of the United States.

Steven Green, historian and attorney, analyzed the intentional myth-making of the aspirations of these people in the United States.[3] He pointed out that there is evidence that early in the eighteenth century, if not before, some people began to justify their colony's growing religious tolerance or even freedom by injecting retrospectively that disposition back onto the earliest European immigrants to the colonies, which was not at all factually true of many of those early colonists. This retrospective altering of certain past history began what historian Steven Green calls the "intentional creation" of the "myth" of the eventual nation having *always* been a tolerant one although of a divinely intended single religion, specifically Christian, with freedom from the outset.

Green analyzes the complex history and different possible understandings and different uses of language during the three periods of the myth's making. The first was the third generation Puritan apologists' attempt to "understand and justify the importance of the Puritan errand." The next iteration of the myth appeared in the Revolutionary period by people searching for validation of the "patriot cause" by a higher or providential meaning. The third form came in the second quarter of the nineteenth century, the National period, as the second generation of "Americans" felt a need to find a providential base for their national identity and mission to the world. But none of these is the aspiration of all the citizens who were not religiously affiliated.

For the discerning historian, many of the present works which continue to propagate the claim of this "religious founding" envision their own task to be to suggest that whatever their present aspirational idea of their own

Christian faith is precisely what they find in all the important figures, whether Washington, Madison, or others, or even in ancient documents such as the "Mayflower Compact." That appears to be a reaching of a decision about a concept or principle as one's identity, then hunting through past history to find some sort of corroboration of it. We will address that retrospective element shortly. But this fails to take seriously the complexity of actual history, the ambiguity of people's actions and speech, for example, that many people in those centuries talked about "fate" or "manifest destiny" or even "Providence" whether they were religious or not. It was simply part of the typical vocabulary and proved nothing about one's religiousness or lack of it. Further, many citizens during the eighteenth and nineteenth centuries, like people today, were not wholly consistent in their theologies or theological reasoning, and even a number of quite religious people were opposed to all creeds and most theology in general, or, at least they talked like they were. Green felt these iterations were intentionally created to provide a quite *simple* identity for the Christian nation and/or for individual Christians, and there is no doubt that such views may have spurred the idea of the United States having a cultural and religious mission to the world by the nineteenth century, later called by some our century of "missions."

The elaboration of such a "myth" whose contents shifted in its various iterations from era to era to meet the needs current at the time, whether it was attracting more settlers into a state or providing a sense of nationalistic unity to engage in the War of Independence, or was a simple "founding" myth of the distinct value and *divine destiny* of the New Nation, it has continually become less historical and more divisive in the country, especially in the last quarter of the twentieth century in which more people became aware of the nation's religious pluralism and of the negative aspects of the U.S. feeling it had a "manifest destiny" in a colonial sense of creating an empire. It has been an intentionally narrow way of reading the past, omitting the religious intolerance of the Puritans, attributing the unity of the Revolutionary and Founding periods to the Christian religion and its scriptures rather than to any Enlightenment influence, even misinterpreting purely rhetorical speech for a literal historical description, and utilizing single religious observances as depicting the religion of a national leader such as George Washington even when the latter was not actually active within any religion. In fact, the present reading goes so far as to suggest that present-day *Evangelicalism* is what the Framers conceived for this nation and its laws, all of which are grounded in the Bible. That is as anachronistic and purely aspirational as those present scholars who see the "historical Jesus" as an egalitarian.

By "myth," Green was not saying every historical detail was wrong but simply that the facts were altered to fit the schema that people created in their minds and felt they and/or the nation needed. This corresponds closely to

Jacob Neusner's description of how "exile/return" became the primary motif of Jewish understanding, which not only legitimated the state of the religion as is, not simply stated as past fact, but rather as an implicit suggestion that if the people find themselves ever again in exile, their God will likely deliver them from it as well. He insisted this motif or symbol was *consciously created* in *retrospect*, with the people arriving *first* at the theme which was based not on actual, obvious history but on their desire or *aspiration* for the present group. But after they decided, then they hunted through history to find events and speeches which would corroborate that theme.[4] That is a very *selective way of writing history*. In both, the creation of a special myth involved a search for a very *simple identity* for the people, a retrospective search far removed from the "historical events" from which it is said to have been derived, as is nearly always the case in ancient religions' identities, as can be seen, for example, in the traditions about the origins of both Christianity and Buddhism.

To hunt for a *simple theme* may be even a *more selective* way of writing history than trying to provide a *simple identity* for a people. Green says he utilized Robert Bellah's definition of "myth" as having the purpose "to transfigure reality so that it provides moral and spiritual meaning to individuals and societies." But, I would qualify that it actually only transfigures a *report* of reality, not reality itself, just as the ancient New Year's rituals and myths which Mircea Eliade described did *not* really re-create a new cosmos, even *if* those ancient peoples thought it did. In any case, the idea of receiving a divinely wrought new cosmos, just as in the Hindu stories about Vishnu, encouraged people to *think* of it that way, even if it never really physically changed.[5] But the people, as Eliade suggested, were convinced that their rituals had elevated them into the realm of divine power and purity or innocence, a new world in which *they could begin over*. One must wonder how basic is such a feeling of a need to begin afresh?

If one intentionally reads things into a history which were not factual, what are the criteria for and limit to such alternate or manufactured "history"? If it were limited merely to the subjectivity of each individual,[6] as renowned New Testament scholar Rudolf Bultmann used to imply, it might be fairly harmless. But when the "mythical" dimension adds the aura of divine authority as a religion attaches it to some specific alleged event or even direction of history, and when the "event" or "history" impress, and the mythical references to the historical are taken as literal rather than merely existential, at that point the story or ritual becomes unverifiable, divisive, and dangerous.

When would a reading of such a myth ever be recognized as contrived or *false* history? Green is careful to say that he does *not* think the people engaging in reading history in such a way have intentionally misconstrued history. Yet he said the myth was intentionally created. What else can it be if the *purpose* and not merely the accidental effect was to "transfigure" reality, to color facts with sheer aspiration—unless it was completely a subconscious process so not really intentional? The most formative period of such aspirational reading Green seems to acknowledge as the last part of the eighteenth century and the first quarter of the nineteenth, the period of the critical and fragile founding of the nation, so a supplying of an *identity* to the citizens of the new, fragile nation which could give them hope and which corresponded to their beliefs. But many political leaders (e.g., George Washington, John Adams, etc.) and Supreme Court justices (e.g., Joseph Story) even in those early years of the nation were as ill-informed of religion as many present-day political leaders and court justices, having only a very simplistic understanding of religion, which we will discover in the following chapters.

If the myth of the religious founding can be based on such uninformed or oversimplified selective readings of history and the institutions, it perhaps will not surprise the reader to hear recent justices speak of the Christian "God" as the *only* God, and the *only* real source for ethics and law in the world. Nor will we be surprised to hear the court insist that any religious observance on the federal level after the formulation of the First Amendment validates the usage of that ritual today as "constitutional" since its continued practice is "proof" that those Framers did not consider it a violation of the First Amendment. Such an argument, however, fails to consider the fact that the process of disestablishment was brand new, trying to root out of people's minds the idea of the merged government and religion, the Christendom, which had been the pattern for 1,400 years, which codependency had been assumed as a vital necessity. It would take a *long time* to overcome in all of its nuances and tentacles, and there is still some residue of this belief today. People in the early nineteenth century were barely removed from religious "establishment," and so accustomed to it, it would take time to see all the various parts of it as unconstitutional.

But it surely would be a surprise to hear a justice of either a state court or of the Supreme Court to say that the First Amendment was a prohibition only of the federal government, so any state can have its own "established" religion. And it would be even stranger to hear two Supreme Court justices insisting in oral argument of the *Perry* case that *government* has a right to express *its own* religion. But in the subsequent chapters, we will encounter this very thing. What seems to be lost on some people today who still insist that separate states can have their own state religion, that the First Amendment was only directed at a national religion, is that the two centuries of "establishment" in the country that preceded the First Amendment experienced "established" religions in separate colonies, and since the Articles of Confederation had been so lacking in federal power that the states were not very united, the First Amendment would have made no sense if it had implied only a prohibited national religion but allowed the states to continue their divisive own particular establishments. The "perfect separation" of religion from government, as described by James Madison, seems never to get read or understood these days.[7]

Green concluded his study by summarizing that the intentional myth-making was short on facts and high on aspiration. Indeed, but Rawls would ask *whose* aspiration, the very question which is implicit in Green's study. Can the aspirations of only a few become the ground for the laws of the whole people? Can a myth that is embraced by only a few be the ground for the ethics and laws of the whole nation? How can a democracy be grounded on a *single religion* yet be expected to be agreed to by any other citizens who are either of a different religion or none at all? It was the very awareness of religious pluralism which was recognized rather late on the scene, which Rawls insisted had to be *owned up to openly and publically* by the liberal democratic structure. Our religious pluralism, as Rawls wrote, poses the problem of the nation having to choose between an unending, sinister, if not deadly conflict and a recognition of freedom of conscience and thought for all citizens. Unless the latter is embraced with continual publicity and recognized as imperative, there will simply be no political conception of justice, but only deadly competition. Political liberalism addresses this problem in its depth.[8] The idea of an "aspirational" myth of the religious founding of the United States by a *single* religion's ethics is extremely divisive, no matter how noble its particular aspirations.

If a religion made no claims about history, then one certainly would not look for history to provide details or proof of its claims. But history was the primary focal point of both Judaism and Christianity. The problem seems to be on confusing myth for history, and aspiration for myth, and in the long run, all that is left is *aspiration*, not real historical facts. That might not be objectionable. Aspirations can be good or evil, appropriate or totally inappropriate. But when Christian ethics or Christian nationalistic *aspirations* sanction conquering people, enslaving them or killing them to get their land, or causes people to kill other colonists in the Civil War because they have decided they *must* have slaves to work their crops, or motivates people to suppress the minority voting in a national election, such aspirations are no more ethical than Hitler's intention of annihilating all Jews. Any leader can find a scapegoat even without any historical text or alleged revelation from God. In fact, it is a real question whether a democratic republic has the right to speak even aspirationally of all men being equal and having unalienable rights of life, liberty, and the pursuit of happiness, when it was granting suffrage *only* to white men who owned property, or for the census to determine how many representatives a state should have, when it did *not* count Native Americans and counted male African Americans only three-fifths of a person (or human?). Expressed aspiration can be good or evil, but it does not deserve our allegiance if it is evil or if it is speaking of noble aspiration as if it were a legal fact when it is not. Aspirations do not make a nation "exceptional"; only exceptional reality can.

There are several other big problems with such a myth-making: (1) the aspirations of those establishing the myth may be based on very few historical facts or a minimal knowledge of the facts, both of the paradigm (Christianity) they are propagating as well as the history with which they are trying to identify it; (2) the quest for simplicity of any identity may be only an *oversimplification* so not credible to most people; (3) the meaning of the myth may not be a meaning obviously important today or convincing in the recited event of its alleged past; (4) the myth may be based on aspirations only of a small group rather than everyone involved; (5) the myth may aspire to a *uniformity* which is not possible, so it creates a feeling of being coerced, or only divisiveness; and (6) the aspiration itself, for example, the ethics presupposed in the expressed desire or idea, may be wholly unacceptable or be prejudicially determined by only a select group of people. That is simply another form of majoritarianism.

Even if the aspiration behind this intentional myth is evangelical Christian, its specific aspiration to be the controlling religion of the United States is not an aspiration of others, not even of other Christian groups. It reflects neither some general consensus of Christian institutions' beliefs nor of the values of other religious or even nonreligious citizens, nor in any way does it manifest any awareness of the objective study of Christian theology of the last three centuries. It remains a special interest group which, in typical majoritarian manner, is trying to force its ideas and values—uninformed of the scholarly understandings of Christianity—on the whole nation, even if it requires *altering* the actual history of religion in the United States and the context of the forming of the Constitution with its Bill of Rights, and ignoring every Christian scholar that was in any way influenced by the Enlightenment.

THE ATTEMPT TO IDENTIFY CHRISTIAN ETHICS WITH THE ETHICS OF THE NEW DEMOCRACY

A vital part of this majoritarian attempt to identify its particular interpretation of the Christian faith and its ethics with the ethics of the democracy of the United States is the belief that the latter's laws *were* fashioned precisely on evangelical Christian ethics, which includes to a degree even Jewish ethics prior to Christianity, such as the Ten Commandments. If Christian churches have utilized the Ten Commandments as necessary moral commands for the present Christian, then they have been given the Decalogue a status parallel to Jesus's "Golden Rule" in the famous "Sermon on the Mount" as the central Christian ethical principles most commonly known—other than the command for one to love God with all one's being and love one's neighbor as oneself. Most religions have some fairly similar rules, principles, or dharma that are quite parallel, such as the prohibition of murder or theft or false testimony, or a command to love others. But some are even more rigorous, for example, in prohibiting the drinking of any alcohol, or they are more lenient, for example, in allowing a man to have more than one wife at a time.

In addition to these similarities and differences in content of the various religions' ethics, which are many, all the ethical codes have gone through changes in peoples' understanding of them, and none professed to be a universal ethic when originally articulated. They were all geared to a particular people in a specific geographical location, all *very limited* within a cultural space and time. They were also *unique* in that their mythical or supranatural claims are *not* interchangeable or reducible to an ethical or metaphysical core that would be acceptable to the nonreligious nor even by other religions, nor are their claims to being God's "final revelation" judged by others as true. So the lines are drawn *between the religions*, making them incompatible, as Rawls observed, which means any nation which has a religious pluralism must include a greater sense of unity than any of the religions can supply.

Ethical Attitudes vs. Ethical Principles Which Can be Shaped into Law

But not every ethical principle can be turned into a governmental law. When the Dalai Lama assumed that our actions reflect our attitudes, he was certainly right in many cases. In some cases such as "conspiracy" laws, actions cannot be weighed and enforced by law unless the prosecutors can convince the jury that the suspect had an attitude that corresponded to it or even motivated the person's actual behavior. Therefore, the Dalai Lama suggested that we cultivate ethical attitudes such as empathy, compassion, trust, honesty, and so forth. That makes sense. He even emphasized that we spend time before encountering possible ethical crises, meditating on precisely how we would show empathy and compassion in certain situations, a definite preparation that is needful. While that is very insightful, I reiterate that no ethical attitudes can *per se* be shaped into civil or criminal laws since the laws depend primarily on enforcing empirical behaviors or perceptible actions. If intention is necessary to either a crime or even any moral act, there must be an obvious nexus between the act itself and the attitude or intention as its cause.

In the 1960s, Joseph Fletcher's little book on *Situation Ethics* suggested that we need to avoid the two extremes in ethics: a rigid casuistry and an antinomianism. Also, an ethic needs to be simple. He felt he had discovered that simple principle in the meaning of "love" as "willing the best for others." But neither "love" nor "willing" is enforceable since it would require mind reading. Civil and criminal laws have to be based on empirically perceptible actions, not attitudes, although certain attitudes may underlie specific empirical behaviors. This was the reason Thomas Jefferson said civil government should not get involved in the sphere of religion, since what people believe is their business, not the governments, and may never be proven even from their actions. This is why certain crimes are difficult to prove since they require a showing of "mens rea" or guilty intent, even though the law has no way into the mind, so we can only *infer*, and that often means any decision is not completely certain. Jefferson said civil government could intervene in the religious person's (or really any person's) life *only* when the person violates general laws applicable to all citizens.

If both Judaism and Christianity contain a command to "love God" but also to "love your neighbor as yourself," that certainly is not enforceable in civil life, and could be interpreted as an enforceable law only if one believed that the "enforcer" was one who could read minds. Some religious people do seem to think "God" can and does that very thing. Yet we do not see any evidence that people's violations in failing to love others are actually punished. Many Christians push that judgment off to the ultimate future, a Final Judgment of all people by God. That, of course, is of no help while we are living in history and the law to love is not being enforced nor is it enforceable by finite humans.

For a very conscientious religious person, that suspended judgment in the present may create considerable doubt about one's own state, even anguish or despair. Notably, although the Apostle Paul painted "love" as superior to "faith" and "hope," he seems to have been bothered personally more from the command to not "covet" than the law to "love" one's neighbor as oneself. He states that once he understood the prohibition of coveting, he discovered that his life was full of coveting. He therefore concluded that such laws themselves cannot be the answer to life, or at least not for his life. Of course, he was speaking here primarily to one's attitude, which can only be known by oneself, never by others, so cannot be made into a civil or criminal law.

Yet this was one of the Ten Commandments, just as was the command to "keep the Sabbath." The difference was that observing the Sabbath as a "holy day" was further defined as requiring certain empirical actions or abstinence from certain things, whereas the prohibition of coveting was rather confined to coveting one's neighbor's wife or property. Those are unethical attitudes that certainly can have disastrous results if not controlled, but civil and criminal law cannot weigh the attitudes, but only the actual behaviors. The same nebulousness was true of the command to "honor your father and mother," although other parts of the Torah emphasized that one is not to "curse" one's father or mother, and if one does, one is to be put to death. That was quite severe. One must understand that this is not a prohibition of using profanity toward one's parents, which itself is deplorable, but involved uttering a "curse" with the ancient mentality of invoking some supranatural power to do something dreadful to the person being "cursed." That was accepted as true in many ancient cultures and their law codes, just as most of those people believed in "witches" who could "curse" people, so they had commands from their God to kill witches, which the early Calvinist Christians in Massachusetts accomplished by their infamous drownings.

St. Paul could say that one who loves God with his whole being and loves his neighbor as himself has "fulfilled" the whole law, but until that "love" is given empirically perceptible content, it cannot be regarded as a civil or criminal law of a nation of diverse people, and even a definition of "love" as "willing the best for the other" is too broad to be of much help, as Fletcher's own examples at the end of his book revealed. How is one sure of what is "best" for the other? So to have enforceable laws which a nation needs, two things seem to be necessary: (1) the ethical principles must be as definite with empirical qualities that it can provide fairly clear understanding and be enforceable; and (2) they must be acceptable to all citizens so can be regarded by them as their own will, that is, it must be a mutual autonomy by all involved parties, not a mere heteronomous edict. This is precisely what Rawls's approach does. Attitudes cannot become laws, but a broad *empirically* involved concept such as "liberty" or "freedom" or "equality" can become a legal concept by a close tailoring. This means that he assumes that each person will know when "liberty" is spelled out as including "liberty of voice" or right to vote, or liberty to not be moved against one's will (kidnapping), or liberty to not have to testify against oneself, or liberty from being defamed, and so forth. "Inequalities" in economic and social status are also able to be detected or are empirically obvious enough that it can be a concept just as can "the least privileged."

Therefore, by one's weighing ethical principles that are based on public reason, one does not have to depend upon attitudes of self or others. One does not have to try to turn into a mind reader, nor to attempt to make empathy or compassion into an enforceable law. Certainly, actions might be judged as more ethical if empathy or compassion were present so that one's actions are not simply a grudging compliance. But Rawls shows that even by a "disinterest in others," which he explained as simply being behind a veil of ignorance pertaining to self and others about anything other than "general goods," principles can *be agreed on by all* even *without* any great empathy, compassion, and without any dictating religion. That enables a democratic society to obtain a unity which cannot be matched by any or all religions as they presently conceive themselves.

Presuppositional Differences between Government Ethics and Christian Ethics

The most enduring problem of this question of ethics for the U.S. law as a whole is the mistaken notion held by some citizens that Christian ethics was somehow the *foundation* for the ethics presupposed in the nation's basic documents of the Constitution and the Declaration of Independence and its extensive common law and codified laws. No religion, including Christianity, simply came in a finished package, fully planned and staffed, with an obvious metaphysical ethics for the world which was completely reasonable and voluntarily acceptable universally to humans. Instead, the various groups we call "religions" all began in specific, limited temporal-spatial conditions, so were not universal in any sense. Many new religions were simply originally dissident individuals that grew into small groups within already-existing religions, for example, Buddhism springing out of the Hindu culture, Christianity originating as a dissident sect of Judaism. In fact, many if not most of the early European immigrants to the New World were themselves even dissidents within the Christian movement.

It is difficult to envision any of these immigrations which brought new cultures with different religions to a new land was all planned by some deity. Hinduism came from an Aryan invasion of India in the mid-second millennium BCE. Even Judaism involved an immigrant people moving from the southeast sector of the Fertile Crescent to the southwest sector through both fortunate and unfortunate events. Hinduism and Judaism had been ethnically defined religions, so eventually both Buddhism and Christianity extricated themselves from those confines, *claiming* to be universal answers to the human problem.

Within a fairly short time, however, each of the "new" religions felt constrained to reach back in time to insist that they were as old or older, and therefore as legitimate, as the religion out of which they sprang. Christianity did not merely claim that Israel's reform prophets had anticipated it, but moved back further. It moved past even the alleged giving of the Torah to the people, to an earlier ancestor, "father" Abraham, some 15–20 centuries prior to Jesus's time, and in one of Paul's letters, he even finds the "first man" (Adam) the vital point of the "second man" (Jesus as the Christ) (Gal. 4; Rom. ch. 4 and 5). This seemed to legitimate the claims about Jesus as the Messiah, giving a sense of religious superiority to this small, dissident group of Jews. In Buddhism, the Hindu dissidents did not merely claim that Gautama knew more than those who produced the Upanishads, but rather, that Gautama knew *all his former lives*, thousands of them, way back in ancient times (prior to any Hinduism), and the Buddhist monks living in the caves at Ajanta and Ellora, depicted his knowledge of such with pictures they painted on the cave walls, thereby legitimating their claims of superiority over Hinduism.

However, what they claimed as historical is impossible to sort from *myth*, and what they *aspired* to be has never been realized yet as historical *reality*. This raises the question of whether the Absolute *itself* is only a subjective *attitude*, desire, or aspiration of one's religion rather than some actual Divine Personal Power or God. But no religion started out as either the obvious universal answer or Absolute. And they all used human language found in the area in which they originated, even if tweaked a bit.

The law of the United States was not only not derived from any religion, but the values themselves are in significant ways even basic *opposites* of the Christian ethic. In the next chapter, we can see how the ethics underlying the Bill of Rights has nothing in common with earlier ethics laws of some of the attempted theocracies of the colonies. But, more broadly speaking, the Christian ethic is heteronomous; God tells humans how to live, and they are not encouraged to be autonomous at all. Their autonomous ethical agreement with each other is of no significance; rather, they are all expected simply to obey God.

On the other hand, the basic principles of the Constitution with its Bill of Rights presuppose a mutual autonomy and responsibility of all the citizens. Even the government is not seen as a heteronomous source or authority but rather the product of all the citizens as a whole. One system has an ethic for a theocracy while the other carries an ethic of a democracy. Reason was the Enlightenment's contribution to our Constitution, but Christianity insisted not on reason but on faith which was considered superior to or above reason. The Constitution did not mark any people as the "chosen" by God but all were considered equal citizens, whereas many Christians have appropriated that Jewish concept for themselves as being the only "chosen" by God. In the colonial theocracies, that gave them *advantages* over other people, *if* there were other people in the colony. Speech that cast doubt on the colony's Christian creeds made the speaker worthy of death under those theocratic laws, but the Constitution and Bill of Rights provided freedom of speech and did not include any punishment for speech which showed the speaker's doubt of any religious ideas or even disparaging remarks he or she might make about a religion.

We will see further that the Framers, led by Madison and Jefferson, did not believe government and religion should be surrogates for each other or lend their authority to each other, but should be separated, whereas since Constantine's day, the Christian church had been for the most part inseparably united with government in what we call "Christendom." The Framers of the Constitution saw the hostilities, bitter and almost endless wars that Europe experienced as a result, eventually not only between competing sects of Christians, but between Christians and their own states, as the religious and secular supreme powers often fought for the place of utter primacy over the other. Who among the Framers really wanted simply to replicate the torturous history of England in its relations between religion and government since Henry VIII? Even the few Founders of our Constitution who were still attached to the idea of a monarchy with its Parliament did not want the United States to be a mere recapitulation of England's divisive internecine strife over religious conformity which forced so much war, including England's Civil War. If the principles behind the Constitution and Bill of Rights as well as the Declaration of Independence spoke of equality and liberty for all people, the liberty and equality even in the New Testament was only *spiritualized* by St. Paul, *not* a real sexual and racial equality or liberty for any slaves.

The Particularity of Judaism's Ancient Biblical Ethics

Judaism, or as Jacob Neusner preferred more accurately called it, "Judaisms," came out of the long history of Ancient Israel which was later recited or included implicitly in the Jewish scripture or Tanach (TaNaK= acronym for the three divisions, Torah, Nebi'im, and Kethabim, or law, prophets, and writings). It was called Judaism of the "dual Torah" in the sense that it eventually professed to have always included oral as well as written traditions, and in its rabbinic form has continued reflection on this tradition, continually mining it for more directions for proper living. It has professed in that sense to have no static "dogma" *per se*, even if it recognizes 613 commands, and has perpetuated certain rituals and celebrations for thousands of years, so much that it can be said that the Torah has meaning primarily, as Rubenstein avers, because of its *liturgical* connection.[9]

If we return to the actual Bible, which many Christians think should dictate the ethics and law to the U.S. government, we notice a cultural and scientific gap of two to four millennia in the mentalities, so much that the uniqueness of either the ethics of Ancient Israel or the ethics of first-century Christianity seem rather to be an *enigma*. Most of the history went through long periods of oral transmission, so many of the written documents in the Jewish Tanach or Christian "Old Testament" were committed to that form more than a thousand years *after* the events they purport to relate.

That being true, it is not remarkable that later situations or conditions are accidently or even intentionally *read back into earlier ones*. As we saw about the need for antiquity of dissident religions arising out of dominant religions, the same process of seeing one's roots in the past seems typical to nearly all religions throughout their history, no matter their size. In any case, "Ancient Israel" marked its beginnings with a group experience of freedom: the Exodus from Egypt and the people's adoption by Yahweh at Mt. Sinai.

This god differed from many of the surrounding regions' deities since they were often associated with specific cosmic elements such as the sun, earth, moon, salt water, fresh water, vegetation, and so forth. Even the polytheism of the Fertile Crescent had been an evolution of a much earlier and cruder form of seeing everything in one's world as having some "spirit" or "life power" which could perhaps affect humans. The conception of power gradually became more specifically delineated and eventually began to take on anthropomorphic dimensions. The gods were often geographically located by certain structures or natural sites which became power centers for the people.

Tradition says it was at Sinai that its God, called Moses to deliver the people from their enslavement in Egypt. He gave them His name, Yhwh or, with vowels, Yahweh, as the God who promised to come to their aid, and from the start was associated with Mt. Sinai because the people escaping Egypt gathered there and were given the intimidating experience of receiving the condensed form of their covenant with Yhwh. Nevertheless, the conception of Yhwh was not confined to a space because the people were commanded to build a portable tabernacle for their journey, which would be the symbol of God's presence with them. But there was *nothing* universal about the experience. It was *not* intended to be shared with others so it would include all people of the area or whole earth. It was *not* even a claim of explicit monotheism. The emphasis was always to keep the people belonging to *this god.*

This god identified itself as the god of the *forefathers* of part of that "exodus" group, the "god of Abraham, Isaac and Jacob," who delivered those enslaved people from Egypt, then adopted them for "His" people at Mt. Sinai. A part of the covenant He made with *only them* included the Decalogue or Ten Commandments which were apodictic laws, totally authoritative, simple, and unconditional. Less than half of those 10 laws, however, could be formed into actual civil or criminal law; the remainder had to do with cultivation of one's attitude toward other people, or, even more importantly, of honoring this Redeeming god by utter obedience, which included never equating Him with anything or making any image to represent Him, and to keep one day a week holy in His honor. Later laws added several other "holy days" that this god expected them to keep.

Idolatry, specifically, the worship of any other alleged deity, was the most heinous sin of all, and thus the most important of their civil and criminal law, carrying with it the death penalty. In fact, people were to report any idolatry so those engaging in it could be killed as an example and warning to others. It was not a matter of being an ethical law, but simply that this god would not be compromised in any way, and that priority continued to be true even among Israel's eighth-century prophets who were later famous for their *ethical* renunciation of the people. Even in those ethical condemnations those prophets issued against the people, however, idolatry still had priority.

For example, in Hosea, all the ethical accusations seem to be of secondary importance, since the whole thrust of the prophetic denouncement was that the people were "unfaithful" to God, even as Gomer was unfaithful to Hosea (Hos. esp. ch 1–4). The same is true in Amos because the famous "let justice roll down like waters" is God's rejection of them and their religious feast days, but particularly because they became idolatrous (Am. 5:18–27), with a promise that the coming "day of Yhwh" will be one of their being punished by God. This focus was the same in the other prophets as well and was even utilized by the postexilic prophet, Malachi, who accused the men of being unfaithful to their wives, which was analogous to his more important condemnation of the people's being unfaithful to God in failing to offer their tithes or sacrifices to Him (Mal. 3:7–9). One gets the picture that the story was all about Yahweh, that the people had never really deserved His love, but he would promise to be with them in crises provided they honored him properly and lived as he told them (Deut. chs 28–29). Because this single people had this specific covenant with this specific deity, they were to obey all of His commands, which originally included conquering a land by His power, making no covenants with those people, but killing the men and all women who were not virgins. Many conquered people were turned into slaves. Fathers could even sell their daughters into slavery, which was quite common in ancient cultures.

The original ethics formed laws applicable to their seminomadic and emerging agricultural life in that conquered land of Canaan, an *agricultural existence* which continued to shape the community's ethics even centuries later in the Mishnah, as a part of the "dual Torah" which dealt with the situation of being a Jew with*out* a temple or even a land (i.e., after the Bar Kochba revolt and war of 132 CE). Their earliest laws replicated many of the civil and criminal laws of surrounding tribes and ancient law codes, most of which were created for the benefit of petty kings. Even Yhwh's adoption of this people at Sinai had, in fact, followed the form of such ancient Hittite suzerainty treaties of that time. In those ancient cultures, men were superior to women, and, even in Ancient Israel, the wife was barely above her maid-servant in personal rights. She was her husband's property, and if she failed to produce children for him, he was free to have children by the maid-servant. Women were not property owners, and we have record only of Zelophehad's daughters who demanded to be their father's heir since he left no sons. Men could bring suspicions of unfaithfulness of a wife, which evoked a strange test administered by the priest and an oath, with the assumption that if she lied in the oath of her innocence, she would be forever barren thereafter. Of course, the women had no parallel tests for their husband's faithfulness. And women's fruitfulness or bareness seems to have been regulated by Yhwh completely.

Regarding any structures of justice from those ancient ethics, the history reveals the development from a loosely organized tribal/family relation, somewhat resembling the ancient Greek amphictyony, after the people settled fully in the land of Canaan. They designated several "cities of refuge" to which one guilty of what we call manslaughter could flee and stay the remainder of his life. If he left, or was found to have committed murder by ambush or specific type of weapon or because of a long-standing hostility, he could not be sheltered in such a city of refuge, but was to be turned over to the family's "blood-avenger" to administer justice.

The tradition tells us that quite early in their relationship with Yahweh, the people would turn to idolatry away from Yahweh, so He would allow them to be overrun by the native people they had failed to exterminate or drive out. The same text of the book of Judges, however, which states the disobedience of the people in not getting rid of all the locals is the very reason God punished them, yet it also indicated that Yahweh himself was intentionally responsible for leaving some of the locals so as to tempt his people to disobey. A strange juxtaposition, to say the least. In any case, the theme of the cycle of idolatry, punishment, remorse by the people, God's restoration of the people by God's raising up some charismatic warriors (the "Judges") repeated itself over and over. Its point was stated that in those days there was no king in Israel so each person simply did what was good in his or her own eyes. That is a very telling statement, implying that humans cannot be self-governing, that they either do not know what is right or they have no power to do it, or both. So much for autonomy![10]

Yahweh reluctantly gave in to the people's desire to have a "king," though taking this as a personal rejection. The structures of justice and its ethic had earlier depended upon the primary leader such as Moses or Joshua or people they chose as surrogate judges, but then became the role of the delivering heroes in the book called "Judges," and was finally the role of the king as the ultimate judge of problems, legal and ethical. The king, however, found himself in competition with the priest who anointed him by the command of Yhwh, and when Yhwh gave an order that was not carried out by even the anointed king, such as in the case of King Saul and his leniency in sparing the Ammonite king, Agag, the priest, Samuel, killed Agag and summarily told Saul he was through being king and his son would not succeed him. During the "united kingdom" and the later "divided kingdom," the kings and priests both were involved in enforcing the laws, therefore the ethics underlying them, and some kings eventually became symbols or paradigms of the "good" king while others were remembered as the "evil" kings. Largely because of the people's faithlessness toward Yhwh, evidenced in their trusting other nations for their security, the Northern Kingdom collapsed in the early eighth century BCE and the Southern Kingdom fell in the late sixth century BCE.

Their explicit assertion of monotheism came about when Yhwh influenced Cyrus of Persia to allow captives from Jerusalem to return to their land some decades later, and this proved to "Second Isaiah" that Yhwh was not only the Redeeming god but the Creating god, since he had created anew this people. In making this equation, the author felt justified in mocking polytheists or idolaters who "make" their own gods.

If, in the postexilic period the people had been taught by Haggai and Zechariah to put their trust in the two "sons of oil" (which was a way of referring to the "anointed" or "messiah" of God), Joshua ben Jehozadak, the new high priest, and Zerubbabel, the new governor, to rebuild the temple and restore the former structures of religion and government, all to the glory of Yhwh, the aspirations never became reality. The temple got rebuilt, but the return of the "golden age" was perpetually elusive. During the following centuries, rabbinic Judaism came to the foreground from the necessities the community had experienced in exile with no temple and for those Jews who remained in Babylon rather than return to the land. The Egyptians and Syrians fought each other, conveniently even using the land of Judah, Samaria, and Galilee as their battleground, and occasionally Judaism which was restored in Jerusalem was punished explicitly, such as when Antiochus Epiphanes blatantly defiled the temple. Eventually, the small surviving nation was taken over by the Roman power.

A "messianic" hope still existed in some circles, a hope of another "King David." But when the people felt the lowest, a new form of thinking developed into a specific literary form, called "apocalyptic." It existed especially during the two centuries both before and after the birth of Jesus and can be seen in canonical books such as Daniel and Zechariah, but in noncanonical apocalypses collected as part of the later *Pseudepigrapha*, especially Fourth Ezra and the Similitudes of Enoch. This literature expressed hope in a future time when God would bring ultimate salvation and vindication to His chosen, the Jewish people, so it created symbolic pictures of a coming "Son of man" or "Man from the sea" a representative of Yahweh who would bring history to a close, initiate a final judgment, and a millennial reign.

The "Christian" movement began within Judaism largely over an apocalyptic hope which the early church was convinced it could trace back to *an aspirational* apocalyptic message by Jesus of Nazareth, and since the earliest Christians were Jews, Christianity quickly appropriated the scriptures of Judaism, with its own emphases and favorite passages. Judaism suffered the terrible loss of its temple in 70 CE, and by the Bar Kochba war in 132 CE, lost its land. During this period, some of its rabbis put together the *Mishnah* which dealt with the question of how to be sanctified as a Jew without a temple. The work imagined a people still within its land, living an agricultural life, achieving sanctification of its *people* in a very utopian sense, looking for perfection at the "end of days." Judaism's status in the world was diminished even further in 132 CE when Constantine made Christianity legal, and then later embraced it as the religion of the Empire.

The different Judaisms' emphases changed within history, but the distinctness, the "holiness," or being such a special or separate people was never lost but only intensified as it continued its history of suffering for refusing to become indistinct, that is, simply part of the assimilated masses. It is this history, from their captivity in Babylon after the destruction of the first temple, to the destruction of the second temple and finally to the Holocaust of the twentieth century that seems to demand the focus of the question of what it means to be Jewish in the world. If the Dual Torah approach continues to be needed today, it is primarily for family life and its moments that require sanctification, but that ancient "exile/return" theme has been superseded by a larger, much more inclusive group by the more graphic "Holocaust/State of Israel" theme, which addresses more one's relationship to the governing structures of justice, political and economic concerns. During this long history, Judaism has had its significant rabbis, theologians, philosophers, and mystics who have addressed its ethics in many different ways, but significantly, it has learned how to function with integrity in a nation even as a minority within a democracy which includes many religions and ethical systems—without desiring to force its ethics or religious beliefs on others or the government, which is pretty much what Rawls and the Framers had envisioned for religions.

The Particularity of Christianity's Biblical Ethics

Christianity arose out of this Jewish setting, at first not as a new religion but simply the fulfillment of Yahweh's promises to the Jews throughout the centuries. The earliest records emerging from this new community probably were letters by a Hellenistic Jew who had a previous short history of persecuting these disciples of Jesus, but through a later mystical encounter he had en route to Damascus, was himself converted to the sect. His was a universal vision of God having planned from ages past to incorporate all the nations into His people, to save all (Rom: 11:32), so whatever rejections occurred in prior years, they were to be overcome by God's plan which had been hidden all this time (Col. 1:24–29), so a very *aspirational* picture, some vindication for the Jews, but more universal and ultimately quite otherworldly. He saw God's calling of the Jews "irrevocable" (Rom: 11:28–32), but by God's decision to have Paul be the "apostle to the Gentiles (or nations)," God was simply becoming totally inclusive. Of course, if the Torah remained the criteria for one's living, one's ethic and one's religion, then the Jewish exclusive possession of the Torah would be violated, and Paul was bright enough to know that his mission to Gentiles would be unsuccessful since they would be so opposed to circumcision and many other Jewish religious customs. But if his opposition to the Torah on behalf of the Gentile inclusion was not qualified by him, then the Palestinian Jews would see him as their enemy.[11]

While Paul's Christ-mysticism could rescue people from having to hope for a radically changed world by rescuing them out of this world, how could Jews vacate their need for vindication *in* this world and at the same time, allow the "chosen" of God to become so broad that it included people in whom God had never shown much of an interest. Even Jesus was later remembered as sending his Twelve apostles only to the Jews, not to Gentiles, since he predicted the Kingdom would come before they could even return to him (Matt. 10:23) and the message of Jesus was given by him with strict instructions *not* to share it with Gentiles. Further, the book of Acts shows the reader that the earliest church leaders in Jerusalem were not keen on the idea of preaching to Gentiles (Acts 10:9–16). But Paul was the man for the job, a Hellenistic Jew from Tarsus of Cilicia, not a Judaean, a person who claimed that he had always lived with good conscience (I Cor. 4:3–4; Phil. 3:6), yet ironically was frustrated with the Torah's command not to "covet" (Rom. 7:7–12). So he was torn by an ethical imperative he felt obligated to keep yet felt powerless to keep, and welcomed finding the answer was instead in faith in the promise given by God to Abraham which preceded the Torah, ironically somehow involving even Christ (as the singular seed to whom God's promise was given)? (Gal. 3:15–18; Rom. 7:14–8:4).

The new plan of God, as Paul saw it, was not to be confined to the Torah which the Jews had, nor was it to be a plan to restore an earthly monarchy and thereby some utopia on earth. It was conceived in more mystical terms as being united so much with the crucified Jesus that the disciple would be one with him also in his resurrection (Rom. chs. 6–8), and that lies *beyond* any civil government, any utopia, any king, any laws. It is created by God's Spirit, which Paul saw as the primary vehicle for human behavior or ethical living (Gal. 5:16–26). Paul was convinced that this union with Jesus the Christ would ultimately "save" one from this evil world, and such was necessary since even the world itself groaned to be redeemed by the Spirit (Rom. 8:18–25).

In any case, Paul was so convinced that Christ would return to his disciples soon for the ultimate turning over of everything to God, that whatever state one was in presently, one should simply stay put and satisfied, because of the "shortness of time" (I Cor. 7:29). This "status quo ethic" was satisfactory only if Christ *did* "return" and bring history to a close with the General Resurrection and Final Judgment. Paul was convinced it would happen probably during his own lifetime, but he still insisted that fellow Christians should live by love for all others (Rom 13:8–10), rather than avenge themselves, and allow the Spirit to direct them to the most noble ethical or moral relations to reaffirm their mystical union with Christ. What he did not resolve was the fact of who was to blame, if one professing to be a Christian had the Spirit, if that person did not live morally? Was it his fault or the Spirit's? Within a few years after Paul's final letters to a church, Jerusalem fell to Titus and his Roman army, and the Temple was once again destroyed. Whoever this Jesus was, he had failed to prevent that disaster even though he allegedly told his closest disciples he would be with them to the end of the age (Matt. 28:20).

While most of Paul's letters probably were written primarily within the decade of the 50s, and they provide almost no information about the historical Jesus (only that he was crucified and was raised from death, and that he shared a "last supper" with his disciples), there were oral and perhaps written traditions about that Jesus that may have circulated prior to his letters.[12] While it is true today that we have four canonical gospels, in the last century we have uncovered more and more accounts of that information about Jesus, now totaling 20 gospels if we include fragments. Because of this, the most recent quest to find the "historical Jesus," conducted by the Jesus Seminar, has traced and studied these sources, attempting to see their relation to the canonical gospels, and then to the writings of Paul and general expectations and teachings of the Christian community. After 20 years of mutual study and sharing, the group generally agreed that not even 20% of the deeds or words attributed to Jesus were likely "historical."[13]

The apocalyptic or eschatological expectation of the early church has been self-evident since Albert Schweitzer's groundbreaking work at the turn of the twentieth century. But it has never been shared with the Christian churches in language everyone could understand. On the other hand, most Christians through history have been taught about Jesus being the "Messiah," the corrective has always been furnished by the church that he was the true Messiah, not just the political, military Messiah for whom Judaism longed. It has been totally spiritualized and pushed into the remote future, except for those who think Jesus is still around in some way.

When one examines the three synoptic gospels, however, the only real equation of Jesus with the "Messiah" is made by the Apostle Peter in Matt. 16:18, but scholars long ago pointed out that this statement of Peter's and even Jesus's reply to Pilate's inquiry as to whether or not he was the Messiah were not likely historical. The latter answer by Jesus was seen by many as evasive, like "Do you say so?" Whatever notions these gospel writers had about Jesus actually being a Messiah, it was a quite unique picture, not of a victorious earthly king or ruler, but quite otherworldly, so it is more the *last part* of Peter's confession when he blurted out that Jesus was the "Messiah, the *Son of God*" which the church emphasizes. Yet these documents were written by Jews and Judaism knew only of one God, who had no Son, no equal, and knew nothing of a "Trinity" or "Triune God" or of a "Son" who was of the same substance (*homoousios*) as God the Father. Even the "Messiah" meant only an "anointed" of God, nothing of the "same substance" as God, as the later fourth and fifth centuries creeds expressed.

Whoever wrote these three synoptic gospels, and whatever their inter-dependence and their usage of earlier materials or traditions, they give the impression that Jesus described himself and his mission in apocalyptic terms, not just eschatological ones as one of the leaders of the "Jesus Seminar," Prof. Crossan, wanted to distinguish. Jesus is portrayed speaking of the coming "Son of man" who will bring in the Kingdom and will do it during the lifetime of his audience (Mk 9:1), even before his Twelve can return from their short preaching mission to the Jews (Matt. 10:23). It is evident that these writers were persuaded that Jesus was speaking of himself as the "Son of man" by several of the passages they cite. Otherwise, when the delay of His return became apparent and embarrassing, they would *not* have inserted it into their gospels as His promise to them if they knew he never claimed that.

In the famous "Sermon on the Mount," the ethical instructions Jesus alleg-edly articulated could not have been formed into any law for a government, since they concern primarily attitudes not actions. They are unrealistically extremely pacifistic and apocalyptically world denying, even to the point of welcoming being defrauded and not giving any thought to one's future. But as Albert Schweitzer saw it, this was only an "interim ethic," an ethic that would be relevant *only if* the Kingdom and end of history did occur *very soon*. But it did not. Of course, this is not to say that none of the statements, if removed from the context, might not provide a principle which could be relevant. But the whole of the promises implied in these gospels and in Paul's early writ-ings explain the expectation of an imminent "return" of Christ, which did not happen, and by the turn of that century, the letters attributed to Peter revealed that was a subject over which opponents of the Christians were using to mock them.

The distinction John Dominic Crossan made between ethical eschatology and apocalyptic was simply that the latter always included vengeance, vio-lence, or brutality, whether it was produced by humans or they hoped God would do it. But the symbolic pictures of "Final Judgment" in the scriptures are not Dante, and justice often requires some kind of sanction, even if cul-tures separated by millennia may not consider the sanctions or punishments in the same way, and to distinguish justice from vengeance is always a fine line to draw. In any case, the imminent aspect of this eschatological or apocalyptic hope dissipated or lost credibility over the years, and as Martin Werner wrote years ago, the church *replaced* the receding Parousia (Jesus's "return") by the sacramental authority as a *present* certainty.[14] Whether that Jesus was histori-cally an enigma to our time as Schweitzer insisted, or was a wandering sage teaching a subversive wisdom in his opposition to Caesar and the Empire as the recent Jesus Seminar concluded, in neither case do the ethical teachings assigned to him provide any system of Christian ethics for all time to come.[15]

Cultural Exclusivism and Aspirations in Subsequent Developments

The history of the ethics of Judaism and of the ethics of Christianity began to take almost opposite and exclusive directions after the Bar Kochba Rebellion in mid-second century CE and Constantine's attachment to Christianity in the fourth century CE. The Bar Kochba revolt put the finishing touches upon Judaism's occupancy of its land until 1948, which meant the ethics of the Torah, which, with the influence of the two Talmuds, sustained the Jewish Diaspora, but was not seen as a possible ethics to shape the laws of any nation. They were a landless people, at the mercy of other governments and other religions, philosophies, and politics. Racism, xenophobia, and anti-Semitism were fueled for centuries by Christian discrimination against them based on their subconscious feeling of the Jews being the "potentially disconfirming other," as Richard Rubenstein noted.

The question of whether or to what degree to assimilate into the different cultures became a life or death issue in many instances in those 18 centuries. Their ethics necessarily became more restricted toward actions only within the Jewish community itself. Lack of assimilation fed into non-Jewish people's xenophobia, especially the Jews' retention of their own language and religious rituals which were so different from those Christians in the various countries in which they scattered. The more the people were marginalized by a nation's dominant group, naturally, the more important their unique history and language became to them for their own existence, which others took as their unreceptiveness to assimilation.

As in most cases of xenophobia such as those Erika Lee documented, this simply forms a continuous vicious circle of hurt for the minority group. In the early decades of Christianity's rise to Western power, the Jews, as the potentially "disconfirming other,"[16] had been accused of deicide by Christians, and within Christendom, they were often deprived of even minimal human rights, suffered immensely in various pogroms and were banned from many countries at different times. Eventually, much of Europe emancipated the Jews. But many emigrated to the United States as "Reform" Judaism, while those who stayed eventually furnished Hitler and other anti-Semites in Germany a scapegoat for their wounded national pride. That culminated in the Holocaust.

Rabbi Richard Rubenstein responded brilliantly to the Holocaust in all his theological, philosophical, and psychological learning, tracing its causes, motivation, and tactics, which leaves no conclusion but that it was a very unethical *religious* war against Judaism. It was religious or specifically a "Christian" war because rather than the Christian religion being blamed for replacing the Teutonic gods, the German Christians were provided the Jews,[17] and Hitler enlisted the Christian church in his attempt to restore the Fatherland's traditions, wealth, and pride in addressing the "Jewish Question." That does not mean that all Christians were aware of what Hitler was doing to the Jews, since he claimed only to be "resettling" them to protect them. But passive complicity is often driven by a fear and inability to trust those in power.

Only since 1948 have they had their own country, but situated by a displacement of Palestinians, creating terrible resentment parallel to that likely evoked by the conquest of the land of Canaan in the thirteenth century BCE. Jews are still scattered throughout the world, so in most cases, have their own religious ethic but are not able to think of their government's ethic as corresponding to it, and, in many cases, even having to endure anti-Semitic discrimination, demonstrations, and violent attacks. Nevertheless, the Jewish culture has furnished a disproportionate share of geniuses to cultures throughout the world, and many of them have provided an ethical impetus to governments and structures of justice. So far as this inquiry is concerned, it has to be said that many of them have illustrated how possible it is to live in a democratic society that includes a religious pluralism without either insisting on specific privileges or exemptions or trying to have the nation adapt to their religious uniqueness, perhaps because they have found themselves in Rawls's category with others of the "least advantaged" because of merely their ethnic heritage and their history of being abused by Christians. But their presence in the United States has been precisely what Madison and Jefferson considered as a necessity for any and all citizens who were religious, except they would have objected to the anti-Semitic elements of the United States which make Jewish people feel vulnerable or as less worthy citizens.

Christianity, on the other hand, found itself being embraced by merged religious and governmental powers, in which the relationships at times deteriorated to one of terrible tension or imbalance in favor of one at the expense of the other. At different stages in the history of Christianity, its ethics had different orientations. At first, once its imminent eschatology faded into the distant future, it was thought by many to be somewhat similar to the ethic of the Stoics. Through Augustine's influence, it became quite NeoPlatonism. Then by Thomas Aquinas and others, it turned to Aristotle and created a "natural law" and "right reason" ethic. In the Protestant tradition beginning in the sixteenth century, it was influenced by Luther's individualism but also his understanding of the "natural orders" and of his idea of "forensic righteousness," and then by Calvin's injection of a stronger sense of being "predestined" by God, of being God's "chosen" people. The earliest and largest group of Protestant immigrants to the New World were Calvinists. Unlike Luther's almost complete dismissal of Jewish scriptures or "Old Testament," the Calvinists had been persuaded of the necessity of following God's law even found throughout the Old Testament, a view considerably different and more legalistic than Luther. Even there, however, it was only a very selective Christian manipulation of a few passages in those scriptures to read them in such an anti-Semitic, uncritical, and unhistorical way.

Protestantism further divided, splintering over and over, always adding new unique ideas to distinguish each new sect. So exclusivism reigned, but often was more a cultural exclusivism than even a religious one. Meanwhile, the break with the Catholic Church did not mean the end of religion's alignment with government, but Christianity simply became splintered also between Protestant governments, according to their preference of Christian views and particular cultures. The religious factions kept governments involved in hostilities that were not altogether their making as well as the opposite, as religious wars and persecution of religious minorities continued in Europe. Although they gave each other an added authority or actual enforcement, both governments and the religion quite often suffered, eventually losing credibility with many citizens which included most minorities in the various countries. Prof. Curry described succinctly what the merger of church and state of "Christendom" *meant* and how it had worked in Europe beneficially for some people:

> Although Christendom distinguished between and separated the sacred and the secular power, it conceived of society as an organic whole and envisaged both as cooperating in a joint task, each fulfilling its proper role. Ideally, both would work together for the common good. The Church, as the spiritual authority, would anoint the ruler and bind subjects to his power by an oath of loyalty. In turn, the ruler, as the secular authority, would protect the Church, promote the true religion as defined by it, and punish dissenters. The two powers would work hand in hand to promote a culture, a legal system, and a way of life based on Christian beliefs. Such a system provided little room for dissenters, and non-Christians existed only on its fringes.[18]

Of course, history does not reveal the two powers always or even usually working "hand in hand," and the world does not have a single religion, nor does the United States, and, in fact, it was mainly those Curry called "dissenters" who came to the New World prior to the late nineteenth century. After that more immigrants were Catholic or of non-Christian religions. In any case, the United States was conceived as a "democracy," not merely a merger of two power brokers, not just an empowering of a single religion as if it were the obvious will of the only god, even if Supreme Court justices in the oral argument of *Perry* mocked other religions, and asserted the Christian God as the only true god and insisted not only that it is only that God who provides authority for human laws and governments, but even that our government has a right to express its own religion.[19] We shall see how the Framers of the U.S. Constitution conceived this nation as a "lively experiment" and *radically different* from the Christendom which had dominated the West, to separate religion from government once and for all, and to create a democratic republic which had a strong enough unity that government of the whole people could extend to any citizens who were religious both the freedom to believe what they wanted as well as to worship with whatever people or religious group, when and how they desired, so long as they did not violate the generally applicable laws that apply to all citizens. This was a monumental achievement which must not be lost by carelessness, indifference, or feeing superior to others in any way.

By the nineteenth century, scholarship had moved far beyond the earlier "metaphysics of infinity," as Foucault called it, not only in the human sciences which was Foucault's interest, but even in the study of religion. It had begun with textual criticism in the late fifteenth and early sixteenth centuries, in an attempt to determine the most valid text of the Bible. By the late seventeenth century, it developed into an early form of literary criticism, asking questions of the various biblical documents, their origins, authors, primary opponents, basic messages, dates, and so forth. Eventually it developed into a historical criticism, form criticism, transmission of tradition or redaction criticism, rhetorical criticism, ideological criticism, and other disciplined approaches. Aside from the concern with the Bible, the religion moved theologically or Christologically from an Absolute Idealism in the early nineteenth century in Schleiermacher and Hegel, to an existential or ontotheological approach in Tillich, finally to a phenomenological ontology in Scharlemann.[20] Despite the Hegelian equation of his era in Germany as the culmination of the Absolute Spirit, of the true work of God, so that history itself was a theodicy, his Lutheran aspirational certainty was not shared as reality by the Catholic Church or many Protestants. By 1864, the Catholic Church published a "Syllabus of Errors" which made quite explicit that no one had a right to belong to any religious group other than the Catholic Church since it is the only true religion in the world, and the church's authority and power is divine so superior to any human authority, reason, or any government.[21] Following this, in 1870, in Vatican I, the Council declared the Pope "infallible" when he is speaking officially on behalf of the church on either faith or morals. In the same period, fundamentalist Christians began to wage their war with Darwinism by declaring the plenary inspiration of the scriptures. Thus, the "absolutizing"—whether of Christian theology by Hegel, or of the Bible by Protestant fundamentalists, or of the structure and doctrine of the Catholic Church—reached its zenith.

But such exclusivism and narrowly defined aspirations, even if wrapped in the garments of heteronomy, ancient tradition, and absolutism, were too precritical, exclusive, and narrow in interest, *not the interest of the entire people of the nation*, and it was too dependent upon simplistic and obviously fictitious caricatures of their opponents. They were all fighting an impossible war against reason based on empirical data, the new sciences, religious diversity, freedom of conscience, and of the United States' novel break with a fourteen-century-old idea of Christendom. A century and a half later, most of their exclusivistic arguments *against* science, the new philosophies and political ideas, and so forth have revealed themselves as quite specious and of little interest to anyone except those at the top rungs of the institutions which propagated the defense of one interpretation of one religion and its ethic. But, unlike science which was shared on a public level, religions guarded the laity from hearing anything of modern critical approaches or the actual development in theology. Thus, most lay Christians were unaware that much Christian theology no longer saw "God" as a specific being at all, but rather as a power of being and meaning which cannot be identified with anything but can be manifest in its "being-other-than-God" in anything. Theism seemed to reach its point of no return.

If we go back just one century, at the same approximate time of the assertion of the Absolute in the second half of the nineteenth century by Protestant fundamentalists and the Catholic hierarchy, the United States found itself caught in a struggle to preserve its democratic republic, finally having to resort to a Civil War to try to keep all the states within the union and to free the slaves, which was the only way to have a real equality of all people. Both sides tried to claim the Christian ethic or at least the Christian symbols and Bible to justify their side, either for or against slavery, but it was more of a cultural argument rather than a truly ethical one, prompted more on an economic question. The fact that the Bible was used by both sides should have put the nail in the coffin about any "perspicuity" of the scriptures of which Luther boasted, or of the plenary inspiration and inerrancy of them as the fundamentalist Christians were insisting. But only the scholarly world saw the contradiction, people who were using new methods of inquiry which depended upon tracing empirical data, historical causality, and development.

Rather than deal with the inherent conflict between the different interpretations of a Christian ethic, many who presupposed it to be infallible simply espoused one of the two sides as the absolute truth. That meant a future of hardened positions, of resentment for any of one's aspirations not being realized. Over the next 150 years, many have seen themselves as the true protectors of the country, of the democracy, while they have undermined democracy with their majoritarian policies, economic theories and lobbying, their gerrymandering and their gross caricatures, and exaggerations of opposing positions.

By the 1970s, many blamed higher education for the nation's problems, while others blamed the "elite" from whom they felt alienated, and yet others blamed various minority groups, and finally many more were influenced by multiple conspiracy theories. These hardened positions of cultural exclusivism developed into a culture war and finally engaged in an insurrection on January 6, 2021, violating the ethics *both* of the religions as well as the ethics and laws of the government in their antigovernment action. They breached the Capitol claiming the president instructed them to do so to stop the counting of the electoral votes. They carried U.S. flags, Confederate flags, Jesus flags, QAnon flags and badges, and Trump flags. Together with the inscription of "Holy Bible" and "In God We Trust" on the breastplate of one of the men, the exclusive package was supposed as a coherent whole: the Bible and Jesus and the United States all stood for the ideals of Trump, QAnon, the Confederacy, and the White Supremacists who were all conceived ironically as victim/savior. The siege lasted around 6 hours, over a 140 law enforcement officers were injured, one was killed, three later committed suicide, legislative offices were ransacked, articles were stolen or defiled, and the insurgents chanted death threats to the vice president and the Speaker of the House, as they searched through the chambers and halls in their attempt to locate a legislator to harm or kill. That was the reality, and the *aspirations* of those ransacking the Capitol were a cultural phenomenon, diametrically opposed to the values and aspirations of the U.S. Constitution and the nation as a whole. It was majoritarianism in its most vile, authoritarian form, completely antidemocratic.

The whole scenario showed a cultural group driven by fear and contempt for a truly democratic republic, attempting to prevent the Senate count of the electoral votes which had made Joseph Biden the new president. If ever an event was both treasonous and sacrilegious at the same time, this was it. But much of the religious element manifest by the insurrectionists was only a hollow use of symbols, no more coherent with the actual religion than are the burning crosses of the KKK. It was not that people were trying to protect something sacred to them, but rather a manifestation of the loss of self-esteem and resentment of people who felt otherwise powerless to succeed in life as they wanted, as Eric Hoffer would describe them.[22] Their aspirations had not been met, but somehow Trump's attempt to fulfill Bannon's agenda to "deconstruct the administrative state" ignited them. The flags and symbols manifest by the group were matched in their incongruity with the weapons they used in beating and killing; they were only used as perverted weapons to give them a feeling of authority and power. The flags and symbols could have as easily all been swastikas.

DESACRALIZATION, DEMYTHOLOGIZATION, AND FREEDOM OF CONSCIENCE

"Desacralization" points to the fading of the consciousness of anything "sacred" or "holy" or even the "divine" in people's lives, or, in more common terms, is the "desecration" or the viewing or violating of the sacred, thus a "profaning." It need not occur by one's intention but can be an attitude within a culture that develops over time, that is, as any consciousness of something "sacred" or "holy" simply *loses meaning.* If a religion regards the name of its god as "sacred," then any common use of it may seem to be a desacralization. For example, my writing "Yhwh" or "Yahweh" earlier may appear to any Jewish person as my being very profane or sacrilegious, although I am only identifying the specific name vis-à-vis any number of other specific and generic names. Any word can be used so commonly that it becomes trite, and "Oh, my God!" is probably a good example. If the term "God" really was understood as signifying some all-powerful source of all being, then it is not likely it would be used in such a common way as a mere term of surprise or consternation.

"Demythologization" is more a technical term coined by New Testament scholar, Rudolf Bultmann, to indicate that the Christian message was originally infused with mythical elements but which can be meaningful in the present age only if the mythical terms can be seen as not assertions about empirical or cosmic entities or actual history, but only if they are taken as "existential" truths. Myths usually are stories about supranatural events or beings which have in some way become involved in history, and in so doing, have divinely established certain *ideas, values, or behaviors* as normative or required. But when a story embraces myth, it is no longer verifiable by historical method or any other scientific method; it basically makes a supranatural, historical claim while dislodging the content from any history we know.

Finally, "freedom of conscience" was a step beyond mere religious tolerance which was explored by John Locke, but became extremely important with the Framers of the U.S. Constitution. They were no longer satisfied that this New Nation would simply tolerate people who were religiously different, but that all people would be valued equally, and all honored in the freedom of their own conscience, provided they all complied with the generally agreed laws with which all citizens are expected to uphold.

What is of note is in the same late nineteenth century in which an absolutizing in Christianity occurred, first in the Absolute Idealism of Hegel, then the Catholic Syllabus of Errors and Dogma of Papal Infallibility, and in the Protestant idea plenary verbal inspiration of the scriptures—an obvious appeal to "freedom of conscience," as well as desacralization, and demythologization, also occurred. In fact, it was the consciousness of the widespread common (i.e., not scholarly, and often not even a person's conscious abandonment of his or her religious understandings) acceptance of "freedom of conscience," desacralization, and demythologization that was itself the impetus for the religious institutions themselves retrenching and trying to negate what they saw as this challenge to their very existence. While Altizer, Hamilton, and others seemed to startle a few Christians with their declaration that "God is dead" in the 1960s, the thought was really not that novel, not even when it had been articulated two generations before by Nietzsche.

In fact, we could probably say that "desacralization" itself has existed since the first person who refused to believe that the world actually is divided between the "sacred" and the "profane" spheres, which means the first person or group that began to disagree with those who were religious, who propagated a message about things or even beings who were "sacred," "holy," or "divine." "Divine" eventually indicated more only certain live beings, not lifeless objects, and "holy" was often similarly circumscribed. But they were all in a category which was opposite the "unholy" or "profane" or "evil" or even the "ordinary." "Sacred" came to indicate not simply items used in one's worship of deities, but the rituals themselves, the words spoken, and this eventually led religious people to thinking of a process by which the *ordinary* or profane could be transformed into or at least treated as something "holy" or "sacred," and the process was called "sanctifying." If it was considered to be a "cleansing" or transcending of the normal or ordinary state, and was usually assigned only to a power that was "holy" or "divine," although within Judaism and other religions, the actual sanctifying depended also on the individual person following prescribed rituals or rules to bring about the sanctifying. This was extremely important in giving special meaning to various days, months, and cyclical events in the year and in people's lives.

In some Eastern cultures, human beings in the present may be referred to as "holy" or even "divine" or as "realized" beings. The person or power who performs this change in the nature of things is not merely changing people's attitudes toward it, but thought to be actually altering its nature. Even the Western or Roman Catholic idea of "transubstantiation" in the Eucharist involved what was believed to be a *real change of substance*, although quite undetectable. Of course, many religions conceived of deities who had the power in such an unrestrained capacity that it could not only change things for the better, but could also permanently wreck them or destroy them. Rudra and Shiva in ancient Indian Vedism had such an ambivalent character. Even Yahweh in the ancient tradition of Israel could destroy at will.

When a people *no longer fear* such potentially destructive and unpredictable powers, that may be called a mentality of desacralization. They may no longer think a certain holy ritual causes what results the authorities believe, or they may no longer worry about using "God's" name "in vain" since they do not see any power implicit in a usage or nonusage of a name, or they may not think they need to drown "witches" since they no longer give any credence to the old claim that she (or he) has some supranatural or evil power. When the stories of such deities are no longer viewed as history, the process of demythologization has occurred. And when people quit viewing their religion as the only absolutely true one, they no longer feel threatened by the institutions prohibiting them from belonging to any other religion.

In many if not most ancient cultures, everything was thought to be alive, to having its own Spirit. In its earliest forms, the religion of Ancient Israel did not seem to view everything as having its own Spirit, but it did conceive of Yahweh as personal and in control of human life. The Deuteronomist knew of no accidents in life: if one experienced the good things, one was being blessed by Yahweh for obeying Him; if one experienced only negative things such as crop failure, illness, and so forth, one was being punished by Yahweh for disobeying Him (Deut. chs. 28–29). So there were no accidents. That came much later, probably first in the book of Ecclesiastes, in which the author spoke of "time and chance" happening in life, often defying one's hopes or expectations. While the "God" of Christianity was more removed from the mundane activities of typical human life on this planet, the scriptures do not release this "God" from having the power to destroy and even, after Final Judgment, to torment the unbelievers endlessly, or at least that was what those Christians believed or hoped would happen to those who victimized them as we see in Revelation.

The ancient Vedas are filled with spells, chants, and procedures for cancelling curses other people have put on a person, and both early Christianity and Islam accommodated a belief in evil spirits or demons or jinn which could invade a person's body and mind. In the 1970s, a movie called *The Exorcist* was built around the idea of evil spirits themselves randomly selecting to inhabit a person's body and mind, and they could be "cast out" only by a qualified "exorcist," which meant usually a person in a religious order who was found to have such supranatural powers. The movie was a sensation. Kurt Anderson described those years of unrestrained beliefs in the most fantastic in his *Fantasyland*.

The movie itself seemed to be a test to find out how "desacralized" a person might be in one's attitude or thinking. There were reports of many people fainting while watching some of the gruesome or nauseating or absurdly imaginative elements of the movie. Many viewers seemed quite impressed, thinking that perhaps it was not sheer fantasy but real possibility, while others derided it as unbelievable and harmless like the old Frankenstein movies, perhaps even a bit stupid. It might have been that after people stood out on the street in long lines all night to get into the theaters, which was very common the first few weeks, this might have contributed to the adverse reactions like getting nauseous or fainting during the movie. But, in any case, it probably revealed that most of the people of the nation were more "desacralized" than they would have confessed, that they were not totally convinced this was a real possibility, not all that unscientific levitating above the bed by the little girl or her turning her head 360 degrees. That was too much.

In the early twentieth century, philosopher Rudolf Otto wrote his *The Idea of the Holy*, in which he emphasized that the mysterium tremendum, which has been attached to the "holy" for centuries, seems to have been neglected in modern Christian theology. That may have startled some theologians or even lay church members who might have found the book. But the loss of the sense of the sacred had been going on for hundreds of years in Western culture. It did not even begin in the Enlightenment, as bad a rap as many ultraconservative Christians want to give to that great movement. In fact, even Michel Foucault—who dated the beginning of the "new sciences" at the end of the eighteenth century, as they founded an empirical element as the very key to their methods of research and analysis which provided new forms of comparison and weighing—called this the demise of the "metaphysics of infinity"—was nevertheless confident that conservative institutions would continue to fight for that metaphysics and their nonempirical or different methods of earlier centuries.

This is not to say that the entire population of the West consisted of Platonists or mere essentialists up to the end of the eighteenth century, or that Aristotle had no influence on the West. The focus on the empirical, first in Aristotle, then others in succeeding generations, did give science a radically different orientation eventually, and also had *progressively* injected itself into analyses of theological and Christological claims which still in the late medieval period had been able to work with imaginary analogies such as the "analogy of being" whereby one could understand the meaning of a word used about "God" by comparing it to what is being said when the same word is used about a human being.

Yet what was said about "God" never stopped at that point, but added what one learned from "revelation" which was given a status far above human reason. Gradually, a greater discomfort in such easy talk about "God" and even things "sacred" set in. Yet even in the fifth century, St. Augustine, who was a NeoPlatonist, had recognized that the analogy of being was quite insufficient, that one could *not* speak literally of God "knowing" something as if he knew or learned things in the way humans do. So what *did* the word mean when used about "God"?

Desacralization came not just from a new focus on the empirical, beginning with astronomy, though that certainly affected people's trust in some of the stories of the Bible, for example, of Yhwh stopping the sun in its orbit around the earth for a 24-hour period so the Israelite invaders could chase down the local rulers and put them to death. But it came from innumerable sources including the unscientific claims made or manifest in most religions' scriptures and dogmas. It also emerged a bit with the voluntarism or autonomy so valuable to generate conversions in the "revivals" of the Great Awakening.

Of course, the success of the Great Awakenings of both the eighteenth and nineteenth centuries was not due to the revivalists or converts *awareness* of desacralization, much less their agreement with it. Quite the opposite was the case as the hellfire sermons and absolute certainty of the evangelists deepened and in many cases, embedded a sense of the "holy" or "sacred" in the minds of many people for the first time. But the *sense of freedom* to make a decision about one's religion was an *extreme* result of desacralization. As we already saw, the Syllabus of Errors of the nineteenth century showed the Catholic Church had not caught up to this sense of freedom for all; to the church, any desacralization was a blasphemous threat to its very existence. Many Christians before and after had been taught that one's religious life depended wholly upon one being "called" by God, and this was true, though in different ways in both Calvin's Protestant message as well as the Roman Catholic control of its message through its catechizing. Richard Rorty, however, described the other element of desacralization as the *end of worship*, just as Rubenstein had illustrated how the criticism of Egypt's gods which was part of the Exodus was bound over many centuries to produce a self-criticism even of Israel's belief in its God, resulting in *atheism*, though he did not become an atheist even though he spoke of the "time of the death of God."[23] Rorty quoted the historical connection historian Hans Blumenberg saw between the Age of Faith and the Age of Reason in the following words:

[O]nce upon a time we felt a need to worship something which lay beyond the visible world. Beginning in the seventeenth century we tried to substitute a love of truth for a love of God, treating the world described by science as a quasi divinity. Beginning at the end of the eighteenth century we tried to substitute a love of ourselves for a love of scientific truth, a worship of our own deep spiritual or poetic nature, treated as one more quasi divinity. The line of thought common to Blumenberg, Nietzsche, Freud, and Davidson suggests that we try to get to the point where we no longer worship anything, where we treat nothing as a quasi divinity, where we treat everything—our language, our conscience, our community—as a product of time and chance. To reach this point would be, in Freud's words, to "treat chance as worthy of determining our fate."[24]

Of course, none of the converts to the revivalists' message would have recognized this, but the desacralization occurred less explicitly on a much broader scale in the brush arbors of the frontier than it did within more scholarly circles. Uniquely, "time and chance" as well as the absurdity or vanity of life feeds into a "desacralization," especially if one is trying to lay hold on anything as Absolute or permanent, and this theme of impermanence, as I said, was the theme of Ecclesiastes as well as of Buddhism—the *impermanence* or contingency or relativity of *everything*.

But that awareness of impermanence of everything or the loss of the sense of an Absolute or intervening God or "desacralization" is *very gradual* since religion invariably introduces itself as the absolute answer, as all or nothing, and for those who have not yet realized that as an exaggeration—that is, have not yet seen that meaning *can* be available even within our utter contingency and relativity of everything—the hold of religion's "sacred" and "holy" remains in lay circles, despite its being equivocal within critical scholarship and consistent science. And that hold on the sacred or Absolute remains as divisive as ever.

By the beginning of the nineteenth century, Christian theology had assigned the meaning of "God" or the "Absolute" to human states of mind about the "whence" of one's being or the totality of all that is (Schleiermacher), the process of Spirit or Reason, as reflections on reflection (Hegel), then later, "God" was an accurate process of speaking about the *human species* itself which was the only "God" (Feuerbach). After Nietzsche panned "God" as the emptiest of all concepts, and had his "madman," "last pope," and "ugliest man" all declare the death of God, Freud called religion with its belief in a Father-God all an "illusion" based on the limitations and fears of being human. Marx decided that the power of Hegel's dialectic of the world process was not Spirit but economics, and Kierkegaard, who also found fault with Hegel, dumped both ethics as well as Christendom as inferior to one's relation with "God" as Absolute, *above all ethics*. That metaphysic of infinity was eventually left in the twentieth century only with Barth's dialectic "wholly other," Tillich's paradoxical and mystical "depth of being beyond being and non-being," and by the end of the twentieth century, Scharlemann's phenomenological-ontological approach of naming *anything* "God," *not* as a being but only as a place or time when "God" might be manifest by God's "otherness" or God's "not being God."

That means the process of "desacralization" necessarily involved the *end of theism*, as I mentioned earlier, which began to make its appearance among even devoted Christian scholars from the late eighteenth century to the present, and that nineteenth century saw the *separation* of Christianity as never before experienced, with the extreme absolutization of it in exclusive forms by certain Protestants and by the Catholic Church on the one hand, and, on the other hand, the desacralizing and relativizing among the professional theologians/philosophers of the Protestant church. That remains the present state although less and less of the newer generations of laypeople are being drawn to the old absolute forms which are so unscientific and heteronomous.

This is one of the reasons for this present study, to try to *bridge the gap*, and it appears that such can be done *only* by Rawls's approach to the unity found in a democratic republic which can allow difference so long as all citizens obey the laws derived from the basic principles all agreed to in the social contract or "original position." Religions have previously given people the impression that their ethical claims *must be absolute* even if many people would consider them only quite relative, contingent, or changing. From ancient times, religions have been accustomed to being the center of culture, *the unity*, the whole from which all parts of communal life found their meaning. But a gradual reconfiguring has taken place through this "desacralization," as the organizing center or unifying element is *now* in political or national structures. Religion in all of its differences is only one possible part of the whole, though most religious institutions continue to want religion as the center or power of the unity of the whole. The unit or whole is now seen to be *in process*, as is a democratic republic's sense of ethical/political agreed unity, as is all life. It is a unity to be sustained with effort, requiring continual reexamination if not restructuring, whereas it used to be that the religious unity was simply conceived to be a static, eternal, incomparable, an unchallengeable institutional unit, one which could not be conceptualized by human reason, but had to be only accepted by faith.

Such a *replacement* of the power that provides the *unity* between humans is remarkable, but it stands not only on the reality of religious pluralism but also on the process of desacralization. The realization of the real power of values and meanings as a voluntary agreement rather than a coerced position is a huge change, even if the values and meanings are still in a process of desacralization and *humanization*, a process of dealing with *empirical realities* rather than invisible or only "postulated" powers. Instead of thinking in terms of static values or a Platonic eternal world of Forms, or Aristotelian "entelechies," or even Kantian "postulates," we realize humans must and do come up with their own goals, values, and aspirations from *their own instinct and reason*, as humans have always done, even when they attributed it to some invisible power or divine revelation.

Now, different nations, many of which include a *variety of religions*, can no longer depend upon any unity deriving from these diverse, competitive, and divisive *religious ideas* and their mythologies. So each nation is eventually being forced to recognize the very contiguity of bodies, the actual presence of the significantly different others, to find *its own universal* in the common instinctual "will-to-live," to create its own sense of unity and identity by a *consensus* of its citizens on basic ethical principles, that is, a government "of, by and for the people," to formulate its structures of justice by "freestanding principles," a unity far *beyond* the diverse, divisive, and exclusive religious claims. This is the future impinging on the present, despite the continual rearing of the inhumane head of fascism across our globe.

This does *not* mean that religions can no longer have stories or speak of ethical principles. But they cannot expect any authority to be seen in these stories either inherently by their being part of a traditional religion nor by any amount of myths that are attached to them. Aspirational stories and symbols can motivate and provide a sense of security and well-being, but they cannot be aspirational if they are spoken of as real facts or history when they are neither. Nor can they be aspirational for a whole nation if they are owned by only a part of the people. We can find a greater social solidarity only when we realize the irrelevance of myths, the limitations of stories, just as we do with moral clichés.

The irony is that most religious people can quickly find fault with the myths and stories of other religions, but they do not see any fault with their own. They can easily sense when the aspirations of others are not their own, but find it difficult to understand why their own desires, values, and aspirations are not readily accepted by others. Most people never think of themselves as persecuting others for their race, gender, social status, or religion, but although many are still discriminated against systemically because of their race, gender, or social status, few if any Christians in the United States are actually persecuted as victims for their religion. Meanwhile, most citizens affiliated with no religion or with non-Christian religions continue to be the objects of discrimination, and often of serious attacks, now in the early part of 2021, it threatens our Asian American communities. This is the *indiscriminate hatred* and fear, the xenophobia Lee wrote about, shifting from one group to another, but even returning, as if some citizens hate all other immigrants other than their own group. To even utter the words E Pluribus Unum seems to be a cruelty-joke.

Even the Supreme Court has fallen prey to the talk about possible "hostility to religion," a slogan used in the United States only by Christians who have experienced favoritism by the law rather than "hostility." In subsequent chapters, we will see how the court seems to tremble at the prospect that it might be accused by religious people of being "hostile to religion." But the *only* people who would bring such an accusation would be different groups of Christians who are engaged in illicit "majoritarian" methods to try to influence the court for their own narrow and exclusive agendas and benefits rather than from a real national concern. We will see the record.

In fact, we will see that this nation moved in its formal stance from its colonial days of trying to have a theocratic colony and a single, uniform religion, to the colonists realizing they had to tolerate religious differences in adjoining colonies, finally even among citizens of their own colony and states, to finally being persuaded by the Framers that mere tolerance of difference is *not* enough. All citizens need to honor differences, to honor the "*freedom of conscience*," rather than to think that one's own conscience should govern others. This was what our Framers understood, and both Jefferson and Madison became quite disenchanted with the way various states, even their own Virginia, continued to harass and overtly persecute minority religions. It is the situation of this "religious pluralism" which Rawls pinpointed as pushing the choice between either an unending conflict between different parties or a freedom of conscience, and he emphasized that the latter can be an answer only if it is publicized and honored proudly, not just snuck in apologetically.

Now that we have seen the myth of the religious founding of the United States, as well as the problem of thinking that the Jewish-Christian ethic is somehow the ethic underlying our Constitution, and we have seen how our world understandings have changed over 2,000 years pertaining to religion, ethics, government, and even what humans are, we need finally to see how the Framers formulated what they did and how the background suggests the proper understanding of what they wrote and said.

DEMOCRACY ARTICULATED WITH A FREEDOM OF CONSCIENCE AND FREEDOM OF WORSHIP

Religion was still *very divisive* in the colonial period of U.S. history. But the new political structures were fragile at best, and usually even based on the particular sect's interpretation of the Christian tradition, as some colonies sought in vain to establish their own theocracies. The mutual antagonisms of the religions in themselves are enough of a social problem, but when any of them seek to be endorsed by and supported by the *government*, that can become offensive to all those who belong to other religions or have chosen no religious affiliation at all. Such a theocracy was attempted in the New World for a very short time. But when people of different sects of Christianity showed up, it created the same tension that was typical of the "Christendom" in Europe from which the immigrants or their forefathers had fled, which had spawned many decades of terrible wars *between* professing Christians.

It was this "Christendom" with which the Framers of the Constitution *broke ties* at the end of the eighteenth century, after it had reigned some 1,400 years. People wanted something different even in the colonies over time when they realized they were just replicating problems by their attempts to "establish" a church with the government of each colony. James Madison,

Thomas Jefferson, and others were determined to not turn the New Nation into the Old World, either to let a single man or select small group have absolute control of the government, or by government aligning with a religious group which creates persecution, hypocrisy, and often a social splitting and perpetual war between religious sects. They therefore insisted that religion and government must be *separated* to do their own work *independently* of the other. Madison insisted that government simply has "no cognizance" of religion, and by "cognizance," he meant jurisdiction. They emphasized that the nation had to be a *potent and "lively" unity* to embrace significant differences without dissolving.

By this time, many colonists, now belonging to the new "states," had realized that a national unity would have to be more neutral, not religious, and it would have to enjoy priority in the minds of all citizens, with self-preserving power, or it would perish quickly. A national unity had to do basically what no religion had been able to do. Multiple religions or even varied sects of a single religion would only war over who was to get control unless the nation's leaders could devise a plan for the democratic republic to embrace reasonable diversity and individual freedoms. That was the challenge. Such would be a *formal* changing of the guard, even a constitutional change with great *aspirations but minus the exclusive myths of the past*. Madison devoted himself to studying all previous forms of government back more than 2,000 years, to the ancient Greek amphictyony, so he could assess the pros and cons of each.[25] This "lively experiment" was too important to fail by lack of due diligence.

Influenced by John Locke, he and Jefferson both emphasized that religion is a matter *only* between an individual and God, and one's mind must remain free in that sense. In his "Memorial and Remonstrance," Madison proclaimed that a government-established religion "is not necessary for the support of Civil Government . . . [and] if Religion be not within the cognizance of Civil Government how could its legal establishment be necessary to Civil Government?" Instead, even the proposed bill of Gov. Patrick Henry of Virginia which was to continue to tax all individuals to *support religion*, but was general so as to support any religious group each person chose, was to Madison still a mark of "degeneracy," even though he was an active Anglican in Virginia's predominant Anglican population. Madison wrote of this bill,

Instead of holding forth an Asylum to the persecuted, it is itself a signal of persecution. It degrades from the equal rank of Citizens all those whose opinions in Religion do not bend to those of the legislative authority. Distant as it may be in its present form from the Inquisition, it differs from it only in degree. The one is the first step, the other the last in the career of intolerance.[26]

He emphasized how a position in law must be consistent and one needs to anticipate how it will be used in the future as a *precedent*, which needs to be heard even by today's Supreme Court:

> The free men of America did not wait till usurped power had strengthened itself by exercise, and entangled the question in precedents. They saw all the consequences in the principle, and they avoided the consequences by denying the principle. We revere this lesson too much soon to forget it. Who does not see that the same authority which can establish Christianity, in exclusion of all other Religions, may establish with the same ease any particular sect of Christians, in exclusion of all other Sects? That the same authority which can force a citizen to contribute three pence only of his property for the support of any one establishment, may force him to conform to any other establishment in all cases whatsoever?[27]

If civil authority can establish Christianity and exclude all other religions, he warned that it could also establish one sect of Christian and exclude all others. That point has not quite arrived in the United States, but by the time the reader finishes digesting the Supreme Court opinions in the following chapters, he or she can be the judge of how close the nation is to that. Madison also pointed out that governments in the past which tried by coercion to reduce different religious groups into some uniformity proved useless and lethal: "Torrents of blood have been spilt in the old world, by vain attempts of the secular arm, to extinguish Religious discord, by proscribing all difference in Religious opinions, Time has at length revealed the true remedy, Every relaxation of narrow and rigorous policy, wherever it has been tried, has been found to assuage the disease." This was not myth, but real history he was analyzing over and over. He was sure that the American experience shows that an equal and complete liberty of the religions from government would, if not eliminate the problem altogether, at least nullify its "malignant influence on the health and prosperity of the State."[28]

Thomas Jefferson agreed that government should not become involved in religions. The human mind is free and

> all attempts to influence it by temporal punishments or burthens, or by civil incapacitations, tend only to beget habits of hypocrisy and meanness. . . . That to compel a man to furnish contributions of money for the propagation of opinions which he disbelieves and abhors, is sinful and tyrannical: That even the forcing him to support this or that teacher of his own religious persuasion, is depriving him of the comfortable liberty of giving his contribution to the particular pastor whose morals he would make his pattern. . . . That our civil rights have no dependence on our religious opinions any more than on our opinions in physicks

or geometry. . . . That it tends also to corrupt the very principles of that very religion it is meant to encourage.[29]

He saw in history that when the Christian religion was even persecuted, it did better in the long run than when it was merged with government. It was simply best for each that they be separated, as strange as that might seem. Instead of one person or a few deciding on the religion to be supported by taxes and the government, government must be *separated* from religion. Rather, "it is time enough for the rightful purposes of civil government for its officers to interfere when principles break out into overt acts against peace and good order."[30]

This same last sentence, as well as most of the content of Jefferson's earlier bill in 1779, Madison copied into the bill "Virginia, Act for Establishing Religious Freedom" six years later in 1785.[31] Then in 1821, Jefferson, in explaining the wording of the Virginia bill of 1785, noted that its words referred to "the plan of the Holy author of our religion" in speaking of the freedom from coercion, and he pointed out that some in Congress proposed an amendment to those words, adding "Jesus Christ" as the "Holy Author of our religion." He insisted that this amendment of such an insertion "was rejected by a great majority, in proof that they meant to comprehend, within the mantle of its protection, the Jew and the Gentile, the Christian and Mahometan, the Hindoo, the Infidel of every denomination."[32]

This matches even Madison's use of "religion" in distinction from "Christian" in his "Memorial and Remonstrance," in which he warned of "all other religions" as being excluded to favor Christianity as being itself *the problem*, not just a skirmish between competing sects within Christianity. It is this "all other religions" that now describes the religious pluralism of the United States and other countries and democracies, which were *not yet* the case in Madison's day, but which consideration he gave, and he supplied the answer: *separation* of religion and government. Even though the United States probably still had only Christians and a few Jews, the separation which Madison later, in 1822, called a "perfect separation,"[33] was the only way people with different religious identities could live together within united states. The government could not endorse one religion and antagonize all other people, nor could it endorse or sponsor or aid all religions equally as the Henry bill for Virginia had proposed. That idea was roundly defeated by Jefferson, Madison, and all the others, including religious leaders such as Isaac Backus. The First Amendment was the result of all of these half measures such as supporting all equally, and it eliminated such ideas. Ten years after his letter to Livingston, in 1832, at age 83, Madison wrote to Rev. Adams that the 50 years of the separation of government from religion had proved the two had flourished without the aid of the other. He admitted that it might not always be easy to "trace the line of separation between the rights of religion and the Civil authority with such distinctness as to avoid collisions & doubts on unessential points," but his advice was that "entire abstinence of the Govt. from interference in any way whatever, beyond the necessity of preserving public order, & protecting each sect agst. Trespasses on its legal rights by others" was by far the best course to pursue.[34]

In that sense, of course, even this vision was largely *aspirational*, as was the democratic republic's very structure that they planned. The federal government had to provide a *stable unity* in very fragile times, a unity which could still allow people to be religious or nonreligious, to have their own personal goals and ambitions. The "freedom of conscience" had not really been tested except in a very narrow scope largely of different sects within Christianity. Even then, Protestant and Catholics still had no use for each other, unless the others' bodily presence could help the colony or state to survive, for example, in the state of New York.

Both Jefferson and Madison, as well as many that supported the First Amendment of the Constitution, envisioned the future government's rightful intrusion into religious matters as limited to only the possible time if and when religious people themselves violated civil or criminal laws, that is, the laws or principles by which *all citizens* agreed to live. But this meant that government's jurisdiction over religious people was only in their *non*-religious activity, *not* in the religious worship or conscience, but only in case they violated generally applicable civil or criminal law. Such a restriction was intended to prevent government from, as Jefferson wrote, the "corrupt" practices of offering special honors, emoluments, or bribes which actually violate the very religious principles they would profess to uphold, and it means that all people "shall be free to profess, and by argument to maintain their opinions in matters of religion, and that the same shall in no wise diminish, enlarge, or affect their civil capacities."[35] For any Justice later to claim the Constitution gave religion a "preferred" position[36] is the *opposite* of what Jefferson wrote[37] and the opposite of what Madison and other Framers had in mind, as we saw.

This formulation of the U.S. First Amendment's freedom of religion, of course, all *began* with the question of religion in the state of Virginia, in the defeat of Gov. Patrick Henry's general assessment bill which would have distributed state taxes to the church of each citizen's choice. In the process of formulating the religion clauses of the First Amendment to the federal Constitution, Madison, Jefferson and others used the same arguments, approach, and even language they had used in defeating Gov. Henry's proposed bill for the state of Virginia. This is evident when one reads the House of Representatives' records for the debates over the religion clauses of the First Amendment,[38] and most of the former quotations from them that came after 1891 were only concerned with the federal law, the First Amendment. It is difficult to see how any Supreme Court Justice could read this and still interpret the Framers as saying all they wanted was an equal treatment of all religions, so government can help them all, as C.J. Rehnquist did, or that the law should never be applied to the separate states, as J. Thomas holds, even though if it had not, the conflict between federal and state laws would have made the whole unworkable. It defies their very words, the history, and the explicit support they received from religious leaders such as the famous Baptist ministers, Isaac Backus and John Leland.

Backus, who, though born into the Congregational Church, by 1756, at age 32, had become a leader among the stricter Baptists, and the Baptists which had begun the century with bleak and dwindling prospects spread like fire throughout New England. He, like so many profiting from the new pietistic revivals, and aligning himself with growing groups which placed an emphasis not on inherited religion and old traditions but rather on personal autonomy and freedom of conscience which could lead to conversion,[39] realized that the entrenched denominations in various colonies becoming states presented a barrier to such conversions. Thus, it was that Backus assisted Madison's and Jefferson's efforts of separating religion from government entirely, beginning with Virginia.[40]

This *aspirational* change can be viewed in the colonies other than Virginia in a similar way, if, for example, one compares the very rigid Massachusetts Bay Colony's laws of 1641 and laws of 1780. In the former, civil law was identified with Christ's law (despite many of their laws, such as worshipping any other god, or laws against witches or blasphemy which were read out of the Old Testament, with nothing in the New to agree with them, which was the Calvinist typical exegesis), and freedom was granted *only* to those who conformed. The death penalty was reserved for those who did not. By 1780, the same colony, now a state, progressed to a tolerance of difference within Christian groups, much as the defeated Virginia Bill, even though within the Christian groups people were supposed to have freedom to worship as their conscience dictated. They felt that religion was still needed for civil government or morality to exist, but people could "invest their legislature" to authorize and require the various towns, and so on to provide for the worship of God and general instruction religiously, and that as long as any denomination of Christians behaved itself peaceably, they would not be subordinated or discriminated against, but rather protected, by the government.[41]

This was still not a complete freedom for any religion in Massachusetts, not a freedom equal to that in Virginia or in the First Amendment, but for Puritans, it was quite a move even over 140 years, but a move prompted by the necessity of being adequately populated and by the voluntaristic emphasis during half of the eighteenth century by the revivals or "Great Awakening."

Their aspirations for the state and country had still not caught up with Virginia and the First Amendment, but they gradually moved as time passed. After all, the religious pluralism was very minor as of yet, even though it had been sufficient in Europe to provide a long history of bloody persecution in the name of one small group or one religion of the world, and had enabled even Massachusetts to drown alleged witches in its sad history.

NATIONAL UNITY AND SOCIAL SOLIDARITY

The debates over how to form a Constitution which would answer the problems of everyone were lengthy and often rancorous, even though the quite frail voice of Madison gave a calming effect at times, especially among those who realized how well prepared he was, having spent probably thousands of hours devouring every book he felt was relevant, attempting to figure out the best possible form of a republic for the New Nation. When he and others gave in to the demand many states had to include a "bill of rights," it was not simply that he became convinced of the correctness of their argument, but that he realized there was already sufficient opposition against the Constitution that without a bill of rights, it might never gain their states' approval.

His expansive and genuinely inquisitive research enabled him to establish workable parameters within the conflicting views the various delegates had on nearly every issue. Others also saw that the Constitution was an absolute necessity since the Articles of Confederation had so many problems, giving almost no enforceable power to the federal government, thereby allowing the separate states to do pretty well whatever they pleased, creating national disunity and chaos in their competition with each other. Yet many delegates felt the entire Convention was a manipulation, since there was no attempt really to improve the articles but simply to replace them.

Given these problems and divisions as well as purely local interests which seemed at times unyielding, something was needed to enable the people's loyalty and sense of unity to be more comprehensive, inclusive of very different others, not simply a grudging accommodation of others, but a real sense of genuine unity greater than could be achieved from either their individual interests or even their states' unique interests. The radical changes that were eventually formulated after many arguments, revisions, and even total rewritings were understandably a threat to many people since they required a new trust without any collateral or reason other than the previous war which they had surprisingly won, almost by sheer default, and many critics of Washington had felt during the war that his tactics were not aggressive enough, too "Fabian," of merely outlasting the enemy but never confronting it in an all-out battle.[42] He had proven his critics wrong, of course, if he had not also just lucked out. But he did discover toward the end of the war that his troops needed not just a national interest but had to be persuaded that if that were secured, it would also be to their own individual benefit.[43]

If Washington had been trusted enough to be given the chance to command the troops, and he had been successful, perhaps he and others even more versed in politics than he could be trusted to "improve" the federal government by a Constitution, provided it included limitations of its federal control in a Bill of Rights. Certainly, not all the states ratified the Constitution, but enough did, a sufficient number to get the new government moving, and some of the strongest opponents to it became supportive, willing to give it a chance once it was ratified.[44]

The country had a long way to go to become credible to other nations, and almost as far to become credible in the eyes of some U.S. citizens. This was truly a starting from scratch, a "lively experiment." Although one can see the parallels between the mistreatment of the colonists by England which Jefferson articulated in the Declaration of Independence and the subjects within the Bill of Rights, there were no parallels, nothing but a big break, in the "disestablishment" the First Amendment created for religion and the state. Some disestablishment had already occurred, but it would be still a few years before the final states followed suit.

On the other hand, the slavery issue had been intentionally postponed since if the issue had been pushed further, the Constitution might not have been ratified. Some leaders of the country were afraid for the slavery issue even to be a part of a national discussion. Thus, the issue rode in limbo, and the problems mounted, and more slaves were imported so the South flourished. Although the Northern colonies owned less slaves and no plantations, they nevertheless made fortunes off shipping the slaves to the United States, transporting the commodities they produced to other countries, and actually *building* the slave ships. More than half a century later, the issue would be formally resolved only by the very uncivil Civil War, and from that loss of 600,000 lives, the South had even less a sense of national unity than before.

This was a costly lesson that a democratic republic must be driven by genuine ethical principles and by the interests of the *whole* nation, not simply the economics of some sector or "majoritarian" group such as those defending slavery. Majoritarianism had been the fear of Madison, Jefferson, and others, yet the lack of resolution of the slavery issue led to a temporary secession from the Union by several states and a terrible war simply because there were still too many who felt their local interests were more important than the preservation of the nation.

This raises the question of how such a strong sense of unity or a devotion to a national interest of all citizens can be created and sustained, when citizens have so many differences in their perspectives, interests, ideas, identities, and allegiances. While Nietzsche and Schweitzer both spoke of a life-affirming disposition or a life instinct as present in all humans, and as the basic moral motivation, they knew that it becomes moral or ethical *only* when it recognizes the same instinctual "will-to-live" in others and responds favorably to it. They both thought one's instinct would somehow motivate one's reason to make such a response, in fact, Nietzsche insisted that it had to be tailored by reason lest instinct simply be unrestrained.[45]

Steven Pinker illustrated how humans find it much easier to respond positively to those who share their own DNA, those within the family bloodline, than they do to those outside it.[46] That may be fairly natural to all animals, yet most of us have witnessed even certain animals treating other animals as if they were their own offspring when they were not of the same species. It is also easy to see competitiveness between various animals, and the human animal certainly has plenty of that feature, so the whole sense of one's needs and another's needs creates a very complex picture, often affected by outside influences that interfere with one's need for protection, food, companionship, or other.

Richard Rorty spoke of the ethical moment being when we develop the sensitivity to hear the "cry" of the other as identical to our own, or to recognize in a play or novel our own cruelty in one of the characters, and determine to change ourselves or respond differently. It is a moment of realization of greater "social solidarity," of moving beyond our egocentrically limited "we" to include others who may formerly have been seen by us as a "they" or "them."[47] Late Christian theologian, Wolfhart Pannenberg, described this as being open to the world and to others, moving from egocentrism to an exocentrism.[48] The unique Jewish philosopher Martin Buber, in his famous *I and Thou*, observed that even the words we use to describe ourselves and others *create* relations. No one wants to be treated as a mere "it" but as a "you," even as Kant described his "categorical imperative" as a rule of always treating all rational beings as ends-in-themselves, never as mere means-to-an-end.

This sense of unity or social solidarity is powerfully portrayed in great novels such as Albert Camus's *The Plague* in the tragic death of Father Paneloux when he finally identified with a dying child and subsequently died himself, but not from the plague. Perhaps Rubenstein was also correct in attributing it to his inability to reconstruct his world since he was so rigidly attached to religious myths since Rubenstein shows how difficult it is to treat people as fully human as long as they are viewed in *mythical* terms. In Fyodor Dostoevsky's great *The Brothers Karamazov*, Ivan Karamazov stresses that his rebellion was not so much against God as it was against the injustice in this world that God made and failed to prevent, in Ivan's poignant illustration of how the suffering of even one innocent child cannot be justified. Yet, I would add, as I noted elsewhere,[49] that the "solidarity" which was so missing within this family of "voluptuaries" was actually discovered after their father was killed, and one of the brothers was unfairly convicted. They found quite late a solidarity of family that had been completely missing.

John Rawls's theory is that the necessary unity of a nation can occur only when we are able to engage in a "hypothetical" "original position" behind a "veil of ignorance." That is the only way to separate our legitimate ethical interests from those which are simply happenstance or accidental, and the only way to move to a society in which we no longer strain to take advantage of each other, but rather reach an overlapping consensus of basic principles to which we all agree, as the national interests which have priority in our lives. While the mythological and aspirational claims of any religious people may remain important, even central, to their identity, freedom to choose to embrace or relinquish these mythological and aspirational elements must be left with each person. As Rawls suggested, what Rubenstein called the "social solidarity" or *unity between all* must have *priority*. Rawls was convinced that metaphysical claims will not deliver people from their own human-produced evils, but if they want to believe that, they may be allowed to do so, as long as they give *priority* to the *basic principles all citizens* have agreed to in the "original position." That choice of special individuals and special groups, because it is *not* inclusive of *all* the people in the group, must be subordinated for the sake of *social solidarity* or the *unity* of the *entire* nation's very *diverse* people. It must be subordinated to the *basic ethical principles* of the nation to which *all have agreed* at least *by proxy* and do agree as citizens.

It is not easy to move beyond egocentrism and narcissism, beyond careless indifference of others' needs, and actually will an equality in the extensive way we all desire, with a principle of "difference" Rawls suggests in social and economic inequities which places the decisions about new laws involving distribution of goods with those "least advantaged." Rawls emphasized that

historically one of the main defects of constitutional government has been the failure to insure the fair value of political liberty. . . . Disparities in the distribution of property and wealth that far exceed what is compatible with political equality have generally been tolerated by the legal system. . . . Thus inequities in the economic and social system may soon undermine whatever political equality might have existed under fortunate historical conditions.[50]

He insisted that universal suffrage, as vital as it is to a democracy, in an "insufficient counter-poise" when parties and elections are not financed by public funds but by private contributions, and for this reason, he felt that the political equality must encourage more participation even if this means that in a system of "private ownership of the means of production, property and wealth must be kept widely distributed and government monies provided on a regular basis to encourage free public discussion."[51] In order to agree to this kind of genuine social solidarity, each voter and every legislator will have to place herself or himself behind Rawls's "veil of ignorance" to see what justice really is when it is not perverted by irrational and/or inherited advantages.

It will not be easy to make such radical changes, but much of the present extreme *inequality* in the distribution of goods was brought about intentionally for selfish motives over a period of more than three decades.[52] So even if it takes time, we really have no choice if we are ever to be a democracy and not mere a motley group thinking we are exceptional and democratic when we are actually unflinchingly selfish and irreparably divided in our most basic interests. If no religious deity or its ethics has created a world unity or even really much of a national unity, and certainly has not rescued this world from terrible wars and tragedies, even the basic national unity seems inconsistent, ragged, and ineffective. We are living in days in which there is no real consciousness of God as some presence in our world, though many still go through motions they have learned that are supposed to show that they truly believe in such an all-powerful and all-loving God, while our tragedies and wars go on constantly, revealing what we value most.

The desacralization or the demise of the "metaphysics of infinity," as Foucault called it, shows the shift of the focus now on the will and power of the people and the nations they are able to form. The U.S. Constitution spoke of our desire to "make a more perfect union" which is the only way the nation will survive. The key word here is "union." So the *aspirations* are *still possible*, perhaps among most citizens, but the realities have been questioning whether such noble aspirations could ever become more realized. Those self-aggrandizing clichés cause people to expect that not only would one's religious or nonreligious identity *not* diminish one's status or equality, as Jefferson said, but neither would one's racial, sexual, or economic identity.

Yet the facts tell otherwise. All of these areas become very emotional issues to discuss, but continue to exist despite the law having created special "suspect" categories and legally defined "hate" crimes. This is especially the case when the problems of divisiveness seem never to get resolved but periodically fester up again to boil the pus of hatred between citizens, or experienced as an illness that one is not sure one will outlive since the possible "cures" seem to be things so many legislators appear unwilling to spend either time or money on.

Thus, the unity and equality remain *only an aspiration* in many individual minds. But in the meantime, that very aspiration is still named, defined, and publicly presented as a *motivation* by some of various media companies and their remarkable staffs, a motivation to improve the nation, to recapture a sense of unity. And they have been motivated by thousands upon thousands of peaceful protesters in the streets. Were it not for them and the important newspapers around the country, the country would have dissolved itself long ago by its multitude of divisive interests, its alternate readings of facts, its fascination for conspiracy theories, hardened positions, and lack of federal leadership. It appears that the *politicians*, of all people, must *reorient themselves* on how to *create or recreate a unity* in the nation that will preserve and *honor difference* rather than refuse to engage in reasonable negotiations with people who see things differently. If they simply cannot reorient themselves and be willing to yield an inch of their absolutized policy presuppositions, they should resign and open the position to others who can and are willing to sincerely reason together. Democracy requires a genuine sense of unity or social solidarity, just as it requires that all political leaders be motivated by the interests of the *people as a whole*, *not* simply the interests of certain *select groups or parties*, and this must involve a greater and more responsible peaceful and respectful participation in the business of the nation by *all* citizens.[53]

NOTES

1. On the relationship of history to the myth, three different religious answers were given by D. F. Strauss, Mircea Eliade, and Rudolf Bultmann. Bultmann's "demythologizing" was existential, but still pointed to the Christian emergence, whereas Eliade's existential answer did not need any historical event, and Strauss's answer was that myth is simply the truth of an idea but not of any single reality or event.

2. See Lee, *America for Americans*, 274.

3. Steven K. Green, *Inventing a Christian America: The Myth of the Religious Founding* (New York: Oxford Univ. Press, 2015).

4. See Jacob Neusner's splendid introduction to Judaism in Arvind Sharma (ed.), *Our Religions* (San Francisco: Harper San Francisco, 1993), 293–355, esp. 306–319.

5. Eliade thought that myth was never intended to provide historical truth but rather existential truth. But the way he sketches their expectation, he makes it sound like they were literal. See Mircea Elaide, *Myth and Reality*, tr. Willard R. Trask (New York: Harper Torchbooks, 1963); and *The Sacred and the Profane: The Nature of Religion*, tr. Willard R. Trask (New York: Harcourt, Brace & World, Inc., 1959).

6. This was very explicit in Rudolf Bultmann, *History and Eschatology: The Presence of Eternity* (New York: Harper Torchbooks, 1962); *Kerygma and Myth* (New York: Harper Torchbooks, 1961); and *Theology of the New Testament* (2 vols in 1), tr. Kendrick Grobel (New York: Charles Scribner's Sons, 11951, 1955) though it was evident as well as he referred to the "Resurrection" not as a material raising from death but as a raising of the image of Jesus into the message of the gospel.

7. "James Madison to Edward Livingston," 10 July 1822, Writings 9:100–103, in Philip B. Kurland and Ralph Lerner (eds.), *The Founder's Constitution*, 5 vols. (Chicago: The Univ. of Chicago Press, 1987), V:105–106.

8. Rawls, *Political Liberalism*, xxvi.

9. Rubenstein, *After Auschwitz*, 237.

10. It is intriguing that the erudite Christian theologian, Wolfhart Pannenberg, moved from seeing autonomy as mutual awareness of self through the other person in his *Anthropology from a Theological Perspective*, to seeing it as a form of idolatry in his final publication of the *Systematic Theology*, based on his assessment of the way moral autonomy after Kant left itself open to a rejection of God as the moral base for human activity. See, for example, Pannenberg, *Systematic Theology*, II: esp.265, also 222–231, 320; also III: 164–165 and 628.

11. According to the book of Acts, this dilemma was never resolved, but rather led to misunderstandings in Jerusalem which caused Paul's arrest, ultimately his appeal to Caesar and trip to Rome where he was incarcerated. Acts 21:17–ch. 28. His explanation of his position was that "I have become all things to all people, that I might by all means save some," which meant being a Jew under the Torah when he was with other Jews, and as one "outside" the Torah to those who were not Jews (I Cor. 9:19–23) or when he said in I Cor. 10:32–33 that he tried to please "everyone"—both Jews and Greeks—in everything he did, or when, after insisting that a Gentile who allowed himself to be circumcised in his conversion to Christianity has severed himself from grace (Gal. 5:1–4), yet somehow nevertheless insists that neither circumcision nor uncircumcision count either way, but only "faith working through love" (Gal. 5:5–6) or "a new creation" (Gal. 6:15).

12. The irony is that the Q Gospel, which may date as early as Paul's letters, differs so radically from him. There is no mysticism in Q, just as there are no teachings of Jesus in Paul's letters, and if the Crucifixion and Resurrection of Christ are the most important aspect of Jesus's life to Paul, the Q document does not include either. Crossan, of course, thinks the Gospel of Thomas also dates just as early, but it is Gnostic and many find it cryptic and unintelligible in places.

13. The general results of the Jesus seminar can be seen in a variety of scholars, but especially two of the seminar's leaders, Funk and Crossan, who have reminded us that the consensus of the seminar was that less than 20% of the acts and teachings attributed to Jesus in the gospels has any likely historical connection to Jesus.

14. Martin Werner, *The Formation of Christian Dogma* (New York: Harper & Bros., 1957).

15. This was recognized long ago by Rudolf Bultmann, and his various books which attempted to demythologize the Christian message, and his recognition that the gospels do not have Jesus providing anyone with an ethical system at all is dealt with specifically in *Jesus and the Word*, tr. Louise Pettibone Smith (New York: Charles Scribner's Sons, 1958).

16. Rubenstein, *After Auschwitz*. In his explanation of a group's need to reduce its cognitive dissonance, history shows that the group may feel a need to eliminate the potentially disconfirming others (84–95). In religious terms, a group may attempt to convert all the others who create this cognitive dissonance, but, in circumstances

in which that is not likely, and the disconfirming other is seen as adversely affecting other areas of one's life such as economics, the alternative method is extermination, especially when the "disconfirming others" are viewed as a redundant population, as a competing "middlemen" minority. He summarizes, "Total elimination of disconfirming others has always been an ultimate theological aim of the Christian Church" (94).

17. Rubenstein, *After Auschwitz*, 33–34.

18. Thomas Curry, *Farewell to Christendom: The Future of Church and State in America* (New York: Oxford University Press, 2004), 10.

19. *Oral Argument of Thomas Van Orden v. Rick Perry*, No. 03-1500, March 2, 2005. 3–5, 8–9, 11–12, 15–17, 23–24, 26–27.

20. See my *Ethics and the Future of Religion: Redefining the Absolute* (Lanham, MD: Lexington/Fortress Academic Press), 2021.

21. Readers not familiar with this defensive action by the church can retrieve it under "Papal Encyclicals Online" or just under "Syllabus of Errors." This was a fairly comprehensive list of everything the church felt threatened by: Pantheism, Naturalism, Absolute Rationalism, Moderate Rationalism, Indifferentism, Latitudinarianism, Socialism, Communism, Secret Societies, Biblical Societies, Clerico-Liberal Societies, Erroneous views of the Church's comprehensive rights, Errors about civil society and especially errors of those who think government and the church should be separated, Errors of Natural and Christians Ethics not Approved by the Church, Errors concern Christian Marriage, Errors about the Civil Power of the Sovereign Pontiff, and the Errors of Modern Liberalism. To a modern reader, these errors (stated in the supposed form of the error) are overwhelming, and it is rather hard to believe that was written only slightly more than 150 years ago. It shows that the desacralization of Christianity was in process, that, as Foucault suggests, even though the "metaphysics of infinity" had been abandoned for better empirical tools for creating the new sciences, including human sciences, but the religious institutions would continue to fight it, to deny the validity of the new sciences. Had the Constitution been framed primarily by Catholics rather than Protestants, they would never have felt comfortable trying to separate the religion from the state, even though this document from Pope Pius IX came a half a century *after* the U.S. Constitution. In 1875, an Amendment proposed by Mr. Blaine received more than 90% approval in the House, but lacked four votes of getting the 2/3 votes needed in the Senate. The Amendment was to make explicit that the First Amendment meant, inter alia, that no tax money could be used in any form for a parochial schools but only for public schools which were open to all students. When the bill was defeated, many states adopted it as their own. Now, in 2020, the Supreme Court struck down that state equivalent of the Blaine Amendment in *Kendra Espinoza, v. Montana Department of Revenue*, 591 U.S. ___ (2020) (slip opinion, No. 18-1195). Such a decision agrees with the position in the *Syllabus of Errors* rather than with Madison, Jefferson, and the other Framers of the First Amendment, and rather than with the Supreme Court itself from 1940 to at least 1983. Is this more of the nostalgia for an imagined utopia of the past, which is now concerned to avoid anything new, but increase one's advantages over others, as Kurt Andersen diagnosed the U.S. economic structural change during the past half century? See his *Evil Geniuses* diagnosis.

22. Eric Hoffer, *The True Believer* (New York: Harper & Bros, 1951).

23. Rubenstein, *After Auschwitz*, 146–147.

24. Rorty, *Contingency*, 22.

25. "Notes on Ancient and Modern Confederacies," in *The Papers of James Madison*, Robert Rutland (editor-in-chief) (Chicago: Univ. of Chicago Press, 1965), 9:3–24.

26. Madison, "Memorial and Remonstrance," in *The Papers*, Rutland (ed.), 301–302.

27. Madison, "Memorial and Remonstrance," 300.

28. Madison, "Memorial and Remonstrance," 302–303.

29. Jefferson, "A Bill for Establishing Religious Freedom," V:77.

30. Jefferson, "A Bill for Establishing Religious Freedom," V:77.

31. Madison, "Virginia, Act for Establishing Religious Freedom," 1785 in Kurland and Lerner (eds,), *Founders' Constitution*, V:85.

32. Jefferson, "Autobiography, 1821," *Works* 1:71, in Kurland and Lerner (eds.), *Founders' Constitution*, V:85.

33. "James Madison to Edward Livingston," V:105.

34. "James Madison to Rev. Adams," 1832, *Writings* 9:484–487 in Kurland and Lerner (eds.), *Founders' Constitution*, V:107–108.

35. Jefferson, "A Bill for Establishing Religious Freedom," V:77.

36. J. O'Connor's suggestion in *Smith (II)*, and *Aguilar v. Felton* was later utilized by two colleagues.

37. The same Amendment that provided citizens "free exercise" of the religion (i.e., worship) gave them freedom of speech, press, of peaceably assembling, and to petition the government for a redress of grievances. There were no special privileges afforded the religious since all of these "freedoms" had limitations.

38. A select portion of these can be found in "House of Representatives, Amendments to the Constitution," 15, 17, 20 August 1789, *Annals* 1:729–131, 755, 766 in Kurland and Lerner (eds.), *Founders' Constitution*, V: 92–94.

39. See especially Sydney E. Ahlstrom, *A Religious History of the American People* (New Haven, CT: Yale University Press, 1972), 292–293. He was one of the very few Baptists in Massachusetts who voted for ratification of the Constitution, and in 1789, he visited Baptist churches in Virginia and North Carolina, and saw how they needed the government to be separated from religion. He supported Madison's and Jefferson's efforts to separate them. He took a public stand in Congress against any government religious tests for anything, against slavery, and against the idea of "nobility." The "religious" tests in general have "been the greatest engine of tyranny in the world." His idea of Christianity repelling slavery and nobility was a convoluted blaming of the covenant of circumcision, although his citation of people being "bought with a price" was generally acceptable to most Christians. In any case, he opposed all three as tied together. Isaac Backus, *The Debate on the Constitution: Federalist and Antifederalist Speeches, Articles, and Letters During the Struggle over Ratification*, Part One (New York: The Library of America, 1993), 931–933.

40. One should not impugn Madison's motives, suggesting that the primary reason he was for separating religion and government was because he knew that was the

only way he could get Baptists to vote for him to retain his position. Instead, as we will see later, he became very disillusioned with his fellow Anglicans in their shabby treatment or persecution of Baptists and Quakers, until he was sick of it.

41. To compare the two sets of laws, see Kurland and Lerner (eds.), *Founders' Constitution*, V: §3 with §38.

42. Thomas E. Ricks, *First Principles: What America's Founders Learned from the Greeks and Romans and How That Shaped Our Country* (New York: HarperCollins, 2020), ch. 8.

43. Ricks, *First Principles*, 162.

44. Pauline Maier, *Ratification: The People Debate the Constitution, 1787–1788* (New York: Simon and Schuster, 2010), 432–434.

45. Nietzsche, *Twilight of the Idols*, 545.

46. Steven Pinker, *How the Mind Works* (New York: W. W. Norton, 1997).

47. Rorty, *Contingency, Irony & Solidarity*. His theme was that contingency is an element in everything we know, so no language or insights will have the final say, but will be superseded mostly by accident rather than purpose. Nevertheless, he felt that we can become more sensitive to the relations we experience and often by those that we see depicted in plays or novels, to improve our social solidarity in a moral way.

48. Pannenberg, *Anthropology from a Theological Perspective*.

49. On solidarity in Dostoevsky, see ch. 4 in my *Will Humanity Survive Religion?*

50. Rawls, *A Theory of Justice*, 226.

51. Rawls, *A Theory of Justice*, 225–226.

52. See Kurt Andersen, *Evil Geniuses*, for a chilling account of this "unmaking of America" in bracketing out any desire for equality and controlling the laws under the guise of equality even when they were the opposite.

53. Rawls emphasized that "historically one of the main defects of constitutional government has been the failure to insure the fair value of political liberty. . . . Disparities in the distribution of property and wealth that far exceed what is compatible with political equality have generally been tolerated by the legal system. . . . Thus inequities in the economic and social system may soon undermine whatever political equality might have existed under fortunate historical conditions." He insists that "universal suffrage" is an "insufficient counter-poise" when parties and elections are not financed by public funds but by private contributions, and for this reason, he insists that the political equality must encourage more participation even if this means that in a system of "private ownership of the means of production, property and wealth must be kept widely distributed and government monies provided on a regular basis to encourage free public discussion." Rawls, *A Theory of Justice*, 225–226.

Chapter 4

The History of Religion, Ethics, and Law in the United States

From Theocracy to a Constitution

If the only choice the reader has for determining the law he or she would desire to live under were the following two sets of laws, which would the reader select?

Whatsoever pson or psons within this Province and the Islands thereunto belonging shall from henceforth blaspheme God, that is Curse him, or deny our Saviour Jesus Christ to bee the sonne of God, or shall deny the holy Trinity the father sonne and holy Ghost, or the Godhead of any of the said Three psons of the Trinity or the Unity of the Godhead, or shall use or utter any reproachful Speeches, words or language concerning the said Holy Trinity, or any of the said three psons thereof, shall be punished with death and confiscation or forfeiture of all his or her lands and goods to the Lord Proprietary and his heirs.[1]

OR

[T]o compel a man to furnish contributions of money for the propagation of opinions which he disbelieves and abhors, is sinful and tyrannical; that even the forcing him to support this or that teacher of his own religious persuasion, is depriving him of the comfortable liberty of giving his contributions to the particular pastor whose morals he would make his pattern, and whose powers he feels most persuasive to righteousness . . . it is time enough for the rightful purposes of government, for its officers to interfere when principles break out into overt acts against peace and good order. . . . Be it enacted by the General Assembly, that no man shall be compelled to frequent or support any religious worship, place, or ministry whatsoever, nor shall be enforced, restrained, molested, or burthened in his body or goods, nor shall otherwise suffer on account of his religious opinions or belief; but that all men shall be free to profess, and by argument to maintain, their opinion in matters of religion, and that the same shall in no wise diminish, enlarge, or affect their civil capacities.[2]

The first choice, from Maryland in 1641, was grounded on an attempted theocracy. The second choice was a statement from Thomas Jefferson, a part of the basic ethic of the U.S. Constitutional Republic from 1779. The first professed a *purpose* of coming to the New Land, quite parallel to that cited by the Mayflower Compact of 1620, which began with "In the Name of God, Amen," and explained that the immigration was "undertaken for the Glory of God and advancement of the Christian Faith and Honour of our King and Country, a Voyage to plant the First Colony in the Northern Parts of Virginia." Even the *aspiration* in the Mayflower Compact which included bringing honor to the King and to England was dissolved within 130 years. Those colonists lost their desire to be such a colony under such a ruthless King and came to the realization through England's negative treatment of the colonies that a theocracy would tend to simply replicate the same divisiveness and persecution from which their kinfolk had to escape but still had to put up with—even when spatially separated from England.

The second author above, later added in 1784, after the bloody Revolutionary War was finally over, and the ineffectiveness of the Articles of Confederation had become obvious, that

> our rulers can have authority over such natural rights only as we have submitted to them. The rights of conscience we never submitted, we could not submit. We are answerable for them to our God. The legitimate powers of government extend to such acts only as are injurious to others. But it does me no injury for my neighbor to say there are twenty gods, or no god. It neither picks my pocket nor breaks my leg. If it be said, his testimony in a court of justice cannot be relied on, reject it then, and be the enigma on him. Constraint may make him worse by making him a hypocrite, but it will never make him a truer man. It may fix him obstinately in his errors, but will not cure them. Reason and free enquiry are the only effectual agents against error.[3]

In Jefferson's strong protest in the preceding text, whatever "God" meant, the author separated citizens' duties to other humans, including the King, from duty to "God." Whether the insight came from John Locke or others or was purely Jefferson's, that meant he thought a people could and should exist with two sets of duties or ethics, as I earlier mentioned, though they did not have to contradict each other. To the reader who may get the impression that Maryland and Massachusetts' laws were strictly some adoption of the ethics and law from the Christian scriptures, to the contrary, the references to the New Testament or to Christian ethics are simply vague. There was no comprehension that the covenant Yhwh made with Israel was *only* with Israel, never with any other group, yet, as Calvinists, many of the Puritans were quite comfortable reading death penalties from the Old Testament as if *they themselves* were that ancient nation of Israel. There was also absolutely no awareness of the eschatological determination of the ethics both in the gospels' recitations of Jesus's teachings as well as in the writings of Paul and other canonical authors of the New Testament. How either an ethic of one specific people in ancient times or an ethic built on the belief of an imminent end of the world could have any relevance for future governments is simply a mystery. Of course, there were common ethical ideas of being kind to others, whether it is the Christian ideas in Matt. 25 or the commands in the Jewish scripture about being hospitable to the strangers, orphans, and widows. But this Calvinist view, like Luther's, came from the sixteenth-century Christendom. It was not so "aspirational" as much as it was simply *un*informed about those religions of Judaism and Christianity, both in their unique origins and separate historical developments. Things have *changed* since then as critical studies in many disciplines, including religion, have developed.

It may be a comfort to feel that one is part of God's "chosen people." But as long as one believes God's "perfect law" must be obeyed, an honest person can hardly think of himself or herself as so flawless as to avoid the disturbing picture of any Final Judgment based on dividing the people between the "obedient" and "disobedient," as one sees in Fourth Ezra, ch. 8.[4] Had Deut. 28 and 29 (and the whole book itself) meant only that one should at least just *try* to follow the commands, or that to obey two-thirds of them would suffice, then the picture would be quite different. Then the people would not divide into two distinct groups at all. But as Ezra objected, *no one* is that essentially different from others that one keeps all the law perfectly. So the distinction between the "obedient" and "sinners" cannot be anything other than unjustified bias, not justice.

Of course, even in IV Ezra, the visionary was overruled by God, and scolded for pitying others who were bound for severe punishment by God. For Christians who want to argue that they will settle for "grace" rather than "justice," that has absolutely no application to the real world once one realizes that injustice exists among humans by their own admission. All the Divine power could reply to Ezra was "quit thinking about it" and "be quiet"; just enjoy *your special treatment!* Any bifurcation of humanity on such preferential or unjust basis cannot found a theocracy or even have any input into a civil government or civil conception of justice.

But the ignorance of the actual ethics of both Ancient Israel (and Judaism) and Christianity as found in their sacred scripture extended even to the lawmakers in the seventeenth century. In King Charles of England's delegation of power in the colonies, although he turned the governance of the "plantations" (colonies) in the United States over to a number of people (any "five or more") including a variety of possible ecclesiastics, there is no citing of biblical ethics to follow or principles from Jesus or Paul. Absolutely nothing. King Charles gave them leeway to *make* whatever laws, civil, criminal, national, or international, to facilitate the operation of the colonies and retain the glory and status of England, anything they saw necessary to governing such an enterprise, never even suggesting that they must copy some ethic from Christianity,[5] and never revealing if he himself had any knowledge of the ethics of Christianity other than simply what his present culture manifest, for better or worse, or what ethics England's civil and criminal laws might have presupposed. Not a word.

THREE CENTURIES OF SURVIVAL AND CHANGE FOR RELIGION, ETHICS, AND LAW

From 1562 to 1648, Europe had engaged in two big religious wars between Catholics and Protestants which claimed more than *11 million* lives by combat, famine, and disease as a result of the wars. This could not have been absent in the memories of those who subsequently came to the New World. But strangely, the truth that the primary cause of the devastation was because of the merged power of religion and government did not seem to dawn on many people. Instead, many immigrants continued to think in terms of re-creating a theocracy in the New World, but one favoring *their* interpretation of *only their* religious group. That was the extent of the "religious freedom" they sought. That was the case with many early colonies, while others simply tried to be a faithful extension of the religious group that was allegedly controlling them from England, as, for example, was the case in Virginia.

Some of the most basic human ethics are the prohibitions of theft, murder, and perjury or false testimony. One would expect these to be fundamental if one were attempting to trace the influence of an ethic into a newly created culture and its basic laws. A most obvious area of examination would be that of the position of the victors who established the government, that is, the European immigrants' actual ethical treatment of *other ethnic groups* they found residing in the land they wanted or those ethnic groups they imported to serve them as slaves. I here must emphasize that each person stands within his or her own contingent culture, not with the retrospect vision from centuries in the future, so I am not judging people in the past for their being limited by their own culture. The vital question is whether the norms and standards they utilized should be accepted *today* as normative in any way. That is the question that has to be answered, and it cannot be answered by glossing over differences or by assuming one's own standard is the Absolute. Neither is convincing.

Citizens of the United States stand more than five centuries from Columbus and more than four centuries from the Jamestown settlement of 1607 and its first imported slaves from Africa in 1619. Even to return from the present to the close of the eighteenth century at the time of the Ratification of the Constitution is difficult to grasp existentially. The distance from the latter eighteenth century back to the beginning of the seventeenth century, to the Mayflower compact or to the Jamestown settlement, of more than 150 years, and then another 115 years back to Columbus's time, shows tremendous changes that make it difficult to imagine those earlier primitive conditions: the terrible voyages without proper navigation instruments and only crude maps, voyages which killed many, the sparsely occupied lands to which those European immigrants came, lands lacking all their normal signs and conveniences of their former European culture. The anxiety must have been gut wrenching over the inability of ever being able to predict whether they would find people already residents on the land, and if so, whether the inhabitants would welcome the ships' passengers, turn them away or try to kill them, and possibly eat them. Although the armaments carried by the crews were significant, they were not always successful, when misunderstandings due to language barriers were so easy.

For the later journeys undertaken with the intent to *settle* in the new land, the difficulties were slightly of a different type, but longer lasting on land. After their arrival, the immigrants had to experiment and assist each other just to *survive*, and many had to learn firsthand over many decades that followed how much diversity of other European immigrants' ideas and values they had to tolerate. Some had to become quite innovative, even inventive, and most became *very interdependent*. There was no overriding purpose or plan, always present, motivating them to establish and found a democratic nation, much less a Christian democratic nation. They came to establish *colonies*, not to create a New Nation. There was no "constitutional" talk in those early days, and if the word ever appeared, it simply referred to a written body of laws they relied on in England or another country, but said nothing more about the actual structure of a new government in the New Land. We must be careful not to read too much into the past by our retrospective desires or oversimplifications.[6]

Among the first to come were many religious dissenters, yet some of these tried to emulate the theocratic forms from which their own families had recently escaped. But it was probably because they and their ancestors had *never* known anything but "Christendom." The exclusion of Catholics in a few of the earliest colonies showed the continuing reaction to the long wars in Europe between Catholic and Protestants that were in their recent family histories. But the "Christian" theocratic attempt so exemplified in the Mayflower Compact and various colonies, several of which were Puritan, whose religious views were as prominent as in the first quotation above, simply failed over time. There was so much *diversity* even among the original colonists that they were not only *unable* to *unite* people sufficiently to form a nation, but also they could not even keep the peace between colonies with such different priorities and irrational local or geographical advantages such as being on a seaport or a major river vis-à-vis being landlocked.

Meanwhile, other nations had become aware of the vastness and possible wealth of the new land, and the colonists began to realize how impossible it was to negotiate anything with foreign powers if they remained a small, vulnerable, and insignificant colony with little local government, no real military, and only a marginal and fragile, if not ambivalent, connection with England. Finally, by the last half of the eighteenth century, the claims of ownership of huge parts of the New World still by Spain and France, and the oppression of England and its military presence within the colonies, made the colonists realize although they had tried to make a go of it with England, they now had no choice but to declare independence. It was liberation through war or a deplorable servitude to England for the indefinite future. Much public discussion sought to justify a break with England, even though the colonial economy was very connected with England as were many select nostalgic memories of a few of the better times and the more sophisticated culture and conveniences.

Even after the war, the idea of any national government of reasonable power was distasteful to many colonists. Had it not been for the chaotic conditions that followed the impotent Articles of Confederation, which had no solution for enforcement of the laws that most states decided to ignore, no resolution would have been sought. These are the facts cited by so many of those writers of the Revolutionary and post-Revolutionary years. Even for those who admitted the various forms of corruption going on unchecked within various colonies-later-states, and the gross failure of some states to make any payments on the war debt, opposition to a new Constitution or new government was very outspoken in some circles. Some claimed it quite an illegal and subversive manipulation through a congressional convention that was called under the Articles of Confederation to undermine those very Articles. They had a point. But without significant change, the disparate colonies, now states, would not last long on their own.

The Constitution's ratification over many months itself was fairly uncertain, uneven, tortured, and manipulated by various sides. It seemed that everybody and their dogs had to express themselves, in pamphlets, newspapers, meetings, often in gross exaggerations of either the positive or negative elements of the proposed Constitution. Madison tried to remind the people that those living on the outer edges of the new states after the war would certainly be less susceptible to some foreign invasion if they could form a strong constitutional republic by which their closest neighboring states would feel a sense of unity with them, enough to help defend them. This representational government was to him the answer: the greater the diversity of interests, whatever they were, the less likely it was that any "majority" would form to dictate narrow and exclusive interests to the new government.[7] A much greater sense of unity could be achieved as such a democratic republic than was possible under the Articles of Confederation. Thus, the checks and balances between the proposed federal powers or branches were matched on a regional level by the checks and balances which diverse interests there created. This he saw as true even in religion, as did Jefferson: the more sects or religions, the better.

When ratification of the Constitution finally occurred, a greater measure of that unity was felt. Even some former radical opponents of it decided to put their support behind it.[8] Probably there was no logical choice of going backward at that point, so that "democratic" or Constitutional republic superseded the earlier theocratic attempts at government by an *acceptance* of *real differences* among citizens, including a difference in their religious allegiances or nonreligious positions. A *free or voluntary unity* had been purchased at the high price of a deadly war, but it had to be a *trusting* unity of a new "free" and *equal* people out of the *diversity* of the *whole people* who had fought for that freedom. That transition and acceptance of considerable differences within a more explicitly embracing sense of unity was a remarkable historical achievement, in which the people of the "constitutional republic" stood light years removed from the exclusive narrowness of even their colonial predecessors in the early seventeenth century. It was a radical break with a 1,400-year-old tradition of "Christendom" in the West, the only thing they had known in Europe.

It is more difficult to appreciate their *lack* of moral treatment of many residents of the lands they "discovered." The "discoveries" of the New World, from the fifteenth century through the seventeenth century, which was the initial mass movement across the Atlantic and even beyond, were driven primarily by the hope for more riches and power for the nations from which these emigrants came and a share of the fortune for the actual ship captains. But as historian Sydney Ahlstrom pointed out, those "discoveries" were as contingent as was the influence of the Puritans on the productiveness of the general culture of the New World.[9] More in the words of philosopher Richard Rorty, "it just happened,"[10] or historian Sidney Mead's statement that the democratic structure itself was something they just "stumbled into."[11] It is not likely that anybody sailed from England with the purpose of establishing a democratic republic.

Since these European immigrants were the agents by which the "Christian" ethic arrived at the New World, it was quite a mixed bag, affirming David Hume's idea that most governments in the world during his day were *not* some mutual voluntary original contract but rather were the rule of the conqueror over the conquered, to which the latter finally acquiesced when facing possible death.[12] Of course, the colonists who defeated England did not want to rule England, but only to be free of it, and some found it difficult to break with even the idea of a monarchy as the ideal, a nostalgia that stood in contrast to their listing of all the abuses they enumerated in the Declaration of Independence, abuses suffered at the King's hand during the previous decades.[13]

Certainly Columbus did not sail to the West to buy land at a fair price or buy products from other cultures, but to find gold and silver for his King and Queen (and himself), even to trade worthless trinkets to the gullible for their gold, which could be camouflaged as his mission to convert pagans to Christianity—to save their souls. Yet, we must not question his motives nor religious devotion too much, even if his methods were completely unethical and inhumane by our present standards.[14] He and his successors over the following voyages and years considered *none* of the local inhabitants as *fully human*, whether in the Caribbean or on the West Coast of the United States, or elsewhere in the New World. If the locals resisted "conversion" (another form of being enslaved or dominated by a foreign power) or were sensed as a threat, they were either killed or enslaved, and the conquerors sometimes helped themselves to some of the attractive females as their own sex slaves.[15]

The distance of the New World from the Old World, as well as the stark and dangerous conditions of the new lands, often staggered the imaginations of the new explorers. It called forth an individualism as well as cooperation that had to be exercised by those who *settled* in the New World, requirements that frequently exceeded their ability to adapt or respond. Those who came with the intention of staying had a more difficult long-term challenge than the "explorers" who were always thankful to make it back home to Spain or another country in Europe. Many died en route to the New World; many settlers died within a year or less after arriving. Since it was a much more difficult trip back across the Atlantic than in coming west, for most except the hardiest sailors, to return was not a feasible option for many years no matter how difficult they found life in this New World. This great distance also made any European control of the lives of those immigrants very unlikely, tardily implemented, and often resented because of an ignorance the people "back home" had of the real conditions of this wild and seemingly endless country. This was true of most aspects of colonial life—whether England was trying to control the religion, economics, social life, or political concerns. Over decades, this created tremendous tension between the immigrants and authorities of the established churches, sponsor-trading partners, and taxing authorities in the Mother countries.

The conditions of 1607 to the War of Independence and the Constitution, as nearly two centuries in length, was a period of radically different uprooted peoples with significantly opposing understandings of their political and religious settling on the same continent and often in close proximity, a constant struggle for sheer survival in which people often became dependent upon others who were close enough to assist, a trial and error of living methods among colonists who had mixed motives in immigrating. That made it more difficult to treat the other immigrants of different religions unethically. Before the middle of the eighteenth century, upper New England's successful "revivals" by John Whitefield, the Wesley brothers, and others unintentionally strengthened this *toleration* among the masses (who had never yet read Locke or others) because they insisted that their audiences should exercise their own freedom or autonomy in regard to their response to God or Christ.[16] By the end of this period, a number of colonies had already disestablished their government from religion, and the population had expanded from about 200,000 in 1690 to more than 2.5 million by the time of the Revolution, the overwhelming majority of this later growth being German and Scotch-Irish immigrants. The Africans imported as slaves grew from 58,850 in 1715 to more than 400,000 by the Revolution, and close to 700,000 by 1790.

By the end of this period, much had been stabilized, at least by the European immigrants' cultural understandings. The early immigrants who sought "freedom" for themselves did not extend that to Africans imported as slaves, nor to the local inhabitants, the Native Americans, or First People, who had preceded these immigrants by *thousands of years*. Eventually, ocean voyages became safer as routes became established, and the trading companies could maintain their connection of trade with the Old World. The commerce then became a staple for all the new immigrants, providing a market for their tobacco, cotton, and other commodities, supplying the colonists with finished products for daily living, and a greater stability and permanence was felt, especially as these shipments brought more armaments for the immigrants, enabling them to continue to subdue the Native Americans in the late eighteenth and nineteenth centuries as the *superior-armed* white people migrated further west across the vast "new" country.

Trade between the various colonies also developed, as had navigation routes within the New World, whether by canal or significant rivers. Since most Native Americans did not think anyone had the right to "own" land, they had no established legal records of lands owned. The white people were quick to divide it up among themselves with official-looking written documents and a cavalry to enforce the newly imported or quickly drawn laws. The new European immigrants *became* by sheer fiat, by power and legal documents *they* constructed, the buyers and even the sellers of the land, by which many second and third generations inherited vast estates of literally thousands of acres, becoming extremely wealthy.

The "equality" as the basic ideal mentioned in the Declaration of Independence became a vital part of the public image the New Nation was pleased to show, but equality within the policies, structures, or actual plans of the citizens remained always *unrealized* and was a topic of the general populace only at short intervals such as national crises. Poverty in both the North and South, even just within the white population, involved in some states as much as half the population, with those actually owning land being as low as 10% of the population.[17] Promises and treaties were made with the nonwhites or Native Americans and broken willy-nilly as often as they were convenient to the well-armed white European immigrants.

David Hume's description that the known governments came from conquest or usurpation or both, and that acquiescence finally followed that power,[18] seemed to fit precisely the "government" of the Colonial period, from the fifteenth through part of the eighteenth century. Only very gradually did new generations begin to see humans more equal, more civil, and more reasonable. Hume's concern was that the idea of a universal awareness of human equality and therefore of the necessity of a government which derived only from a voluntary, reasonable "original contract" was unhistorical and unrealistic. He did not contend that there was never any willing or voluntary subservience by the ruled, but it was the option by coercion, the choice of accepting the conditions or being overpowered or annihilated by the ruling power. Nietzsche later thought he had found the origin of morality in ancient cultures in which people got so used to being commanded by a ruler that they eventually equated the principles of such with the "good." With this analysis, he thought he discovered the "ressentiment" that was originally behind the morality and grew especially under "priests" and was reflected later in the quest of the "herd" for equality. Both of these appear at first to challenge either Rawls's idea of the need for equality and/or his insistence on a voluntary "original contract" to which all can agree.

Hume was right in describing what seems to be the facts behind most present governments in his day, and he admitted that one cannot go far back into the primeval times to see how it all came about. But the important element in their different positions is that somehow Western culture began to *change*, at least on the surface. The aristocratic value which was still associated with the leaders of many countries, and the royal families that still governed much of the world, was gradually being undermined by a sense of a need for equality, which was accentuated in the last half of the eighteenth century especially in the colonies and their War of Independence and in the subsequent French upheaval at the end of the century.[19] Its recognition of what a "human" is changed radically, finally seeing certain "natural rights" as life, liberty, property, and the pursuit of happiness.

None of that traces back to either ancient Jewish or Christian ethics; neither knew of any "natural" rights but only what they thought God told them, whether it was to love one's neighbor as one loves oneself, or to commit genocide to inherit the land of Canaan as "God's gift," or it was to simply retain the "status quo" since the Final Judgment was imminent. The *application* of the insights of the "natural" rights of life, liberty, property, and the pursuit of happiness, with equality at their base, however, came quite *slowly*, from the fifteenth century to the present in finally accepting different ethnic groups and women. These ethical ideals even of the modern democratic society of the United States *remain only* "aspirational," not reality, as we see the way ethnic minorities are treated by the "white" people, and the double standards or worse in the area of any sexual equality in both freedom and distribution of general goods.

So far, then, we have seen that there has been a basic *mis*information or intentional myth spread over centuries that (1) the civil and criminal laws of the United States were adopted from the Christian ethics and laws which were derived even from the Jewish Torah, especially the Decalogue; and (2) the United States was also intended to be a nation of a single religion, namely, Christianity, even though it has also always been tolerant of others. We analyzed the second point in the previous chapter. We also described the ethics of Ancient Israel and early Christianity, To summarize the latter, however, the ancient ethic found in the Jewish scriptures was (a) intended only for Ancient Israel as the ancestors of later Jews, never for other people; (b) it was geared toward a very agricultural/seminomadic people, centered around a sacrificial worship system in a temple, where priest, prophet, and king determined what was "God's" will, and the people had no voice; (c) there was no human autonomy or equality, but rather a theocracy and inherent inequality racially, sexually, and even economically; and (d) the only general ethical principles such as opposition to false testimony, murder, theft, and bribery were always subservient to the terrible sin of idolatry, even though the prophets showed that the sacrificial system itself had little effect on stemming either idolatry or the violation of these rather universally recognized ethical principles. Everything rested upon "God's will" and whoever could claim to know it, but the latter was often a severe and deadly contest.

The ethics of early Christianity as reflected in the New Testament was basically eschatologically driven, as simply an "interim-ethic" or "status-quo" ethic, simply biding the short time prior to the Parousia and Final Judgment. If many ethical instructions attributed to Jesus in the "Sermon on the Mount" seem hyperbolic, drastic, or unreal in their approach, such as lopping off one's hand to prevent one from stealing, or gouging out one's eye so it won't cause one to want to commit adultery, it also reflected a sense of irresponsibility toward the future, simply reassuring that God will supply, period. Yet Jesus instructed disciples to allow anyone who wants to defraud them. That can make sense *only* if Jesus is truly overwhelmed by the conviction that the coming Kingdom and Final Judgment are very, very imminent; otherwise, it is sheer irresponsibility. He does present what is called the "Golden Rule," but it was well known by Jews of his day in its more cogent form (which was given by Rabbi Hillel) as a command to *not* do to others what you would *not* want them to do to you. One actually learns more what Jesus opposed such as greed than what he approved in ethics, but in one gospel at least he is reported as saying that he is not doing away with the Torah at all.

Yet Paul came along and dismissed the Torah or law from having any relevance for Gentile converts. Instead, he substituted the power of the Spirit as the ethical motivator.[20] Yet, ironically, he for some reason thought it was important to point out that the person who loves others as himself has "fulfilled the law" (Rom. 13:8–10), and the "Spirit's" result of fruit in one's life is defined largely in ethical categories taken from the Torah. The double irony was that he insisted every disciple had received the Spirit to make them moral, yet for some reason he felt a need to write numerous searing condemnations of many of the disciples regarding their lack of morality,[21] while he also insisted that the "shortness of time" required that people simply remain in the state in which they were "called" (by Christ). By the latter, he intended to be understood as saying the slave remain satisfied to be a slave, and if one is married, one is even to live as if one is not married? (I Cor. 7:17–35, esp. 29).

This latter is a surprising instruction, all built on his idea that the world is soon "passing away," but probably also reflects his feeling of his own superiority in a celibate state in which he did not have to always be concerned for the welfare of a wife and/or children. Basically, Paul's fight against the Torah as a threat to his being an "Apostle to the Gentiles" left much ethical instruction simply hanging, and, had it been managed by the Spirit as he said, he would not have had to reprimand anyone who had the Spirit for suggesting they could just sin to receive more grace. His ethical injunctions are nearly always directed only at how the converts must behave only toward other Christians; it can hardly be said that "love" is more inclusive in Paul's letters. Otherwise, his ethics pick up the common Greek vice lists, but basically insist that the disciples must *imitate him as he imitates Christ*, yet he never tells how Jesus related to anybody, so details of how to imitate ethically remained extremely vague.[22] If this was part of the ambiguity by which early Christian missionaries promoted some sort of ethic among different cultures, the difference in cultures in immigration to the "New World" was even more difficult, and the ethics nothing like even what St. Paul had propagated.

THE CHRISTIAN ETHIC'S ENCOUNTER WITH
THE ETHNICALLY DIFFERENT OTHER

For those who contend that European immigrants brought the true religion to the New World, but were very tolerant, the real test does not come by what people have professed to believe, but how that caused them to *act toward others*. *Not* what they aspired to, but how they *related* to others, as the profound Christian theologian, Hans Küng, emphasized, the focus of Christianity is not merely of believing but on *"being* a Christian."[23] The European immigrants' evolving view of themselves was split into a variety of gradations. On the one hand, each immigrant was either religious or not, and if he or she was, it was the Christian religion, predominately Protestant (with small settlements of Catholics) he or she professed, and that means the ethic which Protestant Christianity propagated. This constituted a very broad kind of identity, with familiarity at least in a professed common name, although the *ethical differences* between Calvinist, Lutheran, Anglican, or the more radical Reformation sects were *vast*.

Most of the religious people also very soon had neighbors that were of a quite different Christian group, either within their colony or adjacent to their colony, and, combined with their awareness that many immigrants had little or no concern for religion, this significant difference could not be simply ignored. Even in Columbus's first journey to the West, though part of his mission was to "convert" people to the Catholic Church, even so he seemed caught off guard at how *different* the people he found were, whose history was unknown by him, and his history was unknown by them. That fact probably came as a rude shock to his system as did the fact that during food shortages on these voyages, the sailors often had to resort to eating some of the stowaway rats, especially before the rats ate up all their decent food and even their leather ropes! The immigrant settlers may not have been concerned with ropes, sails, and rats, but they were completely in the dark about the people they found already inhabiting the land.

The Indians' or Native Americans' lengthy story in this land took place as innumerable migrations of a Mongoloid people from Asia crossed the Bering Strait to what was later known as Alaska. It was so early that by 8,000 BCE the descendants of those immigrants had traversed the entire Western edge of both continents of North and South America, all the way down to the Patagonia region of South America. Over the many centuries, as the temperatures changed with the melting ice, the immigrants spread throughout the warmer zones such as the Pacific Northwest first and then beyond, through North, Central, and South America. In many countries, this people created remarkable cultures and sophisticated cities, and many religious sites of the ancient Incas and Aztecs remain well preserved today, attesting to their culture.

When Columbus had encountered these people in 1492 in the Caribbean in a settlement he named "San Salvador," he thought he had made it to India so called them "Indians." We know little of their history, but they developed communities in various pockets of the continent of North America, where they were later seriously confronted by the Spaniards in what became known as Florida and California. The Spaniards came to the Caribbean and North America with any number of motives, originally sent by the King and Queen, initially under an Italian captain named Columbus who had great personal ambition in such a voyage, and whose confidence allowed him to promise the monarchy great wealth and international power if they sponsored him. The exploration was obviously motivated by the lure of Spain becoming the dominant trading power of the world. Columbus was to establish a trading post colony in China or Japan, probably similar to the one he had seen in West Africa. But government and explorers alike were also on a hunt for instantaneous wealth through discoveries of caches of gold or silver or other precious metals as well as acquiring new land masses by conquest.

In fact, immediately following Columbus's first voyage to the Caribbean, the Spanish and Portuguese marked off a certain line on the maps, dividing the world between them. Shortly thereafter, the line was moved 260 kilometers further west to satisfy Portuguese interests, but most of it was unknown territory as both sought to get to India to lay claim on it. When the Spanish explorations failed to find obvious gold mines awaiting their ownership, they at least tried to trade noisy, cheap trinkets for the little gold the locals possessed privately, and the Spaniards were not altogether unsuccessful. For the explorers, especially the captains of the ships, there was promise of rank, recognition, wealth, perhaps marriage into wealth because of one's fame. There was also a downside, however, including the prospects in such a venture of not living through the experience, of ship trouble or even shipwreck, of being annihilated by local tribes wherever they made land, of starving to death en route or resorting to eating the ship's ropes, dried leather straps, or stowaway rats to survive, the danger of mutiny if conditions on the ship became too unbearable, and later the problem of contracting venereal disease by intercourse with one of the Caribbean women (or taking such women back to Spain as great prizes, only to learn that they subsequently spread the disease in Spain!).[24] So it required courage in the face of tremendous odds, as well as a bit of ingenuity and basic intelligence. But *what* were their Christian ethics?

Of course, there were many, including Columbus, who were motivated by the idea of spreading the influence of Christianity, "saving the heathen," and although they used strange methods including coercion and threats to bring about this "conversion," no doubt many still were convinced that their exploration was truly the work of the Christian God. Many voyages carried priests or other "religious" with them. Columbus even interpreted his first return to Spain (unlike his third return trip when he came back in chains!) as being wrought by God's continuous and bountiful miracles. This religious motivation of the Spaniards, assisted by Franciscan and Jesuit clergy, eventually spread Spanish influence along the edge of the country abutting the Gulf of Mexico all the way to California, later the Baja Peninsula, and finally up the Pacific coastline of California. As the Spaniards planted or built missions in various spots along the Pacific Coast of California, they "converted" thousands of local Indians to Christianity (mostly by force), and simply enslaved or killed the Native Americans who were not dissuaded to abandon their "pagan" ways. The subdued local Indians served the Spaniards in their ranching enterprises and building projects of missions and presidios, but were always regarded and treated as *inferior*, which was admittedly only a little more humane than the option of the Spaniards simply slaughtering the Indians as they had done elsewhere. (The Spaniards had even killed other Christians that differed from them such as the French Huguenots in Florida.)

Eventually, the European immigrants who came to the New World encountered a more radical difference as they found themselves actually *living among* Native Americans and then among African Americans who had been shipped over here as slaves. Of course, it was not simply a passive accident into which they stumbled. None of these slaves were white or Christian, so their labor was cheap;[25] Africa had been turned into a hunting ground by the slave traders from England and other countries, which became an extremely lucrative business.

The European immigrants were simply not interested in any specific religion of *other* ethnic groups because of skin color and difference in culture. Most never learned anything about the others' religious beliefs. The reality of their everyday lives showed how incorrect was the later retroactive aspirational myth of religious tolerance of the Puritans and others, as we saw in the prior chapter. It also raises the question of the ethical validity of the principles behind the immigrants' treatment of the other ethnic groups. Was this what was meant by "Christian ethics"? Their treatment of the different ethnic groups was a form of "White Supremacy" even if they never used those words. It was deeply embedded in the Europeans' psyche as they faced the Native Americans and the Africans who were imported as slaves, despite the irony that many of these immigrants themselves had been marginalized in the society from which they came. But in the new land, they generated sufficient *religious-cultural superiority* (or at least superior weapons) to treat the different others as less than human. This form of xenophobia periodically later shifted to different immigrant groups such as the Germans, Irish, Chinese, Japanese, and Mexicans, but when the whiteness of a group or their adoption of the English language, or their stringent work ethic was sufficient for some to see them as assimilating into the culture, the xenophobes always turned back on the original nonwhite groups of Native Americans and African Americans.[26] In addition to being xenophobic, it was obviously a form of "majoritarianism" since it did not include the interests of all the people, but only the white people.

This white supremacy image has persisted since. An early twentieth-century U.S. president was reported as saying, "I don't go so far as to think that the only good Indians are the dead Indians, but I believe nine out of every 10 are." He was thought to be an avid reader of his Bible, and also convinced that Indians were *quite inferior* to the "white man," and their only hope for survival was to replicate the European culture, to assimilate entirely, even though they were not full citizens. When Indian delegations and even a chief rode horseback all the way from Oregon to Washington, D.C., to talk with this president, neither the president nor his staff spoke to them. He later wrote a scolding letter, accusing the chief of acting like a "headstrong child," but seemed unaware that he was treating the chief in an inhumane way. He was not the last president of the United States who had such an unjustified and ignorantly dim view of nonwhite people.

The earliest immigrants from Europe after Columbus and the subsequent Spanish mission to North America considered *all* the Indians as *nomadic*, which, of course, was far from true. They simply had a sophisticated culture quite separate and different from any European highly structured government or capitalistic economics. They did not conceive that Mother Earth could be owned by any mere humans. Rather, there had to be a reciprocal and caring relationship between the humans and the earth. Those European immigrants who came to replicate their European culture naturally viewed Indians as horribly naïve about the land, as illiterate (since they did not speak a similar language), and embracing a "pagan" religion rather than the true one.

They proudly informed the Native Americans that they needed to become Christian and as European as possible. In many writings of those times, it is easy for the reader to get the impression that to be "civilized" meant first to be Christianized, second to be organized exactly as Europeans would be. They could not penetrate far enough into the Indian culture to perceive the intricacies of its actual organization and certainly not its religion. But even the cannibalistic Caribs, as inhumane as they were at times, hardly surpassed the Christianized Spaniards for brutality when the latter had the upper hand as conquerors of their islands. Certainly, the *furthest* thing from any of the Christian European immigrants' minds at that time was that religion should be one's actual individual choice, or that the local Indians' religion had any validity, or not even much more value than their existence which was next to none. Yet an equal number of European immigrants came with no religious incentive at all and almost no knowledge of any religion.

In any case, this is the first *major exception* to the European immigrants' aversion toward any kind of *religious persecution*. The European immigrants did *not* view *their* abusive and even homicidal treatment of the Indians, or inhumane treatment of their African slaves as "persecution." Why? Was it because they conceived of "persecution" only if inflicted on those who belonged, as they saw it, to the true religion or faith, that is, Christianity, so for those Indians who refused to convert, their conclusion was that God wanted them disposed of? That is certainly found in some white men's notes, as Brian Dippie documented.[27] But might it also have been because they, as settlers and explorers, regarded persecution as only something that *government* can do, so whatever their responses as *individuals*, they would not be "persecuting" but simply protecting themselves? Perhaps even their soldiers would be simply defending the immigrants rather than persecuting the Native Americans? In fact, might they not even be doing the "will of God" in "disciplining" the pagans, since "discipline" was so central to John Calvin's theology? Or was it simply that the only real persecution of people's religion that they recognized was when and if *they themselves* as white people were persecuted, and all other was simply commonsense prohibitions to preserve the peace among the pagan? The former was unethical and inhumane even if they perhaps saw their behavior merely prudential.

In any case, that inconsistent or self-centered way of understanding "persecution" of people's religion has not changed much over time. In the early nineteenth century, the U.S. Supreme Court had to settle a case between the Cherokee tribes and the state of Georgia. The United States had insisted on always treating the Indians as if they were "foreigners," that is, only by treaties, in considerable distinction from the way the government treated the separate colonies and later states. This was a blatant nonrecognition of their occupancy of the land. When the land was conquered by subduing the Indians, the government eventually confiscated their lands, by graciously volunteering not to kill them but rather protect them and furnish certain necessities. That, of course, is what contract law would *never* recognize as a legal contract but rather coercion or bribery, or both.

In the process, the lands over which the Indian tribes had ranged with only the restrictions of encountering other hostile Indian groups now had many more restrictions, and they found themselves ceding more and more land to the white man for *sheer survival*, as treaties were modified by the U.S. agents over and over, leaving the Native Americans small, often fairly useless parcels, while also quite often giving them *only* hunting rights—unless the Indians agreed to give up all their lands and thus be swallowed up by the states. But when the state of Georgia desired to possess more of the land occupied by the Indian tribes, the latter finally refused. To respond to this, the state of Georgia prepared its armies to evict them by force. This, in turn, made the tribes request from the government an injunction to stop the state. Ironically, in *The Cherokee Nation v. The State of Georgia*, 1 Peters 5, 1 (1831), the Supreme Court simply *refused to do anything*, insisting it had *no jurisdiction*.

The Court held that the Cherokees were neither a state of the United States nor a foreign state, so the Court was unable to judge or issue the injunction. In dissenting, however, J. Thompson insisted that "foreign" is not determined judicially or politically by geography or land but by jurisdiction itself, and that from the very beginning, the ceding of the lands to the United States or even state of Georgia was accompanied by the right of the United States *to govern* the Indians' trading or its commerce, despite the fact that the federal government made the tribes responsible for keeping their own laws. He insisted that the treaties the federal government made with the Cherokees, like all of its ties with other foreign nations, did *not* dissolve the sovereignty of either side, yet both were thereby "foreign" to each other. Yet, like the *separate States* in the United States, in their relationship with the federal government, they are both sovereign in their own right, *but form a unity as well*. The same was true of the Indian tribes, as citizens of the nation but having their own sovereign nation.

The *majority* of the Court, however, insisted that the Cherokees, after being conquered by the U.S. forces, were always *treated as conquered*, as *inferior*, so *not* really sovereign, and certainly not as sovereign and foreign. The descriptions these Justices gave of the Cherokees were that they were uncivilized, unorganized, restless, warlike, cruel, lacking in real stability. Their hunting state had implicit seeds of self-cancellation or else radical improvement since when the game fled from one area, the hunters moved from it to where they could find game once again. The conclusion to this was, since the legal conflict could not be resolved by a Cherokee court that would be honored by Georgia, nor could a Georgia state court resolve it since the Cherokees would not honor it, the only judicial body that could hear the case was the U.S. Supreme Court, which said it was simply *not* the court to hear such, so there could be no resolution.

That means, in short, that the Cherokees simply had *no Court* to vindicate *any* wrongs various states of the United States wanted to inflict on them. Was this Christian ethics made "law" as they experienced it? But that was not the end of the story. The president of the United States, Andrew Jackson, resolved the situation by *forcing* those members of the five tribes who did not leave willingly, finally removing more than 16,500 Indians to the Oklahoma Territory, a journey in which so many thousands died en route by starvation, violent weather, disease, and mistreatment, that it was called the "Trail of Tears."[28]

It is this history of the government's dealing with the Native Americans and the *Court's abandonment of any moral or natural law* in its adjudication by the end of the nineteenth century that allowed legal decisions to be based merely upon *written*, Constitutional law, *starkly separated* from any *moral* consideration, thereby treating nonwhites as less than human.[29] Was this the European immigrants' utilization of Christian law and its ethical base? Or was it more parallel to Ancient Israel's conquest of Canaan in the book of Joshua, one of the goriest books of any religion's sacred scripture? But the court was henceforth too embarrassed over the unethical consequences of the legal actions to want to ever hear of the ethical issue again. And so it was.

The early efforts of the Spaniards to conquer the New World permanently actually failed.

In fact it was only much later repeated immigrations of the Spanish to the Southwest (Texas, New Mexico, and Arizona) that finally created permanent, relatively peaceful Spanish communities in those regions during the seventeenth through nineteenth centuries. Over the centuries, the one element *essential* to any relationship, any ethic or law or nation—the element of *trust*—became next to impossible for African Americans and Native Americans or First Peoples, with the U.S. government continually neglecting, altering, or disavowing its promises, treaties, and the alleged bestowed "rights" without any justification.

Time and again, the European ideas or format of religion have prevented U.S. citizens from appreciating the ancient possession by sheer residence on the lands by these Indian tribes. The Dust Bowl days of the 1920s and 1930s occurred not simply by lack of rain but primarily because of the white settlers whose tractors and plows destroyed the natural vegetation of the High Plains which the Native Americans had left untouched so it could sustain the wild animals including the buffalo, which the white immigrants nearly completely obliterated. The white hunters were light years removed from Albert Schweitzer's understanding of the instinctual "will-to-live" as common to all living creatures. In the early twentieth century, these white immigrants with their new tractors and plows turned the soil over and over, turning it into a fine powder that would fill the sky and human lungs with the least amount of wind, something the High Plains never lacked. The abuse of the natural elements paid back in kind as many people in the Dust Bowl years died of dust pneumonia.

If we skip ahead to the late 1980s and 1990s, we will see Supreme Court cases in CA and OR in which the white culture simply refused to accommodate these Native Americans, refusing to honor their sacred places or religious worship, even when the government had a long history of honoring parallel Christian practices and sacred Christian sites. More recently, the profit motif of large corporations forced the construction of the oil pipeline which endangered the people's water supply in North Dakota in 2016–2017, which, despite exaggerated claims of the safety of the pipes, has already leaked severely by 2021. Even when the Indian tribes insist it was about water rather than their religion or spirituality, corporations were still allowed to ignore their claims, parallel to the way a whole state ignored the claims of contaminated water in Flint, Michigan, much of which poisoned African American families. But this brings up that *other* "different" group which also has never yet been allowed equality with the white European immigrants to the New World, the "African Americans."

After five centuries of the European discovery and immigration to the "New World," was David Hume right, that most if not all government is simply a matter of coercion, force, might, or conquest, including the United States? That certainly describes the encounter between the European immigrants and these two other ethnic groups, a matter of "might makes right." Or was there ever any reality to the idea of an "original contract" between equal people, a totally voluntary arrangement of government, such as the one Rawls has proposed? I must remind the reader that Rawls insisted that he was *not* speaking of a *historical* contracting but a "hypothetical" contracting which is presupposed by any society which considers itself "democratic." The question is only now whether the nation of the United States, with its Constitution of 1787 and its Bill of Rights of 1791, changed that inhumane rule of "might makes right" or not, or whether Rawls is correct that *justice cannot* be built on the exercise of irrational, accidental, or inherited advantages, including sheer coercion?

I believe the Constitution and Declaration of Independence spoke of *aspirational ideals* but not reality, so those articulations of "equality" and "natural rights" simply postponed the legal correction, practically *changing very little* if one views the present status of both African Americans and Native Americans in 2021. That should become more obvious as we view what occurred to a *second ethnic group* prior to the Constitution, and then continued even to the present. It is a story of whites importing African slaves as *nonhumans*,[30] exploiting them for the white man's economy for generations, finally freeing them, even promising them legal equality through the Civil War Amendments, but not allowing their assimilation into the culture. The nation's first Civil Rights Act of 1866 came on the heels of Thirteenth Amendment which was followed by the Fourteenth and Fifteenth Amendments which extended equal protection and due process to all citizens.

These were followed *not* by more laws of equality but rather by "Jim Crow" laws, "separate but equal" (e.g., in *Plessy v. Ferguson*) slogans for *another century* until the Civil Rights Acts of 1964 under the Johnson administration.[31] The momentum of those 1960s in civil rights was, however, lost as the negative prophetic self-criticism of the nation's ethics irritated some, which resulted in three assassinations toward the end of 1960s. By the mid-1970s, a conservative recoil grew tired of every national problem, the nation suffered defeat in the terrible Vietnam conflict and in its selection of its president. Kurt Andersen has shown that in the 1970s a small group, at first only four men, who were very wealthy heirs of large corporations were influenced by a new long-range strategy written by Lewis Powell to increase the wealth of businesses and their owners while pretending to stand for the middle class. They were able to turn the economic clock backward again in the mid-1980s and the Reagan administration as new policies radically changed not only the income tax system but also the estate tax structure to favor the wealthy via a "trickle-down" pseudo-philosophy, and pockets of resentment against civil right advances were generated and festered by many whites.[32]

The African Americans were, *un*like the Native Americans or Indians, *strangers* to the new land, but they were *not voluntary* "immigrants." They had been brought bound from Africa by armed, enterprising slave traders, who opened up markets throughout North, Central, South America and the Caribbean. The slaves were bought and sold as mere *nonhuman merchandise*. Does this mean the Christian culture of England and other European countries, the European immigrants in the New World and South America, had no laws pertaining to "kidnapping" or moving people against their will? Did Europeans view Africa as open and free for the taking, whether minerals, diamonds, rare wild animals, or semihumans, as they judged those people?

If this was "capitalism," Luther's objection to it as "buying cheap and selling dear" was a pretty anemic objection. It was grand theft, kidnapping, illegal imprisonment, the most heinous form of antihuman actions imaginable. Most white people still cannot even conceive of the terror of being turned into a slave and hauled off to a foreign land for the rest of one's life. This slavery was Christian ethics at work, an ethic that was defended by many American Christians as they prepared to fight for the right to have slaves in the 1860s, even using the Christian scriptures to try to justify it. Of course, slavery was such a "touchy" issue a century prior, that the Constitution had to avoid it, postponing any action for at least 20 years just to get the Constitution ratified. But the Civil War came in the 1860s, whereas the Constitution was ratified at the end of the 1780s.

Slavery not only was *not* legally stopped by the U.S. Constitution, but continued on until by the nineteenth century it was not uncommon for these traders to sell slaves for between 1 and 2,000 dollars each (which in 2021 dollars would be around $30,000–$60,000 each) far beyond the reach of any except the very richest of plantation owners. Some "slavers" (the ships transporting the enslaved) boasted of delivering as many as 1,000 or more slaves to a locality in one delivery. A Charleston, South Carolina newspaper, ran a headline on New Years' Day in 1808 that acknowledged that as of that day, the importation of slaves from Africa ceased, according to the act of

Congress. Yet in years 1804–1807, the slave *importation* had *increased each year*, to 15,676 during the final year, for a total in those years of 39,310.

Then, in the same issue of that Charleston[33] paper in 1808 "there were six notices of the sales of recent cargoes of 'Prime Africans.'"[34] It almost sounds like the way one would advertise to sell beef. In North America, profits were realized not simply in the cotton fields and tobacco farms. That whole burgeoning cotton and tobacco industry, through exports, involved not just the southern colonies but also the northern colonies who built and outfitted the slave ships ("slavers"). The industry needed cheap or free labor. Slavery was the demonic answer. If these humans could be reduced to mere merchandise so they did not count as persons, certainly neither could their religion or ethics be acceptable or valid, whether it were an African tribal religion or African form of Islam.[35] Of course, we do not learn of these African religions from the slaves. For self-survival, many of them converted to the Christian religion, and most suffered from the greatest indignities a human can receive, continually raped, robbed of self-respect and autonomy, if not of life itself by some lynching or fatal beating.

The slave trade involved millions of Africans to North and South America, and in modern currency equivalent, billions of dollars, over dozens of decades. In 1790, it was estimated that, even with many of the colonies and general population turning against slavery, there were perhaps still 700,000 slaves in the colonies, that is, *after* the Constitution and Bill of Rights were ratified. In fact, it has been suggested that American ship captains of slave ships as late as the 1840s knew how to switch around their English and American flags on their vessels, when encountered by other ships that might be trying to prevent the prolific but recently outlawed (by England) African slave trade. So the industry blossomed even more within those two decades *prior* to the Civil War. The prospects of profit can produce the most inhumane of practices, and enable people to justify it all to themselves,[36] even with *specious* religious (specific Christian) justification as it documented.

In any case, what we see during all of these years is that the distasteful persecution of people for their particular religion, which had been the historical background of many of the European immigrants to the New World, *never* became a factor of which they owned up to in *their own* inhumane treatment of these two major groups of the Indian and African populations. On the other hand, it became historically obvious to the discerning that each group contributed significantly to the Europeans' attempt to survive and settle the new country, growing and harvesting its cotton and other essential commodities, and even building the White House.

A contrast is sometimes painted between the alleged story that many of the African slaves *willingly adopted* the Christian religion and were "happy" in their relationships with their slave owners, while on the other hand, the

Indians did *not* adapt to the European and Christian ways, but rather grew discouraged and died off. Both sides of the description are untrue; it is simply another white supremacy myth (the negative side of an unhistorical-ethnological story of the *origins or faults* of those who are "different") based on an *un*realistic caricature of the African slaves' contentment on the plantations and the myth that the Indians were so pagan they could not adapt to the European culture and religion, and therefore were destined by God to die off.[37] But no slaves overall were either content or happy, and their music reveals that, even if much of it was influenced by their necessary conversion to Christianity.[38]

Nor was the Indian population incorrigibly heathen and therefore destined by God to die off. The latter myth of this "vanishing" breed was created very early in the immigrants' attempt to explain their failure to convert the Indians and to justify their brutal treatment of the people, but the myth still prevailed even when the general Indian population was actually *growing*. In fact, estimates have shown that the "vanishing American" (Indian) was very resilient in the European attack upon its civilization, despite their general lack of immunity to smallpox the European "white man" brought them, so much so that the population figures of the Indians in 1960 were the approximate equivalent of the lower of the estimates of that population way back in 1500, around 900,000 in the United States and Canada. So even if the Europeans brought more negatives than positives into the lives of the Indians and Africans, neither their inhumane mistreatment of them nor the Christian God obliterated them. The Indians were not a "vanishing" breed after all.[39] They were simply *dehumanized* by religious and unethical bias and treatment by people who called themselves Christians.

Of course, the simple story-turned-myth of our religious founding, once it was conceived, was widely propagated, never explaining how the Christian religion and its ethics allowed such inhumane treatment of two other large groups of residents. The ethnically others were always painted in unrealistic colors, as barbarian, as uncivilized, as the aggressors, as "painting" their bodies and faces, as wearing feathers (of all things!!), as "dancing" in uncouth and immoral forms, but just fortunate to have the white Christians come to their rescue, and even perhaps to share "Thanksgiving" celebration together. The traditional Western movie in the United States would often depict the barbarian Indian as scalping the white families, never bothering to document that scalping was an ancient method of trophy-taking in war, which probably superseded keeping the entire head, and had been used even by the colonial governments in New England, by offering bounties on Indian scalps! But from the movies one can draw a distinction between crudely scalping an enemy and shooting him full of holes by a Henry or Winchester. Is that really a significant *ethical* distinction or merely one based on whether the instruments for killing were technologically different? Should not the ethical judgment be against those who were aggressors rather than the residents who were being unjustly invaded? Or is it just "might makes right"?

In any case, the myth of the religious founding and tolerance did not mention the hundreds of thousands of Africans imported as slaves or the thousands upon thousands of Native Americans the immigrants killed or were driven from one area to another by the white man's superior armaments and always-revisable treaties. The myth preferred to focus primarily on the Pilgrims and Puritans of New England as the model of our religious freedom, no matter how far-fetched the image was, which is still often used to connect their Christian commitment and religious freedom with the First Amendment and from there to the present, from which some continue to assert that the United States was intended by God to be a Christian nation from the outset.

What we did not mention in the previous chapter was that Steven K. Green pointed out that this is a *strange myth*, strange because the *most* diversity and tolerance of religions among the early colonies was in the South, or Rhode Island (and perhaps the colony of Pennsylvania), though even it had its severe limitations. The myth originally arose, Green avers, from the Congregationalists rereading their history, and thereby re-forming their Puritan forefathers (who were in fact *not* famous for their religious tolerance) in their own image. Amazingly, it took. Many people bought the connection and moved to Pennsylvania where they could stand in line for an alleged real religious freedom while able to be a Christian of the particular type they chose. But *real* religious freedom came only by the First Amendment, from people such as Madison and Jefferson in the late eighteenth century.

THE SECULAR NATURE OF THE
CONSTITUTION AND "BILL OF RIGHTS"

By the end of the eighteenth century, it actually made sense to speak of "human rights," and to articulate a "Bill of Rights" as Amendments to the U.S. Constitution, even if the view of who was "human" was still imperfect. This shows the connection between ethics and laws in the base of the Constitution itself. The Constitution never mentioned "God" or the Christian religion or the "Bible," nor did the Bill of Rights. The Bill of Rights was largely reactionary to many of the "inhumane" abuses the Founders accused England of committing against them, which were documented by the Continental Congress on October 14, 1774, and again in the Virginia Declaration of Rights of June 12, 1776, the Virginia Constitution of June 19, 1776, and the federal Declaration of Independence of July 4, 1776.[40] They, of course, assumed the fairly universal ethical-legal basics such as prohibitions of theft, murder, and false testimony, which were known worldwide, even if the history of the colonists' treatment of the nonwhite ethnic groups placed even those basic ethical/legal restraints in doubt.

But the Bill of Rights, as the Constitution, was more concerned with the social contract or the structures and institutions of justice than explaining the ethical ground upon which any of the laws depended. The ethical principles of equality and justice for all, of liberty of conscience, and freedom from restraint of speech, of government based upon the whole people, of the freedom from taxation without representation, or the right to own property, the right to trial in the locality where the offense was alleged to have occurred, and so forth, were *not* derivable from the Christian scriptures or tradition. Here one need to only compare the Massachusetts' Constitution of 1780, with the early Massachusetts' theocratic law of 1641 that even gave Old Testament scripture references with its religious laws which included the death penalty. The U.S. Bill of Rights, attached as Amendments to the Constitution, opposed the tyrannical changes in laws that were so arbitrary and of which the subjects were not informed or in cases in which the laws did not exist until a colonist was accused. They now saw innumerable areas where the ethic of what we have called the mutual autonomy and trusting equality based on the "common will-to-live" demanded articulation of individual protections of persons, their papers, and possessions. Even the single idea of mutual human autonomy or equality stood in terrific contrast to the heteronomy of most religions, including Christianity, in which God is *the* authority, and women are subordinate to men, so religious ethics and its law are totally heteronomous; even humans are not equal since God has His "chosen."

This Bill of Rights had an ethical conception of the *inviolability of the person* which necessitated protecting citizens' bodies, movement, speech, beliefs, integrity, reputations, even their real property and personal property from any presumptuous "taking" by another. It went so far as protecting them from unreasonable searches and seizures, and from "general warrants" issued by the government that had been so abused by the British during the period preceding the Revolutionary War. Warrants now had to be specific and had to show "probable cause" given under oath. The Bill of Rights legislated against restricting not simply people's speech, but their writing, peaceful assembling, religious belief, and even worship (as an extension of speech and conscience). It prohibited a foreign government from depriving them of their arms (as had even happened by deceit shortly before the war) and their right to defend against that foreign government, as well as prohibited the foreign government from housing its soldiers in private quarters of the colonists without consent of the owners, whether in time of war or peace, which the British also had done over and over. It also protected citizens from being indicted for capital crimes without a grand jury, protected them from "double jeopardy," from forced confessions of guilt, or a lack of due process, including any taking of property for public use without just compensation. Each accused person was to have the right of a speedy impartial jury trial by his or her own peers, in the district of the alleged offense rather than being hauled thousands of miles back to England. The person also had the right to be informed of the specifics of the charges, to be able to confront as well as call his or her own witnesses, and even a right to a "public defender." Many of these, such as the right to a "public defender," show the common sense of justice that was defined in Rawls's second principle, the "difference" principle, because it placed social and economic inequities to be compensated to benefit the "least advantaged," which would be agreed to by anyone behind the "veil of ignorance" in the hypothetical "original position."

Since humans are dependent upon functioning reasonably by their own physical and mental capabilities, the Bill of Rights also prohibited "cruel or unusual punishments" which had been so commonly inflicted on their bodies or minds of citizens in England, nor could bails be "excessive." All of this was a very reasonable ethical expectation based upon the value of the *human being's life and integrity*, his or her right to think on his or her own. People should be given the freedom to be autonomous in the sense of directing their own lives toward their preferred goals and ends *so long as they do no harm to others*. The latter was the key for Madison and Jefferson, so much that even any religious profession should be honored by government unless and until the time the religious person hurts others or creates disorder or breaks the generally applicable laws by which *all have agreed* to live as citizens, as cited in the prior chapter.[41] Jefferson spelled out, as we saw earlier, that no one gains exemptions from those laws. No one is to receive *more or less* civic benefits for being religious or for not being religious, any more than bald people should get more civic benefits or less than people who have lots of hair. If there are no special benefits for being religious, as Jefferson insisted, one does not suffer legal or civic disadvantages either. He insisted that he suffered no harm if his neighbor wanted to worship 20 gods or none at all,[42] and, like Madison, he was terribly upset over the Virginia Anglicans' legal persecution of Quakers in their state. He became extremely agitated later when he read of an act that was going to be passed in the New York legislature that was going to nullify the marriages of any "Shaking Quakers" and remove from them all their children and property.[43] On the other hand, any government which thinks it can coerce a religious uniformity is sadly mistaken, as Jefferson wrote:

> Difference of opinion is advantageous in religion. The several sects perform the office of a Censor morum over each other. Is uniformity attainable? Millions of innocent men, women, and children, since the introduction of Christianity,

have been burnt, tortured, fined, imprisoned, yet we have not advanced one inch towards uniformity. What has been the effect of coercion? To make one half the world fools, and the other half hypocrites.[44]

Most of these laws manifest the ethical qualities we elaborated earlier of a trusting, mutual autonomy of equals which presupposes a common "will-to-live"[45] and were established by Rawls's process or its equivalent basic two principles of equal liberty and the "difference" principle where inequities exist in social and economic areas, the benefit of any proposed law must be for the "least advantaged." But, notably, *none* of these have any base or ground within the Jewish or Christian ethics *per se* (with the possible exception of the admonition to help the orphans, widows, and strangers), or any explicit or implicit connection to the Christian faith, but rather only connections to the much more recent "Enlightenment" philosophy of such equality and freedoms which came from a variety of human sources such as Baruch Spinoza, David Hume, John Locke, Montesquieu, Jean-Jacques Rousseau, Immanuel Kant, Roger Williams, James Madison, Thomas Jefferson, William Hamilton, Benjamin Franklin, Tench Coxe, Isaac Backus, John Adams, John Hancock, John Trenchard, John Jay, Thomas Paine, John Marshall, and many others.

Back in 1721, Thomas Gordon (Cato's Letters, No. 38) wrote of the "right and capacity of the people to judge of government," and his emphasis of government as a "trust" is brief but unexcelled. He spoke of a trust (whether by all the people or most) in one or more people "to attend upon the Affairs of All, that every one may, with the more Security, attend upon his own," is a "great and honorable Trust, but too seldom honorably executed" as those so trusted are more interested in exercising and increasing their power rather than making it useful for the whole people. Gordon emphasized that it does not take extra-human power to execute such a Trust, but rather only "honesty, diligence, and plain sense."[46] No words are more needed in the United States today.

By the end of the eighteenth century, outstanding insight as to the moral value of autonomy, and therefore of mutual autonomy, as the mark of "enlightened" or reasonable people, was articulated by philosopher Immanuel Kant's works on ethics which pointed to a democracy in which all rational beings saw themselves as involved in the forming of the law. In the same spirit in the United States, in September 1787, Tench Coxe provided us with an analysis of the advantages of a president, a House of Representatives, and a Senate, in comparison to their typical counterparts in the English government, and the voice of the "people" again surfaced as the remarkable determinant of the advantage of the "constitutional republic" of the U.S. Constitution.[47]

Madison's writings not only emphasized the protection from any abuse of majorities by the broad diversity of interests in such a "republic," but also defined over and over the distinction between a republic in which the whole people's interests are represented by people they elect as opposed to a pure democracy which can only operate in a very small geographical area with a minimal population, but also distinctions between hybrids of monarchies and aristocracies or of aristocracies and parliamentary governments such as in England.[48] So the themes of the diversity of people and their interests, the voice they have in electing those to represent them, stand in contrast to inherited positions by a sense of real equality and fairness. Certainly, the "will-to-live" with the maximum possible equal liberties with others—the two main emphases of Nietzsche, Schweitzer, and Rawls—is what was at work in the genius of those people and many others who furthered the negotiations of the Constitution.

Again, notably, none of the intricate ethical reasoning that went into negotiating the different branches of government and its power and limitations had any direct grounding by any religion whatever. The checks and balances between the various branches were to serve as a vehicle for maintaining a sense of unity yet diversity, a unity that could be inclusive of substantial diversity so long as it did not threaten the public order, as Jefferson said. Within that slight limitation, which should not be a limit at all, since every citizen embraces the basic principles of the social contract or Constitution, as Rawls pointed out, people are free to be religious or not, but religion can*not* be used as a law by the government which would restrict who can qualify for public office, or affect one's civic protections or benefits in the least.

The Constitution and new government were not "hostile" to religion, but provided citizens a freedom of conscience or even of worship, without in any way playing favorites among religions by endorsing one or allowing citizens to be led to think that only one religion was acceptable to government or even that religion was preferred to nonreligious affiliation. As Madison said, government simply has "no cognizance" of religion.[49] This insight is much older but light years ahead of the thinking of two Supreme Court Justices, who, in the oral arguments of the *Van Orden v. Perry* (2005) case, insisted that "government" itself has a right to express *its own* religion.[50] *Government*'s own religion? But if Jefferson is right that "religion is a matter which lies solely between man and his God" that one perceives his or her own individual duty to God to which he need not give account to any other, and God created the human mind for it to be free in this respect, free to this "natural right" of conscience, he was right in also saying that the separation of religion from government in the First Amendment *restored* to man his "natural rights," and "he has no natural right in opposition to his social duties."[51] At that point, he obviously was implicitly saying the ethic upon which the social duties are grounded can*not* be violated by one who thinks "God" gives him the right to do so. This is the equivalent to Rawls saying the "original position" of the social contract and its principles is a "political" conception of justice which has *priority* within the structures of justice over any alleged "metaphysical" duties or rights. Otherwise, one simply has chaos since there is no public recognition agreed to that any single person or group has the true interpretation of the only true religion and its ethics.[52]

Fortunately, over time, ethics applying to a people's relation to other peoples, or nation to nation, also began to change to a degree from its former position of thinking that land and possessions could be taken by any kind of "conquest" if a nation or group had the power, to a position of viewing aggression or interference against another legitimate sovereign as ethically *un*acceptable. A preemptive aggression has only recently arisen because of covert terrorist activities, but its justification in recent wars has left it as extremely questionable, no matter how covert various countries operate. Very gradually, the realization has come that each person is different, even if related by blood, that no one thinks exactly the same way. So the *relativity* of human opinions and even of what we call "objective" reason is recognized, including an ethic rule that nations can*not* simply invade other lands to create their own empire. Of course, that has not prevented aggression from taking a more *subtle or covert* route to overthrowing weaker states.

For those philosophers such as John Locke who were convinced that the human conscience is free so cannot be relinquished by a human nor deprived a human by someone else, Locke based this on his belief that one's conscience was answerable only to "God."[53] Thomas Jefferson, as we saw, used similar words, even though he and Locke were miles apart on what they thought "God" was as well as what Christianity represented. With the "desacralization" of the Christian culture over the past three centuries, even its theological abandonment of "theism" at least since the middle of the twentieth century by some of its most influential theologians, there is no universally agreed single party (formerly a theistic "God") to whom one's conscience answers. We have found ourselves returned to Kant who said a person cannot ever escape his or her own *conscience*, which is more certain than any symbol of "God." But one's conscience cannot be Absolute. In Rawls's embracing of Kant, he was intent to show that government's concern for the "good," the "right," or for "justice" means the government "of the people" *answers to itself*, "to the people." It is that *basic agreement* or hypothetical "original position" of the negotiating of the social contract, behind a veil of ignorance, the resulting "overlapping consensus" or the basic principles and a constitution, which amounts to an overlapping of the consciences of all involved, *for which we become answerable* to each other, to the whole people, as responsible agents of the public reason and a shared nation.

This means the "social contract" is continually updated, never becomes static or fixed for all time in one temporal manifestation which is so limited, and this means we need to *leave completely behind* former ideas of who is "human" and who is not, or of an "equality" which we all knew was "separate but (NOT) equal." The radical changes in human thinking that occurred between the time of Columbus and the present were more radical than any similar 500-year period in human history, and we do not live at the front part of that, but are moving quickly into more expansive models of interdependent unity, of a globalism that cannot be left up to ancient ideas that would destroy it by some exaggerated cliché of libertarianism, nationalism, antiglobalism, or unreasonable isolationism. We are entering a stage of an awareness of an interdependence and spirit of cooperation by which the population of the *entire* Earth can and must address the terrible threats of pandemics, global warming, and human pollution, as well as nuclear, cyber, and germ warfare or terrorist-led weapons.

In the future, the basic *unity of humans and the basic rights of all living beings* will be exponentially more important than mere national interests, state priorities, regional problems, or family traditions. It will necessitate the recognition of *science's validity* as well as the *values* of the "liberal arts" to a culture. It will educate toward independent thinking, but cooperative spirit, toward trust and trustworthiness, in which "ethics" is not a mere side dish after the important things are settled. There will be *no* room for *special exemptions* from universally applicable laws simply on the basis of some people belonging to one specific religion, or race, or sexual identity or social group, not in any country or any state, but that also includes no room for special exemptions for nations from universally applicable laws simply on the basis of military power, wealth, international status, name-recognition, or ethnic group.

Without such an effective sense of national unity and world unity, humanity will simply *not survive*. A single pandemic, hideous nuclear war, or radical climate change with its raging fires, droughts, and famines and its flooding of shorelines and whole cities can annihilate humanity, whether by constant incursions which grow over time to the point of extinction or by some short-term crises that bring humanity down. The problem with any religions or other comprehensive schemas of nonpublic reason is *not* their existence, but their attempts to influence laws if not nullify public reason by their "faith," their specific metaphysics and myths, which are all *outside* the political conception of justice and absolutized by them rather than allowing all arguments from public reason to be open to negotiations and compromise.

Typical of such restricted perspectives are the fairly recent attempts to rewrite history, including the history of religion and government in the United States as we have already seen, but also the militant opposition to the theory of evolution and especially its being taught in any public schools. But these mythical absolutes also place a protective halo around any Christian symbol erected even on government property, so as we will see, people ironically have gone to great lengths recently to deny any *religious* significance to these religious symbols (since that would be such a blatant violation of the Supreme Court's own *Lemon* standard), to instead say the symbol is simply a reminder of death or of the rule of law or of freedom. If the absolutistic reactions of both Protestant and Catholic positions in the second half of the nineteenth century tell us anything, we should probably *expect* public reason, scientific theories and methods, obvious historical facts to be summarily altered, belittled, or even painted as the "enemy," the more people's absolute is disappointingly experienced as self-betraying or difficult to defend.

EQUALITY'S ELUSIVENESS DESPITE BEING THE BASIC ETHICAL PRESUPPOSITION

When John Rawls posited a people negotiating hypothetically their social or political contract, and arriving through freestanding principles at an overlapping consensus of two primary principles in a lexical order, he also presupposed an ethical element behind these. The two principles were the principle of the maximum equal "liberty" for all and of compensation for any "difference" in social and economic equality by placing the benefit of the "least advantaged" as the primary concern. Those, he believed, would be voluntarily chosen by all people if they were behind the hypothetical veil of ignorance, divested of any knowledge of what their actual situation in life would be. The *presupposition* was that the negotiating *process itself* would be *fair and just*, between people who valued life above all, who wanted to cooperate, and thus use only "public reason," so in the initial position all parties would be *equal* or have equal voice. But he also presupposed the supreme value of life, as I said, the common "will-to-live," and those who know anything of life experiences realize that grounding.

"Equality," however, has proven not to be unequivocal, but quite elusive, but I believe Rawls knew that it must be qualified, which he did. The great culture critic, Jacques Barzun, just prior to the twenty-first century, wrote the following:

> So difficult is it to define equality and nail down its conditions that in dictatorships where it is proclaimed and enforced in dozens of ways, the needs of government and daily life re-introduce distinctions; as Philip Guedalla observed early in the Soviet regime, "some are more equal than others." The paradox

reminds us that international law has no option but to assume, in the teeth of the evidence, that all sovereign nations are equal.

There is but one conclusion: human beings are unmeasurable. It follows that equality is a social assumption independent of fact. It is made for the sake of civil peace, of approximating justice, and of bolstering self-respect. It prevents servility, lessens arrogant oppression, and reduces envy—just a little. Equality begins at home, where members of the family enjoy the same privileges and guests receive equal hospitality without taking a test or showing credentials. Business, government, and the professions assume equality for identical reasons: all junior clerks, all second lieutenants, earn so much. In other situations, as in sports and the rearing of children, equivalence based on age, weight, handicap, or other standard, is computed so as to equalize chances. That is as far as the principle can stretch.[54]

When he said that talk of equality "prevents servility, lessens arrogant oppression, and reduces envy—just a little," Rawls had shown that when the basic principles are agreed to behind the veil of ignorance, there are no grounds for envy. Each person has voluntarily selected the same principles out of self-interest in the *general goods*. The only place "envy" could then occur would be over vested, irrational inequities that do not involve the general goods but very specific or unique traits, attributes, or assets which one would *not know* in that original position of the veil of ignorance. His whole point was that the two principles themselves should eliminate envy since such unique traits, attributes, or assets are attached to a complex of unique elements that simply are not and can never be the "general goods." For example, one does not envy a virtuoso violinist when she plays so beautifully, since one realizes that one has not spent the immense amount of time practicing to play that repertoire, not to mention that the person might even have been born with perfect pitch or other abilities well suited especially to playing the instrument. Despite what perhaps some white people think, black people do not envy them for being white, but only for being treated differently than black people are. The skin colon is part of the inherited and nonrational or happenstance uniqueness over which the individual has no power. In similar manner, it would be ridiculous to envy people for being bald or for having tons of hair, or for being genius, or for being 7 feet tall, or for running faster than everyone else. That would make no sense. We might envy others being *given advantages* when we never had any equality of opportunity to even get in the race. But Rawls is saying that there would be no envy when all of us have the same fair process to shape the basic ethical principles of our social contract, and if we do not have that fair opportunity, then the laws need to change. Democracy requires that our basic concerns for the general goods can be met while allowing for differences, but if the equality of general goods does not exist, then the standard of justice as fairness has not been met but rather abused.

Notably, Barzun points out my earlier emphasis, that this ethic outlined by Rawls which focuses on equality, maximization of liberties, and *compensation for differences or social and economic inequalities*, especially if rooted in the ethic of mutual trust and recognition of the universal, common "will-to-live," applies to *all human relationships*, even as small as the family. Within the typical family, there have to be adjustments based on maturity so that equality is not given to minors who cannot yet responsibly handle it. But that does not justify never allowing them to mature and become independent of the parents. Nor does it imply treating other mature adults as *un*deserving of equality or *more deserving* of equality because of their height, health, sexuality, political party, ethnicity, religious affiliation, wealth, fame, political power, color of their hair, or their DNA or other nonrational or inherited elements.

Barzun says we figure out forms of "equivalence" in order to better "equalize chances." When he said that equality is a "social assumption independent of fact," that seems to contradict his later use of "equivalence" and "equalizing" chances, since there could never be any sense of equivalence or equalizing chances if the whole concept is "independent of fact." What he seems to have meant is that the *value* we give to equality is the "assumption" devoid of fact. But the distribution of general "goods" are not invisible things but *empirically perceptible* entities, as also many political liberties such as being able to vote, or sensing that a political leader is not concerned with the interests of the nation but only of himself. This idea of the "equitable" is, like the idea of "fair," pretty obvious even to children, even before they learn to count or use these specific words. So his observation that we tend to attempt to "equalize" things to resolve tension, and this was matched by Rawls's emphasis that economic and social inequalities can be *accepted only* if there is equality of opportunity and only if the "least advantaged" are actually benefited from it. That does *not* mean that they are merely *promised* that the benefits will "trickle down" from those who have the major benefits of the inequality, but that the inequality *actually* works to their benefit as *the least-advantaged rather than the privileged judge* the situation.

"Circumstances," as Mark Twain recognized, work with "temperament," but an individual does not affect the former at all, and can only temporarily modify even his or her own temperament.[55] They were called by Rawls the "happenstance" or "accidentals" of one's life, again, *beyond one's control*. Of course, one can say that *perverted* and inhumane political systems have still spoken of equality, as Barzun gave an example. One often also hears that the natural effect of different circumstances in which people live and their different ways of responding to them mean that even when they begin as equal, over time they will become unequal. There is nothing very profound in that observation; it certainly does not justify people taking advantage of others or wanting the game's rules to be rearranged if they ever have less than they feel they deserve.

It was the uniqueness of Rawls's system that he saw people as *being able* to *hypothetically* bracket out those irrational or accidental elements so that one *can* gain with others a reflective consensus of what "justice" would look like (a "reflective equilibrium" as he put it), realizing that one can*not* base justice on mere accidents, happenstance, irrational, or absurd aspects of life. To try to do the latter would mean one would *never* understand "justice" and would always be at the mercy of anyone who had any kind of advantage, no matter how unfair or irrational it was. It would be a never-ending conflict since it was conceived as a zero-sum contest. Rawls's "difference" principle stepped in here to "equalize chance" as Barzun described it, that is, to *offset* in advance the accidental advantages that occur in real life in social economic distributions, *not to force* everyone into possessing exactly what everyone else possesses, but, in modern parlance, "to level the playing-field," or to determine and agree to *fair rules* to be applied equally to everyone participating in the game, and having "referees" or "judges" who are certified as reasonable, fair, and neutral.

Equality of opportunity is how Rawls described the "difference principles," that the political equality in voice in the original contracting would settle only for an equality of opportunity for all in social and economic realms, and no lesser goods would be considered a fair trade for being deprived of such equality of opportunity. But an ideal of equality of opportunity, experienced only by a handful of citizens, does not create a state or nation of equality of opportunity. In fact, a nation, *aspiring* toward equality, is not a nation of equality, nor is one that finally goes so far as to write equality into its actual laws.

As Martin Luther King Jr. wrote in his letter from a Birmingham jail, "unjust" can mean laws which are unjust on their face, but it must also include those laws whose *application* is unjust or unequal. This might involve an inequality among the different ethnic, sexual, religious, political, and economic groups, and when it does, the nation cannot even brag of having political equality of voice, or equality within its written laws, much less of equality of opportunity in social or economic areas of life. What many have come to realize is *not* that equality is demanded by people who are *un*successful in life, but by people who have been systemically and structurally *denied the opportunity to succeed* in a variety of forms.[56] The current financial inequality in the United States and so many other countries is *not* due to some laziness on the part of those who are destitute but rather on the influence on the political structures, especially legislation, a literally determining or causal influence including rates and "incentives" in the tax code, a killing of the power of unions, the pejorative language used in speaking of "entitlement programs," and so on, to keep the wealth limited to those who presently have it, to protect only *vested* interests, no matter how irrationally or accidentally vested, *rather than* offer an equal opportunity to succeed or to be equal.[57] Some companies are judged "too big to fail," but that is true only because of the disproportionate power they have accumulated by the disproportionate and skewed methods of lobbying favorable laws for themselves over decades, a form of legal bribery since running for political office costs so much, offering the most privileged the continual opportunity to buy their politicians who will do their bidding.

Under Rawls's schema, *no one* behind the "veil of ignorance" would ever negotiate to keep wealth so restricted if he or she had no idea where on the economic scale he or she would be. They would demand Rawls's second principle. This is very crucial to the future of the United States, not limited simply to economic status but also to one's social status, which includes one's sexual, racial, and religious identity, so is very pertinent even to the present discussion of the relation of religion to government in a democratic society. But those with significant vested interests who cannot conceive of their being in any other situation in life (different economic level, race, sex, religion, etc.) find such a suggested "veil of ignorance" laughable, unrealistic, pathetic, or terribly threatening. That simply shows how far the country is from a sense of "justice" which includes "equality." The word is a sham. People who mistakenly read Rawls as *preferring* a system of *inequality* simply choose not to read him closely enough to understand him or even to try to make his different ideas fit together coherently.

Long ago, the United States came to the realization that the majority of its citizens would never have this equality of opportunity if they were unable to receive a *significant education*. That brought about the "public" school system, which was seen not only as the leveling of the playing field but as the way to have a productive and satisfied citizenry, of being sure they would be educated not only in self-sustaining disciplines in school but also learn the significance of the unique form of government under which they are living. It would be a method of making people informed and critical rather than uninformed and uncritical, enabling them to grow and change, but in the process remain patriots as well as thoughtful and empathic citizens. Thomas Jefferson was so set on government and schooling to be *nonsectarian, therefore secular*, that as he and others were laying plans for what became later the University of Virginia, he disclosed his proposal to make education in Virginia *totally public*, supported by the state, in distinction to the education which had been only private schools which were largely religious in nature.[58]

Yet, the twentieth century has shown that once the public coffers are opened for a particular common need, people come "out of the woodwork" to qualify for funds even when they do not qualify, and the two most popular

areas of our recent history are the prolific increase in "nonprofit" organizations or corporations which allege some public service they can do, and
private and parochial schools, especially private colleges and universities,
with or without campuses, with or without a professionally degreed faculty,
and with or without any long-term plans on educating the public. Many
are definitely "for-profit" organizations with that as the primary goal, but
if that can be hidden, they may find access to funds of which they never
even dreamed. Even famous politicians have established scam universities
to make money, and federal administrators of public education have taken
public funds to fund private and parochial schools, and public school super-
intendents in certain states have been seen on TV instructing citizens to send
their children to private and parochial schools, as if public schools would
not sufficiently do the work if people quit bleeding off their tax dollars for
parochial schools.

   Instead of this reversion to the discredited *Plessy v. Ferguson* "separate but
equal" institutions, the government needs to fund the public schools more and
help *equalize the taxing base* in various districts instead of allowing it to work
to only place greater advantage in the richer districts. This is a concern for the
"least advantaged," Rawls's second principle, the principle of social and economic inequalities, which demands that change, and requires that the *determination* of whether *it actually benefits* the "least advantaged" be made by those
who really *are* the "least advantaged" rather than some wealthy administrator
who does not believe in public education at all. Public education remains
the *primary nondiscriminating vehicle* of *creating equal opportunity for all*,
since education is almost the only viable way of improving one's social and
economic status in a rigidly capitalistic country in which so many have associated any form of social benefits with "communism," which itself reveals
their own great lack of education. That is the irony of not being able to think
of justice *detached* from *accidentally vested interests*, even though the vested
interests are the very thing which so many in the lower rungs economically
speak of as the "elitism" which they oppose.

   If "equality of opportunity" seems basic, the question arises naturally of
what kinds of opportunities should be equal so the equality continues past
simply having a one-time effect. In certain European cultures today, a "just"
society is one that provides for *all* citizens publically funded or sponsored
health care, formal higher education to equip all people for jobs that pay a
very livable wage, adequate public housing at affordable prices, and even a
fulfilling kind of work or employment that gives a person a sense of pride
and accomplishment.[59] There are manifold aspects to each of these areas
which would have to be addressed to make them equal in opportunity, which
would be equal pay for similar work, paid vacations, paid sick leave, paid
unemployment insurance, paid dependent care when the employee is at work,

paid refresher educational courses to keep employment, and so forth, and paid long-term care and retirement programs.

In the United States, the mistreatment the colonies received at the hands of the British government seemed to make an indelible imprint, especially the idea of "taxation without representation." Then why is that "representation" *not* understood as the equivalent of "opportunity" in these broad forms in today's U.S. culture? Unfortunately, even after the Revolutionary War, many former colonies, then states, still showed *little responsibility* in paying the debt the totality of colonies had accumulated through the war. They failed to realize "no benefits without taxes," which is always easier to overlook after one has received the benefit rather than the straights one feel one is in prior to receiving the benefit. But at least a sufficient number of them realized that the New Nation would *have to share*, would have to *tax itself*, that individuals would have to *discipline themselves*, if there was ever to be any sense of equality and therefore a viable unity among the people. Yet to this day, the false political campaign claim of decreasing everyone's taxes still attracts some voters who evidently think one can receive *something for nothing*, that one's nation can provide great national defense, a fabulous infrastructure, and infinite conveniences with only minimal, if any, taxation.[60] It is not possible.

Most European countries realized the relation between benefits and sense of real unity within a nation and the taxes necessary to have the benefits, whereas the mentality of some of the European immigrants to the New World seemed to be expecting something of value for nothing, first free or almost free land, then a free war, then a free government, and how much else could they expect—free defense of the country? Free shipping of products from other countries? Perhaps free clothes? Almost free labor by importing slaves from Africa? But how would *they* be free, or who was to labor and sweat to do the work to pay the taxes for these benefits for whom? Little that is of real value has come free.

The question of social and economic *equality* is subservient to its natural prior principle, that of *equal political liberty* for all citizens, as he said, standing in a lexical order. Rawls insisted that the value of equal political liberty is the most neglected area, which carries into not simply political rights but equality in "participation" in this area. This raises all kinds of considerations which we cannot take space to discuss, but much of the inability or lack of interest in participating is due to economic controls, the whole being shaped by donors whose wealth determines the agendas and subjects for discussion. Other areas, which might also play into this truncation of the political discourse, which he did not really spend much time analyzing, would be the question of term limits on all political and appointed positions, which would give turnover which the Framers conceived of especially in the House of Representatives, preventing the caricature of the "professional politician" who seems to seek a lifetime position. The reasonable mentality of the Supreme Court which Rawls emphasized is perhaps more aspirational than real since neutrality has not been more evident there than among the legislators, and has little or nothing to do with lifetime appointments. A greater political opportunity needs to be made available, a wider participation in actual governing of all citizens, with definite term limits for all, in order to represent the diversity of the nation, and to prevent decadence.[61]

Meanwhile, we need to realize that although we often think of the "Framers" of the Constitution as being only a select few, well-educated men, they went through months and years of long discussions of the possible structures of justice for the nation, with a tremendous variety of participants. They had their moments in which the different positions seemed irreconcilable and the war for naught. But through the selfless and difficult, strategic brilliance and determination of this handful of leaders, the hundreds of others and various new state legislators were finally able to ratify the Constitution in order to form a new country. The political participation during those years was probably more fluid than it is in the United States today. It was the mature insights of several that were so constructive. For example, Madison had projected that the country's inner mobility would greatly improve quickly with all the waterways, and the roads would be considerably upgraded once the new Constitution was in place since the Article of Confederation had so many flaws. But at whose expense would these developments occur, if only a handful of the brighter minds like Madison saw the need for taxes? And what kind of taxes would everyone consider fair? He asked the *vital question*: Without taxes, how could any country in the world have any respect for the United States, which would be essentially hamstrung and defenseless, a poor allay and pitiful trading partner? Fortunately, Madison's reasoning was convincing. It should be rediscovered today by people whose primary political principles is "less tax" and maybe even "no tax." It simply is not possible, without federal taxes. The nation would long ago have *dissolved*. But the *possibility* of *dissolution* never sleeps, needing a national sense of unity and equality of basic liberties and opportunities, all based on truth, mutual autonomy, and the common "will-to-live."

Jacques Barzun thought it was a real irony or paradox that with governments such as England's which seemed to be so proud of its ideal of being able to vote, their equality of voice, yet after they elected officials, they often' expressed nothing but contempt for those elected, showed a low percentage turnout for the vote, and then they allowed their legislation to be directed by lobbyists.[62] It is perhaps even more of an irony that President John Adams, who was one of the Framers of the Constitution, thought it was the role of government to provide formal education for all as a part of the equal opportunity, yet found any idea of equality for women, African slaves, or Indians quite *unreasonable*. He even mocked his wife as if they both knew she was really his "Master," and he the slave.[63] Perhaps he thought he was funny, but slavery was no joke to those who experienced it as slaves. Was even inequality in a marriage such a joke?

Over a century and a half have passed and we have realized how ethnic "hate" crimes are rising, how intolerance and discrimination against different ethnic, religious, and sexual preferences has increased, how economic inequality has accentuated greatly over the past 50 years, and how arrests without probable cause but only a reasonable suspicion[64] (or even unreasonable suspicion), racial profiling, abuse, incarceration, and unjust Court decisions and penalties have been disproportionately experienced by African Americans and to a lesser degree other nonwhite minorities. In 2020, when an African American journalist was awarded the Pulitzer Prize for the *New York Times* magazine "1619 Project," the same superiority complex by white conservatives was seen in the backlash by guest editorials in various papers against her and her work. TV images have been burned into our psyches, images of a white father and son chasing down a young African American man jogging for his health, and shooting him to death on groundless suspicions. For the past three years, racism has grown more violent in the United States, more public, more armed, and more overlooked by the administration, as police break into homes and kill people who have been sleeping, or place their body weight on the person's neck for nearly 10 minutes to kill him for allegedly trying to pass a small counterfeit bill, or the politically aggrieved surround a state's official in charge of the election of 2020, and, some armed, intimidate with chants and totally illegal demands. Where is the sense of unity?

Even more importantly, where is the instinctual value of life or the "Reverence for Life" as Schweitzer saw it? That instinctual "will-to-live" is ignored when there is no real sense of equality and unity within a democratic republic. Where is the sense of unity of the nation in which the *agreement* is to have elections by *all* the citizens, with the results being graciously accepted by *all*? As the year 2020 came to a close, where was the sense of *loyalty to the democracy* when most federal Representatives of one party signed on as "amicus" ("friends of the court") to undermine a national election by overthrowing the voices in four states with which they happen to disagree? Where is the sense of reasonable political equality and reasonable political participation of which Rawls spoke, where the voice of the "least advantaged" is provided the real opportunity to *decide* whether a proposed law is to the benefit of the "least advantaged" or not, while the legislators, during a pandemic, cannot be impressed enough with others' poverty and lack of resources as to offer them the assistance they need to survive, as if the public taxes were not paid by that very public, as if those taxes are owned by the legislators themselves in their comfortable jobs and salaries, as if it is more just to have the most privileged make the decision rather than those who are "least privileged"? Rawls would be truly horrified today if he were still living. So would Schweitzer and even Nietzsche.

Today when white and especially white male supremacy is becoming so vocal, when fundamentalist religious opposition to any sexual activity other than strict heterosexual activity is so strident, and in which we are uncovering more and more examples of male sexual assault against females, even underage females, which has gone *un*reported, as well as priestly pedophilic crimes that have been covered up by the Church for decades, whether in the United States or European nations or Chile or other, the laws or *equality of all* need to be emphasized in their *inclusiveness*. There can be no insertion of some supposed Absolute divine law that enables one religion, one ethnic group, one sexual group, to treat all others such as nonwhites, women, transgender people, and others as "second-class citizens," whether that Absolute is Shari'ah law or the Jewish scriptures or Christian scriptures or any other *religious tradition or racist or other ideology*. These are not from the "public reason" and are narrow interests of a few who try to impose their interest on the entire nation.

None of these religions consistently proposed *real equality among people*, and none have on their own ever actualized it, but instead have implicitly—even if limited only to their preservation and reading of their sacred scriptures—encouraged exclusiveness, superiority, and divisiveness within a culture and often even within their own religious ranks. Fortunately, more and more are freeing themselves from such "metaphysics of infinity" to the empiricities of real life and the human sciences, as Michel Foucault called them.

In the midst of a pandemic at the end of 2020, although there were great acts of compassion, empathy, sharing of risk and pain, even voluntary sacrifice of lives among medical professionals, we saw more *formal inequality, even blatant inequality*, forced on people by those who saw themselves superior or above the law. The virus had its most deadly effect on the most vulnerable, older people, especially those who were separated from family in private commercial "homes" for the convalescent, chronically ill or hospice facilities, as well as those incarcerated in prisons throughout the country. In normal cities, the virus showed a *disproportionate* deadly effect on *minority ethnic* groups who lacked sufficient shelter, nutrition, and medical insurance, or who suffered from "preconditions" that disqualified them from government assistance. People working in meat-packing plants, in many localities consisting of minority workers who were willing to work for inferior salaries with no fringe benefits or even medical care insurance, were *forced* to continue to work when tests are either not made available to them to see who had the virus, or the company tested but was not legally pressed to disclose the truth to the public or the employees. While some boasted of tests being available to whoever wanted them, it was untrue. Then the majority leader of the Senate showed his primary interests were not on helping individuals in the pandemic or even to help prevent states from going bankrupt, but really only in supplying funds to immunize corporations from any liability during the pandemic, no matter how inhumanely they subjected their workers to the disease from which many died.[65]

This is *not* "equality of opportunity," and it requires no genius to detect such. It is not ethical or humane. It is the precise opposite of the schema of "justice" as "fairness" which Rawls elaborated. Can anyone imagine any *reasonable* person who, behind a "veil of ignorance," as Rawls demanded, would argue for protection from a pandemic *only* for a *select group of citizens*, perhaps only those between ages 20 and 25, or only for the Hispanic women, or only for those born in the state of Texas, or only for those who are plumbers, or only those who are Baptists, or only those who are Pure Land Buddhists, or only for those who wear size 14 shoes, or only for those the president approves—if one had *no idea* about what one's *own being would involve*? To fail to consider where one might fall on that scale would be a risk *no one* would ever take. The response would be unanimous, as Rawls emphasized, unanimously *to protect everybody equally*.

To spend time discussing a pandemic when, by the time the book is published, the pandemic may be totally behind us, may seem a superfluous example, too contingent. But Rawls's objective was to provide a *hypothetical standard* to which we could agree precisely for the purpose of dealing with *real life* in its manifold expressions which are *all contingent*. The *measurement of the success or failure* of whether the hypothetical exercise has been understood is the degree to which people's actual responses have manifest such elements as the "veil of ignorance" of the hypothetical "original position," or whether one has applied the principle of difference with its necessary "equality of opportunity" and determination by the "least advantaged" at all. As Rawls reiterates, "The force of justice as fairness would appear to arise from two things: the requirement that all inequalities be justified to the last advantaged, and the priority of liberty. This pair of constraints distinguishes it from intuitionism and teleological theories."[66]

The "rule of law" helps provide a sense of trust much more reliably than a rule of a single person or select group. However, trust is undermined when the rule of law is violated. Rawls suggested the violations of the rule of law are best illustrated not from "gross violations" such as bribery and corruption or "abuse of the legal system to punish political enemies," but rather in "subtle distortions of prejudice and bias as these effectively discriminate against certain groups in the judicial process."[67] It tends to dissolve the equality of political liberty but also the equality of social and economic expectations. He saw the extreme of judicially created problems if judges are not impartial and completely *independent* in their determinations. Trials must be fair and open, not prejudiced by public clamor, and it goes without saying that "no man may judge his own case." The trust can be maintained only if the precepts of natural justice insure their continued validity and the trustworthiness of the system itself.[68]

The basic trust can be dissolved in a society by a handful of its leaders, that is, when the "rule of law" is no longer observed by leaders, as Rawls says, no authority can suffice since it cannot be trusted. When that happens, only pure force is left, no longer any legitimate authority. There remains no possibility of equality either in the structure of justice or the applications and enforcement. To think this is the result of the nation being a Christian nation from its very contingent beginnings even to this day, would be blaming Christianity far too much. But one must understand that no ideology of what Rawls calls a "nonpublic" group can be the voice or power which shapes the ethics and structures of justice of the country. It belongs to *all the people* as a constitutional republic, as built on an "overlapping consensus" of "freestanding" principles of "public reason."

That being the case, the basic values of that process of a trusting mutual autonomy of equal people utilizing their "public reason" to form a system of justice that upholds and accentuates the common "will-to-live" in its unanimous selection of basic principles of justice which give priority to the maximum liberty possible to all, *will succeed*. But the vital "difference" principle must be honored as imperative, as it addresses any accidental inequalities by using the criteria for new laws of whether they benefit primarily the "least advantaged" or least benefited by the first principle.

We now turn to examine the history of the specific relationship of government and religion, especially as it has been shaped by the Supreme Court through its "incorporation" of the Religion Clauses of the First Amendment into state laws. Does that history reflect the insights of the Framers of the Constitution, of Madison, Jefferson, and others, or of the recent philosophy of John Rawls? What does this suggest for the proper ethical grounding for a religiously pluralistic democratic society, the proper relationship of government to religion in a democratic society such as the United States? That depends upon how the First Amendment is read since it was "incorporated" into state law by the court's decisions in 1940 and 1947.

NOTES

1. "The Body of Liberties of the Massachusetts Colonies in New England," 1641, MYS Collections (3d ser.), 8:216, 226, 2331, 232, 2234–2236; "Maryland Act

Concerning Religion" (1649), *Maryland Archives* I:244–247 in Kurland and Lerner, *Founders' Constitution*, V: 46–48; 50–51. The Massachusetts laws of 1641 included many of the same death penalties for any form of blasphemy or denial of "God," as well as for all witches, and utilized the pattern of Ancient Israel and *specific passages* from the Pentateuch as the authority, alongside vague references to the "word of God," the "discipline and censures of Christ" and the "rules of Christ," without ever citing anything specific in the New Testament. See note 9 on the ambiguity in the Massachusetts laws which seem to provide "liberty" to many Christian groups, but *only* if they were true to the "word of God" as judged evidently by Massachusetts' leaders.

2. Thomas Jefferson, "A Bill for Establishing Religious Freedom," 12 June 1779, *Papers* 2: facing 305, in Kurland and Lerner (eds.), *Founders' Constitution*, V:77.

3. Jefferson, "Notes on the State of Virginia," *Query* 17, 157–161 (1784), in Kurland and Lerner (eds.), V: 79–80. Jefferson and Madison both emphasized how religion suffered when it was merged with civil government. Roger Williams was more blunt, that "the doctrine of persecution for cause of Conscience, is proved guilty of all the blood of the Soules crying for vengeance under the Altar," that God's intention was for people who differed religiously to reason things out together, but civil government has no place in the discussion, no more than some small "corporation" in London has a right to interfere with the government of the city itself, and the city will remain long after the little corporation has disappeared from the scene. His main point is that "uniformity of religion" is simply not possible, was never approved by God, and cannot be achieved. See Roger Williams, "The Bloody Tenent, or Persecution for Cause of Conscience," 1644, *Stokes* 1:196–197, 198, 199, in Kurland and Lerner (eds.), *Founders' Constitution*, V: 48–49.

4. See chapter 2 in my *Will Humanity Survive Religion? Beyond Divisive Absolutes* (2020).

5. "Royal Commission for Regulating Plantations," 28 April 1634, *Bradford 422–425*, in Kurland, and Lerner (eds.) *Founders' Constitution*, I: 611–612.

6. As Kurland and Lerner (eds.) wrote in the introduction to §17 on "Constitutional Government," *Founders' Constitution*, I: 607, even though "constitutions" were identified with the Enlightenment, that meant nothing about what was understood by the term. "Today, every nation-state hardy enough to issue its own postage stamps sports a constitution. Rarely does one not lay claim to being governed according to the rule of law; and more rare is the tyrant who cannot point to his shiny little constitution." But it is the specific content of such constitution that actually is important, and the Framers of the U.S. Constitution saw the content they put into it—its division of power, checks and balances, limits but comprehensive representation—as giving it a very unique stature in the world. Here the publication by Tench Coxe's *"American Citizen" (I-III) in The Debate on the Constitution, Part One* (New York: The Library of America, 1993), 20–30, are quite instructive even though many of the limits he articulated have been altered, ignored, or violated subsequently by the branches of government without repercussions.

7. Madison, *The Federalist Papers*, X and LI (122–128, 318–322) in which the diverse interests help diminish the power of "factions"; in which both state

governments and especially the federal government will be broken up into so many different "parts, interests, and classes of citizens" that its diversity can prevent majorities from emerging which threaten the interests of the minorities.

8. Pauline Maier, *Ratification: The People Debate the Constitution, 1787–1788* (New York: Simon and Schuster, 2010), 432–434.

9. Sydney E. Ahlstrom, *A Religious History*, 97, where Ahlstrom quotes Tawney and suggests that Puritanism in the New World was a "recapitulation" by "remarkable happenstance" of the English Reformation. R. H. Tawney's *Religion and the Rise of Capitalism* (New York: Mentor, 1953) shows how the Calvinist rather than Lutheran or Catholic theology gradually shaped the emphasis upon economic production in the New World at least in the minds of the Puritans. But even in the quote from Tawney, the relationship between government and religion was not resolved by the Puritans in any sense. It took the influence of the Enlightenment and Locke, which provided the idea of the natural freedom of each person's conscience.

10. This is the "contingency" of all history, including language, as the late Richard Rorty emphasized in *Contingency, Irony and Solidarity*.

11. This author's lecture notes from Prof. Mead's class in "The Genius of the American Religious Institutions" in the Fall of 1968 at the University of Iowa. See also Sidney E. Mead, *The Lively Experiment: The Shaping of Christianity in America* (New York: Harper & Row, 1963), and Mead, *The Nation with the Soul of Church* (New York: Harper & Row, 1975).

12. This great Scottish philosopher died less than two months after the United States signed its Declaration of Independence.

13. Congress's early draft of the Declaration was sent to a committee for editorial suggestions, and many statements, Jefferson, explained, were deleted from it because they were obviously too offensive. The deleted sections included a long paragraph in which the Declaration accused the King of kidnapping Africans, sailing them to America (which voyages themselves killed many of them), and forcing them on the colonies, a quite inhumane practice, and then, when relations between the colonies and the King became strained, he encouraged the African slaves to turn against their masters and kill them, so a doubly inhumane plot. Jefferson notes that it was not accurate to paint all the colonies as innocent of slavery, since South Carolina and Georgia had never opposed it, but quite the opposite. Further, he noted that many in the northern colonies also had slaves, but even more blatant, many were involved in the shipbuilding of the slave ships or in the actual importing itself. See Thomas Jefferson, "Note on Debates in Congress," 2–4 July 1776, *Papers 1:314–19*, in Kurland and Lerner, *Founders' Constitution*, I:522–524.

14. The same year he sailed with his three ships, 1492, his King and Queen drove all Jews from Spain, so the inhumane practices were not limited to Christian "explorers" mistreating people they saw as "pagan." Portugal followed suit just five years later.

15. As Morrison documents, free sex slaves were offset on some islands when the local Caribs ended up eating the explorers rather than trading with them or being converted by them. One even expressed that he hoped the next explorers were less salty than these Spanish men. See Samuel Eliot Morrison, *The European Discovery of*

America: Vol. 1: The Southern Voyages, 1492–1616 (New York: Oxford University Press, 1974).

16. I do not mean to imply that "revivals" are basically a positive thing because I am no longer convinced of that. But at least the structure of trying to get people to make their own decision about what religion they wanted to be affiliated with, if any, furthered the autonomy and theme of freedom of conscience of the Enlightenment. For a very readable and thorough analysis of religious conversion, see Susan Jacoby, *Strange Gods: A Secular History of Conversion* (New York: Pantheon, 2016).

17. J. R. Pole, *The Pursuit of Equality in American History* (Berkeley: Univ. of California Press, 1978), 33. When the Revolutionary generation utilized their relation to England as their being turned into "slaves," that term gradually turned in their minds back to begin raising the question why they themselves had any right to own "slaves." Pole emphasizes how the white population was dependent upon the nonwhite slave population, without which it could not have resolved its problems between its economic situation and its representative government: "The free sector of society could never have achieved its way of life without the support of the unfree" (33).

18. David Hume, "Of the Original Contract," 1752, in Kurland and Lerner (eds.), *Founders' Constitution*, I: 49–52.

19. Montesquieu was very influential on the Framers of the Constitution. See his "Spirit of Laws," Bk. 2, ch. 2, 1748, in Kurland and Lerner (eds.), *Founders' Constitution*. I: 47–49. Despite his emphasis of the people being both the sovereign as well as the subject of the laws, and the peoples' voice must be heard in determining the magistrates, based on obvious empirical evidence of the candidate's success militarily or economically, or some other way, he still seems locked into a "class" system from ancient governing, so those in the "lower class" realize (or at least *should* realize) that while they may be able to *detect* a good ruler by his economic or military success, they themselves are not equipped to govern.

20. For example, Gal. 2:15–3:5; 3:11–14; 5:1–6, 13–26.

21. Col. 3:5–4:6; I Thess. 4:1–8; I Cor. chs. 5–7; Rom. 1:18–3:31; Rom. chs. 6–7.

22. I Cor. 11:1; 7:7; 4:16; I Thess. 1:6; 2:9–10; II Thess. 3:7, 9. Of course, his description of the *kenosis* of Christ in Phil. 2:1–11 is used to encourage people to "be of the same mind" as others, to have others' interests at heart. But to use a myth of a divine being to illustrate an ethical principle is hardly useful as a parallel or example.

23. Hans Küng, *On Being a Christian*, tr. Edward Quinn (New York: Wallaby Book, Simon & Schuster, 1978).

24. All of this is documented carefully through his descriptions in Morrison, *The European Discovery of America: Vol. 1: The Southern Voyages*, 1492–1616.

25. The earliest law in the religion of Ancient Israel treated slaves also as mere property, for example, in Exodus 21:20–21: "Whenever a slave owner strikes a male or female slave with a rod and the slave dies immediately, the owner shall be punished. But if the slave survives a day or two, there is no punishment; for the slave is the former's property."

26. See Erika Lee, *America for Americans: A History of Xenophobia in the United States* (New York: Basic Books, 2019).

27. Brian Dippie, *The Vanishing American: America's White Attitudes and U.S. Indian Policy* (Lawrence, KS: University of Kansas Press, 1982).

28. President Andrew Jackson had pressured Congress to pass the Indian Removal Act in 1830 which violated all the former U.S. treaties with these five Indian nations (Choctaw, Seminole, Creeks, Chickasaw, and Cherokee). The Court decided against the Cherokees in *The Cherokee Nation v. State of Georgia* of 1831, but reached a different position in *Samuel A Worcester v. The State of Georgia*, 6 Peters 515 (1832), emphasizing that the Cherokee nation is a distinct community occupying its own territory in which the laws of Georgia have no force. But President Jackson ignored this and simply offered to provide transportation to the Oklahoma territory, and then, when the Cherokees and others refused to go, he forced them out militarily. The total removal was around 16,500 Indians from the Southeast to Oklahoma, freeing up around 25 million acres to be taken over primarily by white people. The removal of all the tribes required more than seven years, in which thousands of the Indians died of disease, terrible weather, starvation, and mistreatment. It was later referred to as the "Trail of Tears." Yet President Jackson had insisted that the forced removal would be best for all parties, including the five Indian tribes, as he said, perhaps they would seize the opportunity under the protection of the government "and through the influence of good counsel, to cast off their savage habits and become an interesting, civilized, and Christian community." To be "civilized" required not only leaving the fertile lands to the white man, including specific new gold mines that had been discovered in the Cherokee land in Georgia, but, of course, becoming submissively Christian. Thus, the First Amendment had not begun to penetrate into the minds of many of the country's leaders, much less the average citizens.

29. White notes that although in C.J. Marshall's Court, the moral and legal principles were still intertwined to a degree, by the end of the nineteenth century "the stark separation of moral and legal principles became an assumption of American jurisprudence." In fact, the American Revolution had accentuated the natural law approach "which had evolved from religious origins to a secular principle" which stood especially behind early contract theory and laws of property. Eventually, "where natural rights had not been expressly codified in the text of the Constitution, their intrinsic appeal did not in itself furnish an argument for their elevation to constitutional status," and this became apparent in Court's cases in the nineteenth century that overlooked the natural rights of personal liberty or right to not be discriminated against because of ethnic or racial origin. G. Edward White, *The Marshall Court & Cultural Change: 1815–1835* (New York: Macmillan Co., 1988), ch 10: 675–76.

30. Actually, the Constitution counted for census purposes of determining the number of representatives a state was entitled to, counted blacks as only three-fifths of a person, and did not count Indians at all.

31. Even after the Civil Rights Acts of 1964, racial discrimination was still practiced in a number of ways, especially in restaurants, hotels, housing, and the like. A sense of white superiority was still so strong, that cases for equality had to approach the facts from alternative positions rather than Thirteenth, Fourteenth, and Fifteenth Amendments. For example, in *Heart of Atlanta Motel, Inc. v. United States*, 379 U.S. 241 (1964), Archibald Cox, for the United States, said prohibiting African Americans

from staying in the motel was not only a violation of Title 2 of the recent Civil Rights Act, and a violation of the Civil War Amendments, but also violated the Commerce clause of the Constitution, hindering people's freedom to travel so adversely affecting commerce in the process. Among other things, he showed that traveling by car from New York to Miami, the distance between motels in which African Americans could stay averaged 141 miles apart.

32. Andersen, *Evil Geniuses*.

33. Jefferson's "notes" on the changes Congress made to the Declaration of Independence included him acknowledging that South Carolina and Georgia had *never protested against* the importation of slaves. See note 33. Thomas Jefferson, "Notes on Debates in Congress, 2–4 July 1776," *Papers* I:314–319 in Kurland and Lerner (eds.), *Founders' Constitution*, I:522–524.

34. Dumas Malone, *Jefferson and His Time: Volume Five: Jefferson the President: Second Term, 1805–1809* (Boston: Little, Brown and Company, 1974), 541.

35. African slaves had the same choice as many Native Americans about religion: either convert to Christianity or be killed. The fact that the Christian church became important to their much later descendants—including black political leaders in the twentieth century, as the community from which they found strength and identity—is more parallel to the spread of the revivals and creation of new Christian communities on the "frontier" in the first part of the nineteenth century. Church meant community. Surely, some stories in the Jewish or Christian scriptures might have given hope as they related an escape from Egypt, but the actual value of equality came from the Enlightenment, not from any religion, even if it was articulated later as if it had come entirely from the religion.

36. Ironically, both Native Americans and African slaves were involved in the eventual "trail of tears" narrative, since not only was oil (or was it gold?) discovered under the surface of the land on which the Native Americans were living, but the plantations owners needed more land on which to grow cotton, thus hiring more slaves. It is a pretty incredibly immoral picture.

37. In December 2017, an Alabama Republican candidate running for the U.S. Senate is recorded as having remarked that the last time this country was great was when it had slaves, and families were so united and happy. Was he so old to have remembered that as a firsthand experience?

38. Many of the African slaves brought to the colonies who later converted religiously had come to identify themselves with the story of the enslaved people of Israel in Egypt. Of course, many of the immigrant Christians from Europe had earlier identified with the same Israel and saw their crossing the Atlantic as "God's people" parallel to Israel's crossing the "Red Sea." But their experiences of oppression were quite different than their slaves, so that the hope in the slaves' Christianized hymns was totally in the *future* beyond death, whereas many of the Europeans, though they may still have talked of being a "poor wayfaring stranger" or exiles in a hostile land, actually lived in a comfort and security totally foreign to their slaves, so to that degree theirs was only a feigned or at most temporary persecution and oppression now far in the past. Their idea of the whole project being God's leading them—their justification of their treatment of both slaves and Native Americans—was as unconvincing as was

Ancient Israel's annihilation of the Canaanites in order to possess their land and those few people they spared as slaves. If this "Christian" biblical ethic is the proposed ethic for the United States' laws, it is bankrupt.

39. Brian Dippie, *The Vanishing American*.

40. An intriguing element surfaces when one compares the Bill of Rights with the Declaration of Independence. If many unethical and therefore illegal abuses by the English government against the colonies were simply recast as negative laws, for example, the prohibition of "general warrants" which could be used as "fishing" expeditions, the Declaration itself shows that many elements of the original were struck out later by Congress so as not to further offend the English unnecessarily. One of these paragraphs was the accusation of the English government violating Africans by kidnapping them, bringing them to sell in the colonies, forcing them on the colonies, and then subsequently inciting them to turn against their masters and others and murder them. See the original draft, then altered draft and explanation. Thomas Jefferson, "Notes on Debates in Congress, 2–4 July 1776," *Papers I:314–319* in Kurland and Lerner (eds.), *Founders' Constitution*, I: 522–524. The Virginia Constitution of June 29, 1776, contained a shortened and undeleted accusation about England forcing slaves on Virginia and then inciting them to take up arms against the Virginians. See *Founders' Constitution*, I:7.

41. By "religious freedom," Jefferson and Madison both meant freedom from government restrictions, beginning with freedom to *choose which religion, if any,* one desired to embrace, and that naturally included freedom to believe what that chosen group believed, either in part or whole, and finally to worship with them, according to their custom and the dictates of one's own heart. They did not have to embrace any particular religion, certainly not one that the government would try to force on them. That is the "religious preference" Berkin notes Madison referencing in his letter to George Eve, of January 2, 1789, 404–406, cited by Berkin in *The Bill of Rights*, note 12, p. 231. That is a far cry from the present Court's recognition of protection for anyone's alleged freedom to *anything* they personally choose to believe and therefore act on.

42. Thomas Jefferson, "Notes on the State of Virginia," *Query* 17, 157–161, 1784 in Kurland and Lerner (eds.), *Founders' Constitution*, V: 79–80.

43. "Thomas Jefferson to Albert Gallatin," in Kurland and Lerner, *Founders' Constitution*, V:105.

44. Jefferson, "Notes on the state of Virginia," in Kurland and Lerner (eds.), Founders' Constitution, V: 80.

45. See my *An Ethic of Trust: Mutual Autonomy and the Common Will to Live* (2021).

46. Thomas Gordon, "Cato's Letters," No. 38, 22 July 1721, *Jacobson 93–95,96, 101*, in Kurland and Lerner (eds.), *Founders' Constitution*, I: 46–47.

47. "An American Citizen" [Tench Coxe] I-III, in *The Debate on the Constitution, Part One* (New York: The Library of America, 1993), I: 20–30.

48. Madison, "Federalist 51," etc. on diversity adequately represented only by a constitutional republic in which all the interests of the people are represented by elected officials, whose turnover is every two years. Madison, unlike other leaders, made an

intensive comparison of "Confederacies" in history, running from the ancient Lycian, the Greek amphictyony which was seated at Delphos, and came through history down through the Helvetic, Belgic, and Germanic confederacies. One problem he saw in most was a lack of a central power, which meant little enforcement or organization to meet crises, but in the ones that were dominated by a single group, the central power worked a disadvantage on all the other members which dissolved its purpose. So he sought diversity and "checks and balances." See especially, Madison, *The Papers of James Madison*, editor-in-chief, Robert A. Rutland, "9 April 1786–24 May 1787" (Chicago: The University of Chicago Press, 1975), 9:3–24. In addition to this study, in preparation for the Federal Convention, he also studied and wrote extensively on the problems of the present political system of the United States under the *Articles of Confederation*. See Madison "Vices of the Political System of the United States," also in *The Papers*, 9: 345–358. My emphasis on Madison rather than other Framers of the Constitution is not misplaced, since his exceptional deep study of *Greek* culture and political system and his finally acceding to a "Bill of Rights" were among the most important factors in assuring the country ended up with a Constitution. See Thomas E. Ricks, *First Principles: What America's Founders Learned from the Greeks and Romans and How that Shaped our Country* (New York: HarperCollins, 2020),

49. Madison, "Memorial and Remonstrance," in Rutland (ed.) *The Papers of James Madison*, 10 March 1784–28 March 1786 (1973), 8: 299, 301. By saying religion is "wholly exempt from its [Civil Society's] cognizance," he was not using "cognizance" simply as the equivalent of knowledge or apprehension, but means religion is simply *not within the legal jurisdiction* of civil society or civil government. Here, he and Jefferson were united in saying that religion is simply between a person and his or her God, however the latter is conceived, a matter only of one "freedom of conscience" which is off limits to civil government. He used "cognizance" the same way as when he argued against C. Mason's objections to the scope of the Constitution that most of the suits in state courts are between fellow citizens, or, in modern parlance, do not concern a "constitutional" issue, so "relate to matters not of federal cognizance." Madison, "A 'Prolix' Comment on Mason's 'Objections'; James Madison to George Washington," New York, October 18, 1787, in *The Debate on the Constitution, Part One*, I: 350.

50. *Thomas Van Orden v. Rick Perry*, No. 08-1500, oral argument, pp. 4, 10, 12, 15–17, 23–26. Is the Court in the twenty-first century turning any abstract group identity as a "person," following the legal fiction of the "corporation"? Does this mean that a corporation or the government is an individual with a brain, or is it going to the extreme of Kierkegaard's day in trying to extend the description "Christian" to everything possible, perhaps even as a thoughtful adjective for brothels? When Jefferson and Madison spoke of religion as being between an individual and God, they did *not* intend to *include the government or simply any business* that wanted to claim its own "free exercise" of religion such as a hobby store or a bakery. And their setting had much less real religious diversity than does the present United States, which means the perspective of some Justices and some decisions of the Court are simply perpetuating *more religious divisiveness* in the nation than is necessary. If not averted, this will soon take its toll.

51. See "Thomas Jefferson to Danbury Baptist Association," 1 January 1802, *Writings* 16:281, in Kurland and Lerner (eds.), *Founders' Constitution*, V: 96.

52. Rawls, *A Theory of Justice*, 216–217, 221.

53. As Dworkin notes, despite Locke's insight on religious "toleration," Locke was convinced that an *atheist* was *not* entitled to be a citizen of the country. So Locke's limitations on *citizenship* prevailed more than his idea of "religious tolera-tion" since he conceived citizenship to be limited to those who belonged to a theistic (if not *only* Christian) religion. Dumas notes, on the prolongation of slavery, at the end of Jefferson's second term as president, after the 20-year period allowed the institution of slavery following the ratification of the Constitution, the president, like many others, was still convinced that the union was so fragile that if the subject of emancipation actually came back on the drawing board, the nation would probably dissolve. So differences were hard for people to accommodate, much less to give such people real freedom.

54. Barzun, *From Dawn to Decadence*, 436.

55. Mark Twain, "The Turning Point of My Life," in *The Family Mark Twain* (New York: Dorset Press, 1988), 1129–1135.

56. It is possible to disagree with Rawls over a difference in "incentives" under the principle of "difference," but one must remember that the *prior* principle of political equality does not allow for any difference in incentives (or sanctions) since it (as well as the second principle) is actually agreed to in the "original position" of a "veil of ignorance" completely *devoid of incentives* that could be advantageous. That "consensus" is arrived at only on the basis of the agreement to equality of the primary "goods" that are the same for all humans. J.R. Pole noted that the focus on equality in U.S. history did not originally come from an ideal of wanting equality for all but rather was provoked from the colonists' realization that England was depriving them of common-law rights by its general warrants, writs of assistance, trial without a jury, or even threat of being carted off to England to stand trial. They became aware first that they were being treated very unequally with their peers who remained back "home" in England. Pole, *The Pursuit*, 15–25.

57. All of this can be seen in Kurt Anderson's *Evil Geniuses*.

58. See Ralph Ketcham, *James Madison: A Biography* (Charlottesville, VA: University Press of Virginia, 1990), 648. The various disciplines and breadth of the education Jefferson proposed for the new university was astounding for his time, combining the liberal arts with sciences.

59. Phillips, *Toward a Just Social Order*.

60. We had a great popular song years back called "No Such Number!" Elvis Presley, 1962.

61. I use "decadence" with the meaning Barzun gave to it, not of something evil, but simply that the West has pretty well exhausted its forms and structures and will need something new.

62. Barzun, *From Dawn to Decadence*, 536. This has an obvious parallel in the United States in 2020.

63. See their letters back and forth to each other, in Kurland and Lerner (eds.), *Founders' Constitution*, I: Ch. 15, Equality, Nos. 9, 10 and 12, pp. 518–520.

64. The standard of "probable cause" to justify a "stop and frisk" was reduced to "reasonable suspicion" that the person had either committed a felony or was armed, by *Terry v. Ohio*, 392 U.S. 1 (1968). It later became the base for racial profiling and disproportionate arrests of African American males in New York City in the early years of the new millennium.

65. The political leader behind this has, for other reasons, called himself "the grim reaper," and that name is quite becoming now that he seems *oblivious to the deaths* caused by an incompetent and indifferent president and greedy corporate leaders. The basic trust necessary for a viable democracy has been undermined within four short years, precisely because too much power lies in hands of those who think only in terms of their own interests rather than national interests, and they cannot conceive of ever placing themselves behind their "vested" accidental advantages, whom Rawls calls "sociopaths" (*Political Liberalism*, 251).

66. Rawls, *A Theory of Justice*, 250.

67. Rawls, *A Theory of Justice*, 235.

68. Rawls, *A Theory of Justice*, 239.

Chapter 5

The "Free Exercise" Clause

Worship *as Beyond*
Government's Jurisdiction

The First Amendment to the U.S. Constitution has two clauses that pertain
to religion: "Congress shall make no law respecting an establishment of religion, or prohibiting the free exercise thereof." They intended to restrict government, as Madison and Jefferson both wrote, since religion was supposed
to be a private affair between a person and his or her "God." The two clauses
were not intended to define different areas since "establishment" as they saw
it, occurred in any kind of support from or pressure from government to join
a specific religious group, or to attend a certain worship, or any explicit governmental support for a certain religious doctrine, pastors, or teachers. One
was not to be treated differently from other citizens for being either religious
or nonreligious; one's civil responsibilities and benefits remained the same.

Religious institutions were to realize they had no jurisdiction other than
persuasive power, and that alone should put an end to their interreligious
squabbling and fighting each other. If they restricted each other by violating civil or criminal laws, such as actual physical fighting, they were to be
punished just as any citizen. No religious people were to be exempt from
civil laws, and no religious laws or religious claims of authority were to be
utilized by government. If many of the values of one were obviously not
transferable to the other, there were many ethical ideals they shared; but
the *purposes* of the religious communion were different from civil government's purposes, and the *authorities* they claimed giving them jurisdiction
over peoples' lives differed radically, one professing to be eternal, invisible,
metaphysical and absolute or incomparable, while the other was subject to
examination and amendment by public reason. We will see that the latter
differences of purposes, uses of reason, scope and authorities, as well as different comportments are seldom considered by the Court which prefers to
look only for "precedent," and the Court seemed early on by its treatment of

the two clauses to think the purposes of the clauses as somehow quite different, so divided the two clauses rather than divide the reason, authorities, and
jurisdictions of the two institutions.

That was the Court's crucial mistake almost from the first cases which
"incorporated" the First Amendment into state law in 1940 and 1947. We
shall see how they delineated the areas of each clause so distinctly that they
contradicted each other when pushed to extremes. That is, it soon was discovered that an overzealous response to either clause ended up violating the
other clause, and we shall show that the very *purpose* necessary to claim for
one's "free exercise" quickly was a blatant violation of the "establishment"
clause test in the 1971 "*Lemon* test." The Court subsequently even in its
post-1980s redefinitions has failed to see the *nonpublic reason* of the limited
and exclusive religions vis-à-vis the *public reason* behind the inclusive and
unanimous adoption of the Constitution by all citizens. So it has found itself
making many inconsistent decisions which have created more divisiveness
and resentment without clarifying the problem. Through its generous and
novel way of recently approving tax dollars as "neutral aid" for religious
education, and extending "free exercise" to include anyone's discriminating
business practices because of their alleged religious convictions, the Court
has not simply opened Pandora's box but actually split the box wide open.
Or, if we could switch and confuse metaphors, the corner the Court is painting itself into may turn out to be a box canyon or perhaps an endless swamp,
despite the very sincere efforts of most of the Justices.

John Locke, whose idea of the separation of government and religion
had so much influence on Madison, Jefferson, and others in that period,
had written in 1689 that a "church, then, I take to be a voluntary society of
men, joining themselves together of their own accord in order to the public
worshipping of God in such manner as they judge acceptable to him, and
effectual to the salvation of their souls."[1] Then in 1695, he clarified that a
bit by suggesting that while worshipping as a group should be completely
voluntary, the *theological and moral content* evoking the worship cannot be
autonomous, but must be a *revelation* of God through Christ which has genuine ultimate authority rather than mere human reason.[2] So "conscience's"
jurisdiction was restricted to the revelation in the New Testament as Locke
read it. That authority to Locke was based on the traditional idea of Jesus
having fulfilled all the ancient prophecies of the coming "Messiah" and his
performing miracles.[3] This authority, Jesus pointed out, came only from his
Father, God, Who therefore is what Locke called the "great Lawgiver" to the
world. Locke saw Jesus's ethics fully disclosed to his disciples, even *absent*
any specific biblical references, so not only their divine authority but also the
incentive of reward and punishment Jesus attached to them, made them, in
Locke's judgment, far superior to any ethics in the world. In addition, Jesus

also taught his disciples proper worship, which meant essentially decent, orderly, and intending to edify.[4]

Although Locke advocated "liberty of conscience" which seemed to be far superior to mere religious toleration, he qualified that as *not* something coming from *reason*, but totally dependent upon the revelation of God through Christ's teachings. He showed no awareness of any other religions, so despite his advances in certain areas, his idea of "freedom of conscience" was too narrow to assist any government which covered *actual religious pluralism* to any degree. His contribution to the future, however, was in seeing one's conscience beyond the jurisdiction of any civil government, which influenced the Framers of the Constitution. But he, like Jefferson, saw no natural or supranatural duty which contradicted civil law. He also seems unaware of anyone in the Old Testament being told by God to do something we all would see as blatantly unethical, such as God's command to Saul to exterminate all the Amalekites, or even the story of God commanding Abraham to kill his son as a sacrifice to God. On the embarrassment of the story of Abraham, Hegel was correct and Kierkegaard's opposition to Hegel was only an old-fashioned dream of an Absolute, by which humans really have no ethical responsibility, but simply will respond when the Absolute connects with them. But Locke was intent to move Christianity beyond not just the Old Testament or Jewish scriptures, so beyond all Judaisms, but also beyond all creeds, to see it as simple. Simplicity is noble, but as we know today, his view of Christianity was too simplistic, aspirational, uncritical, and even *un*informed for its own day.[5] Anything may often seem "simple" when a person knows very little about it.

But, if we move past Locke's influence, just prior to the Revolutionary War, Isaac Backus, a Baptist minister representing 20 Baptist churches of New England in September 1774, advocated the cause of the "Antipaedobaptist" (opposed to infant baptism) churches. He reviewed how they were persecuted in England, insisting they should have "free and full enjoyment" of equal rights as other Protestants, "in the support of religious worship." He argued that since Christ's Kingdom is not of this world, religion is a concern only between "God and the soul," which "no human authority can intermeddle . . . [therefore] we claim and expect the liberty of worshipping God according to our consciences, not being obliged to support a ministry we cannot attend, whilst we demean ourselves as faithful subjects."[6] He argued that this means, among other things, that for the Baptists to violate their consciences in allowing the state to assess taxes from them for a religion they do not approve and have no representation is gross injustice and the state would be *preempting God's jurisdiction* in the process.

In 1779, Thomas Jefferson, in his *Bill for Establishing Religious Freedom*,[7] insisted that "Almighty God both created the mind free, and manifested his Supreme will that free it shall remain, by making it altogether insusceptible of restraint." He pointed out that history is filled with various attempts by human agencies to restrict one's freedom, even with penalties, and they have all failed. He argued "the [religious] opinions of men are not the object of civil government, nor under its jurisdiction," so to allow a civil magistrate to "intrude his power into the field of opinion," thereby restricting people's freedoms including even forcing them to pay taxes to support religious opinions they disapprove, "is sinful and tyrannical." Instead, "it is time enough for the rightful purposes of civil government for its officers to interfere when principles break out into overt acts against peace and good order."[8] He was confident that "truth is great and will prevail if left to herself; that she is the proper and sufficient antagonist to error, and has nothing to fear from the conflict."[9]

On the "*State of Virginia*," in 1784, he wrote among other things that "our rulers can have authority over such natural rights only as we have submitted to them. The rights of conscience we never submitted, we could not submit. We are answerable for them to our God. The legitimate powers of government extend to such acts only as are injurious to others. But it does me no injury for my neighbor to say there are twenty gods, or no god. It neither picks my pocket nor breaks my leg." On the other hand, "millions of innocent men, women, and children, since the introduction of Christianity, have been burnt, tortured, fined, imprisoned; yet we have not advanced one inch toward uniformity. What has been the effect of coercion? To make one half the world fools, and the other half hypocrites."[10]

Finally, the religious pluralism of the New Nation was not seen only in terms of many different Christian "churches" as was Locke's limited view, but James Madison referred to both diversity within the Christian ranks as well as *diversity of world religions* in general. He wrote:

> Religion is wholly exempt from its [i.e., civil government's] cognizance. . . . Who does not see that the same authority which can establish Christianity, in exclusion of all other Religions, may establish with the same ease any particular sect of Christians, in exclusion of all other Sects? that the same authority which can force a citizen to contribute three pence only of his property for the support of any one establishment, may force him to conform to any other establishment in all cases whatsoever? . . . If Religion be not within the cognizance of Civil Government how can its legal establishment be necessary to Civil Government?[11]

We saw in the previous chapter that Jefferson even named various non-Christian religions in his autobiography of 1821, as he insisted that the Virginia Congress overwhelmingly *opposed* adding "Jesus Christ" to the expression "holy author of our religions" in the "Virginia, Act for Establishing Religious Freedom" of 1785, as he said "that they meant to comprehend, within the mantle of its protection, the Jews and the Gentile, the Christian and Mahometan the Hindoo, and Infidel of every denomination,"[12] not just Christians.

THE DISESTABLISHMENT AS REAL SEPARATION RATHER THAN ACCOMMODATION

This maturing of thought in the colonies from the seventeenth century to the end of the eighteenth century was summarized by the Court in 1982, with brilliant J. Brennan writing the Court's opinion in *Larson v. Valente*:[13]

> Before the Revolution, religious establishments of differing denominations were common throughout the colonies. But the Revolutionary generation emphatically disclaimed that European legacy, and "applied the logic of secular liberty to the condition of religion and the churches." If Parliament had lacked the authority to tax unrepresented colonists, then by the same token the newly independent states should be powerless to tax their citizens for the support of a denomination to which they did not belong. The force of this reasoning led to the abolition of most denominational establishments at the state level by the 1780s, and led ultimately to the inclusion of the Establishment Clause in the First Amendment in 1791.[14]

J. Brennan cited the new "logic of secular liberty," that is, of freedom from being taxed for something that is not for one's benefit and in which one has no voice or representation. To this, as suggested earlier was added (1) the voluntary aspect of religion, as one's autonomous choice, which was so vital to the Great Awakening, reshaping the constituencies of most churches in the colonies; (2) the influence of the "freedom of conscience" as more than mere religious tolerance, but a natural right of all, which itself shows religion to be a matter only between individuals and whatever deity they profess, if any; (3) the impractical or unworkable scenario that would be created if different states could have their own religious establishments, thus conflicting with their neighboring states, which simply recaptures on a smaller scale the terrible situations that the contiguous nations of Europe experienced that caused such tragic wars just between Christians; and (4) the idea that being assessed taxes to support a pastor (priest, minister) even of one's chosen denomination still deprives one of his or her *autonomy* of contributing to the person from one's own religious conviction. Obviously, this fourth element may seem to have been the weakest of the four, but it is not once one agrees that religion is strictly beyond the "cognizance" of civil government, by which Madison meant "jurisdiction," just as he divided the jurisdiction or "cognizance" of state and federal courts.[15] It was *separation* of jurisdiction that he proposed.

Thus, Madison warned against even the least incursion of one's liberty in this regard, remembering the religious travesties such as the Inquisition. Madison was opposed to chaplains in Congress and in the armed services, and saw these not only as residual forms of religious establishment, as if patterned, like in so many other nations, after the *theocracy* of Ancient Israel, but he even opposed the church incorporating in order to hold real property since he was afraid that over the years, such holdings would give the religion far too much power in the nation.[16] As he and Jefferson viewed the history of Christendom, it was not a checkered history with plenty of benefits or good as well as some problems, but only a negative merger, bringing out the worst in both institutions of church and state.

By the late 1780s, not only did formerly established churches feel the negative effect of the revivals which were drawing many members out of their communions, almost turning the statistics of the constituencies upside down, but the possible nonreligious competitions on Sundays for entertainment, as well as the "enthusiasm" of unrestrained subjectivity in religious experiences threatened all institutionalism, including the various states' taxing schemas for their churches. Persecution broke out even among the Virginia Anglicans against the Quakers, so much that Madison said he had become worn out trying to correct the situation.[17]

As we noted earlier John Locke's lack of any critical understanding of any religion,[18] he nevertheless was convinced that government and religion need to be *separated*, that one's religion and *worship* is *only* a matter of one's own *autonomous* decision, a "natural right," depending upon no other people and no government nor even on government's laws. Civil magistrates' powers extended to religious people's lives, but only in the laws common to all, the civil and criminal laws, that have no religious basis. He obviously did not feel that religious people could force their religious views on others, but did this mean that religious people could be exempt from the nation's civil and criminal laws if their religion differed with those laws?

The separate religious institutions, he believed, as institutions, were voluntarily chosen by each individual, but so long as the individual wanted to be considered as a member of any of them, the member would have to observe whatever expectations, rules, or laws the institution had, provided those laws did not contradict the common law of the civil government. This seems to be his answer. Kant took this one step further, insisting that the Enlightenment's emphasis on autonomy had both a public and private reason side, so although a pastor has an obligation in his private profession of satisfying the religious institution's expectations, he also must honor his public role and pursue the truth and share it wherever it leads.[19] That still makes sense, but Rawls has made Kant even more precise in the autonomous or voluntary selection of principles of justice which are derived from either a democracy which tolerates differences but formulates its basic justice from freestanding principles which form an overlapping consensus—or from a hypothetical original position behind a veil of ignorance—which accomplishes the same thing.

It might seem that our entire thesis of the heteronomy so common and absolute in religions is overblown once people in a particular country such as the United States realize that they have autonomous power in choosing their own religion or no religion at all. Yet by far the majority of Protestants, Catholics, and Jews espousing those particular religions at the end of the eighteenth century were *born* into a family embracing that very same religion, despite the success of the Great Awakening in New England. They did not feel they really had any autonomy in the matter. Even in those revivals, although some were actually converted from different Protestant denominations, almost none converted from a radically different religion other than a few of those African slaves and coerced Native Americans. But whether they were born into it or converted, it invariably presented itself as incomparable, as the Absolute, not to be questioned. So autonomy was very limited in Locke and even in the U.S. revivals, since "God" was thought to be dictating things and in control. Prior to Locke and even in his mind, any real "toleration" of such different people existed *only* for those who belonged to the Christian faith, and in the seventeenth-century colonies this had quite stringent theological, ritual, "covenant," and ethical demands (including one's speech, leisure activity, and associations) for any slightly different Christian, as in Massachusetts (1641), Maryland (1649), Pennsylvania (1682), and Carolina (1669), even if Locke *felt* he could tolerate all of them. So did Maryland, though until 1961, it still demanded that anyone running for public office had to affirm their belief in God, and, of course, this was only in the Christian's "God," no other.[20] So "freedom of conscience" had its different gradations in the minds of different people, but there is hardly any doubt that Kant's autonomy was more consistent, even if he thought morality required postulating "freedom" or even "God."

Even in the mind of Jefferson, as he described it, Virginia still divided up between the Anglicans and the "dissidents," and he estimated that by the time of the Revolutionary War, after approximately one hundred years of Anglican domination of Virginia, due to the "indolence" of Virginia's clergy, as much as two-thirds of the population of Virginia was now comprised of religious dissenters. Governor Patrick Henry attempted but failed to restore the state taxes for the established Anglican church after the war. Jefferson tried to make sure that Anglican clergy got paid, but also that dissenters did not have to pay that tax. Henry then tried to pacify everybody by proposing a bill in Virginia that would be a "general assessment," as we saw earlier, allowing every church member to specify *which* church would be the recipient of one's taxes.

One might have anticipated that all the Virginians would have been pleased with such a "general assessment" bill. But Jefferson insisted that the "exercise of religion" had been decided by Virginia Convention of 1776 to be a "free" exercise, a "natural" right. He further argued in his "Notes on the State of Virginia," that "our rulers can have authority over such natural rights only as we have submitted to them. The rights of conscience we never submitted, we could not submit. We are answerable for them to our God. The legitimate powers of government extend to such acts only as are injurious to others."[21]

Without any clear answer about what would replace "assessments" for the churches if there were to be no "established" religion, there was nevertheless a widespread rejection of Gov. Henry's Bill. Some very conservative Christians who opposed Virginia's proposed general assessment bill had a very different reason for their rejection of it: they saw such an assessment a violation of or intrusion upon the Spirit of the Gospel. In any case, they decided to support Madison and Jefferson in opposing the general assessment bill. Madison, by the earlier and continued influence of Jefferson, and with the desperate support of some of these dissidents such as the many Baptists, and two of their leaders, Isaac Backus and John Leland, quashed that proposed bill of general assessments with Jefferson's *A Bill for Establishing Religious Freedom* (1779), Madison's own influential *Memorial and Remonstrance* (1785), and Madison's *Virginia, Act for Establishing Religious Freedom*, October 31, 1785, which was a slightly longer treatise than Jefferson's Bill with the same position and often similar wording.

It must be admitted that Thomas Jefferson left behind his early repulsion of ecclesiastics to the point of being at peace with anyone's religious opinion, so long as it remained only that—a private affair. As his emphasis of the *separation* of religion from the state became more extensive, his convictions of this *necessity* even more solidified with the passing of his years. He stood adamantly *against* what today is called an "accommodative" posture of government toward religion, speaking instead of a "wall of separation" between them, though he was *not hostile* toward religion, but simply asserting that a person's religious opinion and duty were between the person and God, no business whatever of government.[22] During his lifetime, he remained interested enough to spend many hours culling through the ethics of the four canonical gospels to form what he considered the essential gospel, which was largely the ethical principles he found therein. In this sense, he was a bit ahead of his time. Jefferson's bill was first written in 1777, submitted to the Virginia legislature in 1779, where it met opposition so was tabled, but then revived after Jefferson was sent to France in 1784, where he published and circulated it widely among legislators and heads of states in Europe who had heard about it. Many European leaders were impressed with that bill.

The Bill was later taken up again in the Virginia legislature by Madison who had meanwhile published anonymously his own *Memorial and Remonstrance* (June 20, 1785) against the general assessment bill.[23] Madison's treatise had also been widely disseminated among Virginians. Eventually, after a few of the most emphatic statements eulogizing reason in Jefferson's bill were deleted or changed by the Assembly, it was ratified by the state in 1786. It subsequently influenced other states to follow the same *complete separation* of church and state, not a mere equal accommodation as proposed by the defeated Virginia bill earlier. This historical chain of events is of supreme importance if one is trying to figure out the *meaning* our Founders intended in the First Amendment or what the "best" interpretation of it would be. Of course, Jefferson's bill was condensed succinctly in the same spirit to form part of the First Amendment of the U.S. Constitution.

Further, although the earlier Virginia Constitution of 1776 had been supplemented with a "Declaration of Rights" which spoke of all men having the right of the free exercise of religion, it had *not* eliminated the possibility of an establishment of religion, but only, like the English Act of Toleration of 1689, simply allowed dissenting Protestants a certain freedom, but not Catholics, Jews, or any other religion whatever. So Jefferson's bill as well as Madison's *Memorial and Remonstrance transcended* the rather nebulous idea of "toleration" or mere government "accommodation." There was no gradation between acceptable religion and unacceptable religion, no criteria for any declaration of "orthodoxy" or special treatment by the government. In contrast, they grounded the religious freedom on one's *natural right*, something unalienable, which was totally *outside* the jurisdiction as Madison said, beyond the legal "cognizance" of government.[24] Both men were persuaded through the sordid history of most religions, including Christian history, that any governmental interference into the private sphere of religion served to cripple both religion and government, and that religion has flourished best when it depended only on persuasion and reason, even ironically doing better through persuasion and reason when it was actively persecuted by government than it did when it became the state religion. That seeming paradox was very important, underscoring the strength of religious faith under persecution.

As Madison and Jefferson opposed even three pence tax assessment for ecclesiastical purposes, and fiercely opposed anyone, including government, trying to force a person to believe some religious idea or attend some religious service, Jefferson showed where he felt the state *did* have an interest, but that was *only* the point at which the religious person or group *overtly* broke the civil or criminal law. That is "time enough" for the government to get involved, as he ends the following: "Whereas Almighty God hath created the mind free; that all attempts to influence it by temporal punishments or burthens, or by civil incapacitations, tend only to beget habits of hypocrisy and meanness . . . it is timeful enough for the rightful purposes of civil government, for its officers to interfere when principles break out into overt acts against peace and good order."[25]

Since he saw the secular civil and criminal laws as sufficient in the nation, there was no reason to inject religion into them which would likely create arguments if not internal, unnecessary, perpetual and disastrous conflict. Otherwise, we saw earlier, Jefferson insisted if his neighbor wanted to believe in 20 gods or none at all, it did him (Jefferson) no injury; the very nature of religion was totally between a person and his or her god, if he or she had such. In any case, he was convinced that even God couldn't save a person from himself. This idea of religion being kept in the private sphere of life, depending only upon one's autonomous decision, and government concerning itself with a religious persons or institutions *only if and when* they overtly violate civil or criminal law, is precisely the equivalent of what Rawls means by the "overlapping principles" or "overlapping consensus" of "freestanding" laws, the difference between "public reason" and "nonpublic reason," and between a "political concept of justice" as opposed to a "metaphysical concept of justice." It is what I analogized to "two sets" of clothes or tools, but here two sets of ethical principles, with different authorities, constituents, scope, and comportment, not necessarily contradicting each other, but *one having priority in civil affairs*.

To allow religion to argue its typically unquestionable absolutes, thereby precluding all reasonable inquiry and argument, would be to make civil life subservient to the religious authoritarianism, squelching others' autonomy, therefore dehumanizing people. Those at the table working out the social contract must have equal voice, which means that any principles have to be arrived at as "freestanding," as autonomously suggested, which, in their different formulations disclose some "overlapping" by which a discussion of principles can reach a "consensus" by the principles' participation in the "public reason" to which *all would agree*. This is how the structures of justice are established hypothetically, but which, then, in actual life should mean that any prosecution of a person could *not* be based upon a religious reason, nor could one claim a religious reason to be *exempted* from the nation's generally applicable laws.

That is the effective "wall of separation" which Jefferson, Madison, and most of the others who ratified the Constitution and the Bill of Rights understood. If the modern Supreme Court eschews the idea of trying to decide what is "central" to a religion, the Court painted itself into that corner rather than *refusing* to hear litigation unless it was based simply upon the universally applicable laws. For decades now, people have thought they can obtain certain privileges, financial support, or exemptions from general laws by making the claim upon the Court that they are *religious*. Once that was thought to be implicit within the clause on the "free exercise of religion," it began to wreak havoc.[26] That is the very opposite of the "separation" Madison and Jefferson conceived. Nor were they simply proposing an *equal accommodation* of *all* religions, which was unjustifiably the interpretation of the Framers' intent given by one of the Court's Chief Justices for years. That was Gov. Henry's proposed bill which Madison, Jefferson, and others *defeated*, then utilized their answer again to form the religious freedom of the First Amendment to the U.S. Constitution, a genuine "separation" of government and religion.

If it be asked why one would find objectionable a secular constitution which allows for people to be free to worship in whatever way they choose or not to worship at all, so long as they all follow the Constitution or universally applicable laws that they expect *all other citizens* to observe, this is difficult to answer. Two different answers are usually given: (1) that there is no such right as freedom to worship, since God has dictated what is to be done, which usually comes down to saying that one particular sect of one specific religion should be allowed to determine the true policy for all; or (2) humans are incapable of being ethical without a true belief in God, so the only government that can offer any ethical laws is the one based on that true belief in one true God. The second answer has been expressed by various Supreme Court Justices over the past few decades, but it also usually folds into the first answer of one specific religion.

Yes, it is true that in President George Washington's "Farewell Address" he emphasized the second point, that humans have to believe in God to be ethical. But he simply underestimated humans and overestimated their mythologies of their gods. He also said that all Americans "with slight shades of difference . . . have the same religion, manners, habits, and political principles." That, of course, was pure political hyperbole, since he was leaving office, and trying to make the people realize the value of the "union" they had established, how unique it was and what it would require to keep it going. Such a rhetorical statement carries no more precedential or logical weight than his yielding to people's request to institute a day of "Thanksgiving." He was a hero in war, but not a deep thinker like Madison, Jefferson, Hamilton, and others. He went along with what he took to be public religious sentiment without seeing the fine nuances of differences and without reflecting on the terrible conflicts of the seventeenth and eighteenth centuries, conflicts caused by Europe's and England's religious "establishments" and their dissenters. If his leadership in the war was now behind him, was the history that prompted that, the theocracy or established religion even in England already forgotten? Not by most of them.

Madison also struggled with the vulnerability of the new Constitution for years, often trying to figure out where the weak points of the new government would likely be, where it might be prone to implode. Since the office of the President was not being given great power, he felt it unlikely that the president would abuse the relations. Nor would the judiciary, despite the lifetime appointments each justice would have. He concluded that it would most likely be the legislature. Nevertheless, he and others hammered away long and hard to try to create sufficient "checks and balances" between the three branches of government so this would not occur. A principle of inclusion and the value of diversity stood at the top of Madison's assurance of the nation surviving and continuing. Thus, it was that he concluded, as I pointed out earlier, that even more powerful than the legislature was the majority, *any majority* in any part of the country that became desensitized to the needs and rights of minorities or the *whole nation*, any majority which put it interests ahead of the interests of the nation as a whole. The way to attempt to prevent this rule by a majority or the unjust treatment of one part of the society by another was to encourage *inclusiveness and diversity*, real diversity, and the more the better.

At this point, Madison's answer for preservation of civil rights was the same as for the preservation of religious rights. By encouraging all views and interests and people, the authority of the government will be so scattered and therefore diffused, embracing all the disparate parts, that it will not experience a united authority which can abuse or practice injustice. In his words,

> the society itself will be broken into so many parts, interests and classes of citizens, that the rights of individuals, or of the minority, will be in little danger from interested combinations of the majority. In a free government the security for civil rights must be the same as that for religious rights. It consists in the one case in the multiplicity of interests, and in the other in the multiplicity of sects. The degree of security in both cases will depend on the number of interests and sects; and this may be presumed to depend on the extent of the country and number of people comprehended under the same government.[27]

The vital ingredient for success was "multiplicity" of interests and of religious sects, genuine and prolific diversity, not as a weakness but as an asset to the nation. But that could be effective *only* if the legislature and judiciary did not overrule the multiplicity of interests and religions by passing laws and judging cases based on some majoritarian premise. Additionally, Madison felt that in the "separation" of religion and civil government, the concern must not only be to prevent either one from *encroaching* on the other, but a third factor must also be considered. This is the *accumulation of wealth by religious organizations*. In his words, besides the danger of any direct mixture of religion and civil government, "there is an evil which ought to be guarded agst in the indefinite accumulation of property from the capacity of holding it in perpetuity by ecclesiastical corporations. The power of all corporations ought to be limited in this respect. The growing wealth acquired by them never fails to be a source of abuses."[28] What should be heard here is that he said the government needed to help prevent such accumulation in any and all corporations,[29] and included religions in this since in many states they were incorporating precisely to be able to hold property, as he said, even "in perpetuity." Over time, the increase in wealth could give them unnatural and undesirable power over the diversity which the *democracy* was supposed to be able to accommodate, but religions simply could not.

In fact, the Court has never defined what it *includes* as "religion," simply leaving that up to the litigating parties to define. Nothing could be more counter to what Jefferson, Madison, and the Founding Fathers had in mind. They were attempting, if possible, to *preempt all litigation* over religion, by insisting the civil government (all three branches) have no jurisdiction over it whatever. For example, in a letter Jefferson sent to Albert Gallatin on June 16, 1817, the author mentions news that the New York legislature is purportedly attempting to pass a bill that will punish "Shaking Quakers," and in his indignation over this, Jefferson contrasts it with the religious restraint and common sense shown by refraining from intermixing civil policy with religious beliefs. He wrote, "This act being published nakedly in the papers, without the usual signatures, or any history of the circumstances of its passage, I am not without a hope it may have been a mere abortive attempt. It contrasts singularly with a contemporary vote of the Pennsylvania legislature, who, on a proposition to make the belief in God a necessary qualification for office, rejected it by a great majority, although assuredly there was not a single atheist in their body."[30]

What Jefferson is saying here is very important, that even though the Pennsylvania legislature likely had no atheists within it, it nevertheless *refused* to coerce a belief in God as a necessity to holding public office. As we saw earlier, Jefferson also alluded to the situation in the Virginia legislature when someone wanted to insert "Jesus Christ" to limit the meaning of the "holy author of our religion," but the Congress immediately rejected it, which he interpreted as meaning the Congress was protecting *all people's consciences*, whether they were religious or atheists. If the present Court were to recognize religion as *not within its competence* or jurisdiction, as Madison insisted, that is, if the Court were to hear only cases that raise nonreligious or "neutral principles" in their "overlapping consensus" found in the civil and criminal laws to which all citizens have agreed, and if the Court were to limit its concern even with *religious* people and institutions to *only if and when* they overtly violate *those civil or criminal laws* and thereby threaten the peace and good order, as Jefferson said, they would not feel they were in the business of trying to determine whether people should be theists or atheists, or monotheists or polytheists, or henotheists, pantheists, pan-en-theists, or monists—much less determine which specific sect of which religion is legitimate, or what is "central" to any religion or religion in general, and thereby much potential divisiveness within the nation could be *averted*. That approach of Jefferson and Madison was not a "hostility" to religion of which our present Court seems to fear such an accusation.

We shall see that progressively over the past 40 years, the decisions of the Court have given many the impression that they can demand special exemptions from neutral laws and can demand billions of tax dollars for their religious purposes simply *because* they are *religious*.[31] Nothing was further from Jefferson and Madison than such a posture or impression. The recent decisions which insist they *cannot be denied benefits* simply on the basis of their obvious religious purpose for the tax dollars or exemption from neutral laws, will, if they stand, force the Court into a very untenable position in granting exemptions, which, as we shall see, Justice Kennedy warned in the *Bourne* case, will have the power to *undermine most law*. The result will be protecting practices which violate neutral laws, or funding religious activities by taking money from nonreligious groups, such as moving educational funds from public education to parochial schools or private religious schools. This is the result of failing to see the *different authorities, constituencies, purposes, types of reason, scope, and comportment* of those involved in governing for the public and those intent to spread a religion by assistance from the government. These five differences we noted to begin with are simply often overlooked.

But this realization is no more noticeable to most Justices than it was to the philosopher, G. W. F. Hegel, in his arguments in his *Phenomenology of Spirit* (or "Mind").[32] This is the reason I have emphasized that how the ethics underlying the political conception of justice or the government differs from the ethics of *any* religion, by the difference in scope, authority, constituents, openness to public reason and argument, and even comportment of those involved—so is somewhat analogical to one's having two or more sets of anything, whether it is clothes, tools, dishes, books, fishing poles, or other entities. The different "sets" have different purposes, different functions and forms of "reason," imply different constituents or people involved, are different in scope, and the one who chooses between them is choosing between different comportments for himself or herself. One does not attend a funeral in a ragged T-shirt, shorts, and thongs, which one might very well wear in mowing one's law on a hot summer day.

Having different specifics of the same general specie does *not* mean one is a hypocrite or has no standards, but simply means that different situations, institutions, and forms of one's identity and allegiance in life require different things as appropriate, fitting, or even necessary. This, I think, is the virtue of the way Rawls describes the differences between religions and governmental structures as well as their many areas of similarity. In fact, Rawls insisted that the actual ethical principles involved in both need not be contradictory, but when they conflict, the priority must be given to that principle to which the whole people have agreed. It is that simple. Without such understanding, no nation, certainly no democracy, can exist.

For this reason, Jefferson, Madison, and certainly Rawls insisted that these institutions or forms of our identity and allegiance had to be *kept separate* in order to best accomplish their specific purposes. Religions should not attempt to supplant the interests of the whole people by the religion's exclusive metaphysics and refusal to be open to "public reason."

If they can be kept separate, the political unity being overarching enough to include people's reasonable comprehensive theories so long as they comply with the political conception of justice and its basic laws, it would mean the courts and legislatures *per se* would not become *concerned with anything religious* whatever, nor have to try to distinguish that which is "central" or essential to any religion, nor be caught up in deciding what was religiously "orthodox," as J. Jackson pointed out for the Court in *Barnette*. J. Jackson was correct about the extent of "difference" which a democracy should accommodate, though he ironically applied it *wrongly*, as noted by J. Frankfurter's dissent, making an *exception* to generally applicable laws by a mere claim of one's being *offended religiously* over such laws.[33]

We must ask over and over, as we analyze the Court's decisions: Should a *religious* person be able to bring a case to the Court which *no one else* is allowed to bring, just because he has religious convictions, for example, that no one can own an auto, or no agencies or people loaning money to others can charge any interest at all, or, everyone must worship with the religious group closest to their house, or, all white women must have abortions, or no one can drink any alcoholic drink, or medical doctors may not perform surgery on anyone of a different sex, or no one may have assets totaling more than one million dollars, or no one may attend any athletic contest if they are bald or pigeon-toed or wear contact lenses? These may seem silly, but *discrimination* presently going on under the special exemptions or benefits religious people are demanding is certainly *not* a laughing matter, for example, demanding exemption from the mitigation procedures the national health agencies put in place to help stop the spread of the Covid-19, so they can worship as large groups, without masks, and so forth. At such points, the lack of any genuine national interest seems obvious, leaving only a narcissistic majoritarianism.

Unfortunately, the Court's decisions for the past eight decades have allowed the concerns of citizens to *pulverize* the "wall of separation," and the

Court has even referred to it not as a straight but a serpentine wall, or *no wall at all*. For those who consider themselves as "Constitutionalists" or dedicated to the "original intent" of the Framers, this feeds into the ultraconservative idea today that belittles the whole concept of such a "wall," which insists that it has "eliminated" Christianity from the public sphere, that Christians have been victimized by the Court's decisions. Nothing is further from the truth. We will see, and each reader will be able to judge in the next few chapters, whether the Court's decisions since 1940 have not *favored* the *Christian religion* in a disproportionate way over all other religions, including Judaism, under both the Religion Clauses of the First Amendment.

We will see that since the *Everson* case of 1947, the Court has approved billions of public tax dollars to religious schools whose primary purpose is to *indoctrinate* in primarily only one particular sect of Christianity, religious institutions continue to pay no tax on their income or assets, including hundreds of billions of dollars worth of real property; and their pastors, priests, and other ordained clergy continue to get free housing allowance by section 107 of the IRS code. When religious groups want help in spreading their religion, they resort time and again to trying to get the government to do it for them with public funds,[34] or with displays of *their specific religious symbols* on public or government property or with inserting *Christian rituals* into the public schools or other public institutions, or to prohibit the teaching of ideas of which they disapprove such as evolution, or to prohibit certain medical procedures such as abortion. When the Court has refused, people have accused it and the government of being "hostile" to *their religion*, so the Court often seems to run in fear of being charged of that hostility. But the results of the Court show a special favoritism for Christianity ever since the "incorporation" of the two religion clauses of the First Amendment into state law, but especially since the mid-1980s, in the ignoring or reversing of most of the earlier "tests" the Court devised.

Our Founding Fathers tried to avoid this obvious confusion and divisiveness by erecting what Thomas Jefferson called the "wall of separation." The line or wall of separation between government and religion as both Jefferson and Madison saw it could be crossed by government only if and when the religious or their principles "break out into overt acts of disorder."[35] But even that did not mean the wall separating them had been crossed, since government in such cases was not stepping in to judge something religious but only the alleged violations of the universally applicable civil and criminal laws of the land. So, even when government had to make such judgments against religious people, the judgments had nothing to do with their religion, but were the standards all were expected to comply with as citizens. The same would be true of Madison's concession that government could intervene to prevent religious groups from hurting other religious groups,[36] but this again involved only violations of the general laws all citizens had agreed to observe, so did not involve any inquiry into religious ideas or doctrines. That's the simple *neutrality* of the government. That's the *equality of all* citizens—no special benefits or exemptions from universally applicable laws just for being religious or nonreligious.

Madison and other Framers of the Constitution did not think that they were defining with precision for all ages to come every possible law that would be needed in future centuries. They showed no inclination to wanting to tie all future generations to the "intent" they had or the "text" they wrote as they compromised with each other in all those lively debates over many months. It was their basic "intent" to *establish a union*, to "experiment" with a constitutional republic which, though democratic, was a republic in which voted representatives could advocate for the multitude of diverse interests, so being able to encompass a greater scope or population than could a pure democracy.

The Constitution and Bill of Rights involved dozens if not hundreds of compromises and unresolved problems as well as intentional ambiguities or vague expressions that left decisions for future generations. So for future generations, it was never just a matter of ascertaining the intent of the Founders or of finding the best or more logical interpretation of the "text" they wrote. The nation would continue to change, they all knew, so would have to adapt. It would be forced to have to create laws that could not even be imagined in that late eighteenth-century atmosphere. The Constitution was not all-encompassing for the indefinite future, so has had to be supplemented with extensive statutory law. It provided only a bare framework.

If Patrick Henry's idea of the government supporting all the Christian sects to which the various citizens belonged in Virginia was insufficient and degrading for its own time, that idea of government providing equal treatment from its tax base is even *more inappropriate* for the future in which the religious diversity and the nonreligiously affiliated population has *grown extensively* among citizens. As Rawls has shown, even equal treatment of *all religions* (which is not possible) *fails to treat all citizens equally* if it provides benefits for all the religious that it does *not* provide for the *non*religious. Those who want the government to extend certain benefits *only* to members of one particular religion (or even *only* to all those who are religious), but not to others, thereby stand among the "intolerant" in Rawls's classification.

If "equal liberty" is truly "final" or the first principle in a *lexical* ordering, no amount of economic or social benefits can be acceptable for one to consent to less than equal political liberty. If equal liberty is itself threatened by those who desire such liberty but are intolerant of others having liberty equal to what they have, an absolutism which is attached to most religions in their unwillingness to compromise, whether with government or even with other religions and their metaphysics, their intolerance itself cannot be tolerated but must be *restricted* to *preserve* the more extensive freedom, the political justice and political morality to which all citizens have agreed. Otherwise, the whole system collapses with its ill-designed favoritism.[37] Favoritism, whether it is of one race over others or of one religion over other religions and the nonreligious, shows a complete failure to hypothesize the "original position" behind the "veil of ignorance."

So the real question is: What is required to unite a very diverse people, not all of whom are religious, a state in which there is great diversity between the separate religions, even completely blatant contradictions, while most of the religious are absolutists that feel only they have the truth? To favor one religious group or even all, to the exclusion of the nonreligious, is to split apart the people, to play favorites with no obvious justification. The choice is simple—either for religious division, resentment, and chaos *or* for a wholly secular structure of justice with only secular laws and standards for government. Only the latter can have priority since the conflict even between merely the different religions has no superior source recognized by them to resolve their conflict. Rawls insists that in such awareness of conflict, it can be resolved only by appealing to the basic principles of the original position and veil of ignorance. This captures what the Founders established, by the historical context of their First Amendment, as they chose a separation between government and religion, a governmental system of secular laws based on ethics from "freestanding" principles rather than from any or all religions, just as Rawls suggests.

Importantly, the choice of the latter does *not* prevent the religious person from being religious; it only means whatever one believes metaphysically does *not* entitle one to benefits that others fail to receive from the government, nor exemptions from keeping the civil and criminal laws that all citizens must keep, nor does it give the person some trump card in any discussion of possible new laws. The social contract must be built *only* on the "public reason," and its principles will possibly "overlap" so as to give a united position, but only within this public reason, in this hypothesizing of the original position behind a veil of ignorance, and *only* if the principles themselves are "freestanding," as Rawls insists.

The Virginia situation is also extremely important for interpreting Madison's and Jefferson's true views, since Virginia was *not* attempting to establish a "national" church despite some Justices insisting that the establishment clause has to do *only* with a "national" church. Such a position ignores Patrick Henry's Bill as well as its opposition by Madison and Jefferson. The bill they fought and defeated was *not in any way* attempting to make the Anglican church the established church of the single state of Virginia, much less of the New Nation. Instead, the governor's proposed bill allowed each taxpayer to designate the recipient church in Virginia, whether

Anglican, Baptist, Congregational, Quaker, or other, to receive the appropriate share of his or her taxes. Even this "accommodation" was clearly too much for Jefferson and Madison since it took one's autonomy of whether to support and how much to support completely out of the individual's control, placing it in the state government's hands. So they defeated it, and the ensuing First Amendment to the U.S. Constitution was framed on the very heels of this *defeat* of the Virginia bill—as most of our Supreme Court Justices know—framed by the same people, following the same principles, just reduced in wording.

Madison and Jefferson belonged to a group of intellectuals. They were avid readers, extremely familiar with the history and literature of Ancient Greece and Rome, and both read Greek and Latin with ease. In preparing for the long policy discussions that they anticipated occurring in the Constitutional Convention, Madison especially spent weeks and months reading and thinking through the philosophy and political uniqueness of those earlier federations, especially of Greece and Rome, as far back as the Greek amphictyony, of distilling important principles out that could help form a basis for this "lively experiment" of democracy or a "constitutional republic." When the Convention met, he translated these intellectual insights into common language so all could understand so they could ask questions, argue, and work together to hammer out a Constitution. This was neither authoritarianism nor pedantry on his part, but a genuine sharing of insights and research which made all the difference in the world.

With the New Nation facing so many other conflicting positions on crucial issues such as taxes, military, banks, slavery, the borders, treaties with other nations, the Native Americans, and the like, unless people could forego having their particular religion in a privileged position, there would not have been great odds that an enduring nation could have been either created or sustained. At least religious privilege had to be transcended in the name of national unity, as the Founders saw it. Above all, they could not afford to rebuild the religiously divisive conditions that had preoccupied Europe's history for so many generations, killing so many people and creating antagonisms that would require not simply decades but perhaps centuries to transcend. Once again, that is what Rawls's hypothetical "original position" does behind the "veil of ignorance"—there simply is no privileged position at the table of the social or political contract, no metaphysical language or "nonpublic reason" could be used since it remains unique to only a particular association,[38] but not to the entire population of the New Nation. Unity requires voluntary agreement, and voluntary agreement requires "public reason," the recognition of significant valid differences between people, and a fair method of working in an interdependent and united way despite the diversity, transcending all irrationally vested advantages.

If they were actually to have a nation, the only way was to acknowledge a diverse people in which a trusting, mutual autonomy could be cultivated and respected, built upon the common "will-to-live," with obvious limits on people's freedoms at the point at which they encroached upon the equal freedoms of others, a position articulated by many philosophers by the early nineteenth century. That, of course, meant, as we have seen over and over, that there can be no absolute held by certain individuals which can be privileged over those who differ. Nothing else could be the reasonable explanation for their actions. But the ratification of the Constitution and Bill of Rights does not imply that all citizens of these states understood *all* the implications of the First Amendment. But at least most citizens did not want (1) to be taxed to support some religion or beliefs of which they did not approve, or (2) continuous hostilities to be perpetuated within a state or between states on the basis of conflicting religious allegiances, or (3) to sacrifice certain common civil benefits because they were either religious or nonreligious.

Within the facts of eighteenth-century history, a merely equal accommodation of all religions was *not* what those Founders had in mind in the First Amendment. After the war, no religious connection really existed between the various states and England, nor was it wise to emphasize that the Virginia church had those roots and former loyalties. Many of the new states knew of the religious diversity from state to state and often within individual states, and realized even state-by-state general assessments might very well estrange states in proximity to each other, ending up causing bad enough relations that different groups within those proximate states might well sour relations between states to the degree of causing them to miss out on otherwise significant economic benefits such as from duties taken in by a contingent state that had seaports or river traffic. Rutland even suggested that disestablishment of religion reached maturity in most states fairly quickly because of a *declining interest* in organized Christianity and the people's fascination for doing other things on Sundays, for example, the Virginians' attraction to horse races and cockfights on Sundays.[39] That is a part of the process of "desacralization" and the "demythologizing" in the culture even without people being fully cognizant of their "loss" of the sense of the "sacred" or their little use for religious myths which we discussed earlier.

There were still some people in the New World who resented the idea of having to tolerate others in a religious denomination that seemed to them so heretical. There were even judges as late as the early nineteenth century who upheld lower court *convictions* of an individual who said "Jesus was a bastard, and his mother must have been a whore." Few people would defend the offensiveness or unnecessary crudeness of such talk, but why was it considered a "crime"? The justification for convicting the person was that these were "false, feigned, scandalous, malicious, wicked and blasphemous" words against Christ, thereby undermining Christianity, which, in turn undermined ethics or morality of the people, which then undermined the very state itself. That's quite a long connection of "undermining," to say the least. No facts were given as evidence of any of this "undermining," that is, actual damage to the state. Chief Justice Kent, writing for the NY Supreme Court, spoke of religious freedom, but insisted that when one maliciously reviles the religion of the state or country, that is a crime.[40] He missed the fact that Jefferson, Madison, and other Framers did *not* think that a *state or country* had a relation with God, not even corporations, but only *individual people*. J. Kent claimed that Madison's statement about government having no cognizance of religion applied only to the "establishment" question, but otherwise does *not* deny that there can be "judicial cognizance of those offences against religion and morality which have no reference to any such establishment . . . but are punishable because they strike at the root of moral obligation, and weaken the security of the social ties." But this simply ignores what Madison and Jefferson both wrote, that neither religion nor state need each other so must be separate and mind their own business.[41]

THE "INCORPORATION" OF THE BILL OF RIGHTS, INCLUDING RELIGIOUS FREEDOM

Amendments, including the Fourteenth (one of the "Civil War" Amendments), which guaranteed all citizens, whatever their ethnic group or status, equal protection and due process under the law, were, just like the original Ten Amendments, originally understood as federal law rather than state law. Yet, ironically, that very war and these Amendments themselves legally *eliminated* any state's claim to exempt itself from federal law on vital issues. Therefore, it was only a matter of time before those very few states who had not yet begun a religious disestablishment were now legally forced to do so by virtue of the Fourteenth Amendment, as the various fundamental protections under the Bill of Rights became "incorporated" into state law in *piecemeal* fashion largely by gradual decisions of the Supreme Court and by specific new state statutes.[42]

This "incorporation" of especially the U.S. Constitution's Bill of Rights into state law was not unique to the religion clauses of the First Amendment. Most of the enumerated rights of the first eight Amendments had already been included in two or more states' own Bill of Rights, and disestablishment was underway prior to the ratification of the Constitution and its Bill of Rights. The debates on whether the Constitution should even include a "Bill of Rights" was lively, prolonged, and quite justified as one views the arguments. Some opposed it since they conceived of people possibly arguing that the limited form in which it would be articulated was the extent of rights left to the power of the states, or others insisting that without an articulated Bill of Rights, states might feel totally eclipsed by the new federal system. On the other hand, how could all the presupposed possible rights of a citizen be encompassed specifically without making a bill tedious, redundant, and unenforceable?[43] Federalism and republicanism were in tension prior to the argument over a possible Bill of Rights and longer after, as the twin dangers to the nation were perceived as either (1) the central government having or developing too much power, thus nullifying the ideal of any independence of the separate states, or (2) the central government having so little power that conditions were not improved over the earlier Confederation whose faults were fairly obviously recognized. The first option would pose the problem of an autocracy or even monarchy which they had just defeated; the second would leave the states as so lacking in any central unity that they would be simply another banana republic, ready for the plucking by any foreign power.

To get a modern picture of the *tension*, the present status of cannabis may be a relevant example. While it remains on a list of federally "controlled substances" which violation produces criminal prosecution, many states have made an exception not only for "medical" use of marijuana but for recreational use. The effect of that is a state of chaos, with uncertainty rather than clarity, and has been defused only by the feds not actively pursuing those violating the federal law. When there is a significant difference between federal and state law, rather than one simply agreeing with the other and perhaps supplementing it in some way, with state and federal courts perhaps even across the street from each other, it creates a confusing and unfruitful *impasse*. In late 2020, the House passed a law decriminalizing cannabis, but the Senate has not taken up the bill, so the impasse remains.

Regarding the effect of equality of citizens and their promise of equal protection and due process via the Civil War Amendment XIV (when seen with Thirteenth and Fifteenth Amendments),[44] there should never have been any question of a difference of state and federal laws regarding individuals' equal status and due process after that point. That does not mean that every aspect of law contained in the Bill of Rights has been "incorporated" formally into state law, but nearly all. The only reason state or federal governments neither one have protested too loudly is because most of those rights were already contained in two or more states' Bill of Rights prior to being in the federal Bill of Rights. And most of those had their precursors in the listed English violations of the colonies within the Declaration of Independence or in the Declaration of the Continental Congress in 1774. So the precise origin of the idea was not nearly as important as the content of each right, and those seem to have been known and accepted quite widely by the Revolutionary and post-Revolutionary generations. Eventually, the protection of rights under the due process clause of the Fourteenth Amendment was understood as not merely procedural but substantial in this same sense. One assumes that whatever rights are posited beyond those found in the Bill of Rights would fit Rawls's understanding of the two primary principles of (1) equal liberty to the maximum achievable, and (2) the "difference" principle which requires in cases of inequality due to happenstance social and economic elements in life that any law pertaining to the social or economic areas would therefore benefit first those who are "least advantaged."

This does not require distinguishing some as "preferred" rights because of some presupposed greater value they have to a well-ordered society, but it also does not relegate all considerations of importance legislatively or judicially as involving only questions of efficiency or an interested majority, either one of which could destroy the equilibrium that is sought. Here, I believe, we are driven back to the basic instinctual "will-to-live" that Schweitzer discovered, which has broader forms of self-assertion which are included in Nietzsche's "will-to-power," as not only a "discharging of one's strength" but of self-assertion or life assertion in the multiplicity of a person's physical and mental capacity, which includes not simply survival of self and the species, but survival of self-expression and growth or fruition of one's ideas and values. If equality is one of "opportunity" more specifically than of assets, possessions, or accomplishments, then, even if a society has espoused a "self-made" image or hypothetical materialistic independence, one quickly understands its myopic vision as one comes to appreciate a greater whole than oneself, an interdependence. Here the hypothetical original position and veil of ignorance need not assume anything more generous than Rawls suggested, that all people possess a basic "disinterest" in the others, since even in that position, each will select the process and principles which *all the others* would, once the "veil of ignorance" is taken seriously.

He was not suggesting that under this hypothetical, or behind the "veil of ignorance," one transforms into a more empathic or compassionate person. That would be fine, but is not necessary, since even in the state of "disinterest," *all freely select the similar option* to protect themselves in their "ignorance" of where they would be in real life. Those equalities of opportunity are assured by the first principle in political realms of equal maximum liberty. This would include not simply equal opportunity to vote, meaning being able to vote for whomever one elected, but to have the *conditions met* under which one is able to vote intelligibly and easily. Rawls points out that it not only precludes voter suppression or gerrymandering to manipulate the value of each vote, but should also prevent the campaign discussions or issues from being dictated merely by the largest campaign donors. As Rawls himself pointed out, as long as campaigns are not funded entirely from a neutral source such as universal tax base, they will unfortunately predetermine which issues and which candidates get the most coverage and thereby get elected.[45] But even more than this, for one's voice to be equal to that of all others in voting, this may well require the end of the "electoral college" which is a residual element of the elitism and aristocratic thinking still in power in the late eighteenth century. Finally, this equality of voice may itself require a certain prior level of "opportunity" achievable only by having sufficient basics of living met, elements such as necessary food, shelter, a profession that is fulfilling and meets the needs of one's family, and an education which enables one to express an intelligible and reasonably informed judgment as well as achieve necessary skills to qualify for a profession which can be rewarding financially as well as emotionally.[46] Certainly that is what the continuation of a democratic society needs and is the only way to cure that elitist view that for some reason not all citizens are qualified to vote. That is the most basic political liberty to Rawls.

Of course, the Court does not refer to these sorts of things yet as "rights." They certainly are not listed in the federal or various states' bills of rights. But in this country, it took centuries for the culture to recognize that "rights" belonged to *anyone other* than white men who owned property. To suppose that most of those who owned property had earned it themselves is to create a meritocratic fiction; most of it was inherited by them, and their fathers, and further back, was basically an unfair bargain their ancestors made with the Native Americans, or it was simply land they took over after conquering or slaughtering the local Native Americans. Such a state of being a "landowner" was in many cases less noble and much less moral than the property-less status of thousands of other citizens, past and present. This might suggest that the most basic "rights" somehow are *not* simply beyond the reach of federal government but also state government, so are found more in Ninth and Tenth Amendments, and the "due process" and "equal rights" guarantees of Fourteenth Amendment. Reparations to those who had their land taken from them or to the millions brought from Africa with their freedom taken from them—seems to be a first step the United States needs to initiate if equity is ever to be more than a trite cliché.

Rights flow more from the content of the actual "overlapping consensus" Rawls elaborated, based on "freestanding" principles, rather than upon litigation of peoples' supposed *vested* rights or a "preferred" nature. Vested rights, behind most litigation, is the most convoluted form of realizing a true system of justice since it continues to be focused on "contingent advantages and accidental influences from the past" producing "bargaining advantages that inevitably arise within the background institutions of any society from cumulative social, historical, and natural tendencies."[47] It simply returns us to David Hume's understanding that almost all government has been based upon either *conquest or usurpation*. That does not make it "right," nor does it bestow "rights," nor does it suggest that those today who advocate that government should be based on a voluntary original contract since all humans are equal are incorrect, as Hume contended.

Any Justice's idea of "religion" being a "preferred" status or involvement is simply a reflection of the weight of tradition, confusing religion with the necessity of ethics to a culture, when, in fact, as Madison and Jefferson pointed out, history has proven that government's *preferring a religion* actually works to the disadvantage and crippling of both institutions. Ethics is not the main benefit religions provide. As Kant acknowledged, it probably should be, but is simply not, since ethics offers a much less extravagant hope than the religion's mythology and metaphysics, which, in many cases removes the effort from the human shoulders entirely, offering a utopia simply on faith, even almost ignoring ethics and effort.[48]

The First Amendment's two religion clauses promising not only that government would *not* make any law pertaining to the establishment of religion nor prohibiting the free exercise of it, at least in the twenty-first century, has to involve the general citizenry's recognition that this means neither federal nor state religious establishments are legal, and neither governments can prohibit one's "free exercise" of religion, that is, "worship." The "separation" and the "incorporation" elements that we have briefly explained assure that much, and that applies to any religion, and, as we will see later, to people who espouse no religion. Neither the religious nor nonreligious are therefore exempt from universally applicable laws, nor do they gain some specific benefits or preferential treatment from government for being religious or nonreligious. They remain only equal citizens, and the Court and Legislature have the obligation to avoid classifying, defining, or judging what "religion" is, since that would be to make a law pertaining to the establishment of religion or prohibiting its free exercise, which the First Amendment forbids. The final question of this chapter is: Precisely what did that term "free exercise" of religion mean?

"FREE EXERCISE": THE COLONISTS' AND FOUNDERS' OPPOSITION TO COERCED *WORSHIP*

As proof of the meaning of "Free Exercise" as "worship" rather than just anything I do at any time, I offer a very brief sketch of historical facts. Many of the European immigrants had come to the New World to escape being taxed for a religion they were not a part of, to support clergy that propagated ideas they did not believe, and to escape being forced to espouse a certain religious allegiance, including a coerced faithful attendance at worship which they did not approve. They were persecuted when they attempted to gather as dissenting groups and worship in the way they saw fit. Even in the early American colonies, many still felt this prohibition of their "free exercise" in that their colony *forced* them to *worship only* with the accepted church and not as they felt convicted in their hearts. While some colonies, as we saw, did early on create similar coercive religious laws, by the time of the Revolution, most realized that the resulting New Nation, in order to survive, would have to mitigate if not abolish this divisive religious approach. Begrudging religious toleration had transformed into freedom of conscience, which itself morphed into real religious freedom being a natural or inalienable right. We can see that by the time of the Constitution and the Bill of Rights, this had become apparent as the only real cure to prevent religious division that could shred the New Nation which was so vulnerable. Many colonies-turned-states had already "disestablished" their government from a religion by 1789.

The primary objective of "free exercise" was being *free to worship whatever, whenever, however, and with whomever one saw fit.* The freedom from being taxed by the government on behalf of the church fell more under the anti-Establishment clause of the First Amendment, but Jefferson still saw it as a violation of one's conscience, a violation of one's freedom of conscience, even if the state did no more than coerce taxes even to supply to pastors of one's own church. Note how in the following few examples of "Free Exercise" the scope changes from a sectarian freedom to a religious freedom, and how often it is defined only as free *worship*.

The "Original Constitution" of New Haven in 1639[49] actually did *speak* of "free exercise" of religion, but in contrast, showed a fairly *homogeneous* community attempting to establish a *civil government strictly* upon what it thought were the principles of God. The document implies that not only were all the townspeople in agreement about their religion, but they quickly, by voting, agreed that their wisest men become the civic leaders, and that both the civil and church government was spelled out in the scriptures. But where in the scriptures and specifically what was said? There was little diversity, so little room for religious freedom other than *their own.*

In the Massachusetts Body of Liberties of 1641,[50] while there was some latitude given within the churches, the civil government, in the Spirit of John Calvin, on the basis of passages from the Jewish scriptures, still retained the death penalty for *worshipping* any god other than the one true God, as well as for blaspheming either that God, or Jesus Christ, or the Holy Spirit, and it extended the death penalty to any woman who was a "witch" or consulted with familiar spirits. They enforced those laws and became infamous for their "witch" trials.

Maryland's Act Concerning Religion of 1649[51] had similar laws of capital punishment and confiscation by the government of all of one's assets for blaspheming God, Christ, the Holy Spirit, the Trinity, as well as severe penalties for speaking disparagingly of Mary, Mother of our Savior, or the Apostles or Evangelists, and as well for using pejorative terms or belittling manners in speaking of any religious person. This was a blatant "establishment" of religion, and there was *no mention* of "free exercise" of religion, to say the least, because there was none.

In 1655, Roger Williams's presented to the town of Providence, RI, his idea of religious freedom. Here "religious freedom" was central, and its "exercise" was seen in "worship." He used an illustration of a commonwealth being like a large boat crossing the ocean in which there were many people, including many of different religious persuasions, such as Protestants and Catholics, Muslims and Jews. He said that *no one* of these groups, whether large or small, had the right to *compel the others to worship* in the manner they did, none had the right to be able to compel the others to pray only the way they did. However, as regards the maintenance and duties of the ship and its general voyage, all had responsibilities to it which were not diminished nor enhanced by any reference to their religion. That was his distinction between people's religious freedom to worship as they choose and their civic responsibility as members of a commonwealth. Of course, he was ahead of his time, but Jefferson, Madison, Backus, and many others in the closing decades of the eighteenth century said virtually the same thing, as does the "theory of justice" of John Rawls in 1971. Earlier, in 1644, in his explanation of the impossibility of founding a civil government on some alleged *uniformity* of conscience or religion, justified by some reference to the Christians' alleged right to persecute others on the basis of their own conscience, Williams emphasized the bloodshed throughout the centuries was the direct result. So uniformity of belief and worship could not be expected but people must learn to live amid real diversity.[52]

The Carolina Fundamental Constitution of 1669[53] included law number "one hundred and nine" which reads: "No person whatsoever shall disturb, molest, or persecute another for his speculative opinions in religion, or his way of worship."

The Pennsylvania Charter of Liberty, Laws Agreed Upon in England, etc. 1682[54] instructed: "XXXV. That all persons living in this province, who confess and acknowledge the one Almighty and eternal God, to be the Creator, Upholder and Ruler of the world; and that hold themselves obliged in conscience to live peaceably and justly in civil society, shall, in no ways, be molested or prejudiced for their religious persuasion, or practice, in matters of faith and worship, nor shall they be compelled, at any time, to frequent or maintain any religious worship, place or ministry whatever." If *worship* was generally understood as what people wanted to protect as their right to the "free exercise" of their religion, the equation here is quite *explicit*.

In the Delaware Charter of 1701[55] the emphasis is upon freedom of conscience and therefore freedom of religious expression, that is, "religious
worship," for any believers in the One God, so long as they "live quietly
under the Civil Government." If they also believed in Jesus Christ, they
could hold any government office as long as they "solemnly promised" their
religious faith, "when lawfully required." When we skip ahead to the time of
the Revolutionary War and years immediately following, prior to the actual
Constitution being ratified with the Bill of Rights, the subject becomes even
more explicit as religious freedom becomes less toleration and more a natural
right, but still *freedom of worship.*

For example, the Delaware Declaration of Rights of September 11, 1776,
included a prohibition of any authority from compelling any person "to attend
any religious worship or maintain any ministry contrary to or against his own
free will and consent . . . or in any manner control the right of conscience in
the free exercise of religious worship."[56] The freedom from "establishment"
meant precisely freedom from constraint in belief and in gathering with others to worship.

The Pennsylvania Constitution of 1776, Declaration of Rights (Thorpe
5:3082-84)[57] similarly read,

> And that no man ought or of right can be compelled to attend any religious
> worship, or erect or support any place of worship. . . . Nor can any man, who
> acknowledges the being of a God, be justly deprived or abridged of any civil
> right as a citizen, on account of his religious sentiments or peculiar mode of
> religious worship: And that no authority can or ought to be vested in, or assumed
> by any power whatever, that shall in any case interfere with, or in any manner
> control, the right of conscience in the free exercise of religious worship.

The New Jersey Constitution of 1776, ARTS. 18, 19 Thorpe 5:2597-98[58]
does not use the words "free exercise" but is obviously describing it:

> That no person shall ever, within this Colony, be deprived of the inestimable priv-
> ilege of worshipping Almighty God in a manner agreeable to the dictates of his
> own conscience; nor, under any pretense whatever, be compelled to attend any
> place of worship, contrary to his own faith and judgment; nor shall any person,
> within this Colony, ever be obliged to pay tithes, taxes, or any other rates, for the
> purpose of building or repairing any other church or churches, place or places of
> worship, or for the maintenance of any minister or ministry, contrary to what he
> believes to be right, or has deliberately or voluntarily engaged himself to perform.

How many times in a single paragraph do people have to use the term
"worship" for a reader to pick up the meaning? They *never* indicated that

almost *anything* they might want to do in their business or personal life should be able to be claimed as their "free exercise" of their religion. That freedom was of their "worship." Their ancestors' history was one of being persecuted for trying to worship as a dissenting group from the orthodox that was merged with government, so they were protesting to be free to worship in whatever way, when, where, and with whomever they chose, as their conscience led them, and most thought God was able to lead their consciences.

The North Carolina Constitution of 1776, ART 34 (Thorpe 5:2788, 2793)[59] covers both the "establishment" as well as "free exercise" clauses as it insists that

> there shall be no establishment in this State, in preference to any other; neither shall any person, on any pretense whatsoever, be compelled to attend any place of worship contrary to his own faith or judgment, nor be obliged to pay for the purchase of any glebe, or the building of any house of worship, or for the maintenance of any minister or ministry, contrary to what he believes right, or has voluntarily and personally engaged to perform; but all persons shall be at liberty to exercise their own mode of worship:—Provided, That nothing herein contained shall be construed to exempt preachers of treasonable or seditious discourses, from legal trial and punishment.

In the Maryland Constitution of 1776, Declaration of Rights, XXXIII reads:[60] "That, as it is the duty of every man to worship God in such manner as he thinks most acceptable to him; all persons professing the Christian religion, are equally entitled to protection in their religious liberty; wherefore no person ought by any law to be molested in his person or estate on account of his religious persuasion or profession, or for his religious practice." If it was still equating the Christian religion with religion in general, it was still far behind Madison and Jefferson who extended the same freedom to people of *any religion* and even *atheists or people of no religion*.

In the Vermont Constitution of 1777, ch. 1, sec. 3,[61] the law stated: "That all men have a natural and unalienable right to worship almighty God, according to the dictates of their own consciences, and that no man ought, or of right can be compelled to attend any religious worship . . . nor can any man who professes the protestant religion, be justly deprived or abridged of any civil right, as a citizen, on account of his religious sentiment, or peculiar mode of religious worship, and that no authority can . . . interfere with, or in any manner controul, the rights or conscience, in the free exercise of religious worship."

The South Carolina Constitution of 1778, article XXXVIII[62] reads: "That all persons and religious societies acknowledge that there is one God, and a future state of rewards and punishments, and that God is publicly to be worshipped, shall be freely tolerated," even though it established Protestantism as the state religion, which was also presupposed in the Vermont preferential treatment of Protestants. "Free exercise" is still only "worship," not one's business activities, hobbies, drunkenness, or other obvious dangers to the public or infractions of generally applicable laws.

The Massachusetts Constitution of 1780, pt. I Handlin 442-48, in article II[63] reads in part that "no subject shall be hurt, molested, or restrained, in his person, liberty, or estate, for worshipping GOD in the manner and season most agreeable to the dictates of his own conscience; or for his religious profession or sentiments; provided he doth not disturb the public peace, or obstruct others in their religious worship."

Finally, the New Hampshire Constitution of 1784, article V[64] states that "every individual has a natural and unalienable right to worship God according to the dictates of his own conscience, and reason; and no subject shall be hurt, molested, or restrained in his person, liberty or estate for worshipping God, in the manner and season most agreeable to the dictates of his own conscience, or for his religious profession, sentiments or persuasion; provided he doth not disturb the public peace, or disturb others, in their religious worship."

This is simply a historical reminder that the peoples' understanding of the "free exercise" of religion was *only* as freedom to *worship* as one chooses (or not at all). It was gradually accepted as the only reasonable approach of civil government toward religion within a religiously diverse society. When one compares all these documents with the various states' ratification of the Constitution and Bill of Rights, and with the U.S. House of Representatives' final consideration of the Bill of Rights, the idea of "worship" as the focus of "free exercise" of religion is simply confirmed even more. The same is true if we view *individual* correspondence of people like Jefferson, Madison, George Mason, and many others who focused on the problem of government *coercing either one's faith or one's worship*, the double focus of John Locke's *Letter Concerning Toleration* of 1689.

For example, in Jefferson's letter of January 23, 1808, to Rev. Samuel Miller, he responded to Miller's inquiry as to whether he or the general government had any power to prescribe "any religious exercise." He answered with the following:

> I consider the government of the U.S. as interdicted by the Constitution from intermeddling with religious institutions, their doctrines, disciplines, or exercises. . . . Certainly no power to prescribe any religious exercise, or to assume authority in religious discipline, has been delegated to the general government. . . . But it is only proposed that I should recommend, not prescribe a day of fasting & prayer. That is, that I should indirectly assume to the U.S. an authority

over religious exercises which the Constitution has directly precluded them from
. . . I do not believe it is for the interest of religion to invite the civil magistrate to
direct it's exercises, it's discipline, or it's doctrines; nor of the religious societies that the general government should be invested with the power of effecting
any uniformity of time or matter among them. Fasting & prayer are religious
exercises. The enjoining them an act of discipline. Every religious society has a
right to determine for itself the times for these exercises, & the object proper for
them, according to their own particular tenets; and this right can never be safer
than in their own hands, where the constitution has deposited it.[65]

For those Justices who are often citing the early presidents' endorsement
of religious holidays and rituals, it is inexcusable that they ignored this and
similar strong statements by our other early presidents.

Once again, the "free exercise" of religion protected by the First
Amendment was *acts of worship such as prayer and fasting.* "Free exercise"
or religion was *never* needed to guarantee acts of worship one might do completely in private, such as even prayer and fasting, but pointed to the "gathering" of the saints in homes or church buildings to worship together with other
believers. It was also *never* conceived as something people could claim about
their business pursuits or other aspects of their lives, totally aside from their
connection to a religious body with whom they chose to *join for worship.*
It was certainly never conceived as a form of exemption from universally
applicable common civil or criminal laws. Jefferson's "Bill for Establishing
Religious Freedom" showed quite the opposite, that "it is time enough for
the rightful purposes of civil government for its officers to interfere when
principles break out into overt acts against peace and good order."[66] Those
universally applicable or neutral laws must be obeyed by all citizens; there
were no exemptions for belonging to any religion.

The meaning of the religion clauses of the First Amendment make more
sense when we see them as a part of a whole picture that includes (1) the
Enlightenment emphasis on freedom of conscience, (2) the successful and
powerful revivals of the Great Awakening in New England which emphasized
autonomy or individual decisions or conversions, (3) the reactions of some
of the established colonial churches to the "dissidents" such as the Quakers
and others, and (4) the defeat of Patrick Henry's general assessment bill for
Virginia. The First Amendment, just like Madison and Jefferson's opposition
to Henry's bill, was *not* a law for an *equal accommodation* by government of
all religious groups, since that was what *Henry's bill was promoting.* It was
to *separate* them because of their different authorities, constituencies, types
of reason used, scope, and comportment. Religion was based on a special
metaphysics not acceptable to many citizens; in contrast, government was
based on freestanding principles to which all citizens would agree. Henry's

bill would invite jealousies over which group was receiving the most public tax dollars while it neglected aiding nonreligious people in the same capacity. The rejection of that bill made no claim on public taxes for support of any or all religious groups. This is most crucial to avoid divisiveness.

After the Revolutionary War, no religious connection really existed between the various states and England, nor was it wise for any state such as Virginia to emphasize that it still had those religious roots, ties, authority, structure, and loyalties to England. Most of all, most citizens of these former colonies wished *not* to make the bloody Revolutionary War merely a sheer waste of lives for nothing. There was no returning in time, and that applied also to political structures and religious institutions. Many disestablished long before any litigation began, even though the "Bill of Rights" had initially begun as a limitation of federal law and jurisdiction. Gradually, people realized that state law and federal cannot be at odds with each other if the intention is to form a "United States."

NOTES

1. John Locke, "A Letter Concerning Toleration 1689," *Montuori* 17–25, 31–22, 34, 45, 65–69, 89, 91, 93, in Kurland and Lerner (eds.), *Founders' Constitution*, V: 53.

2. John Locke, *The Reasonableness of Christianity* (Stanford: Stanford Univ. Press, 1958), 5–65.

3. These two proofs sounded fairly credible on the surface, though "miracles" had become a touchy point and more so with the divisions in theology between the rationalists and supranaturalists, until D. F. Strauss gave them a way out in the nineteenth century. But earlier than Strauss, Friedrich Schleiermacher had definitively examined the two "proofs" and shown how absolutely unreasonable they both were in his classic *The Christian Faith* (1832), which he defined as an explanation of the teaching of current evangelical church of his time. See Strauss, *The Life of Jesus Critically Examined*, tr. George Eliot (Philadelphia: Fortress Press, 1972) and Schleiermacher, *The Christian Faith*, eds. H. R. Mackintosh and J. S. Stewart (Edinburgh: T. & T. Clark, 1960).

4. Locke, *The Reasonableness of Christianity*, 68.

5. For example, he based his simple idea of "Jesus being the Messiah" only on the sermons he found in the book of Acts, but never showed any awareness of the Messianic problem occurring between the gospels when one compares them. In this sense, he was even behind Luther, who basically avoided the synoptic problem, preferring the Fourth Gospel which was later recognized as the least historical, but to Luther at least supplied the reason for the Crucifixion. Locke was a philosopher but not a theologian, so showed no concern for even the quest for reconstructing the best Greek critical text of the New Testament which Erasmus published in its second edition in 1522. Hermann Samuel Reimarus, son of a Pietist pastor, Nicolaus Reimarus, was born even *prior*

to Locke's publication of *The Reasonableness of Christianity*, and H. S. Reimarus's conclusions about Christianity, revelation, and Jesus, although published posthumously much later, were exact opposites and better documented and informed than Locke's. Locke misjudged the dating and influence of Paul's theology entirely. For more, see Samuel Reimarus, *Reimarus: Fragments*, ed. Charles H. Talbert, tr. Ralph S. Fraser (Philadelphia: Fortress Press, 1970), and the last part of ch. 3 in my *Will Humanity Survive Religion? Beyond Divisive Absolutes*. At least Locke influenced Jefferson and others toward a "separation of church and state" by his social contract theory.

6. Isaac Backus, "A History of New England," 1774–75, *Stokes* 1;307–309, in Kurland and Lerner (eds.), *Founders' Constitution*, V: 65.

7. Jefferson, in Kurland and Lerner (eds.), *Founders' Constitution*, I: 77.

8. Rawls conceded that liberty of conscience might be limited, but only when there is a "reasonable expectation that not doing so will damage the public order which the government should maintain." *A Theory of Justice*, 213.

9. Jefferson, in Kurland and Lerner (eds.), *Founders' Constitution*, I:77.

10. Jefferson, in Kurland and Lerner (eds.), *Founders' Constitution*, I: 79–80.

11. James Madison, "Memorial and Remonstrance, against Religious Assessments," 20 June 1785, *Papers 8:298–304*, in Kurland and Lerner, *Founders' Constitution*, V: 82–84.

12. "Thomas Jefferson, Autobiography," 1821, *Works*, 1:71, in Kurland and Lerner (eds.), *Founders' Constitution*, I:85.

13. *Larson, Commissioner of Securities, Minnesota Department of Commerce, v. Valente*, 456 U.S. 228 (1982).

14. *Larsen v. Valente*, at 244–45.

15. Madison claimed that religion "disavows a dependence on the powers of the world" and no civil magistrate is a "competent Judge of Religious Truth," and for the magistrate to use religion "as an engine of Civil policy" is simply "an unhallowed perversion of the means of salvation."

16. See "James Madison, Detached Memoranda," ca. 1817, W. & M Wu., 3d ser., 3:554–60 (1946) in Kurland and Lerner, *Founders' Constitution*, V: 103–105, and "James Madison to Rev. Adams," 1832, Writings 9:484–87, in Kurland and Lerner (eds.), V: 107–108.

17. He wrote to William Bradford that the "diabolical Hell conceived principle of persecution rages . . . [which] vexes me the most of any thing whatever. . . . I have neither patience to hear talk or think of anything relative to this matter, for I have squabbled and scolded abused and ridiculed so long about it, [to so lit] tle purpose that I am without common patience. So I [leave you] to pity me and pray for Liberty of Conscience [to revive among us]." In "James Madison to William Bradford," 24 January 1774 *Papers 1:106*, in Kurland and Lerner (eds.), *Founders' Constitution*, V: 60.

18. For more analysis of Locke's position, see my *Will Humanity Survive Religion? Beyond Divisive Absolutes*, ch. 3.

19. Immanuel Kant, "What is Enlightenment?" in Carl Frederick (ed.), *The Philosophy of Kant: Immanuel Kant's Moral and Political Writings* (New York: The Modern Library, 1949), 132–133.

20. This Maryland law was overturned in 1961 in *Torcaso v. Watkins*, 367 U.S. 488 (1961).

21. Jefferson, "Notes on the State of Virginia," *Query* 17, 157–161 (1784) in Kurland and Lerner (eds.), *Founders' Constitution*, V:79–80.

22. The expression "wall of separation between Church and State" is found in his message to the Danbury Baptists. See "Thomas Jefferson to Danbury Baptist Association" 1 January 1802, *Writings* 16:281, in Kurland and Lerner (eds.), *Founders' Constitution*, V: 96.

23. For more details on the death of Henry's general assessment bill, which meant Jefferson and Madison prevailed in Virginia in defeating any taxation for any religious group or even all of them, see Ralph Ketcham, *James Madison: A Biography* (Charlottesville: University of Virginia, 1990), 162–168.

24. Levy notes that Madison continually read the First Amendment more broadly than many others in that he quoted it prohibiting Congress from making any law pertaining to "established religions," which went beyond merely the idea of a government-sponsored "establishment of religion." So that erected the "wall of separation" further back than if the phrase were interpreted only to prohibit government from making any laws with the intent or effect of establishing a religion. It simply reinforces his idea of "separation" or of government's complete lack of cognizance of religion, as Madison put it. His analysis of "establishment" and the mistaken "nonpreferentialism" are chapters of "must" reading. See Leonard W. Levi, *The Establishment Clause: Religion and the First Amendment* (New York: Macmillan Pub. Co. 1986).

25. Jefferson, "A Bill for Establishing Religious Freedom," in Kurland and Lerner (eds.), in *Founders' Constitution*, V: 77.

26. Most recently, people have learned to claim that they are being deprived or prohibited certain general benefits that are available to all, discriminated against just because they are "religious." The Court has bought this argument. But since *Everson* to the present, this kind of pursuit for public taxes for churches, for taxes for the church's religious schools to indoctrinate students, for public land to display a particular religion's symbols, for special exemption to a public health plan's minimal requirements, for special exemption to treat customers in discriminatory ways, to allow churches to ignore health requirements of the state during a pandemic—all of which we cover in the following chapters, are all suits for *special treatment because* one is "religious," which was precisely what Jefferson, Madison, and other religious leaders were against, which blatantly violates Rawls's conception of "political justice" attained through a hypothetical "veil of ignorance." Would *anyone* behind the veil of ignorance agree to such? It is significant that the Court never discusses the ethical principles behind the conceptions of justice.

27. James Madison, Alexander Hamilton and John Jay, *The Federalist Papers*, Number LI (New York: Penguin Books, 1987), Number LI, p. 321.

28. Madison, "Proclamation," 16 November 1814, *Richardson* 1:558 quoted in Kurland and Lerner (eds.), *Founders' Constitution*, V: 103. He repeated the same warning in his letter Madison to Rev. Adams, in 1832, *Writings* 9:484–487 in Kurland and Lerner (eds.), *Founders' Constitution*, V:107: "Under another aspect of

the subject there may be less danger that Religion, if left to itself, will suffer from a failure of the pecuniary support applicable to it than that an omission of the public authorities to limit the duration of their Charters to Religious Corporations, and the amount of property acquirable by them, may lead to an injurious accumulation of wealth from the lavish donations and bequests prompted by a pious zeal or by an atoning remorse."

29. We will see how Rawls also showed the negative impact an unequal distribution of wealth has on political justice when it controls political campaigns, often the very subjects being discussed, stands behind the formulation of most laws, sponsors gerrymandering and other voter suppression methods. *A Theory of Justice*, 225–226.

30. Thomas Jefferson to Albert Gallatin, 16 June 1817, Works 12:73, in Kurland and Lerner (eds.), *Founders' Constitution*, V:105.

31. See note 26.

32. The extensive argument shows Hegel's failure of reaching certainty because of his presupposition that "the referents for the principle or ground of totality and for the principle or ground of intelligibility are one and the same." The very particularities of the "world" as "given," however, become impossible of providing intelligibility or certainty of the totality under this presupposition. The scope and different comportments possible within different wholes which are only partial totalities do not satisfy what is expected of the intelligibility of the totality. This "presupposition" mistake in Hegel was pointed out in detail by Joseph C. Flay, *Hegel's Quest for Certainty* (Albany, NY: State Univ. of New York, 1984), 249–267.

33. *West Virginia State Board of Education v. Barnette*, 319 U.S. 624 (1943), at 642, 653.

34. Regarding the mandatory education required by states, when the Court approved of a child meeting that requirement by attending a parochial school, that did not mean the government was thereby forced to foot the bill for it since free public schools were an option. The latter question was not even raised. *Pierce vs. Society of Sisters*, 268 U.S. 510 (1925), yet ironically, in *Everson v. Board of Education*, 330 U.S. 1 (1947), the plaintiffs actually demanded the state pay for the parochial school students' transportation, while *not* extending it to other private schools.

35. Today's Religious Right's idea that the "wall of separation" was only an off-handed remark of Jefferson that does not reflect his or Madison's true views suggests those holding this have not read closely either Madison's *Memorial and Remonstrance* or Jefferson's *Bill on Religious Liberty* or their many other writings that reinforce this *explicit metaphor*. In the very quotation I ended this sentence in the body, quoting Jefferson, he spells out the "wall" quite precisely.

36. The benefit to *both* government and religion was considered by the Founders, not as one-sided, as merely protecting religion from government, but by freeing each side from the other, protecting both, so both could go about their proper business, and the nation could avoid the sordid history that preceded our ancestors' immigration from Europe.

37. Rawls argues that the principles arrived at through "public reason" are formative of "political justice," and religious or theological arguments are not based on "public reason" since "public reason" is open to argument, compromise, correction,

and cooperation, which religion, theology, and other comprehensive systems are not. He clarifies that "What is essential is that when persons with different convictions make conflicting demands on the basic structure as a matter of political principle, they are to judge these claims by the principles of justice. The principles that would be chosen in the original position are the kernel of political morality. They not only specify the terms of cooperation between persons but they define a pact of reconciliation between diverse religions and moral beliefs, and the forms of culture to which they belong." *A Theory of Justice*, 221. See also 211–220.

38. Rawls, *Political Liberalism*, 212–226. Some think the veil of ignorance makes any kind of negotiating of a social contract vacuous of any meaningful content, and others argue on what they see an unclarity about why "comprehensive doctrines" are not acceptable in the negotiating process yet can be judged as "perfectly reasonable" as Rawls does refer to them. See *Political Liberalism*, 24–25, esp. note 27 on those pages, as well as 10–11, and 243, 253, where he states that the "only comprehensive doctrines that run afoul of public reason are those that cannot support a reasonable balance of political values." One must be reminded that Rawls is saying the whole of this is *hypothetical* and abstract, not *historical*, so one surely can recognize the need to move the bargaining process beyond a mere contest between accidental or happenstance advantages which appeal to egocentrism. He clarified it more by saying the *representative* knows those he represents likely have reasonable comprehensive theories, and they may be firmly fixed, but he himself does *not* know the "content" of these conceptions of the "good" or how they relate to the peoples' aims or loyalties (*Political Liberalism*, 310–15). The bargaining of the social contract is still a hypothetical original position behind a veil of ignorance.

39. In an editorial note attached to James Madison's "Memorial and Remonstrance" of June 20, 1785, Rutland and others note that disestablishment had already become "an accomplished fact, a social system of declining interest in organized Christianity." That is, among those who emigrated as religious, the attraction of it dissipated in the New World once they got here. In their words, "Church-going in Virginia had long been on the decline as communicants found more reasons for attending Sunday horse races or cock fights than for being in pews." Rutland, *The Papers of James Madison*, 8: 295. This is the history of which so many Christians today are completely ignorant, the real facts. Interestingly, in the ancient "Pennsylvania Charter of Liberty, Laws Agreed Upon in England," etc. 1682, *Thorpe 5:3062–63*, in Kurland and Lerner (eds.), *Founders' Constitution*, V: 52, warns people that what offends God has been turned into law, so is not only "discouraged" but "severely punished" including "swearing, cursing, lying, prophane words, incest, sodomy, rapes, whoredom, fornication . . . treasons, misprisions, murders, duels, felony, seditions, maims, forcible entries . . . all prizes, stage-players, cards, dice, May-games, gamesters, masques, revels, bull-baitings, cock-fightings, bear-baitings, and the like." I guess "cock-fights" did not lose their attraction between 1682 and 1784, so still had more appeal than sitting "in pews."

40. *People v. Ruggles*, 8 Johns. R. 290 (N.Y. 1811), as cited in Kurland and Lerner (eds.), *Founders' Constitution,* V:101–02.

41. In Madison's *Memorial and Remonstrance*, he emphasized that "religion is *wholly* exempt from ['Civil Govments'] cognizance" (emphasis added), and that

being true, he argued, it certainly is wholly exempt from any legislative or judicial body. To imply that a "Civil Magistrate is a competent Judge of Religious Truth, or that he may employ Religion as an engine of Civil policy" is an "arrogant pretension" and an "unhallowed perversion of the means of salvation." Kurland and Lerner (eds.) *Founders' Constitution*, V:82–83. He warned again in his "Act for Establishing Religious Freedom," of October 31, 1785, "that to suffer the civil magistrate to intrude his powers into the field of opinion, and to restrain the profession or propagation of principles on supposition of their ill tendency, is a dangerous fallacy, which at once destroys all religious liberty, because he being of course judge of that tendency will make his opinions the rule of judgment; and approve or condemn the sentiments of others only as they shall square with or differ from his own." This, of course, is precisely what the Chief Justice Kent did, whereas Madison continued by using the same words Jefferson coined in his earlier Bill, "that it is time enough for the rightful purposes of civil government, for its officers to interfere when principles break out into overt acts against peace and good order." See *Madison Papers*, ed. Rutland, 8: 399–401.

42. It is an irony that some Justices have insisted that the religion clauses of the First Amendment applied only to the federal government, not to the states, but they have not insisted that all the other amendments are also only for the federal government, so that the separate states need not protect people's right to be free from unwarranted searches and seizures or from self-incrimination, and people in various states do not have freedom of speech, press, freedom to bear arms, and a right to trial by jury. When it became evident that any great variance between federal and state law could lead to chaos, the Bill of Rights *had* to be incorporated into the laws of the separate states; otherwise we would have a system of states fighting the federal government, simply placing the citizens of both in a confusingly, chaotic mess. This "incorporation" did take time with many of the "rights" of those amendments, just as the "equal rights" of the Fourteenth Amendment has still not been fully *actualized* in every state, even in its hypothetical theoretical presence. States like Alabama have still insisted they are free to establish their own religion if they desire, and any number of other laws have upset various states so much that some of their vocal legislators or leaders have suggested they might as a state just secede from the nation.

43. The difference between negative and positive laws becomes obvious at this point. For example, if one said "whatever you don't want others to do to you, don't do to them," it might take much less defining, if any, than if one said "whatever you want others to do to you, do so to them."

44. Whereas Thirteenth and Fifteenth Amendments are concerned with slaves or racial issues, Fourteenth is not so limited, but speaks of "persons" who are born or naturalized in the United States, so supposedly includes all women. Unfortunately, the sexist "servitude" was not yet recognized in the same magnitude as the racist servitude, so they had to wait another half a century. But if Fourteenth included women who were still not allowed to vote, it is unclear how they were "equal," receiving "due process."

45. See Rawls on the problem of money in campaigns, etc. *A Theory of Justice*, 226.

46. What is required for a "just social order" or for an equality of opportunity to exist is far beyond that usually conceived the U.S. culture. Its citizens need seriously to look more closely at many European nations who have been willing to have much higher taxes, not in order to build the world's best military, but to provide for the real needs of every citizen. See Derek L Phillips, *Toward a Just Social Order*. But, instead, even the people who often claim to suffer the most from the "elites" in the U.S. system continue inconsistently to run scared of the very word "socialism." It is a matter of priorities.

47. Rawls, *Political Liberalism*, 23.

48. See my *Ethics and the Future of Religion: Redefining the Absolute*.

49. In Kurland and Lerner (eds.), *Founders' Constitution*, V: 45–46.

50. Kurland and Lerner (eds.), *Founders' Constitution*, V: 46–48.

51. In Kurland and Lerner (eds.), *Founders' Constitution*, V: 49–50.

52. In Kurland and Lerner (eds.), *Founders' Constitution*, V: 48–52, #4 and 6,

53. Kurland and Lerner (eds.), *Founders' Constitution*, V: 51–52.

54. See note 53.

55. Kurland and Lerner (eds.), *Founders' Constitution*, V: 55–56.

56. Kurland and Lerner (eds.), *Founders' Constitution*, V: 70.

57. Kurland and Lerner (eds.), *Founders' Constitution*, V:71–72.

58. Kurland and Lerner (eds.), *Founders' Constitution*, V: 71.

59. Kurland and Lerner (eds.), *Founders' Constitution*, V: 71.

60. Kurland and Lerner (eds.), *Founders' Constitution*, V:70–71.

61. Kurland and Lerner (eds.), *Founders' Constitution*, V: 75.

62. Kurland and Lerner (eds.), *Founders' Constitution*, V: 76.

63. Kurland and Lerner (eds.), *Founders' Constitution*, V:77–78.

64. Kurland and Lerner (eds.), *Founders' Constitution*, V: 81–82.

65. Kurland and Lerner (eds.), *Founders' Constitution*, V: 98–99.

66. Kurland and Lerner (eds.), *Founders' Constitution*, V: 77.

Chapter 6

Religious "Free Exercise" to the Religious Freedom Restoration Act of 1993

The First Amendment's two-clause statement of religious freedom, like all the other Amendments, was paradoxically a federal law prohibiting the federal government ("Congress") from making laws which would limit or prohibit certain freedoms. So the Bill of Rights included not simply free exercise of religion but free speech, press, peaceable assembly to redress grievances against the government, and also freedom from coerced self-incrimination, from unreasonable searches and seizures, excessive bails and fines, and so forth. Several of the Amendments were positive laws in that the "right" was defined or circumscribed with some specifics, whereas the prohibitions of the First Amendment were pretty "bare bones."[1]

To make a law forbidding the making of a law in a certain area may seem a contradiction, but it must be remembered that many people lived in states that had all kinds of laws that restricted one's speech or religion, or redress of grievances or had excessive fines and punishments. Was this only a maneuver to prohibit the federal legislators from doing what some of the states still thought was good law, which, of course, would set federal law and state laws at odds with each other? That cannot be the case. When any Supreme Court Justice in the last 80 years has contended that the Bill of Rights was never meant to apply to the separate states, that was saying the Framers of the Constitution were merely trying to sow discord with it. But they were aware of the laws of various states, and they knew what they were doing, trying to *unify law* and a nation, even if that meant consolidating. No one wanted that to reduce the states to complete powerlessness, but a nation cannot exist with significant powers having opposite laws.

Despite the disestablishment that many states had already initiated, there were still state restrictions which the Constitutional Convention could understand as opposed to the federal standards. For example, the New York

Constitution of 1777 still prohibited a "minister" or "priest" from holding any political or military position, which itself violates the Constitution, Article VI (3). The Vermont Constitution of 1777 also spoke glowingly of religious liberty, freedom of worship, but felt it could require that as only being on the "Sabbath," and was sure it could also require the people to "support" financially such religious worship. The South Carolina Constitution of 1778 spoke of "freely" tolerating religious groups, but only as long as they were monotheistic, believing in a future state of rewards and punishments, and were Protestant. The Massachusetts Constitution of 1780 was seemingly more liberal with its religious freedom, so not limited to Protestants, but definitely still limited to Christians who were monotheistic. But some states such as Virginia and New Hampshire did not force specific rules onto the alleged "free exercise" of religion, but left it totally up to the people's consciences.

If the content of the amendments had been explicit counters to the specific mistreatment the colonies had to endure at the hands of the British, such as Amendments II through VI and VIII, even all the other Amendments of the first 10 had their roots in the *authoritarianism* the colonies had to put up with for which they blamed the King of England. None of the Amendments were intended only as a facade or a mere principle which most of the citizens were willing to cast aside. The people as a whole still felt completely vulnerable to foreign powers. The New Nation had no military, no funds to support one, and little desire to create one since they had seen how abusive it could be to its own citizens. The country was still trying to pay off the huge debts it incurred to fight the Revolutionary War. But no one wanted religions divisions to rack the New Nation, replicating the history of Europe from which their ancestors had fled. Hopefully, that inhumanity was behind.

The First Amendment's protection of the separation of government from religion was *not* intended to provide guidelines for litigation from either side, but to *preempt it*. Religion was *not* within the cognizance or jurisdiction of government, so the Founders were convinced the courts could not adjudicate anything of a religious nature. But many states not only still had laws which were definitely "religious laws" (among which the Sabbath or "blue" laws continued to exist even into the twenty-first century in a few states), but they had religious rituals from earlier Christian "establishment" whose violation of the First Amendment many citizens failed even to notice. That is only to have been expected since the separation of religion and government was new in the West, after 1,400 years of Christendom. But Jefferson's and Madison's specific words, with the Virginia "religious freedom" background which we have mentioned, pushed the freedom *beyond* a mere tolerance of different Christian sects to a freedom of conscience for people of *any* religion of the world or of nonreligion and atheism, as we previously saw, and opposed not only the accumulation of wealth by religious groups but also any administrative law to continue any residual religious habits, rituals, or forms of worship from any single religion.

The ideal was for civil and criminal laws to be framed and adjudicated from a complete *ignorance* of or legal indifference to anyone's religiousness or nonreligiousness, that no citizens would either experience less government benefits or more benefits by being religious or nonreligious. It was that simple. It was precisely the requirement Rawls injected into a hypothetical "original position" behind a "veil of ignorance." The government's laws have *nothing* to do with people's religious beliefs or worship, but, as citizens, all people, religious or nonreligious, are under the obligation of strict compliance with the nation's civil and criminal laws. The democratic government was formed as the will of the whole people with enough sense of unity and stability to provide for considerable differences among citizens, so long as all complied with the basic political conception of justice.

Thus, the Founders were trying to *avert any litigation* over religion. Otherwise, they surely would have defined what they meant by "religion," and whether any litigation could be resolved in state courts rather than federal courts. The Founders of the Constitution did not explicitly claim to have the authority to dictate to the states any law of the states, but the Articles of Confederation had revealed a toothless federal government which was unable to provide any stability to the nation, while diversity created colonial and state conflicts which lacked any method of resolution. This weakness was the main one prompting the Constitution. On the other hand, if the states would necessarily have to align their standards with the federal, rather than split the nation, and no "Congress" was allowed to make laws pertaining to the "establishment of religion or prohibiting the free exercise thereof," that simply meant *no laws would exist* pertaining to religion.

That was possible only so long as no litigation arose, but when that occurred, it placed the *Court* into the unenviable position of being not just the adjudicator but also the lawmaker since most decisions actually do *create new* common law. But how could that be if Madison and Jefferson were correct, that civil government had no cognizance (or jurisdiction) of religion since the latter was only a private matter between a person and whatever deity, if any, in which she believed.

At first, the Court could have avoided this by approaching the litigation only from the neutral laws or ethical presuppositions it saw behind cultural legal standards or practices. But when it began to judge the cases by the other elements of the First Amendment, the freedom of speech or right of assembly, neither one of which had any more specific definition than did the religion clauses, the temptation of consistency between the different phrases was perhaps too much. Of course, the Court usually addresses the issues specifically raised in the lower court, which means the appeal to the "free exercise" of religion was used by the party claiming actual damage.[2] Thus, the problem was intensified not only by vagueness, but by conflating "religion" with speech rights, and that with actual damages which implied vested interests, the latter of which is simply not a vehicle for determining justice since it ignores Rawls's "veil of ignorance."

Once the Court distinguished in this sense by separating the "free exercise" clause from the "establishment" clause and adding it to the "freedom of speech," it was only a matter of time until people realized that perhaps "establishment" and "free exercise" were not just opposite kinds of words but actually *separate spheres*. Once referred to that way, rather than being viewed as a *single* "freedom from religious establishment," the separation of them quickly developed in litigation as having an *inverse effect* on each other. Perhaps it was not apparent to the Court that a distinction should *instead* be made between the *government and religion* in terms of authority, claims, reason, scope, and comportment, which could have eliminated any need for making laws about "religion." But once Pandora's box was opened, despite the Court's continual reluctance to further define "religion" or what was "central" to it, it eventually did measure what was "central" to it in cases of non-Christian religions such as the Native American and the Santeria religions, and based many decisions on that over which Madison and Jefferson said the civil government simply had no cognizance or jurisdiction.

In order to get the most from the little summary of cases I present in the following chapters, it is important to remember not only the basic elements of Rawls's theory of justice, including (1) his "veil of ignorance" to eliminate all advantages of accidental inequality of economic or social status over other people by a compensation through equality of opportunity and any law in question being for the benefit of the "least advantaged"; and (2) his distinction between public reason of the social contract or basic principles of the "original position" and Constitution vis-à-vis the nonpublic reason of associations. But it is also important to judge a case by seeing what was the primary motif in the approaches by the Framers of the Constitution such as Madison and Jefferson, and what was the underlying meaning and unity of the two religion clauses of the First Amendment for which they fought. It is also necessary to recall that Rawls, Madison, and Jefferson were all attempting to form a democratic society which would provide a sense of unity, trust, and stability while allowing maximum liberty of conscience or mutual autonomy—valuing "life, liberty and happiness"—so long as the primary principles underlying the structures of justice have priority to which all citizens strictly comply.[3]

The reader should bear these in mind, combined with the historical fact that the "free exercise," as background to the meaning of the First Amendment, always meant *only* "worship" until the past few years.[4] Finally, one should recall the implicit values of "mutual autonomy," "trust," and the common *instinctual* "will-to-live" (Schweitzer) or "will-to-power" (Nietzsche) and Rawls's theory of the necessary agreement or social contract in a democratic society, all of which help update and clarify the positions of the Constitution's Framers—as we progress quickly through the various "Free Exercise" cases in this chapter and chapters 7 and 8. In the final three chapters, we will focus on the "establishment" cases. Thus, the intention of the Framers is important, but ultimately, if the United States is attempting to have a democracy, the present generation must always subject all earlier interpretations to its own unique situation, since all interpretations come from different perspectives with unique and even unspoken, if not unrecognized, presuppositions. What is ultimately important and normative is what *each generation agrees to*[5] since the final authority in a democracy ends up being only those presently living citizens, as they struggle to interpret their present in the light of their inherited political foundations such as their Constitution, including the disparate interpretations the latter has received over the years.

Prior to the twentieth century, the "Civil War Amendments" (Thirteenth, Fourteenth, and Fifteenth, 1865, 1868, and 1870) added a new dimension of law. They abolished slavery de jure, though not de facto, recognized all persons born or naturalized in the United States as citizens both of the United States as well as the state in which they reside, and prohibited any state from making laws or enforcing present state laws which in any way "abridge the privileges or immunities of citizens of the United States; nor shall any State deprive any person of life, liberty, or property, without due process of law; nor deny to any person within its jurisdiction the equal protection of the law." The final Amendment provided the right to vote to every citizen, not to be abridged by the United States or any State "on account of race, color, or previous condition of servitude."[6] This surely remains basic to the democracy of the United States, having priority over the "big lie" that the 2020 election was fraudulent, as several states now frame laws to suppress voting, despite the fact that those in charge of the security of the 2020 election have found nothing fraudulent, and it was declared by the Republican placed in charge of its security, as the most secure election on record.[7]

Between the Civil War Amendments and 1940, when the "Free Exercise" clause was said to be "incorporated" into state law *explicitly*, many aspects of other federal laws were already "incorporated" into state law through especially the "equal protection" and "due process" clauses found within the content of the Civil War Amendments, though it was a gradual process, since some feared it would overrule states' sovereignty to enforce a "total incorporation."[8] But who really supposes that responsible legislators or judges would think it was best to have conflicting state and federal laws? The "incorporation" obviously was intended to unify the law just as the Constitutional Convention called under the Articles of Confederation was intended by many to supersede the Articles with a valid Constitution to unify. That is not duplicity but common sense.

Two religion cases appeared in 1879 and 1890, both of which involved the issue of polygamy and the Mormon church. The church was originated by Joseph Smith. Upon his death in Illinois, he was succeeded by Brigham Young. The people seeking a land in which they could flourish finally arrived in Utah in 1847. Five years later, the "secret" of Joseph Smith about the necessity of the revelation of plural marriage came to light. Five years after that, U.S. president Buchanan replaced Brigham Young with a non-Mormon as the territorial governor, and a territorial war broke out with the slaughter of a "peaceful group of California-bound settlers."[9]

In the first polygamy case in Utah, *Reynolds v. United States*, 98 U.S. 145 (1879), the Court ruled that the Act of Congress in 1862 that made polygamy illegal was not a violation of people's "free exercise" of religion. The Bill was judged as having a legitimate interest in "good order" or "social order," so the test was not the strength of the religious person's conviction but whether to grant such freedom to have more than one wife would violate the legitimate police powers of the state, the health, safety, welfare, and morals of the citizens. The Court argued that obviously the state cannot allow each person to become a law to himself, or it could even condone religiously induced suicide or human sacrifices.

Eleven years later, in *Davis v. Beason*, 133 U.S. 333 (1890), the Court again ruled in an Idaho case that it was not a violation of one's "free exercise" of religion to require its electors to swear that they were neither bigamists nor polygamists, nor belonged to any organization that encouraged such. Again, it had nothing to do with worship, so the case should have come only from state prosecutors based on state civil and criminal law, not religious belief. Appellants had perjured themselves and obstructed justice. The Court was adamant that "[f]ew crimes are more pernicious to the best interests of society." It saw this claim of the practice being a part of religion as an offense to the "common sense of mankind." Religious beliefs are free, but religious action must be subordinate to the criminal laws of the country. This was clear enough: anything that violates civil or criminal law which *all* citizens must comply with cannot be overruled by a person's claim to "free exercise" of his or her religion. So the decision seems correct but sadly opened up more possibilities of litigation over one's "free exercise" of religion rather than the state squelching it by insisting government law has priority in a democracy.[10]

"CONSCIENTIOUS OBJECTORS" AND DRAFT
LAWS BUILT ON RELIGIOUS CONVICTION

As we will see when we examine the cases after the "incorporation" of the religion clauses into state law, a "free exercise" claim could have been based strictly on neutral civil and criminal law without ever mentioning religions, as Madison and Jefferson seem to have intended, without getting into what kinds of "free exercise" of religion would be protected and what would not. But the early cases mixed "free speech" rights with the "free exercise" of religion, thereby giving the impression that decisions could be based strictly on either one, so "free exercise" claims would be sufficient in themselves. Jefferson and Madison had seen it as the reverse, the government could intervene in religion *only* when it could make a case of the person violating generally applicable neutral laws that *all* must obey. But then, if the Court's decisions themselves could form new law, if the Court separated the religious element from the generally applicable law for all citizens, this means Congress would be *making laws* that had strictly a religious purpose or content, which would explicitly violate the First Amendment.

In fact, Congress did this very thing. For example, Congress passed laws relating to the military draft which would enable *only religious* people to object to carrying arms, and therefore exempt them from such, allowing them to serve instead as "conscientious objectors" in noncombatant roles if they met Congress' requirements. Yet, by 1971, the Court's own "*Lemon*" test for Establishment adjudication would have made all these laws pertaining to the "CO" status in the armed services quite illegal, but for some strange reason, they were never seen that way at all. The "*Lemon*" test by 1971 had insisted that in order not to be an illegal establishment of religion, the law must have a primary *secular purpose*, primary *secular effect*, and must not create an *excessive entanglement* between government and religion (such as continual monitoring by the government). Thus, under Establishment criteria, a law having a strictly religious purpose or effect would be *illegal*, yet, ironically, within Free Exercise criteria, a claim by an individual *had* to show his intended and effected religious exercise was being violated by some governmental law. To resolve the latter problem meant a Court decision or governmental decision which would serve as a *religious law* to nullify some conflicting religious law or an antireligious law. That is fairly convoluted. One can quickly see that a sharp attorney who wanted to serve his religious client well would move a case out of the establishment area into the free exercise sphere, especially after the Court found that people lost in Establishment cases when the Court was able to detect an actual religious purpose instead of the sham purpose which they otherwise claimed.

Even though the nation no longer has a military draft, the process of the evolution of this particular issue has relevance even today since the Selective Service still enables people to serve in an "alternative" nonmilitary service or in a military noncombatant service. The former requirement of one having religious objections to the type of service he designates has been broadened to religious *or* moral, and cannot be determined by political preference or for merely personal reasons. But the broadening of the *source* of the conviction into one that might be moral instead of purely religious came through a very gradual evolution. The Court heard cases in 1929, 1931, 1934, and for a variety of reasons, ruled against all these men who were conscientiously opposed to bearing arms.[11]

Finally, in *Girouard v. United States*, 328 U.S. 61 (1946), which was six years after the "free exercise" clause had been "incorporated" into state law by *Cantwell v. Connecticut*, the Court overruled the three earlier cases in finding for Girouard.[12] It decided that it was an illegal violation of a person's "free exercise" to construe the Naturalization statute as requiring those applying for citizenship to promise to bear arms so that even a willingness to serve as a noncombatant would not satisfy the oath they took. The Court argued that the oath they were required to take was only to defend the country, but *not* necessarily as an armed combatant, and had the petitioner in this case served as a noncombatant in the previous war, he would now have been awarded citizenship.

By the time of the next "CO" case, the United States had become embroiled in the Vietnam War which was a very divisive event for much of the U.S. population. Many saw the U.S. involvement in it as unjustified or manipulated, and the massive use of napalm an indiscriminate form of killing and defoliation of the country. Thousands of young U.S. men fled to Canada to avoid the draft. The Selective Service required that the person applying for "CO" status had to have been trained in some *religious institution* to believe both in a "Supreme Being" as well as that bearing arms was wrong. The Court, in *United States v. Seeger*, 380 U.S. 163 (1965) found these requirements, however, as an unlawful violation of Seeger's "free exercise" of his religion. Instead, it emphasized that the exemption should be available to anyone whose belief occupies a place in his life that would be parallel to the effect of the orthodox belief in God. It even cited Christian theologian Paul Tillich's idea of "God above God" or "ultimate concern" as having a similar function, and perhaps even being superior to a mere theistic belief in a "Supreme Being," which I have designated as the "Absolute."[13] The idea of "free exercise" of one's religion here never addressed the former limitation of "worship," even if it no longer required a "religious" affiliation but simply an ethical conviction that was as absolute as that of a typical religion.

Five years later, in *Welsh v. United States*, 398 U.S. 333 (1970), the Court again found an unlawful violation of Welsh's "free exercise" since his belief was similar to Seeger's in the above case, but the only difference was that he insisted that he was *not religious*, so he derived his opposition to war from the sum total of his experiences. Since, however, the regulations *forbid* that the opposition to war could come merely from political, sociological, or philosophical areas, which was precisely what he was claiming, and that would have prevented him from gaining the exemption, the Court insisted again that his belief *is essentially religious* since it *functions* in a way similar to religious belief. The original draft laws in the CO classification were totally biased for *religious* people in allowing *only* them to be exempt from the draft, although the Court did not argue or admit that bias. Rather than the Court decide that the law did not treat citizens equally and fairly, that the law must be religiously neutral, that the same civil and criminal laws must be applied equally to *all* citizens, and when it is not, it must be struck down, whether it is religious or not—they simply *exacerbated the problem* once again by extending Free Exercise privileges further, but merely on the basis of the Court's redefining "religion" to make it *opposite* to the meaning it had in the law in question, to people who even considered themselves *nonreligious.* If this person could be exempted from the war because he was "religious" despite the fact that he said he was *not*, then *anyone* opposed to the war could have qualified as "religious," whether they claimed to be religious or not, so all should have been exempt.

But the Court failed to recognize the precedent it was setting. Had the Court, instead, decided that the *religious base of the law* was itself in violation of the First Amendment which was never intended to release people from neutral, generally applicable laws, never intended to give religious people special favors or status for which nonreligious people could not qualify, the Court would not have had to wring such a tortuous meaning out of a statute which was obviously the very *opposite* of its exact words and explicitly originally intended meaning. This points out the problem between the two religion clauses of the First Amendment, once they are separated from each other, especially once the Court in *Lemon* in the following year of 1971, would decide that a religious purpose of a law can make the law an illegal establishment.

Finally, in *Gillette v. United States, and Negre v. Larsen*, 401 U.S. 437 (1971), the Court ruled that it was quite legal for CO applicants to be required to object to *all* war, but *not* simply to object to one particular war as being "unjust." The Court saw the latter's focus on the "justice" of a war being far too subjective, nonconscientious, and even political rather than religious. In all this, it becomes obvious that the entire discussion of what is ethical was submerged for the most part, covered up by the question of whether one's convictions had an objective "religious" base or the equivalent function.[14] That seems to have meant the function of an "Absolute" again, so was *not* something subject to one's own reason or reasonable alteration by "public reason" over time, which is precisely why religion, as Rawls saw it, can*not* be involved in dictating the policies of structural justice. Those standards or laws must be based on "freestanding" ethical principles which come from public reason and can be finally seen as "overlapping" enough to enable a consensus to be visible from which the social contract's basic principles are articulated and appeal to *all* without any favoritism, coercion, or negative bias.

JEHOVAH'S WITNESS, AMISH AND KRISHNA CASES: "INCORPORATION" OF THE "FREE EXERCISE" CLAUSE

We must return back to 1940, to see the actual time of the "incorporation" of the "Free Exercise" clause for the first time to state law in *Cantwell v. Connecticut*, 310 U.S. 296 (1940), through the equal rights of the Fourteenth Amendment's "due process" rule.[15] One specific aspect of this form of litigation of Free Exercise involved parties that were outside mainstream Christian circles or even of non-Christian status. In the *Cantwell* case, a man and his two sons, ministers of the Jehovah's Witness Church, were arrested in New Haven, Connecticut, for soliciting without a license and for inciting a breach of the peace. They had been going door to door with pamphlets, books, and records with a turntable, requesting to play a record which followed one of the books they wanted to sell, a record which was very anti-Catholic. The Jehovah's Witnesses requested permission to speak and play a record for two men, who, upon hearing the anti-Catholic dogma on the record, were deeply offended and turned the three Jehovah's Witnesses away. They were convicted by the lower courts.

Upon examination of the statute they allegedly breached by the solicitation without a license, the Supreme Court simply insisted that to give not just ministerial but discretionary power to a local government employee to decide on his or her own—without any government criteria, which groups applying for licenses to canvass the town qualified as "religious" and "charitable" and which did not—comprised a "previous" or "prior restraint" on speech, and in this case, religious speech or his "Free Exercise" of religion.[16] The discretionary power exercised by the clerk was illegal. The Court emphasized that the

constitutional inhibition of legislation on the subject of religion has a double aspect. On the one hand, it forestalls compulsion by law of the acceptance of any creed or the practice of any form of worship. Freedom of conscience and freedom to adhere to such religious organization or form of worship as the individual may choose cannot be restricted by law. On the other hand, it safeguards the free exercise of the chosen form of religion. Thus, the Amendment embraces two concepts—freedom to believe and freedom to act. The first is absolute, but, in the nature of things, the second cannot be. Conduct remains subject to regulation for the protection of society.[17]

The Court held that this clearly did infringe that freedom, and additionally, his actions did not in any way incite any breach of the peace, so reversed the holding of the lower court. The case was actually solved as a prior restraint on free speech and could have been left at that.

Other cases decided in 1940, 1942, and 1943 were later *overruled* by subsequent cases which we analyze below. In 1941, in *Cox v. New Hampshire*, 312 U.S. 569, the Court easily ruled that it was *not* a violation of parties' Free Exercise rights to require a special license prior to their forming any parade or march on the public streets. The license requirement here was seen as a reasonable time, place, and manner restriction on free speech from the state's strong interest in public safety. It had no need of bringing up people's "free exercise" of religion.

Ironically, two years later, in *Murdock v. Pennsylvania*, 319 U.S. 105 (1943), the Court vacated the *Opelika* decisions of 1942 and 1943. The *Murdock* Court found that to require expensive licenses for the door-to-door canvassing, while *not* requiring others such as Fuller Brush salesmen to buy the license, *was* an illegal flat tax on *religion*. Whether the expense of the license was the issue, or its singling out of religious solicitation, the Court bought the idea that canvassing was the Jehovah's Witness' *preaching*, a form of *worship*. The latter opened up Pandora's box for the future, when the Court could have left it as simply a Free Speech decision.

In the same year, *West Virginia State Board of Education v. Barnette*, 319 U.S. 624 (1943) also involved the Court's overturning of a rather similar case in which it had ruled against the Jehovah's Witnesses in *Minersville School District v. Gobitis*, 310 U.S. 586 (1940). In *Gobitis*, the Court insisted that religious freedom *never* gave a person a right to violate nonreligious social and political concerns of the society, and since the flag is a symbol of ordered society, thus of national unity, it has to be protected and honored. But in *Barnette*, the justification of the law as a symbolical claim of national unity was rejected by the Jehovah's Witnesses as a form of *idolatry*, only exacerbated by the legal coercion. The Court pushed the protection of religion even further, insisting that *any* law that infringes upon one's "free exercise" of religion must meet a "compelling interest" test, not simply a "rational basis" test. This became crucial for later litigation.

The Court attempted to justify this high standard by emphasizing that people's rights to life, liberty, property, free speech, press, freedom of assembly and of worship were all beyond the reach of majorities or officials, open to no vote.[18] The Court also insisted that government could not decide what was "orthodox" in religion, and the freedom to differ had to include "the right to differ as to things that touch the heart of the existing order."[19] It noted that if the law in question had the purpose of trying to build patriotism, it likely actually had the opposite effect here.

While J. Jackson wrote profoundly about tolerating difference which a democracy requires, did this mean that now *anyone* could define *legally* what true "worship" was and what "idolatry" was and the Court would be bound by that? Surely not. The Court held that if these rights were infringed by state law, it could *only* be to "prevent grave and immediate danger to interests which the state may lawfully protect." But there were no such articulated "grave and immediate dangers" to the state in these prior "free exercise" cases. This raises the basic issue between "public reason" and "nonpublic" reason in Rawls, whether anyone in the original position and its veil of ignorance would have been willing for a nonpublic reason to have priority over the "overlapping consensus" of the social contract built on "public reason."

If the Court could distinguish freedom to believe from freedom to act, it surely also could have argued as Jefferson and Madison that government has no power *to increase or diminish* a citizen's general benefits, status, *or responsibilities* depending upon whether the person claims to be religious or nonreligious. Instead, now the door was open to religious people claiming an exemption to a strict compliance of facially neutral laws by their claim of "free exercise" that had *nothing* to do with worship. The lawmakers themselves were possibly at fault, shortsighted, thinking they could mandate a national flag salute, but this was in the middle of WWII and the raised-arm salute in the United States was similar to the "Heil, Hitler!" salute with raised arm.

But what possible interests could be so "compelling" as to segregate the population into the "religious" who were *exempt* from the universally applicable neutral laws that all others had to follow, and where would this claim of "free exercise" request for exemption end up?

Prince v. Massachusetts, 321 U.S. 158 (1944), added to the Jehovah Witness religious canvassing the presence of a nine-year-old child accompanying the parent. If the canvassing was truly their form of "worship," so deserving free exercise protection, it should have been also determinative here. But instead, the activity was placed under the heading of "police powers," and the health, welfare, safety, and morals of the child became paramount and were not diminished by the mere presence of the parent. Yet there was no showing of any potential danger to the child. Instead, it was sufficient to insist that the state's child labor laws prohibited a nine-year-old child from selling books on the streets although in the continual presence of the parent and despite the fact that there was no showing of the child *actually* involved in the selling or being in any danger as regards its health, welfare, safety, or morals, but the police powers prevailed as "compelling."[20]

The Amish, who came from the more radically conservative branch of the Reformation, lived in communes, as farmers, often conspicuous for their refusal to consume the most up-to-date clothes, styles, conveniences, or even necessary tools, and were people who actually tried to be inconspicuous as they attempted not to be "conformed" to the evil world. By *Wisconsin v. Yoder*, 406 U.S. 205 (1972), the Wisconsin law of mandatory education of all children up to the age of 16, which was facially neutral and universally applicable, was *rejected* by the Court. The Court insisted that any law prohibiting or even significantly burdening one's "free exercise" of religion could be constitutional *only* if the state could prove that it had not merely a reason but was protecting its interest of the "highest order," which usually meant the typical police powers of the state: health, safety, welfare, and morals of the citizens, the equivalent of a "compelling" state interest. Mandatory education, of course, *was* a part of the "welfare" if not also of the "morals" the state was protecting, so in most situations should have been considered an interest of this "highest order" or "compelling state interest."

But not so here. The focus on the need for further education, and the means by which to accomplish it, was solved by the Court's assumption that the vocational training the girls would receive *at home* during ages 14–16 would be most appropriate and effective in their fitting into the adult Amish community. The Court said that evidence showed the Amish to have achieved a self-reliance which has sustained the community for more than two centuries without them becoming a burden to the nation or without their young people's vocational (farming) expertise depriving other non-Amish adults of jobs. This makes the whole case sound as if it were decided strictly along economic lines, with little or no consideration of what the lifetime goals of the students might be. What seems to count for the Court is that the community is self-sustaining and not a burden to the government nor causing any unemployment of other citizens. This means the Court assumed that all the students would simply continue on the family farm and never want anything different. In a country that saw the public as well as individual value of a liberal education for all students, this is a *strange approach* to the issue of extensive public education, including "higher education," especially for Supreme Court Justices to manifest. During this same time, many if not most young children throughout the nation were, upon high school graduation, leaving the farms either to go to college or to work in the more exciting cities.

Dissenting J. Douglas emphasized that the children's own interests in education should not be so ignored, and their education so tunneled in vision, since one could *not* assume they would all simply stay forever on the family farms. If their education were allowed to end with the eighth grade, they might be ill fitted to compete for jobs in other settings once they left the farm, especially if they ended up in metropolitan areas. The Court, however, discounted both the suggestion that they might leave the farm, and if so, might be ill prepared educationally to compete in the job market, insisting that the children's interests were *not at issue* in this case, but only their parents' interests in their children's futures, and that the children were being taught to be self-sustaining and productive. The Court *referred* to the interests of the parents and interests of the state requiring this "balancing test."

By the state's failure to show its interest as truly of the "highest order," or "compelling state interest" which could not be met by any less restrictive means, the Court felt justified in "accommodating" the religious group. The Court decided the case *without* any in-depth "balancing" of possibly competing interests. Of course, the Court was also warned that to overturn this Amish scheme of education for their children might actually lead to the breakdown of the whole religious group over time, and that prospect of possibly inducing a factor which could be the ultimate *demise of this religion* was unthinkable to the Court. It did not want to be accused of being hostile to a religion. So we see that the "free exercise" decisions quickly became progressively further removed from a mere *freedom to worship* as one chooses.

In the Amish case of *U.S. v. Lee*, 455 U.S. 2552 (1982), Lee was a self-employed minister, Amish farmer, who employed other workers for his farm. The Court pointed out that as a minister, he was self-employed and could *elect not* to have or pay into Social Security for himself, but he could *not* refuse to pay Social Security for his farm workers who were not ministers. The Court insisted in *Lee* that the "state may justify a limitation on religious liberty by showing that it is essential to accomplish an overriding governmental interest." Even if this law burdens the Amish way of life, not all social concerns can be eliminated or dictated by particular religious groups. Renowned Constitutional scholar, Laurence Tribe, noted that *Lee* seems to have weakened both aspects of the required state's showing, that is, that the law pursues a compelling state interest and that the "state's means of pursuing that interest present the lowest possible burden on the claimant's religion." More specifically, he explained, "previous cases required the state to show that it was pursuing a compelling interest, *narrowly* defined, and that an exemption would defeat that interest; *Lee* seems to require the state to show only that it is pursuing a compelling interest, *broadly* defined, and that an exemption would 'unduly interfere' with that interest."[21]

But why were there *any* exceptions given to the Social Security mandate and coverage, that is, why were *only religious leaders* given the option of either participating in Social Security or not, and given only a short period of their early professional years to decide permanently one way or the other? Was that original exemption only for the religiously ordained, a law to appease their religious institutions which did not want to have to pay their part of the Social Security taxes, or was it based upon some theological reason the clergy itself had about such a program, or was it because clergy were paid so little that the legislators who framed the rules of Social Security figured most of them would not be able to afford it? In any case, this decision by the Court is clear regarding employees and their employer submitting to the requirement of Social Security as a facially neutral, generally applicable law for employees.

The Krishna Consciousness Group has experienced much less success than the Jehovah's Witnesses in a similar attempt to confront people directly with their religious beliefs and literature. In *Heffron v. International Society for Krishna Consciousness*, 452 U.S. 263 (1981), the Court ruled that the state of Minnesota law restricting their attempts to proselytize was *not* a violation of their "free exercise." The regulation in question permitted them to talk with people at the state fair but to confine their activity, as all others did, to a booth. The state claimed the safety of the sizable crowds required this kind of regulation rather than simply allowing any group that wanted to wander around freely, involving one-to-one confrontation all over the fairgrounds, and the Court accepted the state's argument.

A few years later, in *International Society for Krishna Consciousness, Inc. v. Walter Lee*, 505 U.S. 672 (1992), the New York Port Authority restrictions on solicitation inside the airport terminals were challenged. In the question of whether or not the restrictions violated free speech and free exercise of religion, the Court, in a 6/3 decision said they did not. The Krishna Consciousness group, an obvious important sect of the Hindu religion, engaged in a similar activity as Jehovah's Witness except they went where there were larger crowds of people, yet the people, unlike many in the Jehovah Witnesses activity, had no expectation of privacy since they were not being confronted in their own homes. The Krishna group claimed their "Sankirtan" as a religious ritual responsibility they had, just as Jehovah's Witnesses claimed their door-to-door solicitation as their form of preaching, ministry, or worship. The Court agreed with the Port Authority that the airport terminal buildings were actually private property and far too busy to be considered as public forums. The rules prohibiting any kind of solicitation within the buildings were quite reasonable, as the Court saw it, since the Port Authority allowed the group to use the sidewalks in front of the buildings to spread their message.

In a related case, which came from the lower court with the opposite result, the question was posed whether the Port Authority's ban on any and all distribution of literature within the airport terminal was a violation of free speech and the free exercise of religion. So, on the same day as the other case, 6/26/92, in *Walter Lee v. International Society for Krishna Consciousness, Inc.*, 505 U.S. 830 (1992), because of the split on the other issue, the Court reached a per Curium 5/4 decision that it *was* an illegal ban by the Port Authority despite dissenting Justices depicting how messy the terminal floor might be with all the dropped pamphlets. Again, why questions which focused primarily on whether a forum was public or not should have any bearing on religion is the problem. It, like most of the earlier cases of "free exercise," could have been resolved strictly by laws pertaining to speech and assembly or the safety hazard if the literature was actually strewn all over the floor, without having to rule anything about religion, and that would have kept religion separated from government as Madison and Jefferson and all the others proposed in the First Amendment, so that government would have "made no law" about religion as the Amendment reads.

Where the Court could possibly draw the line on religious speech once it had made it quite legal in door-to-door solicitation which is never considered a "public forum" – "became uncertain." Surely, even the great divider of the airport terminal doors could not have provided anything significantly different in the situation if the real problem was the congestion, haste, and inconvenience to airline passengers, nor could the content of the speech or the pamphlets have made any difference, whether the people were trying to convert people to a religion, sell raffle tickets from a local club to win a new car, or trying to give free advice on proper dieting. General, neutral, universally applicable laws should have been able to handle everything, *except* the Court, through *former decisions*, had unnecessarily *enabled* religious people to gain *exemptions* from those kinds of laws by pleading their "free exercise" of religion.

But rather than ending the specious claims for exemptions, they continued to expand from 1982 to the present. Would it be disingenuous to suggest that Madison and others had been able to envision a similar situation if the government got itself involved in an area of which it had "no cognizance"? The next thing on its agenda seemed to be whether the Court should determine whether to call a day "holy" or only "secular," and similar sorts of decisions. In the following determinations it had to make, it predictably contradicted itself time after time. The only thing that might have been predicted was that the Court would rule primarily *for* Christian litigants and not often for others unless such ruling would at least indirectly also benefit Christians. But let the following Court decisions speak for themselves.

Once the Court had determined that a "free exercise" can require a show-ing by the government that it has a "compelling state interest" or interest of a "higher order" rather than simply the law's "rational basis," as it asserted in *Barnette*, the question was unsettled as to what specifically could comprise that "higher order" of interest by the state. Would any and every generally appli-cable law of the government be this "compelling interest," and, if not, would it be only a few? Specifically what principles would enable any drawing of a line between laws that had only a "rational basis" and those that had a "compelling interest"? One would think that the common police powers of a state *would* be of the "highest order" of interest, yet the terminology worked the other way. The interest the state had to show was only a rational basis when it came to such areas as the typical police power of the health, safety, welfare, and morals of the citizenry, which means that here the government's interest was so great that one did not have to show anything more than a conceivable rational basis since few if any people would contest those particular interests of the state.

This means that the "compelling" or "higher" order interests would be interests which the state could explain which were *not* as widely known or recognized as the legitimate police power, so it required much more specific argument and proof to convince. This meant that the government would have a *more difficult* time defending its laws that restricted the "free exercise" than it did other laws which required only a "rational basis." Though the "compel-ling interest" test was also called a "balancing test" in which the individual interests and those of the government were weighed against each other, it still put more of a burden on government than did laws that needed only a show-ing of a "rational basis," since nearly any law could be justified by some form of a conceivable reason.

The question was what would constitute a showing of a compelling interest if the law being challenged by the individual was an obvious *neutral, gen-erally applicable law* with which *all* citizens are expected to comply? That remains the real question even today. But how could a law be considered applicable to all citizens while still being open to anyone to challenge, but *only* if the person claimed the law violated her "free exercise" of religion? Why would such not be a *preferential* treatment for religious people, relegat-ing all others to the status of "second-class" citizens? That was explicitly opposed by Madison, Jefferson, and their peers.

SUPREME COURT DECISIONS ON "FREE EXERCISE" FOR HOLY DAYS, SITES, AND SACRED RITUALS

In 1961, several "Blue law" cases were decided, which focused on the observance of the Sabbath. Before explaining them in their complexity, another case in the same year, though not related to holy days, shows how some state laws still conflicted with the Federal Constitution. In 1961, in *Torcaso v. Watkins*, 267 U.S. 488, the Court had to deal with the Maryland state law which required a candidate for the public office of a Notary Public to declare his belief in the existence of God, an obvious residual law from former times. The *Maryland Constitution* of 1776, number XXXVI *did* require a public officer to swear his support and fidelity to the state but also supply "a declaration of a belief in the Christian religion," of a belief in one God. But Torcaso was an honest atheist. While the Court of Appeals ruled against him, saying he was not being forced to take the job, the Supreme Court unanimously overruled the Court of Appeals, insisting that the Federal Constitution explicitly prohibited any such test to hold public office.

Even more unexpected and weird were four "Blue law" cases, which I will generalize with primary reference to only one of them: *McGowan v. Maryland*, 366 U.S. 420 (1961).[22] All the cases involved Orthodox Jewish merchants, especially those who were developing department or discount stores. They had to observe their Shabbat (sunset Friday to sunset Saturday), the original and real Sabbath, but they were prohibited by government from doing business on Sunday by the "blue laws" which came from Christian misappropriation of the Jewish Shabbat many centuries prior, extremely old laws that existed in Christendom long before the establishment of the Colonies, and these laws even in England were part of an official "established" Christian religion. By 1961, after 200 years of living under the First Amendment, the United States did *not* have an official "established" religion. Or was the "establishment" merely more subtle, a residue of former theocracies?

Because the Court chose *not* to discuss the *historical fact* that these Sabbath restrictions were *always* a part of an "established" religion, a presupposed "theocracy" of some sort, whether in Ancient Israel or in sixteenth-century England or some of the early colonies in what became the United States—the very thing the First Amendment legislates *against*—the Court *rejected* the Jewish allegations that the Christian bias of the "blue laws" was an unconstitutional "*establishment*" of religion. It instead switched gears in the analysis and insisted that the "*free exercise*" of religion by the Jewish merchants was *not* being affected by any law governing Christian worship. The latter was mostly true—so long as the Jewish merchants did not mind going bankrupt. All the Court could reply was that it could not help it if people's religion made it more expensive for them to do business. Strangely, the dissent by J. Brennan, which said people should *not* have to choose between their religion and their work, became the new rule in *Sherbert v. Verner*, just *two years later*, revealing the *anomaly and Christian bias* of these decisions *against* these Jewish merchants in 1961 while it was *for* a Christian worker in 1963.

In *McGowan* and its parallel cases, the Court ruled that the "secular" purpose in the Sabbath laws had always been recognized, so they were not simply religious laws, which would have violated the "establishment" clause had they been simply religious laws. Further, the Court opined that the secular purpose of a day of rest and relaxation needed to be a *uniform* day throughout the country, an argument they propounded without any proof, and they more specifically determined that the uniform day of rest should be Sunday or the Christian Sabbath. The Court never acknowledged the strictly Jewish understanding of the Shabbat, but instead gave preference to the Christianizing of the particular day, and therefore said *it* (Sunday) should be seen as no longer having any primary religious reference but only secular.

The Court would have been surprised to have seen the ancient Christian writing, the *Didache*, of the second century, in which the author insisted that the Christians must *not* be mistaken for Jews, so therefore must meet only on *Sunday*, "the day of the sun," and the day Jesus was raised from death, *rather than the Jewish Shabbat*. Eventually the Christians began to refer to Sunday as the genuine Shabbat, just as some of them spoke of Christians as the "true Israel." It was *totally religious*. So *when* did Sunday lose its religious significance enough to be understood only as the "day of rest" for all people?

The Court *admitted* in all these cases that *originally* the Sabbath restrictions were religious, but it was convinced that the Sabbath had now evolved into being totally secular. It completely overlooked the religious overtones of the actual Blue laws which *insisted* on restrictions primarily during the Sunday worship hours of the Christian churches, but otherwise allowed all kinds of commercial transactions and recreational behavior in the afternoons. The Jewish merchants here were being accused of violating a law for selling innocuous items on Sunday such as a loose-leaf binder, a can of floor wax, a stapler, staples, and a toy. Had they instead sold tobacco, liquor, gasoline, drugs, newspapers, certain groceries, or tickets to amusements parks or to bathing beaches with all kinds of concessions, souvenirs, flowers, as Christian merchants did, *that* would have all been *quite legal* by these laws.

But there was no consensus or uniformity in the lists of the actual forbidden items from county to county. No one could have known or guessed what to expect or how to behave or what could be sold on Sundays. Any kind of *enforcement* proved to be totally selective and *arbitrary* since the prohibitions were so varied, that is, except for their protection of the geographical area of any Christian church buildings, and especially during times of their worship services, from midmorning till noon. The test was *not* simply that whatever relaxes one is okay nor was the test to maximize one's health and morals, as part of the "police powers."

The forbidden items and the tests were illogical, and the Jewish merchants had been innovative enough to open up huge department and discount stores.

In one of the other three cases, the *Two Guys* litigation, the owners of the business had purchased more than a 90-acre plot of ground that had a building already on it, and they added a parking lot for 4,000 cars, which was the beginning of "malls," which began to provide people an opportunity to shop discount even on Sundays when they were free from work. The opening of that store in *Two Guys* marked the beginning of real economic development of the community for which the community remained very grateful.

So the deciding factor of the cases, rather than logic, or specific objectionable objects that had a connection to the prohibition was simply the warning that the *Christian* merchants gave that *they* would go bankrupt if the Jewish merchants were allowed to sell things on Sundays. So it was virtually a contest between the two religious groups, each warning of its imminent bankruptcy should the case be decided in favor or the other. But the protection of the Christian church building and its environs as well as its Sunday worship services was too obvious. The law and Court both went "majoritarian." In his strong dissenting opinion, J. Douglas wrote,

> The issue of these cases would therefore be in better focus if we imagined that a state legislature, controlled by orthodox Jews and Seventh-Day Adventists, passed a law making it a crime to keep a shop open on Saturdays. Would a Baptist, Catholic, Methodist, or Presbyterian be compelled to obey that law or go to jail or pay a fine? Or suppose Moslems [*sic*] grew in political strength here and got a law through a state legislature making it a crime to keep a shop open on Fridays. Would the rest of us have to submit under the fear of criminal sanctions?[23]

While the Court ended its long opinion, holding against the Jewish merchants, it tried to have it "both ways" by the following: "Finally, we should make clear that this case deals only with the constitutionality of #512 of the Maryland statute before us. We do not hold that Sunday legislation may not be a violation of the 'Establishment' Clause if it can be demonstrated that its purpose—evidenced either on the face of the legislation, in conjunction with its legislative history, or in its operative effect—is to use the State's coercive power to aid religion."[24]

In contrast to this rather duplicitous approach of the Court, J. Douglas (dissenting) was quite straightforward, insisting that the First Amendment "admonishes government to be interested in allowing religious freedom to flourish—whether the result is to produce Catholics, Jews, or Protestants, or to turn the people toward the path of Buddha, or to end in a predominantly Moslem nation, or to produce in the long run atheists or agnostics." On matters of this kind, "government must be neutral." This means people have freedom to espouse any religion or to be free "from religion," citing the *Barnette* holding. This was almost precisely the approach of Madison, Jefferson, and then Rawls in the twentieth century. J. Douglas further clarified that the "establishment" clause "protects citizens also against any law which selects any religious custom, practice, or ritual; puts the force of government behind it; and fines, imprisons, or otherwise penalizes a person for not observing it. The government plainly could not join forces with one religious group and decree a universal and symbolic circumcision. Nor could it require all children to be baptized or give tax exemptions only to those whose children were baptized. Could it require a fast from sunrise to sunset throughout the Moslem month of Ramadan? I should think not. Yet why then can it make criminal the doing of other acts, as innocent as eating, during the day that Christians revere?"[25]

J. Douglas cited to *Barnette* especially emphasizing that the proper test in a Free Exercise case is not some rational basis but the question of whether the state really had an interest of a higher order, a compelling interest, to justify such a burden on the person's free exercise of religion. There was *no* such *compelling* state interest in these incoherent and self-contradictory Blue Laws.

Many states still retain majoritarian "Blue laws" on their books. Their U.S. origins were back in the seventeenth century, the same time when many of the colonies that had such Sabbath laws also refused Catholics and Jews to reside in their colonies and were still drowning witches and persecuting people for the slightest religious difference. The Constitution and Bill of Rights were geared to change all that legally, although the Court's Christian bias preferred Jewish merchants go bankrupt rather than Christian merchants.

Interestingly, by the time of the next "Free Exercise" case of significance (1963), the "wall of separation" which the Framers thought they had established between religion and government had been first observed, then admitted that their decisions seem to make it only a "serpentine" wall, so the changing attitude was that the relation between government and religion was not merely a negative relation, but instead, government and the Court could "accommodate" religions without violating either of the two First Amendment Clauses. It was later sometimes spoken of a "benevolent neutrality" since after its Establishment decision in *Everson* in 1947, the government had been quite benevolent, providing millions of tax dollars to parochial schools.

But to continue with the question of a religious holy day, with *Sherbert v. Verner*, 374 U.S. 398 (1963), the Court did not come to the aid of a Jewish litigant and it did not overrule these holdings in these four "Blue-law" cases. Instead, it favored a Christian Seventh-day Adventist, no matter how incongruous such a decision was after the "Blue Law" cases against the Jewish merchants just two years prior. The Court argued that *she* should *not* have to choose between her job and one of her most important religious beliefs and practices of worshipping on Saturday, the Sabbath.[26] It utilized the "compelling state interest" test which had become the higher standard through *West Virginia v. Barnette.* The Court argued that unemployment benefits (which she had applied for when she left her job after her employer changed her schedule to include working on Saturdays) were not mere "privileges" but "rights" having quasi-property status.[27] Further, it noted that the South Carolina law *already* exempted people who opposed work on *Sunday,* so the law itself discriminated. So here do two wrongs make a right; double discrimination against nonreligious people make the two laws right? Where was the "compelling state interest" test in the four Jewish cases just two years prior? J. Brennan, dissenting, warned against the obvious majoritarianism of this decision, for the same reason he objected to the decisions against the four Jewish merchants two years earlier.[28]

The Court, however, ruled the *opposite* way in another Christian's case whose church met on the Saturdays in *Trans World Airlines, Inc. v. Hardison,* 432 U.S. 63 (1977). The Court ruled it was *not* a violation of his "free exercise" of his religion. Why not? He had requested to work on days other than Saturday, and the company accommodated him as much as possible, which worked out when he was in a department in which he had seniority. When that changed, TWA agreed to permit Hardison to seek a change of work assignments so he could be free, but the union declined to overrule its seniority system for such. He sued under the *Civil Rights Act of 1964, §703(a) (1),* but the Court decided the employer had sufficiently attempted to find a *reasonable alternative* to accommodate him, so TWA had no alternative but to fire him.

The test of "compelling state interest" with no less reasonable alternatives then became a double-edged sword, as people seemed to expect that their religious "freedom" should *extend* more and more, giving them *special exemptions.* Yet most employees come to realize that the exact nature of one's job cannot be guaranteed for life. At least the case still was concerned with freedom to *worship,* not simply a wide-open freedom about just anything one wanted to do.

Another employment compensation case arose for a Jehovah's Witness in Indiana in *Thomas v. Review Board of Indiana Employment Sec. Division,* 450 U.S. 707 (1981). This action was brought not over some holy day, and certainly *not freedom to worship,* but basically his religious conviction against war. As a sheet metal fabricator, he found himself being transferred to constructing turrets for military tanks which he found violated his conscience. He requested a layoff, but was denied, so he quit his job and filed for unemployment compensation. The Supreme Court overruled the lower court in an 8/1 decision that this substantial pressure upon his "free exercise" could only be justified by the compelling interest, but such interest was *not* shown, so he could *not* be forced to choose between his faith and his work, as both *Everson* and *Sherbert* had ruled. "Free exercise" now encroached on a freedom of conscience which was traditionally seen under the Establishment Clause, that government could *not* force a person to *believe* certain things. Yet the Court had earlier acknowledged that one's freedom could not be so extensive or unlimited when it comes to one's *actions or behavior*. Now that was challenged.

In 1986, an Orthodox Jewish Air Force officer/psychologist found the Court ruling 5–4 against his controversy with the service over his insistence on wearing his yarmulke as his *religious necessity. Goldman v. Weinberger*, 475 U.S. 503 (1986) involved several years of service that was hassle free, but when appellant was called to testify in a court-martial case as a witness for the defense, the opposing counsel complained to Colonel Gregory, the Hospital Commander, and the attitude of reprisal grew against Goldman as his Commander quit accommodating his yarmulke and shortly thereafter withdrew a recommendation for Goldman to extend his active service, even submitting a negative recommendation.[29] The Court ruled that Air Force regulations were designed to provide uniformity, proper functioning of authority, even esprit de corps or military morale, which was being opposed by his demand for special treatment. The Court said the "free exercise" rights do not carry the same weight in the military as in civilian employment, and the "compelling interest" was met by the Air Force's objectives and rules.[30]

The year 1986 saw the first of several Court decisions related to Native American beliefs and practices, pertaining to their spiritual existence, the sacred places, and their rituals that utilize peyote. In *Bowen v. Roy*, 476 U.S. 693 (1986), the Court ruled on their *spiritual existence*. That is, it ruled the Native American family could *not be exempt* from the statutory rules for the government supplying aid and food stamps to needy families. One of those rules required not just parents but their children to have a Social Security number. Roy argued that their religion protected the Spirit of each person, and to place an arbitrary number on their small daughter might very well destroy her identity and even rob her of her Spirit. The Court insisted that the law was not a violation of their "free exercise" since one simply cannot "dictate" to government how it must *run its business*. What accounts for this difference between the unusual conviction of this Native American family and the strange conviction of the family in *Barnette* who insisted the flag salute required of their child constituted idolatry? But the Court had yielded to the Jehovah's Witness family and denied the Native American family.

Was the Court saying implicitly that some religious beliefs are more credible than others? The *Barnette* Court denied that government had any capacity to define what religious "orthodoxy" was, just as Madison had insisted government had no competency, no role, no "cognizance" or jurisdiction over religion, period.[31] In the same state of Pennsylvania, the Court, as early as 1972, had yielded to the Amish who felt their children should *not* have to attend public schools after age 14, and the Court honored them completely. Both sets of parents were requesting exemption from a neutral, generally applicable law of the government which offended their beliefs. Why the difference in the decisions by the Court? Was there some different conception the Court had of these two groups, perhaps a stereotype that the Native Americans were not as *industrious* as the Amish? It does not come out in the decision of *Bowen v. Roy* but it was certainly an *emphasis* in the Amish case, *Wisconsin v. Yoder*, which made the Court favor their request.

Why one's convictions about a certain day of worship should carry more weight than convictions about one's spiritual state is not clear, since such a judgment would place the Court in an unenviable position of having to decide what made for a valid claim of what was "central" to a religion and "free exercise" and what was only peripheral, a role the Court often rejected explicitly but implicitly utilized over and over. Overall, a neutral generally applicable law intended for all citizens should be expected by all to be observed by all. This was a part of the beauty of Rawls's insistence on the necessity in a democracy of an agreement by all on the basic freestanding principles of the "original position." It creates a posture of mutual trust and trustworthiness. Consistency must be a paramount concern. But the law must be reasonable and relevant to its declared purpose, not a majoritarian or biased law, and not based on any religion. Just those simple elements would have alleviated much of this litigation, although the *priority* must be finally given to "public reason" rather than some religious "nonpublic" reason, and *if* it is strictly "public reason," then Rawls's "difference principle" should be applied in some way to give voice to the "least advantaged."

Another unemployment case, this time from Florida, came to the Court as *Hobbie v. Unemployment Appeals Comm'n of Fla*, 480 U.S. 142 (1987). In this situation, a woman was *converted* to the Seventh Day Adventist church while working for a jewelry company, and after requesting not to work on the Sabbath (Saturday), she was forced to work then or resign. She resigned and was refused unemployment compensation. The Court decided that *Sherbert* and *Thomas* dictate the result: this law was a *violation* of her "free exercise." But the principle being given priority in *Sherbert* and *Hobbie* is not one of "public reason," but one of a "nonpublic" reason in which one places an absolute value on a certain day, which people outside that religion could never be expected to live by. Does the decision here mean all the employees can suddenly convert to the same church, and when they get fired for refusing to work on Saturday, they will justifiably be able to draw unemployment compensation? How could employers have any assurance that employees who originally accept employment which calls for them to work on Saturdays will not change their religion and their mind, and leave the employer hanging? No contractual law could accommodate this arbitrary alteration of the "consideration" involved.

In the same year, in *O'Lone v. Estate of Shabazz*, 482 U.S. 342 (1987), the Court ruled it was *not* a violation of "free exercise" if one class of minimum security Muslim prisoners, assigned to work *outside* the prison, thereby had to miss attendance of the weekly Muslim religious services which others were able to attend. Institutional concerns for security, logistic personnel problems and resources, and so on justified the rule, especially since these prisoners could attend other Muslim services. Here, the Court saw "compelling state interest" and insisted that officials did *not* have to demonstrate that there were no less restrictive reasonable alternatives. Yet, that very qualification of there being no less restrictive reasonable alternatives was explicitly attached to any use of "compelling state interest" test and was crucial in deciding numerous other cases. So why not here? Would it have made any difference if he had been a formerly successful white Christian Wall Street trader who had been convicted of some insider trading so was in a minimum security prison and was having to work outside the prison on Sundays which made him miss the Christian worship services on Sunday? Because of the preferential treatment the Court was giving to Christian litigants, we can only ask the question. Here Rawls's "veil of ignorance" is crucial as is consistency, but incarceration always involved certain limitations of one's freedoms, of which every citizen is aware.

Another Native American case, *Lyng v. N.W. Indian Cemetery Protective Association*, 485 U.S. 439 (1988) focused on the sacred *place of religious worship* that was assumed protected under one's "free exercise" of religion, from Madison and Jefferson to the present. Here, the U.S. Forest Service desired to make some money off timber harvesting in an area of the National Forest in Northern California which had been used by the local Native Americans for about 200 years as a sacred place of spiritual generation. The Forest Service commissioned a study of the feasibility of connecting a "G-O" road, a 6-mile strip, in the center of this sacred high place, in order to bring the logs out. The study they commissioned and received was that it was *not* feasible, and that to violate this sacred space of the Native Americans would simply show a lack of understanding of their culture and religion, their view of the Earth itself. But the Forest Service ignored the study and pushed ahead.

While the case was pending appeal to the Ninth Circuit, Congress passed the State of California Wilderness Act of 1984 which preempted any further cutting of timber or commercial activities of the area. The separate parts of the unpaved existing road were within the Wilderness Area so were closed to general traffic. The *only* part *outside* the Wilderness area was the proposed

6-mile connection between the unpaved existing parts, but both ends of the road were *within* the Wilderness area. Studies had shown that the completion of the road would *not* have made logging more convenient, and logging within that designated area was always of very minimal income to the Forestry Service in comparison with the general logging in those coastal mountains, and now prohibited by it being wilderness.

˙ Nevertheless, the Forest Service pursued and the Supreme Court finally had to hear the case. The Court ruled that the Native American's "free exercise" of religion would not be violated by the proposed road and timber harvesting up to within one-half mile of their sacred sites (where they hoped to have an undisturbed scene and silence of the natural surroundings). When the Native Americans emphasized that the noise of the harvesting and logging trucks would still completely disrupt their sacred atmosphere, the Court (evidently including no Justices who were ever around chain saws and logging trucks!) rejected this, telling them that they could *not* dictate to the government how to *run its own business* (like the *Bowen v. Roy* decision).[32] But the Court became even more offensive in speaking of the land as the government's own land, with the implication that the government could do with its land whatever it pleased. The Court claimed that the Forest service had gone the extra mile in minimizing the impact on the area, in staying back one-half a mile from the most sacred sites, so that even if this made their worship more difficult, it did *not coerce* them into acting contrary to their beliefs. Truth to be told, it promised not to make it merely "more difficult" but rather *quite impossible*, negating entirely any validity of their beliefs, nulling their "freedom" to *worship*.

Ten years prior, the *American Indian Religious Freedom Act*, 42 U.S.C. #1996 (1978) had attempted to bridge the cultural divide on "land issues," directing the government to protect and preserve the American Indians' free exercise rights, their unique ceremonies and traditional rites, and access to their specific sacred sites. It also directed governmental agencies to consult with Native American religious leaders before taking actions that might impair the Native American religious practices. But the Court here in *Lyng* insisted that the AIRFA contains not even a "hint of any intent to create a cause of action or any judicially enforceable individual rights" since it "'has no teeth in it.'"[33] So that meant that the original contracting process of the AIRFA was basically worthless, a pseudo-contract, completely preferential to the whites and discriminatory against the Native Americans. If the Court was correct, that "Religious Freedom Act" for the Native Americans was simply typical of the treaties the European immigrants made with the Native Americans through the centuries in that they were often ignored or were unenforceable because the U.S. government drafted the treaties in their special English legal language and seemed to violate them at will with little repercussion.

The sacred area, called "Chimney Rock," was already designated a "Wilderness Area," but the Court speculated that to concede to the wish of the Native Americans would give them "de facto beneficial ownership of some rather spacious tracts of public property . . . an area covering a full 27 sections (i.e. more than 17,000 acres of public land."[34] The Court spoke of "their" beliefs many times as if to call attention to how strange they were. It admitted that even if the G-O road did not "doom their religion," as the lower courts had both held it would, "we can assume that the threat to the efficacy of at least some religious practices is extremely grave." In fact, the Court insisted that "even if we assume that we should accept the Ninth Circuit's prediction, according to which the G-O road will 'virtually destroy the . . . Indians' ability to practice their religion.' . . . the Constitution simply does not provide a principle that could justify upholding respondents' legal claims."[35]

But the Native Americans were *not* claiming ownership of the land, because they did not believe in any person or agencies owning the land. Nor were they demanding exclusive possession of it, but simply requesting that it would continue to be available in its pristine state for their practices during different parts of the year as it had been for so many generations. They were not asking to live there permanently or to exclude wilderness hikers; they lived further toward the Coast in the Three Rivers area.

Nevertheless, the Court presented a groundless caricature that they "might seek to exclude all human activity but their own from sacred areas of the public lands."[36] They had, in fact, *encouraged hikers* to come enjoy the wilderness area and never claimed sole use of the land, nor was that their request here. But the Court demanded, "Whatever rights the Indians may have to the use of the area however, those rights do not divest the Government of its right to use what is, after all, *its land*."[37] This was hyperbole with no substance, a gross misrepresentation of what the Native Americans were requesting. As a Wilderness area, they wanted it simply to remain such so they and others could experience its natural and spectacular peacefulness. The idea of insisting it was the "government's" land was simply an obnoxious reminder that evidently "might made right" when the European immigrants took it all away from the Native Americans by their superior weapons.

The Court asserted that the reasonable, neutral, generally applicable laws in this case, as in the *Bowen v. Roy* decision, did *not* require the "compelling state" interest showing which would include also proof that there were not any less restrictive reasonable alternatives for the government to take. The Court asserted it simply *did not need to* if its decisions about the road were reasonable and it had attempted to mitigate the most obvious burdens to the Indian spiritual leaders. But how was the decision approving the road *reasonable* if there now could be no timber harvesting? *Bowen v. Roy* did not involve one's freedom of worship, whereas this case here was explicitly about only that worship, which the government was being allowed to trample.

Perhaps the government and Court felt a need to make a point even if it could never be used for timber harvesting? That becomes a valid question since ironically, after they made the Native Americans lose the contest, the Forest Service *never built the road*. Was this long fight due to a complete inability to see any validity in a different culture and different religious forms of "worship," or a mere economic decision, or a mere put-down by the party that has the most power? Rawls's "second principle" of difference, which makes any economic and social inequality acceptable *only* if the laws provide equality of opportunity and *only* if the benefits accrue to the "least advantaged" party, as determined by the "least advantaged party," was certainly *missing* here. One side had an obvious irrational advantage over the other, and exercised it insultingly, instructing the other that it had *no voice* in telling the government what to do with the *government*'s property. One can hardly overestimate how offensive such words would be to *any* citizen, especially coming from the Supreme Court. Who, behind Rawls's "veil of ignorance" would ever have bargained for this kind of inequality and exercise of a happenstance or accidental advantage (of the white European immigrants taking the land from the Native Americans by their superior weapons), if one did not know on which side of the litigation one would be? Rather than exemplifying an impartial or blind justice as U.S. symbols manifest, this was vested, accidentally vested advantages controlling. It was obviously a blatant "majoritarian" decision.[38] Unlike many of the "free exercise" cases, this one *did* concern the freedom to worship as one chooses.[39]

Another unemployment compensation case came before the court in 1989, this time about one's refusal to work on Sunday. In *Frazee v. Illinois Dept. of Employment Security*, 489 U.S. 829 (1989), the Court ruled it was a *violation* of one's "free exercise" when he was deprived of unemployment compensation benefits when he refused to work on Sunday, based on his religious conviction, even though he did *not* profess this as any teaching he derived from a religious denomination or body. This was consistent with the Court's evolving views toward conscientious objection to war by this time, since it allowed men to be exempt even when they said their refusal was social and ethical but *not* a religious reason. Of course, none of these involved "free exercise" in the sense of "worship," so the Court continued to open Pandora's box to allow exemption to neutral, generally applicable laws merely when people *said they objected*, either for an ethical or religious reason, whether they were affiliated with any religion or not. Were the general public really aware of such decisions, the generally applicable laws would have become irrelevant since anyone could object to it violating one's sense of ethics.

In Oregon, a case arose a year earlier than this, but was not decided then, but only in 1990. Its focus was on the actual *religious rituals of worship* by a religious community. Two Native Americans who worked as drug rehabilitation counselors were fired from their jobs for ingesting peyote at their Native American church's religious services. The legal ordeal of *Smith v. the Employment Division of Oregon* went back and forth between state and federal courts for six years, twice to the U.S. Supreme Court, *Employment Division v. Smith*, 485 U.S. 660 (1988), designated "*Smith I*" and 494 U.S. 872 (1990), designated "*Smith II*." It is a very convoluted case, but the Court's 6/3 final decision was that their being fired from their jobs was *not* a violation of their "free exercise" of religion, but a firing "for cause," so their denial of unemployment compensation was correct.[40]

In *Smith II*, the Court said that if minorities' religions have to suffer because their desires sometimes clash with the majority's neutral civil and criminal laws, well, that was just the price they would have to pay.[41] That repeats the Court's line in *Lyng*, that they, as Native Americans or Indians, simply asked for that to which they were *not entitled*. But the question is why peyote was even listed as a "controlled substance" of level I and how it could have been considered "neutral civil and criminal laws" since *no one* ingested peyote for recreational purposes, and the only people who used it at all were the Native Americans for whom it was part of their religious ritual and was very well regulated by the church itself. This fact alone negates the Court's insistence that the law was a neutral, generally applicable law since it had no application or relevance for the population, none but the Native Americans who used it in their religious worship. Instead, it was a narrowly drawn law discriminating against Native Americans.

In that sense, *despite* what the Oregon court said about the general applicability of listing peyote as a Schedule 1 "controlled substance," it was *parallel* to the later Santeria case in which the group worship insisted on animal sacrifice while ignoring all the really generally applicable health laws. But in the Santeria case, the Court was sure it found the City of Hialeah forming a law which had only a *primary religious purpose* of preventing the group's right to "free exercise," so found the law a violation of their "free exercise."[42] Why else was peyote a controlled substance in Oregon law other than its primary religious purpose of preventing only the religious from using it? Both cases involved a *form of worship* utilized by only one specific minority religion, in one case finding *against* the religion (*Smith*) and for the state, while in the other, finding *for* the religion (*Church of Lukumi*) and against the city.

The free exercise of worshipping when, where, how, and with whomever one chooses surely did not conceive of including acts which were prohibited generally of all citizens. But here, *no one else* was involved in these actions. It was not a generally applicable law. The Court did not show any evidence that the use of peyote was harmful or dangerous, which might have justified it as a part of the state's concern for the health, safety, and welfare of its citizens, which might have justified it being considered a "neutral civil and criminal law." But since it was used only in *religious services*, it simply was *not a neutral law*. Further, J. Blackmun noted:

> carefully circumscribed ritual context in which respondents used peyote is far removed from the irresponsible and unrestricted recreational use of unlawful drugs, and it is used only in religious ceremony; any other usage is regarded as sacrilegious. Further, the values of the Native American community are, as they were in *Yoder*, congruent for the most part with those values the State seeks to promote through its drug laws, promoting brotherly love, care of family, self-reliance, and avoidance of alcohol. The usage of the drug strengthens the ego of the participant, helping him to become more sure of himself and no longer to see his world as gone, but as a people whose way can be strong enough to change and meet new challenges.[43]

Finally, he insisted, there is no drug trafficking in peyote for the state to fight. Between 1980 and 1987, the DEA seized over 15 million pounds of marijuana as opposed to only 19.4 pounds of peyote! He argued in dissent that it simply is not a popular drug for a variety of reasons, so if the state were to make an exception for the religious usage of peyote, as more than half of the states already have, it would not affect the drug traffic one way or the other.[44]

Not only was it a very undesirable thing to ingest but it was not shown that the state of Oregon *ever* actually prosecuted anyone for using peyote. But the Court opposed the higher level of "strict scrutiny" or "compelling state interest," insisting that all the state needed to show was that its laws were rational, and therefore generally applicable to all citizens. It objected to citizens thinking they could be exempt from such neutral laws simply by asserting their "free exercise" of religion, and in this it was certainly correct, though it was not in its estimate of how little use the Court had made of the "compelling interest" test, as J. O'Connor later proved.[45] But to include peyote in the list was not "neutral" since it was used by only a single religious group, only in their religious services.

J. Scalia, for the Court, here formed a new category he referred to as "hybrid" cases, which he asserted, added a *second level or right* in order to be able to carve out any exception to the rule. That is, "hybrid" meant that some right *in addition* to one's religious right to "free exercise" had to be shown, and he was sure it was, as he listed several cases. As we pointed out in the early Jehovah's Witness cases, they could have and should have been resolved only on their "free speech" criteria, not adding in "religion" as if the Court could determine what religious practices could qualify. Unfortunately, most of these he cited proved nothing and he was called on this by J. O'Connor. For example, he listed *Wisconsin v. Yoder*. Here he saw the right of "free exercise" of one's religion *combined* with parents' right to determine how to educate their child. To this, he used the usual scare words that to grant this exception would simply allow each person to be his or her own law. In any case, the conviction stood since even J. O'Connor, after all of her attempt to correct J. Scalia's argument, agreed that the state had the right to include that prohibition of peyote as a controlled substance.

She, on the other hand, like J. Scalia, went too far in her argument, finally even emphasizing that the "free exercise" of one's religion gives a person a "preferred" position via the First Amendment, which surely blatantly contradicts what Madison and Jefferson insisted, that religion neither enhances nor detracts from one's civil status, benefits, and responsibilities. This, of course, was also Rawls's point of the place of religion as an association with a nonpublic form of reason but which, so long as a citizen complied with the basic principles of the structure of justice to which all citizens agree, *need not* be deserted or changed any more than any other association's beliefs and practices. But being religious does not provide a person a preferred status with the government; as Madison, Jefferson, and Rawls all insist, *all citizens* must strictly comply with the generally applicable or universal laws.

In *Church of Lukumi Babalu Aye, Inc v. City of Hialeah*, 508 U.S. 520 (1991), 20 years after *Lemon* and the Court's continual usage of its "three-pronged" test, the City of Hialeah would have lost easily simply by those first two elements of the *Lemon* test, since the laws enacted by the city had both an *illegal religious purpose* as well as *illegal primary religious effect*. But it was addressed from the standpoint of the laws crippling the Santaria's "free exercise" of religion instead of pushing the idea of an illegal religious "establishment" that had affected their freedom. The Santerias won.

The Court approached it from the standard it had used in the recent *Smith I* and *II* cases, that a burden on one's free exercise of religion need *not* be justified by a compelling interest if the law is "neutral and of general applicability." Upon close examination, it found the three specific laws the city had enacted hastily when it heard that the Santeria were moving as a group to Hialeah were *not neutral* but obviously focused on this particular religion. The Santeria religion, begun in the nineteenth century, was the product of members of the Yoruba people being brought from Africa to Cuba as slaves, who adopted from the Cuban form of Roman Catholicism a number of Catholic elements including various Catholic symbols, the iconography of Catholic saints, and Catholic sacraments. But why was the city's law *less neutral* than Oregon's law which added peyote to the list only from its new awareness of that part of the Native American worship services? *Neither law was neutral*, even if both city and state contended their laws were.

Central to the worship of the Santeria is ritual sacrifice, which involves a ritual killing of a number of different small animals, and the ritual in most cases involves eating the cooked "sacrifice." Their belief in spirits or orishas includes the idea that the sacrifices somehow sustain the orishas themselves, and they believed that humans' destiny is determined by God and depends upon the humans receiving help from the orishas. By this time, there were estimated to be about 50,000 Santeria in the state of Florida, due to their exile from Cuba. When the Santeria in Cuba had faced widespread persecution, they resorted to practicing their religion in secret, and the citizens of Hialeah were persuaded that such a secrecy in Florida would make any enforcement of laws extremely difficult, so they had to preclude all possibility of the services occurring by prohibiting any form of religious or ritualistic sacrificing or killing of animals, whether eaten or not. The three laws attempted to foreclose the Santeria possibilities but not adversely affect other people in the area, whether Kosher markets or even individuals who occasionally slaughtered animals on their own premises, animals they intended to consume.

Although it seemed that the Court could not make up its mind as to whether the laws were "underinclusive" or "overbroad," so they used both expressions, there was little question as to the group for whom the legal prohibitions were intended. That, of course, meant that the laws were not facially neutral and generally applicable but quite discriminating and specific, which, in turn, meant that they could be justified, by the Court's standard, *only* if the city could show that the laws were narrowly tailored to accomplish its compelling interest and there were no less restrictive alternatives by which they could protect that compelling interest.

Safety, sanitation, and animal anti-cruelty arguments were unpersuasive to the Court, so it found the laws a violation of their "free exercise" of religion. The Court appeared united in its "result" but the Justices split radically over the various parts of the argument. The most problematic element in the Court's decision seems to be that despite the fact that the Court over and over insists that *it cannot and will not* give any consideration in a case to arguments about some element being "central" to the religion, that is *exactly* what it blatantly did, even using the word "central" as the Court determined that the object of the city's ordinances was to suppress the central element of the Santeria worship, the sacrifice of the animals.

A second argument by the Court is almost as untenable when it suggests that the city devalued killing for religious reasons, seeing a religious reason as less valid than nonreligious reason for killing animals, which means it was the city's discrimination against religion. What would be a legitimate "religious" reason for killing? To feed the orishas or spirits, as the Santeria believed? How does one believe in such spirits which demand such material sacrifice, as if they actually depend upon them to exist? Is this parallel to thinking that God as Spirit is enriched and satisfied only by the Sacrifice of the Mass, in which elements are supposed to have some transformed composition, but wholly spiritual benefit? If it all depends upon the believer having the idea that such killing is required by God, would this justify ISIS's construal of Islam vesting on them the right to kill in the name of Allah any and all infidels? Does such an idea not return us to the most ancient religious beliefs millennia back, which were pervasive around the globe, that humans were at the mercy of the gods, and must therefore try to appease them with sacrifices, originally human sacrifices, then animal sacrifices which were simply surrogates for humans? Is the Court suggesting that such a view of reality still includes that "value" of killing for "religious reasons"? If so, we have left "public reason" far behind when we begin to distinguish religious reasons for killing people, and our attitudes toward killing animals are even more anthropocentric and bizarre, even *indifferent* to animals' instinctual desire for life as Schweitzer elaborated. Religious sacrificial rituals, as Kant noted, are "pseudo-religious" (by which he meant irrational "superstition") since they *value sacrifice above morality.*

Finally, the Court went to great length to show the hostility the city and many of its leaders manifested toward the idea of the Santeria moving there and practicing their religion, even the derogatory descriptions they used of the people and their religious practice. While the decision seems obvious in its being grounded on a negative discrimination against a religion, it is not clear how the final ruling by the Court would have resolved any of the community's problems. It would have simply *intensified* the *religious divisiveness* that the First Amendment was intended to heal. We are drawn back to Madison's and Jefferson's idea that the government takes no legal cognizance of religion until such times that it breaks out into overt acts of disorder, and precisely what constitute those overt acts may change from time to time.

Instead of formulating city laws or resolving Court cases of such city laws that are based on obvious divisive religious views, both city, state, and federal legislatures and courts must cleanse the discussion of all religious, metaphysical ideas, and formulate and adjudicate purely civil and criminal laws based on the "public reason" with its "overlapping consensus" of principles. Necessarily this means they address animals' rights in a more exhaustive and comprehensively consistent way, based on the inherent value of the animals rather than on an anthropocentric view of animals, whether it is merely as human food or offered in religious sacrifices as divine food.

A few months later, Congress passed the Religious Freedom Restoration Act of 1993, in reaction against the Court's position in the *Smith* cases in 1988, 1990. It clarified that the "free exercise" litigation had to honor the standard it had articulated in *Sherbert v. Verner* and *Wisconsin v. Yoder*, the "balancing" or "compelling interest" test that it had abandoned in *Smith*. It required not only a showing of "compelling governmental interest" but also that such a law in question was "the least restrictive means of furthering that compelling governmental interest."

The Court countered this four years later in the *City of Boerne v. Flores, Archbishop of San Antonio et al.*, 521 U.S. 507 (1997), which was called a "landmark" decision by the Court on Congress' power, but then in 2000, Congress enacted the Religious Land Use and Institutionalized Persons Act (RLUIPA), 42 U.S.C. §§2000cc. et seq. which obviously was countering the *Boerne* decision among other things. So now the question was whether Congress or the Court would win the battle, made all the more ironic since Congress was actually using the standard the Court itself had articulated in 1943 in *Barnette*, and abandoned only in 1990 in *Smith II*, though without saying it was abandoning it.

NOTES

1. To see this contrast, one only need compare the freedom of religion from the freedom of the Fourth Amendment. The first mentioned only freedom from government establishing the religion or attempting to regulate people's worship. But the Fourth Amendment defines (1) what items are at stake (one's security in one's person, house, papers, and effects), (2) what is prohibited activity (unreasonable searches and seizures), (3) what makes such searches and seizures "unreasonable" (their lack of warrant based on probable cause, supported by Oath or affirmation, without any particular description of the place to be searched or person or things to be seized). It did not say Congress shall make no laws further qualifying these elements, but it was quite obviously provoked by the abusive "general warrants" the British had used against the Colonists.

2. The five words at the beginning of the First Amendment, "Congress shall make no law . . ." applied to *all* of the areas listed: religion, speech, press, assembly, and petition of grievances against the government. This seems to suggest that in such brief form, the Bill of Rights was actually more of a formality than a definitive prohibition just to satisfy the Anti-Federalists in order to get the Constitution ratified, just as Berkin suggests in her *The Bill of Rights* (2015).

3. Ronald Dworkin, who found "integrity" in law more correct than either "conventialism" or "pragmatism," in arguing against Tushnet's criticism of "liberalism" as an unfair caricature, insisted that Rawls's system does not create a bunch of isolated individuals, thus lacking any form of adjudication or legal coercion, but rather is open to a mutual autonomy and trust that, working with a ground of political rather than metaphysical principles, arrives at a constructive picture of justice which is a politically organizing tool rather than merely a key to a way of life for individuals. Ronald Dworkin, *Law's Empire* (Cambridge, MA: The Belknap Press of The Harvard Univ. Press, 1986), 440–441 and note 19.

4. It has always been assumed that the religious freedom of the First Amendment included a freedom of conscience or belief, but also that by the nature of things, it did not include an absolute freedom of actions or even absolute freedom of what one actually did in one's "worship." No one ever asserted that one had freedom to worship by offering up human sacrifices, or worship by killing people, or even worship by having sex with a temple prostitute which was quite common in ancient times. The question is what all can be included under the rubric of "worship."

5. It may seem simplistic for me to emphasize merely present agreement, but when one realizes the contingency of all institutions, including that of language, ethics, and law, the discussion must involve different perspectives, rather than viewing some documents, whether sacred scriptures or a Constitution, as if they were absolutely fixed for all time and beyond any perspectives. It must involve then a reasonable discussion of the present "horizon" as well as those pasts, and all the presuppositions or unnoticed elements that were causally instrumental in a particular position being taken. Laurence H. Tribe, *Constitutional Choices* (Cambridge, MA: Harvard University. Press, 1985), 8, also noted that no past intention can be normative just because a text originated there. Further, he insisted that "constitutional choices, whatever else their character, must be made and assessed as fundamental choices of *principle*, not as instrumental calculations of utility or as pseudo-scientific calibrations of social cost against social benefit" (viii). This is a classic formulation and certainly in agreement with Rawls's focus on agreed principles vis-à-vis intuitionism and utilitarianism.

6. Women were still not given the right to vote, and Indians not taxed were not to be counted in the census which determines the number of Representatives each state should get in Congress.

7. After Republican Chris Krebs had been appointed to head up election security by President Trump, he was summarily fired by the president on November 17, 2020, after declaring that the election was the most secure in U.S. history, and the talk of fraud was misleading and baseless.

8. In criminal procedure, the incorporation came in *Powell v. Alabama*, 287 U.S. 45 (1932) and *Palko v. Connecticut*, 302 U.S. 319 (1937). See Yale Kamisar, Wayne R. LaFave and Jerold H. Israel, *Basic Criminal Procedure* (St. Paul, MN: West Publishing Co., 1980), 28–35.

9. Ahlstrom, *A Religious History*, 507.

10. For those who felt this was a correct decision because polygamy was so prohibited by the Jewish, Christian, or Islamic scriptures, none of those scriptures actually forbid polygamy at all. Divorce, yes, but not polygamy, as beloved King David showed, and men were allowed in Ancient Israel to have children by household female servants or slaves. It was very common. The New Testament is simply totally silent on the issue, but the Qur'an allows a man to have up to three wives, provided he treats them all equally. So these laws against polygamy were based more on the English and European *cultures* rather than on any "Holy Scriptures."

11. *United States v. Schwimmer*, 279 U.S. 644 (1929); *United States v. Macintosh*, 293 U.S. 605 (1931); and *Hamilton v. Regents of the Univ. of California*, 293 U.S. 245 (1934). In the first two cases, the person applying for citizenship was denied the CO status, and in the third case, the person was expelled from the University for not enrolling in ROTC.

12. It overruled *U.S. v. Schwimmer*, 279 U.S. 644 (1929); *U.S. v. Macintosh*, 293 U.S. 605 (1931); and *U.S. v. Bland*, 283 U.S. 636 (1931).

13. If the Court really took this seriously, the question has to be raised as to what the limits might be of the power or jurisdiction of this alleged "ultimate concern" or "Absolute," which was pushed to an extreme of having *no limit whatever* by Soren Kierkegaard in his opposition to Hegel. See Kierkegaard's *Fear and Trembling* which attacks G.W.F. Hegel's ethical criticism of Abraham in his *The Spirit of Christianity* we mentioned earlier.

14. Was the Court willing to say that the entirely of any single entity or event must always be judged exactly the same, that if one auto of a certain brand turns out to be a "lemon," one must also hold that all cars of the same model are "lemons," that if one senator is found to be corrupt, that must imply that all senators are; otherwise the single one cannot be? Such defies logic.

15. As we saw earlier, the Court had earlier made "free exercise" decisions in its antipolygamy decisions based on the "police powers" and sheer Western tradition in *Reynolds v. U.S.*, 98 U.S. 145 (1879) and *Davis v. Beason*, 133 U.S. 333 (1890), with*out* alluding to the Fourteenth Amendment.

16. The real issue was why *Cantwell* and *Barnette* were not resolved simply by keeping the focus on "freedom of speech" laws, rather than making a new law about "religion."

17. *Cantwell v. Connecticut*, 310 U.S. 296 (1940), at 304.

18. *West Virginia State Board of Education v. Barnette*, 319 U.S. 624 (1943), at 638.

19. *Barnette*, at 642.

20. Cases involving the Jehovah's Witnesses have continued from state to state over the subsequent years: *Jamison v. State of Texas*, 318 U.S. 413 (1943); *Tucker v. Texas*, 326 U.S. 317 (1946); *Watchtower Bible & Tract Society of New York, Inv, v. Village of Stratton*, 536 U.S. 150 (2002). They always have the same result with the law being found a violation of "free exercise."

21. Laurence Tribe, *American Constitutional Law*, 2nd ed. (Mineola, NY: The Foundation Press, Inc., 1988), 1261–1262.

22. *McGowan v. Maryland*, 366 U.S. 420 (1961) was decided with three other cases, *Braunfeld v. Brown*, 366 U.S. 599; *Two Guys from Harrison-Allentown, Inc. v. McGinley*, 366 U.S. 582; and *Gallagher v. Crown Kosher Super Market of Mass., Inc.*, 366 U.S. 617. In the *McGowan* case, the Court made the remark that it was not even sure what religion the litigants belonged to, yet to award damages, litigants had to *show what religion they espoused* and *specifically how* they were damaged. This is ludicrous since the Court recognized over and over even the Jewish origin of the Sabbath as well as the present litigants' religious affiliation.

23. *McGowan*, at 565. It is interesting that at the time J. Douglas gave this example (1961), nothing seemed more unlikely to most U.S. citizens. It still does. Yet, since the growth of ISIS, now in 2017, many have heard the word, "Shari'ah," and without knowing Muslim civil/religious law, they speak of their fear since they equate it with what they see ISIS doing. J. Douglas's point stands.

24. *McGowan*, at 453.

25. *McGowan*, at 564–565.

26. The Court could not make up its mind which was the Sabbath, Saturday or Sunday, but certainly this litigant should not have to choose between her religion and work, as the Jewish merchants did two years earlier.

27. We will see that J. Scalia later insisted that the "compelling state interest" requirement was limited to unemployment compensation cases, as *Sherbert v. Verner*, but *Barnette* was where it started, which did not involve employment at all.

28. J. Brennan warned how many people of different religions in the United States hold different religious scruples than the majority of our citizens, and their free exercise rights can often be trodden on by the majority, that a majority in a community can mistakenly think they can "compel a minority to observe their [the majority's] particular religious scruples so long as the majority's rule can be said to perform some valid secular function." *Sherbert v. Verner*, at 411.

29. *Goldman v. Weinberger*, 475 U.S. 503 (1986), at 505.

30. *Goldman*, at 507–510.

31. Would Christians really have been willing to subject their professed beliefs such as a "Virgin Birth," "Resurrection," or "Ascension" to a "credibility" test against the teachings of Buddha?

32. Is it peculiar that when the Court differed earlier, it never reprimanded a litigant for trying to tell the government how to run its business, but here in two Native American cases, that was the primary message?

33. *Lyng v. N.W. Indian Cemetery Protective Association*, 485 U.S. 439 (1988), at 455.

34. *Lyng v. N.W. Indian Cemetery*, at 453.

35. *Lyng v. N.W. Indian Cemetery*, at 451.

36. *Lyng v. N.W. Indian Cemetery*, at 452–453.

37. *Lyng v. N.W. Indian Cemetery*, at 452–453, italics added.

38. Mark Tushnet mentioned the "majoritarianism" which was a conservative Christian reaction against the Court's decision against prayers in the public schools, but here the majority defeated the minority under the guise of neutral, generally applicable laws which were applied in a very discriminatory and useless way just to put down the minority. See Mark Tushnet, *Red, White, and Blue: A Critical Analysis of Constitutional Law* (Cambridge, MA: Harvard Univ. Press, 1988). Tushnet writes "an unelaborated majoritarianism suffers from several flaws: it is anticonstitutional, noncomparative, and inconsistent (in its usual incarnations)," p. 168.

39. Had this been a Christian church built in the pristine area to manifest to worshippers God's wonderful Creation through the natural beauty and silence of the high country, would the decision have been the same with all the hyperbolic caricatures? The hidden presuppositions of "White supremacy" that came from Europe centuries ago, then manifested itself in the Colonists' treatment of both Native Americans and African slaves they purchased, are still pervasive in the incarceration of African American men and in the treatment the government provides for the Native Americans on their "reservations" during the Covid-19 pandemic.

40. During Prohibition, the Catholic Church and a handful of others who used wine for the Eucharist or Lord's Supper gained exemption from what was otherwise a neutral, reasonable, universally applicable law to stop the consumption of alcoholic drinks. J. Scalia, who wrote the decision for the Court here, took two contradictory

positions. On the one hand, he suggested that the Native American church and these litigants should try to seek special exemption from the state so they could use peyote legally. Yet, quite on the other hand, he insisted that people should *not* expect to be *exempt* from just any or every universally applicable law because their "religious" beliefs happen to differ. So which was it? Both could not be the answer. Why was the Court demanding that people could not "be a law to themselves," yet upholding many people who did sue from their religious convictions to "be a law to themselves"?

41. Notably, it did not include the possibility of a clash between a religious majority and the nation's "majority" laws, only a religious minority. But this was explicitly a repudiation of Madison's conception of the *protection of minorities* from any form of majoritarianism.

42. We will examine this case later, *Church of Lukumi Babalu Ave, Inc. v. City of Hialeah*, 508 U.S. 510 (1993). If the Oregon Court was more aware of the negative consequences of admitting that the inclusion of peyote was relevant only to one religious group, and the City of Hialeah was so naïve that they were not able to hide its religious motivation, that does not change the facts that in both cases, the practice in question was specifically aimed at only *one group's religious worship*. Either *both* should have been a violation of their "free exercise" or *neither*.

43. *Smith v. the Employment Division of Oregon*, 494 U.S. 872 (1990), (II), at 915.

44. *Smith II*, at 918.

45. J. O'Connor labeled a misreading of judicial history J. Scalia's insistence that the neutral principles/universal application approach was always the correct standard, articulated even prior to the Native American cases in the Amish case of *U.S. v. Lee*. She expressed shock at his misconstrual of facts when he argued that the "compelling state interest" was *only* applied in unemployment cases or only in "hybrid" cases in which *at least two or more* constitutional rights were involved. She insisted that she agreed with the sentiment of the *Barnette* Court that the Bill of Rights was designed to protect minorities, not just majorities. She reasoned that the Court's "strained reading" of its history of Free Exercise litigation unnecessarily contradicts the Court's *usual preferred test* of "compelling state interest" or the "balancing of interests" rather than a mere "rational basis" test. She said this despite her decision in *Lyng*, that the case did not require such a showing of any "compelling interests." J. Scalia later admitted exceptions to his "hybrid" rule, and even later yet, faulted the Court for using tests which would most easily determine the result it wanted at that specific time. But in *Smith*, he insisted that in *Wisconsin v. Yoder* there was both the religious "right" to free exercise but *also* the right of the parents to determine the education for their children. These, however, were the *same right* since all the Amish families followed their religious idea of separation from the world by withdrawing their daughters from school at age 14. Even this had *nothing* to do with "free exercise" of worship. This was only a freedom to *believe*, but that in itself does not validate exempting anyone from general, neutral, universally applicable laws, such as the educational laws of the state of Wisconsin.

Chapter 7

The First Amendment

Who Guarantees "Free Exercise"?

Barely two centuries after the ratification of the Constitution and Bill of Rights, the antagonism within the Court and between the Court and Congress shows how religious "free exercise" jurisdiction had attained very little consensus among the legal authorities of our government. When Congress saw what happened in the *Smith* case (1988, 1990), it insisted on "restoring" the religious freedom which it was persuaded the Court had deserted after earlier defining it by utilizing the test of requiring a state to show its "compelling" interest if it substantially burdened one's "free exercise." Congress formulated the statute in extremely sweeping terms, formalizing the earlier Court criteria that in order for a "compelling" interest to be valid, it would have to be shown that there were no other less restrictive reasonable alternatives to meeting its interest. Further, Congress applied this new law to all forms of government, and "to all federal and State law, and the implementation of that law, whether statutory or otherwise, whether adopted before or after the enactment of this Act." This Religious Freedom Restoration Act took effect in November 16, 1993, and is found in 42 U.S.C. §§2000bb through 2000bb(4). Subsequently, various states have enacted similar laws.

Congress specified that it found the remedy in the compelling or highest order interest the Court had utilized in *Sherbert v. Verner* and in *Wisconsin v. Yoder*. This is the reason the Act was called a "Restoration," since Congress viewed the "compelling" state interest test as the primary if not predominant test used by the Court in Free Exercise cases. It saw *Smith* as the abandonment by the Court of that compelling state interest test, though the Court actually had abandoned it in all three Native American cases, as we have seen, *Roy*, *Lyng*, and *Smith*. So the statutory law Congress enacted was not considered by Congress as an innovation.

Because the RFRA professed power to "restore" that standard even in past cases, thereby aligning itself with the First Amendment of the Constitution, and applying to any agency, statute, or case, with additional subsequent statutes in 1994, Congress *did* make an exception for Oregon's sacramental use of peyote, and even extended the peyote exception to all members of every authentic Indian Tribe (42 U.S.C. §1996a(b)(1)). This was a rejection of the Court's standard that it formulated in the Native American cases that disallowed people's religious free exercise to have any impact on facially neutral, generally applicable laws, in *Roy*, *Lyng*, and *Smith*, despite J. Scalia's oscillation we mentioned earlier, suggesting that Smith tried to get the state to grant an exemption to the Native American Church.

What the Congress failed to do in the Act was to give any significant definition of "religious exercise." Its mere redundancy in 42 U.S.C. §2000cc, etc. of the expression "religious exercise" is too vague to offer any legal understanding of what would distinguish "religious" exercise from *any other* kind of exercise, or what even constitutes "exercise" as opposed to acts that evidently are not an "exercise." Undoubtedly it may have refrained from being more definitive simply to show deference to the First Amendment's own lack of definition. That meant that the RFRA simply *intensified* the problem, opening the door to more and more claims being made of *religious uniqueness or particularity*, of *exceptions* to criminal or civil laws possibly being justified as a valid religious sacrament or protected religious free exercise because of laws which could be seen as "burdening" the person even though the laws were simply facially neutral, generally applicable laws.

THE COURT'S *BOERNE* COUNTER
TO CONGRESS' RFRA

The *City of Boerne v. Flores*, 521 U.S. 507 (1997) provided opportunity for the Court to take back its territory or authority which it felt was imprudently and illegally encroached on and appropriated by Congress. However, the Court split within itself in *Boerne* as it had in *Smith*, with three dissenting justices requesting a reargument of the *Smith* case which they regarded as incorrectly decided by the Court, as well as a subsequent reargument of the *Boerne* case. Since the Court majority denied that, J. Souter went on record suggesting that the Court should at least "dismiss the writ of certiorari as improvidently granted"[1] which the Court also refused to do. The extremely detailed dissent by J. O'Connor not only insisted on *Smith* as wrongly decided, but traced the history of the "meaning" of "free exercise" prior to the expression being incorporated within the First Amendment. J. Scalia, on the other hand, devoted his entire space in the case to counter J. O'Connor's reading of that history and he defended the *Boerne* decision by insisting that *Smith* was correctly decided, which was natural since he himself had written for the Court in *Smith*.

Now it became more apparent than it had been earlier that the "religious purpose" that would be necessary to protect a person under the Free Exercise clause might very well force the *Lemon* test to be negated or at least totally ignored by the Court since this antiestablishment test's very "first prong" had regarded the presence of a "religious purpose" as prima facie evidence of an unconstitutional Establishment. Yet any decision the Court made from a litigant's claim of his "religious exercise" being violated ended up being a "law" with a religious purpose behind it. The skirmishes persisted between Congress and the Court from the Religious Freedom Restoration Act of 1993, through the *Boerne* decision in 1997, to the RLUIPA of 2004. The congressional resentment of the Court's *Smith* decision in 1988, 1990, drove the origins of this conflict back to that point, as some people evidently felt their religion's future accommodations by the Court might be curtailed by *Smith*.

The conversation temporarily moved away from any concern that the "Free Exercise" claim might be used to exploit the law by gaining tax funds or credits or exemptions to a contest between the standards of "compelling interest" vs. "rational basis" (or neutral, generally applicable law), which some members of the Court thought had been resolved back in *Barnette* in 1943, only to discover the majority of the Court abandoning it in *Lee*, *Roy*, *Lyng*, and *Smith*. The discussion ensued not only about which "tests" were correct, but about which principles were to be involved, the limits of the different branches of government, the meaning of the Fourteenth and Fifteenth Amendments in conjunction with the First Amendment, as well as the history of the meaning of "free exercise" both pre- and post-Constitution and its ratification. But for the average person, the concern was still more the issue of how one might be restricted by the government or how one could be sure of the government still accommodating one's free exercise, that is, a question of *exemptions or benefits one could expect* through making *religious claims* against certain laws. We must examine this process in more detail.

The Court was able to counter Congress, accusing it of misreading the Court's decisions and tests, and therefore striking down the RFRA in *City of Boerne v. Flores*, 521 U.S. 507 (1997). St. Peter's Catholic Church was built in 1923 on a hill in Boerne, Texas, a city located less than 30 miles northwest of San Antonio. The building, which is in the old "mission" style of earlier Texas history, was now insufficient in size to consistently accommodate those in attendance, so the Archbishop of San Antonio gave the parish permission to expand the building. A few months later, the city of Boerne passed an ordinance authorizing the city's Historic Landmark commission to prepare a preservation plan with proposed historic landmarks and districts, which placed it in charge of granting any permission for any construction affecting these landmarks in the historic district.

When the Archbishop applied for a building permit shortly thereafter, the city denied the application since the present church building was within the zoned historical district. The Archbishop subsequently brought suit against the city, utilizing the RFRA as grounds for claiming the denial of the requested permit was unconstitutional and a violation of the RFRA. The District Court decided that Congress, in formulating the RFRA, exceeded its scope of delegated power under section 5 of the Fourteenth Amendment. The Fifth Circuit, however, reversed, finding the RFRA constitutional. The Supreme Court granted cert and found, as had the District Court, that Congress had *exceeded* its power in the RFRA. *Boerne* simply articulated the Court's "neutral principles" approach as the standard for "Free Exercise" cases, as opposed to the earlier "compelling state interest" standard which had granted tremendous privileges to certain litigants for being religious, especially for being Christian. The Court was not turning "hostile" toward religion, but trying to resolve its disparate grounds for its "free exercise" decisions of the previous half-century.

By virtue of the RFRA requiring a showing by the state of its "compelling" interest, and that its means or law to meet that interest is the "least restrictive," the Court insisted that Congress was in error. It had misread the *Smith* case as well as the pre-*Smith* Court decisions and tests, so the RFRA, operating from such misreading, added to Congress' presumptuousness by preempting the powers delegated to the states as well as the primary power of interpretation of the laws delegated to the Supreme Court by the Constitution. The Court insisted that Congress' power under the Fourteenth and Fifteenth Amendments was only *remedial and preventive*, not power to interpret the laws or to change the substance of the Constitutional protection, a power the Constitution itself had vested only in the Court.

When the Congress is given only remedial and preventive power, it must manifest "congruence and proportionality" of the means used in their relation to the ends sought. But the Court insisted that Congress had far exceeded a mere remedial and preventative power, and by its sweeping scope, of all cases and controversies as well as statutes, by any and all possible parties, both future as well as past, it moved beyond congruence and proportionality into the area of making substantial changes to the protections which the Constitution had vested only in the power of the Court.

To show the legitimate distinction between being entrusted with the substantial interpretation of the law and being entrusted only with doing what is necessary, once given the Court's interpretation of the law—to remedy infractions or to prevent excesses or avoidance of the law as interpreted by the Court—the Court used the example of the issue of voting rights and the threat of racial discrimination. Several states struck down literacy laws as a remedy for or prevention of racial discrimination as pertaining to voting rights. This was the correct use of their power. The substance of the law pertaining to voting rights is interpreted by the Court; Congress or the separate states may, within the parameters of that interpretation, devise remedies and preventive measures to assure compliance with the substantial element as determined by the Court. The *Boerne* Court presented much history to illustrate this distinction, citing especially to *South Carolina v. Katzenbach*, 383 U.S. 301 (1966); *Katzenbach v. Morgan*, 384 U.S. 641 (1966); and *Oregon v. Mitchell*, 400 U.S. 132. It agreed with J. Stewart in *Oregon v. Mitchell* as saying that to interpret *Morgan* as giving Congress the power to interpret the Constitution would be an unjustified extension of the *Morgan* Court's rationale.

The Court insisted that it *intentionally* did *not* utilize the compelling state interest test in *Employment Division v. Smith I* (1988) and *Smith II* (1990), which it had used primarily in *unemployment* cases such as *Sherbert v. Verner*. The reason it did not was because it would have produced an anomaly in the law, providing incentive for religious people to challenge neutral laws of general applicability with which they disagreed on strictly religious grounds. The problem would have been intensified, the Court reasoned, by the difficulty of determining whether a particular practice was central to an individual's religion which the Court was unqualified to make. Yet the Court in earlier cases felt quite capable of judging a case by first distinguishing the "centrality" of a certain element in the religion, such as in *Barnette* (1943) (true worship v. idolatry); *Yoder v. Wisconsin* (1972) (abstinence from worldly values), *Church of Lukumi v. Hialeah* (1993) (ritual sacrifice), *Murdock v. Pennsylvania* (1943) (solicitation as preaching); as well as *Sherbert, Hobbie,* and *Frazee* (observance of Sabbath); plus the CO cases of *Girouard* (1946), *Seeger* (1965), *Welsh* (1970) (moral objection to taking up arms).

While the Court insisted that the "least restrictive means" was not required in pre-*Smith* cases, which is true, some of those cases *did* mention that the law in question had to be "narrowly tailored" to the compelling state interest. It seems far too late in the day for the Court to say the Court has *always* recognized its lack of qualification to judge some claim by a religious person about an element that is "central." Similarly, it is far too late to try to come up with reasons, in retrospect, for *different criteria* used by the Court when they contradict each other as the Court did in suggesting that the "compelling interest" or "balancing" test was used *only* in cases in which other constitutional protections were also at stake, for example, in *Wisconsin v. Yoder,* which involved not only the "free exercise" right of religion but the right of parents to determine their children's education. We have already seen this was basically only a *single* right in *Yoder*.

In the unemployment compensation cases of *Thomas v. Review Bd. of Indiana Employment Security Div* (1981), *Sherbert v. Verner* (1963), *Hobbie v. Unemployment Appeals Comm'n of Fla* (1987), the *Smith* Court had acknowledged that where the state laws had "already in place a system of exemptions, it may not refuse to extend that system to cases of religious hardship without compelling reason."[2] Can one assume that all of these therefore fit into what J. Scalia had called "hybrid" cases?[3] What the Court strangely omits is any reference to the very point in history—the *Barnette* case (1943)—at which the "compelling state interest" test was defined as the correct test for "free exercise" cases rather than the "rational-basis" or "facially neutral, generally applicable" law test.

Additionally, *never* in these cited cases did the Court insist that precisely because a *second right*, in addition to the Free Exercise right, was involved, or because exceptions to the law were already given, it justifiably and necessarily raised the test to the "highest order of interest" or "strict scrutiny" or "compelling interest" test. Those reasonings appeared *first* only in *Smith*, by J. Scalia himself, then again in *Boerne*. Nor did the Court reexamine the entire scope of its "free exercise" adjudications to distinguish *which* test was used for each—for obvious reasons. Could it be that the "exemptions" the Court had made to people's responsibility to comply with neutral, generally applicable laws did not begin to be seen in their possible *negative* consequences until the *Lee* and *Smith* cases arose? Then consistency with *Smith* required a compliance with those kinds of neutral laws so long as they were not intended to burden disproportionately religious people or institutions, so this accounted for *Boerne*. Yet that was exactly what *Smith* did since by accepting the inclusion as "illegal" something which was used *only* by the Native Americans, *only* in their religious services, that "disproportionately" burdened only one particular religion.

But *Boerne* was also the Court's attempt to protect its authority as an equal branch of the federal government, the only branch given authority to interpret the law substantively, which, requires a separation of powers, and was unfortunately breached by Congress as it usurped authority which it did not have by the RFRA. The Court read Congress's legal power of "enforcement" of the constitutional right of "free exercise" as only preventive or remedial, *not* substantive as in changing the criteria or tests.[4] Finally, the Court reminded Congress that the "least restrictive reasonable means" requirement had *not* been formally attached by the Court to the "compelling interest" test, in fact, not used in *pre-Smith* jurisdiction. It also argued for J. Scalia's idea of the "hybrid" cases, that the "compelling interest" test was not used prior to *Yoder* and then only in the various unemployment compensation cases, in which the litigants all had a "second right" in addition to their "free exercise" right. We have seen this argument as quite questionable.

The Court argued in *Bourne* that the Free Exercise cases it has dealt with for the past 40 years have *not* involved laws which had a *religious bias*—and this is the reason it can abide by the facially neutral, universally applicable standard rather than demanding the stricter scrutiny that is required, for example, in racial discrimination litigation. That, of course, is a misrepresentation of some of the laws that have been challenged. Many of them have had a very obvious *pro-religious bias*, usually Christian, from *Cantwell* on, in the CO cases of *Seeger* and *Welsh* in the 1960s and 1970s, and in the extension of unemployment benefits from *Sherbert* (1963), to *Thomas* (1981), to *Hobbie* (1987), to *Frazee* (1989), and *very obvious* in the four "Blue-laws" cases of 1963. Was the Court concerned only with discrimination *against* a religion but not bias *for* a religion?

More accurately, the "compelling" interest test was normative from 1943 until *U.S. v. Lee* in 1982. With the exception of *Lee* in 1982, it continued to be consistently used even *after* that in *all* the Christian cases, and in the lone Jewish and Muslim cases in which the religious person lost, as we have seen. Despite the inaccuracy of the Court's reading this history of its decisions, the Court significantly argued in *Boerne* that one's "free exercise" of religion *may legally* be significantly burdened by a law so long as the burden is incidental and not disproportionate, the law is facially neutral and generally applicable (the very thing the *Yoder* Court *denied*), and does not single out the "religious" people to burden, so shows no religious bias. That reverts precisely to the "rational basis" test in *Boerne*, the very standard that was *explicitly rejected* by the *Barnette* case in 1943 but which in *Boerne*, the Court 54 years later tells us *is correct*.

Why could the Court not admit it had been wrong in most of those earlier cases rather than ignoring them or trying to supply a specious "second" right that each allegedly involved? Nearly all the "free exercise" cases involved a "second right" of at least "freedom of speech" or "freedom to assemble." But in each case, it is the latter that is what is claimed as "religious," so only really one "right" being claimed. Even if the Court finally found its way to the separation of the "political" conception of justice and the "metaphysical" conception of justice, as Rawls put it, the priority of the former because it is unanimously agreed to by all citizens whereas the later are not, many of these arguments of the Court are only half correct, as we saw above.

At least the Court seemed on the right track here, according to what Madison, Jefferson, the First Amendment, and Rawls with his "theory of justice" would accept, a unity and equality of treatment, not of making special exemptions. But religious people were not finished with litigating for special exemptions from neutral, generally applicable laws. Significantly, the following statements of the *Boerne* Court by which it decided this case should be quoted since within a dozen years, the Court would forget them in exempting people from more and more neutral, generally applicable laws just because they claimed "free exercise" of religion:

> It [the RFRA] appears, instead, to attempt a substantive change in constitutional protections . . . [as its] sweeping coverage ensures its intrusion at every level of government, displacing laws and prohibiting official actions of almost every description and regardless of subject matter. . . . Any law is subject to challenge at any time by any individual who alleges a substantial burden on his or her free exercise of religion. . . . If 'compelling interest' really means what it says . . . , many laws will not meet the test. . . . [The test] would open the prospect of constitutionally required religious exemptions from civic obligations of almost every conceivable kind . . . [which is] a considerable congressional intrusion into the States' traditional prerogatives and general authority. . . . When the exercise of religion has been burdened in an incidental way by a law of general application, it does not follow that the persons affected have been burdened any more than other citizens, let alone burdened because of their religious beliefs.[5]

In *Boerne*, J. O'Connor, dissenting, agreed with the Court's analysis of the limited power of Congress, and therefore that it had overstepped its bounds. But on the question of the legitimacy of the Court's construal of the reason for rejecting the RFRA (that the Congress misunderstood the *Smith* decision), her strong dissent insisted that she felt *Smith* itself was *incorrectly* decided at the time, so it needed to be revisited before the Court could make any judgment about Congress's reaction to *Smith* in the RFRA. She also argued that the entire ethical structure behind the laws of the nation was understood as *requiring religious conditioning*, and without that, there would be no sense of the rights our Constitution protects. She was correct in showing "worship" as the primary elements protected under the FE clause in the pre-Constitution days and those immediately following. She, however, missed the point in suggesting that where there is a conflict between the civil and religious laws, Madison emphasized the religious must have priority. It was exactly the *opposite*. He and Jefferson both *separated* the spheres of the individual religious duty and the individual and societal political duty. As they both said, government could and should step into the private sphere of one's religion *only* when one breaks the general civil laws or attempts to interfere with others' religious freedom. There was *no point* in their writings in which they said that religion should overrule civil laws if they conflict or that religious people should be exempt from strict compliance of the civil and criminal laws. Religion is certainly *not* given a "preferred" status by the First Amendment as J. O'Connor alleged in *Smith (II)*, unless she was just thinking of the ethics of a religion. But religion did not have a preferred status and cannot since it *divides* the population rather than unites, by its Absolute which is always attached to specific cultural and mythical elements of the past.

But the Founders, as many states, grounded the whole relationship of religion and state on the *natural right* of freedom of conscience that came from the Enlightenment rather than from any religion, so to posit the necessity of religion in order to establish law and government is to *misunderstand* the role of religion by the end of the eighteenth century, to give the mistaken impression that the Constitution did not establish a secular government.[6] We cannot repeat the history we have already documented of pre-Constitutional and post-Constitutional views, and the general abandonment for the most part of even any state maintaining an "established" religion. But even the long history of Christianity shows it is not an unambiguous good, but spawned division, hatred, and wars century after century, justifying economically enslaving people who were racially different, if not killing them, and Christians' immigration to the New World did not end this sectarianism except by the *secular* construction of the structures of justice in the Constitution, which was largely due to the influence of the Enlightenment and the voluntarism of the revivals in New England. But many religions still do battle against the government as if it should have adopted their exclusive metaphysics for the base of its law, no matter how other citizens felt about it. Had that been the case, the United States would have dissolved as a nation many decades ago. The religious pluralism has become exponentially greater the past 50 years.

The actual confrontation of this pluralism, the presence of the *very different other religions*, as Rawls said, only *recently* presented itself to people in the United States, posing to them the choice of fighting a continual war against each other or honoring a mutual freedom of conscience in a social contract.[7] The latter is not supplied by nor encouraged by any religion. The feeling of religious superiority continues in the minds of many who have never seen the real unity of the democratic society, just as a feeling of white supremacy occupies the minds of some who cannot realize the "happenstance" or "accidentals" of life as being no basis for a definition of either what it is to be "human" or of "justice." But, as I have shown, this is not unique to one democratic group, but is found just as militant and divisive in present-day India, and to a degree within most pluralistic cultures simply because of the *absolutized* claims of most religions.

For our Founders, there was *no point* at which their worship was justified as *exempting* them from civil and criminal laws that were facially neutral and generally applicable, and there was *no point* at which public taxes were to be shifted to benefit special religious indoctrination, whether through religious institutions' schools or other private or charter schools, when the government finally established public education for the benefit of *everyone*. The two spheres of religion and government were to be separated. The government should *never* need to show any "compelling" interests by which to justify its facially neutral, generally applicable laws, for the latter come from the "overlapping principles" or consensus of the Rawlsian negotiating from the *hypothetical* "original position" behind a "veil of ignorance" which gives *priority* to the civil/criminal laws of government which are founded on the public reason's "freestanding" and finally "overlapping" principles. If government needs never to prove a compelling interest, religious people cannot expect to take shelter in and find exemptions or special benefits by arguing that the government was unable to prove such compelling interest. The social contract binds all equally. It is not a sieve full of holes through which many can slip through by claiming the government failed to show a compelling interest, not when it comes to "political justice."

Why should there be *any exemptions* from a facially neutral, generally applicable law for *anyone*—whether one is religious, or nonreligious, or bald, or weighs only 110 pounds, or works in the local grocery story, or is a trader on Wall Street, or is unemployed? "Political liberties," as Rawls said, belong to the first principle and have priority over the "principle of difference" in social and economic realms. In his idea of the fair reasoning with public reason and "freestanding principles," there is no room behind the veil of ignorance in which one can assert some happenstance advantage over others. The playing field is level, so there are no special exemptions and no special rewards and no special categories by which one can expect either exemptions or rewards.

It is a more difficult question, however, if we ask whether it is even possible for the majority's law to be *applied fairly*, or whether the Court upholds a "majoritarian" interpretation as equivalent to a "constitutional" interpretation even if it adversely affects minorities? Madison himself recognized that it might not always be obvious where that "separation" must be seen, but it nevertheless *must be* or the New Nation would disintegrate in more religious divisiveness.[8] Rawls's second principle dictated that the law had to be assessed by whether it benefited the "least advantaged" and presented an equality of social and economic opportunity.

Perhaps it was unfortunate that the RFRA was called a "restoration" of religious freedom. If it was an attempt to get the Court to clarify its standards, that was one thing. But if it was an attempt to *reinstate special privilege*, either unavailable to other religions or at least unavailable to the *non*religious, that should *not* be available because it violates the first basic principle of equal liberty which Rawls articulated and upon which the Constitution rests. The Court's *Boerne* standard of a facially neutral law that has universal application is logical and fairer than the special benefits the Court itself had earlier bestowed on religious people by its more stringent standard and more specific than some mere "rational basis" test which the "compelling state interest" test seemed to supplant. It certainly comes closer to corresponding to what people under Rawls's suggested "veil of ignorance" in the hypothetical "original position" would agree on, rather than agree to special benefits for anyone that happened to turn up "religious," or, more specifically, "Christian."

Even so, the Court had *not* given the Native American claim its "Free Exercise" of its *worship* rituals involving silence, meditation, communing with the Spirit, and power of Nature or Mother Earth any religious credibility in the *Lyng* case in 1988, since the action the government brought affected only a single religious group as everyone knew. Yet the primary and often only meaning of the "religious freedom" embodied in the "Free Exercise" case was "worship" which was also the issue of the *Smith* case in 1988 and 1990, the Native American sacramental use of peyote in their *worship*. There was *no* substantiation of the inclusion of peyote within the list of "Controlled Substances" applied to *anyone* other than those Native Americans, since, in fact, no one else used it. But the Court determined that it was not placed in the list just to prohibit the Native Americans, yet had *no evidence* that any-one else was the least interested in it. So these were strained decisions by the Court, with its inability to accept other cultures' religions as of equal value to Christianity to protect. Congress's reaction of the RFRA in 1993 and its specific later laws allowed them peyote for religious worship after all.

CONGRESS DOUBLES DOWN WITH THE RLUIPA

After the Court found Congress's RFRA as a misreading of the Court's posi-tion and faulted it for failing to include in the RFRA considerations of both the Commerce and Spending clauses, Congress reasserted itself again in 2000 with the RLUIPA, in 42 U.S.C. §§2000cc-1-5. This modified the RFRA of 1993 which *Boerne* had overruled, now explicitly broadening its scope espe-cially where commerce or government funding was involved ("land use" or "institutionalized persons"). The latter (e.g., in prisons or mental hospitals) especially needed attention since this group of people had been deprived of their autonomy, so were entirely at the mercy of the government if they were to enjoy any free exercise of religion. The bill also concerned zoning or limitations or restrictions attached to any land uses, whether they were abso-lute prohibitions of religious groups, or discriminated more against religious usage than other proposed uses. The standard of compelling interest and the least restrictive means to meet that interest remained the "test" carried forth from the RFRA.

The *RLUIPA* states that "government shall not substantially burden a person's exercise of religion *even if* the burden results from a rule of general applicability" (42 U.S.C. 2000b-1(a)). If such substantial burden does occur, the government must utilize the old test, the compelling state interest with the least restrictive means of furthering that compelling interest. Of most significance of this *RLUIPA*'s modification of the *RFRA* was that it explicitly made the religion more individualistic by saying that this compelling state interest must apply to "any exercise of religion, whether or not compelled by, or central to, a system of religious belief" (42 U.S.C. §2000cc-5(7)(A)) and it must "be construed in favor of a broad protection of religious exercise, to the maximum extent permitted by the terms of this chapter and the Constitution" (§2000cc-3(g)). It still did not define more closely what was meant by "religious exercise" though the emphasis seemed intent on providing opportunity for such institutionalized people to worship according to their own consciences. In any case, it restored the compelling state interest test, which has also been referred to as the "balancing" test, since the law being challenged as prohibitive or burdensome of one's "free exercise" must be shown to have no reasonable alternative methods that would be less restrictive on the religious person in the state's pursuit of its compelling interest. Inasmuch as the two areas were land use and institutionalized persons, its focus was centered more on the "free exercise" of just "worship" than was the more general RFRA, but the word "any" still left it very open if not wholly ambiguous.

We have already in the previous chapter shown the ubiquity of this understanding of "free exercise" as freedom to *worship* as one sees fit, so that the "exercise" mentioned in the First Amendment protects individual choice of people's method, place, and religious group for their "worship," something that had been hotly debated in England for decades and was at the heart of the religious persecution by the English government. It included freedom from taxation for the building of churches in which to worship as well as to support the clergy in such worship. Sadly, in some cases, various colonies, as we saw, did the same quite early in U.S. history—insisting that they could punish people who failed to come to worship services on Sunday or people who held different beliefs or customs manifest in their specific group worship sessions. The Quakers required a silence, very different from most churches, as they waited for the Spirit to move them; the Shakers danced and "shook," which was also quite different from the more typical types of religious "exercise." These were novel to many Christians so for several years both groups were viewed suspiciously as troublemakers by the traditional Christian churches.

The positions Jefferson and Madison explicitly put into writing were already accepted sufficiently so their positions on the *separation* of religion and government were impressively and overwhelmingly accepted. Since the First Amendment emphasized that religion is a totally private, individual thing, it *never* spoke of government having a religion (in fact, actually prohibited it), nor did it speak of any groups such as businesses *per se* as having a religion. It was a matter of a person's individual conscience, not an institution, especially not an institution which attempts to escape any personal liability by being a "corporation."

UNREALISTIC EXPECTATIONS OF FREE EXERCISE

During the year of 2004, two cases came before the Court under both Establishment and Free Exercise Clauses, *Locke, Governor of Washington, et al. v. Davey*, 540 U.S. 712; and *Elk Grove Unified School District et al., v. Newdow et al.*, 542 U.S. 1. In both cases, the Respondent seemed unrealistic in his expectations, asserting his own "free exercise" (either of religion or atheism) as strong enough to overturn the obvious neutral law. In the first case, *Locke v. Davey*, Davey sought to enroll at a small religious college in the state of Washington, and use a state scholarship award for the one explicit thing the scholarship could *not* be used for—following a degree program in Christian ministry (called "devotional theology"). In the second case, *Elk Grove v. Newdow*, an atheist father sought to shield his child from any religious influence either from his estranged wife who had sole custody of the young daughter or from her school which expected children to recite the Pledge of Allegiance which included the clause "under God."

It is hard to believe that either of these men were the least surprised by the Court's decisions. In Davey's case, there should have been no surprise since WA state's scholarship program spelled out certain qualifications the candidate had to meet in applying, as well as the fact that one could not use the scholarship to pursue a degree in the ministry or theology, with the intent of becoming a religious leader. Once at the college in the Fall semester, he was required by the Financial Officer of the college to sign papers that he was not using the funds to pursue a degree in the ministry or devotional theology, and because he refused to sign, he received no award. He then sued. Did he think that because he declared a "double major" in business administration as well as in the prohibited "devotional theology" or "ministry" that somehow he could fool the rules? He stated that his only interest in pursuing higher education was to become a minister.

In the other case, Newdow should not have been surprised at the outcome since he knew that his daughter, like other students, was allowed to be *exempted* from reciting the Pledge of Allegiance if she objected to it, and he knew that his daughter's mother was a Christian and disagreed with his atheism, and she claimed the five-year-old daughter was also a Christian, and was quite comfortable with the "under God" phrase in the Pledge. But even more importantly, Newdow knew that *she* had sole custody of the child, for the welfare and education of the latter, and to the degree that the estranged couple had any conflicts over what they thought was best for the child, the ultimate authority was hers. Yet after she intervened in the case, he still continued to pursue his rights, basing his claim to standing, not on being her father (since that was subservient to the ultimate authority of her mother's decisions) but being her "next friend."

On the surface, to a person unfamiliar with the Court's history of the interpretation of the two religion clauses of the First Amendment, what Davey and Newdow both wanted might well have seemed reasonable. Why should the government be able to tell a college-bound student what he or she had to study, or more precisely, promise to help him financially if he would refrain from seeking a degree in one specific discipline? This seems very discriminatory on the government's part. And why should Newdow, the noncustodial father, be deprived of his natural rights of sharing with his daughter his convictions about religion, even in trying to get the school to change its requirement about the "under God" part of the Pledge of Allegiance? So we must look more closely.

In *Locke v. Davey*, J. Scalia strongly dissented against the Court's holding for the State of Washington over Davey, insisting that this was a general government benefit that involved a blatant discrimination only on the basis of religion. He deplored that "Davey is not asking for a special benefit to which others are not entitled."[9] But he was, in fact, even asking for a special benefit explicitly prohibiting anyone, including himself. J. Scalia further insisted if the state gave scholarships in which it allowed students to select their field of study in preparing for a profession, it *must* do the same for Davey to pursue the ministry. He cited to *Lyng*, 485 U.S. at 453, and began a tirade using *Everson* (1947) as the proper key: "New Jersey cannot hamper the citizens in the free exercise of their own religion. Consequently, it cannot exclude individual Catholics, Lutherans, Mohammedans [*sic*], Baptists, Jews, Methodists, Non-believers, Presbyterians, or the members of any other faith, because of their faith, or lack of it, from receiving the benefits of public welfare legislation."[10] The basic problem is that what J. Scalia is advocating is *exactly* like Gov. Patrick Henry's "general assessment" bill, which would have allowed citizens of Virginia to select which religion their taxes could support, the very bill which Madison, Jefferson, and all the Baptist and other leaders *soundly defeated* in Virginia, and then copied the same "separation" of government and religion into the U.S. Constitution's First Amendment.

The problem with *Everson* in 1947 was that the Court's 5/4 decision supplied funds *only* to parochial or Catholic schools, *not* to any other private schools. So even the case itself discriminated between people completely on the *basis* of their religion "or lack of it." A general benefit for all citizens, when denied, J. Scalia argued, constitutes a violation of one's Free Exercise. But here the government scholarship explicitly was not a "general benefit," but honored the anti-Establishment definitions by Jefferson, Madison, and others who began the process by prohibiting even "three pence" of tax dollars to be used in that way. Unfortunately, by the time J. Scalia finished his dissent, he was arguing that the Court here joined in the modern popular culture in which many have nothing but disdain for religious conviction.

He asked rhetorically if the next step might be to deny priests and nuns their prescription benefits on the ground that tax payers' freedom of conscience forbids medicating the clergy by public taxes. This raises a red flag, since priests and nuns receive such government help *unless they elect* to be exempt from it and therefore never pay into the fund, just as all "religious" have that option. So why all the straw dummies? J. Douglas later lamented having wrongly voted with the majority in *Everson*, which would have reversed the decision. But the camel's nose got under the tent in *Everson* and made it progressively more difficult for the Court to find a violation of the Establishment Clause in any public funds that could be used either *directly or indirectly* to *indoctrinate religiously* (*Nyquist* (1973), *Levitt* (1973), *Meek* (1975), *Wolman* (1977), *Grand Rapids v. Ball* (1985), *Aguilar v. Felton* (1985), *Tilton v. Richardson* (1971), and *Roemer* (1976)). Even on the college level, *Tilton* allowed funds for buildings to religiously oriented colleges, but *only* if none of the classrooms were *ever* used to teach any religion or for devotionals. Nothing could be more pertinent to Davey. The gift of the general public's taxes for *indoctrination* or training on how to indoctrinate was a negative "bright line" if there ever was one.

But J. Scalia avoided mentioning most of the Establishment cases since they reveal the billions of tax dollars annually that have subsidized parochial instruction and indoctrination since the *Everson* case in 1947. Ironically, he proclaimed that the *Everson* case should control in *Locke v. Davey*. J. Scalia even used a similar example in his rhetorical statement, "No one would seriously contend, for example, that the Framers would have barred ministers from using public roads on their way to church."[11] Of course not. But the roads, police and fire services, and so on used as analogies were *not true analogies*, as we will see when we cover the Establishment cases in detail and notice the dissent. These were general services or benefits, but the scholarships in *Locke* were *not general*, just as the funds appropriated in *Everson* were only for a select group of parochial schools, *not* a *general* benefit, as the dissent pointed out.

C.J. Rehnquist, writing for the Court in this 7/2 decision, countered J. Scalia's dissent, insisting that this was *not* the Court's hostility to religion or a discrimination against religion. It utilized the tax exemption offered to religious institutions that was upheld in *Walz* to emphasize that "there are some state actions permitted by the establishment Clause but not required by the Free Exercise Clause." The Court had subsequently used a term to describe this, that is, it was called room for a "play in the joints" between the two religious clauses of the First Amendment. The Court noted that nothing about the Free Exercise clause required that the state include such degree candidates. This scholarship program was *not* a *general* benefit offered by the state, but was *qualified* in *many* respects, only one of which was the state's rigorous constitutional antiestablishment respect.

Whereas Davey argued that Church of *Lukumi Babalu Aye, Inc. v. Hialeah* should control since the Washington law was *not* facially neutral, similar to the law in *Hialeah*, the Court argued that the burden incurred was *not the same* at all. Hialeah had made the church's usage of ritual sacrifice a criminal offense. But in the Washington case, Davey was not prohibited from going to the school of his choice, even a religious school, a very conservative Christian college. Nor was he prohibited from taking courses in ministry or (devotional) theology. In fact, it was acknowledged that all students were required to take a minimum of four such courses, regardless of their degree program. He could have still received the funds of the scholarship, so long as his *degree* was sought in *another* field, and this requirement is not against Davey's religious free exercise, but is one of the ways the state of Washington sought to *avoid any religious establishments.*

But it is not illegal discrimination any more than any other antiestablishment law is, which, of course, includes the First Amendment itself. The Court argued correctly that there is no facet of religion that was more essential to the Founding Fathers and early states in their disestablishing than their explicit prohibition to any *funding for clergy or the training of such*, the "three pence" that Madison thought was itself too much which I mentioned earlier. No tax dollars were to be used for such religious training period. In light of the obvious limits placed on government funding of religion in all the Establishment cases the Court has decided, this should have been a unanimous Court. Subsequent litigation, on the other hand, has found it easier to obtain a sought government benefit or exemption by moving potential Establishment cases into the Free Exercise realm, because of the *Lemon* criteria, and then approach the whole issue from the negative side, that is, that the person is being discriminated and prohibited their "free exercise" precisely *only because of their religion.* We earlier saw how this blossomed into daily or business activities which have no relation whatever to the "free exercise" of "worship," and, as Justice Kennedy warned in *Bourne*, this could undermine most of our generally applicable laws by requiring a showing of compelling interest to avert it.

In the *Newdow* case, the Court ultimately decided *only* Newdow's "standing" issue, and in *denying* that he had standing, it did not have to go further to resolve the First Amendment issue about the legality of the "under God" phrase in the Pledge. It turned out a decision by five Justices, with three others concurring only in the result, and J. Scalia not involved in the case.

Newdow had requested J. Scalia recuse himself from the case since Scalia had unprofessionally already *publically* expressed *his disapproval* of the Ninth Circuit Court which had heard the case three times. The Court went to great lengths to show that its general policy through the years has been to avoid making constitutional judgments unless they are really necessary, except for J. Scalia's very unprofessional lack of restraint. By the time it finished examining his claim to standing, it had eliminated the necessity of analyzing the constitutional issue.

The Court also explained that in the area of domestic disputes, such as are involved here, it has always deferred to the state law, thus here to the Federal Circuit Court (which here meant the Ninth Circuit) because it was more familiar with California law than was the Supreme Court. It noted that while the relevant laws do not preclude Newdow's influencing his own child, there is nothing in this case that shows that he was being hindered or prohibited from doing that. But on the other hand, the Court insisted that the relevant cases do not provide any basis for his desire to extend his "free exercise" rights to the point of dictating to others what they can or cannot say to his daughter, or of eclipsing the rights of either the daughter or mother. By California law, he did not qualify for standing as her "next friend," and as her father, he obviously did not have the same interests as she, nor did he have a right that equaled her mother's over her education and welfare.

Although C.J. Rehnquist concurred in the judgment, he faulted the Court for improvising a new "standing" doctrine, misinterpreting the way the Court of Appeals had read the relevant two most important CA cases on the subject. He insisted that, contrary to the Court's idea, Newdow did not seek to restrict what others (the mother and the classroom) were saying to the daughter; he was only insisting that his personal right to indoctrinate his own daughter with his atheism was being infringed on by the Pledge in class. Rehnquist thought the Court was wrong saying that the daughter was the only source he had for possible standing. It was not his daughter *per se*, but his *relationship* to her that provides standing, so the "California court did not reject Newdow's right as distinct from his daughter's, and we should not either."[12]

Despite C.J. Rehnquist's rejection of the Court's impromptu "standing" doctrine, that is, he felt Newdow should have had standing, but would have lost on the merits of the First Amendment question anyway. Here he presented the same argument as J. O'Connor, that the "Pledge of Allegiance" is *only* a patriotic exercise, *not religious*, that the mere insertion of a word or two that are religious does not change the character of the Pledge. Despite the attempts by both C.J. Rehnquist and J. O'Connor to make the "Nation's history" one of being *generically religious from the start*, the "under God" phrase was not added to the Pledge until 1954, and as C.J. Rehnquist admitted, quoting President Eisenhower, the insertion of the two words was "to contrast this country's belief in God with the Soviet Union's embrace of atheism."[13] One could not find a more "religious" purpose, but the Court was not summoned to evaluate whether the Establishment Clause was implicated in the case.

But this is no "generic God" that J. O'Connor posits. "Under God" is as specific as the other examples given ("under Jesus" or "under Vishnu" which are very specifically attached only to a single religion), and the only reason she fails to understand this is because she has simply become accustomed to the "God" of Israel and Judaism, being the same as the "God" of Christianity, but which in Judaism was "Yahweh," with very specific identification, and in Christianity, "God" as Incarnate in "Jesus" as the "Christ," with just as specific and exclusive identification. Since Islam claims its "God" is the same as the Jews' and Christians' "God," would it still be considered "generic" by J. O'Connor if the Pledge read "under Allah" and Muslims speak of Allah also as "God"? The usual way of distinguishing between the generic use of the word is to use only small letters, "god," and capitalize it only as proper name of a religion's specific deity.

There simply is no "generic" God except in the minds of people who know nothing about particular religions and their unique histories of ideas, and maybe not even there.[14] History and ubiquity of usage of religious symbols or words will not by themselves prove anything about what is meant by "under God," even though J. O'Connor thought this really would be the key for the "reasonable informed person" approach. Many Hindus over the centuries have had a particular deity they were devoted to, and in whom they even consolidated some of the powers attributed of other deities, but it was still a very specific god or deity, not a "generic" one—and it was always attached to a particular cultural mythology and history, never outside it or without it. They could speak of it as "God," not simply a "god." If some think that "deism" is the belief in a "generic God," in the Christian tradition, it is specifically *only* the "God" espoused by Christians, whether the particular deist thinks of "God" as a "person" or only as Supreme Power of Creation and Design or "Providence."

Despite the United States' most common term of surprise or indignation, "Oh, my God!" this trivializing certainly does not reveal a "ceremonial" or "generic" God but only a "trivialized" God, a point in history in which the former specific sacred names are not only not sacred but even meaningless. The Western conceptions of deity have never been any more generic, even when Christians referred to "Providence" or other such terms. Even Tillich's "being-itself" or the "abyss beyond the polarity of being and non-being"— even here he is speaking *only* of the Christian God, of the one who engages in "forensic righteousness" or "justifies" the person who is therefore *simul justus et peccator*, and its *particulars* are *never close* to Vishnu, Shiva, Allah, or any deified Buddha, not even to Tillich's contradictory idea of "pan-en-theism," certainly not if "God" to Tillich was the "God beyond the God of theism."[15]

It is *not* sufficient to say that the Establishment Clause is intended to treat all religions *equally*; Madison and Jefferson opposed that "equal" treatment in defeating Gov. Henry's Bill, and they said Congress is to make *no law* respecting the establishment nor prohibiting the free exercise, but, even as earlier courts have elaborated, this means not only that no religion has an advantage over any other religion, but that religion does not get special exemptions and benefits that the nonreligious do not get. Yet that "preferen-tial" treatment is precisely where such a defense of the "under God" phrase in the Pledge leads, even if it is called a mere "patriotic" expression, reminding citizens of their heritage, or even as a "nonpreferentialism" by using the idea of "God" as generic and universally known as "unitary." Does that assume all citizens came from Europe, were white Christians "under" the Christian "God"? The atheist is presented with the option to play the hypocrite, feel as an outsider, the one who does not belong, the one who is not patriotic? J. O'Connor's test from *Lynch* becomes too inconsistent; her "reasonable observer" ends up being limited to a fairly reasonable, but uncritical, undem-ocratic *Christian* observer.

In *Barnette*, the Court said the Pledge was a dubious way to try to build patriotism, and to insist on it being recited might well defeat its very purpose. So the Court exempted Jehovah's Witnesses who saw it as idolatry. Then it had no religious reference within the words whatever. Now, the "under God" is a symbol of a "theocracy" as even C.J. Rehnquist's speculation about what it means shows, though he does not use the word "theocracy." To say that this nation was founded on "God" or by "God" or only by God's laws and author-ity, or stands "under"[16] God's rule and dominion would make it a *theocracy*, *not a democracy*. The only mitigating factor is that in *Newdow*, the school allowed children to be exempt from reciting it if they were opposed to it. That seems like it might suffice. Yet the Court in *Schempp*, which we shall exam-ine in a later chapter, did *not* accept that option as sufficient since it *singled out* the students who opposed it.[17] They became more noticed by others, creat-ing a divisive situation. While a few legislators in Congress might have felt that was a good tactic during the "Cold War" with Russia, *forcing* a student either to engage in something that involves a specific, theocratic symbol or being possibly discriminated against by fellow students as an "atheist," it is not the best way to build a sense of patriotism, and probably was no more effective than McCarthyism of the 1950s.

In 2005, the RLUIPA received a unanimous defense by the Court in *Jon B. Cutter, et al., v. Reginald Wilkinson, Director , Ohio Department of Rehabilitation and Correction, et al.*, 544 U.S. 709 (2005). Prisoners belonging to nonmainstream religions, namely, Satanist, Wicca, and Asatru religions and of the white supremacist Church of Jesus Christ Christian,[18] brought suit against the Department of Corrections for discriminating against them, violating 42 U.S.C. §2000cc 1(a)(1)–(2). This provided that "no government shall impose a substantial burden on the religious exercise of a person residing in or confined to an institution" unless the burden furthers the state's "compelling" interests and is the "least restrictive means" of meeting that interest. Contrary to this, petitioners argued that their free exercise of religion rights had been violated by the prison discriminating against them for exercising their faith, by denying them access to religious literature, denying them opportunities to worship that were equal to that given to prisoners who belonged to "mainstream" religions, by failing to provide them a chaplain trained in their faith or even withholding religious ceremonial items necessary for their worship, items which were identical to those supplied to or permitted those in mainstream religions.

Since Respondents objected that the RLUIPA was itself a violation of the Establishment clause, they argued they were exempt from following it. That became the central question before the Court. The District Court had held that the RLUIPA was *not* a violation of the Establishment clause, but the Sixth Circuit had reversed, holding for the Respondents that it *was* a violation. Here J. Ginsburg, for a *unanimous* Court, *reversed* the holding of the Sixth Circuit.

The Court rehearsed the history of decisions by the Court and attempts by Congress to enable people to enjoy the free exercise of their religion without that enabling being counted as an illegal establishment of religion (i.e., *Smith*, RFRA, *City of Boerne*, RLUIPA). It appealed especially to *Hobbie v. Unemployment Appeals Comm'n of Fla.*, 480 U.S. 136; *Locke v. Davey*, 540 U.S. 712, and *Walz v. Tax Comm'n of City of New York*, 397 U.S. 664. Most pertinent was the expression it used from *Locke* that "there is room for 'play in the joints' between [*Walz*, at 669, cited by *Locke*] the Free Exercise and Establishment Clauses, allowing the government to accommodate religion beyond free exercise requirements, without offense to the Establishment Clause."[19]

The Court opined that the RLUIPA corrected the deficiencies of the former RFRA by invoking the Commerce and Spending Clauses, and the history of treatment of institutionalized persons was studied considerably by members of Congress, showing "frivolous or arbitrary" barriers imposed on such people, preventing their free exercise of their religion. So the Court held that it was following the *Locke*, *Walz*, etc. decisions, and that *Smith* had enforced the idea that there is, as J. Ginsburg worded it for the Court, "some space for legislative action neither compelled by the Free Exercise Clause not prohibited by the Establishment Clause." The *Smith* phrase that allegedly was understood as suggesting that last sentence was "[A] society that believes in the negative protection accorded to religious belief can be expected to be solicitous of that value in its legislation."[20] This supposedly justified the Court's conclusion that section 3 of the RLUIPA that is central to this case "fits within the corridor between the Religion Clauses: On its face, the Act qualifies as a permissible legislative accommodation of religion that is not barred by the Establishment Clause."

The Court necessarily compared the lack of autonomy for institutionalized persons with the lack of autonomy of the military, which makes their position totally dependent upon the agency in charge of their well-being to provide for them if they are not to be deprived of their free exercise rights. The Court attempted to strengthen its decision by emphasizing that the compatibility of the RLUIPA and Establishment Clause "alleviates exceptional government-created burdens on private religious exercise." It also emphasized that this approach assumed that the institution would of course coordinate this accommodation of free exercise with the policies and procedures necessary to the institution itself. It minimized the possibility that other prisoners would find they could feign being religious, so it was doubtful the accommodation itself could be used fraudulently. In any case, the RLUIPA was not in conflict with the Establishment Clause.

Necessarily, of course, the *Lemon* test was never mentioned. Rather, the Court argued the virtue of the RLUIPA in that it did not discriminate between bona fide faiths or religions. However, it neither showed how the legislation, the Court, nor the legislature could ascertain what a "bona fide faith" was,[21] much less to show why only religious prisoners would receive this benefit while there was no counterpart benefit given to all nonreligious prisoners. This is a decision which raises great unanswered questions, and simple unanimity based on precedent cases does not answer those questions. The issue of equality under the law has to include the nonreligious, so the whole idea of giving preferential treatment to people who are religious in whatever ways they choose to exercise their religious rights is a problem, a problem not anticipated within the specific clause, but is addressed in Jefferson's statement that one does *not* receive enhanced benefits by being "religious." This case at least should begin a new dialogue for the future about *real equality* and the "wall of separation."

By 2006, the religious sacramental drug exemption whittled out in the RFRA for Native Americans because of the negative decision by *Smith II* (2000) was extended to an imported Brazilian religious group which had only 130 members in the United States in *Alberto R. Gonzales, Attorney General, et al. v. O Centro Espirita Beneficente Uniao do Vegetal, et al.*, 546 U.S. 418 (2006). It sued to enjoin the government from preventing its importation and use of the components it used to make a special sacramental tea for its religious observance. The tea ("hoacsa") was made from two plants, *Psychotria viridis* which contains dimethyltryptamine (DMT), which is hallucinogenic, and *Banisteriopsis caapi*, which augmented the hallucinogenic effect of DMT. Since it had no recognized medicinal use and was a hallucinogenic drug that could be quite dangerous, and although used for religious ceremonies, might be diverted to a recreational use, DMT was listed as a Schedule I Controlled Substance.

U.S. Customs officials intercepted a shipment of the hoasca in 1999, and UDV, prior to trial, sought declaratory and injunctive relief, arguing that since it was strictly for sacramental usage, it was legal under the RFRA of 1993. The RFRA act required government to show that the burden it placed on the religion was due to the government compelling interest, and that there were no less restrictive means by which the government could meet that interest. The District Court, on hearing the evidence of both sides, reckoned that it was in a state of "equipoise," that basically neither side overpowered the other, but since the burden was upon the government to prove its compelling interest, and it did not, it issued a preliminary injunction and laid certain requirements on the UDV in its use of the hoasca. The government appealed the preliminary injunction, but the Tenth Circuit agreed with the District Court.

The Supreme Court insisted that the government did not even get to the second "prong" of proving its compelling interest, much less proving that it had no less restrictive means of meeting its interests. When the government argued that it would have proven these at trial on the merits, and that the religion had the burden of proof resting on it in the pretrial injunctive stage, the Court ruled that incorrect. The government also argued that it had to maintain a uniformity with the drugs listed under Schedule 1, that there could be no exceptions, which the Court also did not accept. Rather, it cited *Yoder* and *Sherbert* as examples of compelling state interests for which specific litigants were made exceptions because of the severity of the burden placed by government, a judgment made on the basis of the particular situation rather than mere uniformity. It rejected the government's "slippery-slope" argument in making exceptions.

The final emphasis of the Court was its observance that if the RFRA had the purpose of enabling the Native Americans to be an exception in the use of peyote which was also a Schedule 1 Controlled Substance, then surely the precedent was established to include also this small group of 130 of the UDV. Therefore, the insistent idea of the RFRA that a burden to one's free exercise of religion can be challenged even if the burden is from a generally applicable, neutral law stands when the government does not meet the burden of proving that its law was compelling and the least restrictive means to further its interests. This argument, now based on the RULIPA, as the post-*Boerne* Congressional revision of RFRA, now by *Hobby Lobby* (2014) and

Masterpiece Cakeshop (2018), which we will analyze shortly, has run to the extreme of allowing exceptions to universal, neutral laws, thereby exempting more and more people from these laws on the basis of their religious convictions, having nothing to do with freeing them to "worship."

It is one thing to protect people from being forced to worship a certain way with a certain group, but to open the "free exercise" up to grant certain exemptions because of any person's idiosyncratic ideas that he or she calls "religious" does raise the question not only of where would the line be drawn but also on what possible basis. The Court used to argue that it would not get involved in trying to ascertain what was "central" to a religion any more than it would judge what was "orthodox," but in this case, at the very outset, the use of DMV for sacramental purpose was spoken of as "central" to its worship ("central to the UDA's faith is receiving communion through hoasca"). To this was added the adjective of "sincerity" or "honest" convictions. In later cases, the latter terms became almost shibboleths, if pronounced just right.

This decision did at least concern "worship." The question of subsequent cases leaves "worship" behind, raising first the question whether an *honest* person with *sincerely* held convictions about something the person thinks to be "central" to its *religious belief* be allowed to exempt the person from *any* generally applicable, neutral law—just on the basis of that subjective assertion? The more extended question would be whether anyone, for any reason one thinks is "religious," be exempt from neutral, generally applicable laws? If a religious person drives down the highway at 100 miles per hour on the way to worship, and is pulled over, if he says it is his sincere conviction as well as the conviction of his religious group that to be late for worship, which is "central" to its faith, implies indolence for which God will punish the person, should he be exempt from a speeding ticket, and allowed to continue his speeding, endangering others' lives? If he is pursued by the highway patrol, and does not slow down, and finally runs into another car and kills all the passengers, should he simply be excused from all of it because of his religious belief, which is not just his but also of all the 150 people of his religious group? One can think of any number of scenarios. Can religious parents be excused for rejecting any blood transfusion which could have saved their infant's life, when the infant dies? Do they not meet the requirement under the RFRA if that refusal is "central" to their faith which they "sincerely" hold, and the government has to exempt them because it could not prove that the child would die without the transfusion, and the parents were honest in this assertion as were all the people of their religious group? Less tragic, but even more likely, how many religious people will expect to be exempt from having to do business with those people their religion considers as hopeless "sinners," a doctrine which is "central" to their faith and existence—whether they reject those others because they belong to another religion, race, or different sexual orientation? Or, finally, if one's pastor or imam or priest or other religious leader is imbued with religious authority, and he or she makes the decision, that, despite the Covid-19 pandemic and the governor's or mayor's health restrictions which limit gatherings to no more than 20 people inside a room, all parishioners must be present for worship, should the "Free Exercise" excuse the religious leader for breaking the law when six members contract the virus and die as a result? Or, does the Court have to wait to see if anyone dies before hearing such a case?

The real question remains: Why does a person claiming to be religious get to act in socially unacceptable ways, that is, obviously unethical ways, or defy public reason and scientific understanding as well as show no respect for general legal authority in his or her behavior, even violating common laws, whereas a nonreligious person does not? Is that really the meaning of the First Amendment? This is the big question when it comes to Free Exercise jurisdiction. This brings us to a strange case of people who wanted to *discriminate illegally* in this precise way *because* they were *religious*, but they accused the school of *discriminating against their discrimination!*

LEGAL ANTIDISCRIMINATION CHALLENGED BY EXPLICIT "FE" DISCRIMINATION?

The concept of "discrimination" stood behind the Religion Clauses of the First Amendment. Under "Christendom" in Europe, many knew what discrimination could feel like. If you belonged to the official state religion, the government discriminated in your favor; if you were a dissident, the government discriminated against you, even persecuted you. To the degree that a few of the early colonies in the New World thought they had power to favor a single religion—that of the founders or administrators of the colony—they discriminated as well. But as we saw earlier, things changed and the freedom of conscience became an overriding theme in the Enlightenment as well as in the revivals in the New World. The two Religion Clauses were attempts to prevent discrimination because of religion by preventing any "establishment" and by protecting people's "free exercise" of their religious conviction to worship the way they chose, so long as they obeyed the universally applicable laws all citizens had to observe.

The question is, is the First Amendment *itself* thereby illegally discriminatory by virtue of those antidiscriminatory clauses? That may sound silly. Few if any legal scholars today would answer "Yes." John Rawls addressed the subject of basic equal liberty at considerable length, and especially the limits of the "toleration of the intolerant" in §35 in *A Theory of Justice*. Rawls emphasized that since religion is a matter between an individual and his God, civil law should be tolerant enough to allow his differences, even if he or his religious sect are intolerant of others. *But* only so long as the universal liberty of the Constitution itself is *not* in danger, the *equal liberty* to which *all* have agreed in the "original position." In that position, behind the "veil of ignorance," all citizens agreed to reconcile their conflicts by reason and those basic principles. None would have agreed to granting that certain people or groups should be able to be intolerant of others or discriminate against others in the sense of taking advantage of others, of some being able to receive benefits and exemptions others did not, or of being able to get certain privileges because of their "faith" which others could not if they not share the same faith. Behind Rawls's veil of ignorance, they would have no idea of what convictions or what religious group they might even belong to.

Rawls is very clear. The "original position" itself serves as a *limiting principle*. The original position and its "principles of justice" or "kernel of political morality" must be the deciding arbiter, and, that, in fact, allows it even to "reconcile" estranged, diverse religions, or prohibit parties from such violating discrimination since religions at large have not agreed to any other authority to resolve their religious disputes, largely because they absolutize their religion.

In 2010, that very issue, of the limit of discrimination or intolerance that the constitutional system has to accept, was at the heart of the litigation between the *Christian Legal Society Chapter of the University of California, Hastings College of the Law v. Martinez, et al.*, 561 U.S. 661 (2010). The Petitioners claimed that the regulations the University established for its "Registered Student Organizations" were, in fact, discriminatory in their antidiscriminatory mandate, and the University also applied this antidiscriminatory or "all-comers" idea in a discriminatory way to different groups. Specifically, the local club argued that the University discriminated primarily if not only against *it* over all the years of the RSO's existence, whereas there were all sorts of groups that were accepted and registered, groups which had obvious agendas that were not content neutral or viewpoint neutral at all. They contended that being discriminated against in this way, simply because of their *religious* views and religious-moral requirements for membership in their club, the University had violated their "free exercise" of religion.

The 5/4 decision of the Court was in the University's favor, however, holding that there was *no violation* of the Petitioner's "free exercise," that, the group knew the antidiscrimination requirement *prior* to applying for the status of being a Registered Student Organization, yet applied anyway, and subsequently persisted in discriminating. Specifically, the Christian Legal Society, following its national organization, required those who want to become members or become officers in the group to sign a "Statement of Faith," assuring the club that one is a Christian and conducts one's life according to the principles of the Bible, the "inspired Word of God," and, specifically, in terms of opposing any form of sexual activity that is not heterosexual between only a married man and his wife. The CLS opposed any other form of sex, classified gay life as "unrepentant homosexuality," and their regulations rejected any such person from being a member if he or she either engaged in or failed to overtly stand against being gay. The discrimination of the club on campus also was fairly detailed in rejecting many who professed to be Christian but were not in full agreement with the fundamentalist position taken by the CLS.

J. Alito, dissented, joined by the Chief Justice Roberts, J. Scalia, and J. Thomas, accused the majority of deciding the case not from its precedents but on the basis of "political correctness." One familiar with Court opinions becomes used to the justices differing in strenuous language, but to accuse the majority of deciding something only on the basis of "political correctness" seems to have set a new low. The dissent was simply embracing a form of majoritarianism. The dissent bought the position of the Petitioners, arguing that the CLS was the only group the School of Law had rejected in 20 years, that a good portion of the 60 present RSOs had agendas that involved speech content that was not "neutral," that the University failed to show the connection between their "all-comers" policy and its Anti-discrimination Policy, and in fact, did not even speak of having an "all-comers" policy when the litigation was underway, so essentially the University had not required any "viewpoint neutrality" in other applications for an RSO. These conclusions were offered without much more than simply a passing reference to several diverse RSOs that *allegedly* were not viewpoint neutral. But the dissent offered *no proof* other than their *names*. It accused the Court's majority of building the whole case on the all-comers policy and Non-Discrimination Policy and the following short stipulation by both parties which was the following as if "stipulation" was of *no* consequence: "Hastings requires that registered student organizations allow any student to participate, become a member, or seek leadership positions in the organization regardless of their status or beliefs."

The earlier District Court's decision for the University emphasized that there was no impairment of the CLS's right to expressive association: "Hastings is not directly ordering CLS to admit [any] student[t] . . . [r]ather, Hastings has merely placed conditions on" the use of its facilities and funds. Hastings denial of official recognition to the group "was not substantial impediment to CLS's ability to meet and communicate as a group." The Court also rejected the "free exercise" complaint of the Petitioners: "[T]he Nondiscrimination Policy does not target or single out religious beliefs," but is a *neutral policy of general applicability*. It argued that "CLS may be motivated by its religious beliefs to exclude students based on their religion or sexual orientation, but that does not convert the reason for Hastings' [Nondiscrimination Policy] to be one that is religiously-based." This is the crucial and credible reasoning. It too noted the stipulation by the parties, so summarized the whole with the following: "The parties stipulate that Hastings imposes an open membership rule on all student groups—all groups must accept all comers as voting members even if those individuals disagree with the mission of the group. The conditions on recognition are therefore viewpoint neutral and reasonable."[22]

If the question arises why a group that knew that its basic philosophy was so at odds with the University would apply to be an RSO, since the group had existed on campus *prior* to applying, and had many different functions to attempt to attract members, the answer could have been the privilege of being "recognized" by the University, of being permitted to use its facilities, of having a certain access to financial assistance, or being able to use the University's name and logo—or it may have been primarily motivated by the national organization to try to win a legal battle, to set a precedent—although the latter is not speculated by the Court since many such "test cases" are brought to the Court in similar fashion even though the petitioners already know they are fighting against a law that may have many years behind it.

But this is unique in that the Court's dissent utilized the Petitioner's argument against the majority of the Court—accusing it of a religious bias in ruling that the discrimination or the Nondiscrimination Policy or "all-comers" policy was *itself* an unlawful discrimination equaling that of the CLS. That is the most alarming element in this case.

The Court insisted this was *not* an open forum but a limited public forum, in which it is *not* unlawful for the sponsor of the limited forum to draw reasonable regulations, and that does not unlawfully restrict Petitioners' speech. It also does not violate "expressive-association precedents" since the rules of Hastings do *not* compel Petitioners to accept into their club unwanted members. All Hastings is doing still allows the CLS to function on campus, to attract members, to publicize itself vigorously, even to use the facilities to a degree that they are available. The official recognition or logo of the University surely cannot be such a huge deal, the Court suggested. The Court noted with cell phones providing easier and quicker access for social contacts, that surpassed the methods of contact the University was offering, so the latter would not be missed. All these benefits were still available, but simply not as an officially recognized student organization of the University. In this way, by not becoming members of an RSO, the club *could still exclude any* person they wanted or require *any* statement of faith they wanted to use, but they simply could *not* expect the University to endorse their sexually discriminating practices. The Court noted that the University had chosen to dangle a carrot of subsidy, but not wield a stick of prohibition; they had simply provided all groups with a choice, and here the students were informed of this *long before* they officially applied, even when they gave the stipulation, and the stipulated facts must be treated as "undisputed."

Three cases were utilized by the Petitioners, *Healy*, *Widmar*, and *Rosenberger*, but the Court argued that they are not dispositive here since in the present case, in contrast, the University's regulations are *content and viewpoint neutral*. It recited the stipulation as follows: "The parties stipulate that Hastings imposes an open membership rule on all student groups seeking RSO status—all groups must accept all comers as voting members even if those individuals disagree with the mission of the group. The conditions on recognition are therefore viewpoint neutral and reasonable"[23] (also p. 8).

The Court notes that CLS argues that Hastings's all-comers condition violates the Free Exercise Clause, but the *Smith* decision "forecloses that argument . . . [since] in *Smith*, the Court held that the Free Exercise Clause does not inhibit enforcement of otherwise valid regulations of general application that incidentally burden religious conduct. . . . In seeking an exemption from Hastings' across-the-board all-comers policy, CLS, we repeat, seeks preferential, not equal treatment; it therefore cannot moor its request for accommodation to the Free Exercise Clause."[24]

Thus, religiously identifiable groups can discriminate in their rules about who can belong, whether they are a law student club at a university or a church, mosque, or synagogue or other. The Court has never tried to dictate limits on who can be a member of a particular religious group. The question was whether a government university utilizing public funds could endorse the group's form of discrimination, and that meant that the public reason—facially neutral, generally applicable laws—would have to govern the public institution, laws which could *not* approve this particular form of discrimination. That is parallel to Rawls's idea of the "original position" having *priority*, principles of public reason agreed on by all citizens. Otherwise, the University extended to the club the same freedom of speech, religion, and association as all other students, but it could *not* fund or specifically endorse the club's mission and discrimination. This appears to be a natural distinction which defeats the litigants' argument that the University itself was discriminating against it.

Rather infrequently, a "Free Exercise" case gets all the way to the Supreme Court which involves decisions the Court long ago said had to be resolved *only* by the religious institution itself. But the issue was whether or not the religious institution's authority could be extended past decisions over the ownership or control of property which was all the earlier decisions involved. While the religious group cannot discriminate on any government laws or constitutions, can it be legally *allowed to discriminate* against its own members that it *employs*, that is, to use its own standards, whether they are compatible with the neutral, universally applicable law and whether they are well defined or not?

In 2012, such a case arose in which a church fired a teacher, after encouraging her, as a "lay" member and teacher, to take the formal training to become one of the religiously approved or "called" teachers. She acceded to their wishes, was trained, and became a "called" teacher. After she had served them effectively in this capacity for several years, she developed narcolepsy and was unable to teach for several months. The case was *Hosanna-Tabor Evangelical Lutheran Church and School v. Equal Employment Opportunity Commission et al.*, 565 U.S. 171 (2012).

At issue was whether the government in its capacity as the EEOC could have *any* role in adjudicating a case of a teacher, trained and recognized as a "minister" by the church's standards, who was fired from her work. The answer was unanimous that the "ministerial" exception had been recognized by the judicial system since the 1970s. Thus, the Court's refusal to have any voice in the decision of her employment or unemployment was based on the consensus that religious groups necessarily maintain *complete control* of their "ministers" to whom they entrust the role of propagating the religious group's message, that government has no authority to interfere. That means that the "ministerial exception" exempts the religious institution from normal facially neutral, universally applicable laws regarding its employment and unemployment. The neutral, universally applicable laws still applied to any *non*-minister employee of the church, someone such as a janitor or musical accompanist or music director, but not to one who was formally recognized as a "minister" by the church.

This principle of the church's power is not a mere exception for autonomous churches but especially for those that have central organizations, so it is especially attached to the idea of the general image of the church, allowing its national leaders to determine rules such as those governing employment and unemployment over "ministers" it wants to propagate its message. To that degree, it harks back to litigation in the post-Civil War years when a Presbyterian church in Louisville split between the antislavery and proslavery groups, each claiming sole possession of the building of the "Walnut Street Presbyterian Church." The Court, viewing the long history of interference between ecclesial courts and civil courts in England, distinguished the U.S. approach by clarifying three different forms of church organization in its ownership of property. The two at issue were the local, strictly autonomous, congregational organization of a church, and the other, the organization that had a national body through which all the local bodies were governed and organized. The latter was the situation of the Walnut Street Presbyterian Church. Therefore, the particular group in the split that insisted on remaining connected with the national body was the legally recognized group, which would enjoy the future use of the property. The Court insisted that the rule was that civil courts would exercise no jurisdiction if the issue was

> a matter which concerns theological controversy, church discipline, ecclesiastical government, or the conformity of the members of the church to the standard of morals required of them . . . [for] it is easy to see that if the civil courts are to inquire into all these matters, the whole subject of the doctrinal theology, the usages and customs, the written laws, and fundamental organization of every religious denomination may, and must, be examined into with minuteness and care, for they would become, in almost every case, the criteria by which the validity of the ecclesiastical decree would be determined in the civil court. This principle would deprive these bodies of the right of construing their own church laws, would open the way to all the evils which we have depicted as attending upon the doctrine of Lord Eldon, and would in effect transfer to the civil courts where property rights were concerned the decision of all ecclesiastical questions.[25]

In the case at hand, a teacher, being requested by the local church in this Missouri-Synod Lutheran Church, had gone through the required training and was therefore a "called" teacher who was successful and effective. When she began to suffer from narcolepsy, she requested disability leave just prior to the beginning of the 2004–2005 school year and was granted it. When she informed the school in January 2005 that she would be able to return to work within a month, she was told there was no place for her since they had hired another teacher in her place for the entire school year. By the end of the month, *school administrators* decided she was not likely physically capable of returning either that year or even the following year, and the church voted to offer her a "peaceful release" from her "call."

She refused, producing a note from her doctor that she would be able to resume work. But the school board refused to offer her more work since *they* had already decided she would not be physically capable of returning either for the remainder of that year or even the entire following year. There is no record of how they determined this, or why their medical judgment would have been better than the doctor who had written a note that she could resume work in February of that year. In the latter part of February, when she was medically cleared to return to work, she showed up at the school, but was asked to leave. The principal later phoned her at home that afternoon to inform her that she would likely be fired, upon which news, she replied that she had spoken to an attorney and intended to assert her legal rights.

The whole case revolves around the Church's claim that it is *not* subject to the EEOC since she was a "minister" and was fired because she violated the Church's policy by bringing a lawsuit rather than settling it with the

Church. But that expressed intent of hers to sue the Church was made *only* in *response* to her being informed that she would probably be fired. The irony of the Church then justifying its firing of her by her violation of Church policy in bringing a lawsuit is that *its* own theological objections against Christians suing one another in secular courts, based likely on I Cor. 6, for which it was determined to punish her, did not prevent *their pursuing her* all the way to the Supreme Court, where they were the Petitioners. Had they really believed Christians should not utilize secular courts, they would have settled with her *outside court* to begin with, unless that "Church policy" is intended only to apply to employees of the church and not to the Church administrators. The chronology shows that the church had already decided on not allowing her to come back, long before they heard she was getting legal counsel.

What is not said, however, is that her threat to sue was as a last resort, since the school and church had already dismissed her and "rescinded" her "call" (from God?). The Church's claim was that as a recognized "minister," she stands as an exemption from the government employment laws and can be hired or fired as the Church sees fit, and it bases this on the premise that the "ministers" of the church are the ones entrusted with evangelizing and representing the Church's position, teachings, and values, so that *it alone* can decide whether or not she does. The claim was that she no longer does, precisely because she brought the suit—her insubordination. Yet they had decided to let her go long before she brought legal suit.

The Court strangely held unanimously for the Church against its former "minister" on the basis seen in *Watson v. Jones* and subsequent cases,[26] for example, of who gets the church's property in case it splits, that certain ecclesial matters simply are not within the jurisdiction of the civil courts. But "insubordination" was *not* a theological controversy, and if firing her was an act of *retaliation* as it appears, that is *not* a legal area from which religious institutions should be *exempt*. Further, there was no record presented of her failing to represent properly the Church's position. She even led the devotionals and worship for the children occasionally.

The irony is that in matters like this the Court would abstain from getting involved, but simply defer to the opinion and authority of the church, while in the Native American cases, the Court felt sufficiently justified in upholding neutral, generally applicable laws against the religious no matter how much it burdened the religion itself, its administrators, and whole organization, even to the point of *making worship impossible*. No recent case better illustrates precisely why Rawls insisted that our social contract with all of its civil and criminal laws must come from a base that is developed out of the "public reason" and "overlapping principles," a "political" understanding of justice rather than merely "metaphysical." And the earlier Court's idea of giving priority to a religious institution's nonpublic reason and noninclusive metaphysics *reverses the priority of the unity of the nation itself* based on principles to which *all* have agreed, quite unlike the religious associations. If the religion itself can decide how to treat its members, especially its "called" or "ordained," and this precludes any interference by government, are there any limits? If the religious institution is not subject to employment and unemployment regulations of states or the federal government, nor to property ownership laws, are there other laws a person or a group could be exempt from or favored by for just being "religious"? If a "called" teacher sexually molested two students, could one's being a "minister" or "religious" shelter one from state criminal prosecution? Where is the line to be drawn once the government allows the authority of the religious person or institution to overrule the basic principles we, as citizens, all agreed to live by? One can only hope that anyone in a similar position of being either a "lay" or a "called" teacher realizes that to select the latter option will enable the teacher to be fired at will by the church without any genuine specified cause at all. This "religious freedom" has nothing to do with being free to worship. So where will the Court draw the line on the "Free Exercise" of religion?

NOTES

1. *Boerne*, at 566.

2. *Smith (II)*, at 884.

3. But anything that one does as "free exercise" of religion will likely involve the right of free speech, or freedom of assembly, and so forth, so one cannot simply add "rights" to finally get a substantial "hybrid" one, such as one's right to exist, one's right to think, one's right to eat, the right to be an adult, the right to be a child, the rights of parents (e.g., as J. Scalia emphasized in *Yoder*, though he was sure there is no "right of privacy"?), the right to sleep, etc., ad infinitum.

4. This reading of §5 of Fourteenth Amendment probably condemns the Court as well as Congress, since the "test" that is in question had been *changed by the Court*, and who gave *it* the power to change the *substance* of a law? On the other hand, this boilerplate statement (in §5) is the way most of the newer Amendments end, but the words themselves do not, without the Court's interference, mean any such restriction. Each is actually geared to the specific content of the *particular* Amendment, and the issue in *Boerne* has nothing to do with the content of Fourteenth Amendment.

5. *City of Boerne v. Flores*, 521 U.S. 507 (1997) (at 532, 534. 535, 536).

6. The "natural rights" emphasis became secularized by the Revolution, the Declaration of Independence and Constitution. See G. Edward White, *The Marshall Court and Cultural Change: 1815–1835*, ch. X. The irony is that while the Court deemphasized natural rights more and more in the nineteenth century, gradually formulating proper adjudication as *not* involving any "moral" considerations, the Court *did* allow under the Free Exercise Clause a primary appeal to one's morality or conscience, but again, *only* if it had some *religious* grounding. The exceptions, however,

were in the CO cases in which the Court gave the exemption to a person who claimed his morality was *not* grounded on a religion at all (*Welsh v. U.S.*, 1970). The moral conviction was in 2020 also added as being sufficient with or without a religious base in *Little Sisters of the Poor* (2020). Though we no longer have a draft, the Selective Service still provides the CO or alternative options for one enlisting. But, as Rawls emphasizes, there is *no consensus possible* in the conflict between *metaphysical absolutes*, so one has to return to the basic political morality of the "original position." Rawls, *A Theory of Justice*, 221.

7. Rawls insightfully wrote the following:

> What the ancient world did not know was the clash between salvationist, creedal, and expansionist religions. That is a phenomenon new to historical experience, a possibility realized by the Reformation. Of course, Christianity already made possible the conquest of people, not simply for their land and wealth, and to exercise power and dominion over them, but to save their souls. The Reformation turned this possibility inward upon itself. What is new about this clash is that it introduces into people's conceptions of their good a transcendent element not admitting of compromise. This element forces either mortal conflict moderated only by circumstance and exhaustion, or equal liberty of conscience and freedom of thought. Except on the basis of these last, firmly founded and publicly recognized, no reasonable political conception of justice is possible. Political liberalism starts by taking to heart the absolute depth of that irreconcilable latent conflict.

Rawls, *Political Liberalism*, xxvi.

8. James Madison to Rev. Adams, 1832, *Writings* 9:484–87, in Kurland and Lerner (eds.), *Founders' Constitution*, V: 107.

9. *Locke, Governor of Washington, et al. v. Davey*, 540 U.S. 712, at 727.

10. *Locke*, at 726–27.

11. *Locke*, at 727–28.

12. *Elk Grove Unified School District et al., v. Newdow et al.*, 542 U.S. 1, (at 24–25, ftnt 2).

13. Citing 100 Cong. Rec. 1700 (1954).

14. The only element of religion that can be called "generic" is its tendency to "absolutize," but even the pictures of "God" as the Absolute in the "Abrahamic" traditions are viewed as different and absolutely exclusive.

15. For a more definite analysis of Tillich's theology, see ch. 4 of my *Ethics and the Future of Religion: Redefining the Absolute* (Lanham, MD: Lexington Books-Fortress, 2021).

16. "Under God" still sounds like "God" is some definite being up above the Earth somewhere.

17. The concurring opinion by J. Thomas began by noting that he agreed with C.J. Rehnquist that Newdow had standing. More significantly, he noted that *by the Court's precedents*, especially *Lee v. Wiseman*, but also *Schempp, Barnette, Torcaso*, and others that these precedents have ruled that one should not be pressured by the government into declaring "a belief," so the Pledge should be unconstitutional by that standard, even if one could opt out of it. But he argues that the Court went off the track by "incorporating" the Establishment Clause, which, in turn, led to an

incorrect decision in *Lee*. (The implication is that all the Court's decisions regarding Establishment are incorrect if it was wrong to incorporate it to begin with, which means the federal government and various state governments can all be fighting each other over the meaning of the First Amendment, if anything.) He is convinced that only the Free Exercise clause supplies an *individual* right, whereas the Establishment Clause supplies a *state* right. That is, he thinks the Establishment Clause was simply prohibiting the federal government from interfering with the various states' established churches (at 45–54). While that might simplify what the Court has to decide, it simply reveals a lack of respect for the whole discussion of the early states as they disestablished upon the adoption of the First Amendment, and the history even of Jefferson and Madison in the state of Virginia alone invalidates J. Thomas's opinion. It is strange that he alludes to Madison's "Memorial and Remonstrance," but not to the Bill he was remonstrating against that Patrick Henry was pushing for the *state* of Virginia (at 53–54). The Founders were opposed to any establishments, not giving separate states the option to preserve an established single religion or even to establish Christianity in general while spreading the taxes to support it according to the various Christian denominations the citizens indicated.

18. The fairly loosely organized "Christian Identity" movement is not an institution but an anti-Semitic, militant, pro-Aryan, racial segregationist, and millennialist ideology of white supremacy.

19. *Locke*, at 718.

20. *Smith (II)*, at 890. The religious people in *Smith* were ruled *against* by the Court, whereas this quote would make it sound as if the legislature went out of its way to defend their free exercise rights!

21. "Bona fide faith" is redundant (a "good faith faith"). Perhaps "honest faith" would be better.

22. *Christian Legal Society Chapter of the University of California, Hastings College of the Law v. Martinez, et al.*, 561 U.S. 661 (2010), at 676.

23. *Hastings*, at 676.

24. *Hastings*, at 694, ftnt 24; also at 697, ftnt. 27.

25. *Watson v. Jones*, 13 Wall 679, 733–34 (1872).

26. *Kedroff v. Saint Nicholas Cathedral of Russian Orthodox Church in North America*, 344 U.S. 94 (1952) and *Serbian Eastern Orthodox Diocese for United States and Canada v. Milivojevich*, 426 U.S. 696 (1976).

Chapter 8

Unlimited "Free Exercise"
"Any Law Is Subject to Challenge"?

By the title of "any law is subject to challenge," I point back to J. Kennedy's warning in *Boerne* against the RFRA, that to allow almost anything as a "substantial burden" to one's free exercise of religion, which forces the government to show a "compelling interest," the door would be open to challenging any law and granting exemptions to "almost every conceivable kind" of civic obligations. He warned of this "change" in standards with the following:

> It [the RFRA, replaced by the RLUIPA] appears, instead, to attempt a substantive change in constitutional protections . . . [as its] sweeping coverage ensures its intrusion at every level of government, displacing laws and prohibiting official actions of almost every description and regardless of subject matter. . . . Any law is subject to challenge at any time by any individual who alleges a substantial burden on his or her free exercise of religion. . . . If "compelling interest" really means what it says . . . , many laws will not meet the test. . . . [The test] would open the prospect of constitutionally required religious exemptions from civic obligations of almost every conceivable kind.[1]

In fact, it may produce "exemptions from civic obligation of almost every [inconceivable] kind," because not many people at the time of the *Bourne* case would have thought it likely that within 23 years, "Free exercise" would be so extensively applied to things which have *nothing* to do with "worship." Attorneys, of course, had discovered that to shift cases away from the jurisdiction of the "Establishment" Clause into the "Free Exercise" Clause, they might obtain for individuals and institutions exemptions from all kinds of facially neutral, universally applicable laws and/or even greatly "enlarge" their "civil capacities."

Rather than their "religious" purpose and effect being something which disqualifies them, as it did under the *Lemon* test, once the argument is shifted into "Free Exercise," one's religious purpose can move mountains in one's favor. Of course, this was what Jefferson and Madison had so *opposed*, people either obtaining exemptions and special benefits (or being denied the general benefits all citizens are supposed to enjoy)—just *because* they *are* "religious." Either way, it also grossly violates the equality of liberty of Rawls's system.[2] This was the danger of continuing to use the "compelling interest" test in Free Exercise cases, that the government would be unable to meet the test, so people would be exempt from a plethora of generally applicable laws. Was it perhaps simply a matter that any test the Court devised for either of the Religion Clauses would over time reveal certain inherent problems, that sheer definitions and new decisions would paint the Court into a corner, or was it a problem created primarily because of the change in the Justices which brought different presupposition aboard in the closing two decades of the twentieth century? Yet both of these clauses are supposed to be quite neutral and reasonable. Or in *Hobby Lobby* was it something more contingent, simply the litigants' opposition to President Obama and the Affordable Care Act, for whatever reason? Or was it all about money, about possibly getting out of having to pay for the health care of all the litigants' employees as seems to be a concern in *Hobby Lobby* as we will see? Or was the "play in the joints" alleged between the two clauses simply revealing itself as an inaccurate metaphor becoming a crippling defect and the whole limb becoming useless since to Madison and Jefferson the two clauses were regarded as merely two sides of the *same* coin, both merely things government can*not* do, either enhance or diminish benefits for being religious?

CORPORATION'S CONSCIENCE VS. RIGHTS OF THE EMPLOYEES

One of the most emotionally wrought religion cases in U.S. history, that negated precedents, so became a "landmark" case in the sense of reversing direction of the Court, was *Burwell, Secretary of Health and Human Services, et al., v. Hobby Lobby Stores, Inc., et al.*, 573 U.S. 682 (2014). Because of its becoming a turning point, though only a 5/4 decision, it requires considerable space here to explain. It consolidated two different cases, No. 13-356 the *Conestoga Wood Specialties* and the *Hobby Lobby Stores and Mardel* (No. 13-354). Whatever the reason, the Court allowed the discussion to move miles away from anything approximating the "worship" which the "free exercise" clause was framed to protect.

Here the Court accepted litigants' claimed religious consciences as being a religious opinion significant enough, even if not based on any authoritative evidence except litigants' own opinions, to give them *also* the *freedom to act on it*, to the detriment of thousands of their female employees. The government's significant interest in providing health care to many people who did not have it and could not afford it, which included a choice of methods of birth control for those women who desired it, was denied by the owners of Hobby Lobby stores. One of the primary tenets of Madison, Jefferson, and even Rawls was that no person, because of his or her religious opinions, can assume the position of placing other religious people at a *disadvantage or decreasing their liberties*, since none of them would have agreed to such in Rawls's "original position" behind a "veil of ignorance."[3] But the consideration of all those employees who were disadvantaged was *never even mentioned* by the Court. Surely the Court was not unaware of repercussion of its decision, since the dissent countered with it.

Owners of the Hobby Lobby Stores had earlier funded health insurance for their many employees, including birth control methods. But they took issue with the Affordable Care Act when they discovered that among the 20 different contraceptives available to their employees were included four that they took to be a form of "abortion." They said their religious convictions were that the fetus is a person from the moment of conception, so they were unwilling to pay for such medical supplies for their employees. The HHS had whittled out exceptions to this contraceptive mandate, exempting *religious employers* which included not only churches or the religious institutions but also *religious* nonprofit organizations (such as religious hospitals, etc.) if they had *religious* objections to providing such coverage, an exemption extended primarily because of the Roman Catholic protest against this part of the ACA. But nonexempt employers, of course, had to pay for the comprehensive coverage. The Appellees recognized the difference, that they were *not* a 501(c)(3) organization, or recognized religious organization, but rather a *for-profit corporation*, but nevertheless sued for a temporary injunction.

Their respective District Courts both *denied* their requests for a preliminary injunction. In *Conestoga*, the Third Circuit agreed with its District Court against *Conestoga*, arguing that for-profit corporations could not "engage in religious exercise" under the RFRA or the First Amendment, and the mandate imposed *no requirements* on the persons who owned the business. The Tenth Circuit, however, involved with Hobby Lobby and Mardel, reversed its District Court, arguing that HHS had not proven that it did *not* have a less restrictive alternative to achieve its compelling state interest.

In *Hobby Lobby*, Respondents sued, using the *RLUIPA* and Free Exercise Clause of the First Amendment. The *RLUIPA* states that "government shall not substantially burden a person's exercise of religion even if the burden results from a rule of general applicability" 42 U.S.C. 2000b-1(a). If such substantial burden does occur, the government must utilize the old test, the compelling state interest with the least restrictive means of furthering that compelling interest. Of most significance of this *RLUIPA*'s modification of the *RFRA* was that it explicitly said this compelling state interest must apply to "any exercise of religion, whether or not compelled by, or central to, a system of religious belief," and it must "be construed in favor of a broad protection of religious exercise, to the maximum extent permitted by the terms of this chapter and the Constitution" §2000cc-3(g). What the statute did *not* say, however, that was claimed as one of Hobby Lobby's main arguments against HHS, was that Congress *intended* by this statute "to effect a complete separation from First Amendment case law," which was supposed to be obvious by the fact that Congress deleted the reference to the First Amendment and defined the "exercise of religion" in the broad terms it did. But how could Congress's reference to the "Constitution" in this section dealing with religious belief and religious exercise have not been a specific reference to the First Amendment? This argument by Hobby Lobby was simply specious.

Therefore, J. Alito, for the Court, insisted this is not a Free Exercise case at all, but only a statutory problem. This is a nonsensical statement since *the very statute itself* emphasizes that the protection must correspond to what the statute *and the Constitution* permit.[4] By its same lack of logic, the Court refused the dissent's understanding that Congress had by this statute and its predecessor, simply forced the Court to return to the Court's own pre-*Smith* test. J. Alito had assumed J. Scalia was correct in his view of "hybrid" cases wherein the Court had, prior to *Smith*, utilized the compelling interest test and least restricting alternative or "balancing" text over and over. J. Scalia had argued that it had been utilized by the Court *very little*, and basically abandoned in recent years since it had been used *only* in unemployment compensation cases or in "hybrid" cases, that is, cases that combine a religious claim with another, such as speech. If it were that simple and consistent, that would be marvelous, but as J. O'Connor argued, that was simply a *misreading* of the Court's Free Exercise holdings over the years. But this way the Court could *pretend* this was not a "Free Exercise" case, but only hanging on a statute.

To the contrary, the RLUIPA phrase "any exercise of religion" was surely what the Court understood in the pre-*Smith* cases, since even in those cases, the Court did *not* ultimately require that particular exercise to be "compelled by, or central to, a system of religious belief," as we can see by the way the Court voided that requirement in the CO cases of *Seeger* and *Welsh*. But the words of the statute itself define the breadth of its protection as having to meet not only the statute chapter but "*the Constitution.*" If Congress did not have in mind by its reference to "the Constitution" the "Free Exercise" cases the Court had decided over the years, there is really no explanation of what such a reference would mean. Yet, J. Alito, for the Court, insisted that Congress sought to establish this *statutory* scheme as "a complete separation from First Amendment case law." That contention simply flies in the face of the statutes' own words, its deference to the Constitution. What choice did Congress have, since it formulates statutes, not judicial opinions? One does wonder how this kind of logic got five votes.

In any case, under the pertinent sections of the Affordable Care Act, employers who had 50 or more full-time employees were required to offer "a group health plan or group health insurance coverage" that provides "minimum essential coverage" *with no cost-sharing requirements*. When the area of "preventive care" was examined, they had failed to include preventive care for women. Therefore, the ACA gave to the HHS, the task of studying what women needed in the way of preventive care and screenings to be included in the plan. Among the various preventive medicines for women only were a variety of birth control methods. The study, introduced as the Women's Health Amendment," was added to the ACA and the HHS was in charge of administering it. After experts in women's medicine and detailed studies were considered, the Institute of Medicine recommended to the HHS that the ACA adopt *all* the FDA-approved birth control methods to provide each woman a choice. The importance of women's health, and the necessity of adequate preventive health, combined with the high cost of many such services, including birth control methods, had caused many women in the past to do without since they could not afford it. To include such preventive health care as part of the package for women appeared to have significant long-term national benefits of a compelling interest.

Because of the trend these days of employers not offering their employees any health care, or cutting their work hours so they did not qualify for such a benefit, the ACA attached severe penalties to any employer of 50 or more full-time employees who failed to provide employees with such a group health plan. If the employer furnished a plan for its employees that failed to comply with the *ACA*'s group health plan requirements, a penalty was assessed of $100 per day for each affected individual, and if the employer stopped providing health insurance altogether and at least one of its employees enrolled in a health plan and qualified for a subsidy on one of the government-run *ACA* exchanges, the employer was fined $2,000 per year for each of its full-time employees. The HHS was given the responsibility to decide on the types of preventive care and how to cover it. As studies pertinent to this delegation of power were presented, they showed that since women's health care could be very expensive, especially significant birth control methods, the government health care had the purpose of making the overall coverage free of cost to female employees. This was the reason the various birth control options were placed within the covered plan. But no woman was thereby *forced* to use *any* of it or to have to pay for any of it. It simply had to be *available* for employees, a totally *private or individual choice.*

With the thousands of employees the three companies had, if they furnished a health plan but refused to pay for the HHS's contraceptive element, Hobby Lobby's estimated penalty for its 13,000 plus employees would be $475 million per year, Conestoga's penalty for its 950 employees would be $33 million per year, and Mardel's $15 million per year. If they instead were to drop coverage altogether, they could face penalties of $26 million for Hobby Lobby, $1.8 million for Conestoga, and $800,000 for Mardel. The disincentive to offer health care was obvious as the Court noted, the "penalties" would be a *substantial burden* on the companies.

The Court simply assumed at the outset that the government had a "compelling interest." It acknowledged that it was government's "interest in guaranteeing cost-free access" to health care and preventive care, such as contraceptives, including the four objected to by *Hobby Lobby.* But if providing optional birth control methods was government's compelling interest, why would the employer think *he* should determine which type of birth control methods qualified as that "compelling interest" rather than the HHS deciding since it is the HHS and ACA, rather than the employer that *define* the "compelling interest"? Why were not these laws as religiously neutral and generally applicable laws as in *Lee, Roy, Lyng,* and *Smith?* Why did not the same rules apply, then, that a person can*not* claim by his "free exercise" right to tell the government how to *run its business?* That is precisely Hobby Lobby's posture toward the government, that it would tell the government that it was wrong.

As J. Ginsburg argued in her dissent, Hobby Lobby's claim was actually "foreclosed" by the Court's decision in *Smith,* that the First Amendment is *not* offended when "prohibiting the exercise of religion . . . is not the object of [governmental regulation] but merely the incidental effect of a generally applicable and otherwise valid provision."[5] Further, J. Ginsburg noted that a "conscience amendment" was attempted to counter the ACA's provision of thorough health care coverage by putting the decision in the hands of employers rather than the female employees, but Congress rejected this proposed Amendment.[6] Certainly, the ACA's policy and intention was *never* to *affect much less prohibit the free exercise of religion.* Of course, since "free exercise," as we showed, meant in the First Amendment, only the freedom to worship, it is not at all clear how "worship" and "birth control" supplies are at all related. At most, what the Appellees suffered was from a purely "incidental effect" of the generally applicable law, and really not even that, since the corporation took the brunt of the burden rather than the persons who owned it. The government wanted to offer certain choices to each woman at no cost, but the owners of Hobby Lobby interfered. Did they do this as the later 2020 case of the *Little Sisters of the Poor,* to escape personal guilt of *complicity* in the case? They could have been a mere neutral conduit of the government, doing their part as an equal citizen in offering women some choices, but now that they *interfered*, they *became complicit*, responsible for any negative results. There was no telling how many of their female employees would have had no means of birth control, no prenatal care, so might now, because of litigants' interference, they were forced to select a regular abortion as the only alternative. Or perhaps they were not as concerned as the "Sisters" over "complicity"?

The Court in the *Lee*, *Roy*, *Lyng*, and *Smith* cases had suggested that for "free exercise" rights to extend *that far* would be like saying one need not pay taxes to the degree that he or she has religious qualms about how the government uses those taxes, so that, as the Court insisted way back in *Reynolds v. U.S.* (1879), to allow that much power in the "free exercise" would simply be permitting each person to be his or her own law, making public civil law impossible. *There* the Court was all for strict compliance to the generally applicable laws each citizen is expected to follow, even though at least *Lyng* and *Smith* involved "worship" which *Hobby Lobby* does not. Similarly, J. Kennedy had suggested in *Boerne*, as we saw, that if the Court forced the government to meet the compelling interest test, *few laws* would be exempt from challenge.

Once the burden was proven, and the compelling interest was admitted, the Court insisted that the government *failed* that *other* part of the test, that is, *failed* to show that the contraceptive choice is the least restrictive means of furthering its compelling interest. Is the Court here looking to sexual abstinence as the "least restrictive means," which, despite its endorsement by the most conservative Christian institutions, simply has not worked? That typical opposition to Planned Parenthood overlooks the fact that if more birth control means which actually *prevent* conception were *encouraged*, many less abortions would ever be requested. Cause and effect is not always seen or admitted. But J. Kennedy (for the Court) in *Boerne* had argued vociferously against this "least restrictive means" being a part of the RFRA, since he insisted that it was not a part of the pre-*Smith* "compelling interest" test.[7]

The Court in *Hobby Lobby*, however, seized upon the law *not* being the "least restrictive means" as primary grounds for its enforcement being illegal. It argued that HHS had not shown that it actually lacked these *other means* that would be less of a burden to Hobby Lobby. The government could itself have covered the cost of the four objectionable contraceptives to women who were unable to obtain them because of their employers' religious convictions. Or the HHS could extend its already existing exemptions for religious nonprofit organizations to for-profit corporations. On this point, the Court insisted that the mere existence of exemptions does not disqualify it from still being a compelling state interest, again, revealing that the Court did not want to approach this under the rational basis standard of a *neutral and universally binding law*, since Respondents had seen the "less restrictive alternative" as the *easiest* way to defeat the negating power of the compelling interest and therefore win the case. After all, the Court had argued that *incidental* restrictions on one's religious exercise do *not* require a showing of compelling interest or least restrictive means.[8]

The concept of "corporation" has two primary benefits over a sole proprietorship business. First, one can thereby gain for one's business greater access to funds from other parties to invest and underwrite the corporate adventure by selling shares. That is a great benefit. Equal in benefit in a litigious culture was the owners-become-directors (or CEOs or managers or equivalent) *escape* from *personal liability* for the enterprise to which they could be held in a sole proprietorship. So corporate law refers to the "corporation" as a "fictive person" or a "legal fiction," *not* a real person at all. It was a "person" in the sense that *it* would be held responsible for its actions or effects stemming from decisions made by its corporate board and administration, rather than the actual persons owning or running it being held responsible. The corporation stood between the general public and the shareholders/managers as a fictive person to the two separate spheres. But a "closely held corporation" makes the "person" of the corporation even more fictitious, more like an LLC.

So here the question is *which* "person" has the religious scruples, the real, living persons who own it or the fictive corporate "person"? If either was absent from the scene, that question would resolve immediately: the fictive corporate "person" is merely a passive, inanimate script on paper. It does not think or speak or feel, and it has no religious scruples as an inanimate product of language. But, of course, the Court had already recognized its "rights" as it opened Pandora's box for unlimited campaign contributions in *Citizen's United* (2010) and *McCutcheon v. F.E.C.*, 572 U.S. 185 (2014).[9] But if the fiction allows the corporation to blunt the connection between the issue and the actual owners or executives, why were not the owners of Hobby Lobby satisfied to be *consistent* and allow it to do the same with regard to what "person" was *responsible for the contraceptives*, that is, the *corporation* only. The corporation is not desiring freedom to go some place to "worship" as it pleases, and even these family members/owners of the corporation are not suing to be free to worship as they please. They are simply using "free exercise" of religion as a weapon to exempt them from having to comply with generally applicable laws about universal health care coverage.

The Court went to great length in *Hobby Lobby* to try subtly to expand the "rights" protected by incorporating. It mentioned that incorporating protected the corporation and all managers and shareholders from government seizure of its property without just compensation, and it extends Fourth Amendment protection to employees of the company to secure their private papers (not the corporate papers or records), and so on from warrantless searches. So because of the Second Amendment, may the corporation arm itself? Because of *Roe v. Wade*, may the corporation have itself a legal abortion under those general guidelines? Because of universal suffrage, may the corporation not only fund political campaigns but *also vote*? To the contrary, the corporation's legal "fiction" of being a "person" cannot be stretched that far. Legal structures, somewhat similar to business buildings, do not themselves think or believe or care—they are only "persons" in a fictional and limited financial sense, only a device by which to escape personal liability where one has failed to do his legal duty.

But here Appellees and the majority of the Court try to equate the real persons' beliefs that ran the closely held corporation with the beliefs of the fictive "person" of the corporation. The Court insists that the purpose of incorporation was "to protect the rights of these people." Admittedly, but only their *financial* rights through separation from the corporation, so they can escape financial liability for any poor performance of the corporation. It simply cannot be both ways, so to escape any financial liability by insisting that they are *not* the same and not connected enough to create any continuity of legal consequences, while simultaneously insisting that the corporation, as "person," *actually has* a belief, a religious belief, which is precisely *identified* with the belief of the controlling family of stockholders, which means by such equation, the people and corporation *gain special benefits not available to others* for the *connection*, while *escaping* from any real financial liability through *disconnection* from the corporate entity. But to equate them or identify the belief or exercise of the corporation as that of the owners is to "pierce the corporate veil" and thereby make them once again liable for any suits against the corporation. The *two* "persons" cannot be equated without them really being equated. Surely citizens are not that determined to gain advantage over other citizens by claiming their religious ideas provide them that advantage, no matter how much it hurts their employees. The Court was not suggesting that an inanimate legal structure of a corporation, merely on some pieces of paper, can now make decisions on its own, think, feel, express itself by funding political campaigns, and finally equate *everything* it does (*not* the people behind it) with *its own* religious free exercise, because it is possible for a corporation to be "religious" and need to *worship*. If that sounds ludicrous, it is. It simply cannot be both ways. The Court's idea of corporation as a "person" had already taken an absurd leap in the issue of contributions to political campaigns in *Citizens United*. To a degree, this was simply the next step in legal fiction, combined with religious favoritism, producing an illegal and illogical fiction.

In addition to this irresolvable contradiction, the Court insisted on reading the institutional "exemptions" to the "mandate" for such medical coverage as reading a specific list in the manner of suggesting that no matter how specific the list, it undoubtedly did *not* exclude *other* possibilities from the list. That is false reasoning in such a very specific holding; it could have been justified *only* if the HHS had said "there may be other legal exemptions to these in additions to those we specify." But it did not. The list of exemptions was complete, not left open to amend. The exemptions were for *bona fide religious institutions* such as churches and synagogues, and so on, and for their religious suborganizations such as religious schools, religious seminaries, and so forth, and it went so far as to include religious nonprofit organizations such as religious hospitals, and many of these had to incorporate within their respective states. But the law has no category of "religious for-profit corporations," or "religious for-profit craft stores," or for "religious for-profit barber shops," or even for "religious non-profit tire stores." The list was complete, not open to being pried open by some corporation's money or influence which could motivate the Court to supply the legal costume. They simply did not meet the qualifications to be exempt, and that was obvious to all.

Yet the Court argued that HHS did not preclude the possibility. But that is simply as untrue as stating that a category called "jackrabbits" might also include "crocodiles" as long as it does not specifically rule that out by saying "jackrabbits which are not crocodiles."[10] HHS made no exemptions for "for-profit corporations" at all or for for-profit sole-proprietor or partnership businesses. "For-profit" corporations were never mentioned by HHS, and by not mentioning it, the law means clearly that such was *not exempt*. In fact, HHS was providing the exemption *only* to "religious" organizations, which did not mean just any people who had some kind of religious belief, but to agencies organized and recognized by a religious institution that were founded as nonprofit, eleemosynary institutions providing a morally beneficial service to the public rather than seeking a profit. Those parameters do not describe Hobby Lobby in the least. Those categories have been maintained legally. All religious institutions qualifying as "religious" in this sense receive certain tax breaks, and all of them are nonprofit, even if that is still residue from the earlier theocratic colonial days, so should have been discontinued long ago.

But by the traditional legal terms, a "religious" institution, while it may be forced to incorporate within any given state, simply cannot be a *for-profit* corporation. Yet the Court said over and over that surely the HHS would not have formed such a cruel choice that people either have to choose between not going into business in the first place, or in doing so have to be willing to violate their religious convictions. But this contradicts the fact that the Senate, in 2012, voted down the so-called conscience amendment which would have enabled any employer or insurance provider to deny coverage by their own religious convictions. By this vote, Congress left health care decisions—including the choice among contraceptive methods—in the hands of women, with the aid of their health care providers, rather than placing the decision into the hands of male politicians, employers, and insurers. Yet the Court capitulated and gave the decision back to the employer here, snatching the decision out of the hands of the women employees needing health care. This is religious coercion via manipulating the government, another form of majoritarianism, as Madison, Jefferson, and Rawls would all call it.

Now it is significant that *none* of these three corporations contended that they qualified for the status of a 501(c)(3) organization; they were *not nonprofit*, nor was their operation eleemosynary. The Court argued that *Gonzales v. O Centro Espirita Beneficiente Uniao do Vegetal*, 546 U.S. 418 (2006), *Hosanna-Tabor Evangelical Lutheran Church and School v. EEOC*, 565 U.S. ___ (2012), and *Church of the Lukumi Babalu Aye, Inc. v. Hialeah*, 508 U.S. 520 (1993) show that a nonprofit corporation can be a "person" within the meaning of the RFRA. But in each of these cases, the corporation *was* a *religious* organization, and in most states, religious organizations are required to incorporate as a formality, but they are *not a for-profit business*. That is a very crucial distinction.

In *contrast*, Hobby Lobby, Conestoga, and Mardel were businesses, *not* religious institutions in any formal or legal sense. They were no more "religious" than likely half of the businesses in the United States if the measure is merely whether the owners or primary share holders consider *themselves* religious in some sense, or have some form of religious faith, and they claim to attempt to live their lives and run their businesses consonant with the ethical principles they have learned from their religion. But that does *not* make their hardware stores, bowling alleys, computer technology business, real estate services, and so on ad infinitum "religious" in the sense of churches, synagogues, temples, or even church schools or church hospitals. Why anyone would argue otherwise is a mystery, other than the possibility that the broader the definition of "free exercise" can be given, even if kept under a statute, the more possible establishment cases can be shifted to "free exercise," which might be needed to defend tax dollars going to parochial schools.

Hobby Lobby, Mardel, and Conestoga Wood Products may have been very principled, even benevolent, but as a *for-profit* corporation, their primary purpose was to make profit, not to be a "service" organization, so their "religion" was no more central or worthy of notice than moral or "religious" principles of many or most other *for-profit* corporations. A business or corporation is not religious merely because the owners believe in something, or say they do, and no for-profit corporation is recognized as "religious" because they stand at opposite ends of the materialistic spectrum from religion. In fact, as we will see when we examine the Establishment Clause, the famous Crystal Cathedral was a *true religious institution*, but when it began charging people for tickets to see its spectacular productions, it had to pay income tax on its *profits*.

To interpret the religious free exercise in the "broadest" sense possible, as the Court here read the RLUIPA instructions, cannot possibly mean that a fictive entity is sufficiently a "person," that it can pray, worship, or believe anything, so that *all of its activity is protected* as "free exercise" of religion. Here the Third Circuit was correct while the Tenth Circuit was clearly misusing the idea of "person" as well as "religious exercise." When the Court emphasized the dominant shareholders' religious convictions and sense of "mission" in its business which it wanted to count as the "religious exercise" of the fictive "person" of the corporation, the equivocation is exposed between the "fictive person" (the corporation) and the owners or managers.

The Court climaxed its argument over "person" by saying "[b]ut no conceivable definition of the term [i.e. 'person'] includes natural persons and nonprofit corporations, but not for-profit corporations." But that was not the argument. The problem was not the statute's use of "person" as much as it was the question of what a "religious institution" is and what it takes to be classed as a "nonprofit corporation," neither of which they were. The lesser problem of the meaning of "person," because of the fictive use of it as applied to a "corporation," nevertheless does not allow the "person" to be *both* fictive (the corporation as sole person) and the *real*, natural persons (owners) at the same time. "Person" cannot be intended to mean both "natural" *and* "fictive" when the whole point in incorporating is to *avoid legal liability* of the "natural" persons by *disconnecting* it from the fictive person of the corporation, so that one *cannot* move back and forth between them to gain exemptions or privileges not otherwise available. But, further, the natural and fictive cannot be equated as we have already shown since there is no way a business thinks or believes, and certainly not engaging in *its* free exercise of *worship*.

The Third Circuit not only pointed this out, but, in assuming that the "person" is the corporation, it reassured the owners that the "mandate does not impose any requirements on the Hahns" in their (separate) *personal* capacity (at 13, citing 724 F. 3d 377, 389). Had they left the law alone, they would not have paid for insurance, and they would not have been personally responsible for any of their female employees' own choices. The ACA and the mandate being questioned pertained *only* to the business or *corporation operations*. That is, by forming a corporation, *it* has become the "person" liable and responsible to the law in its operations, which includes proving medical coverage for its employees. The whole mandate issue does not even touch the owners, and it will not do to simply point out that it is a "closely held" corporation so the owners' convictions and worship can be said to be the conviction and worship of the business. Still all they do is manage the corporation, so the *legal fiction* of the corporation being the "person" involved *released* the issue from the *conscience of the owners* and shareholders personally. But the logic is lacking when the Court says that if "person" included *both* natural persons and the fictive person of the nonprofit corporation, it would have to include also the fictive person of the *for-profit* corporation. How can that be and there remain any distinction between the nonprofit and the for-profit corporations?

An even larger problem is the scope of their "free exercise" they were claiming. Respondents wanted their First Amendment protected "Free Exercise" to include "all" they do *as a company*, not simply as a family of persons. Yet they defined that religious guidance in *everything they do* for the company in very personal terms, as things *each employee does*, *not* in terms of what the corporation does.

The Founding Fathers, on the other hand, were trying to protect a *person*'s (not a corporation's) freedom to *worship*, and certain traditional "acts" or "rituals" of worship are noticed as we read the various states' Constitutions, Bills of Rights, and Ratification of the U.S. Constitution. The people were *not* using "free exercise" of religion to say that it covered them in *everything* they do, or *everything their business does*, for that would have made a mockery of the "right" and the "religion." If ever taken seriously, it would have placed one's *religious convictions over any and every law* as the Court pointed out in *Reynolds* 150 years ago. This is the very thing the *Boerne* Court also warned against.

That, of course, was pointed out also by the dissenting justices in *Hobby Lobby*. But the majority of the Court bought Hobby Lobby's insistence that Hobby Lobby's own statement of purpose is the rule for the case, that it "commits the Greens to 'honoring the Lord in all [they] do' by operating the company in a manner consistent with Biblical principles." So *everything* they do, with, by, and for the business is the corporation (person's) protected Free Exercise of religion? These days, the Court has recognized a "person's" rights of privacy, but they do *not* extend to include the corporation's "rights of privacy" as a "person" so that one could claim the corporation's records exempt from any government regulation since it is a "person." The corporation as a "person" does not thereby gain freedom from self-incrimination under the Fifth Amendment. The Bill of Rights was explicitly speaking of individual peoples' rights, not some "fictive entity."

The owners of Hobby Lobby emphasized that all family members had to sign pledges to run the business in accordance with the family's religious beliefs and to use the family assets to support Christian ministries. So they closed on Sundays, even though this allegedly cost them millions of dollars a year in potential sales. They further sacrificed by not selling or promoting the use of alcohol. Of course, most hobby and craft stores actually do not sell very much alcohol to drink, nor do religious bookstores. They insisted that they contributed profits to Christian missionaries and ministries, and bought "hundreds of full-page newspaper ads inviting people to 'know Jesus as Lord and Savior.'" Yet they admitted that they did not affiliate with any particular Christian group, but this was simply their own personal faith. But they obviously knew who they were marketing to and tailored it all by the correct clichés and key claims. So perhaps the company gained more than it sacrificed in these areas. Were these paid for and deducted as the corporation's business expenses or out of the family members' personal income?

In these specific ways, but *especially* in their rejection of certain birth control pills, they claimed they were simply following Jesus and Bible. What the Court never thought to ask was specifically *where* in the Bible and in the *teachings of Jesus* one finds (1) this opposition to birth control, (2) the instructions to close their businesses on Sundays, or (3) their opposition to selling alcohol? Nowhere in the Jewish Bible (or "Old Testament") or the Christian "New Testament" are *any* of these three things found. There are no restrictions about drinking alcohol. The Jewish imperative to keep the Sabbath day holy pertained only to the Jewish people, the people "chosen" by Yhwh at Mt. Sinai after the Exodus, and it is our present Saturday, not Sunday. Finally, the *only biblical passage* ever used to oppose birth control is an ancient story of Onan in Genesis. But in the story, he is *not* punished for his method of birth control, but because he refused to honor the Jewish *law of Levirate marriage*, refused to accept his deceased brother's wife as his own wife and raise children by her to honor his brother. That was part of the religious-cultural ideas of Ancient Israel. To think the Catholic Church is the only group that has specifically mentioned this, and to believe that their scholars and theologians did *not know* that the problem was the law of Levirate marriage not being honored, is incredible. Does this mean the church expects *Levirate marriage* to be followed by Christians today?[11] Or is that what the owners of Hobby Lobby wanted people to follow?

What this decision means is that virtually *any idea* that one *seems* to hold *sincerely* may *overrule any general law*, even if the idea is totally uninformed, ignorant, or untrue. The criterion is simply the strength of the conviction, or at least the *strength of the assertion* of the conviction. But what if people of *non*-Christian religions assert similar irrelevant and *uninformed ideas*, attaching them to their religion, so demanding "free exercise" no matter what generally applicable law they seek exemption from? Or is the criteria now only for people who claim to be Christian?

If the Court's decision was correct, then the distinction between the "for-profit" and "nonprofit" corporations is no longer valid, and that could qualify them all as "religious institutions," entitled them all to other tax exemptions on both their buildings as well as their income, yet they did *not* press for these because they *knew* they did *not* qualify.[12] Well, actually, the Greens who had by far the largest stake in the litigation (Hobby Lobby and Mardel) did not indicate that they had any affiliation with any official religious group, no particular building to try to exempt, but they asserted that they were Christians, they knew Jesus and followed Jesus and the Bible. At least the Hahns acknowledged that they belonged to an actual Mennonite church and were not just deciding on their own what they would call "Christian." The decision, in light of the Green's lack of connection to any religious group, indicates that one's religious convictions need not be rooted in anything other than one's own uninformed opinions or imagination or wishes or even perhaps economic concerns. Yet, all of this was unnecessary had they just allowed the government to include these employees by its own standards.

One only has to ask whether the Court would have gone to this length to protect an owner of a closely held corporation who objected to the same thing, if the owner were a Muslim, or a devotee of Krishna, or a Sikh, or anything other than a "Christian"?

But Appellees and the Court were dissatisfied with that three centuries' understanding of what "Free Exercise" of religion means, which we have shown earlier in detail—that it was only *freedom to "worship"* as one chooses or with the specific religious group's worship to which one elects to belong. Some members of the Court seem largely interested in the meaning of words, even in the "original" in the First Amendment, yet the Court never analyzed what "Free Exercise" meant to the Framers of the Constitution and Bill of Rights, and felt they circumvented it all by saying Congress meant for the statute to remove the whole discussion from the Constitution. Would the Court have honored such a procedure of the Congress on statutes that concerned the subject matter of other parts of the Constitution or other Amendments, for example, would the Court have said that in a bill Congress was passing on owning firearms, it expected its statute on firearms not to have any relationship with the Second Amendment? Or would that be a bit absurd? Strangely, the majority of the Court never defined or limited that concept of "free exercise." Nor did the RLUIPA define "free exercise" at all.

The ACA was *not coercing* anyone to choose to take any pill, much less any of those four that the Greens and Hahns rejected. The primary purpose in the ACA and even this mandate was to provide at no cost to the employee what otherwise could be very expensive for a woman, perhaps even prohibitive, as dissenting J. Ginsburg pointed out. What is missing is any recognition by the Greens, Hahns, or the Court of this burden, thereby placed on the thousands of female employees who may have wanted one of those four pills, and the broader burden on *all* the employees if the employer decided to totally drop the health care in favor of his paying a fine. Who is to say whose religious convictions have a right to negate other people's religious convictions or other facially neutral, generally applicable rights? Or is this just a stereotype that people who are opposed to abortion on religious grounds often make that anyone who has an abortion is obviously not religious, so is not exercising her religious rights, so the truly religious can overpower them and deny them anything the religious ones please as long as it carefully insists that such an action that the others would want would violate or prohibit *their* own "free exercise"?

Such would be a terrible judgment to make on people, since few women view abortion as a pleasant or indifferent or unemotional choice. In the late J. Ginsburg's dissent (joined by J. Sotomayor, J. Breyer, and J. Kagan), she found the majority's opinion truly incredible:

> In a decision of startling breadth, the Court holds that commercial enterprises, including corporations, along with partnerships and sole proprietorships, can opt out of any law (saving only tax laws) they judge incompatible with their sincerely held religious beliefs. . . . Compelling governmental interests in uniform compliance with the law, and disadvantages that religion-based opt-outs impose on others, hold no sway, the Court decides, at least when there is a "less restrictive alternative." And such an alternative, the Court suggests, there always will be whenever, in lieu of tolling an enterprise claiming a religion-based exception, the government, i.e., the general public, can pick up the tab.[13]

We have no estimate of the number of employees who were of the same conviction as the Greens and Hahns, nor how many religiously *disagreed* with them. But as the dissent notes, they were never a consideration by the Court, but the decision of the Court had the effect—if "free exercise" really extends this far astray from "worship"—of allowing the "free exercise" of religion of the owner of a business (even a *for-profit corporation*) to *overrule* the religious "free exercise" of any and all female employees. Quite on the other hand, what the ACA was attempting to do was make preventive health care *accessible* at no cost-sharing requirements; it was *not* attempting to tell *anyone* what kinds of medicines or procedures to utilize, much less constrain them to a certain product. What the Court's decision did was to make health care for these women more *inaccessible* by deleting a vital part of it for female employees of Hobby Lobby. Was *this* accessibility not itself the "compelling interest" of government, admitted by the Court? Or did the prejudice against the ACA know no limits, so pushed the infinite possibilities of "less restrictive reasonable alternatives" as sufficient to *remove* the employees' health care system entirely?

It is not merely the result of the decision but the *reasoning* of the Court—its very arguments of justification of its decision—that is so questionable here. For example, the Court's utilization of the four "Blue-law" cases of 1963 is a *complete refutation* of its own argument in *Hobby Lobby*. It was *not* merely, as the *Hobby Lobby* Court states, that the Jewish merchants all lost on the *merits* of the case. They did not. The Court never got to the merits of the case. That would be to suggest that they lost on the basis of their "Free Exercise" of religion not being a legitimate enough claim to be exempt from the arbitrary Sabbath rest, enforced by Christians on Sunday, which itself was an illegal "establishment," to prevent them from doing business on Sundays. That is not true at all. The Court simply said their Free Exercise was *not affected nor the issue*. It *totally secularized* the case, as we have already seen, insisting that *any religious intentions* behind the laws had *dissipated over time*, but now were legitimately superseded by a *secular* purpose in the laws. Neither did the Court show that a uniform day of rest was a "compelling" state secular interest, or certainly an interest that had no less restrictive alternatives. In fact, the Court's judgment was *not* made on *either* the tests the Court had used for Establishment Clause or Free Exercise clause litigation.

Certainly the Court said the law was not hindering the Jewish merchants' "free exercise," because they could still attend Sabbath services on Saturday by closing their stores as they did, but in those four cases, the Court did *not* rule on the basis of recognizing the Jewish merchants' *religious* claim at all, much less to show what the *Hobby Lobby* Court insisted, that the *Braunfeld*, *McGowan*, etc. were dispositive for Hobby Lobby. The Court failed to recognize the legitimacy of the Jewish claims that the Shabbat was a holy day (Saturday) that these merchants felt they had to observe. The earlier Court did *not* hold that a sole-proprietor for-profit business could "assert a free exercise claim."[14] That is an argument made out of whole cloth only in *Hobby Lobby*, far beyond the ken of the Blue Law cases in the 1960s. The merchants would have won under that, just as they would have won under the Establishment Clause *Lemon* criteria, but for the Court's maneuver to say there was *nothing at all religious about the law* any longer. Had the Court actually recognized their business as "persons" having a "free exercise" claim, they would have had to rule that to force the merchants with a choice between violating their faith by staying open on their Sabbath (Saturday) or going bankrupt by closing on Sunday, was a terrible choice, which they in fact did rule just *two years later* in a decision for a *Christian*. But they glossed over the actual *religious* implications, supplanting them with strictly the *secular issues* of whether a uniform day of rest would be beneficial, and, if so, that it necessarily *had* to be Sunday rather than Saturday or it would bankrupt the *Christian* merchants who insisted on being open on Saturday.

There was the deciding factor which favored the Christian merchants of the area. But the Court in those four cases did not emphasize even the religious element in the Christians' case, but merely the economic and secular and "uniform day of rest" element. So how can the *Hobby Lobby* Court read its earlier Blue Law decisions so *in*accurately? The Court in those Blue law cases tried desperately to *minimize* even the religiously intolerant Christian

purpose behind those old Christian Sabbath laws in its select historical readings. But the Blue Laws themselves betrayed their *pro-Christian bias* by
prohibiting certain activities during the worship hours of the local Christian
churches or prohibited people doing certain things within a specified proximity of the Christian church buildings. To have honored those Blue laws was to
uphold laws which had a primary, obvious, illegal, religiously discriminatory
purpose and illegal primary religious effect, violating the decade-later *Lemon*
test but even *pre-Lemon* understandings of the purpose and effect of any law
in question by the Establishment Clause.

If those cases mean *anything* today other than manifesting anti-Semitic and
pro-Christian prejudice of the Court from a business viewpoint, they appear
to mean that business must stand on its own, *unable to* assert *any religious
claim* for special benefits.[15] Yet the Court somehow *reversed* this in *Hobby
Lobby*, that a *business can* be protected precisely by asserting *its* religious
freedom is being violated. That is the reason it is *very strange* that the
Appellees had to resort to those Jewish merchant cases, which said *nothing*
about a business having a religious conscience and therefore being entitled to
its "free exercise" rights. It simply said it was a secular day, a secular case,
and the Jewish merchants' "free exercise" was not prohibited.

In addition to using the Blue Law cases to try to prove what did not adju-
dicate, the *Hobby Lobby* Court cited *Smith II* (1990). But *Smith* had *nothing*
to do with *any business* whatsoever, for-profit or nonprofit. It was strictly a
Native American religious sacramental or worship ceremony, as was also
Gonzales vs. O Centro Espirita Beneficient Uniao do Vegetal, 546 U.S. 418
(2006) which we noted already and which the Court also cited here in *Hobby
Lobby*. So all the space the Court gives to expounding the Blue law cases,
Smith, and *O Centro* actually worked *against its argument* in that they were
not analogous at all, therefore not dispositive. They were *religious institutions and their sacraments*, not for-profit corporations and the preservation
of profits.

The validity of the party's religious objection, that a "person" exists at the
moment of conception, or that God creates each person from the moment
of conception, is all *metaphysical* or mythical, a form of the *metaphysical
divisiveness* that our Founders hoped to eliminate by separating religion
and government, and that Rawls hoped to preclude by emphasizing the
concept of justice has to be worked out *politically, not metaphysically*,
and in matters of public justice, the political principles of public reason
unanimously agreed on in the "original position" must *prevail* over any metaphysical or nonpublic reason since there is no way the conflicting absolute
claims of the different religions can be otherwise resolved. It is really that
simple.

One of the primary questions Rawls's understanding presents would be on what grounds would people in the "original position" of socially contracting behind a "veil of ignorance" be willing to have others' liberties nullify one's own? It would *not* be some appeal from one's special knowledge of one's uniqueness since the veil of ignorance eliminates that, so the bargaining is only on the basis of the general of common goods that all need. It also could not be an appeal to a metaphysical absolute or nonpublic reason that gave the other person an advantage over anyone who was just utilizing public reason. To allow the argument from the nonpublic or the metaphysical is to threaten the unity of the nation which, as a democracy, is a shared experience, where differences can be accommodated only so long as the basic principles *all citizens agreed* to are *strictly complied with*, which does not allow for the eclipsing of liberty based on those agreed principles by some metaphysical liberty the religious person may profess to derive from invisible, supranatural sources. To settle an issue extending certain special privileges or exemptions to people which results in so many thousands of their employees being denied a general benefit from government merely because the company owners *claim* to be Christian (or any other religion) is certainly to promote an "established" religion. This is the extreme example of the Court leaning over so far to grant "free exercise" that it violates the "Establishment" clause when it humors them.

In *Hobby Lobby*, it is obvious that the Court placed primary weight on the burden the owners would have if they refused to yield to the government since the penalties were so significant. But how does that financial burden for disobeying the government mandate, which the Court admitted as a "compelling interest," differ from the burden of one who objects to having to pay income tax to the government if on religious grounds one disagrees with many of the things the government spends the money on? Ironically, if, in fact, the Greens and Hahns had to pay any personal income tax, that would be part of what was used by the government to pay its bills, so would *still be used* to help the government *provide* for the preventive care of the ACA, for other employees of other companies, including paying for these birth control pills for millions of other women employees, including allowing them to choose which pills they desired, even the *four* to which the Greens and Hahns objected. How would they not be still "enabling" the "sin" (as they judged it) in those cases, just as surely as if they obeyed the general laws and gave the same opportunity to their own employees? The ACA was not intended to allow corporations to leave their employees completely without medical coverage; quite the opposite.

If one accepts this philosophy or mission statement of their business, once the Court approved this, as J. Ginsburg opined, the door is opened to any owners of *any business* to declare their refusal to serve others as their own private, protected religious conviction, a protected "Free Exercise" of *their* religion. This was the explicit agenda of the Christian evangelistic lobby to fight against both abortion as well as gay marriage,[16] to allow business owners to decide and be able to refuse service to anyone on the basis of either of these issues. But once it receives that legal protection, there is no limit to the types of things a religious person can refuse since the Court has insisted over and over that it is *not* in the business of ascertaining what or who is to be "orthodox" or what beliefs or religious exercises are to be regarded as "central" or "essentially" religious in any sense. But they just did, based on a mere *strong assertion* of people's belief in one single family interpretation of only one religion. The Court emphasized that the "free exercise" must be broadly conceived, as insisted by the RLUIPA, that it was to include "any exercise of religion, whether or not compelled by, or central to, a system of religious belief" §2000cc-5(7)(A). We will see that J. Ginsburg was almost precisely prophetic in her anticipations of the future.

The Court's "broad" interpretation of "free exercise" is itself unreasonable not only because it stands in direct contradiction of what the First Amendment's term "free exercise" meant—*worship*—but also because *Hobby Lobby* makes it so extensive that it can mean *everything one does* or *one's business does*; virtually anything can now be legally protected under the Free Exercise clause. It potentially dislodges the validity of any neutral and universally applicable law. It necessarily negates the Court's own decisions in the Native American cases of *Bowen v. Roy*, *Lyng v. Northwest Indian Cemetery Association*, and *Employment Division of Oregon v. Smith (II)*. Fairness of application seemed missing in these Native American cases, so their being overturned might be welcomed, but not by opening protections and exemptions up to anything anyone wants to claim as his "Free Exercise" of religion. Meanwhile, Hobby Lobby stores (the Greens) had been very busy acquiring what were alleged to be illegal ancient artifacts for their planned religious museum for at least the five previous years, were caught, claimed innocence but quickly paid off the $3 million dollar fine and returned back to Iraq and Egypt over 11,000 items that were smuggled out of those countries or had been previously stolen or were even fake items.[17]

This "bifurcated" mentality of which historian Sidney Mead resurfaced[18]—of a person wanting a benefit from government that has certain requirements which are not based on religion or lack of it, but also wanting their religious convictions to overrule the government's requirements when they desire—which was evident in *Hastings* (2010) and now again in *Hobby Lobby* (2014) was bound to resurface over and over. But there were also other cases which utilized the broader guidelines of the RLUIP.

MOVING BEYOND *HOBBY LOBBY,*
THE RLUIPA PUT TO THE TEST

In the following year, 2015, the RLUIPA of 2000 was naturally the guide-line in the Muslim prisoner case in Arkansas in *Holt v. Hobbs*, 574 U.S. 352 (2015). The prisoner in Arkansas wished to grow a ½ inch beard to meet his religious obligation. The Dept. of Corrections allowed a maximum of ¼ inch beard only to those who have a skin condition. The Court found this a substantial burden on the prisoner. But the state's interest in regulating contraband to force the shorter beard or by its arguing that a ½ inch beard would create identity problems—both *failed* to be a compelling interest. The Court suggested the identity problem could be remedied by the less restrictive means of a dual-photo method that other prisons have.

In the same year, in *EEOC v. Abercrombie and Fitch Stores, Inc.*, 575 U.S. ___, 135 S.Ct., 2038 (2015), the Court, following the Civil Rights Act of 1964, Title VII, Stat. 253–42 U.S.C. §20000e–2 (a) ruled *in favor* of a Muslim woman who applied for a job and was not hired because the employer decided her head scarf violated their dress code. The Court over-turned the decision of the Tenth Circuit Court which had ruled that the woman was not protected by Title VII unless she made the employer aware of her need for them to accommodate her head scarf. The Court insisted such awareness is *not* required, since Title VII provided categories of race, color, religion, sex, and national origin, which are protected from *any* discrimina-tion by an employer, which includes all aspects of religious observance and practice, *unless* the employer can demonstrate that it is unable to reasonably accommodate the person without incurring undue hardship for the company.

The difficult project seems to be to prove that any law can be both facially neutral and universally applicable but also accommodate the *preferential* treatment of Title VII's listing of "religion" alongside "race," "sex," and so on as requiring an *elevated* standard, *not* simply some conceivable rational basis. Inasmuch as the fair application of law to all citizens is what one means by facially neutral and universally applicable, could the "suspect" categories in Title VII be seen as merely negative indicators of a law's past tendencies toward specific unfairness, but *not* thereby require an elevated standard which the Court seems to suggest? Does not "facially neutral" and "universally applicable" itself enable laws to be *validated* but also *invalidated* by a "ratio-nal basis" which Rawls would call "public reason"?

This would correspond more closely to Rawls's hypothetical "original position" of the social contracting process, since the "veil of ignorance" is that which *transcends or nulls* all considerations of race, sex, national origin, religion, family wealth, education, and any other element that one might use as a vested *advantage over others* or to try to *exempt oneself* from general civil laws. These and other factors of one's being that are largely determined aside from "public reason" must be "veiled" so the social contract can be bargained *reasonably* (which is what Rawls meant by "public reason" and "political") rather than becoming horribly divisive over vested interests or metaphysical conflicts. This means that the law and government are neither for nor against *any* particular race, religion, sexual orientation, and so on vis-à-vis others, not simply because to a degree some of these are part of the irrationality of being born into a specific family, culture, and so forth, but also because even the choices one feels one makes on one's own, even within that culture, such as one's religion, are still deeply influenced by the irrational or "absurd" facticity and contingency of one's very being over which originally one had no voice. Obviously, religion's greatest disqualifier is its insistence on being a vested Absolute.

On the other hand, in *Reed v. Town of Gilbert*, 576 U.S. 155 (2015), the Court disagreed once again with the Ninth Circuit's choice of standards. Gilbert, AZ, had laws relating to the placement of signs in the city, restricting three classes of speech—ideological, political, and temporary directional signs. A church, meeting in different places in the city, used directional signs and had allowed the signs to stay up a few hours too long, violating the city's regulations. The Ninth Circuit ruled these *restrictions* were content neutral so it was not illegal. The Supreme Court ruled they were *not* content neutral, so the city could have prevailed only if it had followed the higher standard of strict scrutiny or compelling state interest, which it did not show. How could a law have no "content," or what makes it "neutral"? This, of course, was actually resolved as a "Free Speech" case more than a "religion" case, though it was applied to a religious group.

In 2017, the Court decided the *Trinity Lutheran Church of Columbia, Inc. v. Comer, Director, Missouri Department of Natural Resources*, 582 U.S. ___, 137 S.Ct. 2012; 198 L.Ed.2d 551 (2017). The Court's decision marked the *first time* the Court has approved a state providing *tax funds directly to a church*. It was not brought under the Establishment Clause, where it obviously would have failed the third element of the *Lemon* test if not also the first two prongs, despite the Court arguing that it would have passed under the Establishment Clause. But it was heard only as a "Free Exercise" case, under the argument that there was *religious discrimination* by the state law which amounted to a hindering of appellants' "free exercise" of religion. Yet it had nothing to do with "free exercise" meaning only "worship." This was the same argument brought by the *dissenting* Justices in *Locke v. Davey* earlier, which presupposes that any benefits the government grants to the general public cannot discriminate against anybody for religious reasons. But the grants were not open to the general public in either case.

The state of Missouri's Scrap Tire Program, run by its Department of Natural Resources, offered reimbursement grants to qualifying nonprofit organizations that install playground surfaces made from recycled tires. Its program prohibited these grants from being given to any group that was owned or controlled by a church or other religious entity, in order to follow the Missouri Constitution which, under Article I, Section 7, prohibited the same. This means it was similar to the Washington law in *Locke v. Davey*. In neither case were the funds simply made available to the general public; both programs specified their limitations in order *not* to violate the Establishment Clause. The church nevertheless applied for such a grant to resurface its playground of its Child Learning Center which was located on the premises of the church itself. Out of 44 applicants in the state, the church's application was ranked fifth, but denied because of their being a religious organization, and 14 applicants received such grants. We will see in a later case why the Court did not examine the Missouri Constitution here and judged it only by the U.S. Constitution's First Amendment.

The District Court dismissed the case, noting that although the Free Exercise clause does prohibit government from restricting appellants' free exercise, it does *not prohibit* the state from withholding an affirmative benefit on account of religion. This last clause is almost the exact wording of the RLUIPA. The Eighth Circuit went so far as to say that although the state could award the grant to the church without "running afoul" of the Establishment Clause, the antiestablishment aspect of the Free Exercise clause in the *state's own* Constitution had to be honored, so the grant could be *prohibited*.

The Supreme Court *reversed*, insisting that to deny a "generally available benefit" on the grounds of the religious identity of the applicant was to impose a penalty upon the free exercise of religion. It argued that the Court has distinguished challenges to neutral laws of general applicability from those that "single out the religious for disfavored treatment." Here it cited *Lyng, Smith*, and *Lukumi*. But *Lukumi* was an obvious Establishment violation, violating the first two if not all three prongs of the *Lemon* test, so there was no way the Court could have considered it anything but a discriminatory favoring or the Santeria religion even when it was brought under the Free Exercise clause. In *Lyng* and *Smith*, however, to say the Court's decisions or laws it approved (to the detriment of the Native Americans) were not a singling out of a specific religion for *disfavored* treatment is to close one's eyes completely. But the Court quoted from *Lukumi* that laws which impose special disabilities on the basis of *religious status* trigger the strict scrutiny test or the compelling interest test. Can the law get around that by *avoiding specific reference* to a religion but nevertheless favoring or disfavoring it since it was the *only group being affected* by the law, as the Court was aware, in both *Lyng* and *Smith*?

In a scathing dissent, J. Sotomayor wrote: "To hear the Court tell it, this is a simple case about recycling tires to resurface a playground. The stakes are higher. This case is about nothing less than the relationship between religious institutions and the civil government—that is, between church and state. The Court today profoundly changes that relationship by holding, for the *first* time, that the Constitution requires the government to provide *public funds directly to a church.*"[19]

In all the earlier cases, the Court had avoided approving such, but making sure the assistance, if any, was given only *indirectly*, as in *Everson* and subsequent cases, since the Court over and over said government could *not directly* fund either a church or a religious school. When the Court *finally recognized* in the "release-time" cases that the religious schools were a significant arm of the church, and that their mission was *religiously pervasive* of their entire programs and quite indistinguishable from that of the church—that is, *religious indoctrination*—there were more limitations on the way aid could be offered to schools. J. Sotomayor emphasized that the playground in this case was as essentially a part of *the religious mission of the church* as the walls of the sanctuary and the pews, as the church tried to indoctrinate not only its own children, but children of nonmembers. If in former cases the Court had tried to protect younger children from possible religious indoctrination because they were more impressionable than adults or teenagers or college students, even in the funding of university classrooms (e.g., *Tilton v. Richardson*), the funds were made available *only* with the guarantee that the buildings and rooms would *never* be utilized for religious instruction or worship. So here the Court wiped clean all that history, all those "precedents." As one law professor we will later quote, it really seems that two or more of the Justices not only were not impressed with the Framers of the Constitution, nor even with more recent precedents.

The Court premised much of its argument on the discrimination of not what the people had done or might do, but simply for being what they are—religious. But J. Sotomayor correctly pointed out that the Court has repeatedly said that it *can* draw lines based on an entity's *religious status*. What else could the Establishment Clause mean if not an entity's religious status? She rehearsed in detail much of the history of the various states' disestablishment over the years, as a precise line drawing. Likewise, *Locke v. Davey* was a recent case where the line drawing by the state of Washington was approved by the Court. J. Sotomayor (dissenting) argued that "a State's decision not to fund houses of worship does not disfavor religion; rather, it represents a valid choice to remain secular in the face of serious establishment and free exercise concerns. That does not make the State 'atheistic or antireligious.' [citing *County of Allegheny v. American Civil Liberties Union*, 492 U.S. 573, 610 (1989)]; it means only that the State has "established neither atheism nor religion as its official creed."[20]

Finally, she summarized: "Today's decision discounts centuries of history and jeopardizes the government's ability to remain secular. Just three years ago, this court claimed to understand that, in this area of law, to 'sweep away what has so long been settled would create new controversy and begin anew the very divisions along religious lines that the Establishment Clause seeks to prevent.' *Town of Greece v. Galloway*, 572 U.S. 565 (2014). It makes clear today that this principle applies only when preference suits."[21]

THE DISCRIMINATING BAKER, THE MESSAGE, AND SUBSEQUENT "FREE EXERCISE"

In 2012, in a bakery in Lakewood, CO, the owner refused to bake a wedding case for a gay couple who planned to get legally married in Massachusetts and wanted to have a reception back home in Colorado.[22] He said it was for religious reasons that he could not bake that cake for them, but he offered to sell them a birthday cake or other items. When the case went to the Colorado Civil Rights Commission, they referred it to a full hearing under an Administrative Law Judge, who ruled in the couple's favor, that the baker's refusal violated Colorado's Anti-Discrimination Act. The Commission affirmed the decision of the ALJ in full and issued a "cease and desist order" on Phillips, the baker, and added remedial actions for him to take, including documenting any future services he denied customers and describing his remedial actions. Phillips appealed to the Colorado Court of Appeals which affirmed both the Commission's judgment and its remedial orders. The law he violated was quite clear, had been in the Colorado statutes for years, even amended in 2007 and 2008 to *prevent sexual discrimination*, whose present form read:

> It is a discriminatory practice and unlawful for a person, directly or indirectly, to refuse, withhold from, or deny to an individual or a group, because of disability, race, creed, color, sex, sexual orientation, marital status, national origin, or ancestry, the full and equal enjoyment of the goods, services, facilities, privileges, advantages, or accommodations of a place of public accommodation. (Colo. Rev. Stat. §24-34—601(2)(a)(2017))

The baker claimed this law was a violation of his rights to "free speech" as well as his "free exercise" of religion. He claimed his baking was artistic, an expression of himself equivalent of his free speech, but also that the "message" of or on the cake was his *personal* message, and he could not in clear conscience give a message of approval to something God condemned. Regarding his "free exercise," of course he was not speaking of his "worship" with a religious group as was the focus originally of the "free exercise" protection, but "free exercise" of whether he could refuse baking them a wedding cake since it was sinful, according to *his* understanding of God's laws.

Phillips could not be blamed from being ignorant of the history behind the framing of the First Amendment, nor of the sole meaning of "free exercise" as being only freedom to worship according to one's own conscience rather than being forced by government. But why members of the Court would not have explored that history is totally inexcusable, after adjudicating "free exercises" cases since 1940. On the other hand, Phillips claim about gay marriage being against the teachings of Jesus simply has no substance, not one word or verse in all four canonical gospels. In fact, the only reference to homosexuality in all the New Testament is in Paul's Letter to the Romans, where he says that those who behave that way "deserve to die." But in this standard Roman vice list that he utilizes, he includes many other people who evidently also "deserve to die" including any form of idolatry or any creation of images to represent the divine, as well as anybody who is guilty of covetousness, gossip, slandering, envy, or is haughty, boastful, rebellious toward parents, heartless or ruthless, and so forth, ending his list with "They know God's decree, that those who practice such things deserve to die—yet they not only do them but even applaud others who practice them" (Rom. 1: 20–32, esp. vv. 28–32). So was Phillips suggesting that the law should be to put all such people to death? There is *no other reference* in the New Testament which even *mentions* homosexuality, and even this one does not speak of gay marriage. So what was the baker's claim other than his unfounded opinion, but *not* attributable, as he thought, to *Jesus* in any way?

Since the Court seems either to know none of the above or else chooses not to mention it in order to have to distinguish *phony* religious claims from *real* ones when they are professing to be based on some figure in past history, it held for the discriminating baker in *Masterpiece Cakeshop v. Colorado*, 584 U.S.___; 138 S.Ct. 1719; 201 L.Ed.2d 35. This simply raises the question of whether the "free exercise" means *any claim* that *anyone* dreams up and attributes to *any* religion must be protected whether it can actually be found in their sacred documents or not? His claim is as specious as was that of the Greens in *Hobby Lobby*: they are all simply following "Jesus," by which they mean whatever they individually want to think about "Jesus."

In neither case did either Phillips or the Greens assert belonging formally to any legitimate Christian group from which they learned about this "Jesus." That is the "metaphysical" approach to civil life that simply cannot succeed in a democracy that includes a religious pluralism, as Rawls insisted. When a Muslim asserts that the civil law should hear what Muhammed, as God's "final prophet" said about men having as many of three wives, what could the Court respond, in light of this decision? Different from Phillips and Green, the Qur'an *does explicitly mention* the three wives. But how does one argue one metaphysics against another, both of which are absolutized, unyielding, and not based on public reason? Rawls supplied the answer which we have mentioned over and over, but the Court seems not to grasp that "separation" which even Madison and Jefferson envisioned and put into the First Amendment.

The Court's decision, reversing all the earlier decisions, was based on the Court's judgment that the commissioners who heard his case were *disrespectful* of him and his religious views.[23] But the Court offers not one shred of evidence from that hearing as proof. Not one. Further, if it was so disrespectful of Phillips, why did the Colorado Court of Appeals not itself reverse the decisions of the ALJ and the Commission? But not a word was said, not until the Supreme Court nullified the obvious violation of a facially neutral, generally applicable law simply on the basis of some disrespect or discrimination *alleged* to have been shown to the baker. Was it really *more discriminating* and disrespectful than Phillips's uninformed bias against gay people which he admitted? Is this not parallel to the *Hastings* case of the club that discriminated sexually against gay people, knowing it was against the contract it signed with the university, and then the club claimed the university was discriminating against them, so the *victimizer claimed to be the victim*?

Or, even more pertinently, why did the baker's sexual discrimination against the gay couple *not* rise to the level of the racial discrimination which violated the government's compelling interest in *Bob Jones University v. U.S.*, 461 U.S. 574 (1983)? The leaders of Bob Jones University felt they had a deeply held religious conviction just as much as the baker here, but the university policy was ruled against by the Court. Was that not a precedent, or are all precedents confined lately only to those cases which come only under the FE clause, whereas in Bob Jones the Court ruled against the university on *both its violation* of FE and the Establishment Clause?

The year 2019 brought more challenges to the world, the United States, and to businesses, religions, and especially families. As of the time of this writing, the U.S. deaths due to the Covid-19 have exceeded 620,000. The dangers involved in people gathering in groups are well documented, but some states, leaders, and churches resented being told to not hold indoor gatherings of many people. One such church in California sued to enjoin the governor from the restrictions he saw as reasonable and necessary. In *South Bay United Pentecostal Church, et al. v. Gavin Newsom, Governor of California, et al.*, 590 U.S. ___(2020) (slip opinion, No. 19A1044), the Court decided 5/4 to *deny* the injunctive relief to intervene, not merely suspend, the Governor's Executive Order. The Order itself was reasonable in its distinctions between smaller and larger gatherings or people, and the power of deciding on how to protect the people is vested in the politically accountable officials of the state. The four dissenting Justices would have granted the request, as they considered the Governor's Executive Order and the various "caps" he drew was a violation of people's "free exercise" of religion.[24]

The year 2020 brought other decisions of religious import, especially in *Kendra Espinoza, et al., Petitioners v. Montana Department of Revenue, et al.*, 591 U.S. ___(2020) (slip opinion, No. 18-1195). Madison and Jefferson fought and *defeated* Gov. Patrick Henry's Bill which would have allowed individuals the "private choice" of which religion they wanted their taxes to go to, and the First Amendment came from the same *disestablishment* from the same two leaders of the country. The much later Montana Constitution, following the U.S. Constitution, and the predominant *theories* expressed by the Supreme Court from 1947 through the early 1980s,[25] strictly prohibited any public funding in any form, direct or indirect, "for any sectarian purpose or to aid any church, school, academy, seminary, college, university, or other literary or scientific institution, controlled in whole or in part by any church, sect, or denomination" (Mont. Const. Art. X, §6(1)).

It is important to understand the history of this part of the Montana Constitution. In 1875, the Blaine Amendment that was proposed for the U.S. Constitution was closely defeated by a lack of four votes to meet the two-thirds required in the Senate. It had received 180 votes to 7 in the House. The Amendment proposed essentially the same thing Madison and Jefferson had, that public taxes could *not* be given to any church in any form. The Blaine Amendment was an attempt to further build a *public school system* which would be completely *nonsectarian*. Catholics read this as primarily anti-Catholic, since in the public schools, some schools allowed Protestant Bibles and prayers, though the latter practice was not widespread by 1875, and remained as only the residue from theocratic days prior to the Constitution, like legislative prayers. When the proposed Amendment was closely defeated, all but 10 states adopted its basic principle into their state constitutions. For our purposes here, Missouri and Montana were two of these that did adopt the principles of the proposed Blaine Amendment, so that part of those state constitutions was still viewed by the Catholic Church as anti-Catholic.

When the U.S. Supreme Court finally became predominately Roman Catholic in the late twentieth century, it defied these parts of Missouri and Montana State Constitutions under its new standards for "Free Exercise," though these involved a Lutheran church and school in Missouri and an evangelistic Christian school in Montana. This way, the decisions would *not* be seen as favoring the Catholic Church, even if its parochial schools were still receiving billions of public tax dollars every year to indoctrinate children in the Catholic faith. Once the reader understands this, then the reader can see why in the Montana decision, the Court was so completely dependent upon the *Trinity Lutheran* decision of 2017, citing it over and over. But the whole scenario will make more sense only in the following chapters in which we trace the development of the Court's jurisdiction under the Establishment Clause.

The Petitioners sued the Montana Dept. of Revenue, alleging their "free exercise" of religion was being prohibited since the state was not willing to include the religious school, Stillwater Christian School in Kalispell, which they wanted their children to attend, a school which taught the "same values" the parents taught at home. The scholarship program of Big Sky offered scholarships in the form of tax credits of up to $500 per student for attending private schools, and the three mothers who were denied this aid alleged this as a violation of their "free exercise."

Notably, the Court did *not* attempt to invalidate the Montana Constitution's law cited above, for obvious reasons, so it should have been an "open and shut" case under the Establishment criteria. But instead, the Court focused on "Rule 1" and by finding that illegal, was able to negate the Montana Constitution's law that forbid taxes being given for a religious school. This is a quite disrespectful approach to states' rights, to negate portions of *their* Constitution without addressing their Constitution directly or even comparing it to the U.S. Constitution. The Montana Dept. of Revenue had formulated "Rule 1" in an attempt to *clarify* how the scholarships were *limited* by the State Constitution, that is, the scholarship could *not* be used to attend a religious school.

The state attorney general objected to Rule 1, even though the Dept. of Revenue replied that it was necessary to reconcile the scholarship program with the Montana Constitution. The Attorney General insisted the Montana Constitution did *not* prohibit such aid to religious schools, and if it did, it was probably in violation of the First Amendment of the U.S. Constitution. Thus, the Attorney General's *opinion* which contradicted the Montana Constitution itself ruled the day, even though he avoided being a party in the case. Petitioners then naturally focused on this Rule 1 as the *illegal discrimination*. The trial court *enjoined* Rule 1, explaining it was not required by the "no aid" provision in the Montana Constitution since the latter provision applies only to "appropriations" to religious school but "not tax credits." This injunctive relief allowed the scholarships, in the form of tax credits, to include religious as well as secular private schools, and the applications for the public dollars increased dramatically.

When it went before the Montana Supreme Court, however, the Court *reversed*, and, considering the program without Rule 1, found the program an *obvious violation* of the Montana Constitution. Because the program itself had no inner mechanisms to prevent the future funds from being a similar violation by being furnished through religious schools, the Montana Supreme Court abolished the entire scholarship program. The U.S. Supreme Court, however, focused *only on Rule 1* and the split in the Montana Supreme Court. But the "split" did not matter any more than it does when the U.S. Supreme Court "splits," so long as the majority rules with its decision. But the U.S. Supreme Court actually gave preference to the Attorney General of Montana rather than the decision of the Montana Supreme Court. In this case, there would be no Court analysis of the relation of the Montana Constitution or comparison of it with the U.S. Constitution's First Amendment, none at all.

From Rule 1, the Court argued its whole case on two related prongs: (1) the supposed analogy between this case and the *Trinity Lutheran* (2017) case; and (2) the most important element, the distinction between a "religious status" and a "religious usage," insisting that what invalidated the approach was that it was based *solely* on the "religious status." It was based on the more universal word, "religion," because it incorporated all kinds of connotations and uses that could not be listed definitively. But the Court insisted, "Status-based discrimination remains status based even if one of its goals or effects is preventing religious organizations from putting aid to religious uses."[26] But that argument would nullify the Establishment Clause in the First Amendment since it does precisely that, since it specified a religious status that was forbidden to be made legal because of negative and exclusive religious usages that legality would produce, usages which would accentuate religious status which was *not inclusive of all citizens.*

The reason the Court makes such an artificial distinction is that if the "usage" of the aid were examined, the *Trinity Lutheran* case would no longer be analogous or in any way "dispositive" as the Court wanted it to be. The primary usage in *Trinity Lutheran* was to pay for a playground, whereas in Espinoza the parents wanted their children to be *indoctrinated* with the same values they heard at home. Of course, the *overriding mission* of the religious school had a religious purpose of indoctrination, and its curriculum and practices had a primary religious effect, so it would also have violated the first two prongs of the *Lemon* "establishment" test. But that "pervasive" element of religious indoctrination the Court had recognized decades earlier was somehow able to be completely *ignored* by the present Court. However, even if we overlook the pervasive religious purpose of indoctrination, there remained the *difference* between a *playground* for exercise and the parents in *Espinoza* citing the *similar values* they wanted their children to hear which obviously were connected to a quite conservative form of the Christian *religion*. Otherwise, the children likely could have received a better education at any *public* school, but it would lack the *religious* element, the "religious" element which was the parents' purpose in selecting Stillwater Christian School.

But the Court insisted that this Rule 1 was illegally discriminating *strictly* by a forbidden focus on the "status" of the school, which was deduced from the word "religion" being used. Would it have been more appropriate for the law to say that the aid could not be given to any organization which teaches an absolute metaphysics, trains and employs priests and teachers in the true doctrine, sponsors worship in a specific form, teaches certain rituals, symbols, and practices as divine and unquestionable, believes in a personal God and personal Satan, heaven and hell, Purgatory, the Immaculate Conception, the Virgin Birth, meets only on Sundays as the true Sabbath, believes that the Bible is the only and final revelation of God, and so forth?

Or would these "uses" suddenly all be quite *legal*, but it would still be *illegal* to supply public taxes to institutions which indoctrinated students in the truth that Muhammed was the "final prophet" of God, or would be illegal to indoctrinate students in the necessity of embracing the "Eightfold Path" of Buddhism, and its trust of "no-self" and "Sunyata" or "emptying," or in the obvious ultimate truth of the Tao, or of the "coincidentia oppositorum" which means that "Satan" is identical with "Jesus"? How would the Court decide between *any* of these metaphysical claims? Would that have covered enough, or too much, or would it not be *defining one particular religion* and its different functions, any of which might be funded if the "religion" itself were, and thereby itself be discriminating against all other religions as well as nonreligion?

Is that perhaps the reason "religion" *was used*, because most people have some idea of the ways religions function and their primary mission which shapes the priorities among their various possible "uses" of their assets and income? Thus, if the primary purpose is to prevent "aid" from being used only in certain ways for only certain uses, in order to avoid using the terrible word "religion," who decides which religious *usages* would be legal and which illegal? Here the Court insists it does not judge "orthodoxy." How would anything prevent public tax money thus submitted simply freeing up more other money to be used for sheer indoctrination? Then, unless any and every possible activity and usage can be protected under "free exercise," would not a more generic or universal word be helpful, such as "religion"? So the Court's decisive distinction is extremely *un*helpful, placing it ultimately in an unenviable position of having to decide to *accept* anything people claim as their "religious" "free exercise" but to *reject* any law that attempts to limit what people can do under the guise of "religion."

The greatest irony, as I already hinted, is that the Court's distinction makes the First Amendment *itself* illegally discriminatory since it reads "Congress shall make no law respecting the establishing of *religion* nor prohibiting the free exercise thereof." According to this Court, the word "religion" is the illegally discriminating word, and the "thereof" refers back to "religion," to the "free exercise" of "*religion*" which in context of the Framers meant only the "free exercise" of "worship" as we have earlier shown. But in a strong dissent in *Everson* (1947) which we examine in the next chapter, four Justices made the following important observation:

"Religion" appears only once in the Amendment. But the word governs two prohibitions and governs them alike. It does not have two meanings, one narrow to forbid "an establishment" and another, much broader, for securing "the free exercise thereof." "Thereof" brings down "religion" with its entire and exact content, no more and no less, from the first into the second guaranty, so that Congress and now the states are as broadly restricted concerning the one as they are regarding the other.[27]

So "free exercise" in Madison and Jefferson's understanding did *not* hamstring government by enabling people to claim free exercise of religion for anything they chose to do or to believe, but only meant government would not in any way prohibit their "worship," that is, unless that worship violated generally applicable civil or criminal laws. Similarly, government would not try to change people's beliefs or religious consciences unless those caused the people to violate the nation's basic civil or criminal laws which govern all citizens equally. Both Madison and Jefferson emphasized that by separating government from religion, no one would have one's civic benefits either increased or decreased; the government would neither interfere with one's conscience about who, what, how, and when to "worship" nor would it support financially, directly or indirectly, anything a religious group did or believed. It would enter the religious sphere only on civil or criminal infractions and only *by those civil and criminal laws*. This way, it would *"make no law" about religion*, either in establishing, funding, endorsing one particular religion, or in prohibiting the religious worship. By keeping the religion free of government tax funds, it avoided violating other people's religious consciences and kept the government from thinking it should have a controlling voice in the religion. But it likewise freed government to operate on its own without having to fear being directed or owned by or obligated to religious individuals or religious organizations for using their Absolute as if the whole world recognized their particular "God" as the Ultimate Authority as was the culturally restricted presupposition in the old days of Christendom.

The irony of the Court's following analysis of history shows that it *admitted* that there was a long history of opposition to using public taxes for paying clergy. But the Court cited several secondary sources to speculate that the opposition to aiding the religious organizations *per se* is *absent* except in perverted forms of anti-Catholic bias in the second half of the nineteenth century, which pointed to the "Blaine" Amendment, which we now understand.[28] What it failed to do was acknowledge that the same argument it provided would be sufficient to say that there was no real opposition to slavery in the last half of the nineteenth century, so we should allow that the same precedential value as the lack of opposition to funding religious organizations during that historical period. I find it incredible that after arguing that the entire violative element of the law was its discrimination via sheer "status"—that is, "religious status"—yet the Court turned to try to squeeze out a difference in "usage" after all.

Disestablishment was very uneven, just as was the realization of racial and sexual equality, and none of these has yet reached the ideal, because most religions still feel they are the true one if not the *only* true one just as some people feel their specific race or sexuality is the superior or only divinely approved one. The residual effects of the colonial theocracies were not abandoned in a week or two, *despite* the direct and *explicit* understandings the Framers of the First Amendment had. There was nothing ambiguous about where Madison, Jefferson, Isaac Backus, and other religious leaders and supporters of the First Amendment stood, just as most people realized that if the nation were to survive, it had to create a stronger sense of *unity* and less disunity, less feelings of being superior or the "chosen" or the "true" religion. It had to be more inclusive, more united, less judgmental, more respectful and courteous to anyone who differed with one's own views.

Yet to this day, those unjustified, rude, discriminating, divisive, arrogant, ignorant, and hateful feelings are still around, as we see in the spreading of the dozens of different forms of White Nationalism, White Supremacist, or Christian Identity groups in the United States. The Court has simply unwittingly *reinforced* their power by decisions such as this one, *Trinity Lutheran* and *Hobby Lobby*. This is one reason for the title of my earlier volume, *Will Humanity Survive Religion? Beyond Divisive Absolute*. It is the equivalent of ISIS preempting the religion of Islam by its arrogant, exclusive, militant objectives, framed in an apocalyptic scenario. And it very well could be "apocalyptic" in the worst sense, but not by any divine intervention. It did, of course, result in the insurrection, initiated by President Trump, to invade the Capitol while it was in session, to prevent the legislature from formalizing the earlier completely valid electoral vote of the various states which showed Biden the winner rather than Trump, and resulted in several deaths and dozens of injured Capitol Police.

Finally, it must be pointed out that the lengthy analysis the Court gave of the public tax support given to private and parochial schools during the nineteenth century really proves too much. By the mid-nineteenth century, the influence and work of Horace Mann and others had initiated *nonsectarian* "public schools" in Massachusetts, supported only by public taxes, which were to include student diversity, but still could study the Bible, although not any specific church's doctrines derived from it. These "common" schools or "normal" schools in Massachusetts superseded the earlier parochial schools, so by their nonsectarian approach could be embraced by all citizens and educate all the children. Disestablishment in reality came more gradually than on paper. One must remember that even the Ivy League colleges were established with the primary objective to train sectarian ministers, although they ended up very quickly turning out as many or more attorneys, and gradually became less sectarian.

The Court's argument seems to suggest that we should allow free reign of public tax dollars being filtered from the public school system to aid the religious education that the poorer families cannot afford and which many approve by their own free consciences. Should we return to "private choice," no matter what schools people prefer, or how it has and may continue to deprive the public school system of needed funds, or which religion is profited by that private choice? But it is not that easy as we will see in the near future if and when those of non-Christian religions began demanding *public funds* for *their* religious schools all over the nation.[29] And what about all those who either are not religiously affiliated or simply see all this as an abusive use of their public taxes since it is so religiously preferential, coercing those who disagree to pay their taxes regardless? No one would select such principles behind Rawls's veil of ignorance.

Once the "status" is mentioned of "religion" and is seen as an *illicit discrimination*, as the Court here insists, there can no longer be the Religion Clauses in the First Amendment as we know them. They were as illegal as the present "Rule 1," *or else* "Rule 1" was no more illegally discriminatory on a "status" basis than was the First Amendment. Perhaps that is what the Court wants, but it seems it actually desires to set them off as if they are opposites. If both were dispensed with, however, it might resolve the problem of so many religious people thinking that "religion" has a "preferred" place in our Constitution, as J. O'Connor expressed in *Smith* (II), in 1990, from which they, being religious, feel they deserve certain exemptions from laws others have to obey, or they deserve certain government aid that others do not. Certainly the Court from 1940 to the late 1970s did *not* see "religion" as "preferred," but on an equal plane with "nonreligion" and even *atheism*, and J. O'Connor's conclusion would make Madison and Jefferson, and those many religious leaders who helped them get the First Amendment correctly worded and supported—all roll over in their graves.

MORE ATTACKS ON THE BIRTH CONTROL MANDATE OF THE ACA

Following *Hobby Lobby*, the barn door was open to flee from the contraceptive mandate of the ACA for those who found it abominable. To briefly summarize a very unnecessarily complex development, within a few days after the *Hobby Lobby* decision, on July 3, 2014, the Court granted a temporary exemption (in addition to exempting the businesses in *Hobby Lobby*), altering the *recipient* of one's "notice" of religious objection to the contraceptive provision through the EBSA Form 700 to the *government* instead of the earlier suggested insurance company, and the government would then notify one's insurer of the notice of one's religious objection to the contraceptive mandate. Because of further objections from certain members of the Court, the actual EBSA Form 700 was changed to provide the eligible organization the alternative of *either* using the form itself *or* notifying the HHS itself as to the employer's religious objection to providing coverage for all of the optional contraceptives. This was referred to as the "self-certification" and seemed *not a substantial burden at all* for anyone to comply with, just to notify the government that one objected to the coverage of the contraceptives, so therefore requested to be exempt from covering it.

But cases began growing, objecting even to the *"self-certification."* By November 2015, the Supreme Court consolidated seven cases from various Circuit Courts, heard their various arguments, requested supplemental briefs from all of them, and finally vacated all their decisions and remanded the cases, requiring them to reconsider in light of the positions asserted by the parties in their supplemental briefs. It noted that since the Petitioners all agreed that their "free exercise" would *not* be violated if they could simply contract to a health plan that did not include contraceptive coverage, each Court should be able to clarify and reach an approach that would satisfy all parties, whereby Petitioners did not have to be involved in providing the contraceptive coverage *but* in which those employees of any of the organizations covered could *still have* seamless coverage of their contraceptives. The Court insisted it was not ruling on the merits of the cases, but the dissent emphasized that the Circuit Courts must honor that statement and not make rulings as if the merit of the case were decided.

A significant turn in the litigation occurred after President Trump passed an Executive Order in 2017 ordering the HHS to issue a ruling that even "for-profit" organizations could claim exemption from the mandate. Of course, the Court had already granted that in *Hobby Lobby*. Shortly thereafter, another "Little Sisters" case came before the Court, this time from the Third Circuit (the earlier one was in the Tenth Circuit) and was decided by the Supreme Court on July 8, 2020, in *Little Sisters of the Poor Saints Peter and Paul Home v. Pennsylvania et al.*, 591 U.S.___ (2020) (slip opinion, No. 19-431).

Petitioners (the "Little Sisters") *objected* to even the *self-certification* since they saw any decision they made to be exempt from the mandate would force someone else to pay for the contraceptives, and that would make the "Little Sisters" *"complicit"* in such, violating their consciences. Pennsylvania originally brought action to enjoin the new rules promulgated by the Departments (the IFRs) and was joined by New Jersey, arguing that the Departments had no authority for such changes, and they had violated established procedures in pushing the rules through without a sufficient period of notice and comment. The District Court issued the preliminary nationwide injunctions against the implementation of the rules, and the Third Circuit affirmed.

The Supreme Court, on the other hand, decided 7/2 to *reverse* the lower courts, which immediately deprived up to an estimated 140,000 women of needed contraceptive care and education during their child-bearing years, women who could not afford paying for such. To the majority of the Court, however, the Departments *did have authority* to extend and redefine any "exemptions" to the ACA coverage, and *they did not violate any required procedures* even if they did not do things in the usual way. Those were the basic questions.

The case is complex only because of all the refusals to comply with the law as it was originally formulated, or even with its innocuous requirement of "self-certification." The basic principle of Madison, Jefferson, and Rawls was that religious liberty would be guaranteed for one's *belief*, but that could *not* guarantee that one could act in *any and every way one desired* since other citizens have similar and equal rights. That meant to all three that, *provided* a person complied with the generally applicable laws based on the primary principles to which all citizens are presupposed to have endorsed, one has a right to worship as one sees fit so long as one does not adversely affect another person's rights or welfare or violate those generally applicable civil or criminal laws in the process. Conflict between parties' religious or metaphysical beliefs *cannot* be adjudicated by *any* metaphysical or religious standard since there is no such, certainly not the courts, but their *actions* or actual relations can be adjudicated by government, but only on the basic principles of the social contract just mentioned.

This means that the government, including the Court, can*not* slip in some metaphysical or mythical position by which to make one specific religious position the answer to a conflict since there is no authority of mediation of religions and metaphysics, but only a weighing of *specific actions* by civic laws based on "public reason" and "freestanding" principles, as Rawls insists, in a hypothetical "original position" behind a "veil of ignorance." This kind of litigation would *never occur* if people engaged in Rawls's hypothetical exercise or even realized that a democracy requires public reason and tolerance of diversity, that *justice* can*not* be whittled out of competitive, contradictory claims of *advantage, even religious advantage*, as much litigation is.[30]

The Departments of HHS, Labor, and Treasury, in light of District Court and Third Circuit and the multiple cases being brought by parties that wanted to avoid the self-certification which they felt would make them "complicit" in the "sin," decided to pass two "interim final rules" which basically offered the option of exemption from the mandate to any employer, even publically traded corporations which object from sincerely held beliefs, either from religious or moral grounds, to "its establishing, maintaining, providing, offering, or arranging [for] coverage or payments for some or all contraceptive services." This was an attempt to fulfill the ACA's goals by providing medical coverage that simply omitted even the reference to such contraceptives so that no party had to take *any* action, to opt for or against anything. These two rules, of course, had the effect of placing the *burden upon any party who wanted* the coverage which the ACA was offering.

However, the ACA had determined that such coverage had to be at *no cost* to the women. But these interim final rules *violated* that, forcing those who wanted coverage to find another provider, that is, either find another government agency willing to provide at its own cost that contraceptive coverage, which, of course, was not credible, or else the women desiring the coverage had to find it and obtain it by *paying for it themselves*, which was precisely what the ACA had explicitly wanted to *avoid*, insisting it was to be of *no cost to the employed women*. The Sisters, as the Court emphasized, were simply being faithful to their Catholic dogma, holding it as a deeply and sincerely held religious belief. In truth, they were demanding to *shape the law* by Catholic dogma, *not* by the needs of people analyzed by "public reason" or even by the ACA's intentions that included contraceptive options for female employees at no cost.

The idea of "complicity" was emphasized by the Sisters. The organization (employer) did not want even to "self-certify" in the sense of filling out a small paper or contacting the HHS to notify it that they objected to the contraceptive coverage, because even that notification would make them "complicit" or "sinful" because such actions of theirs, in their own terms, would "directly cause others to provide contraception or appear to participate in the Departments' delivery scheme."[31] But what did they think *bringing legal action* would do if not that very same thing? In fact, their appeal to not want to be complicit was only a "red herring" since they *became more complicit* in *forcing others* to provide the coverage by pursuing it in Court than they would have had they been willing merely to self-certify, allowing *all* parties to be *free to choose at no cost to anyone*.[32] But they *eliminated* any role of other parties' free choice by reshaping the medical preventive offerings, influencing the *excision* of anything about contraceptives in the provisions, and forcing other women to either do without the coverage or find a different way of paying for it.

But as much as the Court wants to make it a "complicity" case, it was *not*. If it were, the Court would have found itself hard pressed to have ever discovered any notion of protection for people's argument that they did not want to feel "complicit," whether they examined the First Amendment or the RFRA or even any precedent decisions made by the Court. The idea that a litigant's feeling of perhaps being "complicit" should determine anything is totally missing. So that really was *not* the issue but a mere straw dummy for *emotional* purposes, whose logic is also totally missing, as I will later show. If the contest was not about complicity, what was it about?

It was to reshape the law to make it yield to Catholic standards, so that no Catholic would even have to speak up or object to the medical preventive care being offered since it would no longer contain even references to any contraception. This way, those who object to contraceptives will not attract any possible repercussions such as the stiff penalties of any employer who failed to comply with the ACA requirements. But they would not even be *known* as objecting so would not even get any negative publicity. It would be like pretending that women's preventive health care is adequately covered without including even any reference having to do with the women's sexual life, potential, or needs, that no women need any education, help in planning, no screening or tests, never any medications or surgeries having to do with their sexuality, that this huge area of being a woman simply need not be addressed, that one can pretend that health care has nothing to do with human sexuality, that perhaps even ignorance of human sexuality is preferable since any and every action is itself "immoral" *unless* one intends to procreate by it, as the Court reminds the reader.[33]

Instead of allowing all female employees to have a choice by their own consciences between the various options their employers present through the ACA, groups like the "Little Sisters" brought pressure on the government to offer the required ACA medical coverage for women's health *without any* provisions for contraceptives, so the decision would not depend upon their actions. But the *lawsuit* was their *more coercive actions to do that very thing* of forcing others on the basis of *only their religious* convictions. The difference was, however, that had they been willing to self-certify, contraceptive coverage could still have been provided the individuals through the provider, whereas by demanding not even to have to self-certify, they forced the Departments to offer a policy which did *not include contraceptives for anyone* who wanted them, so did *not* accomplish the goals of the ACA. And they did not avoid actions. The difference was they chose actions which coerced others, deprived others, which the "self-certification" would have not.

When the Court tried to prove that IFR were *within* the authority of the Departments, it *failed* to show any *real connection* between a Department's being given authority to define what the specifics and scope of the care should be and any "exceptions" that might be made for any employers. Those are two different areas. The Court simply redundantly emphasized the "broad" power the ACA gave to the HRSA. It accused the dissent of wanting to insert words, to "supply" or imply the actual words of authority mean less than they appear (i.e., "It is a fundamental principle of statutory interpretation that 'absent provision[s] cannot be supplied by the courts.'").[34] But it was *not* the dissent but the Court itself that wanted to *add provisions* such as the *unlimited scope of power* the Departments had which gave them the right to whittle out more exemptions which not only had *not* been approved by the ACA but which *violated* one of the primary purposes of the ACA, to provide thorough preventive health care coverage for *all women without cost to the women employees*. That is, the argument failed particularly because the IFRs spelled out "exemptions" which changed the specifics of the care and especially thereby changed the *party* that would have to foot the bill. These changes and exemptions deprived thousands of women who needed the coverage but could not afford it. But it was approved by the Court, in order to assist the Sisters to avoid any possible feeling of guilt, or feeling that they had helped facilitate abortions.[35]

The Court made it unintentionally obvious that the decision was to conform only to the "Catholic faith" as the Court made quite explicit reference,[36] and it worked to the *detriment* of those who were not Catholic, people whose religious or moral convictions allow them to use contraceptives but who cannot afford them. The ACA sought to provide this preventive health care for all, giving all female employees a choice—all female employees, not just those within one particular religious association—a choice among *free options* the government would offer through the employer. As originally conceived, any individual woman should have been able to select whether or not to request contraceptive coverage, and, if so, which specific contraceptives she and her doctor wanted, which were approved by the ACA and FDA. Everyone would have had the *same freedom* and been *responsible for her own choice*, and no one individual woman or association would have had any responsibility or *complicity* in the decisions made by any other person. The decisions were for each individual woman, not something to be decided by the employer or decided by one religious organization's dogma, especially by nuns who ideally had no need for the services.

But when certain employers themselves decided *they* did not want to allow others to choose, they placed themselves in a position of eliminating that freedom of others.[37] At *that* point, they *did became complicit*, complicit for any continued ignorance any woman had about her body, complicit for any illnesses related to the women's sexuality of which she remained unaware, any unwanted pregnancies, and even any unwanted abortions that later resulted from not allowing the employees *themselves* to make the choices that included contraceptives. The contradiction is twofold: (1) by *removing the choice* from the needy individuals, the *employer* becomes quite responsible and complicit, and ironically the results of making the contraceptives so difficult to attain might result in *many more abortions*, the very thing the employers allegedly were so religiously opposed to; and (2) the bringing of the legal action is a much more *explicit act* and much *more coercive* on others than simply any self-certification as it was arranged.

While J. Thomas, writing for the Court, wanted to reduce the whole "analysis" to only three words—"as provided for"—which he resolved by a mere dictionary, the analysis involved a whole lot more, or else he just wasted space and time. In fact, if one wanted a *key* to the whole problem which is at issue, it might just be three words "free exercise"="worship." Once Congress or the courts open up the "freedom" of religion to protect not simply "worship" but any and everything anyone *wants to claim* as their deeply felt or sincere religious conviction, then, as J. Kennedy wrote in *Boerne*, any generally applicable law can be challenged and overcome, and the whole civil and criminal structure will *dissolve* under the subjective priority given to claims about "free exercise" of "religion." This is the brunt of the decision.

J. Ginsburg's dissent which insists that the ACA's "exemptions" were limited only to "houses of worship" is correct, though belittled by the Court since it had already decided *Hobby Lobby* which had nothing to do with the religious claims even having any connection to any religious group, but simply the uninformed opinions of the owners of the closely held corporation—a far cry from a "house of worship." If "worship" were the real and circumscribed scope of the protected "free exercise," then there was no room for *any exemptions*. This case again had *nothing* to do with "worship" or "free exercise" protection. No one was being forced to use contraceptives. That was *not* what the "mandate" was.

This is not only light years removed from protecting people's "free exercise" of worship, which was the concern of the Framers of that First Amendment, but it is obviously, religiously named form of *depriving* others of benefits they were supposed to be able to *choose* under the ACA, or at least *forcing them* to pay for those benefits which were supposed to be furnished free of charge by the government—while *attempting* to feel that those who demanded this did not really act at all, were not involved at all, in forcing or *prohibiting* others from having an *equal* choice. It was to be the choice only of the employer to try to preserve its innocence and innocence of all its employees to extreme lengths, an attempt at innocence which logically collapsed, as we saw.

After all, a taxpayer is simply *not* complicit in every expenditure the government makes; nothing would be more absurd. One does not have the option to refuse to pay taxes because one disapproves of the country going to war, and one disapproves of all war, and can feel innocent only by withholding one's taxes. Our laws simply do not allow that. If one disapproves any of the legislature's expenditures, the Court has never allowed the party to have "standing" to challenge that "spending" by Congress. Never! One can, of course, try to influence a change in the law, but to argue to change it so it will create more inequality or provide special benefits to some while depriving others of a certain liberty they have, will not work in a democracy, as the Framers saw, and will not be perceived as "justice" as Rawls noted.

Another part of the problem is that those objecting to the contraceptives do not want to have to object, do not want others even to know they object. They just want the law changed so they do not even have to object, even though the law gives them the legal prerogative to object and thereby avoid the penalty. But most laws are not shaped that way, by any or every party saying they do not want to have to do anything, perform any action, sign any papers, go on any records, either for or against anything, but just remain passive and *anonymous*, yet they expect the law to do *precisely as they want* even in the absence of their self-expression. That is an impossible scenario. Instead, legislators utilize "public reason," not metaphysical or mythical authorities or a "nonpublic" reason, and they reason and negotiate over "freestanding" principles until they reach some consensus, and their votes *are recorded* for transparency.[38]

Thus, what the Little Sisters wanted are precisely the special favors Madison and Jefferson said religious people should *not* expect to receive just because they are "religious." They are the special favors or exemptions that would not even be *known* in Rawls hypothetical "original position" of a "veil of ignorance," in which, as he said, one would know one had values, but one would *not* know *specifically what they were*, whether one was religious or not, would not know whether one would be male or female, which race, rich or poor, and so forth. Under such a veil of ignorance, the basic liberties would *not* be shaped by anyone's particular religion, whether it was autonomous or strictly heteronomous and authoritarian, but people could believe anything they want to, and worship however they want so long as they comply with the generally applicable laws that all citizens have agreed to. *Behind* the "veil of ignorance," no one would bargain for any *exemptions* to general laws since one might well find oneself actually *disadvantaged* by such. Is it really so hard to place oneself into the situation of others, to identify with their specific needs, to empathize with their pains?

CONCLUSIONS ABOUT "FREE EXERCISE" OF "RELIGION"

We saw that in *Cantwell v. Connecticut (1940)*, with the very beginning stages of the First Amendment "Religion Clauses" being "incorporated" into state law, that the most natural way of approaching many of the cases was through Free Speech or some other basic right rather than through religion's Free Exercise. That was undoubtedly what Madison and Jefferson and the other Framers had in mind in the First Amendment. Congress was to "make no laws respecting the establishment of religion nor prohibiting the free exercise thereof." We saw at length the meaning of the "free exercise" in that Constitutional Era, that it was simply that government could not prohibit or dictate in any way one's "worship" with a group. The variety of laws prohibiting a prior restraint on speech or on speech that presents a "clear and present danger," would handle many of those cases, and the legitimate reasonable "time, place, and manner" restrictions on speech, including the forming of parades or gestures such as the flag salute as a form of speech, suggest a huge list of the cases which could have been decided *without any* reference to religion. The speech element would have included the question of content neutrality and viewpoint neutrality, and could have been combined with child labor laws or others if necessary. But the "content" questions would have had nothing to do with religion. This would have been the case in *Jones v. Opelika* (1943) (later vacated), *Murdock v. Pennsylvania* (1943), *Minersville School District v. Gobitis* (1940) (later overruled), *Cox v. New Hampshire* (1941), *West Virginia State Board of Education v. Barnette* (1943), *Prince v. Massachusetts* (1944) (speech and child labor laws), as well as all the significant Krishna Consciousness cases (1981–1992). The accessibility of "Free Speech" laws has been the primary consideration in many later "Establishment" cases such as *Healy*, *Widmar*, and *Rosenberger*, which we will cover in the next chapters, as well the Free Exercise case of *Christian Legal Society Chapter of Univ. of California, Hastings College of Law v. Martinez* which we covered.

If "religion" were simply dropped as a category, most of the cases the Court has heard as "Free Exercise" litigation could have been adjudicated by laws involving only another area such as "Free Speech," or property laws, or laws of contracts, public health, and so forth. None of these other areas prohibited the making of any law on the subject. Only the subject of religion. The centuries of religious persecution of nonmembers or of disastrous religious wars spell out the reason for the Framer's different treatment of "religion" than other areas of general laws. With such an approach of not making any religious laws, the property laws would honor both local zoning laws as well as corporate laws in case of disputes within any religious organization. The same would be true in multiple legal areas. If the law mistakenly had an obvious religious reference, purpose, or requirement to receive a certain benefit, the courts could simply have refused to hear it as a violation of the First Amendment religion clauses which disallows the government to take legal cognizance of religion.

Instead, once the Court began hearing such cases, the *Lemon* test in 1971 provided keys to adjudicating whether Congress had made any "religious" laws since the first two prongs required a *secular* purpose and primary *secular* effect, and a predominant religious purpose or effect was enough to make the law illegal. So the Court could strike it down. But we will see in the following chapters that the Court became dissatisfied with the way the "aid" to religion and religious schools was meeting with restrictions which were not always consistent, perhaps because the history revealed the bulge in the tent was the camel's nose and head rather than a consistent application of a standard as early as *Everson*.

Of course, what we have seen is that for civil authorities or government to have no legal cognizance of religion may seem itself to make the Religion Clauses of the First Amendment an impossible law, since in its broadest sense "legal cognizance" could mean that it does not even notice legally the religious element in society. But if that were its meaning, the Court or Legislature could not be active in *preventing* an "establishment" of religion or in *protecting* people's "free exercise" of religion. In the context in which Madison used that term, he simply meant, as did Jefferson, that the civil government has no jurisdiction, even though it may certainly notice religion, and could defend the free choice that people make either to worship or not to worship, to be religiously affiliated with a group or not. That is, as they both put it, government can neither aid (whether by taxes, government endorsement, or even by allowing exemptions from universally applicable laws to religious people), nor could government punish people's religious beliefs and worship, and really is unconcerned with them *unless* the religion causes people to violate or ask to be exempt from the facially neutral and universally applicable laws that all citizens must follow. And when that arises, they would be judged *only* by the same secular laws by which all citizens are judged, not anything based on religion. To be religious is not to get special civil or criminal favors. All must be judged under a single commonly applicable law.

This keeps the two clauses of the First Amendment both negative, *not* requiring courts to try to divine what is the most authentic religion or which religion embodies the most truth, or what is orthodox, what is central or essential to the religion, and certainly not to decide on its own that religion has more value than a secular or humanistic approach to life and culture. Madison, Jefferson, and Rawls were all optimistic about preserving political and religious diversity in the nation. Certainly it far surpasses living in a theocracy that is not one's belief or choice, or a tyranny by leaders one does not approve. But how religious diversity is kept within civil bounds, how its divisive tendencies can be mitigated or blunted, how conversation can involve "freestanding" principles rather than metaphysical absolutes, is not clear unless we can *dislodge* ourselves at least hypothetically from our *vested* interests to conceive justice that way.

The series of unemployment compensation cases should always have been decided on the basis of whether the refusal for unemployment compensation was reasonable and based on law which was facially neutral and universally applicable. If people's religious scruples about holy days or specific dress or unique religious customs or ceremonies or their location or method are important enough to the person that he or she would consider suing the government if it interfered, then the person needs to ask the pertinent questions *prior to taking the job* rather than objecting to the governmental regulations he or she finds intruding on those scruples much later. "Religious" freedom should *never* have been the central issue in these unemployment cases, since that gives exemptions to neutral and universal laws, and the same was true when government whittled out exceptions to the military draft for "religious" convictions.

But Congress and the HHS were pressured by Christian churches to make an exception in the regulations of the ACA and its inclusion of "birth control" access. Access or free choice was what the ACA promoted; it did not mandate individual use of any form of birth control. For religious groups to coerce the government to change the law so to exclude other people's choice is what Rawls saw a democracy needing to forbid, a utilization of a few people's freedom to nullify the freedom for all. That was the majoritarianism we discussed earlier. But this does not mean anyone is complicit (by allowing the law to stand and still paying one's taxes) when they observe other people's utilization of the government's funds and judge them as sinful choices. That distinction is extremely important. The Vietnam War and the Iraq War cost hundreds of thousands of lives, but no U.S. citizen gained an exemption from federal income tax by insisting that he or she objected to the inhumane conflicts. A more universal health care system that provides a choice through access to options does *not coerce* any specific conduct other than universal taxes over which individuals have no voice other than the ballot box or reasonable discussion with actual legislators.

To reshape the law to include *agencies* as having religiously "free exercise" rights rather than individuals is to *misread* the Framers who saw "free exercise of religion" meaning *only* freedom to decide whether, when, where, and how to "worship" one's "God" or "Absolute," *only* an *individual* relation and responsibility. To see religious convictions within a corporation is like seeing the corporation itself worshipping, absent any humans. It is fictitious, as the law knows, and cannot be taken literally. Perhaps it raises the deeper question of the legal fiction of a corporation itself which may eventually need to be revisited since it appears to be a law determined to gain for the corporation and its leaders and shareholders certain *advantages* over other people. Under Rawls's veil of ignorance, one would bargain for the basic principles *without knowing* whether one was connected to any business, much less a corporation, and one would not know if one were going to be affiliated with any religion or not, so one would have been irrational to have approved of such a shelter from liability which others could not acquire.

What becomes apparent after culling through most of the Free Exercise cases the Supreme Court has heard is (1) rather than "religion" and "state" being separated and able best to accomplish their unique work that way, they have intruded on each other, substantially increasing the divisiveness that the Founders hoped to dilute if not eliminate altogether; (2) religious "free exercise" was meaningful when it points to "worship," but when it is opened up to mean any act from any belief one calls religious, the whole category implodes; (3) once it became evident that the government can be forced to make exceptions by one "religious" case prevailing in the Supreme Court over some facially neutral and generally applicable law, many people have attempted to get their own personal exemptions or benefits by pushing the litigation for *their religion* to the highest Court; (4) because the diversity of religions in the United States has grown exponentially during the past half-century, the Court's earlier quasi-intuitive understandings of what constitutes "religion," "religious freedom," "religious establishment," "religious exercise," without any clear definitions, have been pushed, twisted, and still do not fit what many think of as "religion"; (5) the Court often has been slow in accepting as "reasonable" some ideas and arguments about religion primarily because the Court has only had justices who were Protestant Christian, Catholic Christian, and Jewish, its predominant membership has been male and white since its inception; and (6) what appear as unfair treatments of radically different religious groups is not resolved by merely appealing to history or to a majoritarian position or finding security in precedent cases which did not have to consider the *breadth* of religious diversity that now exists in the United States.

Most citizens have often wanted everybody to be governed by generally applicable laws, but religions have confused them into thinking that one's religion must have the prior authority in human life. Since that is not possible in a nation or state that has a *number of religions* who all feel that way, as Rawls said, the choice is between "mortal conflict moderated only by circumstance and exhaustion, or equal liberty of conscience and freedom of thought" because it is otherwise an "irreconcilable latent conflict."[39] Some religious people have desired on occasions to be exempt from certain generally applicable laws, although there is no indication they would accept other people choosing what general laws they would be exempt from. Some continue to see their religion so absolute as to be certain they are right in expecting government to accept their positions as the law of the land, and they expect the government to allow them to discriminate against any citizens who differ. Thus, we have seen the Court, attempting to preserve people's "free exercise" of religion yield, little by little, then more and more, over the years, so that the

Free Exercise jurisdiction has become more blatantly a majoritarian position when its past four decades are compared with the first four decades of the "incorporation" of the First Amendment into state law.

Most of the problem lies within the absolutized positions that religions propagate. With any significant diversity among the population, a democratic republic must assist people to recognize that they must become *more united*, that their social contract has to be built on "freestanding," "overlapping" principles rather than their historical inheritance and ancient metaphysics. Public education must be able to educate its citizens of the role that "public reason" has played, from the days of Ratification of the Constitution to the present, that it must have *priority* in all matters of justice and structure of justice, that justice cannot be erected on anyone's happenstance advantages or any contests or conflicts between different people's irrational or accidental advantages, nor can it be built on a religious metaphysics which operates with faith or a "nonpublic" reason, not open to challenge or modification. No citizen wants the nation to breed more extreme religious divisions. Even when the Free Exercise is confined only to its original meaning of one's being able to meet with a chosen group to *worship* as one sees fit, it still has to have qualification. That freedom was *never* conceived by the Framers as making one exempt from civil and criminal laws that are to be obeyed by all citizens. No matter how much some Christians and Jews venerate "Father Abraham," no society of the United States will tolerate a father taking his son to a mountain to kill him, while insisting that God instructed him to do it, and no religion will be tolerated if it regards others as "infidels" or "socialists" worthy of being killed.

In addition to religious people realizing the social contract can protect their religious free exercise only if it is built on public reason, there is also a job for the lawmakers who must realize the same and quit yielding to pressure to grant special favors to one religion or more. When the nature of religion is fully realized, and people become aware that they all compete against each other for the most part, with absolute dogmas and myths that can *never* be examined through public reason, then legislators can consciously avoid making laws to give any religion a preferential place in our culture.

"Free exercise" of religion assumes that one's "worship" does *not* violate the generally applicable civil and criminal laws, so it has the same protection as any other citizens' worship through these civil laws since government cannot infringe upon one's worship *except* where one might be violating those civil or criminal laws. There *are no other special benefits or exemptions* from any of these general laws that can be expected since all citizens have agreed to live by a single standard of justice found in the Constitution and its structures of justice, its single "rule of law"—all of which are built upon *human* "public reason," reasonable negotiation of the social contract, and unanimous consent to the most basic ethical principles upon which the entire structure is built, a consent which therefore requires, as Rawls insists, *strict compliance*. Since these civil and criminal laws govern most of one's activity in one's relations to other people, religious "free exercise" is seen in its *very limited* arena, as originally recognized, only one's "worship." There are other laws that limit which acts or behavior of each citizen will be protected under these other broad categories

The United States, by its very name, hankers after no enforced homogeneity or uniformity, but instead values diversity as Madison insisted. It claims "E Pluribus Unum." To make the absolutized metaphysical claim *denies* the *actual origin* of our laws and increases the divisiveness inherent in a pluralistic society once the metaphysical assumptions and absolutized, unquestionable doctrines are allowed to call the shots. A democracy must be above that, and if it is, there will be no need for exceptions or exemptions from the common law.

"Dispensatio est volnus, quod vulnerat jus commune"

(Eng. Tr.: A dispensation [relaxation or exemption] is a wound which wounds common law.)

NOTES

1. *City of Boerne v. Flores*, 521 U.S. 507 (1997), at 532, 534 (also citing *Smith II*, at 888).

2. Rawls, *A Theory of Justice*, 212–221. Rawls is clear that when someone's freedom is being impinged on by another in the name of the latter's freedom, the only resolution comes not from some theological source or resolution but only from the very principles of justice they arrived at in the "original position," which would begin with the two principles he formulated to which all would agree.

3. Rawls, *A Theory of Justice*, 220; and Rawls, *Political Liberalism*, 157.

4. In a specific case built upon religious convictions, as this is, it surely is obvious that the Congress felt the reference to the "Constitution" would suffice, so "First Amendment" would be redundant. No one would think the use of "Constitution" would probably mean the Second Amendment, or Fifth Amendment or Second Article. So this avoidance of redundancy is not an argument that Congress meant to circumvent the First Amendment any more than it was trying to circumvent the Constitution.

5. *Hobby Lobby*, J. Ginsburg, dissenting at 744–745.

6. *Hobby Lobby*, J. Ginsburg, dissenting at 744. As she argued, the exemption sought by Hobby Lobby and Conestoga would override "significant interests of the corporations' employees and covered dependents." "It would deny legions of women who do not hold their employers' beliefs access to contraceptive coverage that the ACA would otherwise secure" (at 746). To the contrary, J. Ginsburg felt that there is an "overriding interest" here, namely, "in keeping the courts 'out of the business of

evaluating the relative merits of differing religious claims'" (at 771, citing Lee, 455 U.S., at 263, n. 2).

7. J. Kennedy appears to be correct if one is thinking about the formal articulation of the pre-*Smith* test, although there were times when references to other alternatives did emerge.

8. This idea was utilized many times by the Court, with different members agreeing to it, even in the Hastings Law School case that we examined above, in which the Court cited to *Smith*, emphasizing that "the Court held that the Free Exercise Clause does not inhibit enforcement of otherwise valid regulations of general application that incidentally burden religious conduct."

9. *Citizens United v. Federal Election Commission*, 558 U.S. 310 (2010).

10. A more obvious parallel to the Court's argument here pertaining to religion would be like insisting that just because Vatican I articulated that the Pope, when he speaks on faith or morals, on behalf of the whole church, is "infallible"—does not mean that Vatican I cannot be said to have closed the list, that perhaps other priests, perhaps even nuns, and maybe even people belonging to other religions could also be included as being "infallible" in the same sense.

11. The Roman Catholic proof-text by Pius XI in his encyclical against contraception stands in the background for this case, decided now in 2014 by a majority of five *male* justices, from the old story of Onan in Genesis 39. But the story's use in the Catholic Church is simply mere ignorance of the Jewish Levirate marriage law, not any law about contraception in general. This negative view of contraception comes from ages past, from the church that learned utter *disrespect for women* from St. Augustine, to blame the evil of sex on Eve and therefore also the plight of universal death as *her* fault, for her lack of rational control of her sexuality. (See Augustine's *Concerning The City of God Against the Pagans*, tr. Henry Bettenson (Middlesex, England: Penguin Books, 1972), 568–589.)

12. This seems to have its parallel in the many people in CA a few years ago who tried to defraud the government by paying a small fee to a certain self-appointed "clergy," so he would "ordain" them "ministers" whereby they could receive the IRS Code §107 "Parsonage Allowance" exemption for all their housing expenses—except the Greens saved millions of dollars, not just a few thousand, and the Greens, unlike those other people, were *successful*.

13. *Hobby Lobby*, J. Ginsburg, dissenting, at 739–740.

14. They were not asking for their business to have a Free Exercise claim, but for the owners who had their religious convictions to be honored by being allowed to do business on Sunday since their religion requires them to not work on the Shabbat.

15. Of course, the pro-Christian bias was so obvious in those 1963 cases, that it is mystery why any Justice would ever quote anything from them, especially when that would require them to have to admit, as their focus here in *Hobby Lobby* (in parenthesis) that the Jewish merchants *lost* on the *merits* of the case. But they claimed that was the decision. They lost, however, but *not* on the merits, but because the *religious* dimension of Shabbat and the Christian "Sabbath" was *ignored*, turned *wholly secular*, which succeeded in obliterating the religious nature of any Jewish claim of either Establishment or Free Exercise.

16. See Robert P. Jones, *The End of White Christian America* (New York: Simon & Schuster, 2016), 66, 119.

17. In 2017, the owners of Hobby Lobby were caught smuggling into the United States illegal, alleged religiously related ancient artifacts from Iraq from dealers in the UAE for their museum they are erecting because of their veneration for the Bible. They had been warned by an attorney about engaging in such a transaction, but persisted since they were able to buy more than 5,000 pieces of such artifacts for such a good price of 1.6 million. They claim the dealer sold them as "pottery" and "samples," but it is not clear why they would have paid such a price for mere "pottery" and "samples." On the other hand, since they had the artifacts shipped to multiple locations of their stores around the United States, that *does* make sense if they were trying to get them past U.S. Customs agents. Much of what they purchased was earlier stolen or was a fake, and most of the articles had little or no documentation of prior ownership. This smuggling had been going on since at least 2009, while they were protesting their Christian values in the midst of being caught in 2014. When they were caught, they claimed absolute ignorance of any possible illegality of what they were doing. Perhaps they should have claimed this also was violating their "free exercise" of their religion, that they were simply doing Jesus's work for God's museum?

18. Sidney Mead, *The Lively Experiment*, and his *The Nation with the Soul of a Church*.

19. *Trinity Lutheran Church of Columbia, Inc. v. Comer, Director, Missouri Department of Natural Resources*, 582 U.S. ___, 137 S.Ct. 2012; 198 L.Ed.2d 551 (2017), (slip opinion) (Sotomayor, dissent, at 1, emphasis added).

20. *Trinity Lutheran*, Sotomayor, dissent, at 24.

21. *Trinity Lutheran*, Sotomayor, dissent, at 26.

22. *Masterpiece Cakeshop, Ltd., et al., v. Colorado Civil Rights Commission et al.*, 584 U.S. ___, 138 S.Ct. 1719; 201 L.Ed.2dd 35, (2018). (slip opinion)

23. If one begins to study the Supreme Court oral arguments, and hear the sarcasm rolling from J. Scalia and occasionally even others, would not this new criterion of the Court invalidate half of the Court's decisions? "Disrespectful" attitudes of judges nullify their decisions in *Cakeshop*?

24. Did this imply that the dissent felt it knew more about the dangers of the pandemic than the medical leaders of the nation, or were they persuaded by various conservative Christian pastors that God would not let anybody that attended worship get the virus, as so many claimed over those dreadful months? Two of the four were appointed by the President Trump. In more recent cases that came after this text was set, the influence of the four dissenting justices caused the opposite result in favor of the religions themselves.

25. As in *Everson* (1947), however, the Court's ideal principle was often contradicted by the Court's actual decision. Over those decades, more aid, without any coercion, was supplied both to parents as well as the actual parochial schools, which was totally against the theory the Court expressed. Illegal "establishment" could exist merely by the public funds, tax credits, and so on being supplied out of general taxes or it could be illegal by any law having a religious purpose or primary religious effect (*Lemon*, 1971).

26. *Kendra Espinoza, et al., Petititoners v. Montana Department of Revenue, et al.*, 591 U.S. ___ (2020) (slip opinion, No. 18-1195), at 11.

27. The dissent in *Everson* said the Amendment's "separation" of government and religion "was broader than separating church and state in this narrow sense. It was to create a complete and permanent separation of the two spheres of religious activity and civil authority by comprehensively forbidding every form of public aid or support religion." See *Everson v. Board of Education of Ewing TP*, 330 U.S. 1 (1947) at 31–32.

28. One can hardly deny the centuries-long antagonism between the Protestants and Catholics from Luther's time in the early sixteenth century. Certainly many early colonies in the New World carried a bias toward either Protestant Christianity or Catholic Christianity. But most did not desire to return to the unending religious wars their forefathers had been involved in. Long-standing bias does not disappear overnight, not even with the First Amendment. When C.J. Roberts speaks of the anti-Catholic bias in the latter half of the nineteenth century, that half-century saw the *absolutizing* and stagnating of both Catholic and Protestant positions theologically in the Protestant opposition not simply to Catholics but to Darwinian evolution, and the Catholic opposition not simply to Protestants and the philosophy and science of the Enlightenment, as spelled out in its Syllabus of Errors, but in the doctrine of Papal Infallibility that came from Vatican I in 1869–1870. The two groups viewed each other as arch-enemies.

29. That might awaken the Court to its pro-Christian bias, but it will be too late, since if certain other religious groups make similar demands that the Christian groups have for their schools, the extreme right hate groups within the Christian ranks will become violent. The Court and Congress need to avert this by stopping the flow of billions of public tax dollars to private and religious schools; they need to reread Madison, Jefferson, and Rawls before it is too late. Even some religious leaders have failed to realize the separation that should prohibit use of public taxes for parochial schools, as for example, when Cardinal Manning belittled Eleanor Roosevelt when she backed the public funds being only for public schools available to all. See David Michaelis, *Eleanor* (New York: Simon & Schuster, 2020), 468–469.

30. One can imagine, however, if S.C. Justices endorse a specific religion as Absolute, and spend their lives reading litigation which is always about vested interests, that they might think Rawls's theory unrealistic, but its vision of "justice" transcends a competition of mere irrational advantages, so is the only way a nation can ever realize a real sense of unity. It is practical.

31. *Little Sisters of the Poor Saints Peter and Paul Home v. Pennsylvania et al.*, 591 U.S.___ (2020) (slip opinion, No. 19-431), at 7.

32. Because of that inherent self-contradiction, assuming their belief was genuine, their choice of a lawsuit appears to make it all a religiously pious protest done for strictly political purposes.

33. *Little Sisters*, at 7.

34. *Little Sisters*, at 16.

35. *Little Sisters*, at 9.

36. *Little Sisters*, at 7. The Court did not put it this way, but cited the dogma of only the "Catholic" church to show this conviction of the Sisters was a "deeply held" religious conviction, based on the church which teaches that "deliberately avoiding reproduction through medical means is immoral." But very few other religions have any such doctrine, and many Catholics do not comply with this one. Most nonreligious people see this as self-contradictory dogma that only results in *more* unwanted pregnancies or abortions, so illogical and unrealistic. It is *not* a "freestanding principle" which should govern civil law, but only a "nonpublic" reason operative within a closed and exclusive association because of an ancient metaphysics.

37. The reason the owners of *Hobby Lobby* made the choice to eliminate their employees' choice is not clear. Here, in *Little Sisters*, the group is comprised of women who compassionately devote themselves to care for elderly poor women. To be recognized as a Catholic religious organization or institute, they had to agree to vows of poverty, celibacy, and obedience, as members of other religious orders, but they also added a vow of hospitality. Obviously, it might seem that the patients being cared for as well as their care-givers might need no contraceptives, but contraceptives were only a small part of sexual preventive health care which comprised the ACA package. It included all kinds of free services such as annual checkups and screenings for breast cancer, cervical cancer, postpartum depression, and gestational diabetes. These services would mean that a pregnant woman covered by the ACA package was more likely to get involved in prenatal care which is so very important to a mother and baby, and the free education and testing can reduce the risk of endometrial and ovarian cancer. To gain such services free of charge can give a woman more of sense of being in control of her own future, can perhaps enable her to obtain a higher education. See dissent by J. Ginsberg, joined by J. Sotomayor (at 1–22).

38. While some legislators seem to view any negotiation with others as "compromise" or being a "traitor" to their party, the democratic republic was formed as a "representational" form, to represent very *diverse interests*, not with the desired end of an unending antagonism but rather of reaching agreements, even with compromising, in a sense of *national unity*.

39. Rawls, *Political Liberalism*, xxvi.

Chapter 9

"No Law Respecting the Establishment of Religion"

In *Abington v. Schempp* (1963), J. Clark, writing for the Court, quoted the following from what J. Rutledge had written in his earlier dissent in *Everson* (1947):[1]

> The First Amendment's purpose was not to strike merely at the official establishment of a single sect, creed or religion, outlawing only a formal relation such as had prevailed in England and some of the colonies. Necessarily, it was to uproot all such relationships. But the object was broader than separating church and state in this narrow sense. It was to create a complete and permanent separation of the spheres of religious activity and civil authority by comprehensively forbidding every form of public aid or support for religion.

This is obviously in total agreement with Jefferson's and Madison's objection to even "three pence" of taxes being given to any religion for any purpose. They and others had shaped the First Amendment after *defeating* Gov. Henry's general assessment bill for Virginia which had proposed to distribute public taxes to churches of people's individual choice, and Madison later emphasized, as we saw, how they superseded Henry's bill with a "perfect separation" which had worked to the benefit of both the religions in Virginia as well as the state government. An illegal "establishment" did not require a showing of formal "coercion" even as it had not in the proposed Virginia bill since each person could direct tax monies to the church or religion of his choice. Even so, the *single* dissenting voice in the *Schempp* decision tried to validate the religious worship in public school by saying it was *not coerced*, while the Court argued that a law could violate the Establishment Clause even *without any formal coercion*.[2]

To say the whole area of "establishment" clause cases over time became emotionally ignited is an understatement. The most obvious manifestations of "establishment" in the colonies had been colonial constitutions which specified which religion one had to belong to, which doctrines one had to believe, which religious ideas or practices one was forbidden to speak against, doubt, or violate, as well as the fact that all citizens of the colonies were expected to be taxed to support both the clergy of the religion, their actual teaching, and other necessary things such as church buildings, and the like. In addition to the *obvious* elements like these, there was the fine line of being able to see that a law or practice which had been a part of a colony's *theocratic* establishment was still being engaged in despite its obvious establishment nature such as any prayers in legislatures; any specifically religious slogans appearing on government buildings, coins, and so forth; any exemptions of religions from real property taxes or even certain exemptions on individual income tax for the clergy.

This residue from former theocracies went unnoticed by most citizens since the religious pluralism in the United States was still confined very largely to an internecine struggle between Protestant Christian denominations, and to a much lesser degree, their toleration of the Catholic and Jewish faiths. That means it was easy to adopt a "majoritarian" posture as a Protestant Christian, and still think one was *not* "establishing" a religion. Yet it was this very majoritarianism that worried James Madison, as we saw, and caused him and Jefferson to establish a "perfect separation" of government and religion by the First Amendment. J. Jackson also saw the sinister danger of "majoritarianism" even in examining "free exercise" claims as early as *Barnette* (1943), so he, writing for the Court, objected strenuously that the freedoms of the Bill of Rights are *not* subject to a majority vote, just as government has no jurisdiction or cognizance to try to determine what is religiously "orthodox."[3]

"ESTABLISHMENT" STANDARDS
WITHOUT DEFINING "RELIGION?"

The first "religion" phrase in the First Amendment is "Congress shall make no law respecting the establishment of religion." We can postulate that likely most citizens in the latter part of the eighteenth century knew roughly what this meant, just as they knew they wanted a "free exercise" or their own choice regarding the religious body with which they desired to "worship," inasmuch as they or their parents, grandparents, or earlier descendants had experienced the government being the civil arm of the given religion of the country in which they lived, or in their recent past of the colony in which they were residents. But, as we saw, the diversity of Christian groups in the colonies who wanted to be *the established religion*, who formerly could not admit the validity of each other's religion, was eroded as most of them lost many members to the "Great Awakening," with almost half century of powerful revivals in upper New England, supplemented with the more philosophical underpinnings of the individual freedom and especially "freedom of conscience" flowing from the Enlightenment.

This made persuasion rather than inheritance or coercion the basis of one's religion among Protestants. Yet among the "converts" of the revivals, the persuasion supplied nothing to actually change people's negative attitudes toward other sects or denominations or religions. If anything, it hardened it, for now one had found the "truth" *for oneself* and *voluntarily* embraced it rather than simply inheriting it or even "confirming" it as a young teenager largely due to parents' influence. The new absolute certainty and new freedom from government intervention in their religion just *shifted* these adults to a self-assurance of being among the *few really* "saved"—from the judgment of an inherited religious group to the promises of an exciting new group now of one's *own choosing*, even the more Absolute or unquestionable than earlier.

By the subsequent battles Christian fundamentalism fought against evolution in the nineteenth century and early twentieth century, many of these Christians did not even see their attachment to a particular Christian group as their own choice. Instead, it was considered strictly as God's doing, His "call" of them. That fit with all the earlier Calvinistic predestination, but was also a very personal element in the pietistic dimension of the revivals which required a *personal conversion experience* by each individual. That being the case, many subconsciously removed themselves even further from any notion of the ethical principles of government being "secular" or based on human reason. God or Jesus was in total charge of their lives. Though they did not use the word "theocracy," they were sure *their brand* of Christianity had shown itself to be nothing less than the ultimate truth, therefore, the most obvious authority for establishing the ethical principles of the government, that is, a "theocracy." The logic was that if their conversion was to the true Christianity and true "God," and true "law" of "God," then there was *no room for diversity*. Therefore, "secularism," "autonomy," and "deism" were simply added to their list of enemies—as they fought Darwinism and belittled what they viewed as the earlier degenerate philosophy of "man being the measure of all things." Most Protestants felt they had "reformed" or "restored" the original, which enabled a simplistic view of Christian history, a view of all the development of Christian theology over the centuries as unnecessary or even a great apostasy, which simply continued the Protestant opposition to Catholicism. Since there were still many less Catholics in the United States at the end of the nineteenth century, the faithful were embraced by extremely anti-Protestant articulation of the grave errors of Protestantism, in the Syllabus of Errors, which insisted that no one has a right to belong to any religion other than the Roman Catholic faith.

As was true of the earliest cases that were adjudicated under the "Free Exercise" clause, the earliest cases decided by the Court dealing with the "Establishment" clause were not actually made on the basis of that first clause of the First Amendment, but on other grounds. *Pierce v. Society of Sisters*, 268 U.S. 510 (1925) was an Oregon case basically answering the question of whether the state mandatory education law could be met *only* by attending public schools, or whether one could satisfy that education law by attending a parochial school or military academy. The Court ruled it could be met by a nonpublic school, that in fact the Fourteenth Amendment gave parents liberty which would include a choice of schools that met certain uniform educational standards for their children, and whatever changes in the state's assets that resulted from their going to a private rather than public school was *not* a "taking" prohibited by the Fifth Amendment.[4] The public schools, supported by public taxes, were accessible to all students, but this decision did not shift public taxes as aid to parochial or military schools. Public schools were viewed as a public investment by the states and nation.

Five years later, in *Cochran v. Louisiana State Bd. of Education*, 281 U.S. 370 (1930), the Court approved using state funds to furnish *secular textbooks* for all schools, including parochial. This, too, was seen as not a violation of due process nor an unconstitutional "taking" of property since, in the state's interest in the education of its children, the textbooks were seen simply as a benefit to the students and state, but not to the schools. The question did not arise till the *Everson* case in 1947 as to whether this was simply freeing up the funds of the parochial school for other things, including specifically religious indoctrination, since the parochial school had primarily a religious purpose and orientation, so that any funding ultimately assisted in achieving its primary purpose, a religious education.[5]

"INCORPORATION" AND THE EARLY ATTEMPTS TO DEFINE "ESTABLISHMENT"

Finally, the "due process" emphases of the Fourteenth Amendment brought about the Court's "incorporation" of the "Establishment" Clause by the famous *Everson* case of 1947.[6] In this 5/4 decision, parochial schools were favored by the New Jersey law that attempted to provide transportation for students who were a considerable distance from the schools. It authorized school boards of townships to reimburse parents of students in *public* schools or *Catholic* schools for the public bus fare they paid for their children. It was *not* made available to other private religious schools or to for-profit private nonreligious schools.[7]

The Court felt comfortable in suggesting that these public funds were used for the public purpose of getting the children to parochial schools *safely*, just as were the funds paying for the local police and fire departments who also assist in *safely* getting them to the school. It decided this was legal since (1) it was not a "taking" of public property for private purposes without due process, since education and safety of the children is a public concern, nor (2) was it a violation of the Establishment Clause since it was a benefit given to aid all the children of the state, equivalent to the universally applied "police powers" such as *safety benefits* including police and fire services. It argued that to remove the benefit of the police powers such as police and fire departments from people just because they were religious would be a terrible thing. But that was never the issue.

In strong dissenting opinions, J. Jackson, and separately J. Rutledge, joined by J. Frankfurter and J. Burton, found the Court's six-page, glowing recitations of the role played in the formulation of the First Amendment by Madison's *Memorial and Remonstrance* and Jefferson's *Virginia Bill for Religious Liberty* totally at complete odds with the Court's ultimate decision, completely and shockingly *incongruous*. After the recitation of the *severance* of civil government and religion in the late eighteenth century by Jefferson and Madison, the *Everson* Court had summarized: "No tax in any amount, large or small, can be levied to support any religious activities or institutions, whatever they may be called, or whatever form they may adopt to teach or practice religion." It emphasized the "wall between church and state," insisting "[t]hat wall must be kept high and impregnable. We could not approve the slightest breach." To this it mildly added "New Jersey has not breached it here."[8]

What was not noticed was that the Court *slipped* from examining a possible "establishment" breach to a strong "free exercise" emphasis two-thirds of the way through its decision, as it wrote, "On the other hand, other language of the amendment commands that New Jersey cannot hamper its citizens in the free exercise of their religion."[9] To illustrate the right of one's "free exercise," Baptists, Jews, "Muhammedans" [*sic*], Catholics, nonbelievers, and "members of any other faith" have to be free to exercise their religion, and the Court converted this from an individual or family decision and interest into public safety and public welfare issue, arguing that to get the children to the Catholic school safely (vis-à-vis the terrible traffic and "hitchhiking" dangers!) was a general public interest as much as the police protection they received en route or the fire protection their school buildings received from the local fire department. To this example, the Court concluded "State power is no more to be used so as to handicap religions, than it is to favor them."[10]

The Court as a whole accepted the idea of "a wall of separation between Church and state." But the majority decided that instead of "handicapping" a religion, it would "favor" it, because, as the majority failed to see, the law in question did *not* really accommodate the school children's welfare in *general* since it made no provision to supply bus money for students attending *non*-Catholic religious schools or other "for-profit" private schools. So it was *not* a general welfare and general safety law at all. The four dissenting justices did not disagree with the Court's bare outline summary of the meaning of the antiestablishment clause of the First Amendment. It was the *actual deci-sion* of the Court, following such analysis, which appalled the dissent. The Court tried to avert the problem connection between the public taxes and the Catholic church and school by insisting "the State contributes no money to the schools. It does not support them." It did not attempt to make the Catholic school a public concern to justify the reimbursements, but under its "free exercise" shift, it added the *public* concern of *secular* education and *safety of the children.*

But there was never any proven danger in the students' travel to the paro-chial schools, no public endangerment put in evidence. As the dissent said, paying the parents out of public taxes for the bus fare did *not* make the travel by any bus any more or less safe.[11] All the students living a distance from the school were either taken by private car or rode the public buses. But the bus was either safe or not, and paying only one select religious group's parents for riding it, but not other parents whose children had to ride the same buses to attend other religious schools or private schools, only discriminated in favor of one specific religion, on the basis of the *character or status of the school, not on a safety issue*, since the bus remained a bus, not any safer or less safe by the taxes given to parents.

As the dissent emphasized (J. Jackson, joined by J. Frankfurter, J. Rutledge, and J. Burton), the real issue was one of enabling students to get to the Catholic school for its *religious education*, that its secular offerings have *never* been the reason for the parochial schools' existence, but only the reli-gious training. J. Jackson quoted a few sections from the Catholic Church's Canon Law, requirements for education of its children showing its rigid emphasis on *indoctrination*. Since indoctrinating its children is likely the *most important* aspect of the Catholic Church's entire program, the dissent insists that these taxes to the parents are as "indistinguishable" as sending the taxes directly to the Church itself.[12] The distinction the Court proffered between "public welfare" and "private" purpose was meaningless.

The real analogy was not that to prohibit funding bus transportation would be like prohibiting the police or fire personnel from protecting the students because the students were headed to parochial school (which was the Court's analogy), but rather, the police and fire department first asking the person in trouble if he or she was Catholic, and responding to help him or her *only* if the answer was "Yes." If it was "No," they received no public assistance.[13] In fact, the dissent noted that anyone of a different religious persuasion than Catholic was, in this use of tax funds, encountering the very thing Madison and Jefferson so strongly objected to—being forced to pay taxes for religious teachers with whom one disagreed religiously. Madison and Jefferson viewed such use of tax funds as being unjust, "sinful and tyrannical" (Jefferson), an "offence against God" (Madison), creating terrible divisions in the society, just as it had in Virginia in their time.

Their prediction has come true.[14] The dissent noted that this aid was a negation of Madison and Jefferson's ideas of a "wall of "separation" As the dissent stated: "Religion" and "establishment" were not used in any formal or technical sense. "The prohibition broadly forbids state support, financial or other, of religion in any guise, form or degree. It outlaws all use of public funds for religious purposes."[15] That was the four justices dissenting. The dissent acknowledged that for parents who insist on the child attending parochial school, the expense may be difficult. But they always have the public schools available, so it is strictly their choice to *get religious indoctrination* by not sending the child to the public schools that presents the great cost to them, *not the public interest* in a secular education or *general welfare of all* students. They would be the first ones to object if in public schools the religious teachings of *another* religious group were presented, the dissent argued. But such objection is to be expected as their right and obligation since "we have staked the very existence of our country on the faith that complete separation between the state and religion is best for the state and best for religion."[16]

Nevertheless, the Court decided that the religious education was after all secular, in the public interest, so it opened Pandora's box, and the very "cognizance" Madison had claimed government did *not* have, the Court had now claimed and appropriated. J. Rutledge's final words are prophetic of the warning given by Madison that even the slightest trifling with our liberties will grow into a massive problem:

> Two great drives are constantly in motion to abridge, in the name of education, the complete division of religion and civil authority which our forefathers made. One is to introduce religious education and observances into the public schools. The other, to obtain public funds for the aid and support of various private religious schools. . . . In my opinion both avenues were closed by the Constitution. Neither should be opened by this Court. The matter is not one of quantity, to be measured by the amount of money expended. Now as in Madison's day, it is one of principle, to keep separate the separate spheres as the First Amendment drew them; to prevent the first experiment upon our liberties; and to keep the question from becoming entangled in corrosive precedents. We should not be

less strict to keep strong and untarnished the one side of the shield or religious freedom than we have been of the other.[17]

But the "corrosive precedents," such as the *Everson dissent* predicted, bubbled up quickly after such a "breach" in the "wall" occurred. In the following year, 1948, the Court, in *McCollum v. Board of Education*, 333 U.S. 203 (1948), had to decide—just as J. Rutledge had said in his dissent in *Everson*—whether the public school students in Illinois could be given religious instruction by religious teachers coming to the *public schools*, and the schools willingly extending "release time" from the normal class schedule to those who desired this religious instruction. The Court, in an 8/1 decision, found this an *illegal* establishment of religion, arguing that the Establishment Clause not only forbids preferential treatment of some religions over against others but also prohibits aid to all religions.[18] Certainly that was Jefferson's and Madison's view when they and others defeated the proposed Virginia bill that would have aided all Christian groups in Virginia. The Court saw this whole atmosphere of the released time was for *religious indoctrination, utilizing a captive audience,* "captive" by virtue of the mandatory public education law, "releasing" them from studying secular subjects *only* in order to study religion. This form of "release time" was used in various states, affecting 1.5 million students.

It was not over, however. New York saw this failure to get "release time" in Illinois, so approached it differently. Their law allowed the students who requested religious instruction to *leave* the public school campus and go to a religious center for their religious instruction. Like *McCollum*, it also was voluntary. Ironically, J. Douglas, who found *McCollum* illegal, wrote for the Court here in *Zorach v. Clauson*, 343 U.S. 306 (1952),[19] insisting that this is mere "accommodation" by the government, not prohibited "public aid" since there was no coercion involved.

Just that quickly, the idea of "separation" of religion and state slid into the background, with Madison and Jefferson's words forgotten, and "accommodation" became the *criterion*.

J. Douglas insisted there was no coercion, and that releasing students to go elsewhere for a period of religious instruction was no different from allowing a student to leave the school to attend some important Holy Day celebration with parents at the choice of their religious group. He then went to the extreme of calling the option here, of disallowing this "release" as a "hostility" toward religion, a preference for nonreligion over religion, a term the Court has continued to use as a "scare" word since. J. Douglas, for the Court, argued that government must be neutral, "but it can close its doors or suspend its operations as to those who want to repair to their religious sanctuary for worship or instruction."[20]

J. Frankfurter, dissenting, was quite perceptive, however, insisting that the "essence of this case is that the school system did *not* 'close its doors' and did *not* 'suspend its operations.'" There is all the difference in the world between letting the children out of school and letting some of them out of school into religious classes. "If everyone is free to make what use he will of time wholly unconnected from schooling required by law—those who wish sectarian instruction devoting it to that purpose, those who have ethical instruction at home, to that, those who study music, to that—then of course there is no conflict with the Fourteenth Amendment."[21]

But students electing not to go for religious instruction were *not* allowed to go home *nor* were they able to have other classes at school as would be the case if a few students were excused to attend some Holy Day celebration. Here they were simply sent to the study hall for that period. So they were *still* a "captive audience" as much as were those in *McCollum*, which, J. Black, dissenting, noted. *McCollum*'s opposition to an unconstitutional manipulating of the compelled classroom hours of its compulsory school machinery so as to channel children into sectarian classes was still the case in *Zorach*.[22] J. Frankfurter, also dissenting, suggested that advocating such "release time" probably was an indication that those pushing it had little confidence that the students would have elected the release time if they had a choice instead of being out of school at that time.[23] So it *was* "coercion" pure and simple, the captive audience, and only a *single religion's instruction* as the alternative to being kept in study hall.

A few years later, a rather anomalous case made it to the Court in *Torcaso v. Watkins*, 367 U.S. 488 (1961). Torcaso was appointed to the office of Notary Public by the Governor of Maryland. But he refused to swear his faith in the existence of God which Maryland law still required, an obvious violation of the Constitution's prohibition of making religion a test for public office so it was easily determined as illegal, since to make religion a "test" for public office was prohibited by the U.S. Constitution.[24]

In the following year, in *Engel v. Vitale*, 370 U.S. 421 (1962), the Court found New York's school prayer a violation of the Establishment Clause, since the prayer was obviously worship and was *formulated by the state*. The Court emphasized that neither the strictly voluntary attendance during the prayer nor the alleged nondenominational nature of the prayer mitigated its unconstitutional import which was simply that the state had formulated the prayer. J. Stewart dissented, insisting this denies our spiritual heritage, so is no more unconstitutional than congressional prayer or "In God we Trust" on our coins. But if these, like the Sabbath laws we saw in 1961, still carried *religious* meaning from days in which people had wanted a *theocracy*, they should *all* be simply illegal under the First Amendment, though the issue dealt only with the state-legislated prayer. This decision received considerable backlash.

The following year, another case involving prayer in public schools arose in *Abington Township School District v. Schempp*, 374 U.S. 203 (1963). A student volunteer was allowed to select some scripture to read, without comment, and lead the "Lord's prayer" over the PA system, piped into every classroom. Further, they allowed the student-reader to choose even between Protestant and Catholic versions of the Bible. If students objected to the exercise, they could be formally excused by permission of the school, and they could stand out in the hall, outside their homeroom while the religious exercise and Pledge of Allegiance were conducted. So it *appeared* totally voluntary on the part of the students, though mandated by the state.

Perceptively, J. Clark, giving the opinion of the Court, found the practice of the state mandating an *illegal* "establishment." It was not a part of the curriculum, but rather a *devotional*. Nor was it justified as improving the morality of its citizens since the scripture selections did not have to focus on morality at all. It could not in any sense be regarded as a part of the general curriculum since it was forbidden even to make *comments* about any of the passages read.

The nonmandatory participation in the religious exercise did *not* mitigate its illegality since by the fact that it was a purely religious devotional, it preferred religion to nonreligion, operated off a captive audience, and those who chose to stand in the hall outside the classroom during this time were subject to feeling *disapproval from peers*. The practice revealed there was *no secular purpose* but only a religious one, and only a religious effect, so by its subtle coercion of a captive audience into a Christian devotional, it was illegal. These two elements of the purpose and primary effect of the law became two of the "three prongs" of the *Lemon* test for Establishment in 1971, but they were already operative in the justices' minds prior to *Schempp*.

The Court insisted that the decision is not hostility toward religion, and with dicta, it even suggested that a well-rounded education might very easily involve historical or literary references to a religion or its history or literature or even to ethics in separate classes. But this was only a *devotional*, so illegal. J. Brennan added an extensive concurring opinion, which buttressed the separation of the state and religion. Both the Court as well as J. Brennan admitted that while this devotional use of scripture was illegal, this did *not* mean that students could *never* be exposed to a religion's history or ethics in other classes. These comments, sheer dicta, were seized upon for a number of years by many professors in higher education, who immediately undertook "religious studies" programs as an "objective" study, devoid of catechetical purposes, in various public colleges and universities throughout the nation.[25] Although J. Brennan traced the devotionals back into the much earlier private schools, as something that itself was not new, he declared that it was the mandating of the exercise every day in every school in the state that was new and made it clearly an unjustified imposition, despite the claim of its being voluntary.[26]

The Court still did not clarify what "religion" itself was or what it included, as applied to the "purpose" or "effects" of any law in question. Nevertheless, in J. Brennan's concurring opinion, he attempted to distinguish this practice from the government legislature practices of chaplains' opening prayers, of religious slogans on our coins and public buildings, by emphasizing the young, impressionable age of the children, including their susceptibility to peer pressure to conform, as well as to the possibility that what was once regarded a religious slogan or symbol could *lose that sacrality* as the Court had decided in the "blue-law" "Sunday-closing" cases of 1963.[27] But, as he and the Court held, the very form of the practices in *Abington v. Schempp* was nevertheless still strongly sacred for most people, so an illegal establishment.[28]

Two significant Establishment cases brought more issues to light five years later. In *Epperson v. Arkansas*, 393 U.S. 97 (1968), the Court found it *illegal* for Arkansas to prohibit the teaching of evolution in public schools since the prohibition stems entirely from a *religious purpose*, namely, to prevent teaching which differs from these people's dogmatic literal reading of the "Creation" in the book of Genesis. This seemed to be a very straightforward decision, although the emotions ran high as it revived the memory of the Scopes trial and the primary foe of Christian fundamentalism—Darwinian evolution.

In the same year, however, more benefits from public taxes flowed to parochial schools in *Board of Education v. Allen*, 392 U.S. 236 (1968). The Court decided that it was *not* a violation of the Establishment Clause for New York to fund parochial schools for their ordering of secular textbooks for specific approved courses, as texts are *loaned* to students of the schools. So it was not funds given to a church, or really even to the parochial school, but books loaned to the students, therefore was only an "incidental" religious benefit, with the primary purpose and primary effect being secular. This was granting more aid than a mere state-selected secular textbook or reimbursement for a bus ride.

The dissent argued, however, that in this case, in considerable *distinction* from earlier cases, the textbooks on the secular subjects were *chosen* by the *parochial schools* rather than the state, which enabled them to select texts best suited to their sectarian, religious goals, or doctrinal ideas. It suggested that books can be utilized *ideologically* in a way that buses cannot, so even certain secular textbooks could be used to teach religion. That seed of thought—that simply avoiding sending money to the church might not prevent the utilization of funds being used by the teachers, with or without texts, for religious indoctrination—sprouted into a confusing series of splitting hairs during the following decades over which supplies or needs of the parochial school or its students could be legally provided by taxes and which could not. Divertibility of funds is still a problem, in fact, more than ever.

In 1968, in *Flast v. Cohen*, 392 U.S. 83, the Court ruled on a more preliminary concern than the Religion Clauses of the First Amendment. The lower courts had denied Petitioner's "standing" under the authority of *Frothingham v. Mellon*, 262 U.S. 447 (1923). Petitioner had objected to the use of tax funds for educational materials for parochial schools as a part of the Elementary and Secondary Education Act of 1965, arguing that either this use of the taxes was a violation of the Act or, if not, then the Act itself was in violation of the Establishment Clause of the First Amendment. The Court's opinion, written by C.J. Warren, found that the Article III requirements for "standing" were actually met by the Petitioner, distinguishing it from *Frothingham v. Mellon*, by the fact that Petitioner alleged that the tax money was being spent in violation of a specific constitutional protection (the Establishment Clause) against the abuse of legislative power. It analyzed the elements that had to be met for "standing," emphasizing that the issue of standing has nothing to do with the merits of the case being brought, but is rather only the question of whether the person bringing suit is the proper party, adequately connected to the outcome of the suit. That he is the proper party and therefore has "standing" is *all* the Court adjudicated.

Of note in this case, however, is J. Douglas's concurring opinion in which he expressed doubt that the Court's present "test" would hold up, and he would prefer that *Frothingham v. Mellon* simply be abandoned now rather than create more frustration. His position emphasized that the federal judiciary should play the role of "guarding basic rights against majoritarian control."[29] He further emphasized that just as we have seen a "host of devices" used by the States to avoid opening to black people public facilities enjoyed by whites, similarly, those who have pushed for federal funds for sectarian schools have done the same: "The mounting federal aid to sectarian schools is notorious and the subterfuges numerous."[30] Was the public aware?

By 1970, many people were certainly aware that religious institutions had various "tax breaks." As nonprofit institutions, they qualified as 501(c) (3) organizations to be exempt from income tax. The rationale was that nonprofit institutions can offer many beneficial services to the general public, so the exemption from income taxation was an incentive to create more eleemosynary institutions. On the other hand, it may not have been very public knowledge how many billions of tax dollars this involved. Nor was it general public knowledge that ordained clergy could also receive exemption on their income tax for their "parsonage" allowance under §107 of the IRS code, whether their institution furnished it or they had to provide it themselves. That had much the same rationale originally but combined also with the tradition that back in the eighteenth and nineteenth centuries, when many clergy were very poorly compensated by their religious institutions, many could pay nothing. Finally, with the same presupposition of the benefit to the general public, the religious institutions eventually received property tax exemptions for their buildings, an *accumulated wealth* Madison had feared would form a majoritarian power. It did.

The latter came to focus in *Walz v. Tax Commission*, 397 U.S. 664 (1970). The three main elements later articulated in *Lemon* as the proper "Establishment" test were already being used here, though had not been formally adopted as the Court's official test. The Court ruled that there was a very large class of nonprofit institutions that shared in this benefit of tax exemption, so this was *not* a *religious purpose*, and the Court was in no position to desire to weigh the "effects," whatever "good works," the various groups did, since churches vary greatly in these, which means the Court could *not* clearly determine that the *primary effect* was illegally religious rather than secular. The question of the element of "excessive entanglement" could be investigated, but the Court emphasized that overturning this 200-year tradition would likely create more "excessive entanglement" than simply continuing it. These three elements became the "three prongs" of the *Lemon* test in 1971.

Interestingly, J. Brennan, concurring in the Court's decision, utilized the "tests" he had earlier elaborated in his concurring judgment in *Abington v. Schempp* (1963), which were that an illegal establishment would be where the involvements of government either "(a) serve the essentially religious activities of religious institutions; (b) employ the organs of government for essentially religious purposes; or (c) use essentially religious means to serve governmental ends, where secular means would suffice."[31] He examined the facts and opined that the tax exemptions, in contrast to subsidies, do not violate any of the three.

In a full dissent, however, J. Douglas insisted that a tax exemption *is* government aid to religion just as surely as would be direct payments by the government to the church. To say, as the Court did, that this is a 200-year-old tradition which therefore cleanses it of any possible flavor of "establishment" actually takes us back to the pre-Constitution years when many of the colonies *did* have *established* churches. It was *those* separate states that had *established churches* that gave the *property tax exemptions*. So *establishment* of religion was the very *ground* out which the practice of the property tax exemption sprang. It therefore is a reference by the Court that defeats its obvious purpose if the Court is attempting to use its age to dilute any charges that it could be an establishment. It began in that very way.

Of course, what it also shows is the significant contrast between any governmental form of financial aid to a religion and the total opposition to that in Jefferson (Jefferson's "three pence," which to him was too much support!)

and his and Madison's total opposition to the Virginia bill for general assessments, as J. Douglas insisted. And, J. Douglas followed that by reminding us that *these* two men were the *primary parties* emphasizing religious liberty that were responsible for shaping the First Amendment shortly thereafter. J. Douglas argued against J. Brennan that the *effect* of subsidies and exemptions is the *same*, and J. Harlan agreed with him, yet many members of the Court have continually used this nondistinct distinction between exemptions and tax credits or other forms of subsidies (as if some are subsidies while others are not), even into the twenty-first century. J. Douglas further emphasized this was illegal since it enabled one's religious belief to merit tax exemption simply not allowed to *nonbelievers*. That means a favoring of religion over nonreligion which the Court had over and over insisted is also a *violation* of the Establishment Clause.

He further gave a rather startling retrospective assessment of his position in voting with the Court in *Everson* in its 5/4 decision, saying "I have become convinced that grants to institutions teaching a sectarian creed violate the Establishment Clause."[32] That meant that he would have reversed the *Everson* decision. He insisted that this case differs from *Everson* in that this is *not* an educational institution but a church receiving the exemption directly, to which he reminds his colleagues of Jefferson's objection to anyone being compelled to contribute even "three pence" to support a church. His standard for the Establishment test is that which the Court explicitly said in *Torcaso v. Watkins*, 367 U.S. 488, that neither the state nor the federal government "'can constitutionally pass laws or impose requirements which aid all religions as against non-believers, and neither can aid those religions based on a belief in the existence of God as against those religions founded on different beliefs.'"[33] As David Currie concluded about *Walz*, "despite its protestations, the majority in *Walz* seemed to have concluded that there are occasions when the state could promote religion after all."[34] The Court usually justifies this as mere "incidental" benefits to religion because the benefits are given to all citizens, yet they often are *not* general benefits and the benefits the religious group experiences are *not* merely "incidental."

THE *LEMON* TEST DEFINED, LATER DILUTED BY THE "HISTORICAL" TEST OF *MARSH*

Finally in 1971, the various loose threads of testing for legality under the Establishment Clause were woven together formally, reaching a clarification in *Lemon v. Kurtzman*, 403 U.S. 1 (1971), which was henceforth referred to as the "*Lemon* test." The Court found it *unlawful* for Rhode Island and Pennsylvania to make direct payments to parochial schools' teachers for their teaching secular education areas to students. Although the purpose of the legislation was secular, the "cumulative impact" of the entire relationship was "excessive entanglement" since there were so many restrictions that required *continual monitoring* by the government. The whole test now was articulated as having three primary parts, the violation of *any* of which would make the law an unlawful establishment of religion. The "test" for it to be lawful was that the law must have (1) a secular purpose, (2) a primary secular effect, and (3) must not create an excessive entanglement between the religious institution being aided and the government. To determine whether entanglement is "excessive," the Court will look at four factors: (1) the nature of the institution receiving aid, (2) the nature of the aid, (3) the continuing relationship between the institution and government (which was basically the question of whether the government would be required by the nature of the law to continually monitor the religious institution), and (4) whether such aid is potentially politically divisive. Each of these four embodied other considerations, for example, the Court had distinguished between aid given directly to churches, from aid given to church schools, from aid given to parents, from aid given to students, and so forth. The question of the age and possible susceptibility to indoctrination had been articulated. "Aid" itself only covered a small area within the "establishment" concerns with others being displays, symbols, rituals, and the like. Some tried to distinguish between cash payments, tax exemptions, and tax credits, and, of course, whether the assistance or exemption was given as a private thing or a genuine public concern. Many other elements attached even to these four elements of the "third prong" of *Lemon*.

In the same year, in the realm of higher education, in *Tilton v. Richardson*, 405 U.S. 672 (1971), the Court ruled it lawful for church-related colleges to receive construction grants from federal government for buildings/facilities used *exclusively* for *secular* purposes, so long as the building was not used for worship or sectarian instruction or used in conjunction with any part of the program that was operated by a department of divinity or seminary. Since the money was strictly for buildings, and the nature of the institutions showed to the Court that the school could separate their secular and sectarian functions, the Court felt there is no religion "seeping" into the relationship with government, requiring some continual monitoring by the latter. One clause in the government's contract with the schools had to be dropped, since it allowed these regulations only for 20 years, after which time, they could be ignored. But the Court insisted the prohibition of using the buildings for religious services or instruction had to be permanent. This seemed oblivious to the possibility that by the school receiving such funds, it was simply freeing more of unrestricted funds for whatever religious indoctrination it might want to engage in within other buildings, and it also never considered adequately the question of enforcement.[35]

Neither the prayer issue nor the desire to indoctrinate students religiously within the public schools ceased, even as the parochial schools pushed for more government funding. In 1973, the Court, in *Levitt v. Committee for Public Ed & Religious Liberty*, 413 U.S. 472, found it *unlawful* for New York to fund parochial schools for administrative costs in the examination and record-keeping for students, since the law failed to distinguish between state-prepared tests and teacher-prepared tests, the latter of which could be used to indoctrinate students. It violated the *Lemon* requirements by its lack of a secular purpose, primary secular effect, and avoidance of excessive entanglement.

In a second case in 1973, the Court, in *Committee for Public Education & Religious Liberty v. Nyquist*, 413 U.S. 756, ruled a *violation* of the "effect" and "entanglement" requirements of *Lemon* when New York provided parochial schools in low-income areas with direct per-pupil money in the forms of (1) unrestricted repair and maintenance funds, (2) tuition reimbursement for parents, and (3) income tax credit for parents not qualifying for #2. Importantly, the Court *rejected* the state's argument that its purpose in the tuition grants was to "promote the free exercise of religion by low-income parents." The Court noted the tension between the Free Exercise and Establishment Clauses, and the impossibility of always being able to satisfy both within a single decision. Here the Court felt it had no choice but to whittle out the most obvious "neutral" course. But in the past 47 years, especially since 1986, the Court has specifically *ignored* this decision and adopted the appeal via "free exercise" to justify tax credits for low-income families who send their children to parochial or religious schools.[36] This case is not used for its value as a precedent, but like so many, was also not overturned by the Court, so the highest Court simply makes the work of the Appellate Courts extremely difficult.

The dissent said it was no more an illegal establishment than *Everson*. This may have been correct, since *neither* situation should have been decided as *legal*. In fact, the limitation in *Everson* of not including students of other private schools in the aid showed that by merely aiding the Catholic schools and public schools, but not other religious schools, it had a *primary religious* purpose dictated by *one single religious* group. But, of course, *Everson* was prior to *Lemon* and its formal test, whereas *Nyquist* was *after*.

What was becoming increasingly apparent was that state legislatures were realizing that if their sponsors or they had any *religious purpose* in formulating a law, they needed to *hide* that and emphasize a *secular* purpose. But what if the Court saw through the deception and called their purpose "sham"? It was not really clear, however, whether a law would fail the test if its main purpose seemed to be religious but it could provide an even *conceivable*, though perhaps unarticulated minor secular purpose in the actual law, or even a quite secular articulated secondary purpose. Obviously, the Blue Law cases seemed to answer with a hypothetical need for a common secular day of rest, but that simply overlooked all the obvious religious elements within the various restrictions, and predated *Lemon*.

Further, how one was able to distinguish the primary effect from a secondary or incidental effect was unclear, since "incidental" or "secondary" would seemingly be discerned *only* by an examination of the "purpose," unless it was simply a matter of calculating sheer numbers of effects or some such quantitative method. Although the Court was incisive enough to give the four indicia to which it would look to determine whether a law created an "excessive entanglement," later analyses by the Court may have been correct in suggesting this *all* concerns the second criteria of "primary secular effect."

The idea of figuring out whether the law is "potentially politically divisive" was very fluid and subjective, since possibly anything *could* be *"potentially politically divisive."* Obviously, by now a law need not actually create an "established" church in the sixteenth-century sense, either national or state, to be ruled a violation of the "Establishment" clause, although several justices continued to utilize that paradigm of "establishment" as the test, and finding nothing exactly corresponding to it today in the United States, they proclaim that any "establishment" test is hardly necessary at all. Earlier ideas of "neither inhibiting nor advancing a religion" were temporarily left behind for the most part by the Court, since the *Lemon* test seemed very clear and objective in comparison to broad categories of merely "inhibiting" or "advancing" a religion.[37] "Accommodation" and "benevolent neutrality" became more oft-quoted ideals of the judicial and/or governmental role. The Court early on said the "politically divisive" test could *not* be satisfied merely by the fact of the litigation itself, which makes sense, but such a blanket rule might seem thereby inadvertently to discount long-standing covert divisiveness that only after many years became overt enough to culminate in litigation.

Meanwhile, on the parochial elementary level, in 1975, the Court ruled in *Meek v. Pittenger*, 421 U.S. 349 (1975), that only *one* part of the Pennsylvania law of government aid to parochial schools was *legal*—the state could only fund textbooks for them. But it could *not* fund instructional materials and equipment since these would have a primary religious benefit, not mere incidental religious benefit. It also could not fund auxiliary service, which, even if it had a secular purpose, created necessary surveillance and therefore excessive entanglement, in addition to being politically divisive. What is not clear is how one distinguishes from the potential religious benefit of indoctrination that instructional materials or equipment have or how they would necessarily be more than textbooks or teachers who are not bound by the words in books.

Five years after *Tilton v. Richardson*, in *Roemer v. Board of Public Works of Maryland*, 426 U.S. 736 (1976), a similar holding involving state funds, rather than federal funds, was approved for grants to private and religious colleges, provided none of the money could be used for sectarian purposes. The Court found it passed every aspect of the *Lemon* test. Its secular purpose was not questioned, nor was its primary secular effect since the schools were autonomous, and religious indoctrination was not a substantial purpose of the schools. The liberal arts were primary, and there were no policy regulations requiring prayer or pertaining to any religious requirements for hiring faculty or admitting students. Neither did the Court sense any "excessive government entanglement" since it required only easy annual business and no need for close monitoring. It was judged that there was nothing politically divisive in the grants since religion played such a minor part in the college functioning.

What the Court seemed oblivious to, which I already mentioned, was that when federal funds are given for buildings only for the teaching of secular subjects, it simply frees up other money of the church-related schools, whatever level and source, to be used to indoctrinate or promote a *single religious* view. Further, it seemed unaware of the fact that teachers of biology or English literature or other subjects are often *more blatantly ideological and evangelistic* than those who are teaching the religion classes *objectively* so *not* attempting to convert students to any position. When the mission of the school is *pervasively religious*, such simple mixing of funds is the most obvious way the school gets the government to help it evangelize or propagate its exclusive message.

To make sure this did not occur, the government would have to monitor expenditures, which would form an "excessive entanglement," prohibited by the *Lemon* test, and any connection between the funds and their actual expenditure could be so *easily hidden* as to be impossible to detect. Church-related colleges could change their mandatory "chapel" or obvious worship services, calling them merely "convocation" or "assembly." But changing the titles would not eliminate the pervasively *religious purpose* behind the mandated attendance. Attempts to religiously proselytize students are never, even in universities, confined to theology classes or classes that are a part of a seminary curriculum, but are experienced by students in many other academic disciplines, depending almost completely upon the *intention of each professor.*

That has been my own personal experience after teaching religious studies and the philosophy of religion "objectively" for 37 years in church-related colleges and universities. In fact, most of the faculty teaching religious studies were more concerned to teach objectively and avoid anything approximating religious indoctrination (as their discipline extended the dicta from *Schempp*, that is, teaching "about" religion rather than "teaching religion") than many of their colleagues in the "secular" disciplines. The Court seems never to have grasped this reality as even a possibility.[38]

The following year, in *Wolman v. Walter*, 433 U.S. 229 (1977), the Court held *Constitutional* portions of the Ohio statute authorizing the state to provide nonpublic schools with secular textbooks, standardized state testing and scoring, diagnostic services, and therapeutic and remedial services. But it found *un*constitutional those portions of the law authorizing payment for instructional materials and equipment, and fieldtrip service, which created excessive entanglement and advanced a sectarian enterprise. The initial biennial appropriation by the Ohio Legislature was $88,800,000 to furnish the approved parts of this program to the 720 chartered nonpublic schools, out of the state's public school budget. Of these 720 schools, all but 29 were sectarian, and 92% of these Roman Catholic.

The line drawn between what was illegal and what was quite legal was so unresolved that some began to blame the *Lemon* criteria for the problem, when the actual problem had begun much earlier with the duplicitous decision of the *Everson* Court in 1947, which, after citing the Founder's opposition to *any kind* of financial aid to any religious institution, *whatever* its form, turned around and provided financial aid to Catholic parochial students' families from tax money, justifying it as if it were as *public and secular* as the state-paid police and fire protection. The services of the *public* schools are the actual equivalent of the *public*-police and *public* fire protection, available to *all people* regardless of their religion, sex, or race. Since to include *all religions* in benefits would create a giant problem because of the lack of agreement as to what kind of religious indoctrination those public schools would teach, such an institution could be sponsored only by private funds. That should not be hard to comprehend.

But it seems difficult for many who belong to the majority religion to understand, especially if they regard Christianity as the *only* legitimate religion for the United States or think that their particular religion is actually generic and therefore universal, even if no other religion recognizes that fact. So the Court had allowed the camel's nose under the tent in 1947, and thereafter found half of its body in the tent, enjoying its new home. In fact, the Court turned *against* Jefferson's expression of such a separating "wall," insisting instead on "benevolent neutrality" or "accommodation" so as not to make government "hostile" to religion.

In *Committee for Public Ed. & Religious Liberty v. Regan*, 444 U.S. 646 (1980), the Court found it *lawful* for the state to pay cash reimbursements to church-sponsored and secular nonpublic schools for performing various *state*-created and mandated testing and reporting. The Court argued this testing and therefore reimbursement for the testing had a secular purpose and effect, which *Wolman v. Walter* controlled, that "a contrary view would insist on drawing a constitutional distinction between paying the nonpublic school to do the grading and paying state employees or some independent service to perform that task." The dissent, however, argued that *Wolman v. Walter* had to be squared with *Meek v. Pittenger*, which had declared the necessity of this very distinction, that any direct cash payments to sectarian schools created risks of furthering the schools' religious mission by subsidizing the *sectarian* educational mission as a whole.

A more difficult case arose the same year in *Stone v. Graham*, 449 U.S. 39 (1980). Kentucky had allowed private groups to place plaques of the Ten Commandments on the walls of the public schools, even with no statements or references nor any utilization of the plaques as educational tools other than a quite small notation that these Ten Commandments are the basis of Western morality and law. We have already shown how grossly uninformed such assertions are.

Of course, *Lemon* required a secular purpose in order not to be a violation of the Establishment Clause, so, aware of that, the state alleged a *secular* purpose. But the Court ruled that despite that allegation, the plaques had an *obvious religious purpose* since half of the commandments are not just moral but *strictly religious*. This was the beginning of the Court's realization that some state legislators were not honest about their purpose being "secular," so the Court had the more difficult problem of trying to see if the alleged purpose was only a "sham." This marked the beginning of parties exploring another way to accomplish the religious purpose, which eventually led to pursuing the cases only under "Free Exercise," as I showed earlier.

It also marked the beginning of J. Rehnquist's novel argument, (here in dissent) ignoring *Lemon*, and insisting that a mere *overlap* of religious and secular purposes does *not* make it illegal, that the Court should listen to the explicitly stated legislative purpose as it usually does, and even if it *is* religious, it may be only a *historical* claim, important to understanding Western culture. This became his position on the Establishment test which he continued to assert, applying it to government's involvement with congressional prayers, Nativity scenes, and Ten Commandment displays for the rest of his tenure on the bench. He was unclear at times about the precise "historical claim" that was being manifest in the display or ritual as well as the connection between any ancient religious text or practice and its possible secular purpose.[39] By 2005, he found company as J. Scalia and J. Kennedy joined him, as we will show in the *Van Orden v. Perry* case.

But, as the Court pointed out in *Stone*, there was no educational utilization of the plaques, no attempt to show the students any historical connections, and the days of the Court simply accepting whatever the litigants claim to be a secular purpose were over, since litigants now knew they had to emphasize a secular purpose even if it were not true. We shall return to much later cases of displays of these Christian or Jewish symbols. But it is best to stick to covering the cases chronologically as much as possible to show the process of the development of ideas, the changes suggested to the tests, the later disclaimers of the *Lemon* test, and the general chaotic view the Court has given with Establishment Clause adjudication, as confusing as its changes in Free Exercise adjudication.

The primary legal objections to having Bible studies and prayers in the public schools had been built around the idea of (1) the mandatory education law which implied a coerced audience; (2) use of public-funded facilities during regular school hours; and (3) the impressionable age/nature of students. When these factors did not come into play in *Widmar v. Vincent*, 454 U.S. 263 (1981), the issue moved to different questions regarding whether the "access" to the public facilities was equal or discriminatory, and what kind of "forum" the school was creating. Those advocating having such Bible studies and prayers in public schools found this approach more fruitful, so it has continued to this day. In *Widmar v. Vincent*, the school was a state university, with students the Court envisioned being able to discern between what was officially the university's position and what was the speech and positions of others.

This case involved the request for use of the facilities after regular hours, and there was nothing mandatory about the group, even if it admitted it desired to proselytize, worship, and teach religion. The Court ruled that once other groups were allowed to use the facilities as a "limited public forum," free speech requires that the school cannot deny such use to a group simply on the basis that it is religious speech. This opened up a new avenue of pursuit for those religious people who wanted to use public schools for their particular religious indoctrination but also for allowing religious groups to get state-funded programs on the basis of their "Free Exercise" being discriminated against (simply because they were "religious" as the Court puts it) by the narrow laws as we saw in the previous chapter.

In 1982, in *Valley Forge Christian College v. American United*, 454 U.S. 464 (1982), the appellate court had ruled an illegal establishment of religion by the government's conveyance of a 77-acre tract of "surplus" government property to a church-related group for the founding of a school. The Supreme Court did *not* judge on the merits of the case, but decided the taxpayer's organization that was protesting the government's gift did *not* have "standing."[40] "Standing," of course, is a prerequisite for the case to be heard by the Court, just as it must be a real case and controversy that is ripe and not moot. But the question of "standing" also seems to be an easy way out of having to resolve what would otherwise be a tough case, when one sees the Court reverting to the "standing" issue over and over in all kinds of cases. Of course, "standing" is a legitimate requirement, but the convolutions created around it seem to be unending.

In that same year, the question of tax exemption arose in a strange form, first in *Larson, Commissioner of Securities, Minnesota Department of Commerce, et al. v. Valente, et al.*, 456 U.S. 228 (1982) then the next year by *Bob Jones*

Univ. v. U.S., 461 U.S. 574 (1983). In *Larson*, the state of Minnesota, in order to protect the public from fraudulent fundraising by groups, including those who might *pretend* to be religious, formulated a law which required registration and then continual disclosures of sources of income, costs of management, fundraising, and public education, along with any transfers of funds to or from out-of-state sources, with sufficient explanation of such transfers. If they showed that their costs of operation were unreasonable, for example, more than 30% of their total income, they were no longer eligible to be registered with the state to solicit funds from the public. For the first 17 years of the law's existence, it was *not enforced*. In 1978, however, they amended the Act, and included that any group wanting to register to solicit funds had to show that it received more than 50% of its income from its *members* or affiliated organizations.

Members of the Unification Church, and later, the church itself, brought suit once it received from the state a notice that it had to register with the state. They argued such a restriction on the religion's necessary door-to-door and public-place solicitation for funding and to proselytize was a violation of their religious Free Exercise, as well as a violation of the Establishment Clause. They received the preliminary injunction, and after examination by a magistrate, the District Court also granted their request for summary judgment. On appeal, the Eighth Circuit Court of Appeals agreed that they met the standing requirement, but also agreed with the District Court that the "fifty-percent rule" was an "inexplicable religious classification" that violated the Establishment Clause. But it disagreed with the District' Court's simple acceptance of the party's claim that they were a religious organization qualifying for the exemption, so remanded it back to the District Court to answer that question.

Eventually, the Supreme Court argued that Respondents *did*, in fact, have standing, that its questionableness arose when—only after all those years of not requiring registration by the Unification Church—the state suddenly did require its registration, and primarily emphasized the "fifty-percent rule." But the "fifty-percent rule" was applied only to churches or religious organizations, so the Petitioners' objection, that Respondents lacked standing since they were not recognized as religious by Minnesota, was incorrect. Further, the state's attempt to impose the "fifty-percent rule" on the Church "amounts to a distinct and palpable injury to appellees" in the sense that unless they can prove they receive more than 50% of their income from their members, they can no longer solicit from the general public in Minnesota. The Court noted that Petitioners' argument is based on three premises: (1) that members of a religious organization can and will exercise supervision and control over the organization's solicitation activities when membership contributions exceed 50%; (2) that membership control, assuming its existence, is an adequate safeguard against abusive solicitations of the public by the organization; and (3) that the need for public disclosure rises in proportion with the percentage of nonmember contributions.[41] It showed how unsubstantiated these were, for example, noting that the need for disclosure actually *increases* in the proportion to the "absolute amount" rather than percentage.

Regarding the merits of the case, the Court had no trouble in citing many of its precedent Establishment cases which insisted that no law could favor any religion over another. So it did not need the *Lemon* test, but the Court saw the state's interests here not "compelling" because their rules were not narrowly tailored, so a violation of the FE test bordering on turning religion into a political issue, and the selective legislation *violates* the "excessive entanglement" requirement part of the *Lemon* test under the Establishment Clause.

Still on the issue of taxes, in *Bob Jones University v. U.S.*, 461 U.S. 574 (1983), the lower court ruled the private religious schools' policies of racial discrimination were a *violation* of 26 U.S.C. §170, causing their tax-exempt status under 26 USCS §501(c)(3) to be correctly revoked by the IRS. This judgment was upheld by the Supreme Court. The IRS ruling against the university did not violate the FE of the petitioners since the government has a fundamental, overriding interest (or "compelling state interest") in eradicating racial discrimination. It also did not violate the Establishment Clause since the law was neutral, not favoring any religions over others or religions in general over other charitable, nonreligious groups. This idea of a law's impartiality or universal application, of not showing preferential treatment, was always in the Court's Establishment language of the government not being able to aid one religion more than others or more than the nonreligious.

But the entire case was largely focused on racial discrimination or preferential treatment, so that was a fairly obvious way to approach it, even if a more "equal treatment" between the *religions and nonreligious* was more the ideal of Madison and Jefferson, who wanted the government not to use religion to become a category either for legal or civil burdens or benefits, to take *no legal cognizance of religion*. This is often forgotten later by the Court, as C.J. Rehnquist helped persuade some of his colleagues that all that is necessary is that government, if it aids any religion, must aid *all* religions *equally*. That very expression of aiding "all religions" is actually included as a part of the Court's definition of the *prohibition* of the Establishment Clause, over and over, as we have seen, since aid only to "all religions" still reveals an aid that the *non*-religious do *not* receive.

Taxes were also the concern in *Mueller v. Allen*, 468 U.S. 388 (1983). In this 5/4 opinion, written by J. Rehnquist, the Court *allowed* the state to give *tax deductions* for tuition, textbooks, and transportation to parents (up to $700 per year per child) for their children's attendance at all primary or secondary parochial schools as well as public schools. Of course, it was no help to parents of public schools since they *had no tuition*, and books and buses were in most cases furnished by universal taxes. If secular textbooks and bus transportation had been approved earlier by the Court, the novel thing here was the tuition, and the fact that the only deductions that were available were for parents of *parochial* school children.

Yet the Court viewed the law as having a total *secular* purpose and effect, since it had left far behind the earlier Court ideas that the religious indoctrination of the parochial schools is their primary if not only purpose in existing to compete against public schools. The *dissent* was simple: the tax deductions, 96% of which were used by parents of *parochial* school students, violated the Establishment Clause which prohibits states from *subsidizing religious education*, which prohibits *any* tax benefit, including deductions. The question that would be asked under Rawls's "veil of ignorance" would be why would anyone ever select a law which would benefit only one religious group since one would have no idea if one was even going to be religious, much less of what religion? So these were vested, irrational interests forming the laws, and the benefit to the parochial schools as indoctrinating agents was far greater than a mere "three pence" forbidden by Jefferson and Madison.

These two sides have yet to be reconciled on this issue of whether any tax deductions or credits or public benefits can be supplied to parochial school students' parents, and if so exactly for what and what the limit would be. Even more critically, the much later Court by the last half of the 1990s, began to read from *Witters* backward to *Mueller* to see what it considers the most lenient standards by which parochial school funding by the government can exist—if litigants can prove the *funding laws were neutral* in the sense of not favoring the religious schools more than public schools, as if the religious schools should have equal claim on taxes as public schools, and if the decision to receive the funds depends upon the *parents' individual private decision* and there is no incentive for them to choose the sectarian route.

The latter's focus on "private choice," of course, easily *removed the cases* from the Establishment realm to "Free Exercise" area which not only tolerated but required the person's or law's *claim to be "religious"* in order to be protected. Whereas earlier decisions seemed to be strangely consistent, forming a bit of a pattern, *Mueller* and other subsequent cases have annihilated even that vague pattern. The decision seems no longer to depend upon the details of the situation *but* more upon the makeup of the Court, and the "voucher" system blended into the alleged "neutrality" and "private choice" the Court eventually used for Free Exercises cases.

Most of these earlier cases had been decided by the *Lemon* criteria, if they came after 1971, a fact *ignored* by C.J. Rehnquist and the plurality in *Van Orden v. Perry* (2005) which we will note shortly. But also appearing in 1983 was a very strange case which simply *deserted Lemon*. By itself, it initiated a *completely different approach* to some Establishment cases. This was the famous *Marsh v. Chambers*, 463 U.S. 783 (1983), which raised a question of legislative prayer funded by public taxes. Prayer in the public school classroom, of course, had been prohibited by the Court over and over, and it would confront another case of the same in 1985.

But in *Marsh v. Chambers*, the Court saw *legislative* prayer in quite *different* terms. Was it only because prayer was religious in a public school classroom but not in a state legislature building? Or was it because the legislators were older, more mature citizens, not as easily influenced? What about chaplains being paid from public taxes to lead such prayers for the legislature, or the question of how the *non*-religious were being honored equally to the religious under the First Amendment? Even the question of *one* particular religion being favored arose here. All of this suggested that one might anticipate the Court would overrule the practice in the Nebraska legislature. So what happened?

THE ORIGIN AND SPREAD OF THE
ELUSIVE *MARSH* TEST

The members of the Supreme Court that provided the *Lemon* test by which to weigh whether a law violated the Establishment Clause would have been shocked had someone been able to tell them that within less than 50 years, the Court would include members on it who asserted that the *government* certainly can express *itself religiously* in *Perry*. In fact, the *Lemon* Court would probably even have been taken aback just to realize how the decision of *Marsh*, only a *dozen* years subsequent, would plant a seed of justification by sheer *selective* "historical" examples that would be utilized by the Court over and over to *approve* the very thing that the *Lemon* test *forbid*. But that is precisely what happened, as justices seemed more and more emboldened to defy the legal standard of *Lemon* and blatantly to attempt to approve *their* particular religion on government property or with government endorsement or fund *their* religious schools with public taxes. But it was a very *selective* reading of "history."

Since the Christian culture and symbols are so ubiquitous in the United States, many Christians saw little or nothing wrong in these blatant attempts to assert a single religion as the religion of the nation. For many, it was *their own* religion, after all. Many Christian fundamentalists began to rewrite the history of the United States, as Steven Green showed, from the standpoint of the myth of its religious and specifically Christian founding. Perhaps it is not an accident that this retrenchment occurred after the critical prophetic[42] years of the 1960s passed, and by the early 1980s, the nation was still tired of those who wanted to be self-critical of our institutions. The nation elected Ronald Reagan for president. Many things began to be "rolled back" including civil rights, highway speed limits (actually the limit increased, no longer at 55 miles per hour), the frugality in fuel usage, the upper brackets of the graduated income tax, the heavy taxes on inherited estates, and so forth. Reagan's time was "roll-back" time.

Perhaps one could only have expected the flourishing evangelistic side of Christianity to make stronger attempts to create its mythical established Christian nation, especially when it began to lose its influence in the last quarter of the twentieth century. From that point to the present, the effort of evangelical Christian leaders has been to nullify the First Amendment clauses on religion, or, more specifically, to equate their particular understanding of Christianity with the purpose behind the founding and development of the United States, so they wanted religious freedom *from* others' opinions and religions, and freedom to establish *their* form of Christianity once and for all. Even a Chief Justice of the Alabama State Supreme Court defied the law by his display of the Ten Commandments, though he was removed from office for it.

Interestingly, the *Lemon* test did not die nor was it *explicitly* set aside by the Court after the strange *Marsh* test, but over time, the *Marsh* "historical" test *spread* to other obvious particular Christian symbols or practices simply perpetuating a more difficult standard because it was so carelessly and vaguely defined. If *stare decisis* was not to become totally meaningless, throwing innumerable cases "under the bus" since they had been decided by the *Lemon* test, the Court had to distinguish the facts enough to provide approval for *both* "tests." It had to clarify *its* position for the Appellate Courts. But it did not.

Led in more recent years by J. Rehnquist, who succeeded C.J. Burger as chief justice, the conservative majority of the Court often found it necessary simply to *ignore Lemon*, claiming it was not a litmus, automatic, or infallible test, but that other sets of facts required a completely different approach. As J. Scalia so honestly admitted in *Lamb's Chapel*, "The secret of the *Lemon* test's survival, I think, is that it is so easy to kill. . . . When we wish to strike down a practice it forbids, we involve it . . . when we wish to uphold a practice it forbids, we ignore it entirely. . . . Sometimes we take a middle course, calling its three prongs 'no more than helpful signposts.'"[43] So is this impartial justice or merely honesty?

So what was significant about *Marsh v. Chambers*, 463 U.S. 783 (1983) and about the "test" it provided for Establishment cases, so significant as to give rise to a vociferous if not verbally militant assault on the *Lemon* standard and earlier understandings of the Court that state and religion were to be "separated"? The Nebraska Legislature had a custom for more than a century of opening each day with a brief prayer by a Christian chaplain, chosen biennially by the Executive Board of the Legislative Council. Robert Palmer, a Presbyterian minister, began a long tenure, being selected over and over from 1965, and *paid out of public funds* monthly that entire time,[44] till the time of the bringing of the action against the practice. The action was brought by one of the members of the Legislature, who was also a taxpayer in Nebraska, Ernest Chambers. He sought an injunction to halt the practice. The District Court eventually found it not an illegal establishment of religion, but the Court of Appeals, examining it on the basis of the existing, honored, and utilized *Lemon* test, found that it *violated all three* aspects of the test.

The Supreme Court, however, *ignored* the *Lemon* test, since using it would force the Court to uphold the Court of Appeals. Instead, the Court based its entire argument on the idea that the very Founders of the Constitution and Bill of Rights had *not* thought legislative prayer violated the First Amendment, so *200 years of history* should show that since no establishment had resulted, that practice was quite exempt. It buttressed its argument by citing to the *Walz* decision in which it had insisted that property tax exemption for religious institutions should not be found an illegal establishment for two reasons: (1) such exemptions were practiced even from the beginning days of the nation; and (2) to find the challenged practice and law illegal after so long would itself create an illegal "excessive entanglement." It is surprising that the Court did not go just a bit further and establish the *theocracy* that some of those colonies tried to create, which accounts for their ancient legislative prayers and tax exemptions, which raises the question of the Court's very selective use of history. Did they understand the several colonies that attempted to develop an "established" religion for the colony, even if it was the very thing their ancestors had fled which caused them to be persecuted in Europe? Or was this fine since now the proposed theocracy was their own, not some other Christian sects? Did the *Marsh* Court read Madison at all or not recognize him and Jefferson as the "Founders" of the First Amendment?[45]

Of course, the Court did not refer even to *Lemon* or prohibitive words of "excessive entanglement" here lest it be more obvious that the Court was avoiding *its own* formulated and accepted test, the most obvious standard the Supreme Court *had furnished* the Court of Appeals. Instead, it ironically *belittled* the Court of Appeals' use of *Lemon* by simply discounting the significance of the chaplain being of only one Christian denomination for so many years, even paid by public funds (equivalent to what the legislators themselves were being paid), and the fact that the prayers were strictly "Judeo-Christian." Indeed, prayers were "Judeo-Christian" about like the dogma of the Trinity and transubstantiation were. Rather than show how ill-informed religiously such opinions were, the Court focused only on the idea that these prayers could not have come from the Framers of the Constitution if the Framers thought legislative prayers violated the First Amendment.

But they simply overlooked the Framers' *explicit comments*, as we've noted above. C.J. Burger for the Court simply insisted "Weighed against the historical background, these factors do not serve to invalidate Nebraska's practice." Yet "conclusory" statements cannot replace legal argument, as every first-year law student quickly learns.

The Court cited the *Cantwell v. Connecticut* (1940) decision as analogous in some way or being a precedent for the Court's newly minted "historical" criteria. But nothing in *Cantwell* can be construed as such.[46] Then the Court alluded to *Everson* (1947) (which was a 5/4 decision with J. Douglas, one of the five, later admitting in his dissent in *Walz* that he had "grave doubts" about the correctness of his position in *Everson*) to suggest that a paid chaplaincy for the legislature is no more "potential for establishment" than public funds to pay for a child's transportation to the parochial schools, or even the tax exemptions for churches in *Walz*. But we have seen what unsubstantiated reason was used by the Court in *Everson* and *Walz*. In addition to the Court's documenting its faithful use of "*stare decisis*" with superfluous if not completely irrelevant quotations from earlier cases that had *nothing* to do with prayer, it obviously preferred to use an argument from the seeming longevity or unbroken practice of legislative prayer in history since the beginning of the nation, but *without* noting much in the way of the more comprehensive history of the Founding Fathers' *actual views*.

It had to counter J. Brennan's statement (utilized here by Respondents) in his concurring opinion in *Schempp* in which J. Brennan warned that we should not place too much weight even on the advice of the Founding Fathers since there is so much more religious heterogeneity today and since history can easily be ambiguous.[47] (J. Brennan, of course, dissented in *Marsh*, as did J. Stevens and J. Marshall.) The Court went further and referred to *McGowan v. Maryland* (1961) in which the Court failed even to realize that the states' "Blue laws" were a carryover from an earlier Christian *mis*appropriation and *mis*understanding of the Jewish Sabbath, as if the purpose and effect of these laws could be seen as *secular* with only a mere accidental or "incidental" harmonizing with religious ideas. The Court insisted that since, in Rev. Palmer's absences, other guest chaplains filled in for him, and since there is also a long history of legislative chaplains being funded by public money, and this has never established a national religion, it is not an illegal Establishment in Nebraska either.

This argument would be parallel to insisting that since the Constitution was ratified, although we have formulated laws that facially discriminated against minority races and we've experienced even neutral laws applied unfairly to minorities, we should not worry since none of that reestablished slavery *per se*![48] Obviously the racial and religious diversity is far greater today, as J. Brennan noted even 60 years ago, than at the time of the Constitution's ratification, but we still have a myth of "white supremacy"[49] *and* a myth of the nation's "Christian founding" as we saw analyzed by Green, creating destructive tension between the races and religions more than ever before. That was true even in 1983.

What the Court failed to *clarify* is why the prayers in both *Engel* and *Schempp* were *illegal*, but here in *Marsh* they were *not*. But C.J. Burger insisted that to have such prayers, "to invoke Divine guidance . . . is simply a tolerable acknowledgement of beliefs widely held among the people of this country."[50] But which people? Why does the government have to be guided by its chief justices to "acknowledge" the specific beliefs of only *one* particular part of its citizens (those who profess *one* particular sect of *one* religion), when the religious and *non*-religious constituency today is even much more heterogeneous than in the days the First Amendment was written? Was Madison that far off when he said civil government has no "cognizance" or "jurisdiction" of religion? Was Rawls incorrect in thinking that the nation has to have uniting principles which are strong enough to allow differences, but the nonpublic reason or metaphysical associations cannot expect to dictate their standards for the law for all citizens?

The Court later suggested that prayers offered only with adults in the room, as opposed to immature school children, justified the disparate legal treatment since children are much more susceptible to indoctrination. Is a prayer only intending indoctrination? But to find an illegal "establishment," the Court has insisted many times over and over that it is *not* necessary that there be explicit coercion *nor* an overt attempt to indoctrinate. Dissenting J. Stevens noted that the Court's *refusal* to look at the *content* of the prayers was because it knew that would show a quite *sectarian* content which is simply more of the divisive *majoritarianism* involved here.

J. Brennan, dissenting, insisted that when the Court minimizes the *content* of the prayers, it seems to be making the prayer only a *device* to call to order the legislators, to get them to get into the room into their seats, to quiet the legislators down, or only as a *solemnizing ritual*. But then the entire significance of prayer as communion with God is trivialized or blatantly contradicted. Nor can the Court say it is innocuous because it is a mere tolerable "acknowledgement" of widely held beliefs of the people of the United States as if it were merely a "museum piece." J. Brennan wrote:

> [P]rayer is religion in act. Praying means to take hold of a word, the end, so to speak, of 'a line that leads to God.' Reverend Palmer and other members of the clergy who offer invocations at legislative sessions are not museum pieces put on display once a day for the edification of the legislature. Rather, they are engaged by the legislature to lead it—as a body—in an act of religious worship. If upholding the practice requires denial of this fact, I suspect that many

supporters of legislative prayer would feel that they had been handed a pyrrhic victory.[51]

He emphasized that the Court itself has in prior cases acknowledged that the Constitution is not a static document "fixed for all time." Rather, "[t]o be truly faithful to the Framers, "our use of the history of their time must limit itself to broad purposes, not specific practices."[52] "Our primary task must be to translate the 'majestic generalities of the Bill of Rights, conceived as a part of the pattern of liberal government in the eighteenth century, into concrete restraints on officials dealing with the problems of the twentieth century.'"[53] This is profound insight into the nature of democratic adjudication.

J. Brennan expounded on a few of the many objections different religious people would have to prayers offered with such official stamp in his dissent, the final paragraph of III (B). His awareness of prayer has not been articulated by any other justice *before or since*. And, on the other hand, J. Brennan's dissent insisted that the Nebraska law and practice of legislative chaplain *violated all three prongs* of the *Lemon* test, elaborating how obvious it was. He upbraided the Court for making "no pretense of subjecting Nebraska's practice of legislative prayer to any of the formal 'tests' that have traditionally structured our inquiry under the Establishment Clause." He noted that during the long tenure of the Presbyterian chaplain, there was considerably more criticism of the practice than represented by the Court, revealing it to be far *more divisive*, and creating "rancor," even splitting the very Nebraska Legislature. He quoted from the *Epperson* Court in *Marsh*: "Government in our democracy, state and national, must be neutral in matters of religious theory, doctrine, and practice. It may not be hostile to any religion or to the advocacy of no-religion; and it may not aid, foster, or promote one religion or religious theory against another or even against the militant opposite. The First Amendment mandates governmental neutrality between religion and religion, and between religion and non-religion."[54]

J. Brennan argued that the "separation" Jefferson intended between government and religion preserves liberty of one's conscience, freedom from direct or indirect coercion in religious matters, preserves the essential autonomy of religious life, prevents trivialization and degradation of religion by such a close attachment to government, and keeps sensitive religious issues out of the political arena when by giving the obvious impression of being "authorized" by the government, they would create "political battles" which the Establishment Clause sought to prevent.

He cited Jefferson and Jackson's explicit *refusals* to declare a national day of thanksgiving or fasting, and Madison's statement about legislative prayer obviously being an illegal "establishment" of religion. If *history* is dispositive for this case, nothing could more dispositive than the direct contradiction by Jefferson, Jackson, and especially Madison. But that did not phase the Court's recounting of its *selective* take on that history.[55] Did Jefferson and Madison, the primary authors of the First Amendment, and others such as John Jay and John Rutledge not count in "history"? The Court assumed that if the prayer was not a "proselytizing" activity and did not place the government's "official seal of approval on one religious view," it was quite constitutional.

J. Brennan objected that this is not a case of merely accommodating individual religious interests, since there was *nothing to prohibit* the various legislators from privately (or even as unofficial groups) engaging in forms of worship such as prayer. To the contrary, this was an *official* prayer by the legislature's chosen clergy, chosen and paid for 16 years, as dissenting J. Stevens noted.[56] J. Brennan remarked "I have no doubt that, if any group of law students were asked to apply the principles of *Lemon* to the question of legislative prayer, they would nearly unanimously find the practice to be unconstitutional."[57]

There is no universally recognized "generic" "God" to whom everyone prays, including the nonreligious, notwithstanding a political/symbolical inclusiveness in prayer-leaders at such things as the Presidential Inauguration Prayer service. Even in the Presidential Inauguration Prayer service of 2017, each rabbi, imam, pastor, priest, and so on represented only *one* religion, and often exclusively only one denomination or sect within that religion, and if they all believed only in one, unitary God that everyone in the world admits and worships, they simply would not still be wholly separate communions, competing against each other in such exclusivistic forms.[58]

The different symbols used in most if not all religions' prayers simply do *not transcend* their unique concreteness, transforming into something universal, much less something "generic," nor had they in Rev. Palmer's prayers for most of his years. To prove that, all that need be asked is how Christians would respond if the prayers in Congress were always or nearly always Muslim or very frequently began with "Hare Krishna, Hare Krishna, Hare, Hare," or were addressed to "Om" or some other Absolute of other religions? Some religions are monistic, others theistic, others quite pan-en-theistic; some deities are spoken of in anthropomorphic terms and others beyond any description (e.g., Nirguna Brahman, as well as the "negative" Jewish theology of Maimonides and the Christian theology of Anselm), and some could be contacted only through mystical practices such as in Sufi methods or other methods in other mystical sects in various religions. "Prayer" is usually thought to be quite "personal," so is often theistic in some form, but is culturally conditioned and circumscribed, not at all something identical or generic in all the diverse religions, and it has no verifiable relation to modern science except as "wish-fulfillment."

If we examine the idea of prayer in legislature or public schools from the approach of the *social contracting* of which Rawls speaks, the government would simply not be involved because religions operate with a "nonpublic" form of reason. While Rawls "first principle" of maximum equal political liberty for every individual guarantees religious freedom, it does so only as long as those freedoms do not limit others' political liberty and everyone complies with the basic principles of the law. If a social inequality results, it can be accepted only if it makes equality of opportunity available and if it is to the benefit of those *least advantaged* by the law in question.

Once the Court's idea of government's separation from religion was breached in *Marsh* (1983), adding to the picture of being *more religiously partial* and not even as neutral as it had purported in *Wisconsin v. Yoder* (1972), *Sherbert v. Verner* (1963), and *Thomas v. Review Bd* (1981), and even in many earlier decisions relating to funding parochial schools and extending property tax exemption to religious bodies, *Marsh* was obviously a new argument Christians could use since they (Christians) admittedly had a longer "history" in the United States than other non-Christian religions since they never gave the time of day to the religion that far exceeded them all in history, the religion of the Native Americans, nor even to the later African Americans imported as slaves.

Marsh was an Establishment case in which the Court *refused* to use the *Lemon* test which had been the standard for a dozen years. Now their religious desires could be met either by insisting a law violated their "free exercise" or by tracing some *selective* "history" to try to show validity of the majoritarian law. What is even more troubling is that the Court now found itself interpreting the meaning and validity of specific *religious rituals and symbols*, as if *it* were qualified not only to distinguish the *true religion* but even to make judgments about religious rituals and symbols, deciding which were constitutional and which were not. It felt it could do that by such a "historical" approach as well, which seemed to imply that *state government* and *federal government* both had the right to express *their own religious beliefs* publically through prayer by tax-paid chaplains, despite using taxes from many citizens whose religious protection was thereby threatened and who were coerced to pay taxes for what they could not accept in good conscience. The Court had forgotten Jefferson's and Madison's main principles which were unmistakable. There is no position more contrary to Madison and Jefferson's idea of the *separation* of religion and the state.

Once such an obvious religious ritual as prayer was ruled as not an illegal Establishment of religion, the door was wide open to try to squeeze other Christian symbols and rituals through the same door of "history." If alluding to history could suffice for keeping Christian prayer in the legislature, perhaps it could find its way into the public schools, even if they do not go that far back in history, and most of them did not include any prayer. Perhaps one could win the fight against teaching evolution in the schools? Perhaps one could keep the Christian nativity scenes as government sponsored or on government land and not an illegal Establishment of religion?

In fact, that *very thing* occurred even in the following year, in *Lynch v. Donnelly*, 465 U.S. 668 (1984). A Nativity scene, *owned* by the city Pawtucket, RI, was erected each Christmas season on nonprofit property as a part of holiday festive display. It was challenged as violating the Establishment Clause, specifically failing the *Lemon* test by its religious purpose, effect, and excessive entanglement.

Although the District Court and Appellate Court, *depending* upon the *Lemon* test formulated by the Supreme Court, found the religious display a *violation* of the Establishment Clause, by a 5/4 decision the Supreme Court *reversed*. The Court, not surprisingly, followed *Marsh* rather than the *Lemon* test, arguing that if the crèche were by itself, it might be illegal, but the *secular* accoutrements in the general park area such as a Santa Claus and other elements made everything simply primarily one of a *festive historical reminder* rather than of religion. Especially the Santa Claus—a historical reminder?!![59] It emphasized that since the Founders themselves accepted congressional prayers, Thanksgiving proclamations by President Washington, and later of the proclamation of a national day of prayer, combined with the explicit Christian art found in the National Gallery, as well as Christian mottos on our coins and etched on government buildings, this also was primarily only an innocuous "historical" reference. But *which* "Founders" of the First Amendment? Not Jefferson or Madison, and they were the *primary authors* of the Amendment.

The Court, however, supplied a very ambiguous and *truncated* "history," *avoiding* the Founders' (e.g., Madison and Jefferson) *explicit statements* which insisted that Christian rituals and symbols were a *violation* of what they had in mind with the First Amendment. Instead, the Court focused on a very small segment of activities and made a blanket statement over these, never considering that they were simply unthinkingly carried over *precisely* from earlier days of colonial *religious theocratic establishments*. Yes, George Washington "recommended" to the people to observe a day of "Thanksgiving," but Washington was *not* the father of the First Amendment. Madison and Jefferson were, as we have seen, because of their role in the Virginia law of disestablishment which they formulated to replace the proposed general assessment bill of Gov. Patrick Henry. They both *opposed* legislative chaplains and *refused* to require some special religious holy days when they were asked. Madison was even opposed, as we saw, to religious institutions being incorporated in order to own real property since he thought the accumulation of wealth by religious groups would end up being a terrible threat to religious freedom.

In the Court's opinion in *Lynch v. Donnelly*, there was also a terrible *ambiguity* over *what* specific history was thereby to be acceptably portrayed. Was it the history of the beginning of the Christian religion, with the birth of Jesus? Or was it simply the history of Christianity being important in the founding of the United States reflected on the coins, the Pledge, the museum art? The Court seemed to be saying *both*—neither one was offensively religious but primarily only a *historical* fact.

It emphasized there was certainly nothing wrong with reminding people of the *historical* origins of this Christmas celebration by including a *crèche* scene. It insisted that mere *accidental* religious references or *incidental* benefits experienced by religion due to a law are *not* sufficient to prove a violation of the Establishment Clause. How a crèche scene could have a merely accidental or incidental religious reference is not any clearer than how a cross could.[60] These were historically the two *most fundamental* religious symbols of only *one* religion, and both of them were enshrouded in *myth*, which the Court has *never* acknowledged, so continues to see any religious reference in either as quite subordinate to or incidental to a sheer historical event, of some human (or God?) being born or some human (or God?) dying. Really?

This diminution of the religious significance of these symbols is a gross insult to those who are Christian. It means the Court is still 300 years behind contemporary Western religious thought, which, if the Court manifested the same antiscientific gullibility in other areas, it would reap nothing but utter disrespect. The crèche was *not* simply showing a baby born in ancient history, but a baby the Christian community later believed to be "Son of God," as coequal with God, *not* of *similar* substance (*homoiousios*) but of "*same* substance" (*homoousios*). The idea of a being who was half-god, half-man, of course, was very well known in ancient Greek mythology, later taken over by the Romans. But the Christian church had insisted that this was *not* a "half god, half man" but had fully both complete natures, fully human and fully divine. If this makes no sense to science or to public reason, the church still does not abandon such antique creeds—fully god and fully human. But no Christian theologian has ever shown this to be true, and some of the church's most brilliant theologians have admitted its unintelligibility.[61] After the idea of Jesus "resurrection" gained momentum, the "historical" or "human" nature of Jesus lost its significance with many. Very shortly, the church did not see Jesus as really fully human since it insisted that all humans sinned, so when the church decided Jesus had *not* sinned, he became only a "Docetic" figure, one who simply "seemed" to be human, but was actually only fully God, only "seemed" to die on the cross, but rose up and returned to heaven. *This* is "history"? By reducing its meaning to "history," the Court did a great disservice to the Christian Church, since no data can provide any proof from history of this one being "God," just as it did a disservice to prayer in the *Marsh* decision. This is not mere "hostility" to a religion, but the religion actually regards such a reduction of Christology as "blasphemy." Why did the Court feel compelled to decide such things in such an *uninformed* way?

The Court here also showed its obliviousness to how much the "Nativity" scene and dogma of Incarnation *offended Judaism* for centuries and *still does*. It also revealed that it had no idea of the way Islam views this strange belief of the Christians, that is, of the supposed "Incarnation" being a belief that God committed adultery with Mary. When one is ignorant of how people outside a given religion view some of its basic ideas, they might naturally think *everybody* worships the same Christian God and none of its dogma is divisive, but is just "historical" fact. How, then, would they see the Islamic claim that its "God" or "Allah" is the *same* God of the Jews and the Christians, and Muhammed rather than *Jesus*, was God's "final prophet"? It too involves a "historical"/mythical dimension in its claim, parallel to the Christian claim about Jesus, but did not go so far as to say Muhammed was raised from the dead. Even in its modesty, the Islamic claim is *offensive to Christians* just as the Nativity scene and dogma of the Incarnation make Christianity *offensive to Muslims*. If religions are to have any place in a *democratic* culture which is *religiously pluralistic*, people are going to have to *separate* government from religion as Rawls showed because of the difference in reason, constituencies, willingness to negotiate principles, scope, and comportment, as we mentioned earlier. What will be required for legislators and justices to become aware of this?

The Court insisted that the benefits to a particular religion by the crèche being maintained by public taxes were much *less* than the money for textbooks, the money for transportation, both to parochial school students, and it was no more objectionable than were the congressional prayers in the Nebraska case of *Marsh*. But two or more wrong judgments do not make a right one. In fact, as one of the two most prominent mythical symbols of Christianity, it was *much more a direct benefit* than mere money for secular textbooks, a more *direct purpose and effect of evangelizing or indoctrinating*. If the display were instead a depiction of Muhammed being called by Gabriel to "Recite" for Allah as his final prophet, would that not be a *direct* attempt to *indoctrinate* or would the Court see that as only a historical but not religious reference? The time *may come* for the Court to be *consistent* about "history" and "religions."

In a concurring opinion in *Lynch*, J. O'Connor attempted to broaden the standard or test to be used (in the neglect of *Lemon*), so raised the issue of whether a *reasonable observer* would think the display an "endorsement" by government and therefore, if the observer were *not* of that religion, he or she would feel an *outsider* in this society. Because of the other aspects of the festive displays and grounds which seemed in their secularity to mitigate the otherwise overwhelming religious connotation or message for the Court, J. O'Connor missed the point I just made about Muhammed. What would the "reasonable observer" think of either display?

She did *not* find that the reasonable observer would take the Nativity scene as a religious endorsement. But her sketch of the "reasonable observer" outside the communion is itself *un*reasonable. To think otherwise is the equivalent of thinking that the festive scene in a city celebrating the end of Ramadan was *not* religious, and all Christians in the city would realize that and not be offended over local taxes paying for the maintenance of the Ramadan exhibit. Would the reasonable non-Jewish person think there was nothing religious about the Jewish observance of Rosh Hashanah or even Yom Kippur, that they are only secular? That very question arose in another case during another Christmas and Hanukkah which we will analyze shortly.

When one sees a cross on the top of a mountain or out in the desert, does one think of it merely as pieces of wood arranged in a strange way in a strange place? When one sees a swastika painted on a wooden fence of an alley in the middle of a city, does one think it is just meaningless scribbling? What does the "reasonable observer" know and what does she or he think? If the members of the Court were to stand beside the Nativity display and give a questionnaire for each person coming by, asking whether this was religious, or whether the secular accoutrements in the area completely desacralized it, so it no longer was religious, that might be a better gauge than the opinions of the justices.

Justifiably, J. Brennan, dissenting, and joined by three other justices, accused the Court of beginning as if it were going to examine the case by the *Lemon* test which was so widely used, but then quickly deserting it by focusing on past history. He said he had hoped that the *Marsh exception* would remain alone, an *isolated* case rather than precedent, but here the "historical" rationale was in fact extended *much further*—to make the most central religious symbol of Christianity an innocuous neutral symbol of a holiday season. As he said, the Court could not see its objectionable Establishment character probably because these justices were *so accustomed* to such Nativity scenes, but that was their *misreading* of its specific religious and nongeneric character of the display which *did* violate *Lemon* and the First Amendment.[62]

Only the next year, another prayer case for the public schools came before the Court, the *Wallace v. Jaffree*, 472 U.S. 38 (1985). Alabama attempted to get prayer into the schools, despite *Engel* and *Schempp* by using a scheme of progression. The first law proposed was to require a minute of silence in all schools, which, of course, was certainly legal. Then the second law would later be passed which mandated a minute for silent prayer in all the schools. The third proposed a minute for verbal prayer led by the teacher. Even in the second stage, one of the young Jaffree children was the object of attempted indoctrination by the teacher for not being willing to voice a prayer with the rest of the class, and the youngest child was being ridiculed by peers.

The Court again easily applied the *Lemon* test, and in a 6/3 decision, with only C.J. Burger, J. Rehnquist, and J. White dissenting, announced that the whole scheme had the *illegal religious purpose* of establishing prayer in public schools, and absolutely no secular purpose. The *deviousness* of doing it in three separate stages over several years alerted the Court that there might be many more attempts to cover the actual *religious* purpose behind a legislature's bill, which, in fact, it encountered again only two years later in a bill for the Louisiana schools in which the Court ruled that the law had only a sham religious purpose. Two of the dissenting justices in *Wallace v. Jaffree* belittled the *Lemon* test, and one of them insisted that Jefferson was *not* one of the Founders of that First Amendment.[63]

However, still in 1985, there was much more financial aid requested for the parochial schools in two more cases. In *Grand Rapids School District v. Ball*, 473 U.S. 373 (1985) the Court in a 5/4 decision found it *unlawful* for the *state to reimburse* parochial school teachers for teaching alleged community offerings after regular school hours in church-related schools, since the *only* students who attended these (or who were admitted) were students of those parochial schools, and the teachers were employed by the parochial schools. Both of the two programs were simply attempts to get public taxes to fund one church's viewpoint. Also, it was unlawful for the state to reimburse *public* school teachers to teach secular courses during regular school hours *at the parochial schools*, many of whom had in fact been formerly employed by the same parochial schools. The Court, using the *Lemon* criteria, held that the primary effect was to advance religion and it excessively entangled government with religion since (1) the pervasively sectarian nature of the religious schools had at least a subtle if not overt indoctrination aspect of a particular religion; so (2) this is subsidizing the religious functions of the sectarian school since it takes over a substantial portion of their responsibility for teaching secular subjects.[64]

In the same year, in *Aguilar v. Felton*, 473 U.S. 402 (1985), a 5/4 decision found the "excessive entanglement" between religion and government *violated* the Establishment Clause. It was a program similar to that in the *Grand Rapids* case, now in New York City, used federal funds to pay salaries of public school employees to teach remedial instruction and offer guidance services in the buildings of the parochial schools. The Court said the monitoring here was not sufficiently less from *Grand Rapids* to distinguish it.[65]

The following year, 1986, the Court discovered a new element to consider in certain Establishment litigation in the case of *Witters v. Washington Department of Services for the Blind*, 474 U.S. 481 (1986). Petitioner had a degenerating eye disease so qualified for the Washington law that offered financial help for the blind to rehabilitate them vocationally so they could be more self-supporting and independent. While he was a student at Inland School of the Bible in Spokane, WA, in 1979, he applied to the Commission (later changed to Department) for such help. The Commission denied him on the basis of the WA state Constitution which forbids using public funds for people seeking a degree or career in theology or related areas. This was challenged by Petitioner, but on appeal, the state hearings examiner agreed with the Commission's denial. Witters then pursued it in a state Superior Court, and got the same result, and appealed to the WA Supreme Court. The latter agreed with the denial but instead of using the WA Constitution, it found such funding would violate the federal law, the First Amendment.

The U.S. Supreme Court *reversed* the judgment and remanded the case back for further consideration pertaining to WA law and some necessary facts which had not been determined. In reversing the judgment, however, it held that the *WA Supreme Court's reading of the First Amendment was incorrect*. It distinguished this from illegal aid by subjecting it to the *Lemon* test, insisting it had only to cover the first two prongs (purpose and effect) of that test since there had been no "excessive entanglement" contested. Its position was that the law itself was *completely neutral*, favoring neither sectarian or nonsectarian stances, and that being true, it was not an incentive for a recipient to attend a sectarian school. Ultimately, the decision about who received the money from Witters was only Witters's choice, a *private choice*, not the government, and no reasonable observer could think differently. "*Neutrality*" and "*private choice*" were keys.

The Court chose the easy route: Reverse the judgment on the basis of the First Amendment to the Federal Constitution since this was the law referred to by the State Supreme Court, and this would allow it to *ignore* the WA state laws entirely which had prohibited using public funds for a theological education. This *ignoring of State constitutions* quickly became a method utilized by the Court since the Blaine Amendment in the nineteenth century, when it barely failed becoming an Amendment to the U.S. Constitution, was then incorporated into most of the states' own Constitutions, but was seen by Catholics as "anti-Catholic" in its prohibition of taxes being used in any way to aid *any* religious organization.[66]

The irony is that on the second "prong" of the *Lemon* test, the requirement that a law must have a primary secular effect, the Court went so far as to say that there was no evidence that this scholarship would have the effect of government funds flowing to religious education or assisting the school in its religious mission. But he was taking a major in religion to be a pastor, missionary, or youth minister, and was taking specific courses in Bible to accomplish that, and he used his government funds to pay for the classes. So the Court's conclusory statements—("nothing in the record indicates . . . any significant portion of the aid . . . will end up flowing to religious education"; "it does not seem appropriate to view any aid . . . as resulting from a state action sponsoring or subsidizing religion"; "[the illegality of public funds subsidizing a religious function] is not apposite to this case")—are all only conclusory statements *defying* the evidence, hardly legal adjudication. It was likely in recognition of this fact that J. Powell, concurring, joined by C.J. Burger and J. Rehnquist, insisted that the case needed to be supplemented with special emphasis being placed on the *Mueller v. Allen*, 466 U.S. 388 (1983) which clarified the two concepts of a *wholly neutral law* and *private choice*.

Since that time, *Witters* and *Mueller* have become two of the favorite cases of several of the justices, a route by which they can justify the government providing billions of dollars a year to parochial schools (or their students to pay to the schools), some of which began to be pursued under the Free Exercise Clause, as we have seen, rather than the Establishment Clause so religious litigants could escape the Establishment prohibition of religious purpose or effect or the obvious religious indoctrinating intent behind the parochial schools. But as we saw in earlier chapters, that was made possible only by expanding the meaning of "Free Exercise" from "worship" to virtually *anything* a person does or wants to do and to claim as his sincerely religious conviction, whether it is his business practices or her objections to birth control. It is not difficult to perceive where Madison, Jefferson, and even John Rawls would stand on all this.

The desire to *religiously indoctrinate* students in the *public school*, however, did not disappear any more than did the insistence to have Christian prayers in the public schools. In *Edwards v. Aguillard*, 482 U.S. 578 (1987), the Court examined Louisiana's law requiring equal time in the public schools to teach "Creation Science" *wherever* the theory of evolution was taught. Upon the application of the *Lemon* test, the Court found that even though the state insisted that it wanted students to see "both sides" of the issue, the *legislator* who had put the bill together admitted that if he had his preference, he would have the schools teaching *neither* side. So it was *not* an enhancement of an *objective educational method* as the school claimed, and Creation Science was *not* recognized in reputable scientific circles as being anything more than a religious interpretation.

Fortunately, J. Brennan was still around, and saw the alleged "purpose" to show "both sides" only a sham purpose. Thus, the Court ruled, with only two dissenters, that the alleged secular purpose of academic openness was *not true*, that the obvious purpose was *strictly religious*, simply religiously opposing the teaching of evolution, so an *illegal establishment*.

What was becoming clearer each year was that if one wanted to win a case because of one's *religious* convictions, one should pursue it *only* under the Free Exercise Clause where obviously the plaintiff legally could assert a religious claim of being overpowered by a law discriminating against religion *per se*, whereas to pursue it under the Establishment Clause would subject it to the three-prong test of *Lemon* which it would immediately fail. Progressively, cases that would normally have been thought as falling under the Establishment jurisdiction were shifted to Free Exercise claims, and the original understanding of "free exercise" being confined to the "worship" of the religious community began to be *transformed* into *any area* where one's *religious conviction was asserted*, which obviously completely reshaped the outcomes to the present. It also opened up sexual *discrimination* along religious lines as never before, as we saw.

But to continue on with cases brought under the Establishment Clause, in the same year, an employment question came before the Court. In *Corporation of Presiding Bishop (LDS) v. Amos*, 483 U.S. 327 (1987) the Court, with no dissent, found it lawful for a nonprofit institution, a church, to dismiss an employee from secular work on the grounds of his not being a member of the church. It ruled that Section 702 of the Civil Rights Acts of 1964 does *not violate* the Establishment Clause since it (1) minimizes governmental interference with the decision-making process of religions by relieving the latter of the burden of predicting which of their activities a secular court might consider religious; (2) a law allowing the church to advance religion is not illegal, where the government itself is not doing so; (3) advancement of religion via the gym in this case is not to be attributed to the government; and (4) no excessive entanglement by 702, but rather a greater separation. This was in line with earlier decisions the Court made regarding religious institutions' authority: basically, even like public schools, the Court has felt the institution itself knows best how to accomplish its goals, so in actions brought before the Court in which the church is an autonomous institution with no higher organization, it is the authority to decide on whether employees must be of the same religion, and if the religious institution has a complex and centralized organization, the *highest authority* in that system is assigned to the role of the central authority of the whole organization. The vital question is whether this highest authority in the religious institution can exempt citizens from universally applicable laws, and Rawls's obvious answer was "No," since all citizens agree to strictly comply with the basic principles of the "original position," and to legislate otherwise would undermine democracy.

The fundamentalist Christian churches by the late 1980s had sexual agendas by which they wanted to regulate the public morality. In *Bowen v. Kendrick*, 487 U.S. 589 (1988), the Court (5/4) found the *Adolescent Family Life Act not* violative of the Establishment Clause, that it met all three of the *Lemon* "prongs," but remanded to the lower court to determine whether its actual practice was a violation of the Establishment Clause. The Court concluded that the Act funded public or nonprofit agencies for counseling and research services involving such things as teenage sex, pregnancies, and so on, but the Act imposed great limitations on the groups involving family planning, and it forbid grants to any group advocating or encouraging abortion.

J. Kennedy and J. Scalia denied the Act was violative simply because it was only "pervasively sectarian" groups that received the aid; they insisted that it must be shown that it *actually furthered* "religion." That is a novel reading, not found in the Court's precedents, and there is no criteria given for judging whether a law *actually* "furthers" religion if religion is a belief and not just actions, and the law here prohibited *certain action, not just beliefs.* Four justices dissented, insisting the Act had a primary religious effect and excessive entanglement, that *could* be *measured,* so was a violation of the Establishment Clause under the *Lemon* test.

In the following year, the *Lemon* test was applied in *Texas Monthly, Inc. v. Bullock,* 489 U.S. 1 (1989). In this case, Texas law provided *exemptions* in sales and use tax to periodicals whose content was wholly a promulgation of a religious faith. With three endorsing the Court, and three concurring, and three dissenters, the Court's plurality found the law a *violation* of the Establishment Clause (and not a violation of Free Exercise) by its lack of a secular purpose and effect, and the excessive entanglement it posed.

That same year, another crèche or Nativity scene case came before the Court, but the ruling involved more than just the crèche and surprised many legal scholars. In *Allegheny County v. Pittsburg ACLU,* 492 U.S. 573 (1989), the Court examined two different displays on the government grounds that were fairly close to each other during the Christmas season. One was Christian, the other was Jewish. The Christian one was a Nativity scene positioned on the "Grand Staircase" in the government building, with no attendant secular accompaniments or other displays but only a large sign, reading "Gloria in Excelsis Deo." The other display consisted of a Jewish menorah and Christmas tree outside in front of another government building, and the menorah had a sign attached to it which read "Liberty."

The Court majority split over the two displays, one majority ruled the crèche an *illegal* establishment, the other majority ruling the menorah quite *legal* on the basis that the first was strictly religious with nothing secular about it or the context in which it was given preferential treatment, but the second was simply a plea for liberty and *historical* reminder of origins of that menorah and celebration rather than a religious symbol. But to think the menorah had *no religious meaning* ignores Jewish history and the Jewish faith. It was a religious celebration of the cleansing of the temple in 165 BCE from its Greek defilement under Antiochus Epiphanes. The Court mentions this, but is influenced by assertions that the celebration is much less religious than secular. There seems to be no awareness with the Court that one *cannot separate* the Jewish identity from the religious traditions and Torah, so when it is told that this is more focused on Jewish identity that supplants the religious dimension. That simply is *not true*.

Four dissenting justices insisted that both displays should have been judged as quite legal, as no violation of the Establishment Clause, but, even though the Court used J. O'Connor's concurring opinion idea of "endorsement" in *Lynch*, "endorsement" is more "support" or "approval" than it is to "proselytize." That is, the dissenters insisted that because neither of the two actually try to proselytize, they remain quite legal, but a reasonable observer can feel a display is supportive of a particular group which makes him feel an "outsider" without having to detect that it is trying to convert or proselytize him. This certainly is *not* a "neutrality" that in any way approximates Rawls's "original position" of a "veil of ignorance," nor does it seem to fit what Madison and Jefferson and the religious leaders that supported them in trying, by creating the First Amendment, to formulate a "wall of separation," even a "perfect wall" (Madison's words) between religion and government.

We see that by the mid-1980s, the growing complexity and inability to decide on even a vague, general standard for "Establishment" cases became as obvious as the parallel problem in "Free Exercise" cases. It made it become even *less likely* that the whole Court could actually view the law or practice being challenged *behind* Rawls's "veil of ignorance." In fact, *no one* seemed capable of removing himself or herself from their particular accidentals of life to discover a *hypothetical original position* from which a *democracy* could arrive at an "overlapping consensus" of basic principles, which was Rawls's answer to the growing divisiveness within a democratic state that comprised a religious pluralism. Old traditions, symbols, rituals, like one's old shoes, seem comfortable and not a threat, so seem to some that they must surely be legal? But perhaps—if one can ever get to the stage of hypothesizing oneself behind that "veil of ignorance" beyond one's irrationally vested advantages, which Rawls suggests—the route to the future may seem clearer. Rawls saw only two alternatives. Yet *Allegheny County* was decided in 1989, so we need to look at the subsequent three decades to see how the Court's standards actually evolved.

NOTES

1. *Abington Township School District v. Schempp*, 374 U.S. 203 (1963) at 217 (*J. Clark, for the Court, citing J. Rutledge, et al. dissent in Everson v. Bd of Ed*, 330 U.S. 1, 32).

2. The emphasis in FE cases now of "neutrality" and "individual" or "private choice" wants to make this the opposite of "coercion," and, lacking coercion,

therefore declares a law quite constitutional. "Private choice," however, was not sufficient in the Henry bill. Government's illegal establishment was not simply avoided by a "nonpreferentialism" but by recognizing that government has "no cognizance of religion" at all. The Court still ignores this difference.

3. *Barnette*, at 225–226.

4. This question of "taking" certainly did not imply that the Court here thought there might even be the question of "taking" in the sense of using public funds to support the private schools or parochial schools, but rather only the mere loss of income to the public school by virtue of the student attending a private school—that *this* certainly was *not legally* a "taking." Nevertheless, the Amendment against the taking of property without due compensation had already been "incorporated" into state law by the Court in 1894, although the religion clauses of the First Amendment had not yet.

5. J. Rutledge, joined by J. Frankfurter, J. Jackson and J. Burton, dissenting in *Everson v. Bd. of Education of Ewing TP*, 330 U.S. 1, 45–58 (1947).

6. See *Everson*, note 5.

7. The inadequacy of "accommodation" of religion, so long as it is *equal* among the religions, continues to overlook the defeat of Gov. Henry's "nonpreferentialism" in his proposed bill for Virginia which Madison defeated. A couple of justices have contended, this late in the day, that the First Amendment was never meant to be applied to the states, so should not be so applied.

8. *Everson*, at 15–16. It provided a fuller quote from *Reynolds v. U.S.*, 98 U.S. at 164:

> The "establishment of religion" clause of the First Amendment means at least this: Neither a state not the Federal Government can set up a church . . . [or] pass laws which aid one religion, aid all religions, or prefer one religion over another . . . No tax in any amount, large or small, can be levied to support any religious activities or institutions, whatever they may be called, or whatever form they may adopt to teach or practice religion. . . . In the words of Jefferson, the clause against establishment of religion by law was intended to erect "a wall of separation between Church and state."

9. *Everson*, at 16.

10. *Everson*, at 17–18.

11. *Everson*, at 20.

12. *Everson*, at 24.

13. J. Rutledge asked whether the Court's *decision* and its analogy of the police and fire department assistance would mean that students would be protected *only if* they were going to and from a public or Catholic school, but *not* any other school, or that the fire department would put out a blaze *only* at the public or Catholic school, but *not* any other school? (*Everson* at 25–26).

14. This decision became a primary precedent, spawning the divisiveness Madison feared, this decision which J. Douglas ironically later said he regretted being a part of the majority. Soon after, in a series of Court cases, public funds could legally provide parochial schools to pay (1) not only for state-approved secular textbooks, but even textbooks selected by the parochial school itself; (2) standardized state-required tests and scoring; (3) diagnostic services; (4) remedial and therapeutic services. The Court

eventually found it legal for a state to allow state tax deductions to parents for tuition, textbooks, and transportation to school, for a state to provide a sign-language interpreter for a student in a sectarian high school, and for religious colleges and universities to receive public money for only secular-use buildings, and on and on. It was not *Everson*'s principles that were used as precedents but only its incongruous decision.

15. *Everson* at 33.

16. *Everson*, J. Rutledge, dissent, at 59, citing Madison's "Memorial and Remonstrance."

17. *Everson*, at 63.

18. Again, this latter prohibition is seldom articulated by the later Court since several of the justices were convinced that the First Amendment prohibited only preferential treatment, so government could lawfully aid all religions equally. That, of course, was what Gov. Henry's bill proposed, which the Framers of the Constitution *defeated*. The Court specified in *Everson* "The 'establishment of religion' clause of the First Amendment means at least this: Neither a state nor the Federal Government can set up a church. Neither can pass laws which aid one religion, *aid all religions*, or prefer one religion over another," 330 U.S. 1, 15 (emphasis added). So how much is precedent, or does it depend only upon how one wants to split up clauses at a later date?

19. There had been such an outcry over *McCollum* showing the Court's "hostility" toward religion, it probably was no surprise that J. Douglas who was regarded as the "liberal" was selected to write for the Court in *Zorach*, a decision that was so uncharacteristic of his position.

20. *Zorach v. Clauson*, 343 U.S. 306 (1952), at 314–315.

21. *Zorach*, at 320.

22. *Zorach*, at 317.

23. *Zorach*, at 323.

24. He was refused the commission since he was unwilling to confess his "belief in the existence of God" which Article 37 of the Declaration of Rights of the Maryland Constitution requires but is a direct violation of Article VI of the U.S. Constitution.

The Court spoke of Lord Calvert whose very hope for Maryland was directly opposed to such a "test" for holding office. Since this case focused on the "test" of a religious oath, the Court's description of the scope of religious freedom in *Everson* was very much on point which ended with "In the words of Jefferson, the clause against establishment of religion by law was intended to erect 'a wall of separation between church and State'" (at 493). To this it added a quote from J. Frankfurter's concurring opinion, in *McCollum* which was "joined by the other *Everson* dissenters,"

"We are all agreed that the First and Fourteenth Amendments have a secular reach far more penetrating in the conduct of Government than merely to forbid an 'established church.' . . . We renew our conviction that 'we have staked the very existence of our country on the faith that complete separation between the state and religion is best for the state and best for religion'" (at 493–494). Then for emphasis, the Court repeated its principle in *Everson* in a shorter paraphrase:

"We repeat and again reaffirm that neither a State nor the Federal Government can constitutionally force a person 'to profess a belief or disbelief in any religion.'

Neither can constitutionally pass laws or impose requirements which aid all religions as against non-believers, and neither can aid those religions based on a belief in the existence of God as against those religions founded on different beliefs" (at 495).

25. The public universities that subsequently opened up religious studies programs distinguished the legality of their pursuit as teaching "about" religion vis-à-vis teaching "of" religion. This was based only on dicta. W. Royce Clark, "The Legal Status of Religious Studies Programs in Public Higher Education," in Frank E. Reynolds and Sheryl L. Burkhalter (eds.), *Beyond the Classics? Essays in Religious Studies and Liberal Education* (Atlanta, GA: Scholars Press, 1990), 109–139.

26. He is said to have struggled as a Catholic with making prayer in public school illegal, but remained convinced that religion and government had to be separated, even as Jeremiah S. Black had described in the prior century. See Hunter R. Clark, *Justice Brennan: The Great Conciliator* (New York: A Birch Lane Press Book, 1995), 187–189.

27. The Court's earlier idea of "Sabbath-observance" being a mere secular need for a universal day of rest was unrealistic assessment of "Sabbath" in both Judaism and Christianity.

28. It has been suggested that it was probably because of the church's indignant outcry against the Court for its earlier ruling in *Engle v. Vitale*, and now in *Abington v. Schempp*, that J. Brennan, as the only Catholic justice on the bench, felt he had to go to such lengths to defend his decision in both cases. Changes in the Court had now reduced him from belonging to an earlier majority to the liberal minority, but his insights justified his lone concurring opinion. See Nathan Lewin, "William J. Brennan," in Leon Friedman (ed.), *The Justices of the United States Supreme Court 1789–1978: Their Lives and Major Opinions*, Vol. V (New York: Chelsea House, 1978), 246.

29. *Flast v. Cohen*, 392 U.S. 83 (1968), at 110.

30. *Flast* at 113.

31. *Schempp*, J. Brennan, concurring, at 680.

32. Almost as significant was J. Douglas's actual switch between *McCollum* and *Zorach*, which made no sense, as if the actual buildings used for the religious instruction made a difference.

33. *Walz v. Tax Commission*, 397 U.S. 664 (1970), at 701–705, citing *Torcaso* at 495.

34. David P. Currie, *The Constitution in the Supreme Court: The Second Century: 1886–1986* (Chicago: Univ. of Chicago, 1990), 528.

35. Enforcement which required monitoring would have triggered "excessive entanglement."

36. As we saw in the last chapter, in *Espinoza v. Montana*, even the Montana State Constitution could not prevent the Court from deciding in favor of parents of students attending a religious school who claimed that to not allow them the tax credits would be a violation of their "free exercise," precisely what the Court here mentioned as illegal.

37. For the sake of brevity, we need not explain in detail several other "minor" decisions, all decided on the same day of June 25, 1973, but the reader may want to

check them out: *Sloan v. Lemon*, 413 U.S. 835 (1973); *Levitt v. Committee for Public Education and Religious Liberty*, 413 U.S. 472 (1973); *Hunt v. McNair*, 413 U.S. 734 (1973); and *Norwood v. Harrison*, 413 U.S. 455 (1973). *Sloan* decided that the program for state reimbursement for part of the tuition for parochial school students was indistinguishable from *Nyquist*, so violated the tests put forth in *Lemon*, by its advancing religion and involving excessive entanglement. *Levitt* found the state's funding parochial schools for administrative costs in examination, record-keeping of students since states did not distinguish the aid devoted to secular from aid to sectarian functions, so was a violation. *Hunt* found legal the new South Carolina law which authorized the use of state tax-free bonds to finance facilities at colleges, including a Baptist college, since it prohibited the colleges from using the buildings for worship or religious instruction (relying on the *Tilton* and *Roemer* precedents). *Norwood* involved Mississippi giving free textbooks to students in both public and private schools, but the Tunica Academy refused to affirm that it had a racially nondiscriminatory admissions policy. The Court ruled this discrimination on the basis of race a violation of the Constitution.

38. Many of the justices have conceived religion as the faith in that which is Absolute, Unquestionable, if not also Unknowable, but have not even seen the basic problem of religious pluralism, if most religions propagate such a belief in the Unquestionable and Unchallengeable or Absolute. They reveal they have never read John Rawls, and not even James Madison very closely. For example, one justice wrote in *Thomas v. Review Board*, 450 U.S. 707 (1981): "There can be little doubt that to the extent secular education provides answers to the important moral questions without reference to religion or teaches that there are no answers, a person in one sense sacrifices his religious belief by attending secular schools" (note 2 at 724). This justice wanted a faith that has every answer, and sees secular education with a ridiculous caricature, so is this the attitude of the Court, that *its* answers are permanent, eternal, beyond ever being challenged? Was he admitting his secular education at Stanford and Harvard sacrificed *his* religious belief? Are not most "answers" as contingent as their contingently shaped "questions"?

39. As renowned constitutional scholar, Laurence Tribe, of Harvard, noted, J. Rehnquist "applied an *usually narrow* approach to *pre-adoption* history (i.e., prior to ratification of the Constitution and Bill of Rights). J. Rehnquist dismissed Thomas Jefferson's contributions to first amendment principles by noting that 'Jefferson was of course in France' when the Bill of Rights was written and ratified" (Tribe citing *Jaffree*, 472 U.S. at 92). He continued, "Justice Rehnquist likewise focused on James Madison's politically motivated support for a bill of rights, rather than his well-established views on religious freedom," which caused M. McConnell to take the *groundless* position that Madison's "activities and statements about religious disestablishment in Virginia should not be applied to the first amendment, because of Madison's belief that factions (including religions ones) were a particular danger in states, but less so in the nation as a whole." Tribe is correct. He noted that Rehnquist focused *very broadly* on postadoption history (contrasted with his extremely narrow focus on preadoption history), on such things as the Northwest Ordinance and early presidents' Thanksgiving proclamations, and the like, to suggest how religious

symbols and references were seemingly acceptable even after the ratification of the First Amendment. Laurence Tribe, *American Constitutional Law*, 2nd ed., (Mineola, NY: Foundation Press, 1986), 1162–1163, and nt. 37 and 38, p. 1163. If J. Rehnquist was correct about the authority of the Constitution's postadoption history, should we still have slaves and women still be denied the right to vote?

40. In ch. 1 of *The God Delusion*, Richard Dawkins noted that religious people in the United States often expect to receive special treatment, to not have anyone question their beliefs. Some religious groups have profited billions of dollars per year and the Court has even refused "standing" to parties who oppose church subsidies such as in the *Valley Forge Christian College* (1982); see also Tribe, *Constitutional Choices*, 103–105.

41. *Larson, Commissioner of Securities, Minnesota Department of Commerce v. Valente*, 456 U.S. 228 (1982), at 248–249.

42. I use "prophetic" not in the sense of predicting something in the future but more in terms of Ancient Israel's eighth century BCE prophets who had the reputation of finding fault with the behavior and lack of morality of the people.

43. *Lamb's Chapel v. Center Moriches School Dist.*, 408 U.S. 384, (1993), J. Scalia, conc. at 399.

44. Recall Jefferson writing that "to compel a man to furnish contributions of money for the propagation of opinions which he disbelieves and abhors, is sinful and tyrannical" and he went further, even saying that it was wrong even to tax him to support ministers he *approves*. "Bill for Establishing Religious Freedom," in Kurland and Lerner (eds.), *Founders' Constitution*, V: 77.

45. For example, his complete opposition to legislative and military chaplains, in James Madison, "Detached Memoranda," c. 1817, W. & M. Q., 3d ser., 3:554–560 (1946) in Kurland and Lerner (eds.), *The Founders' Constitution*, V: 104. See also "James Madison to Edward Livingston," July 10, 1822, Writings 9:100–103, in *Founders' Constitution*, V: 104–106, which he ends by saying: "We are teaching the world the great truth that Govts. do better without Kings & Nobles than with them. The merit will be doubled by the other lesson that Religion flourishes in greater purity, without than with the aid of Govt."

46. Could C.J. Burger not see legislative prayer accepted in federal Congress as simply a carryover of the "established" church custom, a residue from theocratic practices now illegal?

47. The Court argued against Brennan and the Respondents that any opposition they might produce in history to such legislative prayers simply strengthens rather than weakens the Court's position since it shows that the "subject was considered carefully and the action not taken thoughtlessly, by force of long tradition and without regard to the problems posed by a pluralistic society" (at 791). Does this mean that Jay's, Rutledge's, Jefferson's, and Madison's opposition to such prayer can be negated by a simple quote from Samuel Adams? Even as late as Vatican II, the Catholic Church did *not* approve Catholics sharing the Eucharist with other Christians.

48. Here, Thomas Ricks's vital book begins and ends (as well as develops the thesis with historical details) with a note that the Framers, though they learned from

the ancient Roman and Greek cultures, gave us a Constitution which failed to resolve slavery, and as a result, we still suffer from the aftermath of that, despite the Civil War Amendments. Ricks, *First Principles*. The reader must supplement Ricks with Erika Lee's *America for Americans*.

49. There is a plethora of very recent books published dealing with racial inequity and "white supremacy," and one that has much relevance and popularity, analyzing its mythical dimensions, is Richard T. Hughes, *Myths America Lives By: White Supremacy and the Stories That Give Us Meaning*, 2nd ed. (Urbana, IL: Univ. of Illinois Press, 2018). One should read also several basic works by Prof. Eddie Glaude of Princeton, and for the historical analysis of the xenophobia that utilized the notion of "white supremacy," see especially Prof. Erika Lee, *America for Americans: A History of Xenophobia in the United States* (New York: Basic Books, 2019). A very unique approach to African American history is taken by Ibram X. Kendi and Keisha N. Blain, eds., *Four Hundred Souls: A Community History of African America, 1619–2019* (New York: Random House, 2020). One quickly sees in these works that "white supremacy" and therefore the xenophobia that underlies racial injustice in the United States was not a "happenstance" occurrence, but was intentional, by white, male legislators over many decades.

50. *Marsh v. Chambers*, 463 U.S. 783 (1983), at 792.

51. *Marsh*, at 811.

52. *Marsh*, J. Brennan, dissenting at 816, citing *Schempp* at 241.

53. *Marsh*, J. Brennan, dissenting at 816, citing *Barnette* at 639.

54. *Marsh*, at 802, citing *Epperson v. Arkansas*, 393 U.S. 97, 103–104 (1968).

55. To view the chief justice's "cherry-picking" of items in Madison's position, see Leo Pfeffer, *Religion, State, and the Burger Court* (Buffalo, NY: Prometheus Books, 1984), 163–170.

56. *Marsh*, at 823.

57. *Marsh*, at 800–801.

58. The ecumenical aspect of such service is *superficial*, not a real religious unity or agreement, as is shown by it inaugurating a president even if he has neither any religion nor sense of ethics.

59. Santa has to cover the whole of humanity in one long night's journey, whereas many Christians think Jesus is always everywhere simultaneously. Which is reliable "history"?

60. By the time we finish the Establishment Clause cases in chapter 10, we will see the chief defender of the majority religion on the Court actually insisting that a cross can be purified of its religious meaning and be completely secular. The present Court can claim the Cross is primarily just a symbol of death. Does it not understand why it is used in cemeteries or why many Christian cross themselves?

61. See Robert P. Scharlemann, *The Reason of Following: Christology and the Ecstatic I* (Chicago: Univ. of Chicago Press, 1993), 196–197.

62. What made J. Brennan such an exceptional Supreme Court justice was not only his impartial brilliance and insistence on personally researching all the cases, but that he was a faithful Roman Catholic and for many years, the only one on the bench.

63. The latter's "historical" recounting of events had great holes in it, and failed utterly to see the strong connection between Jefferson and Madison during that period of Ratification, and failed to understand that Madison's "Act for Establishing Religious Freedom" for Virginia in 1785 came some six years *after* Jefferson's Bill for the same purpose, and Madison's was almost verbatim from Jefferson. Of course, Madison was more involved in the actual debates in Congress over the First Amendment, since Jefferson was out of the country, but that does not diminish Jefferson's connection and Madison's dependence on Jefferson.

64. It is significant that Justice Brennan, although a Catholic, wrote for the Court against the interests of the Catholic Church in several cases, which showed his impartial approach to justice.

65. Twelve years later, it was overruled by *Agostini v. Felton.*

66. It came up again in 2017 in the Lutheran school case in Missouri and in 2020 in the Clearwater Christian School case in Montana, as the Court ruled against the state constitutions without explicitly examining them but rather by other means, avoiding a direct confrontation since the Blaine Amendment was almost verbatim from the positions of Madison and Jefferson.

Chapter 10

First Amendment

A Very Selective Reading of History

The Court's appeal to history in *Marsh* and *Lynch* isolated certain rituals and symbols from their actual attempted-theocratic support system in the early colonies. The Court did not advocate that a "theocracy" or established church or religion should be the norm. But, instead, it singled out certain traditions within those desired theocracies, and said these should nevertheless be normative, because of their age, their longevity, their historical value. Once several Justices realized that by *appealing* to those customs being continued in *post*-constitutional days, that is, *after* the First Amendment, therefore repeating certain religious customs, such as legislative chaplains, many religious practices, rituals, slogans, and holy days which had their actual origins in the United States in the earlier *theocratic* attempts in various colonies, even if simply continued on as fairly unnoticed, the Court could tell us these should *never* be considered today as an illegal Establishment, prohibited by the First Amendment. As I noted earlier, to make that argument is parallel to *approving* the Jim Crow laws as also post-constitutional, even post-Civil War Amendments, so those Jim Crow laws surely should still be legal since they were still in effect in the early twentieth century and not disapproved by the Framers of the Constitution.[1]

But few people would accept such a "selective reading of history," an unhistorical logic to address changed cultural conditions and justify gross discrimination in the present just because it existed after it was declared illegal. The principle of *separation* of religion from any attachment to government was articulated as the law of the land, just as was the *equality* of the Declaration of Independence and the *abolition of legal slavery* several decades later via the Civil War and subsequent laws. But old habits, customs, and identities which give people any sense of superiority do not die overnight. To cite such residual "hangovers" as now proposed as good law is simply inexcusable and wrong in principle as well as application. Madison, Jefferson, and Rawls would all be wondering what happened to this "lively experiment" in democracy.

That is a form of repristination or trying to turn the clock back to justify present practices. But we do not live in the seventeenth century and neither did those who spawned all the Jim Crow laws. The racial and religious *pluralism* in the United States in the twenty-first century has a variety and numerical intensity not even conceivable to the Framers of the Constitution. The diversity is much greater, demanding a spirit of national *unity* that is *much deeper* than that required at the end of the eighteenth century. We cannot simply read small parts of our national history as if they are to be normative for all time even though our laws have prohibited such for centuries. All law from the past must be viewed in a more comprehensive and developing historical context, and, finally, as having significance today *only* if the *present democratic republic* can accommodate the law as it maintains an "overlapping consensus" from "freestanding principles" which maximize diversity within the stronger and *prior unity* of the nation as a whole.

The Founding Fathers would ask no more. They did not envision themselves as changing the world overnight, not just in theory but practice, nor did they believe that the nation would always view things as they did. They enabled the Constitution to be amended since they viewed it as a "living" document, always dependent upon the general populace basically *agreeing* with it, and altering it where need be so the *unanimous agreement of its citizens can continue*. They were as aware as we that individuals' personal lives do not always measure up to the principles they publically espouse, nor do institutions always abide by the original intentions and agreements of the various parties. But that does not justify trying to reinstate *discriminatory* principles and hateful prejudices to match our weak wills, selfish attitudes, or lack of personal ethics, as if those forms of discrimination are acceptable in our democratic society. Once again, a vision of justice does *not* come from *competing irrationally vested interests* but only from being able to *hypothesize* an "original position" of working out a social contract behind a "veil of ignorance"—or without any vested interests which would give one an advantage over other people. This would be the obvious way of devising even a simple game for children. One would not allow the rules to articulate that certain players could begin with a definite advantage over the others, or that only certain players could revise the rules when they found the agreed rules to their disadvantage. *No one* is exempt from the basic rules, not even the president of the nation or those appointed by him, not even Supreme Court Justices. They all *know* that.

A very obvious example of that principle involved the issue of state sales and use tax, which finally came before the Court in 1990 in *Jimmy Swaggart*

Ministries v. Bd. of Equalization (of California), 493 U.S. 378. Swaggart, who was a traveling Christian crusade minister in the middle of the twentieth century, had his headquarters in Louisiana, but held crusades throughout the United States. In the years of 1974–1981 he held approximately 52 crusades within the state of California alone, and paid no sales or use tax to the state on his roughly two millions in retail sales there. These sales involved dozens of different religious items such as books of his sermons, hymns, and the like, but also subscription to his periodical, and sales of trinket-class items both of a religious and nonreligious nature. When the California Board of Equalization requested payment as early as 1980 of more than $118,000 dollars in tax, plus penalty fees, totaling more than $166,000, Swaggart objected that he was *exempt*, that to tax these items was to hinder his Free Exercise of religion as well as violate the Establishment Clause, making the items less attractive since he had to add the tax into the sales price. He finally registered as a seller in the state, and paid the tax, but then filed to get the money back alleging he was religiously exempt.

J. O'Connor, writing for the Court in an unanimous decision, and agreeing with the lower courts, held that this sales and use tax was a generally applicable law, was not a tax on the right to disseminate religious information or ideas or beliefs, *per se*, so his organization was not being burdened in a special way but simply in the same capacity as all retail sellers, whether selling out-of-state goods under the "use" tax or selling within the state under the 6% sales tax, so did not violate his Free Exercise. There was no evidence that paying the tax *per se* was a violation of the group's religious beliefs, and the taxing did not violate the secular purpose, primary secular effect, or excessive entanglement prongs of the *Lemon* test.[2] Below the surface, however, there was a different kind of "very selective reading of history" by certain members of the Court, which no longer wanted to hear about the *Lemon* test of 1971, nor even about Madison and Jefferson, and the General Assessment proposed bill of Gov. Patrick Henry that they defeated, but to listen only to its (the Supreme Court's) own decisions of the past few years, the decisions most of the members made in only the *previous five years*. This tunnel vision quickly spread.

HOW MUCH "EQUAL ACCESS" MAY A RELIGION HAVE BEFORE IT BECOMES ESTABLISHMENT?

If we were to ask whether the idea of "equal access" applies to either of the Religion Clauses of the First Amendment, the first thing that might come to mind would be that Jefferson and Madison emphasized that one's religion does *not change* one's civil benefits or obligations to the state. It neither enhances benefits nor reduces them. That means they remain the same. If one does not expect to receive 50,000 dollars a year in public taxes to refrain from being religious, one who is religious does not expect 50,000 a year from the government just for adhering to a religion. Nor does one get excused from generally applicable or universally neutral laws for being either religious or nonreligious. All this was intensified by the "Civil War Amendments" which required the various states not to contradict the federal Constitution and its Amendments in basics such as equal protection and due process. The individual's speech rights are speech rights, whether one is religious or not.

How the Court ever progressed through the "speech" and "religion" clauses of the First Amendment to arrive at being able to *separate* private from government speech, giving the latter *unrestricted* opportunity to "express" the "government's religion," is a convoluted labyrinth, which began in earnest with *Widmar v. Vincent* in 1981, then was extended in a decision in 1990, in *Board of Education of the Westside Community Schools (Dist. 66), et al., v. Mergens, by and Through her Next Friend, Mergens, et al.*, 496 U.S. 226 (1990), ultimately making it more difficult for school boards to restrict private speech, including religious speech of its students. Yet, ironically, this route of "free speech" finally included permanent monuments of the Ten Commandments (*Van Orden v. Perry*) and Crosses (*Capitol Square v. Pinette*, and *Salazar v. Buono*), even when the cross was sponsored by the KKK in its hate-based program.

In January 1985, Bridget Mergens, a student at Westside High School in Omaha, Nebraska, met with the principal and requested to establish a Christian club at the school. The school had already established regulations allowing "limited public forums" for students, providing them access to the facilities for nonschool hours. Numerous groups presently used the facilities such as the chess club, photography club, scuba club, French club, as well as student clubs related to Rotary International, National Honor Society, and so forth. The school required that membership in these be open to all students, that no club could be sponsored by a political or religious organization, that each club would have a faculty sponsor, and that permission had to be requested through the administration, and the only other pertinent school policy regarding religion and the students in general was that all students were to have equal respect whether they had a specific religious belief or none at all. Mergens specified that she and others wanted a student-centered group, open to all students, in which they could study the Bible and pray as they chose, but that they would have no faculty sponsor.

She was turned down by the school administration, so when challenged, she appealed to the board of education, which likewise denied the request. Mergens then sought relief in the District Court, which also denied her cause, emphasizing that the school did *not* have a "limited public forum" since all the clubs were actually *curriculum related*, so Westside's denial of her request was reasonable since her request, unlike the other clubs, did not meet the pedagogical concerns of the school. The Eighth Circuit reversed the lower court in 1989, insisting that the court erred in its judgment of all the clubs as *curriculum related* or part of the school's pedagogical plan, stating that the lower court's "broad reading" would make meaningless the Equal Access Act, 20 U.S.C. §481 (1984), so with its requirement if at least one club was *not* curriculum related, then other such noncurriculum-related clubs could not be denied. It emphasized that the Act had extended *Widmar v. Vincent* from colleges to now include public secondary schools and had evidently considered the age difference in the groups in so extending it, and the Act did not violate the Establishment Clause as the school held.

The Court accepted the reasoning of the Circuit Court, affirming that the high school had created a "limited public forum," and the Court had found *Widmar v. Vincent* a violation of the Establishment Clause and free speech for prohibiting students access for purposes of religious worship or teaching after applying the *Lemon* criteria to it. Further, it argued that the Equal Access Act simply extended that principle of the school's inability to regulate content to a limited public forum of secondary schools, so it could not, by that combination, be a violation of the Establishment Clause. The Equal Access Act required that the meetings be voluntary, student initiated, not sponsored by the school, the government, or its agents or employees, not directed, controlled, conducted, or regularly attended by "nonschool persons," not interfering with the school's orderly conduct of educational activities. Further, if it was a religious group, the school could not influence its form or require anyone to attend, and the school personnel could attend only in a nonparticipatory capacity.

Strangely, the issue of "noncurriculum related" as the criteria for acceptable clubs was debated, focusing only on 10 of the 30 clubs, all 10 of which Petitioners argued did *not* qualify since they were connected to the curriculum. The Court countered by saying that by the Petitioner's standard, anything would be disqualified because one could stretch the idea of the curricular purposes of the school to such a length. To the other extreme, the Court knew that if it could ascertain that one single club out of the 30 was truly noncurriculum related, then it was thereby a "limited public forum," and it was sure that the chess club and the subsurfers were *not* curriculum related, therefore the "limited public forum" was established, therefore the school could *not refuse* the students who requested a religious club.

When the School District argued that the primary effect of allowing the club would be the public school or government advancing religion, J. O'Connor, writing for the Court, replied that "there is a crucial difference between government speech endorsing religion, which the Establishment

Clause forbids, and private speech endorsing religion, which the Free Speech and Free Exercise Clauses protect. We think that secondary school students are mature enough and are likely to understand that a school does not endorse or support student speech that it merely permits on a nondiscriminatory basis."[3] This is a very significant division between government religious speech which is *forbidden* and private religious speech which is *protected*, as we move into later cases such as *Van Orden v. Perry* in which two of the Justices in the oral argument insist the government has a perfect right to speak about *its religion*, which was also affirmed in the *Summum* case later.

Finally, it must be pointed out that the *purpose behind* the Equal Access Act that is at the heart of the decision was even a more blatant violation of the "secular" purpose requirement of *Lemon*, as the Court here quotes that the Committee Reports "indicate that the Act was intended to address perceived widespread discrimination against religious speech in public schools." So the *explicit purpose* of the Equal Access Act was *strictly religious* which itself *violated* the first "prong" of the *Lemon* test. But, once again, the majority of the Court decided *not* to use the *Lemon* test which examined the purpose, effects, and whether the effects might even become excessive entanglements between government and religion.

What if the group was several Muslim students requesting to have access to the school facilities to pray, to study the Qu'ran, and to teach and hopefully "proselytize" as was the goal of these Christian students? Would the decision have been identical? We can only ask, but the answer is likely pretty obvious.[4] Does a religion's "equal access" to the public school facilities after hours therefore also entitle the latter to utilize prayers for public school graduation?[5] When confronted with such, what would control, the *Engels v. Vitale, Abington v. Schempp, Wallace v. Jaffree* line of decisions which prohibited prayers in public schools, or would *Marsh v. Chambers* be utilized to include not simply legislative prayer but even school prayer?

In 1992, *Lee v. Weisman*, 505 U.S. 577, J. Kennedy,[6] writing for the Court (5/4) had to adjudicate another prayer at a public school. Deborah Wiseman's father attempted to stop the prayer at her *middle school graduation* in the state of Rhode Island, but she felt forced to attend anyway when the school said it did not have sufficient time to discuss the matter. He then quickly brought the suit to prevent her having to experience the same at her future high school graduation. The Court held that it was a violation of the Establishment clause for the public middle school to request ministers and rabbis to lead an invocation and benediction at the school graduation. The prayer on this occasion was given by a Jewish rabbi, and it was worded as neutrally as possible, at the suggestion of the principal of the school. Nevertheless, the Court insisted, the state cannot engage in sponsoring religious activity or worship such as prayers, especially for such a young age at such an important event in their lives. As opposed to J. Scalia's dissenting view, the Court insisted, very importantly, that the First Amendment *disallows* even a very neutral or general or alleged nonsectarian form of religious expression as a "civic religion." It remains an illegal involvement of the state in that the principle decided to have the prayer, selected the person to give it, and provided him with a pamphlet of guidelines for prayer, a *government interference* in religion totally abhorrent.

Even if students were not literally coerced into being present, the pressure was of such a nature, as was the rite of passage itself, that it was the equivalent of a mandate by the government. The Court insisted that the state may *not* use social pressure to enforce religious orthodoxy any more than direct coercion. So despite the graduation appearing as voluntary, it really was not, since no middle school student should have to choose between such an important celebration of accomplishment with her parents (and peers) or her religion. An alternative of the student absenting herself for the "invocation" and "benediction" but being present for the rest of the program does *not mitigate the coercion* or peer pressure of being singled out, just as it did not in *Schempp* for the students who had the option of standing in the hallway during the school devotional. It was still *a state-sponsored religious activity*, not some *de minimis* act. Thus, this case falls under the *Engels* and *Schempp* decisions, rather than *Marsh* which the Court insisted is distinguishable since it involved adults who were free to come and go during the process of the legislative prayer, and there was little chance of any kind of religious coercion or religious influence of those adults, even as the *Marsh* Court distinguished that case from *Engels* and *Schempp*.

J. Souter, in a concurring opinion, joined by J. Stevens and J. O'Connor, did a masterful job of rehearsing the actual history of the Founders, utilizing their writings that were so instrumental in formulating the Constitution and the Bill of Rights. He showed that there was not always a flawless consistency in the early days of the nation in following the laws exactly, much of which was due to the lack of public debate over issues that were not even real yet, and others inconsistencies due to one's inability to follow through in a way that would not be too upsetting to the young nation. His and the Court's dependence upon the actual writings of Madison and Jefferson preempted the sarcastically critical dissent of J. Scalia, who was joined by C.J. Rehnquist, J. White, and J. Thomas in his very selective readings of history and insistence on government "accommodation" rather than a "wall of separation."

By *Van Orden v. Perry* (2005), oral arguments by J. Kennedy and J. Scalia eventually showed they really had no use for the *history* they preached about but only for a *symbol* that they could interpret as a symbol of a generic but universal and obvious "God" who is the foundation of all U.S. law, the same God that everyone on the globe worships evidently even if they disagree, since it is the only God, the "unitary God" as J. Scalia called it.[7] This lack of understanding of existing religions and their history and thought is far removed from any honest acceptance of significant religious differences or government abstention from entering into the fray to decide what is "orthodox" or "true." It is simplistic "cherry-picking" of historical scraps to buttress a religious prejudice which morphs into a discrimination against other religions and the nonreligious citizens of our country.

One step further and the question is raised whether a particular religious group itself can *demand* "equal access" to a public school's facilities, either for worship or for showing religiously indoctrinating films? One of the few religion cases in which all the Justices concurred in the result though not for the specific reasons given by the Court occurred in 1993 as *Lamb's Chapel v. Center Moriches Union Free School Dist.*, 508 U.S. 384. It involved a local church bringing action against the school district for refusing to allow it to show films from James Dobson's "Focus on the Family" at the public school after school hours. New York law allowed public school districts to formulate reasonable regulations to permit after-hours use of the school property for 10 different purposes, but *not* including *religious* purposes. The local school district did issue such rules on after-hours access to its facilities, following NY state law, of which rule 10 prohibited use of the facilities for any religious purpose.

The church first requested that the school district allow it to use the high school facilities for Sunday worship and Bible classes. When they were turned down, the church requested to use the facilities of the school to show the Dobson films, conceding that it had a *religious purpose*. That alone would have made it illegal under the *Lemon* test. When the church was denied this, the church brought suit, claiming a violation of the Freedom of Speech and Assembly clauses, and a violation of the Free Exercise and Establishment clauses of the First Amendment, as well as the Equal Protection clause of the Fourteenth Amendment.

The District Court found summary judgment for the school district, rejecting all of the church's claims. It held that the school district had created a "limited public forum" for its facilities, which, following state law, prohibited use for "religious" purposes, and the church conceded the showing of the film had "religious" purpose. That was very straightforward meeting of the criteria. It further held that by denying the application by the church, it was upholding the law, not showing a hostility to religion, that denying use for religious purposes neither advanced nor hindered religion, since religious purpose did not qualify for such a limited forum. The Court of Appeals affirmed the District Court "in all respects." All that was necessary was for the school district to show that its exclusions for its forum were reasonable and viewpoint neutral, which it did. It viewed the denial of showing the films as a "content" regulation corresponding to the state law, not a "viewpoint" regulation.

Yet, now the entire Supreme Court *reversed* the lower courts' decisions, calling them "questionable," even though those courts were utilizing *precedent cases decided* by the Supreme Court itself. The singular approach of the Court faulted the Circuit Court for thinking that Rule 7 met the test of being reasonable and viewpoint neutral because the Court of Appeals "thought that the application of Rule 7 in this case was viewpoint neutral because it had been, and would be, applied in the same way to all uses of school property for religious purposes."[8] But the Court argued that merely treating all religions alike does not itself satisfy; it must also show viewpoint neutrality which it failed to do, since the films were primarily of social and civil purposes on child rearing. However, the lower court saw the school district and state's legislation as justifiably regulating "subject matter" or "content" *rather* than "viewpoint," thus to put it more in line with the First Amendment's anti-Establishment clause. If any social or civic purpose would give a group access, then any religion could qualify, as could any antireligious group or political or antipolitical group since all that would be necessary is to simply emphasize its social and civil purpose. Does this make the idea of limited public forums a useless farce?

There is tremendous confusion here as the Court admits that the argument of the church was that since the school allowed such a wide variety of communicative purposes (social, civic, and recreational), this made it more like a traditional (open) public forum such as parks and sidewalks. So any communication that involves anything about humans or their relations turns a venue into an open public forum. The *Church* argued this denial of its request was therefore a restriction on "subject matter" which could be justified only by showing a compelling state interest and laws narrowly drawn to achieve such an end. The *Court* said this argument "has considerable force," especially since the school district had already allowed others to use its property for religious use, *but* in truth, the groups it refers to were only *bands* that performed, not a series of religious lectures or indoctrination set on *restoring power to one specific religion* as Dobson advertised his films.[9] But for some reason, the Court ran with this, confusing "subject matter" with "viewpoint," and reversed the lower court decisions. Obviously, no one on the bench knew anything of Dobson's explicitly stated intentions or else did not care that he was speaking only for a very narrow ultraconservative sect within Christian evangelicals or fundamentalists, and cared not how unenlightened he was in his fight against governmental interference, abortion, and pornography.[10] When the Court says that this subject matter would qualify under "social or civic" purposes, the Court broadly opens the door for *any kind* of subject matter, including sheer religious indoctrination from any religious group, since *nearly all speech* has at least a modicum of "social and civic" purposes, as Dobson's intended *indoctrination*.

This reveals how the Court has grown used to treating the various religions unequally, even in its utter confusion over "content" (or "subject matter") and "viewpoint." Common sense sees the latter as a mere subcategory of the former or a subset. So, for example, a local bookstore might invite young people to come by after school and bring "board games" to play, but no others. So the content or subject matter would have been "board games." Anyone showing up with a chess set or monopoly game or similar type of "board games" would be permitted to play, whereas those coming in with portable race tracks, small race cars, dolls, dogs, or horses would not qualify. Would their exclusion have been because of subject matter (content) or viewpoint?

Or suppose a Buddhist wanted to speak and show films on how following the Eightfold Path can alleviate all human suffering. Or what if he requested to speak on the *social and civic* benefits of realizing anatta and Sunyata? Or, what if a Muslim imam wanted to encourage people to embrace Jihad or to be true monotheists to bring true peace on earth? Would these not have had enough social or civic value to have made the school's exclusion of "religion" to be an illegal "viewpoint" discrimination? If the Court had paid attention to *Dobson's advertisement* of his program as a focus on restoring Christian values, would Dobson' description be of content (or subject matter) or a viewpoint? If a viewpoint, was it "viewpoint neutral"?

Could it not be that the state's and school district's limitations of access in the areas of "religious" or "political" purposes had a very *legitimate* intent of trying to avoid *political and religious divisiveness* in the community? Is that not what Jefferson's "wall of separation" was attempting to avoid—an overlap of religion and government which creates favoritism, suspicion, coercion, insincerity, hostility, and religious wars? If a democratic society presupposes a unity based on unanimously agreed basic principles, but which allow freedoms within those principles derived from "public reason," but all associations' "nonpublic" reason must give priority to the principles of the unity which actually provides certain liberties of conscience, as Rawls articulated, does the Court *ever* think like this? Is it possible that it can conceive of a structure of justice that can be developed that is superior to what Rawls proposed, built on a hypothetical original position behind a veil of ignorance? Rawls knew that no justice can be derived merely through a clash of unresolvable accidental advantages certain people have over others, not in a democracy. But at least the case gave J. Scalia an opportunity to vent his spleen against the *Lemon* test, as if he had better standards. In his words,

When we wish to strike down a practice it forbids, we invoke it, see, e.g. *Aguilar v. Felton,* 473 U.S. 402 (1985) (striking down state remedial education program administered in part in parochial schools); when we wish to uphold a practice it forbids, we ignore it entirely, see *Marsh v. Chambers*, 463 U.S. 783 (1983) (upholding state legislative chaplains). Sometimes, we take a middle course, calling its three prongs "no more than helpful signposts," *Hunt v. McNair*, 413 U.S. 734, 741 (1973). Such a docile and useful monster is worth keeping around, at least in a somnolent state; one never knows when one might need him.[11]

But then his talk of *Lemon* as a "monster" became more explicit, "I will decline to apply *Lemon*—whether it validates or invalidates the government action in question—and therefore cannot join the opinion of the Court today."[12] Justice Scalia went further, insisting that he wants to part ways with the Court's consideration of whether something is an "endorsement of religion." He insisted that the Constitution "itself gives 'religion in general' preferential treatment," so to even think government should forbid religion in general is "a strange notion."[13] "Preferred treatment"? Was he trying to mend fences with J. O'Conner? He cited *none* of the Founder's significant writings on the topic. Instead, he suggested that the Northwest Territory Ordinance expressed the idea that "religion, morality, and knowledge" are "necessary to good government and the happiness of mankind." So this statement also gives "knowledge" a "preferred treatment" or "morality" a "preferred treatment"? Special privileges and certain exemptions from general law because one has a certain morality or a certain knowledge? It is the First Amendment that is at issue here, *not* the Northwest Territory Ordinance. No comment by a Supreme Court Justice is more contradictory of the explicit statements of Madison, Jefferson, and the system of John Rawls.

The question of equal access was broadened further in a case asking whether or not a student in a parochial school could have equal access to benefits provided in the public schools but not by his parochial school—now at *public* expense? The question came in a different form, but this is what it amounted to. The Court decided (5/4) in *Zobrest et al., v. Catalina Foothills School District*, 509 U.S. 1 (1993), that the student *could* have a public-tax-paid sign-language interpreter when he transferred into a Catholic high school. James Zobrest, deaf from birth, had been furnished a sign-language interpreter by the Respondent while he attended the *public* schools. But then his parents, for religious reasons, enrolled him in Salpointe Catholic High School for his ninth grade, and requested Respondent, the public schools *he had just left*, to furnish the interpreter there.

The Respondent, after consulting the county attorney, concluded that it would violate the Establishment Clause of the First Amendment. Then the Arizona state attorney-general concurred in the county attorney's opinion. Petitioners brought suit in the District Court under 20 U.S.C. 1415(e)(4)(A) which gives district courts jurisdiction over disputes arising over services due disabled children under the Individuals with Disabilities Education Act. Petitioners asserted that the IDEA and Free Exercise Clause of the First Amendment *require* Respondent to furnish the interpreter at Salpointe. The Court, however, denied their request for a preliminary injunction, noting that providing an interpreter as requested would likely violate the Establishment Clause. The Ninth Circuit affirmed the District Court's holding, showing that even if the IDEA had a secular purpose, so satisfied the first prong of the *Lemon* test, it violated the second prong by having a primary effect of advancing religion, so would *violate* the Establishment Clause. Since the statute gave the District Court jurisdiction over such disputes, and the District Court ruled against providing an interpreter to the Catholic school at public expense, that should have been the end of it. But then it was appealed and Petitioners lost again in the Ninth Circuit. That certainly should have been the end of the dispute or the statute giving the District Court jurisdiction for such meant nothing. But Petitioners pressed it further.

Then Supreme Court *reversed* the Ninth Circuit decision with divided 5/4 Court over two basic issues, one of which was procedural and the other was on the constitutional merits.[14] The procedural question was whether the case should be approached from the Court's usual "judicial restraint" rule in which it looks to resolve cases on bases other than constitutional claims if at all possible. The merits of the case would seem to require a consistency with precedent cases, and cases in which the Court had distinguished a situation in which there was little or no chance of any religious indoctrination being done by the state, from a situation in which the requested aid to the parochial school was judged too risky because it was so easily morphed into indoctrination.

The Court raised the procedural question, but insisted that although Respondent had raised "several issues unrelated to the Establishment Clause question," since even the Ninth Circuit noted that Petitioner's appeal raised only First Amendment issues, the "prudential rule of avoiding constitutional questions has no application." However, J. Blackburn (dissenting, joined by J. Souter, Stevens, and O'Connor) in Part I argued that "[t]he obligation to avoid unnecessary adjudication of constitutional questions does not depend upon the parties' litigation strategy, but rather is a 'self-imposed limitation on the exercise of this Court's jurisdiction [that] has an importance to the institution that transcends the significance of particular controversies.'"[15] The dissent noted not only *this* procedural preference the Court usually follows, but also emphasized that whatever the judgment on the constitutional issue, the statutory and regulatory issues would still need to be resolved. So the dissent insisted that the judgment needs to be vacated and the case remanded to work through these "weighty nonconstitutional questions that were left unresolved."[16]

On the merits, the Court, consisting of five Justices who had no use for the *Lemon* criteria, insisted that "we have consistently held that government programs that neutrally provide benefits to a broad class of citizens defined without reference to religion are not readily subject to an Establishment Clause challenge just because sectarian institutions may also receive an attenuated financial benefit."[17] It emphasized "attenuated" or "incidental" benefits, stressing the benefits were given here only to the student upon the *request of the parents*, rather than benefits given directly to the parochial school, so the decision of the financial aid *cannot* be attributed to the state, and emphasizing that the IDEA distributes benefits neutrally, without regard to the "sectarian-nonsectarian, or public-nonpublic nature" of the school the child attends. Finally, it argued against the Respondents' reliance on *Meek v. Pittenger* and *Grand Rapids v. Ball*, that although the Court saw the "direct subsidy" to the religious school there, there is no such in the present case since "Salpointe is not relieved of an expense that it otherwise would have assumed in educating its students."[18] This statement is inexplicable. Does the Court mean that Salpointe simply would *not have paid for a translator*, therefore would *not have provided a translator* for Zobrest? So how would they have educated him?

Perhaps the most telling precedents, however, come in the *dissent*'s long recitation of the way the Court distinguished cases on the basis of which had the greatest risk of enabling the religious indoctrination:

> The Court has upheld the use of public school buses to transport children to and from school, *Everson v. Board of Ed. of Ewing*, 330 U.S. 1 (1947), while striking down the employment of publicly funded buses for field trips controlled by parochial school teachers, *Wolman,* 433 U.S., at 254. Similarly, the Court has permitted the provision of secular textbooks whose content is immutable and can be ascertained in advance, *Board of Ed. of Central School Dist. No. v. Allen,* 392 U.S. 236 (1968), while prohibiting the provision of any instructional materials or equipment that could be used to convey a religious message, such as slide projectors, tape recorder, record players, and the like, *Wolman*, 433 U.S. at 249. State-paid speech and hearing therapists have been allowed to administer diagnostic testing on the premises of parochial schools, id., at 241–242, whereas state-paid remedial teachers and counselors have not been authorized to offer their services because of the risk that they may inculcate religious beliefs, *Meek,* 421 U.S., at 371.[19]

The possibility of a sign-language interpreter continually communicating religious ideas in this pervasively sectarian atmosphere was certainly a much *more direct aid* in *inculcating religious beliefs* than slide projectors, record players, field trips, or remedial teachers. It was a much more obvious violation of the Establishment Clause than many the Court had already ruled against in this list of precedents. The Court simply had no reply to these precedent cases.

The dissent concluded that in this parochial school in which religious mission permeated every facet of the program, the sign-language interpreter would be continually conveying religious instruction and information to *Zobrest*. It noted that *Witters* and *Mueller v. Allen* also are important, since they dealt only with the payment of cash or a tax deduction, "where governmental involvement ended with the disbursement of funds or lessening of tax," whereas here the employee of the government (the interpreter) is involved "daily, and intimate governmental participation in the teaching and propagation of religion doctrine," and it would be a daily visual at least for his impressionable classmates, of the *government support* of the *religious* pursuit of their school. This merging of state and church can actually be a problem for both, and the dissent quotes *Illinois ex rel. McCollum v. Board of Ed. of School Dist. No. 71, Champaign Cty.*, 333 U.S. 209, 212 (1948), to the effect that the Establishment Clause rests upon the premise that both religion and government can best work to achieve their lofty aims if each is left free from the other within its respective sphere. This was precisely the sentiments of Madison and Jefferson long ago. But these arguments fell on deaf ears in a 5/4 decision.

If the special needs of a single student in a parochial school could require the state to furnish the deaf student an interpreter with public tax dollars, would a religious group who feared being *tainted* by public schools also have "equal access" to public funds which would provide for their "special needs" students as a large group from many different schools?

This case, also not strictly one of demanding "equal access" yet basically being built upon that concept, involved the *Board of Ed of Kiryas Joel Village School Dist. v. Grumet*, 512 U.S. 687 (1994). The Satmar Hasidic sect of Jews migrated after WWII from their home on the border of Hungary and Romania to the Williamsburg section of Brooklyn, New York, then in the 1970s purchased an undeveloped subdivision in the town of Monroe, incorporating in 1977. Since they preferred isolation and nonassimilation in the secular world, as they began to build their homogenous community, they ran into zoning laws as they altered single-family homes into accommodating extended families. This was eventually resolved by a general New York law which allowed different groups to found their own towns or cities.

Their children first had to attend the local public schools of the Monroe-Woodbury Central School District, which caused the families much emotional consternation because of the cultural differences between the Satmars and the other families. Although they were allowed to have their own private religious schools, funding special education students was very expensive, so at first their only choice was to keep the special needs children in the public school, or pay for private special education, or not meet the children's special needs at all. The majority of the children went the latter route.

Finally, in 1989, the New York legislature carved out a special separate public *school district* that followed the *precise boundaries* of the Satmar's territory, that is, was a tax-funded public school limited only to Satmar families and students (or other Hasidic students from outside the area), and was a school which offered *only* special education needs. The new school ultimately had barely 13 full-time local students, while two to three times that number stayed with their parochial school but attended the new school only on a part-time basis. The lower courts found it a violation of the Establishment Clause, not only by entangling or fusing government and religious functions but by thereby being incapable of guaranteeing this power delegated by the state to the community would be used exclusively for secular, neutral, and nonideological purposes as required by *Schempp*, *Lemon*, and *Nyquist*.

With only J. Scalia, J. Thomas, and C.J. Rehnquist dissenting, the Court found in *Larkin* that "a State may not delegate its civic authority to a group chosen according to a religious criterion." Although the "qualified voters" of *Kiryas Joel* were the ones vested with this power which was a bit different from it being a group's officers or leaders, it is only a difference in form, not of substance, since all the citizens or voters in the district were of a *single religion*, and could not be otherwise, so the law fixing the boundary of the new school district, funding it with public money, was based *only* on a *religious* requirement or preference in direct *violation* of the Court's consistent judgments against this.

More specifically, because the educational trend in New York at the time was for more and more consolidation of small districts, the general laws of New York were not applicable to give the Satmars the isolation they required. Thus, it required a "special Act" of the legislature, to enact a law which "ran counter to customary districting practices in the State"—chapter 748—to accommodate the group. Had it been a general and neutral law which provided this possibility for *any* religious or nonreligious group, that is, to grant them state funds to establish and govern their own small public school for the advantage only of their religious group, that would have required a different level of scrutiny. But there was no such law. The new law granting the new district for them was singularly *religious*, which makes that law an anomaly, and it lacked any guarantee that the legislature would provide similar benefits to any other religious and nonreligious groups, that is, if this is what a *neutral* law or approach means. The Court emphasized that "accommodation is not a principle without limits, and what petitioners seek is an adjustment to the Satmars' religiously grounded preferences that our cases do not countenance." In fact, "we have never hinted that an otherwise unconstitutional delegation of political power to a religious group could be saved as a religious accommodation."[20]

The Court pointed out alternative ways that could have been pursued by the Satmar and the state which would have been *un*objectionable. Finally, the Court insisted that Scalia's sarcastically exaggerated dissent (joined by C.J. Rehnquist and J. Thomas) was simply fighting figures of his own imagination. It wrote, "We do not disable a religiously homogeneous group from exercising political power conferred on it without regard to religion." The religious homogeneity was intentional in the establishment of the community's legal boundaries, and J. Scalia's failure to understand is simply because he seems *incapable* of accepting "the fact that this Court has long held that the First Amendment reaches more than classic, 18th century establishments."[21]

Otherwise, J. Kennedy's (concurring in the result) primary emphasis was that the two cases of *Aguilar v. Felton*, 473 U.S. 402 (1985) and *School Dist. of Grand Rapids v. Ball*, 473 U.S. 373 (1985), which seem to have forced the State of New York to go in the direction it did turned out to be problematical so in the future the Court may have to revisit those cases to be able to formulate a consistent test for Establishment. Finally, J. Stevens' short concurrence (joined by J. Blackmun and J. Ginsburg) suggested that the state could have met the Satmar community's concerns of the emotional trauma or fear their children felt by "teaching their schoolmates to be tolerant and respectful of Satmar customs, to promote diversity and appreciation of differences within the public schools. But instead the state chose the route of allowing the Satmar group to become even more isolated, which would assure the parents that the children would remain in that religious group rather than learning how to live with diverse people whose ideas might enrich them." This is precisely the sense of unity of a democracy that can embrace differences that Rawls's approach proposed.

In 1995, the idea of "equal access" brought a very strange case to the Court in which a known public forum established the legal speech parameters, and the question was whether by following these, the party would violate the Establishment Clause. This was a case involving the grounds of the Ohio state capitol: *Capitol Square Review and Advisory Board v. Pinette*, 515 U.S. 753 (1995). The "speech" was a religious symbol, a cross. The request was to place an unattended *cross* at this public forum site. The party requesting permission to do so was the Ku Klux Klan.[22]

The Capitol Square Review and Advisory Board accepted formal requests for any displays at the forum, and over the years had allowed a wide variety of groups, including the United Way and even the Klan, to use the space with few restrictions other than general safety and health considerations. On this occasion, however, the Board turned the Klan down, so it sought and received an injunction through the District Court, which was later affirmed by the

Sixth Circuit, on the grounds that the city had no justification for denying the display. The Supreme Court heard the case since the question itself of a religious symbol on public grounds had been given different opinions in different Circuit courts.

The Court felt it easily could determine that since everyone familiar with the site knew it was a "public forum," there would not be any possibility of some reasonable person thinking this cross was endorsed by the government or was the government's message. It was simply private expression. On the distinction of government speech and private speech, the Court insisted that "there is a crucial difference between government speech endorsing religion, which the Establishment Clause forbids, and private speech endorsing religion, which the Free Speech and Free Exercise Clauses protect."[23] Private speech rights include religious speech as surely as secular speech. The right to use government property for one's private speech is not an unlimited freedom, but in the case that the site was given the status by the government of a public forum, the primary restrictions that the government can impose are reasonable content-neutral time, place, and manner restrictions. So far as regulating the content of the private expressions or speech in such an open forum, government can do so only if it can show compelling interests that require it, and only if its regulations are narrowly tailored to accomplish that interest.

The Court saw *Lamb's Chapel v. Center Moriches Union Free School Dist.*, 508 U.S. 384, *Widmar v. Vincent*, 454 U.S. 263, and the two crèche cases of *Lynch v. Donnelly*, 465 U.S. 668, and *County of Allegheny v. American Civil Liberties Union, Greater Pittsburgh Chapter*, 492 U.S. 573, as the crucial precedents and therefore dispositive cases. The first two, the Court insisted, were the only two times the specific question arose of whether the government, in a public forum, could regulate the content of private religious speech, and in both cases the answer was that it could *not*. The Court saw the same characteristics of the present situation and *Lamb's Chapel* and *Widmar*, namely the site was open to a variety of uses or broad spectrum of groups, as a public forum; the government was not directly involved in sponsoring the religious expression, as all groups had to obtain permission in the same way to engage in such expression on the site; and any benefits that accrued to the religion in question were strictly incidental. In the crèche cases, the nativity scene on the Grand Staircase in *Allegheny* was strictly religious and not available to other displays, so was the county's favoring of a particular religion. Had it been open to other religious displays during that period, the Court suggests it would have been no violation of the Establishment clause because it would not have been a preference of one religion. *Lynch*, however, was *not* decided because of the presence of other religious displays to reduce the preferential appearance, but by the secular, celebratory atmosphere which reduced the nativity scene to a merely historical reminder and reason for celebrating.

J. O'Connor, in her concurring opinion in *Lynch*, had formulated a new test of the perception of a reasonable person being that the display or message was one of government endorsement. Her concurring opinion in *Capitol Square* focused on the "endorsement" test, and she and J. Scalia (writing for the Court) crossed swords on this issue, with his insistence that to force such government neutrality on private speech at an open forum would be to hamstring the government, but she contended that *his* test had, in fact, no precedent in the Court's decisions.

There was a concurrence in *Capital Square v. Pinette* so far as the decision, since it was narrowly focused only on the question of whether the Board had sufficient grounds for turning down the KKK's request to set up the cross in order to honor the Establishment Clause, but the justices split like crazy on the reasoning behind the decision, so it was only a plurality opinion, *allowing the display*. But as J. Thomas so aptly pointed out in his brief concurrence, although perhaps a few of the members of the KKK are interested in Christianity, the *actual use* of the cross by the KKK is *not* a religious but a *political* message of *white supremacy and racial hatred*. He concluded that their appropriation of the cross, which reminds others of their "cross burning" (accompanying the execution of a former slave), is simply to transform a sacred symbol into a symbol of hate, so this was really not an Establishment issue at all. Why did the KKK's statement of its purpose not seem as a "sham" purpose as had the purpose and effect of the law regarding teaching Creation Science only eight years before, in *Edwards v. Aguillard*?

Here all the Justices said they were going to examine was the question of the "cross" only from the Establishment angle, since that is the way it was brought to the Court, therefore abstaining from any political analysis which the Petitioner had raised.[24] But *why? Edwards v. Aguillard* was brought by the litigants as a question of a "balanced scientific education" rather than one-sided approach, which the *Court rejected* as a "sham" purpose. Was the Court really *unaware* of the meaning and use of the cross with the KKK? That is the real question that went unanswered. Even very few reasonable citizens of the United States think that a cross erected by the Ku Klux Klan is primarily a religious symbol since the organization has always used it as a symbol of themselves, that is, of *racial hatred*. Is their white supremacy really that powerful in the United States that it dictates what a symbol means which is so different from the way a reasonable observer would see it?[25]

The question of limited public forums vs. open public forums, and specifically what either can or must be allowed or cannot be allowed under the Establishment Clause, not just under "Free Speech," arose also in 1995 in *Ronald W. Rosenberger, et al., Petitioners v. Rector and Visitors of the*

University of Virginia, et al., 515 U.S. 819. It was another 5/4 decision in which both sides accused the other of misrepresenting precedent cases and overlooking the obvious. In a nutshell, the Court decided the case on "Free Speech" grounds rather than religious grounds under the Establishment Clause, and the dissent argued that the precedent ignored by the Court was its many cases of Establishment Clause issues in which it had articulated that the one absolute of the Establishment adjudication is that government cannot *provide money or benefits directly* for the *propagation of a religious* message. But it *can* on Free Speech grounds? That is the point of the shifting of cases from the Establishment clause to the Free Exercise clause, since the latter tradition even *required* one to have a religious purpose, where the earlier adjudication at the time of this case under the Establishment Clause promised to find it a violation.

J. Kennedy, for the Court, emphasized that the university was at fault in discriminating against a Christian student group since it had allowed a student forum for a variety of interests with the proviso that they would pledge not to discriminate in their membership, that the majority of their members are students and all of their managing officers are full-time students, and their written materials would include a disclaimer about their activity and purpose, namely, that it was their private speech and not that of the university. The University of Virginia allowed these groups to use its facilities including rooms and computer terminals. The groups were referred to as "Contracted Independent Organizations," and any CIO could exist and operate at the university.

But some CIOs were also entitled to apply for funds from the Student Activities Fund (SAF). University guidelines specified that any groups applying for these funds must be "related to the educational purpose of the University," must be administered not only within the purpose of the university but also consistent with state and federal law, and it articulated 11 categories that would qualify for such funds. It also specified that certain kinds of activities of CIOs would *not* qualify for these funds, and this included "religious activities, philanthropic contributions and activities, political activities, activities that would jeopardize the university's tax exempt states, those which involve payment of honoraria or similar fees, or social entertainment or related expenses."

Petitioner's organization, Wide Awake Productions (WAP), formed by Ronald Rosenberger and other undergraduates in 1990, qualified as a CIO. Its purpose was to publish a magazine "of philosophical and religious expression" to emphasize its idea of Christian commitment, admonishing readers to proclaim their faith and encourage others to embrace Christianity, in its words, to have a "personal relationship with Jesus Christ." The magazine's primary advertisers were Christian churches, Christian bookstores, and

Christian study centers. So WAP was a recognized CIO but *not* entitled to SAF funding. They nevertheless *insisted on being funded* and were turned down when they presented a $5,862 bill from their printer.

Their recourse was to take their case to the District Court, alleging that the refusal by the university to pay their printing bill was based solely on its "religious editorial viewpoint." The District Court ruled it was not impermissible content or viewpoint discrimination, that the university's Establishment Clause concern over "religious activities" of the group justified its denial for payment for the group's magazine. On appeal by the group, the Fourth Circuit acknowledged that the guidelines actually did discriminate on the basis of content, but it affirmed the District Court by insisting that that the alleged discrimination by the university was justified by its compelling interest in maintaining a strict separation of church and state.

J. Kennedy, writing for the Court (5/4), acknowledged that the university had a right to establish a "limited public forum," but insisted that when government (here the university) targets *not* subject matter but particular views, it wrongly engages in *illegal viewpoint discrimination.* He admitted that even in *Lamb's Chapel,* which he utilized to condemn the university's guidelines, the Court had acknowledged that the body establishing the limited public forum has the right to preserve that forum for the use to which it dedicated the forum. He also acknowledged that *content* discrimination which limits speech content to that for which the forum was established is *not illegal* unless it goes further and manifests a "viewpoint discrimination" which is "presumed impermissible when directed against speech otherwise within the forum's limitations."

What he does *not* show is that the religious speech was ever *within* the forum's limitations so far as qualifying for funding. He insisted that the guidelines were used to discriminate only against a Christian "viewpoint," so here he uses *Lamb's Chapel* to buttress his argument, yet he ironically *confuses* in the same paragraph a "Christian perspective" with a "religious perspective." The guidelines did not single out "Christian" but "religion," the much broader subject of *content,* as not qualifying for funding. Since the Court said that the "viewpoint" was only a narrower subset of "content," it should not have confused the two this way.

Further, the Court had earlier in its recitation of the facts, made the inaccurate statement that WAP was never recognized by the university as a "religious organization" or it would never have been given the CIO status by the university. Unless J. Kennedy had grounds for distinguishing between "religious organization" and "religious activity," there was nothing in the application to be a CIO that had anything to do with either. Rather, the guidelines simply prohibited *funding* a "religious activity" which is used interchangeably with "religious organization" as a group whose "purpose is to practice a devotion to an acknowledged ultimate reality or deity." Such a group was *not disallowed* from being a CIO, but simply unqualified for any university (government) funding since it clashed with the university's ethical stance.

This all revealed the fact that the Court never specified what the *distinction* between "viewpoint" and "content" *must be* although it based its decision on its contention that what the university engaged in was *illegal viewpoint discrimination.* Of course, "content" seems the broader category (and the Court admits that the guidelines drew lines based on content, not viewpoint, and the distinction is "not a precise one"), but nevertheless it was convinced that the WAP was turned down for the illegal purpose of "viewpoint discrimination," despite the fact that the guidelines list only "religion" as the broad subject matter or general content, similar to the way the First Amendment does not prohibit *merely* the "establishment" of certain "viewpoints" within a religion, but rather establishing the religion, including *any* religion.[26]

Finally, the Court emphasized what it thought was its best "Free Speech" argument to show that the university was engaging in "viewpoint discrimination." It quoted the university's guidelines that specified groups that would be denied funding as those that "primarily promote or manifest a particular belief in or about a deity or an ultimate reality." From this the Court insisted that were this rule followed, it would bar the writings of any student who mentioned in his article anyone who spoke of a deity or ultimate reality, including such great minds as "Plato, Spinoza, and Descartes. . . . Karl Marx, Bertrand Russell," and so on and sarcastically concluded that "Plato could contrive perhaps to submit an acceptable essay on making pasta or peanut butter cookies, provided he did not point out their (necessary) imperfections."[27] But the guidelines denied funding only to those who "primarily promote[d] or manifest[ed] a particular belief in or about a deity or an ultimate reality."

Here the Court's logic dropped out of its bag. Sarcasm could not substitute for logic. The Court seemed unaware that the typical large university itself has a philosophical curriculum that includes all of these great thinkers and many more from quite different religious and philosophical traditions. The difference between the university's approach to them and what WAP was doing is the difference between day and night. University curriculum is geared to making people think, to question, to analyze—*not to indoctrinate.* The WAP magazines were clearly and blatantly instruments to *indoctrinate,* to propagate a *single* view, even by young people who have *never* actually studied historically what they are propagating. Did the Court really think the faculty at the university could approach any of the great thinkers of the West (or East) with the goal of converting all the students to that single thinker, totally uncritically and uninformed? When Plato, Descartes, or others are read, discussed, analyzed by the university's qualified professors, it is an *objective* analysis, working critically with questions underlying the author or scholar, questions dealing with the author's presuppositions and/or arguments he or she used to buttress his or her epistemology, phenomenology, ontology, and so forth. It is offered to teach the students *to think on their own, to learn to be critical* in their analyses rather than accepting any and every claim that they hear. It is to enable the students to *become autonomous* individuals, to make their own judgments rather than being enslaved to a single view or single content, no matter how authoritative the latter was experienced.

How the Court can create such a *false equivalence* is difficult to see, especially since even legal minds are supposed to be able to analyze, compare, contrast, and ask *critical questions*—none of which was what the journal of the WAP did. It was an indoctrinating and uninformed student magazine. The dissent noted how little of the contents of the magazine by WAP were even mentioned by the Court, and even those quite superficially. WAP's content and viewpoint was to propagate only *one view of one religion*, not to approach any religion from a scholarly, historical, or objective way. That was where the "skewing" which the Court mentions took place, not in the guidelines' limiting funding to avoid divisiveness, but perhaps also by the Court's inability to distinguish unscholarly religious propaganda from higher education's methods.

J. Souter, dissenting, was joined by J. Stevens, J. Ginsburg, and J. Breyer. He documented the Court's history of recognizing and honoring an invariable or absolute regarding Establishment jurisdiction: "using public funds for the direct subsidization of preaching the word is categorically forbidden under the Establishment Clause." He insisted that the Court here ignored the obvious by its "erroneous treatment of some familiar principles of law implementing the First Amendment's Establishment and Speech Clauses, and by viewing the very funds in question as beyond the reach of the Establishment Clause's funding restrictions as such." The Court misread Madison and Jefferson to begin with, then misconstrued *Everson*, *Grand Rapids*, *Wolman*, and *Nyquist*. But the Court also failed to read various issues of Wide Awake's magazine in its uncritical preaching of the Christian message. The Court's utilization of "evenhandedness" was only a part of the test of neutrality. When government's neutrality ultimately benefits a specific religion, "the Establishment Clause requires some justification beyond evenhandedness on the government's part; and that direct public funding of core sectarian activities, even if accomplished pursuant to an evenhanded program, would be entirely inconsistent with the Establishment Clause and would strike at the very heart of the Clause's protection."[28]

J. Souter noted that the three most recent cases that permitted indirect aid to religion (*Mueller v. Allen*, *Witters v. Washington Dept. of Services for Blind*, and *Zobrest v. Catalina Foothills*) are *quite different* from the present case in the fact that the funding was only indirect, reaching religious institutions "only as a result of the genuinely independent and private choices of aid recipients." In the present case, unlike those three, there is here no "third party" standing between the government and the ultimate religious beneficiary to "break the circuit by its independent discretion to put state money to religious use." Finally, J. Souter, in his dissent, argued that "evenhandedness as one element of a permissibly attenuated benefit is, of course, a far cry from evenhandedness as a sufficient condition of constitutionality for direct financial support of religious proselytization."[29]

Finally, among other arguments, the dissent notes that what justifies the university's funding content limitations is simply that it is a university in which people are challenged to become critical in their analyses and weighing of claims, so what obviously *does not fit* this purpose of the university is speech that is *sheer advocacy*. The school simply denies "funding for hortatory speech that 'primarily promotes or manifests' any view on the merits of religion; they deny funding for the entire subject matter of religious apologetics."[30] But the Court ran roughshod over the university's educational, critical purposes to approve a singular, uninformed and uncritical defense (or apologetic) of *one view of one religion.*

CHALLENGES OF "NEUTRALITY," "PRIVATE CHOICE," "DIVERTIBILITY," AND HISTORICAL LONGEVITY

The reader must understand that just because the Supreme Court makes a decision on a case does not mean that states who were not involved in that case will accept or follow the decision. Of course, they are *legally expected to*, but many simply ignore it and go on engaging in the newly prohibited practices or with illegal state laws until such time that *they individually* get challenged. So where people were accustomed to having public prayer at football games at the public high schools, they might not be deterred from that practice merely because of the Court's earlier opinions in *Engle, Schempp, Wallace v. Jaffree*, or even *Lee v. Wiseman*. Certainly not in a state such as Texas where high school "Friday night football" is so big, so vital a part of the culture! If a District Court had actually asserted in the *Wallace v. Jaffree* case in 1985 that Alabama could legally establish its *own state religion* (which the "Civil War" Amendments had made illegal a century before, and the First Amendment was explicitly "incorporated" into all state law by the 1940 *Cantwell v. Connecticut* and 1947 *Everson v. Bd. of Education* decisions of the Supreme Court), the same must have been the thinking of those Texans who continued to promote prayers at the football games despite all the Court decisions against prayer in the public schools.

When a state or party obtains a negative result from the Court on an Establishment case, if people want to get a different decision on a similar practice, they may easily attempt to disguise the "purpose" or "effect" of their law they want to be legal, or they may approach it from a Free Exercise slant, or they may find the "seam" in the fabric of the Court. In cases where a state is insistent on getting its way after the Court has ruled even against it directly, it may attack that "seam" or weak point by new arguments or by insisting that the Justices who sided against them earlier exaggerated precedents of the Court, or by insisting that the facts have changed, or by finding Justices who express a discontent against a former criteria of judgment—especially if it is the one that caused their earlier loss.

Changing Law Not by Overruling Past Decisions but by Challenging Presumptions

Thus, it was that in 1997, New York State *brought back* a case from 1985 (*Aguilar v. Felton*), challenging the earlier negative judgment it had received from the Court. Now in *Agostini v. Felton*, 521 U.S. 203 (1997), the state sought relief under Federal Rule of Civil Procedure 60(b)(5) from the earlier injunction issued by the District Court upon remand by the Supreme Court in 1985. In 1966, federal funds began to be channeled through Title 1 to local education agencies in New York State who were authorized to spend these funds to provide remedial education, guidance, and job counseling to eligible students. To be an eligible student, one had to live in a low-income area and be at risk of failing student performance standards. Funds were provided both to public schools and private schools without any discrimination, which the Court took to mean that there was no financial incentive for parents to switch schools, placing their children in parochial schools.

As early as 1966, 10% of these funds were used for students in private schools, and more than 90% of the private schools were religious schools, as was the case in 1985 when they were almost entirely Catholic schools. Prior to 1985, New York tried to resolve the problem by bringing in portable housing close to the parochial school to alleviate the negative impression of public school teaching taking place on the premises of the parochial schools since that had been earlier prohibited. It limited the services to private school students who were eligible for the aid rather than on a school-wide basis, and required that the Local Education Agency be entrusted with the funding and remain in complete control over the funds, retaining ownership in all materials used.

The earlier Court was aware that even though a large majority of the public school teachers who volunteered for the program to teach in the parochial schools (especially in *Grand Rapids v. Ball*) had earlier actually taught in the parochial schools, the present Court now insisted that they ended up in parochial schools whose religious affiliations were *different* from their own.[31] Further, all services had to be "secular, neutral, and nonideological," all services had to be supplemental, in *no case* simply supplanting or *substituting* the public-funded services for parallel services already offered by the private schools,[32] and all religious symbols had to be removed from the classrooms in which the Title I services were to be offered.

Finally, the public school teachers offering the remedial services were prohibited from any team teaching with faculty of the private school, although the rules recognized that the Title 1 teachers might have to consult with students' regular classroom teachers, and the guidelines ensured "compliance" of the rules by having a field supervisor make at least one unannounced visit to teach Title 1 teacher's classroom each month. But this was challenged in 1978 and resulted in the *Aguilar v. Felton* case of 1985, in which the District Court granted summary judgment for the Board (the LEA), but the Second Circuit reversed, by using *Meek v. Pittenger* and *Wolman v. Walter*, to rule that it created an illegal "excessive entanglement," which was the third prong of the *Lemon* test, to which the Supreme Court agreed in 1985.

Because of the negative decision in *Ball* and *Aguillard* in 1985, on remand, the District Court issued a permanent injunction *prohibiting* the use of public funds even under Title 1 for providing public school teachers and guidance counselors to provide their services on the premises of the sectarian schools in New York City. The school board (LEA) abandoned using parochial school sites, reverting to its earlier use of public school sites, leased sites, and mobile instructional units parked near parochial schools. It also offered expensive computer-aided instruction "on premises" at the parochial schools since the public school teachers did not have to be present there. After initial expenses of over 100 million, and averaging thereafter 15 million per year, since these "alternative delivery systems" did not qualify for other state funds, forcing the Title 1 grants to cover everything, including all the nonteaching logistical aspects of the services, the state had to cut back on the number of students served since they claimed they had to deduct 7.9 million "off the top" to comply with the *Aguilar* decision of 1985.

In 1995, the Board and new parents filed motions in District Court for relief from this injunction under Federal Rule of Civil Procedure 60(b). They argued that the excessive costs justified some relief as "changed circumstances," and relief from the injunction, via rule 60(b) according to *Rufo v. Inmates of Suffolk County Jail*, 502 U.S. 367, 388 (1992). They also argued that the law had also changed since five Supreme Court Justices in *Board of Ed. of Kiryas Joel Village School Dist. v. Grumet* (1994) had expressed a need to *reconsider Aguilar*, since they did not feel the 1985 case was any longer good law. So this further justified relief. But the District Court and

Second Circuit *denied* their motion on the merits, declaring that *Aguilar* (and its companion case in 1985, *Grand Rapids v. Ball)* had not yet been over-turned by the Court.

The Court now made much out of the appropriate reluctance of the lower courts to overrule what was still good law, since the Court itself had not explicitly overruled it. However, it went further by disagreeing with the lower courts by ruling that relief can be sought under 60(b)(5) when either the factual conditions or the law has substantially changed, and the Court's "Establishment" criteria and approach has changed so much since 1985, that a new examination under the Court's present criteria gives the opposite result. Not surprisingly, the same Justices that divided 5/4 in the *Rosenberger* (1985) case we've just summarized, divided with the same Justices in another 5/4 split, ignoring Court precedents prior to 1985 as well as the continual usage of the *Lemon* criteria up to the turn of the new millennium.

J. O'Connor, writing for the *Agostini* Court, noted that the appeal to the great costs of the present program, as well as the reference to five of the Justices favoring a reexamination of the case, has no bearing on the merit of the case. The only question is whether the Court's Establishment cases subse-quent to *Aguilar v. Felton* and *Grand Rapids v. Ball* have themselves in fact undermined that law's criteria or tests, making it no longer good law. For the Court to say it discovered some new criteria that were better in deciding what was "Constitutional" than it had utilized before means that the Court itself *does* "make" law. Its development of any "criteria" for judging something alleged as "Constitutional," as well as any *changing* of that criteria becomes a *super-law* the Court devises for evaluating laws of a lower order. That's what "criteria" or "tests" mean. How it thought it could distinguish its *constant principles* from such *"criteria"* is not at all clear since the criteria then would have had to be based on the *same principles as before*.

In any case, the Court itself *had changed*, with only two Justices of the 1985 decision still on the Court by 1997. But the *Agostini* Court said the real question was only whether the Court's "later Establishment Clause cases [i.e. post 1985] have so undermined *Aguilar* that it is no longer good law." Thus, the task is to ascertain what was the "rationale upon which *Aguilar . . .* and *Ball . . .* rested."[33] J. O'Connor, for the Court, presented her view of the rationale first of *Ball*, then *Aguilar*, in 1985.

Since the Court had used only two tests, the *Lemon* "three prongs" and the "historical" test of *Marsh*, did the Court move to the "historical" one to avoid *Lemon*? No. Because any "historical" approach would have taken the Court back to days when there was no such thing as public schools, when only the wealthy could get an education. And those parochial schools were not funded by the government, nor did they offer remedial classes, guidance, and other services.

Instead, J. O'Connor, for the *Agostini* Court, attacked the "*presumptions*" of the *Ball* and *Aguilar* Courts, which had utilized the *Lemon* test. It was all a matter of insisting that the Court went too far in its "presumptions" in those cases, but J. O'Connor *exaggerated* these in order to make them appear nonsensical and therefore vulnerable. The Court emphasized that the *Ball* Court had been decided by the *Lemon* test especially the "effects" prong, since the *Ball* Court saw its effect was not primarily secular but rather obviously advanced religion. J. O'Connor alleged the *Lemon* "effect" test saw the effect *not* secular which caused the negative decision. She insisted the *Ball* Court "rested on three assumptions" which are no longer judged as credible: (1) that any public teachers working on the premises of a parochial school which has an "atmosphere dedicated to the advancement of religious belief" could either intentionally or inadvertently get involved in inculcating that religious belief;[34] (2) the use of public school teachers in the parochial school is a "graphic symbol of the 'concert or union or dependency' of church and state" especially to children in their formative years, a symbolic union which would "convey a message of government endorsement"; and (3) the arrangement "impermissibly financed religious indoctrination by subsidizing" the primary religious mission of the school since the aid was "direct and substantial" rather than merely "indirect, remote, or incidental," and the Court, in many opinions had upheld the aid if it was "indirect or incident," whereas it invalidated it if it was "direct and substantial."

Grand Rapids v. Ball fell into the latter category.[35] The *Ball* Court was following *Meek v. Pittenger* in the first and third assumptions, and following *Zorach v. Clauson* in the second. J. O'Connor, for the Court noted that in *Ball*, the Court thought the aid of instructional materials could themselves be used to teach religion, and it also advanced religion "by freeing up money for religious indoctrination that the school would otherwise have devoted to secular education."[36] She emphasized for the Court, however, that the *Ball* Court did not give any weight to the fact that the student received the aid, not the school, nor did it note that the aid was only a "supplement" to existing courses. The problem with the latter is if it were only supplemental rather than supplanting or substituting public funds for the funds the school already used for the existing classes, then the Court would never have mentioned the problem of "freeing up money" that we just quoted.

The Court analyzed the rationale of the earlier *Aguilar* Court as following closely the same as *Ball* (utilizing the *Lemon* test), it added the third prong of the *Lemon* test, noting that the level of monitoring required to be certain of a secular effect rather than religious indoctrination would "inevitably resul[t] in the excessive entanglement of church and state," that is, a "comprehensive, discriminating, and continuing state surveillance" (*Lemon*) or "excessive monitoring . . . to be certain that public school officials do not inculcate religion" (*Meek*). The Court said the New York case (*Aguilar*) was like *Lemon* and *Meek*, involving a "pervasively sectarian environment" which required "pervasive monitoring" resulting in the "excessive entanglement" prohibited by the Establishment Clause.

After analyzing the rationale in these specific ways, J. O'Connor, for the Court, then "distilled" the "essence" of all this alleged impermissible "effect" to "three assumptions: (i) any public employee who works on the premises of a religious school is presumed to inculcate religion in her work; (ii) the presence of public employees on private school premises creates a symbolic union between church and state; and (iii) any and all public aid that directly aids the educational function of religious schools impermissibly finances religious indoctrination, even if the aid reaches such schools as a consequence of private decision making." Then she noted that *Aguilar* added a fourth assumption, that the New York program "necessitated an excessive government entanglement with religion because public employees who teach on the premises of religious school must be closely monitored to ensure that they do not inculcate religion."[37]

The reason I am listing these sets of "rationale" which J. O'Connor formulated, and doing so in her own words as much as possible, is to show that the sets are not identical at all. We must be clear of what seemed to be at stake. If J. O'Connor, for the *Agostini* Court, was correct in emphasizing that *Ball* and *Aguilar* were based on incorrect presumptions (which were themselves not simply concocted out of whole cloth, but were derived by reasonable Justices from the Court's precedent cases), then not just *Ball* and *Aguilar*, but all the relevant earlier cases that formed the base for these incorrect presumptions were themselves faulty decisions which all needed to be corrected. If the presumptions, however, were only *harmless*, then *none* of the earlier cases need be overturned, nor would the Court have any present reason to change the standards and their presumptions behind them.

But the Court took *neither* of these logical alternatives. Instead, it ruled differently in the revisiting of *Aguilar v. Felton* in the present *Agostini v. Felton*, but *never* admitted being *significantly wrong* in its earlier decisions, so no further corrections were made. The lower courts were simply left hanging since none of those Circuit Courts could state what J. Scalia did that the Court uses *Lemon* when it will give the result the Court wants, and when it will not, the Court simply does not use it, as we saw earlier. Scalia's words spoke volumes to Circuit Courts, especially if the Circuit Court could read the minds of the Supreme Court Justices.

But back to the way the Court here manipulated the alleged false "presumptions." From the first group, J. O'Connor suddenly exaggerated elements to form the second group, elements which were not at all in the *Ball* or *Aguilar* decisions she was examining, nor do they square with her first set. Beginning with the "(iii)" of the second set, it is *not true* at all that the *Ball* or *Aguilar* Court held that "any and all aid that directly aids the educational function of religious schools impermissibly finances religious indoctrination," since the Court has approved aid such as secular textbooks (*Bd of Education v. Allen*, 1968), state-mandated tests, diagnostic services, therapeutic and remedial services (*Wolman v. Walter*, 1977; *Committee for Public Ed. & Religious Liberty v. Regan*, 1980), and even state tax deductions to parents for cost of tuition, textbooks, and transportation to parochial schools (*Mueller v. Allen*, 1983; *Everson v. Bd of Education*, 1947).

Nor is it true that this form of blanket impermissible effect was *ever* held by the Court or in *Ball* and *Aguilar*, even if the aid was due to "private decision making," as the Court says. "Private decision making" had not yet been clarified by the Court. If the decision that is the focus is that only of the parent of a student, then any and all students attending any private schools (religious or secular) would qualify since the parents are usually the ones responsible for that "private decision." But that surely would not mean that because a parent made a decision about where the child was to attend a school, the *government was never involved* in making any pertinent *decisions* regarding the school or its programs or funding, which decisions themselves might have induced or even totally persuaded the parents to make their own "private decision"—not as long as parochial schools are continually asking the government to fund more and more of their programs.

Rather, those "decisions" are made *first and foremost by the government*, without which a parent's or student's decision to attend a certain school would mean nothing regarding any aid from the government. The "aid" comes from the *decision* made by the *government*; only the "receiving of the aid" comes from a decision made by parents, but whether they receive any aid is *totally dependent* upon the *government's prior decision* to *offer the aid*, and the parents might or might not need any "incentive." The government's actual aid made available does not depend upon a showing of it being an "incentive" to parents unless the Court is to interview every parent who sends a child to the school to make the inquiry and set some criteria that if met would make the incentive too much and therefore illegal. While the Court does not try to totally dismiss the "excessive entanglement" prohibition of *Lemon*, to have to engage in this kind of procedure (not to mention what the legislature would have to do to make sure the aid was not too much an incentive) would certainly be such an illegal entanglement. To suggest that the *parents' decision itself* to place their child in a parochial school entitles them to public taxes is to ignore the fact that the tax expenditure comes only from a *decision made by the legislature*. It was Madison and Jefferson who said even three pence of public taxes going to any religious organization, whatever its function, is illegal. As we saw, Rawls said we have a choice, and funding one particular religion was the choice for unremitting controversy and hostilities rather than unity.

Even the *Witters* case, which some members of the Court have become so intent to use as an example of a "private decision," which thereby *precludes* any possibility that anyone would think the aid was a government endorsement, is *fictitious*. The primary "decision" to fund the scholarships was made by the state of Washington, without which, the student would have been left high and dry, no matter what his decision. He was already enrolled in the school in a program to become a pastor, missionary, or youth director in some church. In *Witters*, of course, the Court insisted that there was no showing that the funds went to *religiously indoctrinate* or that they assisted the school in its religious mission, but that obviously is false when one examines Witters's own program of study and intended vocation as well as the school's religious mission. So the distillation of the primary question to whether any aid can reasonably be thought as a government's aid to religious indoctrination is simply a conclusion which *contradicts the evidence*.

To return to J. O'Connor's two lists, if we compare (1) of the first list with (i) of J. O'Connor's second list which "distilled to essentials," the *Ball* Court did not presume that "any public employee who works on the premises of a religious school is presumed to inculcate religion in her work." The Court had, however, acknowledged on several occasions that indoctrination would be *less likely* from a secular textbook chosen by the state than it would be a teacher, whose actual words are not confined to fixed print. That argument always seemed to make sense to the earlier Court. This problem area, however, the likelihood of indoctrination of the less restricted teacher (as compared with a written text) would be *exacerbated* by virtue of the fact that the *majority* of the "public school" teachers now volunteering for the service with the parochial schools had *earlier been faculty at the parochial schools*, nearly all of which were Catholic. That is a crucial factor that J. O'Connor skips over for the Court.

So the *Ball* Court did admit that a public school teacher as a Title l teacher in the parochial school *might* either intentionally or inadvertently inculcate religious tenets or beliefs. It was the possibility, *not the presumption* of inevitability, that required monitoring as the earlier Court saw it. So J. O'Connor simply mutilated the former decisions in *Ball* and *Aguilar*. Even in *Meek*, admitting that funding textbooks was lawful, both funding of instructional materials and equipment has a primary religious benefit, *not* merely incidental one, so was *illegal*, and funding auxiliary services which had a secular purpose nevertheless created necessary surveillance so created excessive entanglement. So the Court here is not simply overturning *Ball* and *Aguilar*, but either ignoring or defying *nearly all the other cases* the earlier Courts had decided regarding parochial schools. The "pervasively" sectarian feature of the schools makes the *indoctrination almost a certainty* by Roman Catholic guidelines even submitted by the dissent in *Everson*.

Finally, comparing (2) with the later (ii), the *Ball* Court quoted *Zorach v. Clauson*, that the problem of the union of state and church was especially important since the issue was how the arrangement would be perceived by "children in their formative years" (*Ball* at 390). Notably, in "ii," J. O'Connor omitted that phrase about the children. Yet the *impression made on children* was always a strong consideration by the Court, especially in cases involving school prayers or devotionals in public schools but also involving, as in *Ball*, public school teachers working for the parochial schools. Were the children actually mature enough to see them as completely separate, to never think that the public school teachers were approving the parochial school's religious agenda? But the Court *omits* analyzing that vital concern about the children.

So, basically, by altering each of the three "assumptions" in the second list, J. O'Connor was able to exaggerate a problem or misrepresent the earlier Court's presumptions and actual decisions. The question is why she did this? Was it so the Court's next paragraph could insist that while "our more recent cases have undermined the assumptions upon which *Ball* and *Aguilar* relied, to be sure, the general principles we use to evaluate whether government aid violates the Establishment Clause have not changed since *Aguilar* was decided."[38] Really?

But *Marsh* changed the general principles for evaluating Establishment Clause cases radically, two years prior to *Aguilar*, totally deserting the *Lemon* test, and *Marsh* then served as a precedent thereafter anytime sufficient members of the Court wanted to approve a certain law. The "majority" would then allude to its "long history" and ignore *Lemon* as J. Scalia articulated in his dissent in *Kiryas Joel*. But the Court does not admit that its decision in *Marsh* was a mistake, a quite arbitrary approval of an established Christian practice, just as it seldom if ever makes the same claim for other "practices" of the late eighteenth century such as the discrimination against women and the discrimination against Native Americans and African Americans and the owning of slaves, and these *persisted more publically for decades* beyond the Constitutional Founding than any governmental prayers. Mere longevity of a practice in history *per se* proves *nothing* by itself, nothing ethically, and therefore hopefully nothing legally.

J. O'Connor, for the Court, insisted that *Zobrest* nullified the "presumptions" in *Meek* and *Ball* that the "placement of public employees on parochial school grounds inevitably results in the impermissible effect of state-sponsored indoctrination or constitutes a symbolic union between government and religion." *Zobrest* disavowed the notion that "the Establishment Clause [laid] down [an] absolute bar to the placing of a public employee in a sectarian school"—the assumption that the mere "presence" of the public school teacher on the property of the parochial school "presumed" the teacher's inculcating religion in the students. *Zobrest* proved that a public school teacher could be trusted not to try to indoctrinate. But *Zobrest* did *not*, as did this case, involve *former parochial school teachers*, turned public school teachers, *returning* to teach as *public school teachers in the parochial schools*. That is a *vital distinction* completely overlooked here by the Court.

As J. Souter challenged the Court, this "aid" in *Zobrest* was only *translating* in sign language what the *parochial school teacher was saying*. The Court argued there was no indication that the interpreter changed any of the message, so no "government indoctrination took place." But J. Souter noted that a sign-language interpreter is quite different from just a teacher who is teaching a secular subject or remedial skills, since the translator is simply repeating what the *teacher* is saying, so is restricted, more like a textbook would be, so is only a vehicle in the exchange, not a party with initiative to add or change content. So J. Souter insisted in his dissent that *Zobrest* held that the Establishment Clause "tolerates the presence of public employees in sectarian schools 'only . . . in . . . limited circumstances.'"[39]

J. O'Connor, however, argued that not she but *he* misread *Zobrest* since J. Souter's idea that a translator presents no opportunity for the injection of religious content, and she insisted that *Zobrest* did not decide the case on that distinction, since if it had, it would not have examined the records to make sure there was no evidence of "inaccurate translations." What did she mean by saying there was "no opportunity for the injection of religious content," when the parochial school teacher was providing the religious content, and the translator passing it along? It was not a question of whether the interpreter added or changed religious content, but that *only* by the *interpreter*'s presence and work was any *indoctrination* or instruction even possible. But one also has to ask why it was so important to examine the records, or why that was not a violation by being an "excessive entanglement"? J. O'Connor, for the Court, argued, instead, that the dissent in *Zobrest* criticized the majority for *straying from the course* of the *earlier five decades* of Establishment Clause jurisprudence. Indeed, it was five decades. This shows, she insisted, that it was *Zobrest*, not the current case, that "created 'fresh law,'" that the Court did *not limit Zobrest* to its facts unique to *Zobrest*.[40] So the Court admitted that *Zobrest* was "fresh law." How did the "majority" in *Zobrest* itself *justify* straying from the course set by nearly five decades of Establishment clause jurisprudence to create "fresh law"? Was that what could be called "judicial activism" and J. O'Conner was simply trying to justify the *Zobrest* decision?

Is all this simply a reasonable "extension" of the *Zobrest* holding, yet *Zobrest* was hanging on the argument that it was simply a "private" decision, which is totally the *opposite* of the present case? Now, contrary to the whole history of the Court's adjudication on public school teachers being paid by taxes to teach in parochial schools, a consistent history of denying their legality, the Court is saying that not just an interpreter for a single deaf student, but *any number of teachers* to offer remedial classes and other services in a parochial school can be funded by state funds, even to include former parochial school teachers as now "public school teachers" being paid by public taxes, and this does *not* constitute an illegal Establishment? Is this to say that all the fine distinctions the Court made over four to five decades of what types of "aid" could be legal and what could not, now are no longer significant because *any kind* of aid, including public school teachers, paid wholly from tax dollars, is in no way illegal, so that *all those earlier decisions* by the Court were simply wrong? Yet the Court does *not overturn any* of those dozens of cases? They are still "good law" even though she is saying they are "not good law"?

The Court further argued that *Witters v. Washington Dept. of Serv. for Blind* in 1986 decided that a state tuition grant which did not discriminate between public and private institutions could be used by the recipient for classes in a sectarian school since the money was given directly to the student and went to the school only by the "private choice" of the student. Of course, as we saw earlier, this is not the whole story since the Constitution of the State of Washington *prohibited* state funds from being used for education in theology or related subjects, and the Supreme Court did *not rule against* the State of Washington or its Constitution, for obvious reasons, but examined *only* the Appellate Court which had redirected the focus to the Federal First Amendment, whose *standards* the Court was *now changing*. By ignoring all the earlier Court decisions from 1947 on (i.e., decisions that were not made by these nine specific present Justices), the Appellate decision was reversed and remanded for further exploration pertaining to the State of Washington's requirements.

The Court here in *Agostini* was not concerned to rehash these details, but simply to assert that this money could therefore not be perceived as "state decision making."[41] If the State intended to include the money going to anybody to attend *any kind* of school, then that *was* precisely *its* decision, to be willing to fund a religious or parochial education, if the recipients wanted to use it that way. But the *individual's decision* meant nothing had not the *State* either *included or excluded* aid for a religious indoctrination. If it *excluded* it, and the individual used it for that, then the individual was also in violation of the state's intention; if it *included* the religious indoctrination, then the state's law is in violation of the First Amendment. The state is involved *either way*. The state's decision prevails over any individual's.

Then J. O'Connor further insisted the state was not "relieving the sectarian school of costs it otherwise would have borne."[42] This is to say that the money was to *supplement* the school's curriculum rather than *supplant or substitute* different funds. So this means that the state can step in to supplement any parochial school for *any programs* the latter does *not choose* to fund, not simply "special" needs services or "remedial" services? But the recipient of funds does *not* make the *decision* to *offer the funds*, but only to receive. Is offering a bribe or offering to conspire to commit a crime not illegal *unless it is accepted?* The decision to offer is the decision which *violates the law by its very "purpose,"* whether the Court wants to honor its decision in *Lemon* any more or not. Even by Madison's and Jefferson's objection to "three-pence" of tax moneys, is the decision that is a violation the *citizen* who actually gives "three pence" or the *government* which determines the "aid" go to the religion?

The second point of difference made by J. Souter, belittled by J. O'Connor, for the Court, was that Title I services relieve a religious school of "an expense that it otherwise would have assumed." The Court simply replied that it would not "speculate" (as it implied J. Souter did) that it is impossible to draw the line between supplemental and general education offerings, nor would it "speculate that all sectarian schools provide remedial instruction and guidance counseling to their students," nor "to presume that the Board would violate Title I regulations by continuing to provide Title I services to students who attend a sectarian school that has curtailed its remedial instruction program in response to Title I" (at 229). J. O'Connor argued that J. Souter's presumption was simply his own speculation, namely, that the sectarian schools already offered these programs so that the Title I aid simply released the schools from having to pay for them out of their own moneys.

But, as already pointed out, that means a religious school could be rewarded for being quite educationally *irresponsible* by deciding not to fund certain important or crucial services, thereby *forcing the government* to pick up the tab since these were *not* substitute funds but for a "supplemental" programs, that is, for a "supplemental" program which *should have been originally included* within the *school*'s purpose and educational *budget*. Could the school also demand that government build a gymnasium for it since it has not assigned any funding or classes yet that would need a gym but its students obviously need a gym? Or can the school feign ignorance that it would ever need remedial classes, and the Court would stand by it to demand the state pay for them when the school finally discovered the need and couldn't find funds for it?

In fact, the Court *failed* to show that the religious schools actually offered *no* "remedial" or "counseling" services because that would have put a black eye on the quality of their educational services. No responsible public educator would think his or her school can exist *without* offering such services. Can the school really be so *unprofessional* and still expect government funding, whether one calls it supplemental or substitutional?

The Court argued the Title I program "does not run afoul of any of the three primary criteria we currently use to evaluate whether government aid has the effect of advancing religion: It does not result in governmental indoctrination; define its recipients by reference to religion; or create an excessive entanglement."[43] The key to this is the "currently," which means only since 1986, yet even *after* 1986, *Lemon* was still used over and over by the Court, as we have seen in this and chapter 8. These are only "current" criteria, which ignore the earlier criteria and dozens of decisions based on those, and even these criteria are not satisfied in this case, as we have examined, and Souter showed so graphically.

The real issue is *who is funding* the parochial schools' religiously indoctrinating educational program, and whether the state is simply picking up the tab for certain necessary programs that the school lacked the educational expertise, funds, or will power to offer? If the omission of such services (which was only asserted, not shown) was true and intentional on the part of the school, it is an unprofessional approach to education which obviously involves "diverting" of funds, the intentional shifting of funds, or substitution of funds, the freeing up of the parochial schools' funds by adding in public tax dollars, thereby allowing more of the schools' funds to be directed toward religious indoctrination by religious faculty, materials, symbols, religious observances, and rituals.

The idea of "governmental indoctrinating" was not the criteria used by Madison and Jefferson, since that sounds like an institution doing something, whereas, their focus was on the government in some way funding the religious *teachers*, and the teachers are the ones who do the indoctrinating. And that was obviously at issue and not answered by J. O'Connor's focus on exaggerating former Court's presuppositions. Perhaps she should have asked what the most general *ethical principles underlying those decisions* were, and whether they were incorrect.[44]

Finally, the argument that the law here in question did not "define its recipients by reference to religion" is only a half-truth. In order to cover the parochial schools with the aid, it was made general or neutral, but even the laws had to spell out that this "neutrality" necessarily had to *include* private or parochial schools as well, since the attorneys knew the former history of decisions made by the Court. They were not dummies.

With this kind of wholesale abandonment of any sense of a "separation" of religion and state, if the major emphasis is upon religious indoctrination, it will be interesting to see what the Court decides when Muslim, Hindu, Buddhist, Native American, and other religious groups' schools become strong enough and adamant enough to persuade their states and the federal government to provide funding in such dramatic forms for any of *their* services.[45] If citizens who wonder why their public schools lack proper salaries and adequate facilities and equipment finally realize the siphoning off of billions of public tax dollars for established parochial programs and for school voucher programs which can be used for parochial education, they might begin to see how the latter cripples public education.

Behind Rawls's "veil of ignorance," one would very likely find *no person* selecting principles which would allow the shifting of public taxes away from the public schools, the very schools one might discover one needed for one's *own* children. Rawls's "second principle" was that inequality in economic and social spheres can be accepted only if there is real equality of opportunity and if the benefit of the proposed law went to the *least advantaged* as *they themselves* would judge it. Why should the voices of the "least advantaged" be ignored or silenced in a democratic republic? Public education has heretofore been the *primary instrument* of *universal education* to build good, reasonable, self-sufficient citizens for the nation. It enabled the "least advantaged" to get an education, which hopefully could level the playing field a bit, that is, by providing the "least advantaged" with one of the tools vital to one's subsistence and self-respect, as well as building responsible citizenship. Certainly the Framers of the Constitution knew the problems in having education of children being only private, that only part of the population received any education, and many of the Framers knew how privileged they had been to have had even a college education provided them by their family. This stood behind Jefferson's ideal that the new University of Virginia would be completely secular and public, as we saw earlier.

But today, we even hear some who want to control the courts talk about even trying to overturn *Brown v. Board of Education*, which reveals the blatant racism that is surfacing under the power of privilege for many who are unwilling to give even a second thought to Rawls's "hypothetical" suggestion of placing oneself behind a "veil of ignorance." To cripple public education this way is not subtle but a blatant form of *economic and racial discrimination*, equal to a reinstating of "literacy tests" and others forms of voter suppression the United States has utilized in such a xenophobic way,[46] a reversion which has potential to undermine the whole democratic structure and its ideals of equality, life, liberty, and pursuit of happiness. *Trust*, which lies as the most essential factor for any human relationship, can be dissolved more easily than it can be rebuilt, and most citizens are aware of this.

Does "Private Choice" Make Public School Football Prayers Legal?

Another public school "prayer case" involving the Establishment clause was decided in the year 2000. In *Santa Fe Independent School District v. Doe, individually and as next friend for Her Minor Children, et al.*, 530 U.S. 290 (2000), a Catholic and a Mormon mother combined to challenge the school-sponsored, student-led prayer at all high school home football games in Santa Fe, Texas. They moved for a temporary restraining order, objecting that the prayers were a violation of the Establishment Clause. The suit began in 1995, first against the prayers at graduation exercises, but eventually included prayers at the football games.

While original proceedings were pending in the District Court, the school District came up with a different policy, not requiring the prayer, but permitting the prayer-program if initiated and led by the majority of the student body. In May 1995, the District Court entered an "interim order" covering several issues which approved of the prayer at an invocation presented by a senior student selected by members of the graduating class, and the text of the prayer was determined by the students, without any input from the school, and the school spelled out that the text of the prayer might even refer to particular religious figures, so long as it was "nonproselytizing."

In the 1995 complaint by the Does, they alleged that the district had engaged in several proselytizing practices, for example, promoting attendance at a Baptist revival meeting, encouraging membership in religious clubs, and even chastising children who held minority religious beliefs, while distributing Gideon Bibles on school premises. They also complained that the district allowed students to read Christian invocations and benedictions from the stage at graduation ceremonies as well as "deliver overtly Christian prayers over the public address system at home football games."[47] The school District revised its policies several times, but its May and July policies governing "graduation ceremonies provided the format for the August and October policies for football games." The district's May policy established that "the board has chosen to permit the graduating senior class, with the advice and counsel of the senior class principal or designee, to elect by secret ballot to choose whether an invocation and benediction shall be part of the graduation exercise. If so chosen the class shall elect by secret ballot, from a list of student volunteers, students to deliver nonsectarian, nonproselytizing invocations and benedictions for the purpose of solemnizing their graduation ceremonies."[48]

The school District followed these guidelines, and the students voted to include the prayer at graduation as allowed. In July, the *school* District modified it, *deleting* the requirements that the invocations had to be nonsectarian and nonproselytizing. Finally, the August revision extended it to invocations at football games, so the October policy was essentially the same as the August one, but adding the terms "messages" and "statements" to the existing term of "invocations." It is this finished policy the Court considered.

The District Court, using *Lee v. Wiseman*, saw the invocations as uniquely Christian and the facts show coercion to participate was present. When the school District appealed to the Fifth Circuit, it used its own judgments as precedents for defining illegal establishment in two of its own cases (*Jones v. Clear Creek School Dist* of 1992, and *Doe v. Duncanville Independent School Dist* of 1995) to say to Petitioners that even the requirements that prayer at graduation exercises be nonsectarian and nonproselytizing are still *insufficient* to make an invocation legal at a sporting event. So it is specifically the question of whether that final policy by the school District, allowing student-led and student-initiated prayer at *football games violates* the Establishment clause, and the Court held (6/3, with J. Thomas, J. Scalia, and C.J. Rehnquist dissenting) that *it did, affirming* the Fifth Circuit.

The Court's line of argument, while accepting the Fifth Circuit's decision, insisted that a graduation exercise and football game are radically different, so that the argument that allows prayer at the graduation, to solemnize the ceremony, is completely inappropriate for the football game. It further argued that, despite the student involvement, this is all done under the watchful eye of the school, in which the school chose to permit the scheme of student-led prayers, the students used school facilities, in a situation that is quite obviously *not* an open forum, which is further exacerbated by the fact that only one student would lead the invocation for the *entire year*. All of this shows it is not really private speech, but is perceived by spectators as "objective observers" as the school's position or therefore public or government speech, that is, sanctioned completely by the school. The failure to involve other religious views by different students shows it is only a *majoritarian voice* that prevails here, defying the holding in *Barnette* which insisted that our individual rights, including religious freedom as defined in the Establishment Clause, are our "fundamental rights" "which may not be submitted to a vote, they depend on the outcome of no elections."[49]

The Court raised the question from *Marsh* of whether the school District was just trying to get the Court to see the practice as only a *solemnization of the event*, quite secular, that is, to see it quite differently from the way all the students themselves understood prayer. Therefore, any citing of its alleged "secular" purpose (in order to avoid failing the *Lemon* test) is only a "sham" purpose. All this maneuvering by the school District accomplished was creating a situation and policy which was extremely *divisive* which was one of the *Lemon* criteria by which one judges whether or not the law or policy at issue creates an illegal excessive entanglement. The students' varied requirements for being at the football game, from cheerleaders, players, band members, or others, when combined with even the tremendous peer pressure for showing up at the game, all show the policy's indirect but *coercive nature*, a definite *violation* of the Establishment Clause.

Can Private Choice and Neutral Law Negate Religious Indoctrination and Divertibility?

A much more complex parochial school case was decided the same year in *Mitchell v. Helms*, 530 U.S. 793 (2000). It was remarkable only in two ways: (1) it is the first time J. Thomas wrote the Court's opinion on one of the two Religion Clauses;[50] and (2) it is extremely long. Its only new ground, which had already been "broken" by *Agostini* so could have been predicted by many, was that the Court had no use for precedents more than 20 years old, and therefore it allowed for government funds now to be supplied *directly* to the local educational agencies who passed them on to the *parochial schools* in the form of "loaned" textbooks but also instructional materials (including audiovisual devices earlier prohibited in *Meek* and *Wolman)*, and including computer hardware and software programs. The Court had avoided this direct government aid for 53 years (i.e., since *Everson*), even earlier insisting that government aid could only be "indirect" or "incidental," and could *not* be "materials" since they could easily be used for religious indoctrination. In fact, originally in 1947, the *only* aid that could be justified was on the basis of a "safety" concern for students en route to school and could be bus fare reimbursement given *only* to their parents. Aid could not be given to either a church or parochial school, and was only to get the children to school safely, even though there was no showing of any danger, and the children were already getting to and from school safely. How far the pendulum had swung, perhaps to a point of no return?

Now "*stare decisis*" became very selective, very discriminating, turning a blind eye on any case more than 20 years old, even if there were many new cases decided on the principles or criteria those older cases elaborated such as the *Lemon* test. The earlier presumptions and "tests" which had worked as best as they could have been expected, given the continual changes in the Court's personnel, were now caricatured (including especially *Lemon* by J. Scalia) and rejected while the Court, fearing losing its credibility by overturning so many older decisions, was careful not to overturn all of them but only insist that the *principles* themselves are *stable*, as we saw in *Agostini*. But specifically *which* principles are stable? The Court did not articulate them.

Were all of those earlier Justices prior to 1986 evidently too strict in their thinking, similar to Madison and Jefferson, thinking there should be a "wall" of separation between government and religion? Perhaps this is the reason the Court no longer quotes from Madison or Jefferson even though some of them think of themselves as "originalists" or "textualists"? Instead of the principle being that government could not in *any form* fund a religion or the teachers of it, the Court here changed that to only a principle that government itself could not *directly* engage in "religious indoctrination," an idea it took over from *Agostini v. Felton.*

But that was *never* the concern of Madison, Jefferson, and the others who ratified the Constitution and the First Amendment. They were concerned about the government funding *other people* who saw *their* mission as indoctrinating religiously, *not the government* indoctrinating anybody. This is simply a "red herring." Whereas the earlier Courts had become aware of the pervasively sectarian nature of religious schools,[51] so in the earliest cases attempted to allow only aid that could *not be diverted,* misused for indoctrinating, or merely as a substitute for the religious school's other funds which allowed it to use more of those others for indoctrination, the Court now was attempting to say that divertibility is *not even a valid issue* at all so long as there is any "neutrality" in the law or any "private choice" involved. Both of those factors are then viewed as *removing the government* from any *responsibility* just in case the funds end up being used for religious indoctrination.

The *Mitchell* Court decided that only the very recent cases, especially *Witters* (1986), *Zobrest* (1993), and *Agostini* (1997), are sufficient precedents, and since the District Court did not consider the issue of "excessive entanglement" nor was the law's secular purpose challenged, the only part of the *Lemon* test application that is here relevant is the second prong, its "effect." Yet there the Court ironically *contradicts itself* by saying the "effect" can be seen as illegally "advancing religion if it (1) results in governmental indoctrination, (2) defines its recipients by reference to religion, or (3) creates an excessive entanglement." The Court's decision to limit "dispositive" cases only to "more recent decisions" was to *avoid* the *Lemon* (1971) test, the *Marsh* (1983) test, and even J. O'Connor's "endorsement" test in her concurring opinion in *Lynch v. Donnelly.* Since the Fifth Circuit court utilized *Lemon* to judge the case, as the most common test in Establishment cases used by the Court from 1971 to 2000, the Court felt it had to refer to *Lemon,* but only to redefine words, reduce or alter concepts, or point out that those ideas were groundless *presumptions* by the *Lemon* Court, and are no longer recognized as valid. Yet it did not have the courage to *overturn Lemon* (1971) which fashioned the three-part test that the Court used for two-thirds of the total Establishment cases during the previous 29 years and is still used by *most* of the Courts of Appeals, since for the Supreme Court to overturn it would also negate all the decisions made on the basis of that test.[52]

So several members of the Court simply *ignored* most of the cases in which the *Lemon* test was dispositive, belittling the *Lemon* test, as J. Scalia admitted. This means the Court has to end up *overruling* the Circuit Courts' decisions in *case after case,* while it dare not overrule *Lemon,* thereby eliminating half of its "establishment jurisprudence" as being *irrelevant* or wrongly decided rather than precedent. Since those Appellate Courts have to make their decisions on the basis of *Lemon*, because it is still "good law," and many of the more recent decisions by the Court simply *cannot be reconciled* in any way with *Lemon*, the lower courts are put into an unenviable position by the high Court. Evidently, only the Supreme Court feels it can ignore *Lemon* when it wants, as J. Scalia explicitly emphasized, ignore it without overturning it, something no lower court is allowed. This means that if the members of the Court get to choose which "test" to use determined by the result they desire to reach, there is no objective law, but only subjective preferences. The whole process has become capricious.

This case involved a "plurality decision," revealing more than ever the diverse if not irreconcilable opinions on the Court, J. Thomas writing for the Court, joined by the chief justice (Rehnquist), J. Scalia, and J. Kennedy. J. O'Conner wrote a concurring opinion, joined by J. Breyer, concurring in the holding, but only agreeing with the Court's use of *Agostini* to a degree and in overruling *Meek* and *Wolman* to the degree that they conflict with the present holding. J. Souter wrote a dissenting opinion, joined by J. Stevens and J. Ginsburg.

Chapter 2 of the Education Consolidation and Improvement Act of 1981 provided federal tax dollars to state educational agencies who distributed it to local educational agencies, who then "lend educational materials and equipment" such as library and media materials, computer software and hardware, to public and private elementary and secondary schools to aid in "secular, neutral, and nonideological" programs. In this case, of Jefferson Parish, Louisiana, about 30% of the funds spent were on private schools, most of which were Catholic schools.[53] The District Court struck it down as a violation of the Establishment Clause since it violated *Lemon v. Kurtzman* with its primary effect of advancing religion since it involved *direct aid* and the schools were *pervasively sectarian.*

When the Chief Judge of the District Court died and was replaced, another District Court judge reversed the decision. Upon appeal to the Fifth Circuit, the Court there concluded that *Agostini* had neither directly overruled *Meek* nor *Wolman*, nor had it rejected their distinction between textbooks and other in-kind aid, so the Fifth Circuit invalidated Chapter 2 aid as prohibited by the Establishment Clause.

Briefly, J. Thomas, for the Court, insisted that aid to private schools is not an illegal establishment just because many of them are religiously affiliated, not even if they are regarded as pervasively sectarian. He insisted that only the second prong of *Lemon*, the "effect" test, was at issue here since neither the purpose nor the excessive entanglement prongs had been challenged. He noted that the idea of "effect" had been recently redefined, even as the idea of "excessive entanglement" had been pared recently to be absorbed into the test of "effect." He insisted, for the Court, that *Agostini* ruled that there are three primary criteria for determining a statute's effect, that it is illegally advancing religion if it (1) "results in governmental indoctrination, (2) defines its recipients by reference to religion, or (3) creates an excessive entanglement." The "(3)," of course, contradicts his contention that "excessive entanglement" was not as issue here.

To determine whether there is "governmental indoctrination," the Court insists that the test will be simply the "neutrality principle," that is, whether the aid is offered to a broad range of recipients without regard to their religion, and the Court can determine this by assessing whether or not the aid results from the "private choices" of individual parents. But that reduces #1 to #2, and with #3 eliminated by J. Thomas at the beginning, there is only one test, which is #2. Needless to say, the Court is sure that this principle, derived from *Agostini*, *Witters*, and *Zobrest*, was met, that no reasonable person would have thought the law was not neutral, nor that aid did not depend upon the private choice of parents. From this, he examines the second criterion, which amounts to the same thing, the neutrality principle, the idea that the aid has to be offered without any reference to religion, and he is sure it was since it was neutral and offered no financial incentive to parents to enroll their children in a parochial school. Would he and the majority of the Court define "neutrality" in this same way if the aid was offered to all private schools in the given area without singling out religion or secular, and 10% turned out secular and the remaining 90% were Muslim? Would they still have decided there was no "establishing" of religion?

The Court insisted that the Respondent's argument that "direct, nonincidental aid" to religious schools is always impermissible is "inconsistent with this Court's more recent cases," that is, the three mentioned above, *Agostini*, *Witters*, and *Zobrest*, three cases between 1986 and 1997. But what about *all the cases* prior to 1986 in which the Court had insisted that aid was confined to secular textbooks, and could not include audiovisual aids, or in which the Court had declared that the aid had to be *only* "incidental" as it was in *Everson*, rather than "direct"? The specific aid (books and materials) here was requested by the parochial schools, determined by their religious values and goals, and those items approved by the LEAs were purchased and then loaned to the schools. The funds were used to provide not simply requested library books, but computers and software, slide and movie projectors, overhead projectors, TV sets, tape recorders, VCRs, projection screens, laboratory equipment, maps, globes, filmstrips, slides, and cassette recordings, *most* of which *violated* either *Meek* (1975) or *Wolman* (1977) or both. The Court *now*, after two decades and an almost completely different personnel on the bench, insisted *Meek* and *Wolman* were incorrectly decided, that even if it is "direct" aid, if it is *neutrally* available, and prior to reaching the school, *passes through the hands* of the recipients so that it is *their decision* that passes the aid on to the school (even if only figuratively, not literally passing through their actual hands), it is still not illegal.

But there were no such private decisions made here. Even in the only cases that involved the "private choice" of parents or the students the aid came directly to the school in *Zobrest*, and in *Witters*, though Witters had already made the decision to attend the Inland School of the Bible, and the money might have passed through his hands to the school, the Court argument was less of the direct/indirect funds and much more its insistence that this money neither advanced the school's religious program nor did it pay for religious indoctrination, both statements of which were *speciously false*.

In both cases, as we suggested earlier, the vital decision was made by the state to provide aid, and had not the government made that decision, no decision by the prospective recipients would have had any effect whatever. In both *Zobrest* and *Witters*, the "aid" was minimal, with only *one student* challenging the prohibition of the aid, so it is not analogous to the across the board school aid or "per capita" school aid supplied in this Parish in Louisiana. The "decision" for any of the different *forms of aid* being offered here *never came from parents or students*, but was determined by the separate *schools*, as they filled out specific requests, based on their sectarian mission, and submitted them to the LEA. The LEA used the federal money to purchase those materials it approved of, which was basically what the *schools* requested. Therefore, the recently articulated criterion of "private choice" is totally *irrelevant* here.

The Court admitted that where money is given directly to religious schools, there might be more danger of possible illegal establishment, but insisted that such direct payments were not at issue here. Yet they certainly were since here the *parochial schools, not* the individual students, were directly requesting and receiving the aid, whatever form it took which was totally *against earlier Court decisions*. The loaned materials were purchased with public tax dollars and were considered valuable assets, the equivalent of money.

Finally, the Court had to deal with the concept of "divertibility" which has been at issue in prior cases. But it insisted that the idea that the divertibility of aid to a religious use as *always* being impermissible is also "inconsistent with the Court's more recent cases." So the same three recent cases are used, ignoring all the earlier ones that *warned of divertibility*, even if they used other words for the practice. Instead, the Court insisted that the real issue is not divertibility but rather whether the aid has an "impermissible content." Yet it offered no clarity on what such content would be or who would judge the content as permissible or impermissible other than to say if it can be used in public schools then it is not impermissible. But there was no indication that the LEA demanded that the lists submitted by the parochial schools had to precisely be the same as the ones submitted by the public schools. There is no showing of these lists to compare. In truth, of course, there had already been problems of the aid being used in illegal ways since computers are even more flexible to input by teachers than prepared videos or filmstrips that the earlier Court had found illegal.

The Court simply mocked the whole concept, however, saying the question of divertibility rather than actual content is endless or all encompassing, even leading to trivia. The Court finally insisted that even if any aid is divertible in the sense that it can relieve the school from certain expenses so that it can spend its other resources on religious ends, *this is not illegal* since the Court has never prohibited such institutions from diverting in that sense.[54] This is simply a *terrible misreading* of many former Court decisions, as the concurring as well as dissenting opinions show. This brings us to the final issue of the dissent's concern over the fourth aspect of the third prong of *Lemon*, the "potential political divisiveness" of certain aid, and the Court insists that since *Agostini*, this test is *rejected*, and the question of whether a school receiving government aid is "pervasively sectarian" is *not even relevant*, as proven in *Witters*.

This is another decision made by the Court that shows contempt for the Establishment Clause as formulated primarily by Madison and Jefferson, as it ignores the situation of the law proposed in the state of Virginia which they defeated as an illegal establishment, a quite *truncated and myopic* view of Establishment jurisdiction. But what can be expected, since the opinion was written by a justice who has *never* been persuaded that the Establishment Clause applies to the *separate states*? So why was he selected to write this opinion? This is strange.

That openness to divertibility of funds or aid has *never* been the Court's position, but only J. Thomas's and (perhaps) C.J. Rehnquist's. Further, the "private choice" of the proposed and defeated Virginia Bill was more a *genuine private choice* than either *Witters* or *Zobrest*, and the "effect" of "establishment" did *not* require a physical connection to actual words of indoctrination, but simply any enabling or any support of the institution that has indoctrination and/or religious worship as its program. But Madison, Jefferson, and others *defeated* it in Virginia and ultimately replicated their Virginia Bill in the First Amendment to the Federal Constitution. Yet the Court insists here that an actual showing of *government indoctrination* must be shown for the aid to be illegal. Does that require that some high government official must be in the classroom preaching religious dogma to the students?

On the basis of this decision of *Mitchell v. Helms*, how could the Court henceforth ever find an illegal establishment if public taxes were channeled to pay for the pews, lights, maintenance, and utility bills of any church, even food and lodging for priests and sisters, and all their needs since it is *not these particular elements* that *indoctrinate*? But as Madison and Jefferson noted, any requirement to fund even "three pence" can end up being a requirement of a much more significant amount and quality. Does this mean the Court views Madison and Jefferson as having too many unreasonable presumptions too? Did Madison and Jefferson and other Framers not know what religious "establishments" can do to a country?

In J. O'Connor's concurring opinion, joined by J. Breyer, she agreed with the Court that the *de minimis* violations of the statutory restrictions that were discovered in the resulting history of these schools were quickly corrected and were a mere aberration which should have no bearing on the Court's decision. She also agreed with the Court that *Meek* and *Wolman* had to be overruled, not *en toto* but to the extent that they conflicted with the decision here. Ultimately she agreed also that the *Agostini* decision which *she wrote* for the Court should control here rather than any other cases. So, despite her defense in *Agostini*, that it was not fresh law, but rather the fresh law was *Zobrest*, she now admitted that *Agostini* was. J. O'Connor concluded that the real test must therefore be whether any *particular thing* was *actually used for indoctrination*. That means it all depends on how any methods or materials are utilized by the teacher, since a science teacher could religiously indoctrinate even by opposing any evolution that was mentioned in a wholly secular science textbook. The problem of religious indoctrination in a *pervasively sectarian* parochial school is much more widespread than any of the Justices want to admit, since, as J. Souter shows (and earlier Courts were aware of), the Catholic church's *explicit mission* for the schools is that *everything* is to be approached from a *Catholic perspective*. Everything. It would be impossible to provide sufficient continual monitoring of all the classrooms to make sure there was no religious indoctrination. This very issue was raised *decades earlier* when the Justices pointed out that even the supposed "secular" textbooks, if chosen by the local school board (or church) rather than the state, would enable them to select those texts most consonant with their religious message, so would be aiding religious indoctrination.

J. Thomas, for the Court, claimed that whether government aid results in religious indoctrination depends upon "whether any indoctrination that occurs could reasonably be attributed to government action," and this is easily resolved by the "neutrality principle," that is, by the criteria of the aid being offered to a broad range of recipients without regard to their religion. But how does the size and interests of the possible recipients have *anything* to do with the question of religious indoctrination? From *Everson* on, the Court has often violated such "neutrality principle" since even there it was only Catholic schools and public schools that qualified for the aid, and the aid was offered to no other private schools, whether they were secular or religious. The Everson majority simply said these other private schools were not being considered. That is not "neutrality" in any sense.

If "neutrality" means only "evenhandedness" in the offer of funds, that is, by showing that similar funds are offered to public schools as well, then can the actual recipients use the funds however they desire? Do the presence of the mere *words* of "neutral" or "nonideological" make it legal even if the *institution* receiving it is one of the *most absolutist ideological* institutions in the world? *No religion* qualifies as "nonideological"; all have their Absolute, whether it is Christian, Judaistic, Islamic, Buddhist, Shinto, Hindu, or other. Precisely because it is ideological and absolutist, it is quite doubtful that a "pervasively sectarian" educational entity will self-report its violations when it utilizes materials for a bit of religious indoctrination, not when indoctrination is its *very purpose* of its schools.

If "indoctrination" is really the issue, then the question must be what kind of connection would have to be shown between the type of aid and some supposed "indoctrination" in order for the "aid" to be a government enabler of the indoctrination? How would one go about documenting any "indoctrination" at all? Certainly the teacher can intend to "indoctrinate" no matter what materials she uses or does not use, and can do it at select times when no auditor from the state is present. It can occur in a biology class as easily as a literature class, which is just as easily done as in a religion class. Yet the plurality here was happy to summarize its position with the following statement: "[I]f the government, seeking to further some legitimate secular purpose, offers aid on the same terms, without regard to religion, to all who adequately further that purpose, then it is fair to say that any aid going to a religious recipient only has the effect of furthering that secular purpose. The government, in crafting such an aid program, has had to conclude that a given level of aid is necessary to further that purpose among secular recipients and has provided no more than that same level to religious recipients."[55]

If a government offered money for all children in any school to learn world history, including the history of the Near East, if the Muslim schools did that, and in the process indoctrinated all students about the final revelation of God being to Muhammed (in Mecca and Medina), who was therefore God's Final Prophet, and this is the only true religion, the fact that the students learned the history the government had in mind *qualifies*, so by the Court's criteria, it would be quite constitutional? That is the effect of that first sentence. Or does the plurality have in mind it would qualify only if it were an indoctrination of the Christian faith? How can the Court simply *assume* that a school applying for funds, alleging its *secular* purpose which is the primary and *only* interest of the government, is *actually going to spend* the funds *only* on the *secular* purpose, and, even if it does, how can the Court assume it does so with the guarantee of not diverting the funds or using them to free up other funds for religious indoctrination? In fact, how can the Court say that if the law is itself neutral, divertibility is not even a legitimate problem?

J. O'Connor wrote her concurring opinion because she could not agree with very much of the actual *justification* of the decision made by the Court. She claimed that its treatment of the concept of "neutrality" almost turned it into the sole criterion of judgment, and the Court has *never* agreed to that.[56] Further, she insisted that the plurality is completely *wrong* in *approving* of the actual diversion of government aid to religious indoctrination; rather, *any* actual diversion has *always* been impermissible. Here, she was absolutely right, so why did she concur in the result if the rationale for it was so far off base? Further, she stressed that a "per-capita-aid program" should *not* be treated as a true "private choice" program as in *Witters* and *Zobrest*, but rather the *Agostini* criteria should control. These are devastating criticisms of the plurality's opinion since it really *undercuts* its conclusion. It is also interesting that here the two who concur with the plurality only in its result or conclusion, see "private choice" in a *completely different way* from the four Justices of the plurality. "Private choice" then remains *unsettled* as to its scope as a criterion.

Finally, J. Souter's warning a few years earlier in his dissent in *Rosenberger v. U. of Virginia* about the meaning of "neutrality" should have been sufficient to have prevented this case being decided the way it was, as he wrote the following: "the Establishment Clause requires some justification beyond evenhandedness on the government's part; and that direct public funding of core sectarian activities, even if accomplished pursuant to an evenhanded program, would be entirely inconsistent with the Establishment Clause and would strike at the very heart of the Clause's protection."[57] One can think of innumerable examples to show this. For instance, the Virginia Bill proposed by Gov. Patrick Henry that was opposed by Madison, Jefferson, and most of the state, so defeated, was a *very* "evenhanded" bill, treating all religions on an equal basis by allowing each person to designate the specific church his taxes should go to. But the bill was *defeated* because neither Madison nor Jefferson saw "evenhandedness" sufficient to preclude strife between religious groups or problems between religious groups and government, despite C.J. Rehnquist's continual insistence that all the First Amendment required is an equal treatment of all religions by government.

The First Amendment defeated Rehnquist's idea of "equal treatment" as the goal of the Religion Clauses. Alleged equality is an insufficient safeguard for both government and for the individual's conscience, as Madison and Jefferson both showed in their defeating of the equality of Gov. Patrick Henry's proposed general assessment bill. They knew that any government support to any or all religions would create terrible division as it had throughout the history of Christendom. No amount of good intentions can modify that terrible history. If one looks to the present, if the government decided it would provide federal tax dollars for any group to administer *programs for the needy* in their community, especially in providing sufficient food for them, and emphasized that they really wanted to give the tax money primarily to "faith-based" groups,[58] that is, churches, mosques, synagogues, and the like, would that be sufficient "neutrality" and "evenhandedness" to be legal? Not by Madison, Jefferson, or all the religious leaders who joined them in writing, defining, and supporting both the Virginia defeat of Henry's bill but also the U.S. Constitution's First Amendment. If a state decided to pay the utility bills of any groups that *claimed* to be concerned with people's welfare, and that included many religious organizations, would that be legal? If it included a variety of Islamic groups, atheist groups, Buddhist groups, would the funding still be legal? Or one might ask why does it become legal primarily if it is a Christian group? Why is "indoctrination" so hard to discover within a parochial school whereas it would be so easy for Christian Justices to see in a Muslim school?

To Madison and Jefferson, "evenhandedness" was *not* the answer; the only answer was a "wall of separation"—a "wall" first honored by our Supreme Court, but then quickly belittled by it, finally allowing many of the Justices to declare that the government itself has the right to express *its own religion*, which, it assumes, is the only true religion, therefore is "generic," by which they mean only Christianity. If one is following Rawls's procedure to arrive at a social contract that provides "justice as fairness," so places oneself hypothetically in that "original position" behind a "veil of ignorance," as Rawls emphasized, one would *not even know* whether one was Muslim, Christian, an atheist or nonreligious, a Buddhist, or other, so one would not contract to give those groups special benefits denied to others. And, if one was interested in the true public welfare or benefits for the general populace rather than simply people of specific associations, then the funds should be supplied to governmental agencies for such uses, which, in the case at hand, would mean giving educational aid (public taxes) to public schools for *all children.*

Now in *Mitchell v. Helms*, J. Souter, dissenting, joined by J. Ginsburg and J. Stevens, crafted the most detailed analysis of the Court's "establishment" jurisdiction available in such short space of 45 pages, quoting prolifically from dozens of cases to show the actual evolution of the jurisdiction over the decades. He refrained from dicta and from his own opinions in cases, quoting the actual Court decision, and then simply summarizing the results as the focus of the establishment jurisdiction evolved in all of its intricate webs of trial and error, of definition and redefinition. It is truly a remarkable analysis, beyond any other that comes to mind, which every reader needs to see. I have space only for a very brief glimpse of his scholarship.

He admitted that the Court has found no single test that has been sufficient to address every factual situation the Court has had to address. But paramount to any analysis is the recognition at the outset that the Establishment Clause bars public funds for religious aid, prohibiting "not only the institution of an official church, but any government act favoring religion, a particular religion, or for that matter irreligion."[59] Yet, he added, the Free Exercise Clause simultaneously bars any prohibition of individual free exercise of religion, "and because religious organizations cannot be isolated from the basic government functions that create the civil environment, it is as much necessary as it is difficult to draw lines between forbidden aid and lawful benefit."[60] That, of course, is nothing new, but has always been the situation, even as conceived and lived by Madison and Jefferson.

So far as government aid or benefits to education, J. Souter noted that "[t]here may be no aid supporting a sectarian school's religious exercise or the discharge of its religious mission, while aid of a secular character with no discernible benefit to such a sectarian objective is allowable." Yet because the secular and religious spheres largely overlap in many religious schools, the Court has tried over and over to identify some elements that would reveal whether the intent or effect was religious or secular.[61] This includes the question of whether the government aid is offered neutrally, what the particular form of the aid is, what its path to the religious institution entails, its divertibility to religious instruction, its potential for reducing traditional expenditures or religious institutions or of supplanting already-existing programs with government funds, and its relative importance to the recipient.

He faulted the Court in the present decision of misinterpreting many previous cases, of failing to recognize the "nondivertibility" of funds to the determination of the legality of the aid, and for placing an irrational weight on a single element as if it were the only criterion, namely, that of "neutrality" which the Court reduced to mere "evenhandedness." Unfortunately, by the plurality's misreading of the Establishment jurisdiction, the Court has now cast aside not only the "no aid" principle and the "divertibility" test, but has included substantial taxes being diverted to religious schools.

He reiterated the *principle objectives* served by the Establishment Clause: (1) that "compelling an individual to support religion violates the fundamental principle of freedom of conscience" which was the main rationale behind Madison's and Jefferson's objection to any such government involvement; (2) "government aid corrupts religion" as Madison and Jefferson also believed; and (3) "government establishment of religion is inextricably linked with conflict," which was also emphasized by Madison and Jefferson, and the reason the latter spoke of the "wall of separation" between the two.

In all three, J. Souter shows that *Everson* (1947) manifested this same awareness, as he cites also cases subsequent to *Everson* that reinforced *Everson* as well as the Founders' views, as we also noted earlier, that *Everson* went to great length to document how Madison and Jefferson and other Founders articulated such a "wall of separation." This is classically given in

Everson, in which J. Souter focuses on the most pertinent part, that neither a state nor the Federal Government can "pass laws which aid one religion [or] all religions. . . . No tax in any amount . . . can be levied to support any religious activities or institutions . . . whatever form they may adopt to teach . . . religion."[62]

In fact, in his extensive analysis, J. Souter's thesis was that the Founders' basic prohibition of aid to religion has *never* been actually denied by the Court. He emphasized that neither the majority nor the dissent of *Everson* denied this prohibition of "aid."[63] Instead, the majority "wisely chose" not to attempt an "argument-proof formulation of the no-aid principle" in light of the tension the Free Exercise clause[64] stood with the Establishment clause, so the Court simply saw the reimbursement of "bus fares" for the parochial students as a general safety benefit available to all, the equivalent to general government services to all citizens, such as police and fire protection.[65] He noted that finding paradigms that are general enough without subsidizing religious favoritism is not easy, as even in *Everson*, the dissent noted that the limits of the general benefits was the fact that they were given *only* to parents of children in Catholic schools, not to parents of children in other religious schools or for-profit schools.[66]

The *Everson* Court's "conclusory" use of the term, "neutrality," as neither aiding nor handicapping religion (which then was not a test or criteria at all) was extended in *Allen* (1968). By this time, a formulated "test" by the Court required a secular primary intent and effect of a law to be legal. J. Souter argued that significantly, neither the majority nor the dissent in *Allen* focused on a single "test" nor upon some "generality of evenhandedness of the state law," but rather was concerned to determine the "true intent inferable behind the law," as well as the "feasibility of distinguishing in fact between religious and secular teachings in church schools, and the reality or sham of lending books to pupils instead of supplying books to schools."[67] Although the books were seen by the majority as analogous to the bus fares in *Everson*, "the stress was laid on the practical significance of the actual benefits received by the schools," and the majority viewed this as parallel to *Everson* with no money or aid going directly to the schools to save them money. J. Souter summarized that after *Everson* and *Allen*,

1. Government aid to religion is forbidden, and tax revenue may not be used to support a religious school or religious teaching.
2. Government provision of such paradigms of universally general welfare benefits as police and fire protection does not count as aid to religion.
3. Whether a law's benefit is sufficiently close to universally general welfare paradigms to be classified with them as distinct from religious aid, is a function of the purpose and effect of the challenged law in all its

particularity. The judgment is not reducible to the application of any formula. Evenhandedness of distribution as between religious and secular beneficiaries is a relevant factor, but not a sufficiency test of constitutionality. There is no rule of religious equal protection to the effect that any expenditure for the benefit of religious schools students is necessarily constitutional so long as public school pupils are favored on ostensibly identical terms.

4. Government must maintain neutrality as to religion, 'neutrality' being a conclusory label for the required position of government as neither aiding in religion nor impeding religious exercise by believers. "Neutrality" was not the name of any test to identify permissible action, and in particular, was not synonymous with evenhandedness in conferring benefit on the secular as well as the religious.[68]

J. Souter emphasized that even at the time he wrote in *Mitchell* (2000), the substantive principle of no aid to religious mission remains the governing understanding of the Establishment Clause (some 35 years after *Allen*) since most Justices realize that there is "no pure aid to religion" just as there is "no purely secular welfare benefit." But he saw the idea of "neutrality" as "the most deceptively familiar" of the many different considerations the Court has utilized to avoid depriving citizens of general benefits without discernibly supporting or threatening a school's religious mission.

He noted that "neutrality" has been used in three different ways by the Court to describe in a conclusory way "the requisite state of government equipoise between the forbidden encouragement and discouragement of religion."[69] The shift from the "conclusory" or "equipoise" level to a second level used "neutral" to describe explicitly "*secular*" benefits as it was defined in *Lemon* and was used thereafter in that sense in *Tilton, Meek, Wolman,* and others. But the Court also in the 1980s began to reinterpret *Everson* and *Allen* and used "neutral" with a third meaning, as a synonym for "evenhandedness," that is, an *allocation to both religious and secular recipients* on some common or equal basis. The question of whether public taxes could be made available *generally without regard* to *sectarian/nonsectarian categories* could be permissible in *Nyquist*, and subsequent cases characterized the Court's basis for its decision in *Everson* as approving a "general program" of paying bus fares, as it examined the "aid" in *Meek, Wolman,* and *Roemer*.[70] "Neutrally available aid" was then first adopted in its sense of "evenhandedness" by *Mueller v. Allen* in 1983.

Witters, Zobrest, Agostini, and *Rosenberger* all emphasized the *general or neutral or evenhanded* aid made available. So the shift was from a mere conclusory statement of the equipoise between advancing or inhibiting religion, to a synonym for "secular" forms of aid, and finally to a requirement *only* of "evenhandedness" or *equal treatment* of religious and nonreligious recipients was completed, naturally with *radically different results*. Despite the fact that "evenhandedness" may point to the fact that where "religion" is not singled out, a general disbursement may be less likely to be construed as "aid" to a religion, it is not the only factor to be considered. If it were, obviously religious institutions could "thrive off public money" as parochial schools could be funded *equally to public schools with tax dollars*.

But since that kind of "neutrality" or "evenhandedness" by itself is obviously insufficient, the Court has pursued other lines of enquiry to complement an "evenhanded neutrality." It has (1) distinguished two types of aid recipients, distinguishing the "pervasively sectarian" from the merely "religious schools"; and it has (2) identified two different methods of distribution of aid of (a) directness or indirectness of distribution, and (b) distribution by independent choice; and it has indicated (3) five significant characteristics of aid that should be considered, including its religious content, its cash form, its divertibility to religious support, its supplanting form in which the aid replaces the traditional religious expenses of the school, and its substantiality.

J. Souter pointed out that parochial schools have been recognized, via the 1983 Code of Canon Law, as "pervasively sectarian," which means that they do *not* accept that secular subjects should be "unrelated to religious teaching" but more "akin to aiding a church service," so although the Court in *Agostini* said it can no longer be presumed that public school teachers will teach religiously, the Court has *never* said that with regard to teachers of the *parochial* schools.[71] This means that the Court has recognized the nonseverability of secular subjects from religious ones in a *parochial school*, so direct government subsidies to such schools are *prohibited* since it *all* will "inevitably and impermissibly support religious indoctrination."[72] The Court has also realized that elementary and secondary school students are more *impressionable* than university students, as *Lemon* and *Tilton* show. And the intertwined secular/ religious functions in the parochial elementary and secondary schools suggest a *more easily divertible aid. Everson, Allen, Lemon, Levitt*, and *Witters* all mentioned that direct aid to the religious school or parochial school posed *greater risks of being diverted* than aid provided only to parents, for example.[73] As far as direct cash aid, the Court has allowed only one exception in *Regan* (1980) for the expenses of administering and grading mandated state-sponsored testing, but otherwise the Court has held to *nondiversion* and opposed direct cash payments for a *pervasively sectarian* school.

Regarding the content of the aid, which the Court wants to use to replace the test of "nondivertibility," where the content was perceived as religious, it was judged as illegal (*Lemon*), but when it was neutral or had no specific content such as a building *per se* (*Tilton*),[74] or an interpreter which was no more religious than a hearing aid (*Zobrest*), it was approved. Yet, obviously, the computers in the present case which were used more by the theology department than all other departments combined *had easily violated* the prohibited content over and over through several years. But the Court and J. O'Connor were persuaded that these years of violation were "de minimum," and quickly corrected.

J. Souter questioned how content can be monitored, as the Court, assumes, without creating an "excessive entanglement" between government and religion. It is not at all clear. The *Lemon* Court itself did *not* presume that all parochial teachers will continually violate the Establishment Clause, but it emphasized that if parochial teachers were subsidized, a mere "assumption" that they would *not try to indoctrinate* students is *not sufficient*; rather the "State must be certain, given the Religion Clauses, that subsidized teachers do not inculcate religion" and this requires continual, invasive monitoring which *disqualifies* it under *Lemon*'s "excessive entanglement" test. The same would be true of the "content" one can utilize through students' having computers, which is more obvious "risk" of indoctrination than were mere "filmstrips" or fieldtrips back in *Meek* (1975) and *Wolman* (1977) which were found *illegal*.

J. Souter summarized the cash payment stance, insisting that the Court has "never relaxed our prohibition on direct cash aid to pervasively religious schools (*Agostini*, at 228–229) and the plurality concedes this."[75] In *Everson*'s famous words against the divertibility of funds, "The State cannot consistently with the 'establishment of religion' clause of the First Amendment contribute tax-raised funds to the support of an institution which teaches the tenets and faith of any church" (330 U.S. at 16, 18). In *Mitchell*, the individual parochial schools filled out requests for the type of equipment they wanted, and no records were shown to reveal that the LEA turned down many specific items if any, so it was *no different than cash*.

J. Souter insisted that the issue of divertibility is not simply a concern with cash payments, anyway, as he compared bus trips used on a scheduled route only to and from school in *Everson* with the bus trips desired for field trips in *Wolman*, the ones in *Everson* being approved, but the busing for field trips denied.[76] He insisted that his reading of the divertibility issue is no more "boundless" as the Court accuses it, than is the Court's reading of "content."[77] Even the issue of mandated testing raised the question of whether parochial schools could be allowed to formulate their own tests and grade them vis-à-vis the state, and thereby satisfying state requirements, but the Court allowed funding state employees for the work but not the parochial school faculty (compare *Wolman* with *Levitt v. Committee for Public Ed. & Religious Liberty*, 413 U.S. 472 (1973)).[78]

Further, the idea of public funds being supplied to a parochial school to enable the school to use its own funds for something else such as religion classes has *never* been allowed by the Court. J. Souter argued that from *Cochran v. Louisiana Bd of Ed.*, 281 U.S. 370 (1930), the Court has not allowed aid that simply relieved the parochial school from using its own funds. So a distinction was drawn between funds that aided the school by "supplementing" its existing program in distinction from those that simply "supplant" or "substitute" government funds for the school's own funds. As the *Cochran* Court said, the parochial school is not "relieved of a single obligation because of them [the government funds]."[79] He admits that this principle was ignored only once—in the *Regan* decision—but he was convinced that the "weight that the plurality places on *Regan* is thus too much for it to bear,"[80] since even *Zobrest* and *Agostini* recently argued the aid in those cases was a "substitute," not a supplemental expense of their already-existing program. We discussed this problem earlier.

Finally, the question of the *substantiality* of the aid has bearing on the Court's assessment, as one can see in *Meek, Nyquist, Wolman, Witters*, and *Zobrest*, so has not been superseded by some other factor nor dropped from consideration. The larger the amount, the more *Meek* saw it difficult to say the school's aid was only "secular" or "incidental," and in *Zobrest*, the Court referred back to *Meek* with the argument that disabled children are a small part of the school's teaching obligation, so can be regarded as only "incidental beneficiaries." But J. Souter argued that such focus on "incidental" aid or minimal aid shows that "we have never questioned our holding in *Meek* that *substantial* aid to religious schools is prohibited,"[81] and the aid here was *quite substantial*.

All of these considerations, J. Souter emphasized, the Court must examine in asking in each case whether the *benefit is intended to aid in providing the religious element* of the education and is it likely to do so—not simply whether the benefit was given neutrally, meaning extended to various recipients? From his analysis, he insisted "the substance of the law has thus not changed since *Everson*. Emphasis on one sort of fact or another has varied depending on the perceived utility of the enquiry, but all that has been added is repeated explanation of relevant considerations, confirming that our predecessors were right in their prophecies that no simple test would emerge to allow easy application of the establishment principle." But, he added, "The plurality, however, would reject that lesson. The majority misapplies it."[82]

J. Souter pointed out that the plurality's emphasis on "evenhandedness neutrality" took on the appearance as the "single and sufficient test" for establishment cases involving school aid, revealing three mistaken assumptions the plurality made: (1) to make the "external observer's attribution of religious support to the government as the sole impermissible effect of a government aid scheme," since even if state aid is not attributed to government, the aid could nevertheless "violate a taxpayer's liberty of conscience, threaten to corrupt religion, and generate disputes over aid"; (2) of assuming that "equal amounts of aid to religious and nonreligious schools will have exclusively secular and equal effects, on both external perception and on incentives to attend different schools," since unrestricted aid to religious schools will support not simply secular but religious teaching; and (3) of assuming that "per capita distribution rules safeguard the same principles as independent, private choices," which is not true if one realizes that for true "private choice," the recipient would have to be presented with the choice of the school receiving the aid or not receiving it, and one of the Respondents in this case actually preferred that the school *not* receive the aid since she and others had seen a negative effect on the school by these ties to the government.[83] But under the plurality's position, *no right of individual conscience* would be left to deter the government funds, which would make government's influence greater on the schools and *more divisive* for any competing religious groups or others.

J. Souter insisted, however, that the real issue of the case was "divertibility," and the "anemic" enforcement of the regulations showed how actual diversion occurred over many years because of the type of the aid and the structure of the program. He pointed out that the school itself "not only was able to determine what kinds of supplies it wanted, but it was itself able to order them directly and have them forwarded directly to themselves."[84] Divertibility of the materials was even more easily accomplished since the materials were to use in parochial elementary and secondary schools in which the Court has judged students are much more impressionable than college students, more easily proselytized religiously. Further, the trial judge noted that the schools operated under the general supervision of the Archbishop of New Orleans and parish pastors. The schools were located beside or even within a rectory, included religious symbols in their classrooms, required attendance at daily religious classes, conducted sacramental preparation classes during the school day, required attendance at mass, and provided extracurricular religious activities. The published St. Anthony School Handbook, cited by the District Court, shows how *integrally religious indoctrination is in the school program*, infusing every aspect of it.[85] Teachers are expected to teach religiously, that when issues arise in the classroom touching on values, morality, or religion, the teachers' answers must "be consistent with the teachings of the Catholic Church."[86]

He pointed out that even the plurality was aware of the *ineffectiveness* of the government's monitoring, which was only sporadic. "State and local officials in Jefferson Parish admitted that nothing prevented the Chapter 2 computers from being used for religious instruction," no technologies were used to minimize divertibility, and "[g]overnment officials themselves admitted that there was no way to tell whether instructional materials had been diverted. No mechanisms were in place for the government to retain ownership of the properties, so officials admitted that when they got old, they were simply left with the schools."[87] J. Souter cited many cases (*Tilton, Nyquist, Wolman, Meek, Levitt, Lemon, Bowen*) to show that "[p]roviding such governmental aid without effective safeguards against future diversion itself *offends* the Establishment Clause."[88]

In fact, *Bowen* set the "correct evidentiary standard when it said, '[A]ny use of public funds to promote religious doctrines violates the Establishment Clause.'"[89] The bar was set this low to prevent any actual diversion of aid. The Court has never had to strike down any diverted aid, even though Madison saw even a "small infringement of the prohibition on compelled aid to religion is odious to the freedom of conscience." To this, J. Souter added, "No less does it open the door to the threat of corruption or to a return to religious conflict."[90] Because the diversion itself was unconstitutional, J. Souter refrained from a close examination of the question of an unconstitutional supplantation, which also occurred. He emphasized that the Court's debate

> makes one point clear: that in rejecting the principle of no aid to a school's religious mission the plurality is attacking the most fundamental assumption underlying the Establishment Clause, that government can in fact operate with neutrality in its relation to religion. I believe that it can, and so respectfully dissent.[91]

The issue is not a matter of what religious ideology, if any, the government shall choose, since the government is not a person and does not have a conscience. The question is whether some basic principles recognized by government and religious people could "overlap"—as J. Souter called it—giving a sense of a unity having priority over all citizens, but a unity that can enable religious free exercise *without* creating a religious establishment? Rawls thought it could. Our final chapter will perhaps provide more specifics to answer to this question as we conclude the survey of the recent Establishment cases.

NOTES

1. The Court's usual argument is "if the Framers of the Constitution engaged in certain practices after they wrote the Constitution and Bill of Rights and ratified them, then certainly those practices were not seen as a violation of the Constitution or Bill of Rights." It is not logical since seldom does actual practice measure up to the Ideal, even for people who believe in the latter.

2. California had become aware of phony religious degrees and ordination papers being sold for high prices to people who sought to avoid certain income taxes as a minister. Others engaged in selling stuff and not reporting it, as Swaggart. Others,

such as the Rev. Robert Schuler, only seven years prior, were given the deadline of August 31, 1983, by the same California Board of Equalization to pay $427,000 in owed back taxes for tickets it sold to its commercial productions over several years in the Crystal Cathedral. Most of these cases settled out of court.

3. *Board of Education of the Westside Community Schools (Dist. 66), v. Mergens, by and Through her Next Friend, Mergens*, 496 U.S. 226 (1990), at 250.

4. By 2005, in *Van Orden v. Perry*, the "government speech" would in fact *be allowed* to endorse religion, as two Justices (Kennedy and Scalia) insisted in the *oral argument*, which is a significant development to prepare for here. Of course, even if the Court thought it applied the *Lemon* test in *Widmar v. Vincent*, the final sentence above would obviously overlook and violate the "potential politically divisive" test of *Lemon*. J. Marshall, joined by J. Brennan, concurring, warned that the Court had relied too much on *Widmar* and had failed to see the problems barely below the surface that since the Christian club was the only advocacy or ideological group. Further, J. Stevens, offering the lone dissent, emphasized that the whole issue of resolving what was a "noncurriculum" activity by mere reference to a *dictionary* was misguided and simplistic; making a distinction which can be made to fit almost any type group, depending upon the desire of the school, which is too expansive, easily manipulatable. Rather, it should be on the basis of whether the forum was initiated with the *intent* of *accommodating any and all advocacy* groups.

5. Many schools had a "baccalaureate" service for graduates, on a Sunday night prior to the week of graduation. Local pastors officiated with in church buildings delivering a spiritual message, and prayers were expected, whereas the "graduation" or "commencement" services that followed a few nights later were held in the school facilities and were totally academic and nonreligious.

6. By 2005, J. Kennedy would be led by J. Scalia into an *opposite* position. See note 3.

7. Actually, J. Scalia was conflicted, insisting that everyone knows there is only one God, yet he emphasized that Christians pray to only one God whereas others pray to many gods.

8. *Lamb's Chapel v. Center Moriches Union Free School Dist.*, 508 U.S. 384 (1993), at 393.

9. *Lamb's Chapel*, at 387. The Court noted in ftnt. 5 (at 391) that three religious groups had already been allowed access to the facilities: a "New Age" group known as the "Mind Center" Southern Harmonize Gospel Singers, a Salvation Army Youth Band, and the Hampton Council of Churches' Billy Taylor Concert. These were either musical concerts or practice sessions, but there is no indication that they were intended to indoctrinate religiously as Dobson's own brochure insisted about his films.

10. *Lamb's Chapel*, at ftnt 3. Allegedly, Focus on the Family is Christian, therefore using the Christian scriptures as its guide, yet these three big faults that it cites, "where a 'civil war of values' is being waged—'governmental interference, abortion and pornography'"—are conspicuously absent in the Christian scriptures. On the other hand, the same scripture and tradition viewed greed, lying, covetousness, and many other things as deplorable "sins."

11. *Lamb's Chapel*, at 398–399.

12. *Lamb's Chapel*, at 399–400.

13. *Lamb's Chapel*, at 400.

14. When one counts all the cases in which the Supreme Court has overruled the Ninth Circuit, it is difficult to think the Republican prejudice against the Ninth Circuit has not pervaded the thinking of the U.S. Supreme Court, as if the West Coast of the United States is in a state of ignorance or "leftist" ideology.

15. *Zobrest*, at 16, citing *City of Mesquite v. Aladdin's Castle, Inc.*, 455 U.S. 283, 294 (1982).

16. *Zobrest*, at 18.

17. *Zobrest*, at 8.

18. *Zobrest*, at 12–13.

19. *Zobrest*, at 21–22.

20. *Board of Ed of Kiryas Joel Village School Dist. v. Grumet*, 512 U.S. 687, 706 (1994).

21. *Kiryas Joel Village*, at 709, citing *Torcaso v. Watkins*, at 492–495.

22. *Capitol Square Review and Advisory Board v. Pinette*, 515 U.S. 753 (1995).

23. *Capitol Square*, at 765, citing *Mergens*, 496 U.S. at 250.

24. Is that implying that the ethical and legal analysis of a known racist, hate group is *irrelevant*? If not, how narrowly was the Court using "political"? Did they have to burn the cross for the Court to realize their speech should not be protected as hate speech?

25. One must ask if the Court would have seen it differently had the KKK asked to erect a huge swastika at the site since that only expresses its religion? Did the Court allow the Cross because most of the Justices consider themselves Christian and have not deeply realized that it can also be a symbol of racial hatred, depending totally upon *who* is erecting it? Or did the Court already decide the "cross" symbolized only "death" as in a 2020 decision which we will later analyze?

26. When one views the "content" vs. "viewpoint" of the First Amendment, it goes without saying that if the general content is prohibited to be established, *any viewpoint of that religion* would *also* be, so the Court's whole argument here is extremely convoluted and without merit.

27. *Ronald W. Rosenberger, Petitioners v. Rector and Visitors of the University of Virginia.*, 515 U.S. 819, 836–837.

28. *Rosenberger*, J. Souter, dissenting, at 878.

29. *Rosenberger*, J. Souter, dissenting, at 882.

30. *Rosenberger*, J. Souter, dissenting, at 896.

31. *Agostini v. Felton*, 521 U.S. 203, 211 (1997). This is incredible since the only religious schools that were mentioned as being involved among the private schools receiving the services were Catholic; the very few others were Jewish.

32. This is later referred to by the Court as the "divertibility" rule, that is, the Court's awareness that public funds provided to a parochial school would have to be spent on the specific secular element, *not diverted* to something that would end up being a form of religious indoctrination. In reality, once the funds were given and mixed, the Court had long before recognized that the funds might simply be used for

something else or substituted for a secular service in one area of the school's program, allowing the school to use more of its funds for its religious mission since its mission was pervasively sectarian. The parochial schools had early on been approved in many states for public funds for public school speech therapists which they did not already have. However, the idea of a school not already providing *remedial* classes for under-performing students is simply poor educational practice. Further, as the dissent noted, now all a school had to do to qualify for the funds or services was to declare a certain needed program was "remedial" and "supplemental," which the school itself could not afford but needed very badly, and it could conceivably name almost anything "remedial" or "supplemental."

33. *Agostini*, at 218.

34. The Court noted the Ball decision suggested the possibility that when a school district chose not to monitor (which violated the excessive entanglement test of *Lemon*) to protect against indoctrination, rather than this exacerbating the chances of indoctrination, the Court's failure to provide specific examples of the indoctrination might have been due more to the irrelevance or difficulty in ascertaining that it really was indoctrination, which decreased any incentive to report it.

35. *Agostini*, at 219–220.

36. *Agostini*, at 221.

37. *Agostini*, at 222.

38. *Agostini*, at 222.

39. *Agostini*, at 224, citing *Zobrest* at 248.

40. *Agostini*, at 225.

41. The only way the Court could say this could not be perceived as state decision-making was by its overruling the state. In the latter's attempt to prevent any violation of the Establishment Clause, it had specified that although a recipient could use the grant at either public or private school, it could not be used as tuition of a program in a religious ministry. That was the state's decision. Overruling the state, the Court claimed that restriction illegal, and turned the whole thing on its head, so the Court could say this was a wholly private decision—which it never was.

42. *Agostini*, at 226.

43. *Agostini*, at 234.

44. The whole tenor of this decision, like her *Lyng* decision, is so far removed from Rawls's idea of "political justice" derived by freestanding principles of public reason by which the "overlapping principles" are reached and agreed to by all, a hypothetical divesting of irrational advantages or happenstance vested interests that have no moral value that could point to justice, that, ignorant of Rawls's groundbreaking work on legal or political justice, her decisions instead embrace a majoritarian position rather than accommodate diversity as a democratic republic.

45. Of course, many of these minority groups attempt to keep low profile, especially with all the racial and xenophobic violence that has occurred prior to and after the 2020 election. It has especially focused on African Americans and Asian Americans, but the anti-Semitism and Islamophobia and discrimination of Hispanics continues. The religious preferentialism feeds into a White Supremacy, and the combination is violent.

46. See especially Lee's *America for Americans*, esp.117–139.

47. *Santa Fe Independent School District v. Doe, individually and as next friend for Her Minor Children*, 530 U.S. 290, 295 (2000).

48. *Santa Fe*, at 296–297.

49. *West Virginia v. Barnette* at 638.

50. The fact that J. Thomas over and over insisted that the Establishment Clause does *not* apply to the *states*, makes his articulation for the Court in this Louisiana case quite unique if not *self-contradictory*.

51. See Everson, J. Jackson, dissenting, quoting Canon Law on Catholic religious education, at *Lemon*, J. Douglas concurring, at 639–640; *Grand Rapids v. Ball*, at 1080–1081, and ftnt 4 (but later overruled by *Agostini v. Felton*).

52. This means the typical scenario for many years was the Circuit Courts would use the Supreme Court's defined *Lemon* test, only to discover the Supreme Court *reversing* their decisions, minimizing the *Lemon* test. This made the whole Establishment jurisdiction a fiasco.

53. In the 1985–1986 school year, 41 private schools participated. In the following year there were 46, 34 of which were Catholic, 5 were nonreligious, and 7 others were religiously affiliated, though we are not told in what way (at 803).

54. This is proof that the Court here did not bother to read any of its decisions behind 1986.

55. *Mitchell v. Helms*, 530 U.S. 793, 810 (2000).

56. *Mitchell*, J. O'Conner, concurring, 836–867, at 829, citing *Agostini* at 226–228.

57. *Rosenberger v. Univ. of Virginia*, 515 U.S. 819.

58. The Executive Order that funded especially "faith-based" groups, beginning with President George Bush, seems to be based on an "evenhandedness" or, in their words, to "level the playing field," but such "orders" have not been sufficiently challenged yet.

59. *Mitchell*, J. Souter, dissenting, at 868.

60. *Mitchell*, J. Souter, dissenting, at 868.

61. It is worth recalling at this point that the Court has never even defined "religion," and the different components of it in different peoples' minds does not lend itself to some unambiguous word which needs no clarification. The closest the court got was when it utilized Tillich in the *Seeger* case to suggest that "ultimate concern" or a belief that "functioned" similarly to the way a belief in God functions would qualify for "religion." But how does one know how a "belief in God" *functions*, or even what people think they mean by the word "God"? This is the reason I have assumed that religion always *presupposes the Absolute*, whether as a being or idea, and is closed to any questioning or relativization of such a being or idea. That a religion usually involves a shaping of character, certain common beliefs or hopes, rituals, and symbols, involving worship, and usually involves ideas of a supernatural world which in some way has commerce with the world in which we live—is all part of this Absoluteness.

62. *Mitchell*, J. Souter, dissenting, at 873, citing *Everson*, 330 U.S. at 15–16, quoting *Reynolds v. United States*, 98 U.S. 145, 164 (1879).

63. *Mitchell*, J. Souter, dissenting, at 874, note 4.

64. I mentioned in the earlier examination of *Everson* that the Court slipped out of the Establishment Clause analysis into a Free Exercise analysis in order not to find the aid illegal.

65. Of course, he notes in passing what we mentioned in our earlier analysis of *Everson*, that the dissent pointed out that it was not a general benefit given to all, since no children attending private nonreligious schools received any bus reimbursement. (*Mitchell*, J. Souter, dissenting at 875).

66. *Mitchell*, J. Souter, dissenting, at 875.

67. *Mitchell*, J. Souter, dissenting, at 876.

68. *Mitchell*, J. Souter, dissenting, at 877.

69. *Mitchell*, J. Souter, dissenting, at 878.

70. *Mitchell*, J. Souter, dissenting, at 881–882.

71. *Mitchell*, J. Souter, dissenting, at 886, note 7.

72. *Mitchell*, J. Souter, dissenting, at 887, citing *Zobrest*, at 12 (discussing *Meek* and *Ball*).

73. While J. O'Connor, for the Court, in *Agostini* emphasized the Court "has departed from the rule . . . that all government aid" that goes directly to the parochial school is illegal, that was only dictum, while the case did not rely on this dictum, but "instead clearly stating that '[w]hile it is true that individual students may not directly apply for Title I services, it does not follow from this premise that those services are distributed directly to the religious schools.' In fact, they are not. No Title I funds ever reach the coffers of religious schools, and Title I service may not be provided to religious schools on a schoolwide basis" (*Mitchell*, J. Souter, dissenting at 888, note 8, citing *Agostini* at 228–229).

74. The Court in *Tilton* significantly forced the state to delete the provision that the building could not be used for religious purposes for the first 20 years, insisting that the funds were a permanent restriction against a religious usage; otherwise, it would have been a diversion of the funds at the end 20 years.

75. *Mitchell*, J. Souter, dissenting, at 892.

76. *Mitchell*, J. Souter, dissenting, at 894.

77. *Mitchell*, J. Souter, dissenting, at 893, note 13.

78. J. Souter also argued that the plurality in *Mitchell* was incorrect in reading *Mueller* and *Witters* as undermining the Court's opposition to divertible aid, while the Court in *Zobrest* did not consider the interpreter as "divertible" but akin to a hearing aid or to the diagnostic services allowed in *Wolman*. See *Mitchell*, J. Souter, dissenting, at 895–896, note 16.

79. *Mitchell*, J. Souter, dissenting, at 896, citing *Cochran* at 375.

80. *Mitchell*, J. Souter, dissenting, at 897, note 17.

81. *Mitchell*, J. Souter, dissenting, at 898, note 18.

82. *Mitchell*, J. Souter, dissenting, at 899.

83. *Mitchell*, J. Souter, dissenting, at 901–902, and 913, note 30.

84. *Mitchell*, J. Souter, dissenting, at 904, citing App. 156a–159a.

85. *Mitchell*, J. Souter, dissenting, at 904, note 23, and 905, notes 24 and 25.

86. *Mitchell*, J. Souter, dissenting, at 906, note 25.

87. *Mitchell*, J. Souter, dissenting, at 907–908.
88. *Mitchell*, J. Souter, dissenting, at 908.
89. *Mitchell*, J. Souter, dissenting, at 909, note 27, citing *Bowen*, 487 U.S. at 623.
90. *Mitchell*, J. Souter, dissenting, at 909, note 27.
91. *Mitchell*, J. Souter, dissenting, at 913.

Chapter 11

"No Law"?

The "Evenhandedness" and "Private Choice" Cure-All?

On January 29, 2001, only nine days after President George W. Bush took office, he signed *Presidential Executive Order 13199—Establishment of White House Office of Faith-Based and Community Initiatives*. This was, in his words, his effort to "level [the] playing field." In Section 1, the order explains, "the paramount goal is compassionate results, and private and charitable community groups, including religious ones, should have the fullest opportunity permitted by law to compete on a level playing field, so long as they achieve valid public purposes, such as curbing crime, conquering addiction, strengthening families and neighborhoods, and overcoming poverty."

Citizens pay taxes and have little recourse over the actual spending of these, to show "standing" to sue. Congress has the power of spending or "appropriating" the billions and billions of tax dollars each year, which no other government body has. It therefore has the power and right to fund programs to address these kinds of community needs throughout the nation. Any bill that the Senate and House both pass that requires funds include the approved appropriation of funds from the House. Yet if a bill passes both bodies, something that is of vital interest as helping the most destitute in the nation, it should be no problem to obtain funds from the same House. So with the billions in revenues at their disposal, they should be the *primary* governmental bodies to determine and administer to needs of the poor, sick, and disadvantaged.

Of course, there are religious groups who have traditionally used some of their voluntary tithes or contributions for such social needs, and some religious groups such as the Salvation Army have been much more responsive to these needs than others. But overall, only a small portion of the total contributions to most of these religious bodies finds its way to address these social problems and community needs. There are also other nonprofit organizations

467

and a few for-profit groups that address such needs. The question for funding any of the groups, religious or secular, with public money, is how would the government be sure its money was actually used for this rather than for other things? Naturally, it seems it would require submission of reports from the groups distributing or using the funds which would then be checked by the federal government.

The problem is more intense, however, if the funds are provided even to (if not primarily to) "faith-based" groups. Now care must be taken to not violate the Establishment Clause requirements. If one applied the *Lemon* test, even if one were to argue that the executive order really had a secular purpose rather than religious purpose (which is not evident by the very title and emphasis), and even if it might pass muster in showing that the primary effect was secular rather than sectarian, the third prong of *Lemon*, the "excessive entanglement" prohibition would likely make it illegal since that "prong" of *Lemon* raises the questions of (1) the nature of the party or organization that receives the aid, (2) whether the relationships will require continual monitoring by the government, and (3) the issue of the potential political divisiveness of the aid. Using "faith-based" groups in such a way seems to violate every part of the *Lemon* test, and the Court has *never overruled* the *Lemon* case or even its three-prong standard, though it has ignored it. But the *Lemon* Court itself did *not* formulate the test as a mere alternative, a possible standard, to offer future Courts a broad choice of "tests" or "standards." As we saw in the last case we just examined, the Court's biased "selective" reading of cases, its intentional ignoring of the earlier "tests" which themselves were formulated by their predecessors on the bench, and the exaggerated and superfluous arguments the Court has used to provide aid in the specific ways and forms explicitly prohibited by the earlier Court leave much to be desired of its jurisprudence. The "standard" or "test" is often produced only by a plurality and has been reduced primarily to "private choice" and "neutrality" which means to them only "evenhandedness," and even then, often that plurality recognizes only the most recent precedent cases, and those justices do not appear to be interested in trying to pull together the whole history of the Court's decisions to discover any unity or coherence, despite the profound work of J. Souter. Neither "private choice" nor "evenhandedness" come close to Madison's explicit statement that government has no "cognizance" (jurisprudence) of religion.

Tax funds are universally compelled by the government. So this would amount to taking funds acquired by government coercion from many people who would strenuously object to the funds being given to *any religious* group, regardless of the alleged purpose. What would prevent a religious group from training its people to subtly indoctrinate the recipients of their aid and funds? With many religious groups, there would be no need for such training, since they would see it simply as "open season" or a "green light" to evangelize at the government's expense, that is, by this public funding. To think otherwise is simply to fail to realize how most religious groups see their "mission." Those religious groups who seem reticent to ask for such funding are in many cases trying not to attract attention to themselves because of the obvious xenophobia combined with some form of Christian religious majoritarianism which has manifested an extremely violent history throughout the past four centuries, despite our Constitution. Even the nonreligious citizens feel the pressure of this majoritarianism.

One might argue that any individual with any community group could do the same indoctrinating or evangelizing. While that is not an impossibility, the difference, however, is that for many "faith-based" groups, their *primary mission* is to *indoctrinate*; and their typical budgets reveal that general community social services are toward the bottom of their funded concerns, more of an aspiration than a significant reality. To include "community" groups who have no religious mission, and think they would be as likely to try to use the funds or opportunities to evangelize is quite a stretch. Even if there was not an explicit nexus between the funds and evangelizing through particular social activity funded to the "faith-based" groups, there is hardly any question that for a religious group to receive tens of thousands of dollars a year for such a cause would "free up" its budget, enabling the "faith-based" group to apply the portions of its own volunteered contributions that would ordinarily have been used for its social "outreach" now to actually *increase* its own evangelistic or indoctrination efforts. That is the very substitution which Justice Souter so eloquently argued is not being adequately owned up to by the Court. By the faith-based groups shifting the funds from one hand to the other, the government would still be *subsidizing* the general *indoctrination* efforts of the religious group, even if there were absolutely no actual indoctrination efforts within the church's community social action work itself. Decades before, the Court had seen this switching of public funds from hand to hand as an illegal establishment in parochial schools. How did it now become legal?

For the Order merely to safeguard against First Amendment violations by saying that everything in the Order is all qualified by the repetitious term, "to the extent permitted by law," is too indefinite to guarantee anything. Even the service itself might well be used to give credit to the "faith-based" group as if this aid were the church's own generous dollars rather than the public taxes. What appears so strange throughout the Order is that there is not one mention of the Establishment prohibition that the work must avoid violating. Instead, it was intended to "level the playing field." Since when were social services for the needy actually "competing" against each other? What is the intent or goal behind "leveling the playing field"? Rather than merely increase aid to the poor, to "level the playing field" sounds like the real concern is about *who gets the credit* for such community services. If tax dollars are used, the credit goes to the public.

To even suggest that the "delivery" of these services will be rooted in the "bedrock principles of pluralism, nondiscrimination, evenhandedness, and neutrality" fails to consider limitations of the Establishment Clause as well as typical forms of discrimination so often a part of the mission of various religious groups. Is it too late in the day for us to *need to be reminded* of the distinction drawn even by the Framers of the First Amendment when they suggested a "wall of separation," in which even "three pence" mixing of funds (as mandated taxes on the public would be when given to a religious organization) was *too much*? As we noted earlier, Jefferson's bill as well as Madison's *Memorial and Remonstrance*, which lay behind the religion clauses of the First Amendment, transcended the rather nebulous idea of toleration or mere government equal "accommodation" of different religious sects.

The Framers grounded the religious freedom on an *individual's natural rights*, something unalienable, which Madison and Jefferson judged totally *outside* the jurisdiction or even legal "cognizance" of government. They and many others were persuaded through the sordid history of most religions, including Christian history, that any governmental interference into the private sphere of religion served to cripple both religion and government, and that religion has flourished best when it depended only on persuasion and reason, even ironically doing better through persuasion and reason when it was actively persecuted by government, much more than after it became the state religion. Was this ever considered by those who quickly passed through the President's Executive Order 13199? What of Jefferson's adamant protest?

> [T]o compel a man to furnish contributions of money for the propagation of opinions which he disbelieves, is sinful and tyrannical; that even the forcing him to support this or that teacher of his own religious persuasion, is depriving him of the comfortable liberty of giving his contributions to the particular pastor, whose morals he would make his pattern, and whose powers he feels most persuasive to righteousness . . . it is time enough for the rightful purposes of civil government, for its officers to interfere when principles break out into overt acts against peace and good order; and finally, that truth is great and will prevail if left to herself.[1]

It is not a small wonder that this establishment of such "White House Office of Faith-Based and Community Initiatives" was challenged, and went to the Supreme Court by 2007, which we will cover later.

"NEUTRALITY" AND "PRIVATE CHOICE" COMPETING
WITH OBVIOUS FINANCIAL INCENTIVE

Only a year after Bush signed the executive order, the Court decided *Zelman, Superintendent of Public Instruction of Ohio, et al. v. Simmons-Harris, et al.*, 536 U.S. 639 (2002). This is a complex story that can be very emotional, and one can easily allow one's empathic response to bracket out any legal analysis of the facts and arguments. Simply put, Cleveland, Ohio's public schools had reached the bottom of the educational rung, with most students dropping out before graduating, and even the few who graduated from high school were unable to show academic skills comparable to others their age. We are not given details of the tax base for the Cleveland City School District during this alleged degeneration of the academic enterprise, nor how many tax dollars had already been diverted to charter or other community schools prior to this action, but in 1995 a Federal District Court placed the Cleveland School District under state control. Ohio's Pilot Project Scholarship Program was initiated for the school year of 1996–1997, providing parents with new choices of schools and funding of their choices.

We are not told where the millions of dollars came from to establish this program to serve the 75,000 students of the District. Nor are we told why the state decided to channel funds to private schools rather than give their public schools the entirety of the projected funds to help shore up the public schools. In any case, the *voucher program* was aimed especially for those families who were below the 200% poverty rate, but it included many families *above that*. On the surface, it seemed intelligent, compassionate, and emotionally approvable. But constitutional questions are not the type that are resolved by emotions. They often require, as the Court says, "line drawing," which can be very emotionally uncomfortable, though legally necessary.

The simple problem was that the Supreme Court had a long history of precedent cases whose decisions articulated that government funds can*not* be given to parochial schools just as they cannot be to churches. But this "no aid" of any kind, this "wall of separation" articulated by Jefferson, was soon compromised, yet the "aid" was deemed legitimate *only* within very limited parameters, due to the obvious "pervasive" religious mission those school followed (*Lemon v. Kurtzman*, 1971; *Committee for Public Education & Religious Liberty v. Nyquist*, 1973; *Levitt v. Committee for Public Ed. & Religious Liberty*, 1973; *Meek v. Pittenger*, 1973; *Wolman v. Walter*, 1977; *Grand Rapids v. Ball*, 1985; *Aguilar v. Felton*, 1985). All the limitations spelled out in these parochial school cases, supplemented by the many cases involving peoples' attempt to get religion into the public schools, were simply *now ignored* by the Court.

The Court acknowledged in the year at issue before the Court, the 1999–2000 school year, that although the plan made available as a school choice between (1) remaining in the traditional public schools, (2) entering a community school, (3) entering a magnet school, or (4) entering a private nonreligious or private religious school, *only the latter* was accomplished by the new voucher system. The results were (1) 82% of the private schools were, in fact, religious schools; (2) no public schools opted to be included except the Cleveland schools, even though adjacent public schools had been included in the plan for tuition scholarships or vouchers; and (3) 96% of the scholarships finally given by the state were to parents who chose a parochial school for their child.

Those results seem very one sided, as if the whole plan was to enhance the parochial school enrollment by public taxes. But it was even more obvious in the way the funds were to be allotted. The awards were divided into two groups—scholarships or tuition aid for the private school students (82% of which were parochial schools), and tutorial aid for the public school students. The disparity in the amounts of aid was notable between the "scholarships" ("tuition aid") given only to students who elect a private school, and the "tutorial aid" given to those students who elect to remain in the public schools. The maximum for tutorial aid in the *public* schools per student was 90% of the total cost up to $360 for the poorest families; for all others it was 75% up to $360—as opposed to 90% of the total cost up to $2,250 for the poorest families receiving a scholarship or tuition aid to attend a *private* (or *religious*) school (with a possible co-pay by parents of no more than $250), and 75% up to $1,875 for all others in the *parochial* schools, with no required co-pay. The reason for this disparity between $360 and $2,250 is not given, but it was considerable *motivation* for parents to move their children to a private (parochial) school. Of course, no parents would have had to pay anything had the money all been given to the public schools to improve them and service all students free of charge.

The Court tried to distract from the obvious disparity by noting that the law required that "the number of tutorial assistance grants offered to students in a covered district must equal the number of tuition aid scholarships provided to students enrolled at participating private or adjacent public schools." Yet the Court admitted that *no* adjacent public schools chose to participate in the program. In addition, there are two more distinguishing and disturbing elements in this quotation by the Court. It did not say that the total *amount* of tax money actually given through tutorial grants must be the equivalent of the total amount given through the tuition or scholarship grants. It is only equating the *number of students* receiving the aid—must be the same. But it really does not even say that, but only that the number "offered" as tutorial aid must equal the number "provided" as the scholarship or tuition aid. Therefore, if one takes a hypothetical figure of 10,000 students, and the tutorial aid was "offered" to all of them, and all of them accepted it, the actual money involved would have equaled giving them 90% of $3,600,000 or $3,240,000. If the same amount of students received the tuition aid or scholarship, so 90% of the $22,500.000 meant the actual money involved would have been $20,250,000.

On the other hand, if all that was required was a showing that the same number of tutorial aid students had been "offered," but *no* particular number had to *actually receive* it, then the actual amounts could have been as disparate as $0 for tutorial grants (since there was no minimum that had to be disbursed) vis-à-vis $20,250,000 for tuition or scholarship aid in the private or religious schools. The Court fails to tell how many students received tutorial aid in the 1999–2000 school year, noting only that 1,400 did in the year prior, and they anticipated much more in 1999—yet they somehow had the figures that 3,700 students in the private (parochial) schools received tuition aid or scholarships. Obviously this number fails to meet the requirement stated by the Court that the number of recipients offered tutorial aid had to equal the number receiving scholarship aid, and we are left wondering why such a vital statistic of tutorial-aid recipients for 1999 would not have been available. It gives the impression that the rules were not followed or the offers were so disparate in amounts that one could only expect that two and one-half times more students would select a private school over a public school, as they did.

The private schools, of which 82% were parochial, had little in the way of requirements to meet, only that they must not discriminate on admissions on the basis of race, religion, or ethnic background, and that they not "advocate or foster unlawful behavior or teach hatred of any person or group on the basis of race, ethnicity, national origin, or religion." These are fairly insipid, since it is unlikely that any religious group would *explicitly* foster unlawful behavior or teach hatred of anyone else. But the regulations leave *any amount of religious indoctrination* by the religious schools as totally acceptable, so long as it does not foster "unlawful behavior" or "teach hatred" of any person or group. The result: millions of dollars would pay for both secular and *religious indoctrination* in the parochial schools.

The Court lists how much the state provides for each public school child ($4,167), and how much the state funds the child who is in a community school ($4,518) which, it observes, is twice the amount being provided to those who enroll in the new programs ($2,250). The community schools "are funded under state law, but are run by their own school board, not by local school districts." They "enjoy academic independence to hire their own teachers and to determine their own curriculum. They can have no religious affiliation and are required to accept students by lottery." On the other hand, the magnet schools are funded under state law for a total of $7,746 per student per year, including the amount all public schools receive ($4,167, plus the $2,250 of the new program?) (which math adds up only to $6,417?). They are "operated by a local school board that emphasizes a particular subject area, teaching method or service" such as the Montessori schools.

In any case, new moneys were infused into a nearly defunct educational system. We are not given any statistics of how things changed, whether it meant academic improvement or not. It would have seemed that such improvement would have been a paramount consideration and important fact to sway the legitimacy of the project. On the other hand, with so many students being bled out of the public schools which were already underfinanced, the public schools had even less money to meet their educational objectives than before. Perhaps this is the reason there are no measurements of achievements due to the project. Certainly this starving of the public schools in favor of private schools and voucher systems in other states has often simply hastened the absolute poverty of the public school system, and in many cases, as one justice admitted on a certain occasion, those teaching in parochial schools ironically do not have the advanced degrees of those teaching in the public schools, nor do they have to meet the same standards in all states.

The Court defensively insisted that what made this *all legal* was (1) that it did not involve any money going from the government to a religion, but only to the parents of the child (who, it admitted then had to endorse the check and turn it over to the school, whether parochial or not); (2) that it was a very "neutral" program, not promoting nor hindering religion, giving lots of choices to the parents; and (3) by virtue that the parents themselves made the choice about where to send their child to school, the disbursement of the tax funds was made by their own "private choice," not by a religious group or certainly not by the government. This meant, as the Court says it, that no reasonable observer, familiar with the facts, could assert credibly that the government was endorsing a religion. As earlier, it all boils down to the assertion of "neutrality."

The first argument is hollow since this is not a mere reimbursement of funds they themselves spent, but a passing of a check from the state to the religious school through the parents, who have *no choice* or control regarding the *money which never was theirs.* So it is government's *direct funding* of tax moneys to religious schools by "private choice" of parents.

The second argument, that the program was totally neutral, ignores the fact obvious to the parents as well as the educators, that by parents selecting a parochial school for their child, they were removing funds from the economically starved public schools, and using it as a scholarship to pay for nearly every expense of their child, including teaching and *religious indoctrination.* This was *not* a mere *un*expected, "incidental" benefit the religious schools received, as the Court would like to parallel it with other "incidental" religious benefits in cases, not when the *enticement* of the money and a knowledge that though there might be more charges later in any private school, that would *not* be in the case in the religious school.

To pay 96% of the scholarships to parochial school families was surely the expected result of the legislators unless they were totally ignorant of the Ohio school system and amount of parochial schools in the state. There was nothing "neutral" or "broad" in the choices, as the actual choices that were made reveal. The Court attempted to dislodge any idea that new money attracted a flourish of activity for religious schools by saying the high percentage of private schools that were parochial (82% in Cleveland) is simply "a phenomenon common to many American cities." Even if true, it meant it would have failed the first prong of the *Lemon* test.

The third argument for the legitimacy of the program by the Court is that it was a totally "private choice" but its "privacy" is precisely parallel to the "general assessment" bill Gov. Henry proposed for Virginia which Madison, Jefferson, and others defeated, and their position then drew up the First Amendment from that *defeat* of mere "private" choice. Madison and Jefferson did *not* see people's private choice under Gov. Henry's Bill as sufficing for legality. Government was not supposed to be involved in the religious affairs and institutions. But the Court did not even mention Madison's *opposition* to that proposed Virginia bill, much less the fact that he won, which was the framework for the First Amendment. How the "strict constructionists" on the Court can read the same text written by Madison and others, after the latter worked with it over and over, and as "strict constructionists" they can ignore the entire process of the framing of the Amendment with its definite contextually limiting language and its Virginia historical setting—and make it mean almost the precise *opposite*—is inexplicable.

The Court, instead, compared this with *Witters*, saying the state was totally neutral, and the decision was made by the individual, not the state. But the most dispositive example is the very Virginia proposal that Madison and others defeated. It is still the funds that *belong to the state*, no longer money that belongs to the person, who pays the tax. In this Ohio case, there were no safeguards that kept the state's funds directed entirely for secular expenditures, which the Court in these earlier cases had insisted was necessary. The Court ignored the question of divertibility and substitution of funds.

J. O'Connor noted that the millions of dollars here involved is only a drop in the bucket when compared with all the tax breaks, and so on that government has given *religion*. She was correct. That simply shows that the Court's decision to "accommodate" religion, *one particular religion* (Christianity), to the tune of billions and billions of dollars since *Everson*, exacerbated the strain already existing between the various religions. Would the Court have even considered possibly ruling this way if 82% of the private schools in Ohio who received the taxes were Islamic schools or Hindu schools?

In this 5/4 decision, the four dissenting justices were all fearful that this decision by the majority would *accentuate the divisiveness* that already exists between people of different religions in the United States, something this nation certainly does not need. J. Stevens's short dissent is very relevant and pungent, defining the question before the Court: "Is a law that authorizes the use of public funds to pay for the indoctrination of thousands of grammar school children in particular religious faiths a 'law respecting the establishment of religion' within the meaning of the First Amendment?" This being so, he avers that the Court has spent its time, instead, hashing over three factual matters that *should* have been *ignored* since they have *no place* in the determination of the constitutionality of the funding of the educational program *per se*. These three are (1) the severity of the educational crisis in Cleveland, (2) the alleged "wide range of choices" made available through the program, and (3) the "voluntary character of the private choice to prefer a parochial education over an education in the public school system." His argument can hardly be gainsaid.

Even so, the most telling criticism of the majority opinion was again in J. Souter's dissent, joined by J. Stevens, J. Ginsburg, and J. Breyer. His argument is a general and slightly briefer analysis of the history of the Court's Establishment jurisdiction since *Everson* which he gave in *Mitchell* in 2000. The thrust of his argument was that since the *Everson* case in 1947, the Court has moved its standard in several stages, without acknowledging how these changes relate to the *basic principle* espoused by the *entire Court* in *Everson*, which, he emphasized, has *never been disavowed* by the Court (despite the incongruous 5/4 decision of *Everson*), which was the following: "No tax in any amount, large or small, can be levied to support any religious activities or institutions, whatever they may be called, or whatever form they may adopt to teach or practice religion."[2]

Legally, that principle still stands, so he asked how the majority could possibly be faithful to that principle while turning neutrality and private choice into the main if not only criteria. But he noted that even the "neutrality" was nullified here by the *disparity* of amounts of state funding between the private schools (predominately parochial) and the public schools, that is, comparing the "tuition" scholarships with the "tutorial" aid. The 96% figure of the 8.2 million in taxes spent by the state on parochial schools shows it was not "neutral." "Private choice" implies real and valid or equal choices (if not equal, they would nullify the alleged neutrality), but few private secular schools participated to any significant degree. There was *"financial incentive"* to influence "private choice," to cause the decision to be made to attend the *parochial* school, to be willing to be religiously indoctrinated, a consideration the *Court articulated* even *prior* to *Mitchell v. Helms* in 2000—*but not here.*

Further, the public school option which did *not* include the state vouchers was only possible tutorial aid which maxed out at 90% of the $360 or $324 per child as compared with the $2,250 of the school vouchers for private schools. That is neither neutrality nor real choice since few private nonreligious options were available, and the public school options were not close in the amount of funding. J. Souter argued that the Court moved from substantive considerations back in 1947 to a pure and vapid "formalism" here, with neither neutrality nor really valid individual choice.

He schematized the Court's gradual dilution of its dedication to the principle of *Everson.* The first period in which the *Everson* principle was followed of no aid ran from 1947 to 1968. In *Bd. of Education v. Allen,* even though the Court allowed local public school boards to *lend* secular textbooks to parochial schools, thinking it was an "in-kind" form of aid, no more objectionable than the bus fares of *Everson,* the dissent, especially both J. Black and J. Douglas foresaw problems in the future as schools would place pressure upon the boards to utilize textbooks more favorable to the church.

Souter said the second stage flowed out of the recognition in *Allen* that parochial schools did have both a secular and religious purpose, so the issue of "divertibility" became *paramount* following *Allen,* for example, in *Lemon v. Kurtzman* (1971), and "excessive entanglement" was added as a valid consideration of constitutionality along with the law's purpose and effect. So long as a valid secular and religious functioning of the recipient of the aid revealed a credible separation which would not require continual monitoring, the Court often yielded to the request for the aid. If, however, stratagems were utilized to dodge the "no aid" idea, the Court insisted on the criteria of the nondivertibility of the aid, and the focus was ultimately on what the funds *actually bought. Nyquist* (1973) found the divertibility obvious, but also ruled that merely payments to the parents through tax deductions is no different from direct aid to parents, but the dispositive element is the ultimate *effect* of the aid on the religious institution. The idea that the originator and sponsor of something can avoid being legally responsible for the *result* because he or she passed it "through the hands" of another party is as incredible as saying that if I provide a gun and $10,000 to a person to kill someone else, I am not responsible. I have been cleansed of any real connection to the killing by that person whose "hands I passed the responsibility and means to do it." It might even be a conspiracy, but it is *not* a dissolving of the connection,

With *Mueller v. Allen,* however, in 1983, a new step occurred in the Court's position, a step, as J. Souter calls it, "down the road from realism to formalism." J. Souter claims the aid in question was not distinguishable from *Nyquist* (1973) (which had been struck down by the court), but the Court insisted that since the law allegedly was *generally for all*, it was not favoring religion.[3] If the law in question in *School District of Grand Rapids v. Ball* (1985) was found illegal, nevertheless, J. Souter averred, the Court clarified that the notions of evenhandedness neutrality and private choice in *Mueller* were not applicable to cases involving *direct* aid to parochial schools, which were still subject to the divertibility test. This is crucially correct.

But *Agostini v. Felton* which involved aid of the same substance as *Ball* (1997) *rejected* the "divertibility" concern or rule, insisting that so long as the aid merely *supplemented rather than supplanted* the existing educational services, it was constitutional. If *Agostini* marked the end of the divertibility test, other cases had arisen during this period such as *Witters* and *Zobrest* in which the recipient of the aid was a single individual, and the Court had approved the laws in both cases on the basis of there being no religious classification utilized, not a substantial governmental expenditure, and the choice of schools was made by the individual or his parents.

From this progression, J. Souter asserted, the Court had now *cast aside* not only the "no aid" principle and the "divertibility" test, but included *substantial taxes being diverted* to religious schools, quite predictably, by no real meaningful choice or evenhanded neutrality of treatment of the public and parochial schools. It is noteworthy that the *lower* courts in *Zelman v. Simmons-Harris* had both found the educational voucher system to *violate* the *Lemon* test. Although J. Rehnquist, writing for the Court, said the "effect" prong of *Lemon* had to be satisfied by examination (he assumed the "purpose" test could pass muster without any testing?), he and the majority otherwise did not even try to counter the evolution of the Court's standard that J. Souter had traced.

All the Court said in reply was as follows: "While our jurisprudence with respect to the question of the constitutionality of direct aid programs has 'changed significantly over the past decades, *Agostini*.' supra at 236, our jurisprudence with respect to the true private choice programs has remained consistent and unbroken." J. Souter shows that it is completely untrue when one studies the crucial test of "divertibility" of the government funds in the school "Establishment" cases the Court decided between 1947 and 1977 as well as *Grand Rapids School District v. Ball*, 473 U.S. 373 (1985) and *Aguilar v. Felton*, 473 U.S. 402 (1985), the latter of which found government funds to the parochial school illegal because of the *pervasively sectarian* nature of the parochial school, in which even the teaching of secular subjects could be used to indoctrinate the students religiously.

The Court simply presumed now that such would never be factual, or, if it were, it would be harmless at worst. The Court turned more a blind eye on forms of illegal divertibility or the actual need to monitor, being persuaded that monitoring is really not necessary, and by *Mitchell v. Helms* (2000), was willing to say that the idea of religious "indoctrination" by a parochial school is a *much narrower activity* than the Court formerly thought; certainly most of the school's work is now viewed as completely "secular" to justify the government aid, yet with no real identification by the Court of the ways in which such schools *actually indoctrinate*.

But how does the Court describe such schools in *Our Lady of Guadalupe* (2020) and *Hosanna-Tabor Lutheran Church* (2012) cases? Is the "mission" of *no concern* to the Court, at least as long as it is a Catholic school or at least a Christian school (unless the Court is adjudicating the school's employment decisions); but what if it were a Muslim, Hindu, or Buddhist school? How does the school have a very pervasively religious mission when it is examined under the Free Exercise Clause but its religious mission to indoctrinate is such a narrow field that it is imperceptible under the Establishment Clause? How could it be *both*?

The Court insisted the solution to the question in this case involved only three precedent cases, and the decision was similar, approving the aid (*Mueller* (1983), *Witters* (1986), and *Zobrest* (1993)), but it was completely silent in trying to square the Court's present decision with all the decisions it made from 1947 to 1983. If precedent means anything, it should have required more than a mere silent treatment on the Court's part. If the Court's willingness to try to answer the *lower court*'s holdings via the *Lemon* test means anything, those *earlier cases* should have been defended and the present decision should have been analyzed specifically as *compatible* with them. Instead, all the Court says is that the crucial decision was "left open" by the *Nyquist* Court.

Does not the Court's approach here leave in the dust, as simply a relic of ancient history, Jefferson's and Madison's and others' ideas of a "wall of separation" between government and religion? The Court had uncourageously nullified *Lemon* without having the nerve to overrule it, and seemed oblivious to all kinds of religious divisiveness which comes as a result of decisions such as these, divisiveness that eats away at the sense of unity so important to maintaining a democratic society. To think that Madison and Jefferson really meant in the First Amendment that the state taxes can be used to support parochial or religious schools if a *parent chooses* it, no matter how much it pays for religious indoctrination so long as the school does not teach hatred of other religions, is to totally misread them and to ignore Madison's expressed fear of "majoritarianism."

It also flies in the face of Rawls's profound *separation* of (1) a democratic government whose citizens honor diversity by formulating their standard of justice from "freestanding" principles of public reason, behind a veil of ignorance, reaching an overlapping consensus with a sense of unity which can accommodate diversity so long as the basic laws, agreed to by all, are kept, and (2) religious institutions and other associations which are *less inclusive* groups, operating with a "nonpublic reason" and no willingness to compromise, often with an absolutized mythical or metaphysical position that is rejected by everyone outside the particular group, which makes them unable to form the law for the diverse population of the nation. Only the broad and stable inclusive unity of a democratic society is able to accommodate differences, but the *basic principles* of justice must have a "political" nature rather than "metaphysical" and must have *priority* if the nonpublic reason of associations or religions conflicts with them. This was Rawls's answer not only to the quest for justice as "fairness" which involves moving beyond majoritarianism as well as individuals trying to take advantage of each other, but also to the problem when a society embraces religious pluralism. No religion can be given an advantage.

U.S. citizens in the twenty-first century embrace many religions that most of the European immigrants to our shores had absolutely no familiarity with, perhaps never even heard of. Yet these days the Court seems ironically to be working in the *opposite direction* we would then expect—allowing more and more a *single religion* to be established, favored, funded by state taxes, while trying desperately to deny it with all kinds of red herrings, as the religious diversity expands exponentially. Some justices seem to be consciously creating new standards or tests for Establishment cases, which allows them to settle into embracing the particular religious group and parochial schools that they were a part of in their own childhood, having never realized the danger of its *absolutism*, and evidently knowing very little of any other religions or even of philosophers such as John Rawls. They were placed in those positions to defend the Constitution and the democratic republic which *assumes and values diversity* and not simply *taking advantage of others*, or protecting one's particular advantage, as Rawls showed.

THE TEN COMMANDMENTS' MOVE: FROM MT. SINAI TO U.S. STATES' GOV'T PROPERTY

Ironically, despite the *Stone v. Graham* decision in 1980, both Texas and Kentucky more recently (2005) attempted to place sculptures or plaques of the Ten Commandments on or inside government property. The Court heard the oral argument for *Van Orden v. Perry*, 545 U.S. 677 (2005), a Texas case, and on the *same day* (March 2, 2005) heard the oral argument for *McCreary County, Kentucky, et al. v. American Civil Liberties Union of Kentucky et al.*, 545 U.S. 844 (2005), a Kentucky case. On the question of whether a display of the Ten Commandments on government property violates the Establishment Clause, the Court issued opposite answers in its decisions to the two cases, again, on the same day of June 27, 2005. How could opposite opinions on similar facts about the same subject be given on the same day? By only a *plurality it approved* the Ten Commandments monument in *Van Orden v. Perry* (the Chief Justice Rehnquist wrote for the Court, joined by J. Scalia, J. Kennedy, and J. Thomas, while J. Breyer wrote a concurring opinion, concurring only in the judgment). Basically the sides simply switched chairs but found a majority to disapprove of *McCreary*. But by all the justices knowing the decisions the Court was rendering in both cases, J. Scalia took advantage in the *McCreary* case and used the Court's opinion in *Van Orden v. Perry* to buttress his vicious and alarming *dissent* in *McCreary*.

Notably, those on the Court who disliked the *Lemon* test, which was fairly decisive in *McCreary v. A.C.L.U.*, *refused to use it* to examine the situation and law in *Van Orden v. Perry*.[4] The question in *Van Orden v. Perry* was whether by the display's *age* (the monument of the Ten Commandments had been on the government grounds for 40 years, which was the primary factor swinging Breyer to concur with the Court's result), and the apparent lack of offense anyone took to it prior to this case, and the idea that its inclusion in a park-like setting with 17 other monuments (though none of these were religious in any sense), *cleansed* the Decalogue of any religiously objectionable feature. Basically, the Court did not deny that it had religious significance, but asserted that it had a *dual reference*, religious and secular, that was *historically credible* as the *founding of law in the United States*.

That was an *incredible historical assertion* and move, from the origin of the religion of Ancient Israel (the predecessor of the various *Judaisms*) at Mt. Sinai in the thirteenth century BCE to place it on the capitol grounds in Austin, Texas, in the twentieth century as *Christian law* but also the foundation of Texas and U.S. law. Otherwise, it was distinguished from *Stone* and *McCreary* in that it was a "passive monument," amid many others on the grounds, and had been given by the Fraternal Order of Eagles rather than a church, with the purpose of reducing juvenile delinquency.[5]

While the Court spoke of some earlier Court opinions to insist that government must not be hostile to religion, what it did *not* do were obvious: (1) it did not explore any real relationship between the *actual content* of the Ten Commandments and the *actual content* and founding of U.S. law or even of Texas law, which we already analyzed in an earlier chapter (except for Texas law); (2) nor did it discuss the *historical meaning* the Decalogue had to *Ancient Israel* and thereby *only to Judaism*, of *their* being God's chosen people of the world, and of *establishing a theocracy* around this covenant God made with them after delivering them in the Exodus, or *how this* would relate to Texas culture; (3) nor did it show how the appropriation of this particular symbol of one particular people was in *any way justified* or true in the sense of *validating any law* for *Christians*; (4) nor did it discuss the historical debate over "law" in general in *early Christianity* in which the position of the Apostle Paul won out and *separated* the Christian faith from all Jewish law (including the Decalogue) and derogatorily saw Judaism as simply inferior to Christianity as its mere predecessor; (5) nor did it show any awareness that some fundamental laws against stealing, killing, an so on in the formulation of U.S. law were simply *common* civil discoveries of cultures and nations as far back as 4,000 years and which were *never* dependent upon nor actually derived from *any specific religious code*, certainly not from the Ten Commandments which were only extant in Ancient Israel; (6) nor did it show that its presence in Austin was not "potentially politically divisive" by merely *assuming* that this single litigant was the *only* person who ever found this offensive or felt it was an endorsement of a particular religion by the state; (7) nor did it show any connection between its presence or even in the generous gifting by the Eagles of similar exhibits elsewhere in the nation and its alleged secular purpose of reducing juvenile delinquency.

Instead, not only was it the *only religious monument* among all the monuments on the 22 acres, but it included on it two stars of David and a Chi Rho Greek symbol for Christ, thus an embracing of Judaism's and Christianity's attachment to the Decalogue, *as if* the two religions have always embraced each other, which showed a *total ignorance of religious history*. If the lower court concluded that a reasonable observer of it would *not* have seen it as *endorsing religion*, then that person would have to be also quite ignorant of the Ten Commandments, as well as completely ignorant of Judaism and Christianity. On the other hand, if the Decalogue was so vital to the law of the United States, one would have expected to find it mentioned specifically in the Constitution and Bill of Rights. But there is *never* any such reference, *not even obliquely*.

Two of the justices saw the Jewish-Christian heritage of the United States as very *generic* and the god of each being the same "unitary" or "generic" or "only" God, thus, *universal and inclusive* (two *incompatible* qualities that are true of *no* religion), so they insisted in the oral argument that we must be careful not to be hostile to religious accommodation. In that oral argument, they both insisted that if someone sees the monument and is offended by it, then he can just turn his head and quit being offended, since it is a legitimate governmental expression of the government's religion. This was shocking, so was not put into the written decision of the Court.

In the written decision, the plurality's opinion, written by C.J. Rehnquist, for the Court, admits it has both upheld and invalidated laws under the Establishment Clause (nothing an informed person wouldn't already know), even recently, but it insists that *Lemon* has not always been useful and is not here. (Here, we must recall J. Scalia's remark about when the Court uses the *Lemon* test.) The Court then reverts to quoting *Lynch v. Donnelly:* "There is an unbroken history of official acknowledgement by all three branches of government of the role of religion in American life from at least 1789" although it seems to equate the ideas of the politicians in the three branches of government with the truth of the event rather than admitting that they were not historians, theologians, or philosophers of religion. The Court then extended the scope by giving the impression that the entire history of the United States from the Mayflower Compact to the present has been religiously pervasive and unifying, whereas the actual history shows neither religion's universal and consistent pervasiveness *nor* religion's unifying work. Certainly not the latter.

The Court emphasized that the Texas legislature specified the 17 monuments and 21 historical markers in this government ground commemorate the "people, ideals, and events that compose Texas identity."[6] Texas identity, Texas history, and its connection to the Ten Commandments? Yet there is *absolutely no explanation* of how this monument which manifests the alleged founding of a *specific ancient theocracy* involving *only* the Jewish people and their "God," "Yahweh," in the thirteenth century BC was *ever* a *part* of the Texas "identity," of Texas history or *Texas* people, which is *not* a theocracy and *not* very Jewish. There was no connection offered in evidence because there simply is no connection.

Christian scholars have long known that the Ten Commandments was not the totality of the Jewish "law," but that is usually the only part of Jewish Torah that lay Christians are aware of, and they think it is Christian theology and morality, while they ignore all the Jewish cultic or ritual or liturgical laws, as if they could be separated from the moral part. But the Torah was not divisible that way. In fact, the Ten Commandments is not even as important as the "Shema," and could not, in the mind of any Jew be separated from the 613 commands or the Torah *in general*, including the Midrash, Mishnah, and two Talmuds. It was and is an *integrated whole*, whether seen as three basic imperatives in Micah 6:8 or in a single command as in Habakkuk 2:4, or the ten in the Decalogue, or the 613, or all the rest, including the extensive Talmuds, not really separable, *and not* really belonging to *any other* religious people.

For Christians, who have used the Jewish Bible only to attempt to prove Jesus was the promised Messiah, the Ten Commandments were also isolated from all the rest of the Jewish Bible or Christian "Old Testament," with the exception of the Psalms. The "messianic" passages, which are only postexilic and very few, have nothing to do with Jesus, so this kind of use of the Jewish scriptures by Christians is to the Jews a blasphemous treatment of their tradition. The Decalogue was only a part of the larger whole. The few American citizens who ever saw the Jewish Bible in a broader form were the Puritans who had been so influenced by John Calvin. But even they mutilated it to make it become a Christian document, and they still completely abandoned all the laws that they saw as cultic or ceremonial, which makes it a presumptuous and abusive use of the Jewish scriptures.

If God never was alleged to have given or passed on the Ten Commandments to Gentiles, is it not presumptuous for Christians to think God gave it to them, and incongruously to establish *their civil law*, especially for a *democracy rather than a theocracy*? Democracy and theocracy are even *more exclusive opposites* than democracy and autocracy. But J. Scalia opined in the oral argument that it was *not* even the actual *content* of the Ten Commandments that was important here, but only honoring the Ten Commandments as a *symbol* that God is the *founder of all civil law*. So it really did not make any difference to J. Scalia what those 10 commands actually say, since he speculated that probably most Christians could not name them anyway. It is all just a *symbol of authority*. But did he mean that the United States has a government—a *theocracy*—by God, of God, and only for God—rather than a *democratic* government by the people, of the people, and for the people? Was he implying that all 10 of the commands should be formed as civil and criminal law in the United States? Or was "God" also for J. Scalia only a "symbol" of authority so he can *avoid* even the theocratic implications of a living God which was always understood as standing behind the Ten Commandments? This is more mere uninformed "formalism."[7]

Instead of analyzing Texas history, hoping to uncover this connection that the Court said justified its decision, the Court limited its analysis to only two things: (1) the nature of the monument, and (2) our "Nation's history" (at 686). That is, it moved from insisting on Texas' history's connection to the Ten Commandments—to speak of the "Nation's history" (in general?) and the "nature" of the monument? So the alleged justifying connection with Texas underlying its decision is completely *deserted*, which made the decision stand without any justification. But even then, there is *no analysis* of the Ten Commandments' as a body of law, or as a *monument* (which itself ironically actually *violated* one of the 10 commands, which no justice recognized), or its *connection* to the nation or to Texas history, and no analysis of the Ten Commandments being misappropriated by Christians so they can claim to be God's people rather than the Jews.

So after the process of stating its two foci by which it would make its decision, the Court actually examined *neither* of them either. Instead, the Court shifted its focus once again, this time to the *Lemon* test which it insisted is not always useful, and declared by fiat and without explanation that it is therefore not useful here, which raises the question of why the Court even *mentioned* the legislature's "purpose" on p. 681 if it was not going to examine it for a *secular purpose* as part of the *Lemon* test. But the four civic laws of the Decalogue—prohibiting murder, stealing, adultery, and false testimony against another—were *not ever* considered "secular" by Judaism. The whole of the Decalogue was thoroughly religious to them, completely apodictic, utilizing no human reason, open to no argument or hypotheticals, *nor* to human autonomy or equality or democracy!

Of course, there is no certain verifiable historical proof of such an event as Ancient Israel's receiving the Decalogue at Mt. Sinai, if the Court is really insisting that its interest is preserving "history." All we have is a retrospective description of such an alleged divine incursion on Mt. Sinai by the writers *many centuries later*. But most Christian institutions have never shared this history of the actual writing and recensions of the texts in their retrospective work. But the Sinai tradition was all built upon the religious idea of this unique God, "Yahweh," appearing to Moses—a theophanic disclosure—adopting this small seminomadic people of mixed ethnicity as his "chosen" who now had to live by this god's law.

While all of the history of the Decalogue and Ancient Israel shows the actual purposes and effects of that original law which would *violate* the purpose and effects elements of the *Lemon* test, this second point as the Court's determined focus—the examination of the "nature of the monument"—is also nonexistent. So the Court was not concerned by the fact that the Ten Commandment display is the only one on the park grounds that is religious, and that the thing symbolized is totally religious, totally theocratic, and that it is only recognized by Jews and later illegitimately by Christians. The latter simply misappropriated it centuries ago in their opposition to Judaism, to assure themselves that it is they who were and are the "chosen" by God.

Further, very few if any of the Christian churches ever recognize that *none* of the canonical gospels ever mention Jesus referring to the Decalogue (Ten Commandments) at all. Never. Jesus allegedly did speak of the Deut. 6 "Shema" so widely used in Judaism, when asked about the "greatest" or most important commandment—to love God (Yahweh) with one's entire being, and he supplemented this with the command to love others as oneself. But the only record of even the most basic civil commands of not to kill or commit adultery were simply grouped by an unknown author ("Matthew") as Jesus's "Sermon on the Mount" in which he equated hating with murder and equated sexual lusting with adultery, hardly workable criminal laws!

Not that our Founding Fathers thought that the basic civil and criminal laws they all agreed to at the beginning of the nation had no connection whatever to Christianity, but by that time, the influence of English civil law used as the ground of the New Nation's laws, and English civil law had for centuries been based on an "established" religion, at first Catholic, then finally Anglican. Its structures and much of its theology were simply still *precritical*, that is, never asking natural historical questions about reports or alleged events and the like in the scriptures. But the democratic basis, and multitude of its civil and criminal laws that emerged in the United States showed no more connection to the Ten Commandments than they do to the Code of Hammurabi or the Ten Precepts of Buddhism, both of which predated Christians by centuries, and neither of which had anything to do with our democratic form of government (or Texas).

So the Court not only commits the mistakes we saw Green articulating in revealing the myth of our religious founding, that is, taking rhetoric as literal, overlooking obvious historical sources that are even more definitive of the question at hand, and overlooking that the myth of such a religious founding with liberty was less factual and more simply "aspirational" as it evolved through a variety of iterations. The Court, as well, completely overlooked the myth behind the Ten Commandments in its original form, treating all that aspirational talk of the most conservative people as if it were objective history, and history that would fit a democracy, which is absurd and to many of those who are religious, it is quite blasphemous. Most crucially, the "history" that the Court insisted was to be dispositive in this case—the history of the role played by the *Ten Commandment in Texas history*—the Court completely *bypassed*, but approved the monument, presuming its offensiveness was only the number of legal challenges it evoked.

In *McCreary County, Kentucky v. American Civil Liberties Union of Kentucky*, 545 U.S. 844 (2005), the Ten Commandment plaques were placed in conspicuous places on walls of the courthouse. They were hung in three slightly different forms, all within one year, as the parties changed counsel, but the surrounding references to the Ten Commandments remained through these changes—all quoting only the King James Version of Exodus. The second and third iterations surrounded it with other plaques of simple fragments taken from documents such as the Declaration of Independence, the Mayflower Compact, and so on which mentioned "God" or "Creator" or similar Jewish or Christian ideas. They included *nothing* from the Constitution since the Constitution never mentioned "God" or "Christian" or the "Bible," or the "Ten Commandments," but simply *forbid* "religion" being a test for any public office.

It was as if Kentucky was unwilling to honor the *Lemon* test or learn anything from it, as it continued to push the "religious" grounding of the Ten Commandments, as well as their present religious significance. Once it was brought before the Court, however, the Counties asked for a *different* approach, hereby arguing that the *official purpose* of posting those commandments on the wall is not only *un*important but also actually *unknowable* and the search for it inherently in vain. The Court, however, spent many paragraphs illustrating that "purpose" stands at the *basis for evaluating* any questioned laws. The Court showed how important it was to discern the *actual purpose* rather than simply give deference to any sham purpose, illustrating this via

Stone v. Graham that had a sham purpose,[8] as did *Edwards v. Aguillard* in the controversy over teaching evolution,[9] and the changes in wording between three sequential laws showed the unacknowledged government purpose to be illegally religious in *Wallace v. Jaffree*,[10] as the government's own action which "bespoke the purpose" which was clearly an illegal religious devotional in *Abington v. Schempp*.[11]

The Court noted how it had become possible for "savvy officials" to disguise their religious intent "so cleverly that the objective observer just missed it," but the Court is obligated to objectively scrutinize even the sequence of events leading to the passage of a law. Further, the Court asserted, in the alternative, the Counties would avoid the District Court's conclusion by having the Court limit the scope of the purpose enquiry so severely only to the *final* display of the Ten Commandments. The Court insisted that this means they were telling the Court to turn a blind eye on the previous history of the *first two attempts* to post the Ten Commandments, which were obviously only done with a *religious purpose*, as if such forgetting would be a responsible approach for the Court. The Court took this as the government saying that any trivial rationalization should suffice, but it would be under a standard totally oblivious to the history of a government's religious purpose being visible in its action like the *progression* of exhibits in this case (at 859). Despite the government's request that the Court *overlook* the first two exhibits, the Court detected the strong "sectarian spirit" *throughout* the sequence (at 872).

The Court noted that many of the "foundational" documents included in the final display were very odd—such as a patriotic hymn, yet omitting the Fourteenth Amendment, "the most significant structural provision adopted since the original Framing." That display also left out any reference to the Constitution, but strangely included the Magna Carta, even to the point of its declaration that "'fsh-weirs shall be removed from the Thames.'"[12] How *apropos!*

Perhaps the most strained (or should I say "seined"?) and unjustified idea of the Petitioners was its contention that the Decalogue *clearly influenced* the Declaration of Independence. It had stated the following:

> The Ten Commandments have profoundly influenced the formation of Western legal thought and the formation of our country. That influence is clearly seen in the Declaration of Independence, which declared that "We hold these truths to be self-evident, that all men are created equal, that they are endowed by their Creator with certain unalienable Rights, that among these are Life, Liberty, and the pursuit of Happiness."[13]

I need not repeat my critique of such a view which I gave above in *Van Orden v. Perry*. If the vital connection is established by a mere use of similar words such as "the," or "that," then both are connected with an indefinite number of texts, with saying nothing in the process. There simply is *no connection at all* between the Ten Commandments and the Declaration of Independence, *neither conceptual nor moral nor legal.* The ideas of equality, of the values of "life, liberty, and pursuit of happiness" have no counterpart in the Ten Commandments. The Petitioners' argument here corresponds more to the way J. Scalia described the Ten Commandments in *Van Orden v. Perry*, as a mere *generic symbol*, the contents of which may *not even be known* by the people—just a symbol of the authority (God) as the base of all civil law on earth. But, again, this is to overlook the limitations of this cultural/religious phenomenon in Ancient Israel, or even in the eighteenth-century United States. It is ahistorical and uninformed.

The *dissent* wrote an opinion twice as long as the Court's majority opinion. It belittled the *Lemon* test, circumscribed the idea of required government neutrality in religious matters, and ultimately, through its extremely selective and prejudiced readings of the Founding Fathers and its mistaken notion that the First Amendment, *allowed the government* to embrace and rigorously espouse a belief in a monotheistic god, with attending incidental benefits for those who believe likewise but *not* to those who are polytheists or atheists.[14]

J. Souter, writing for the Court, however, closed with his critique of J. Scalia's stinging dissent (which was joined by the Chief Justice, J. Thomas, and with whom J. Kennedy joined only to Parts II and III, dissenting). J. Souter wrote:

[T]he dissent says that the deity the Framers had in mind was the God of monotheism, with the consequence that government may espouse a tenet of traditional monotheism. This is truly a remarkable view . . . [which] apparently means that government should be free to approve the core beliefs of a favored religion over the tenets of others, a view that should trouble anyone who prizes religious liberty. Certainly history cannot justify it; on the contrary, history shows that the religion of concern to the Framers was not that of the monotheistic faiths generally, but Christianity in particular, a fact that no Member of this Court takes as a premise for construing the Religion Clauses. . . . The Framers would therefore, almost certainly object to the dissent's unstated reasoning that because Christianity was a monotheistic "religion," monotheism with Mosaic antecedents should be a touchstone of establishment interpretation. Even on originalist critiques of existing precedent there is, it seems, no escape from inter-pretative consequence that would surprise the Framers. . . . Historical evidence thus supports no solid argument for changing course . . . whereas public dis-course at the present time certainly raises no doubt about the value of the inter-pretative approach invoked for 60 years now [i.e. government neutrality]. We are centuries away from the St. Bartholomew's Day massacre and the treatment

of heretics in early Massachusetts, but the divisiveness of religion in current
public life is inescapable. This is no time to deny the prudence of understanding
the Establishment Clause to require the government to stay neutral on religious
belief, which is reserved for the conscience of the individual.[15]

The Court had no alternative but to strike the law down by its sheer lack of
any real secular purpose as it read the Establishment Clause requiring government neutrality on religion.

EXECUTIVE ORDERS AND *FAITH*-BASED *NEUTRALITY?*

How could a law that was "faith based" actually be "neutral"? Bush's "White
Office of Faith-Based and Community Initiatives" failed to answer this.
Perhaps it was unaware of the "neutral" criteria, but it was bound to receive
a challenge all the way to the Supreme Court, and it did so in *Hein, Director,
White House Office of Faith-Based and Community Initiatives, et al. v.
Freedom from Religion Foundation, Inc., et al.,* 551 U.S. 557 (2007). Here
Respondents argued that Petitioners violated the Establishment Clause by
organizing conferences that were designed to promote, and had the effect of
promoting, *religious* community groups over secular ones, that is, applying
the law or executive order in a religiously discriminatory rather than neutral
way.

Specifically, the "faith-based organizations" were "singled out as being
particularly worthy of federal funding . . . , and the belief in God is extolled as
distinguishing the claimed effectiveness of faith-based social services." Thus,
Respondents claimed the content of these conferences sent a message that the
"faith-based" groups were insiders and to be favored, whereas the religious
nonbelievers were outsiders, and not full members of the political community. The District Court dismissed the claims for a lack of standing; the
Ninth Circuit reversed, holding that *Flast v. Cohen* grants taxpayers standing
so long as the activities are financed by a congressional appropriation, even
where there is no statutory program and the funds are from appropriations
for general administrative expenses, and this applies to expenditures by any
federal agency so long as the marginal or incremental cost to the public of the
alleged Establishment Clause violation is greater than zero.

A *plurality* of the Supreme Court plus two concurring justices who
agreed only with the *result* rather than the ground for it, *reversed* the holding of the Ninth Circuit. It argued that the Appellate Court's broad reading
of *Flast* is "incorrect," so the Respondent does *not* have standing. It went
through the usual delineation of elements of real case and controversy,
actual injury in fact that is traceable to the Petitioner's unlawful conduct,

which injury could be redressed by the requested relief. The plurality saw *Flast* as making a single exception to the "*Frothingham*" principle, that is, that to have standing in an Establishment Clause case, one must show that the alleged violation was funded by a specific *congressional* appropriation and was undertaken pursuant to an express *congressional* mandate. It opined this focus on congressional action has *no application* or extension to the executive branch, such as Presidential Executive Orders. If it did apply to the executive branch, then any discretionary expenditure of the Administration could be challenged by a taxpayer, including many speeches by the president or his Cabinet officers that "touch on religion" such as at Thanksgiving time, which is simply not logical nor legal. The plurality said that *stare decisis* does not require always extending precedents to their extreme limits. Although J. Scalia, joined by J. Thomas, concurred in the Court's judgment, they faulted the Court for attempting to make a factual distinction between this case and *Flast*, arguing that "it is past time to overturn *Flast*."

The dissent by J. Souter, joined by three other justices, in this 5/4 decision, insisted that Madison's protection of every citizen's conscience against incursions by the government should resolve this alone. Madison's "three pence" is emphasized again as too much government support for religion. The "separation of powers" which the Court emphasized as the crucial, determining factor disallowing extending *Flast* to include the executive branch, is seen by the dissent as *specious*, since there is no difference between a judicial branch review of the Executive and Legislative branches. Further, the Court, in *Bowen v. Kendrick*, had recognized that the funds flowing through the Administration rather than Congress did *not* merit different criteria for taxpayer standing. Rather than getting bogged down trying to distinguish "Wallet Injury" from "Psychic Injury" as J. Scalia and J. Thomas did, the dissent noted that the injury required to give standing is not always strictly quantifiable. For example, "being forced to compete on an uneven playing field based on race—without showing that an economic loss resulted, or living in a racially gerrymandered electoral district—have both been honored as a basis for standing." Instead, *Flast* "speaks for this Court's recognition (shared by a majority of the Court today) that when the Government spends money for religious purposes a taxpayer's injury is serious and concrete enough to be 'judicially cognizable.'"[16]

Yet, the Court, by its strange plurality, *never got to the merits* of the case, to discuss whether or not it was legal under the Establishment Clause for the federal government to establish and fund such "faith-based" groups. The question of whether or not it would meet the *Lemon* requirements was never determined by the Court. It certainly seems on the surface that it would violate especially the "excessive entanglement" test even if not violate all three prongs of the *Lemon* test. Even without *Lemon*, how can funding that is "faith based" really be "neutral"?

On February 5, 2009, the Obama Administration, by Executive Order 13498, amended the Executive Order of Bush's which established the "White House Office Faith-Based and Community Initiatives." The name was changed to "President's Advisory Council for Faith-Based and Neighborhood Partnerships," and considerable restructuring of it took place, including the establishing of the "President's Advisory Council on Faith-Based and Neighborhood Partnerships" consisting of a maximum of 25 members, appointed for a year, and serving at the pleasure of the president. It also specified that it would coordinate the efforts of federal, state, and local governments, and it attached the Council to the Department of Health and Human Services, from which it would receive the administrative support and such funds as were necessary for the functioning of the Council. It added other qualifiers including the fact that nothing in the Order would "impair or otherwise affect (1) authority granted by law to a department, agency or the head thereof; or (2) functions of the Director of the Office of Management and Budget relating to budget, administrative or legislative proposals." Even more significant to the Obama Administration, it became more inclusive in the types of community or social problems it addressed, to "deliver vital services . . . from providing mentors and tutors to school children to giving ex-offenders a second chance at work and a responsible life to ensuring that families are fed."

In my analysis of these Executive Orders and the social needs that have allegedly been met by pubic taxes, I am not suggesting that nothing good has been accomplished. Of course it has: a great amount of assistance has been provided to people in need. The real question is why this work could not have been accomplished with*out* having to invite the problem of including religious organizations which operate with a "nonpublic reason" they call "faith"? Had that been done, there still would be people willing to be employed in such social action and helping in various ways to improve citizens' lives. In fact, if the religious people are really that interested in helping those in need, they surely would be open to helping some community organization do that even if it was not their religious group. Or their religious group could have used its own funds for helping, which would have supplemented what government was doing.

Decades ago, J. Brennan[17] suggested a violation of the Establishment Clause in his delineation of *three forms*: "Equally the Constitution enjoins those involvements of religious with secular institutions which (a) serve the essentially religious activities of religious institutions; (b) employ the organs of government for essentially religious purposes; or (c) use essentially religious means to serve governmental ends where secular means would suffice."

It is "(c)" in Brennan's "tests" which fits specifically the questionableness of this commingling of religion and government in this work of the "President's Advisory Council for Faith-Based and Neighborhood Partnerships."

The amended Order did mention that it had to avoid violating the Constitution's prohibiting both any "establishment of religion" as well as citizens' "free exercise" of religion.

What it did not do, just as the original Order 13199 did not do, however, is explore and explain how it would *avoid* any possible violation of the Establishment Clause. The attorneys who put it together may have simply taken for granted that the 2007 Court decision involving the "faith-based" initiative which we just reviewed would prevent any challenges from arising since they would be nipped in the bud on the basis of a lack of "standing." But that was a case which involved only an opinion by the "plurality," and almost the entire case was an unresolved argument about "standing," Of course, to admit it over that initial hurdle would open the issues that would present an obvious outcome of being an illegal establishment under the *Lemon* test, but there were also no other tests it could pass if it was being applied as charged, giving *preference* to the religious groups. Madison, Jefferson, and Rawls would all be appalled.

MORE RELIGIOUS SYMBOLS OR DISPLAYS:
WHICH ARE "GOVERNMENT" SPEECH?

In the same year, a very different "test" to distinguish legal government actions from illegal Establishment emerged in *Pleasant Grove City, Utah, et al. v. Summum*, 555 U.S. 460 (2009). Pioneer Park (public) in Pleasant Grove, Utah, had at least 11 permanent, privately donated displays, including a Ten Commandment monument given to it by the Order of the Eagles. Summum, a religious organization, also located in Utah, requested to donate its monument of the Seven Aphorisms of Summum, but the city rejected it. The city *only then* articulated a formal written policy of its criteria for inclusion in the park, that a display had to be directly related to the city's history or donated by groups with long-standing community ties.

The Respondent then renewed its request, but did not describe how it was involved in the points of these criteria. When Summum was rejected again, it brought suit, claiming that the city had violated the Free Speech clause of the First Amendment by accepting the display of the Ten Commandments, but refusing the display of the Seven Aphorisms of Summum. The District Court denied Respondent's request, but the Tenth Circuit reversed, holding that the display of the Ten Commandments had been accepted as legal as *private* speech rather than government speech, that public parks traditionally are regarded as public forums, and the exclusion of Summum's monument would likely not survive the test of strict scrutiny.

J. Alito delivered the opinion of the Court, and remarkably there were no dissenting opinions. The Court *reversed*, finding for the Petitioner. It acknowledged that the Court had not made any prior decisions addressing the "application of the Free Speech Clause to a government entity's acceptance of privately donated, permanent monuments for installation in a public park." Petitioners and Respondents utilized totally different precedent cases to make their arguments. Rather than have to systematically work through all of these, the Court decided the basic question is on the "nature of petitioners' conduct when they permitted privately donated monuments to be erected" in the park. Was the city doing it as *its own* expressive conduct, or were they merely providing a forum for varieties of *private* speech?

The Court's basic argument was that the placements of *permanent* monuments in a public park is *not* private speech but rather *government speech*, so is *not* subject to strict scrutiny under the Free Speech Clause. That Clause regulates private speech, not government speech. That, of course, did not explain how the Ten Commandments was in the park as "private" speech. The Court repeated that government "is entitled to say what it wishes," citing to *Rosenberger v. Rector and Visitors of Univ. of Va.*, 515 U.S. 819, 833. Yet almost in the same breath, the Court admitted that this does *not* mean there are no restraints on government speech, since, for example, among its restraints, it "must comport with the Establishment Clause." Yet, again, in almost the same breath, it cited cases to quote that the government speech "is exempt from First Amendment scrutiny," that "it can say what it wants," even that it is the very "business of government to favor and disfavor points of view." That phrase and approach would seem obvious to any reader as a *total contradiction* of the First Amendment's insistence that *government* shall "make no law respecting the establishment of religion."

In its extensive belittling of the opponents' argument that the government had to be "viewpoint neutral," the Court insisted that was *ridiculous* because it would require either removing many monuments already accepted as the government's decision about the image of itself that it wanted to convey, or it would result in "an influx of clutter" in the park. If the city had to be viewpoint neutral in its self-expression, and these were the alternatives, the Court insisted that the city would be forced to refuse accepting *any* monuments from anyone.

This seems to suggest that government may express *any viewpoint it chooses*, or make any law it wants about religion? Yet the Establishment Clause never was a restriction of private speech but *only* of government speech and actions: "*Congress* shall make no law respecting the establishment of religion." The Court cannot interpret this phrase both ways—in cases in which Christian groups sued in order to use public school facilities to indoctrinate, the Court says it is *protected private speech*, not government speech—yet in cases of religious monuments on government land, the Court can say it is *protected government speech*, not private speech. Since the Court emphasized the "permanence" of a monument vis-à-vis the transitory nature of an actual speech, is the key only the duration of the speech, even if the club meets weekly for the school year, and the monument exists that year but is hardly ever noticed?

If all citizens know that murder, stealing, and bearing false witness are part of the law of the land, what is the purpose in erecting a monument such as the Ten Commandments, except to place some alleged *absolute religious authority* behind the laws? Are these four laws better principles than the principles of mutual equality, mutual trust and respect, truthfulness, and "Reverence for Life"? If the latter are actually better, and they carry no specific religious connections that many would object to, why erect a monument of the Ten Commandments which are religiously divisive and are *not universal* or specifically democratic in their context? The Supreme Court insisted that allowing private parties to speak in a public park is one thing, but when the local government allows a permanent monument to be placed, that is quite different. Since the Court emphasized that the city had "taken ownership of most of the monuments in the Park, since they were permanent, including the Ten Commandments," and the point is that government has a message in each monument, precisely *what government message* was the city giving by allowing the monument of the Ten Commandments there? The Court gives no answer. Or was *Perry* the answer—to turns one's head so as not to be offended? Or was it the groundless assertion of two of the justices in the oral argument of *Perry*—that only the Ten Commandments suffices as the authority or base for law—even if, as J. Scalia said, no one could tell you what those ten commandments were?

The Respondent's basic argument was that if the city *has adopted* the message of a particular monument, it must *explicitly affirm* that, rather than the private parties who donated it suggesting that it is the city's message. But the Court would have none of that, insisting that there is no reason for imposing a requirement of this sort. Instead, the Court argues not only that by the city's acceptance of a privately donated monument, it does *not* thereby agree with the donor's message, but it went so far to emphasize that there does *not* have to be a *single* meaning, but a monument can have quite different meanings to *everyone*. More than that, it admitted those meanings could change over time. So the government speech can include any and every possible meaning and one may never be able to ascertain the message the "government" is promoting or not promoting? This being the case, if this is really true, what purpose would any restrictions have, or what purpose would any monuments have if their purpose is not obvious to all viewers? When the Court warned that even the government "message" may be altered by the subsequent addition of other monuments in the same vicinity, that makes no sense at all if symbols[18] and monuments can legally be used by the government as its *self-expression* while they can carry any number of even conflicting interpretations or meanings, and the government can be spared from having to say what its message in any monument really is.

This is all the Court's circumlocution to try to escape from having to nail down *any specific* "message" of the government, even though the crux of the case is that government, unlike private parties, can decide on *its specific message* without having to meet *any criteria* or consider other laws or expressly say what its message is. It just does not have to tell anyone what its message is! If J. Scalia was correct in his oral argument for *Van Orden v. Perry*, that probably most people could not even tell you what the specific Ten Commandments say, it made no difference to him in that case since they are simply a symbol that "God" establishes all law. Was this, then, the case with any monuments in this city? The whole idea of government providing a message, which it cannot even articulate through a symbol it has little historical knowledge of, is truly incredible. Yet the Court had admitted that it had to "comport" with the Establishment Clause as well as the protections of the Fourteenth Amendment, but that required *nothing* since the Court thought it *unreasonable* that the city be required to *articulate what message it was presenting* in the cases of the existing displays.

Obviously, the Court was simply allowing the city to *arbitrarily* decide to accommodate whatever it liked, totally ignoring dozens of former Supreme Court decisions dealing with Establishment and turning a deaf ear on the First Amendment through its slippery argument. The *articulated criteria* by the city which the monuments had to meet, of course, came *after* the Summum group proposed giving their display to the city. They did not exist before. J. Alito, writing for the Court, *never* examined the relation between "government speech" and the Establishment Clause, which should have been the most obvious element in this decision, given the parameters drawn by the Court. Nor did the Court examine the *retroactive criteria* the city had established for permission to erect a monument, namely, that the display had to be *directly* related to the *city's history* or donated by groups with *long-standing community ties*. There was *no showing* that the Ten Commandments were directly related to the city's history nor that the donors of that monument had long-standing ties with the community.

In truth, both the Ten Commandments and the Seven Aphorisms monuments are *wholly religious* and do not lose that by simply assuming they serve some secular purpose. Some secular purpose can be seen in most religious ethical ideas. The continual contesting between absolutized religions or even strenuously competing religions can only result in creating the *divisiveness* that Madison, Jefferson, and the First Amendment, as well as Rawls, intended to avoid.

Just one question remains: What significance did the Court attach to its placing in ftnt #1 the information, supplied by Respondents that Summum "incorporates elements of Gnostic Christianity" which emphasized spiritual knowledge rather than anything of a physical nature, even to the point of this special knowledge modifying human perception? But *all religions* make a similar claim of having some *special knowledge* or some "revealed" faith that is beyond natural or "public reason." In fact, the Seven Aphorisms of Summum are an attempt at an ontology, combining alleged physics principles with metaphysical presuppositions, which, if anything, is less strictly religious or less mythical than the Ten Commandments which alleged simply to be transcribing commands (rather than principles) straight from a personal, living deity. For those who were Christian on the Court, the reference of "Gnosticism" may well have been intended as an *immediate red flag*, since *Gnosticism* was by the last half of the second Christian century declared by the Roman Catholic Church as a dangerous heresy.[19]

Then the Court adds in the same footnote the Respondents' claim that the Seven Aphorisms were the content of the original tablet God gave Moses, tablets that Moses shattered because he believed the Israelites were incapable of receiving them. When he returned to the top of Mt. Sinai, God then gave him what we call the "Ten Commandments." That idea of Summum may very well offend not just the Christians but any Jew on the bench.[20] Summum's very recent origin on the world stage, combined with its unverifiable beliefs and alleged connection to Ancient Egypt and to the theophany at Mt. Sinai, seems more like desperate imaginings to give its Aphorisms some otherworldly authority. Yet, on the other hand, there may well be some truth in several of the Aphorisms. But even if *none* of its claims have any real history or truth behind them, one has to ask *if* the Court is really in the business of deciding what is really "historical" and which is religiously "true," is "orthodox," or the ultimate "good"? How does the Court prove the Ten Commandment came from some theistic or "unitary" (or Trinitarian) generic "God" which is the only true god which J. Scalia thought is obviously universal as a fact? How does one move from a retroactive writing of an alleged supranatural but historical event on Mt. Sinai to some eternal, universal principles," or does one instead fall into Lessing's "ugly ditch"? The *Barnette* Court seemed to *settle* that in the fashion of Madison ("no cognizance") some 80 years back in 1943 when J. Jackson wrote,

If there is any fixed star in our constitutional constellation, it is that no official, high or petty, can prescribe what shall be orthodox in politics, nationalism, religion, or other matters of opinion.[21]

The later Court, has created such confusion over the Ten Commandments that it has filtered down to the states, so in 2017, the Court actually refused to grant cert to hear a New Mexico case (14-2149) involving the Ten Commandments, City of Bloomfield, *New Mexico v. Jane Felix, et al.*, November 9, 2017.[22] The District Court had found the monument illegal, as had the Tenth Circuit Court. Many states' attorney's-general sought *clarification* by the Supreme Court through this case (since the Court does not offer "advisory" opinions), but the Court denied cert. Rather than clarify anything, this simply added to the confusion.

But we are getting ahead of ourselves on the religious symbols and displays. The unanswered question was why the Court *ever* wanted to get involved trying to decide why, how, and what kinds of *religious speech* would be allowed to the *government* but not to individuals on government property? But the year following *Summum*, the symbol at issue was the *primary Christian* symbol and the *property* question become *central*, making a justifiable credible exit from the labyrinth of this kind of jurisdiction more desirable but even less possible. The Cross came before the Court again, and was decided on April 28, 2010, in *Salazar, Secretary of the Interior, et al. v. Buono*, 559 U.S. 700 (2010). A Latin cross was erected by the VFW in 1934 on federal land *without* permission in the Mojave National Preserve, at a rock outcropping called "Sunrise Rock," in memory of the fallen U.S. soldiers. From 1935 on, the site was used sporadically for Christian Easter services, and since 1984 its use has been very regular for such religious services.

It originally had a sign indicating it as a memorial in the honor of those deceased soldiers, but the sign and the original cross long since deteriorated and were removed, although replacement crosses later reappeared. The most recent replacement occurred in 1998, when Henry Sandoz, a private citizen owning some private property within the Preserve, created an iron pipe cross, filled it with concrete, and anchored it into the rock itself, which would make it extremely difficult to remove. It had no accompanying sign to indicate its purpose for many decades, so the cross stood completely alone without any memorial signs or statements of purpose or even donors. The site was used primarily for Christian religious services, but it was on government property.

When a request was made in 1999 to the National Park Society to place also a Buddhist stupa at the site, not far from the cross, authorities turned down the request. That plus subsequent threats made to remove the cross caused the National Park Society to undertake an examination of the cross at the site and its history and purpose. The NPS decided that neither the cross nor the property location qualified it for the National Registry of Historic Places, since the original cross was gone as well as its accompanying plaque, and the place had no real historical significance since it was now used *only* for *religious* purposes and commemoration. Because of this, NPS decided to remove the cross. However, in 2000, Congress stepped in to prevent that. Its first law of December 2000 was to prohibit the use of government funds for removal of the cross.

Frank Buono, a retired Park Service employee who made regular visits to the Preserve, filed suit in 2001 in the Federal District Court of Central California, alleging that the cross's presence on federal land was offensive to him as a reasonable observer, as a *violation* of the Establishment Clause, and he sought an injunction to have it removed. The litigation went through several stages. During the first phase (*Buono I*), as noted above, before the case had been filed in District Court, Congress passed an appropriation bill forbidding public funds to be used for removing the cross. Then while the case was pending in the District Court, Congress designated the cross and its land as a National War Memorial honoring the American veterans of WWI, and directed the Secretary of the Interior to expend up to $10,000 to acquire a replica of the original cross and its memorial plaque, and install the latter at a suitable nearby location. Then *Buono I* was decided (2002) by the District Court, holding for Buono by utilizing the *Lemon* standard, especially its illegal primary religious effect as perceived by a reasonable observer.[23]

The government appealed to the Ninth Circuit, and three months after *Buono I* was decided, Congress again prohibited any spending of government funds to remove the cross. While the Ninth Circuit was deciding *Buono II*, Congress passed a *land-transfer statute*, trading the small 1-acre parcel of federal land on which the cross was situated for a 5-acre parcel of private land close by owned by Henry Sandoz, who had built the most recent cross. This way the cross would be on *private ground* within the huge National Preserve, not government land, and the Court in October 2009 claimed Congress thought this should satisfy all parties.

Because the Ninth Circuit had no idea how long the proposed land transfer might take or whether it would be successful, it simply affirmed the District Court's holding for Buono in *Buono II* (2004), staying the injunction. Since the government did not seek review by the U.S. Supreme Court, Buono won both on the standing issue and on the merits, as admitted by the Supreme Court when it finally heard the case.

Buono returned to the District Court, seeking an injunction to prevent the land transfer, either through enforcement or modification of the 2002 injunction. That District Court examined the question of whether the land transfer was a bona fide attempt to comply with the injunction which was already permanent, and could not be challenged, or rather a "sham aimed at keeping the cross in place," and decided that it was obviously the latter, so the transfer was itself *invalid*. The Court rejected Buono's request to amend his original injunction, insisting that the *land transfer violated the original injunction*, so there was no need to amend. The Ninth Circuit again affirmed the holding of the District Court.

The Supreme Court, however, *reversed* in a 5/4 decision. But the opinions were so diverse that it is impossible to reconcile them. First, on the issue of "standing," only three of the "plurality" who reversed the lower courts' decisions admitted Buono had standing. The other two, J. Scalia and J. Thomas, who concurred in the reversal decision actually insisted that he did *not* have standing, and that being true, the Court should *never* have heard the case. Of course, the four dissenting justices admitted he had standing from the start, and it did not change, but their decisions did not count since they dissented in the result or holding of the reversal of the lower court judgment. All J. Scalia and J. Thomas agreed with the other three (J. Kennedy, joined by the Chief Justice and J. Alito) was in holding the Ninth Circuit in error for enjoining the transfer of the property, but these two said since Buono did not have standing, the Court could not decide the merits of the case.

The question is, how did he have standing on the basis of only three people of the plurality, and those three did, in fact weigh the merits of the case? That was the only reason they could have *reversed* the decision. They did not reverse the decision merely to remand, since the decisions of the lower court had not been challenged by the government until after the land transfer was opposed by Buono, so that decision was res judicata. Also, how could J. Scalia and J. Thomas have said they concurred in the plurality's judgment on the *merits*, and turn around and say that the Court could *not so judge the merits* since Buono had failed to prove that he had standing? Chaos?

But it gets worse. There was absolutely no agreement about what *legal question* was before the Court. Whenever a case remains that clouded with the Court, how could there be any agreement of a decision, a decision on what? So there was not. J. Kennedy (joined by the Chief Justice and J. Alito) defined the question the Court had to resolve as to "whether the District Court properly enjoined the Government from implementing the land-transfer statute." On the other hand, J. Stevens (dissenting, joined by J. Ginsburg and J. Sotomayor) insisted that was *not* the question. It was rather "whether the District Court properly enforced its 2002 judgment by enjoining the transfer." J. Breyer, also dissenting in a separate opinion, insisted against the others that this case had to be resolved only by the *law of injunctions* rather than opening up the Establishment issue, since the injunction was the vehicle that was utilized for the relief sought and became res judicata. For him, the question was even simpler but more general: "whether the law permits the District Court so to interpret its injunction." He documented how the law of injunctions is fairly clear, so there is no justification to proceed to some federal question. That is, the Court "improvidently granted" cert, when it should never have heard the case, so at this late point, the best thing to do is affirm the Ninth Circuit's judgment.

The other two (J. Scalia and J. Thomas) who concurred in the judgment on the merits felt that the particulars of the entire situation had changed with the land transfer, so Buono would have to show he had standing to challenge that particular statute, which was an "extension" of any standing he had been given in *Buono I*, and, until that requirement was satisfied, the court could not really weigh the merits of the case. The other three justices reversing the lower court decision insisted that he *did* have standing since in both the question prior to the land transfer as well as after, this was not an unjustified extension of standing of the 2002 decision, but rather involved the same parties, same land, and same cross, so those opposed to his standing were simply confusing their view of the merit question of the case rather than standing.

The plurality held that the big problem with the lower court decision was that it felt free to rule against what it posited as Congress' intent, without in any way substantiating such an important deciding factor. The plurality insisted to the contrary, that it was more evident that all Congress sought was a preservation of the original intent of those who placed the cross there in 1934, that is, to honor the fallen U.S. soldiers of WWI. The land-statute element completely changed the nature of the question for litigation, so the District Court and Ninth Circuit *neither* one considered whether the statute *per se* violated the Establishment Clause.

The plurality argued that "a court must never ignore significant changes in the law or circumstances underlying an injunction," and the circumstances had changed radically since the land transfer meant that the cross was now on private land, now owned by the VFW, so could not possibly be remedied by an injunction issued against the cross on government land. In both oral argument as well as the dissenting opinions, however, the Respondent's attorney and then the dissenting justices argued significantly that the land transfer did *not*, in fact, turn the parcel into private land, since the government retained a *reversionary interest* in it. This is quite crucial. Further, the dissent argued that the very transfer of the land by the government had no other purpose than to keep the cross intact *at that place*, which meant the transfer itself was not permanent, but rather a violation (if not a red herring?).

The plurality emphasized that Congress had, by its ingenious statute of "land transfer," attempted to accommodate both sides, rather than show hostility either toward religion or total disrespect for fallen soldiers. But what the Court did *not* do was *justify* how the *primary usage* of the site was for *Christian worship* which it was so intent to "accommodate." It did not explain what the "historical meaning" of the cross was that it attained, but simply quoted its earlier questionable decision of *Van Orden v. Perry* in which it had emphasized that the religious aspect of the message was only part of a broader moral and historical message reflective of a cultural heritage. This was a vague and specious conclusion with no substance supporting it. The predominant usage of the area and the Cross was for *Christian worship* services.

The religious divisiveness was *already present*; it did not begun with the litigation, and it is only the divisiveness created by the litigation itself which the Court has ruled cannot disqualify it under the criteria of "potential political divisiveness" of the third prong of the *Lemon* test. Already, a Buddhist group had requested another space in the area to build a stupa but was not allowed. That was *prior* to any litigation. So, despite the Court calling this Congress's way of "balancing opposing interests," those were only between the Christians (represented by the government) and Buono, not involving any other religious people or any of the millions of citizens of the United States who are not religious. It clearly violated *Lemon*.

J. Scalia also showed in the oral argument that he thought a cross is the primary symbol used for places of burial, worldwide, a symbol that *satisfies all religions* including Jews.[24] He was quickly shown that he was imagining things that were untrue when he suggested that Jews would not be uncomfortable with the cross as their grave marker. He even tried to draw the parallel of the cross at Sunrise Point with a cross beside a highway, marking where someone was killed, to suggest that to disallow such just because it is government land is a pure hostility to religion. But they are not parallel. By allowing those crosses that might be placed in the ditches along the highway, the government is neither involved in the construction, land transfer, maintenance of the little crosses, nor were these used as sites for public worship by a particular religious group. There is simply no analogy. Nor does the multitude of crosses at Arlington Memorial Cemetery parallel Sunrise Point, since, as Buono's counsel pointed out in the oral argument, each family is given a choice of religious symbols accommodating any religion it can place on its cross in Arlington to specify the religion of their deceased military son or daughter.

But there was no accommodation of any other religion at Sunrise Point—only a bare Christian cross (not Jewish, Muslim, Buddhist, Sikh, Hindu, symbols, but only a Christian cross), period. Meanwhile, J. Scalia continued to broaden his idea of the government's right to embrace religion, attempting to extend his conception of some imagined generic religion. In *Van Orden v. Perry*, he had insisted that government could legally use symbols or texts (such as the Ten Commandments) to express *its (government's)* belief in a "unitary God" as the author or Chief Lawgiver behind all human laws. In

McCreary v. A.C.L.U. (decided the same day), he was angrier since he was on the "losing" side of the Court, so insisted that "monotheism" is the *true* religion, so *any expression* of a monotheistic God by *government* is very legal, and he was sure the Establishment Clause does *not* give that privilege of religious expression to polytheists or atheists. That obviously was J. Scalia's religion speaking, not any legal documents or history.

Now in *Salazar v. Buono*, he moved beyond his earlier position that government must confine its expression only to this monotheistic God, never using the name "Christ," which he insisted even in his dissent in *McCreary*, and but in Buono, he emphasized that government *can* in fact use the more *specifically Christian* symbol of the Cross, and he tried to make *it* also *generic* or acceptable to other religions as well. So he never understood that the Ten Commandments originated with Judaism, as only a covenant and law between the Jewish God, Yahweh, and the people of Israel, just as the Cross was the central symbol *only* of the Christian religion, *never any other religion*. Nor was he willing to give atheists or nonbelievers *any voice* in the question, despite the Court having emphasized over the decades that the Establishment Clause means that government cannot favor one religion more than another, nor can it favor religion over nonreligion. It is no wonder that in *McCreary*, he twisted Madison and Jefferson, missing their emphases, highlighting only expressions which he could interpret to say they were in favor of government expressing its religious belief. But we have seen quite the opposite in our earlier chapters. Rather, government *has no belief* according to Madison and Jefferson; only *individuals* do.

In *Buono*, the plurality insisted that the lower courts neither one examined either the secular purpose nor the excessive entanglement prongs of the *Lemon* test. But a violation of *any* of the three *Lemon* prongs has always been sufficient to show a law or practice an illegal Establishment, so by the Court's implication that the *primary secular effect test* of *Lemon* was considered and failed, is quite sufficient to make it illegal. The third prong—of "excessive entanglement" between the religion and government—which included the potential political divisiveness as part of the way of determining whether there was excessive entanglement, was very obvious in the history of the site *prior* to any litigation, and the *reversionary interest* the government retained in the property transfer *increased the entanglement*, suggesting even occasional monitoring by the government.

But the Court was not interested in *Lemon*. It accused Respondent of utilizing only the "endorsement" test, originated by J. O'Connor in the *Lynch* decision. Interestingly, however, as it emphasized how much the reasonable observer would have to know to utilize this test, the obvious answer such a reasonable observer who knew the history of the place (as the Court as well as dissent emphasizes) would have was the Congress had been simply determined to *keep the cross on that property*, whatever it had to do, so it was totally an illegal religious purpose by *Lemon*, an obvious government endorsement only of Christianity.

The plurality emphasized that this case was chiefly about the location of the cross—whether it was on private property or government property. Had that been true, it would have appeared reasonable that the property exchange turned the little parcel into *private* property, so there should have been *no reversionary interest* given to the government and no further Establishment Clause objections. That is crucial. The Court delighted in quoting from Buono that he would not object to a cross on private property. Would that the case had been that simple!

But it was not. There are several problems. First, although the land transfer was designed to trade 5 private acres a couple of miles away (within the federal Preserve) for the 1 acre of Sunrise Point on which the cross stood, the exchange was (1) initiated by the government from the start, combined with the government's passing a law prohibiting any federal funds to remove the cross; (2) the government declared the *1 acre*, prior the exchange, to be a National Monument, and demanded that it *remain so after* the exchange, which meant that the government was still controlling the disposition and use of the property, so it *never* became actually private; (3) the government insisted on a *reversionary interest* in the trade, so that if the VFW failed to maintain the one "private acre" with the cross for the designed purpose, the property would revert back to the ownership by the government. All of these were actions, as the dissent points out, positive actions by the government by which *it* was *sponsoring and controlling a religious symbol and site*, not merely an accidental or incidental religious benefit along with the predominant concern to keep the war memorial in place.

A second problem, as the dissent noted, was that even the transfer itself was a violation of the District Court's injunction, and that was the real question: Whether Congress could be allowed to overrule the District Court's injunction, that is, by the land transfer which made the relief sought by the injunction impossible? In addition to this, a third problem seems to be how the perception of the "reasonable observer" would be altered? How would such a person visiting the site know that it was on a little *private* acre inside the millions of public acres, so was not an endorsement of religion by the government? In the oral arguments before the Court, there was even a discussion of what signs might be used to let people know that the property was now private, not government, and there was no consensus. But the observation was obvious, that although there were many private ranches amid this huge geographical area, most people saw the whole as *government property*, and if the "reasonable observer" was required, as the Court has instructed, to know of all the years that this was government property with the cross, few, if any people, knowing that history of the area and of Sunrise Point's usage would think it was *not* being sponsored still by the government, especially for anyone who was aware that Buddhists had been denied to erect anything like a stupa in the area or anyone who knew the various ways in which Congress held onto control of the land with its cross, even with a reversionary interest.

A nagging question remains in one's mind—that had location in the sense of ownership of the land been the real issue, why could not the Congress have resolved the issue more easily by suggesting that the cross simply be removed to part of the five private acres of Henry Sandoz, which he was so willing to swap, which was so close to Sunrise Point? That simply confirms the obvious conclusion, that Congress wanted the cross to remain at Sunrise Point, where the Christian worship was historically known, and where it would continue, and it did not want any other religious competition.

The concrete-filled cross had been spoken of as difficult to move. Yet, in the aftermath to the Court's decision, only 10 days after the decision, the Sandoz cross was removed overnight, and never found, despite the large rewards offered ($100,000). Does this not show the potential political divisiveness of getting government involved in religion as the *Lemon* test tried to prevent? A different cross later appeared at the site, also without any permission and was soon taken down, so the situation remains unresolved. And the Court continues to discount the "potential political divisiveness" of such a pro-religious ruling?

WHEN "PRIVATE CHOICE" AND "NEUTRALITY" STILL ALLOW SPECIFIC RELIGIOUS FAVORITISM

In 2011, the Court judged a case as *not judiciable* by the Court since it *lacked standing*. Arizona Christian School Tuition Organization v. Winn, 563 U.S. 125 (2011), the Court (5/4), utilizing the *Flast v. Cohen*, 391 U.S. 83 (1968) decision and following the decision of *Valley Forge Christian College v. Americans United* (1982), in insisting that the Respondents showed only a general taxpayer connection, which has not been recognized by the Court as involving sufficiently specific injury to suffice for standing. The Court interpreted *Flast* to make the sole exception to the general requirements for standing in Article III of the Constitution requiring (1) a "logical link" between the plaintiff's taxpayer status "and the type of legislative enactment attacked" and (2) "a nexus" between the plaintiff's taxpayer status and "the precise nature of the constitutional infringement alleged." It further explained that to ascertain whether these two requirements exist, one must realize the distinction between tax credits and governmental expenditures.

In government expenditures to a religious organization, one's taxpayer connection is direct and particular; in a tax credit, in which the "state simply declines to impose a tax," that connection is absent, so any injury is only speculative. In the first case, the money is collected and spent by the government; in the mere tax credit arrangement, such as the one in this case, the government does not receive nor spend the money. The money remains completely in the hand of the person, and the choice of giving it to such an educational fund is strictly that person's choice. Interestingly, two of the five justices that arrived at the judgment that the Respondent did not have standing, rejected the decision being based on *Flast*, yet admitted that the other three had based the decision on *Flast*.

That phenomena of such a split leave the reader in doubt on what possible basis those two (J. Alito and J. Thomas) arrived at their agreement of the conclusion of the other three to form a majority. As the *Buono* case, it is also very strange. What is just as strange is why the Court went to such length to describe the role of Madison being the chief architect of the First Amendment Religion Clauses by his *Memorial and Remonstrance* which opposed the general assessment bill that was earlier before the Virginia Court, which we described earlier in detail. Madison's opposition to even such an indirect support by the government, by allowing each taxpayer to designate which religious group was to be the recipient of his share of his taxes, was no more direct than the Arizona scheme which allowed the taxpayer to choose among qualified religious or nonreligious, nonprofitable institutions which he would donate within the allowable amount that would be then entered on his tax return as a "credit" against his tax liability. The Court *missed* the fact that "private choice" did *not* satisfy Madison, Jefferson, *nor* the First Amendment. That was simply Gov. Henry's idea, but his bill was *defeated* by the opposition including Madison and Jefferson, the minds behind the First Amendment.

The only difference is that in one case, the state actually received the money, and then expended it as directed by the taxpayer, and in the other, the state simply relinquished its claim on the limited amount which the taxpayer has used—which *legally already was owed to the state*, although they may or may not have yet received it. As the dissenting opinion (of four justices) notes, the *effect* is the *same* either way; the *distinction* of such government expenditure and a tax credit is completely *unreasonable* and never recognized or utilized by the Court in such challenges to the Establishment Clause. The dissent simply saw such a rejection to hear the case on the merits of the case as an oversimplification, and that its reading of *Flast* was a stretch never utilized by the Court by overemphasizing the idea that the state must first extract the precise money from the taxpayer before spending it, under which the taxpayer would *only then* be granted standing.

Instead, taxpayer here met the *Flast* test completely when it stated, "[W]e hold that a taxpayer will have standing consistent with Article III to invoke federal judicial power when he alleges that congressional action under the taxing and spending clause is in derogation of the Establishment Clause."[25] The AZ state income tax still lists in 2021 *dozens* of different groups that offer public services, many of which have definite *religious* roots and missions, to which one can give money and receive credit from the state, up to $400 for each person or $800 for a couple, while the state wonders why it has so little money to pay its *public school teachers*!

The issue of government prayer arose again in *Town of Greece, N.Y. v. Susan Galloway et al.*, 572 U.S. 565; 134 S.Ct. 1811 (2014). One might easily have predicted that because of *Marsh* in 1983, the Court would end up approving the situation in this case even though it was not a legislature but the Town of Greece's monthly board meeting. But there was no real "neutrality" nor "private choice" to dilute the government connection to the religion. For some years the monthly board meetings had been opened with a moment of silence, but with a new supervisor coming aboard in 1999, he changed it, and had his employee phone local clergy to see who might be willing to lead an invocation. Nearly all of the religious institutions in the town of 94,000 were Christian, with most non-Christian religious meeting places outside the town. From 1999 to 2007, all of the participating clergy were in fact Christian. The clergy were allowed to determine the content of the prayer entirely; the city board gave no guidance nor reviewed the prayers before they were given. Many were very explicitly Christian by their references to Christian symbols, doctrines, and Christian holidays.

Respondents, Susan Galloway and Linda Stephens attended two board meetings to speak about current local issues, and they objected to the prayers as violations of their religious and philosophical views, actually admonishing the board members for how offensive they found the exclusively Christian content of the prayers. In response, the town invited a Jewish layman, also a chairman of the local Baha'i temple, and when a Wiccan priestess requested to lead the invocation, she also was granted the opportunity. Respondents brought suit in District Court, charging that the prayers were too Christian, that they would not object to prayer if it was inclusive and ecumenical, referring only to a "generic God," so long as it did not associate the government with any single faith. The District Court, upon the city's request for a summary judgment against Respondents, granted it, insisting that the Town had invited anyone from the town to lead the invocation, and could not be required to seek participants beyond the town's borders. In utilizing *Marsh*, that Court claimed that there was no requirement that the prayer must be nonsectarian.

The Second Circuit Court of Appeals *reversed*, holding that when one considers the entire picture, a reasonable observer would think the Town of Greece was endorsing Christianity. Further, there was no reason why clergy of non-Christian religious groups whose places of worship were just outside the border of the town could not have been asked to participate. When the clergy often asked the board and audience to rise for the prayer or to bow their heads, and when some members of the board crossed themselves at the end of the prayer, one could not but conclude that the *Town itself* was endorsing Christianity.

The Supreme Court *reversed* the Second Circuit Court, basically agreeing that the arguments of the District Court were correct. It added its usual "historical" reference that prayers in Congress have been *religion specific* for more than 200 years, which is proof that the Founders did *not* think such a practice violated the Establishment Clause. This is J. Kennedy's stock proof, which shows he never read Madison and it seems to suggest that the law can never be read differently no matter how different the culture and circumstances become.

But the Court also insisted that no faith was excluded by law here, and there was no coercion, since it was only the board members that *had* to be there. The Court further discounted the two arguments of Respondents: (1) that *Marsh* did not approve of sectarian prayers, and (2) that actual social pressures of the setting and conduct of the town meeting forced nonadherents to remain in the room and even feign participation so as to avoid offending board members who sponsor the prayer or will vote on matters citizens bring to the board.

Regarding the issue of sectarian prayers, the Court emphasized that *Marsh* did *not* indicate that the prayer had to be nonsectarian, and history and tradition have shown that prayer in this limited context could coexist with the principles of disestablishment and religious freedom. The question is what did it mean by "coexist"? What would "coexist" look like in a nation that had as much religious pluralism and nonaffiliation with religion as the United States has in the twenty-first century? Erika Lee's recent book on the history of xenophobia in the United States shows how it "coexisted" even beside the proud tradition of the United States being a nation of "immigrants," even while the most influential xenophobes passed law after law against many different groups of immigrants, persecuting them endlessly. The xenophobes themselves coexisted with other people, though not willingly or very peacefully, and the violent racism was barely below the surface even when the immigration laws professed to be color-blind.[26]

The Court further insisted that the obvious Christian nature of these prayers must not be dismissed as the relic of a time when the Nation was less pluralistic than today. Really? This is among the weakest arguments the Court has ever made in Establishment cases since it is a fact that the Nation was *much less* religiously pluralistic 200 years back, so the practice might very well be such a "relic" or residue from those earlier theocratic days. The proper resolution of the case should have required more than merely saying it is not such a "relic." One would expect to see some proof or argument, but there was none. The *colonial theocracies* whose religious customs were still hanging on in some minds were assumed to be *uniform, not diverse,* since the government was explicitly expressed (even by scripture quotations) *only* by its "God," while a democracy, on the other hand, which the Founding Fathers were creating, was to be a government "of the people, by the people, and for the people," which, as Rawls has emphasized, means it was assumed to *include diversity.*

To this, the Court added that Congress itself has invited Jewish, Buddhist, Hindu, and Islamic clergy. That, of course, is basically only a formality which still presumes too much by assuming the prayers would be in the Christian format, style, or even content, even when led by clergy of the non-Christian religious groups. That's the way a subtle or unofficial theocracy works. And even that diversity was *not* the case in either *Marsh* or the *Town of Greece.* The Court admitted that in *Marsh* Rev. Palmer did remove all references to Christ after hearing the criticism, and the Court was positive that the *Marsh* Court did *not* say that Rev. Palmer had thereby made the invocations legal as opposed to its illegal status as long as the prayers were very religion specific. Instead, the Court further claimed that it does not and will *not consider* the *content* of any prayer in order to judge its legality.

The irony, of course, was that within a single page of the written decision, the *Marsh* Court emphasized that *Rev. Palmer's content in his prayers* was *appreciated* by people of *all faiths* as was his asking God for the blessing of "peace, justice, and freedom." So the specific religion references might have been any or many, but the Court is somehow certain that the *content* of his prayers simply pointed to "universal truths" so was legal. In fact, people could easily be tolerant enough to hear people of other faiths express their prayers for such things as peace, justice, and freedom. That is all the Court's defining what would be acceptable "universal" *content* of the prayer just after *denying* that it ever has or ever will measure the content! But there were objections to Rev. Palmer's prayers long before the *Marsh* Court.

Finally, the Court here in *Greece* said there was absolutely no coercion to participate in the invocation, and Respondents have no constitutional guarantee to never encounter others with whom they disagree. They are adults who are less likely to be indoctrinated than children (as in the school prayer cases), so cases involving children are not dispositive for these adults. This is more of Kennedy's and Scalia's response in the oral argument of *Perry,* that those who were of another faith, should just "avert their eyes" or turn their head and quit taking offense,[27] but the Court simply did *not* consider the *religiously intimidating nature* of the religion-specific prayers within such a small group, among which were people who, because they were present to address the board with their concerns or requests, they had to avoid irritating the board which might occur if they did not follow the chaplain's instructions to stand and/or bow their heads.

What the Court seemed oblivious to is the fact that the *particular metaphysics* separating most specific religions from each other do not simply drop out, leaving a single generic, universal religion which every culture would espouse. The specific metaphysical claims that *divide* the religions from each other *remain intertwined* with the specific religion's values and ethics, and do *not* become generic just because of a *government setting*. Further, if peace, justice, and freedom are the universals that should be the content since they are not offensive, *why make them offensive* by attaching them to a *particular* "God" or specific, exclusive "Christian" form of attaining them or of being "saved?" But then the Court suggested that there should be no objection to "ceremonial prayer," and that means just using prayer as a device to give "gravity" or solemnity to the situation which included the flag salute. Yet it is just as likely to convey a religious Absolute which is promoted by the government and is still *incompatible* with other religions and with nonreligious people. The Court will hunt long and hard to find any religion which gives permission to use its prayers as purely ceremonial, or a tool by which to inject seriousness or gravity into a situation or to think of its particular god as only generic.[28]

Did the "historical" appeal of the Court here suggest that the law, once articulated, *already anticipated every possible argument* testing the limits of its meaning, so that the eighteenth-century Founders, even if they were *not* as aware of religious diversity as we are today? Did the Court think the Framers could anticipate it since they were more aware of the divisiveness and danger of especially religious conflicts, so they made the decision that even religion-specific prayer was *compatible* with all religious and nonreligious people? Did they reach this decision after such long analysis and deliberation among them—just like they understood completely where *we stand on race today* which they also had *all fully analyzed*, yet they decided to *leave slavery in place* for another 20 years (which turned into 70). What is being assumed here of the Framers' knowledge and values that necessarily makes them normative still today?

Of course, these are both foolish suggestions. The Founders could not possibly have anticipated the future that is our present, either with our racial, sexual, or religious situation. Of course, if the Court is not assuming this, then the proof from that ancient historical past may be quite *irrelevant*, since if the only value an ancient reference has is its mere age, it really has nothing commending it. But the ideals of Madison, Jefferson, and others leaders surely are worth considering, even if their ideals were more noble and consistent than their own personal actions, as are most people's. But Madison and Jefferson were the primary definers and shapers of the First Amendment, and they did *not* approve of government officials leading prayers or of establishing religious holy days, or even of religions incorporating in order to own land. They knew of religions other than the Christian religion, although most of their peers did not, and they distinguished between sects of Christianity and of other religions, and *all* fell under their idea of religion needing to be separated from government. In the twenty-first century, the democratic republic requires an equality, diversity, and liberty totally *unknown* to the original formulations of most religions' ethics, but their principles articulated still shape a *separation* credibly. Yet, to be binding law, those principles have to be *agreed to* by all citizens today, as Rawls insisted, and no religion has ever been acceptable to all people, certainly not accepted by all to govern them.

Concurring J. Thomas, joined by J. Scalia, insisted that the "coercion" in the present case has nothing in common with the "coercion" in the days prior to the First Amendment when it involved actual force, both doctrinally and financially. This is part of J. Thomas's usual insistence that the Establishment Clause was always intended *only* as a *federal restriction*, prohibiting a national church, and that the First Amendment "was simply agnostic on the subject of state establishments," concluding that "the decision to establish or disestablish religion was reserved to the States."[29] Was any Framer or justice so naïve as to think all the states would agree and disestablish or that their chosen establishments, which would be a continuation of the same problems they had as colonies, would pose no problems to the New Nation? Were the Framers of the Constitution unable to see what would happen if the states simply went their own way, a pattern which made the Articles of Confederation so ineffective? How can that be squared with the very history of *Virginia* with Madison and Jefferson and others moving to a complete and *"perfect separation"* (Madison's expression, as we saw earlier) of religion and government?

The primary argument from the *dissent* in *Town of Greece* is that the Court of Appeals did not say the *Town of Greece* could not have a nonsectarian prayer, nor did it say there were not other ways the invocation could have met muster, such as informing those in attendance that the invocation was open to volunteers, or suggesting to those leading the prayers that they are acceptable so long as they are not used as attempts to convert or disparage others' beliefs. So the dissent simply emphasized that the *Town of Greece* was too exclusive, showing a complete *disregard for the diversity* of the religious community comprising the *Town of Greece*. Only 4 prayers in 11 years of monthly meetings ($11 \times 12 = 132$), so only 4 out of possibly 132 occasions had been given by non-Christians. There was a list drawn up from the Community Guide or Greece Post, which basically did not include any religious groups outside the city limits, and the board made no effort to contact any groups outside that city limit. Would the resulting Court's decision have been the same, had a Buddhist, Jewish, or other non-Christian led the prayers for all of the 11 years except only four occasions?

As J. Kagan said in her dissent (joined by J. Breyer, J. Sotomayor, and J. Ginsburg), the *Town of Greece*'s practice "does not square with the First Amendment's promise that every citizen, irrespective of her religion, owns an equal share in the government." In *Larson v. Valente* (1982), the Court held the "clearest command of the Establishment Clause . . . is that one religious denomination cannot be officially preferred over another."[30] J. Kagan noted that Jefferson's *Virginia Act for Establishing Religious Freedom* (1785) had the vision that "when a citizen stands before her government, whether to perform a service or request a benefit, her religious beliefs do not enter into the picture." "They all participate in the business of government, not as Christians, Jews, Muslims (and more), but only as Americans—none of them different from any other for that civic purpose. Why not, then, at a town meeting?"[31] From the earliest days of the "incorporation" of the Establishment Clause into state law (1947 on), this list also included not preferring religion to nonreligion, or theists to atheists, as we saw.

What this potent criticism shows is that the Rawls requirement for the contracting process itself, as hypothesized in an "original position" behind a "veil of ignorance" has to be complemented to a degree by a similar "veil of ignorance" *on any adjudication* of actual situations, a veil which removes by illuminating the absurd, nonrational, accidental, or "happenstance" *advantages* certain people have over others which has *no place* within the justice of the social contract. That is the only way to an impartial justice. It surely is as difficult for a judge to ignore these *irrational particulars* in order to issue a "fair" judgment of "political justice" rather than vested-interest-justice or metaphysical justice, as it would be in any contracting party's expectations of the "fairness" of the social contract to which she was originally agreeing. The realities of the actual case and controversy still exist, but if the irrational or accidentally vested advantages interfere with the basic principle of equality or equal, maximum liberty for all, then there has to be a readjustment of laws, since *no one* would contract to be taken advantage of. That is what the Bill of Rights or Amendments were all about.

As wholly distinct from the *Marsh* case, both in the content of the prayer (since Rev. Palmer, because of public pressure, eventually deleted much or all of the Christian-specific references in his prayers) as well as the audience, the *Town of Greece* does not fall under the exception of the *Marsh*, but remains a very exclusivistic, Christian practice, and the majority failed to understand the potential for divisiveness the actual religious differences can cause when used preferentially (citing to *Perry*).[32] All of this might suggest that the Constitution and its Amendments' *anti*-incorporation spokesmen have finally won, that the Court will "turn back the clock" to preincorporation days. But as Leonard Levy noted, that is not likely to happen since the Court feels so compelled to manifest its coherence with its past decisions, and because it can find easier ways to ignore the "incorporation," in his words, "it is quite likely to reinterpret precedents, distinguishing away some, blunting others, and making new law without the appearance of overriding or disrespecting the past."[33] That is the method we have seen it use, although its present incoherence with decisions prior to 1986 is extremely obvious.

PERVASIVE INDOCTRINATION AUTHORITY YET THE CENTRAL SYMBOL IS ONLY A SYMBOL OF DEATH?

The most recent Establishment cases reveal the tension in the logic of the Court between the church's Absolute Authority over its teachers while its most central symbol is primarily read by the Court as a symbol of the "meaning" of death. It raises the question of whether that which is "pervasively religious" or "pervasively sectarian" or "pervasively indoctrinating" is an entity that can change its character back and forth. Either the Cross is "pervasively religious" or it is not, as even a parochial school is either "pervasively religious" (or sectarian or indoctrinating) or it is not. They do not change their character back and forth, especially when the Court characterizes the same entity or symbol as pervasively sectarian or religious in one case (a Free Exercise case) and simply secular in another (an Establishment case).

So, another place and another cross, and another reason is given by the Court for *not* viewing it as an illegal "establishment" of religion. This was decided in *American Legion et al., v. American Humanist Assn, et al.*, 588 U.S. ___., 139 S.Ct 2067 (2019). The 32-foot high monstrous Latin cross, completed by the American Legion in 1925, was found *not* a violation of the Establishment Clause, even though it sits on government property and government funds are used to maintain it. J. Alito, writing for the Court, obtained a 7/2 agreement of *reversing* the lower court decision, but there was *no agreement about why*. He articulated "four" principles that he thought crucial, but his entire approach actually presupposes *four slightly different principles* he articulated that supposedly sealed the case. These presuppositions he tried to invoke as if they were obvious principles are as follows: (1) the symbol of the Cross (just as the symbol of the Star of David), even though it originally (*sic*!) had religious meaning, after WWI, can mean simply basically something secular, namely, the "meaning" people who died in battle attached to *death*; (2) no Establishment tests were really valid from 1971 to at least 1986 since 1971 marked the overly ambitious *Lemon* Court's attempt to define a "test" to connect the disparate criteria that preceded it; (3) since "original" meanings of symbols often can*not* be ascertained, we must depend upon the subsequent history, and the passage of time gives rise to a strong presumption of constitutionality; and (4) a removal of the Cross, after so many years of it being there, would be viewed by the locals as hostility to religion rather than following the First Amendment.

J. Alito, for the Court, went to considerable length to emphasize how ecumenical if not universal the symbol of the cross is, that at the initial dedication of it in its particular location, both a Catholic priest and Baptist pastor participated. But why were only *Christian clergy* used, if the symbol used to be religious but is more secular today? Then he analyzed that the lack of any protest of Jewish families who had lost a son in WWI, whose grave was marked with a cross, is proof of the "meaning" of the cross which goes far beyond the Christian meaning. Does he think the Jews, who comprised around 3% of the U.S. population at the time of WWI, would have wanted to upset the Christian majority, to experience more anti-Semitism from alleged Christians? The absence of protest, however, was an exaggeration. Why did those in charge insist on changing the ways the graves were marked, from a rectangular marble slab to a Cross or in some cases to a Star of David? Why did they repatriate those bodies of soldiers to the United States for burial with a marble slab for a marker if they could not determine that the deceased was either Christian or Jew? Was not the whole question of markers revolving around the specific *religious affiliation* of *each soldier*, and nothing more? Did they not recognize how insulting it would be to mark a body with a religious affiliation which was not his or her religion?[34] Why do people wear crosses on chains around their necks?[35]

The "original" meaning of a cross back in the days of Ancient Rome was the most hideous punishment the government could inflict on a criminal. Once the Christian Church chose to accept the fact of the Crucifixion which had been such an utter shock, it then could hunt for a meaning to it, and, on the idea, especially of the influence of St. Paul, the church was able to use the Resurrection to offset the negative aspect of the Cross, to see the Crucifixion as the sacrifice of "God's Son" for human sins.[36] But it was not a lasting punishment of Jesus's death, but only less than three full days, as the accounts seem to say, which could not really be any comparable "paying of a debt" or redemption, when the Jewish apocalypses, as well as Christian ones, saw sin as deserving a brutally unending, torturous death, not any three-day one with a glorious resurrection afterward. The Apostle Paul was able to move the Christian community beyond the sphere of Judaism only by changing the focus, by preaching a mystical union disciples have with the risen Christ, but by this he was able to isolate the Torah (including all the law in ancient Judaism, even the Decalogue) as at least *irrelevant* to non-Jewish Christians. Paul's view of the Cross, from at least that point forward, eventually drove a wedge between the Christians and Jews, so non-Jewish Christians soon began to accuse Jews in general of deicide.[37]

Christianity changed the pure negative of the Cross, but only over time and a very novel view of a *sacrifice* of God (or "God's Son") for all human-ity (or really only those who become disciples). It was an *exclusive* symbol, *not* applied to just anybody that died in war, but *used only by Christians*, for centuries and centuries. But the Court, uninformed of the entire history of the earliest church, fails to realize this, so speaks as if all Jews have accepted the symbol of the Cross without objection for their deceased soldiers.[38] In truth, the history of Christian anti-Semitism has been so blinded to reality that the canonical gospels themselves long ago gave deplorably unfair caricatures of Jewish people, especially the Gospel of John.

The Court here hated to be reminded that it allowed the erection of a KKK cross on government property because the latter was a "public forum," the organization which had used burning crosses for generations in its racial hatred and homicides of black people, so the Court tried to align the time period of the dedication of the Cross in question with the KKK march down Pennsylvania Ave. in the nation's capital. But for what purpose? Was it to show that the KKK was a group of "very fine people," a respectable Christian group? Or was it to show that our country really does not care how much hatred and death various white supremacist groups produce, and other Christians should not be distressed that the KKK can exhibit their symbols, making a mockery of the Christian Cross, and march down in force in the nation's capital to show how "respectable" they are when they have their hoods off? Do such inferences actually not offend Christians?

Yet J. Alito suggested a primary *generic, secular* meanings of the Cross—that people *die*—and the Court bought it, enough to reverse the lower court decision but without any real agreement about the reason why. Lower courts still do not know what the real arguments for or against in a case involving monuments are, but only that certain *Christian* monuments and symbols must be preserved for "historical" reasons. Those Courts must learn how to read Christian religious symbols as only generic, universal, secular symbols, but see other religion's symbols as primarily religious and to be excluded from government property? Is this the same "historical" reasoning that would require the maintenance of statues of Confederate leaders who attempted to secede from the Union as traitors, over their economic boon of having slaves work for them and whatever feeling of white superiority was required for them to engage in that?

The United States is slowly moving on from that racist discrimination, and it is probably time that people began to imagine themselves in Rawls's "hypothetical" original position behind a veil of ignorance to realize what real "justice" looks like in principle, so we can begin to dissolve the *presumption* that the Christian religion is the only true one, or that its "God" is generic and universal, recognized by all people on earth, or that its institutions, symbols, rituals should be retained precisely as they were in *ancient Christendom*, prior to the founding of the democratic republic of the United States, or that they should be retained *as if* they have a *secular* meaning that is more prominent than the religious meaning? But these conflict with each other since ancient Christendom never viewed the symbol of the cross as only a secular symbol of death. When the *presumption* of "constitutionality" is based on merely historical *residual elements* from that Christendom or even colonial attempts at a theocracy, without being recognized as to their true nature as such *residue* from prior Christian "establishments," their theocratic and therefore *undemocratic* nature—their sectarian Christian nature will *continue* to be divisive and resented by all citizens who are not Christian.

Here, the two systems Rawls delineated, the "political" definition of justice and the "metaphysical" definition of justice, stand in contrast, and if a nation is to exist, it must have a basic ethical agreement which is grounded on "public reason" rather than a metaphysical or mythical faith that is perpetuated as "above" reason or superior to human thinking. Rawls said religions can certainly be free to believe what they want, but when the questions of justice and the structures of justice arise and there are conflicts, they must be resolved not by some alleged superiority of a single religion's metaphysics (since there is no such) but by the principles *all citizens agreed to under the original contract*. If one is truly behind the "veil of ignorance," Rawls insists that one would not even know whether one was going to be religious, much less a Christian, so would one have selected for the government to maintain such a Christian symbol which makes all other people feel they are lesser citizens, lesser valued, or don't really belong?

The Court's second principle, of the ineptness of the *Lemon* test, ignores the fact that the District Court *used* the *Lemon* test to find the Bladensburg Cross constitutional, but the Fourth Circuit reversed that lower court. Yet, instead of examining the principles of *Lemon*'s three-pronged test which had been the *criteria used for the prior decisions*, which had worked so well from 1971 until 1985, and was utilized by the Court even subsequently (J. Alito, for the Court, lists only cases from 1993 to 2018 that utilized novel standards),[39] the Supreme Court did not actually honor either of the lower courts, but utilized *its own novel test*.

It further mocked the *Lemon* test as did concurring justices, as if to say that any test which a Court created prior to *their* joining the bench could not have been right because it lacked *their* insights.[40] The whole process began to dislodge *Lemon* once J. Scalia was appointed to the Court, but the Court has still not overturned all those earlier decisions which would seem to be the consistent and honest thing to do. Is it possible that it did not overrule all of those earlier decisions because so many of them gave and continue to provide so much money to parochial schools? Or, is it just because the Court fears destabilizing things which too much overturning of earlier decisions can produce?

But a severe problem arises when the Court leaves intact all the decisions its predecessors made on the basis of the *Lemon* test and its criteria that were recognized several years even prior to being articulated in *Lemon*, because, as we saw, the result is to make lower courts look foolish, while the Supreme Court refuses to resolve or clarify the problems. It used to be unheard of for the Court *not* to examine the case by the tests and arguments by which the issue was adjudicated in the lower courts, especially when those very tests had been formulated by the Supreme Court itself, such as the *Lemon* test.

But instead of clarifying, the Court simply added to *Lemon*'s three prongs the "historical" test beginning in *Marsh*. It only occasionally utilized the "reasonable observer" or "endorsement" test suggested by J. O'Connor in her concurring opinion in *Lynch*, and basically *ignored* the profound criteria provided by J. Brennan in his concurring opinion in *Abington v. Schempp*. The Court *never clarified* the relation between the *Lemon* criteria and the *Marsh* criterion, nor did it explain how the more recent tests of "neutrality" or "private choice" were related to either *Lemon* or *Marsh*.

If J. O'Connor's "reasonable observer" and "endorsement" test has occasionally been cited and added to other criteria, it has been neglected for the most part, probably because it seems too nebulous and subjective. The "historical" test, begun in *Marsh* in 1983, continued in *Lynch*, but has never been unambiguously defined, as the Court *oscillated* back and forth between ancient history of a religion, colonial history, post-constitutional history, history of a particular state, history of some symbol's usage in a particular state, and so forth. This "history" test was used as selectively or more so than *Lemon* ever was, since it was *neglected* in *Lyng*, *Smith*, and many others.

Uniquely, here the Court selects President Washington's Farewell Address and the Northwest Ordinance to emphasize how a nation needs religion in order to have ethical order on which to base law. But Washington, whatever his reputation as a military leader, was *not* the ethical mind behind the Constitution or the First Amendment. Madison and Jefferson, the authors of the Religious Freedom Bill for Virginia, were, and they were also the authors of the First Amendment, yet they get overlooked, so much that J. Thomas, in his usual tirade that the First Amendment was never to be applied to the states, simply draws a blank from history, as if Madison and Jefferson really thought the nation could hold together by the First Amendment with various states establishing their own religions? It had not worked in colonial days at all. But there is never any awareness shown by the Court that the basic symbols such as the Ten Commandments and Cross were used by Christians in Colonies to try to *"establish"* religion, that is, their specific read of it, their own form of a "theocracy."

Quite on the other hand, it was a "democracy" the Framers sought to establish, *not a theocracy*. It was a break with 1,400 years of Christendom, despite earlier colonial attempts at specific theocracies. The nation would never have survived had individual states finally been free to establish their own religion, as J. Thomas prefers.

J. Alito's third point, which is his overall point, that a practice that exists for a *long period of time* surely increases the presumption of its "constitutionality," is simply too broad to be legally meaningful. Would such a presumption be ethical in the areas of racial and sexual discrimination? How long a period of time gives a practice the presumption of constitutionality? He fails to realize that most of the slogans on our money, within our government buildings, and many practices such as a legislative chaplain, do presuppose something. But it is not their "constitutionality" but rather the fact that they presupposed a *theocratic* government, a *single* religion, an *"established"* religion which was the *background* for the *disestablishing* that the later First Amendment required. But the different arms and relics of "establishment" were not all apparent to every citizen in 1789, not even to President Washington.

J. Alito, for the Court, finally objected to any practice or monument being *removed* if the people have grown accustomed to its presence, since he thinks that would be "politically divisive" (but I thought the *Lemon* test was not to be used?). He evidently thought he can draw a significant distinction to a practice which has been around for a long time and one that is just created. But practices brought by the European immigrants came from a history of *religious wars* within the *Christian* ranks because of the Absolutes each side maintained, and *many* rituals, symbols, and primary doctrines of Christian churches today in the United States are *identical as residue from those theocratic days* of ancient Christendom, those years of terrible religious wars. Does the longevity of these rituals, symbols, doctrines, or ideas give them "constitutional" status?

Since the Civil War was much more recent than the practice of slavery and racism in the New World, does that negate the Civil War Amendments. If "longevity" of a practice means that the practice should continue lest its removal or discontinuance create a "political divisiveness," slavery should be continued as constitutional? But if "longevity" is the criterion, should not the longevity of the *Lemon* test sustain its preservation and honoring today rather than allowing it to be compromised and ridiculed and deserted by the

Court? But what should one think of ideas, symbols, or rituals that are of very *recent* vintage? The "under God" was added to the Pledge of Allegiance in the 1950s. How could that qualify as constitutional under J. Alito's criterion of "longevity" unless "under God" is just another *secular* term so it would not be politically divisive? But it simply is not secular. Would the statues in the South of the Confederate leaders (whose cessation from the Union was treasonous) be kept in perpetuity since they are *older* than the Civil Rights Act of 1965? What is it that is needed to give the preservation of a statue, monument, symbol, and so on *value* other than its mere age? This decision, more than any prior to it, seems to *presuppose* that all U.S. citizens are *only* Christians, and/or there really is only one God, and *everyone* knows that is the Christian God, just as J. Scalia said in the oral argument in *Perry*, even if the various religions have different names, attributes, involvements, mythologies, and the like—which they feel very exclusive about and even condemn others for not accepting—they are all to be subsumed under the universal rubric of "Christian." If not, what else would explain this lack of logic?

To this fourth presupposition J. Alito added the scare tactic: if the Court decided to have the Cross moved to another locality close by which had a number of memorial monuments so it would have made sense, if that move created *more divisiveness religiously*, it would give the impression of the Court being *"hostile" to religion.* But such an argument is built only upon his narrow focus of people who have been persuaded by right-wing propaganda that someone out there is trying to destroy all religion in the United States. That is a fairly common trope today, built upon ignorance of the law and of the facts.

Despite that propaganda, the Cross is *not* a "neutral" or "secular" symbol in *any* sense of the word, whether it is a huge concrete structure, a wooden or pipe cross, or even if it is small and in 18kt gold, hanging around someone's neck. It belongs only to *one* religion which is *neither universal nor generic.* Nor did the Constitution's Framers think it was to be endorsed or established by government in the U.S. democracy which embodies religious pluralism as well as multiple, varied "comprehensive schemas." The *only answer*, as Madison, Jefferson, and even Rawls saw, is for the *unity* of the people to be *stronger* than their *disunity*, their inclusivism more potent than their exclusivism, which means, in Rawls's terms that "justice" has priority in all questions of structures of justice, a "political" (or reasonably bargained and compromised) conception of justice which we *all* have *agreed* to rather than one select "metaphysical" conception of justice held by a few people but rejected by other citizens.

Finally, I will not try to repeat the remarkably tolerant, scholarly, and respectful dissent of J. Ginsburg, but encourage the reader to look it up, and then wonder, as I have, as a retired professor of objective religious studies, how any justice could have actually faulted her argument or endorsed J. Alito's reversal of the lower court. The late J. Ginsburg was a courageous and brilliant champion for equality within our democratic republic, though too often that meant that she was only a dissenting justice with from one to three of her colleagues joining with her. We can only hope that the logic within her dissents will be seen and treasured and become more influential in the coming years.

The reader should also study the final paragraph of p. 7 of the Court's "Syllabus" to see how the members of the Court *splintered* on the major *arguments*, even without looking at the dissent. This kind of lack of guidance from the Court shows more of a problem than the *Lemon* test ever evoked in decisions, since here there are *no two opinions* that agree on *anything* except *reversing* the lower court decision or not doing so. If this provides any picture of the future, perhaps we will soon have not only these 100 page decisions as standard, but a splintering over every paragraph or perhaps every sentence? Surely, what Jefferson, Madison, and even Rawls conceived for this democratic republic can reach a *more wholesome sense of agreement* or perhaps finally admit that, as Madison said, the civil government simply has "no cognizance of religion." And this includes the Court. The Constitution did *not* provide the Court the power of funding *any* institution or entity. Yet its decisions often do precisely that, despite the legislature having the power of the purse as well as the power of *formulating* law, especially since the House of Representatives, by Madison's estimate, would adequately represent the plethora of the various interests as they change, thereby arriving at the interests of the *nation*, which he thought was essential to avoid majoritarianism, which by definition, *never* represents the interests of the *nation* as a whole.

PERVASIVE INDOCTRINATION AND ABSOLUTE AUTHORITY IN EMPLOYMENT

Finally, *Our Lady of Guadalupe School, v. Morrissey-Berru*, which included *St. James School v. Darryl Biel*, as personal representative of the *Estate of Kristen Biel*, 519 U.S. ___, 140 S.Ct, 2049, (2020), involved two faculty members of Catholic elementary schools in the LA area who were terminated. When they challenged it, the District Court agreed to the schools' request for summary judgment, but the Ninth Circuit *reversed* on the grounds that the recent *Hosanna-Tabor Lutheran Church and School v. EEOC*, 565 U.S. 171 (2012) was *not* dispositive since neither of these women fit the "ministerial" exemption from antidiscrimination employment law, so their termination was illegal employment discrimination.

The Court opinion, written again by J. Alito, overruled the Ninth Circuit, emphasizing that the guidelines in *Hosanna-Tabor* were *not* to be used as a rigid test, as the Ninth Circuit did, but rather simply reduced to the question of what the teachers *actually did*, how specifically they functioned. Therefore, the fact of their *not* having the title of "minister," or their *not* having extensive formal training in the Catholic faith, or their *not* being seen by others as the religious leaders of the local church, or their *not* giving themselves out to other as "ministers" or "leaders" of the faith—though in these ways they seem to differ from the teachers in *Hosanna-Tabor*—there are *more general ways* in which the facts prove they *were* included in the "ministerial exemption," even if they neither one ever utilized such a status for tax relief or other advantages.

The question was what *did* they "do"? J. Alito insisted they gave themselves wholly to the pervasively religious mission of the school in every conceivable way, or teaching their secular classes but also religion classes, or modeling the Catholic faith in real life to the students and assisting them to do so. That is, *every facet* of the school program is geared around its religious priority of *indoctrinating* these students in the Catholic faith, and *both did this*, even praying with their students and testing them over their religious knowledge.

That comprises the whole argument, that two earlier cases established that the Court would not interfere in a religion's matter of "faith and doctrine," but would grant the religious institution to determine that. Although those earlier cases had to do only with settling *property* disputes,[41] the *Hosanna-Tabor* extended the church's sole authority to being able to decide who would represent the faith and true doctrine, so the Court figured it should leave that totally to the church. We saw the problem of *reprisal* utilized in the *Hosanna-Tabor* case which had arisen only because a teacher who was vital to the program got ill and had to miss several months. In the present case, Morrissey-Berru was in her 60s, but very conscientious. She claimed she was cut to part-time one year, then not renewed thereafter, enabling the school to hire a younger teacher. The school had given her no reasons, but in Court, they cited that she had not adapted to a new program they had. Biel was younger, so in Court, the school claimed that she had kept a messy homeroom. Does that really mean she failed to represent adequately the Catholic faith?

Interestingly, the Court argued *for* this *pervasively religious* and *pervasively Catholic*, sectarian or indoctrinating mission of the school, but failed to mention that in *Hosanna-Tabor*, the teacher's role was *distinguished* from the roles of the more *ordinary faculty* members, whereas in the present case, the Court's description of what the two teachers *actually did* was *not* different from what *all other teachers also did*—teachers who were *not* considered "ministers," just as they were not. But, as J. Alito bragged to the Court, *all* teachers were required to teach religion classes, and the Archdiocese considered all the teachers as "catechists."

So *Hosanna-Tabor* was *not* dispositive at all. The Court's final insistence was that one must not get hung up on mere formal titles and their absence, but, as the dissent notes, this is the Catholic Church which is very strict on its formal titles. So what these two faculty *actually did* at school was essentially what was expected of *all faculty*, and *no more and no different*. If they were necessarily "ministers," so were all their colleagues. It really is that simple.

Yet they were not even required to be practicing Catholics, and Morrissey-Berru was *not*. So how could the church have considered her one of its chosen "ministers"? Biel found her job disappeared because she had to request time off to have surgery for her breast cancer. To terminate in such a way at such a time in a person's life is difficult to square with the schools insistence that the teachers must be role models for the students to emulate the life of Jesus. What about the administrators? Evidently, empathy was not part of that requirement.

The effect of such a decision, of course, as the *dissent* noted,[42] is to place in jeopardy *every* teacher in *any* parochial school, to put them on notice, that from now on, even if they do not have *any* formal religious training or ordination or title, the school—because the Court has given it carte blanche in hiring and firing—can discriminate over age, race, sex, or *anything else*. The double irony, of course, is how such a Court, in admitting the "pervasively sectarian" or religious or indoctrinating character of the parochial school to provide this discriminating employment power to the church, can, in cases involving public funding to the schools, argue that the funding is all "neutral" and "private decisions" and the divertibility of the funds is *never* an issue since the schools are *not pervasively sectarian*. They either are or are not. The degree to which the Court attributes any wisdom to James Madison, it should reflect on his momentous words: "We are teaching the world the great truth that Govts. do better without Kings & Nobles than with them. The merit will be doubled by the other lesson that Religion flourishes in greater purity, without than with the aid of Govt."[43] But Madison is no longer with us, though some of his reasonable ideas still are.

Finally, Rawls's high opinion of the Court suggested to him that the Supreme Court should be regarded as the body most entrusted to distinguish and protect the "ordinary" power or law of legislative bodies from the higher law the people as a whole form, from which the entire schema originates. In his words, "By applying public reason the court is to prevent that law [the 'higher law'] from being eroded by the legislation of transient majorities, or more likely, by organized and well-situated narrow interests skilled at getting their way."[44] But in addition to this defensive posture, the Court is exemplary, the "institutional exemplar" of the proper use of this "public reason," since public reason is the sole reason the court exercises. It is the only branch of government that is visibly on its face the creature of that reason and of that reason alone. Citizens and legislators may properly vote their more comprehensive views when constitutional essentials and basic justice are not at stake; they need not justify by public reason why they vote as they do or make their grounds consistent and fit them into a coherent constitutional view over the whole range of their decisions. The role of the justices is to do precisely that and in doing it they have no other reason and no other values than the political.[45]

I reiterate that by that last word "political," Rawls did not mean partisan politics, but rather the basic principles of the original position and the constitutional essentials that are based on that by the consensus of the whole people. He, however, admitted that the Court does not always measure up to judging strictly by public reason but quite often falls into the traps of positions espoused by various comprehensive schemas, including religion, which are *not* public reason.[46] Surely one must ask whether some of these recent decisions manifest that public reason derived from behind the "veil of ignorance," or instead are based on specific associations the justices themselves embrace which are *not* built on public reason and do *not* include the agreement of the whole people which the "original position" must. That is the distinction Rawls drew between the "political conception of justice" and any "metaphysical conception of justice."

NOTES

1. Thomas Jefferson, "A Bill for Establishing Religious Freedom," in Kurland and Lerner (eds.), *Founders' Constitution*, 77.

2. *Zelman v. Simmons-Harris*, J. Souter, dissenting at 687, quoting from *Everson*, at 16. The Court insisted in both *Aguillar* and *Mitchell*, by J. O'Connor and J. Thomas, that the Court had changed some of its ideas but not its basic standard over the years. Yet if it subjected its Establishment jurisdiction pertaining to aid to parochial schools since 1971 up to 1986 by the criteria it established in *Aguillar* and *Mitchell*, it would have to *overturn them all*, along with most or all cases in which it gave a negative judgment against parochial schools prior to 1971. So the basic standard itself *has* changed, from "no aid" which might be divertible to "any aid" even when divertible, so long as the law was neutral or included a wide variety of recipients and/or involved private choice, while not explicitly favoring merely religion.

3. We should add to his list, that in 1983, the Court came up with its anti-*Lemon* test in *Marsh v. Chambers*, now willing to look only to see if there was a historical practice of some religious nature that existed from the late eighteenth century to the present—as if that in itself validated it, which, of course, it certainly did not do for slavery or the denial of women's rights!

4. This kind of utilization of different standards or tests to arrive at completely different decisions on a similar issue makes a farce of possibly the litigation, the laws themselves, or the Court.

5. The idea of it being a "passive" monument made it *parallel* to *Stone v. Graham*, since the plaques on the school walls in the latter were not utilized for propagating religion or even as a part of the curriculum. The declared purpose of the monument was to reduce teen-age crime. But more teenagers would have been exposed to the plaques on the wall of their school in *Stone v. Graham*, so that purpose would have a better chance of being met in that circumstance than in *Van Orden v. Perry* where the display was sitting out on 22 acres of the capital grounds in Texas amid many other displays.

6. *Van Orden v. Perry*, 545 U.S. 677 (2005), at 681.

7. If my criticism appears severe, the reader may change his or her mind if the oral argument of this case is read. One can only ask what if the Court, in adjudicating an intricate medical question, showed a similar ignorance to medicine and science? Can *uninformed* and *ancient ideas* about the issue and subject at hand be allowed to determine what is *legal*? The ignorance manifest in *Perry* is only slightly removed from legalizing the "drowning of witches" in Massachusetts centuries ago. This is precisely the problem Madison and Jefferson feared.

8. *McCreary County, Kentucky v. American Civil Liberties Union of Kentucky*, 545 U.S. 844 (2005), at 857.

9. *McCreary*, at 862.

10. *McCreary*, at 862.

11. *McCreary*, at 862.

12. *McCreary*, at 872.

13. *McCreary*, at 856.

14. *McCreary*, at 885–912. This is the same emphasis on the religion of the "majority" which the Court gave preference to in *Van Orden v. Perry*. In the oral argument of *Van Orden*, J. Scalia mentioned that both religious majority and religious minorities must accommodate the other, yet he showed no way the majority actually did so, but rather gave it the upper hand by allowing government to endorse *only it*, or, in other cases, to *fund only it*, that is, the Christian view.

15. *McCreary*, at 879–881.

16. *Bd. of Education v. Allen*, at 752.

17. In *Abington v. Schempp*, at 232.

18. Ironically, the Court was so desperate to cite authorities, that it pulled a *dissenting* opinion from J. Lucero, 499 F. 3d, at 1173 to say "one would be hard pressed to find a 'long tradition' of allowing people to permanently occupy public space with any manner of monuments." And this quote from a dissenting appellate justice is the key to the Supreme Court's decision?

19. In the last 40 years, the scholars of religion have realized that the gnostic ideas among Christians go far back, perhaps as early as the 50s, found in both the Gospel of Thomas as well as in the Apostle Paul's emphasis of having a special, secret, or spiritual knowledge, unavailable to those who are entwined with worldly ideas or emphases. This means the opposition by the Christian church to Gnosticism in the

last part of the second century was a rather arbitrary decision the church felt forced to make, but its exclusion of the gnostic ideas by marking them "heresy" vis-à-vis those making that decision, was a terrible oversimplification from vested interests.

20. From a historical examination, however, the actual facts claimed by neither can be proved. It may be thought historically likely or even probable, by modern valid, objective historical methods, that a group of people left Egypt in the thirteenth century BCE, and perhaps also went through the Sinai area, ending up in what had been Canaan. But the details in Exodus 20 that recite Moses literally meeting with God on top of Mt. Sinai and literally being given tablets with the Ten Commandments—from God—are at best a symbolic mythology, originating back in the cultures that thought their gods actually intervened in their history. They also thought the sun rotated around the earth, and most of them recorded nothing approximating our objective historical conclusions today.

21. *Barnette*, at 642.

22. J. Gorsuch "took no part in the consideration or decision of this petition," since he had served on the Tenth Circuit Court which made the earlier decision, but even there, he considered the materials but did not take part in the decision.

23. There were various ways the Court had construed the *Lemon* test since 1971—its secular purpose, primarily secular effects, and no excessive entanglement of the government with religion—since after *Lynch v. Donnelly*, the Court utilized at times J. O'Connor's "endorsement" test involving what an informed reasonable person would perceive the exhibit to be, whether or not such a person would see it as religious, or would feel it was a message of the government endorsing a religion, and if he were not a member of that religion, might feel that he did not belong to the nation. Of course, meanwhile, certain of the justices sought to ignore the *Lemon* test and to weigh everything by their new "historical" longevity test which remained ill-defined and failed to recognize not only that religious diversity has increased much more since the Founders' days, but also their choice of historical materials created false impressions.

24. This was matched by his oral argument in *Perry* in which he said that Jews accepted the commandments as given in that monument, but he was corrected by opposing counsel.

25. *Flast*, at 105–106.

26. See Erika Lee, *America for Americans*. The xenophobic caricatures of those "others" or "strangers" they feared showed peaceful coexistence could not be expected since those caricatures usually described the others as unassimilable, inhospitable, violent, lazy, criminal and worthless. The xenophobes among those white who emigrated from Northern-European countries felt whites from the Southern or Eastern parts of Europe as a threat.

27. *Thomas Van Orden v. Rick Perry*, Oral Argument, No. 03-1500, March 2, 2005. On p. 12, lines 8–10, J. Kennedy said "This is a classic avert your eyes. If an atheist walked by, he can avert his eyes, he can think about something else." On p. 17, lines 8–9, J. Scalia sided with him, "As Justice Kennedy said, turn your eyes away if it's such a big deal to you."

28. J. Scalia's was right about one thing in his participation in the Oral Argument of *Perry*: Religions do not propose their prayers, formulae, icons, and the like to be

used for any and every secular purpose where people or even the government want to create "gravity" or "solemnity."

29. *Town of Greece, N.Y. v. Susan Galloway*, 572 U.S. 565; 134 S.Ct. 1811 (2014), at 1836.

30. *Town of Greece*, at 1843.

31. *Town of Greece*, J. Kagan, dissenting, at 1845.

32. *Town of Greece*, J. Kagan, dissenting, at 1853.

33. Levy, *The Establishment Clausem*, 171–171.

34. J. Ginsburg correctly saw the *totally religious* nature of both the Cross and Star of David, and noted that eventually the committee in charge, started using crosses even for some of the bodies whose religious affiliation was not known, since the committee evidently felt that would arouse less objection than placing a Star of David above their graves, more than any proof that a cross was a universal symbol. But this again shows the anti-Semitism and the unrecognized "majoritarianism" presupposed by so many Christians in the nation, despite the statistics showing much less religious affiliation of citizens today, less Christian affiliation, and more diversity of religions as Islam, Hinduism, Sikhism, Judaism, and so forth.

35. Can we infer from the Court that people who have crosses on chains around their necks are only reminding themselves that they will die, and those who cross themselves in church are only involved in a secular gesture of stretching their arms, or thinking about dying? Did Jewish families who had their loved one's grave marked by a Star of David simply like stars? Is that all?

36. Once the Council of Chalcedon in 451 decided that Jesus, as Christ, was not merely of "similar" (*homoiousios*) substance to the "Father" (i.e., God), but of "same" (*homoousios*) substance, the question of who was killed on the cross became a question the church has never answered. Instead, it became Docetic, so the death was just of a human being at most, or, if Jesus was "God" he just "seemed" to die but did not. It was not until the late nineteenth century that people raised even by Lutheran-pastor fathers, such as Nietzsche, saw that "God is dead," not just by the mere logic of the Creed of Chalcedon, but as a cultural phenomenon, that is, there is no real consciousness of a personal God interacting in the world except in the most *superficial* senses, but never to rescue anybody or to end wars or raging forest fires, genocide, or pandemics.

37. The irony was not seen that if the Crucifixion (the Cross) was essential to God's plan, then any part anyone had in getting Jesus crucified should have been appreciated by God.

38. It is as uninformed as a justice was in the oral argument in *Perry* when the opposing council had to tell him that he was incorrect in assuming that all Muslims accept the Decalogue.

39. J. Alito took his place on the bench in January 2006. But the Court began its intense and honest work on religion cases back in 1940 and 1947, and to refer only to the most recent simply shows that precedent does not mean precedent, but only *one's choice* among the "precedents" unless the earlier ones are actually overruled. What criteria exist for *properly* selecting among precedents?

40. With the loss of its only Jewish member, and now its lack of *any* non-Christian justice, the Court simply *does not represent* the religious diversity or the number of

citizens who are *unaffiliated* with any religion in the United States in the present, and these are still lifetime appointments. It is a detrimental majoritarianism so feared by Madison and John Rawls, so antidemocracy, even as Court appointments have become totally partisan.

41. *Kedroff v. Saint Nicholas Cathedral of Russia Orthodox Church in North America*, 344 U.S. 94 (1952).

42. J. Sotomayor dissented, joined by J. Ginsburg.

43. "James Madison to Edward Livingston," 10 July 1822, *Writings* 9:100–103, in Kurland and Lerner (eds.), *Founders' Constitution*, V:104–106.

44. Rawls, *Political Liberalism*, 233.

45. Rawls, *Political Liberalism*, 235.

46. Rawls, *Political Liberalism*, 236–237.

Chapter 12

Conclusion

The Inclusive *Will-to-Live in a Democratic Republic*

Dear Reader: In the preceding chapters, we have taken you on a long journey, requiring you to imagine how those Europeans who first settled in this land envisioned what they were doing. Columbus's journeys are very hard to conceive of, given all the advances in geographical, astronomical, oceanic studies since, not to mention the advances in modes of transportation. The planting of Jamestown in 1607 and the importation of its first slaves from Africa a dozen years later are even harder to imagine from where we stand. When we as children studied our history of our country, it had to compete with the depiction of the "wild west" of the many movies we saw in which the First Peoples or Native Americans were usually shown as the offensive aggressors, the barbarians. With that slant, the millions of their people that our European-immigrant ancestors slaughtered seemed so justified, to some, even ordained by Providence. But the actual facts were quite different. They were neither barbarian, nor destined to vanish from the Earth. The actual white man's inhumane treatment of them still remains despicable in its lack of respect shown to descendants of those earlier residents of the country.

Many U.S. citizens have never realized how close this group of colonies came to failing to establish a nation, or of how unique the idea of a democratic republic was, or how unthinkable it was to people in the days prior to the Constitution to try to conceive of religion and government each going their own separate ways. But those were hard times of trial and error, and most of the citizens of the various colonies worked hard to try to improve their lives. The eight years of the Revolutionary War that cost a rough estimate of 25,000 soldiers on each side was a difficult process of self-sacrifice, on one side even a sacrifice only for a *prospective* nation. Most of the early immigrants to the New World and their progeny were illiterate, but even so, they were smart enough to perceive that a spirit of cooperation and unity had to prevail just for them to survive in those difficult years. The same sharing or cooperation became necessary during and after that war that freed the immigrants from their subservience to England and was still vital for life to continue in this New Nation. They were respectful enough and reasonable enough with other white people to argue through dozens of issues that concerned all of those involved, and reasonableness prevailed in the long run as the Framers of the Constitution as well as the states that ratified it, decided to share their lives, and experience a common fate together.

They had been intelligent enough to listen to Madison's wisdom which he had gained through a long study of republics in the history of the West that covered more than 2,000 years. The "lively experiment" of the democracy, or democratic republic, obviously cost many people who had gained irrational advantages over others even through the ineffectiveness of the Articles of Confederation. This was the reason many Framers emphasized that any new structure would have to be "lively." Many people personally sacrificed financially, ideologically, and even their personal pride, in finally ratifying the Constitution and the Bill of Rights. But this was only the beginning, since so many vital issues were not resolved, not even addressed, and some that were addressed were not understood in their full meaning till many years later. The one thing that was evident was the people's decision to have a genuine nation with its own Constitution and unique form of a balanced government with checks and balances, in which representation of all significant interests that were of a national concern could be addressed. It was *inclusive*, more so than any government any of those people had ever experienced, but still not consistently inclusive in its ideal of equality and liberty and justice for all. Those would be driving aspirations which could only be realized by constant dialogue and consistent problem-solving.

Our primary concern in this long journey to the present was to address the question of whether there might be an ethic which could unite these people, since it had become evident over generations that the most obvious institutions espousing ethics were religions, and their wars, even among different sects of Christians, revealed their *incompatibility.* So we asked whether it is possible to "reconcile" what seem to be "opposites"—not simply the opposites of different religious positions, but the opposites of any religious ethic when compared to what ethic would be necessary for a social contract of a nation intent to develop a democratic republic.

The earliest answer to this, supplied by Madison, Jefferson, and other Framers of the Constitution, was that the institutions could function ethically and positively only when they were *separated.* But this opposed 1,400 years of the tradition of "Christendom." On the other hand, no theocracy had actually been established by the efforts of several different colonies. And the history of European Christendom was a story of unending conflict, seemingly not eliminated but only exacerbated by the Protestant Revolution in the sixteenth century and its emphasis on individualism.

What was at first only a slight splintering of the Christian faith into four or five major bodies in the sixteenth century quickly multiplied, as tradition and authority were reinterpreted, and pietism found its power in experiences of personal conversion. That inevitably emphasized "freedom of conscience" and this experience of pietism moved from Continental centers such as Geneva and Amsterdam to England and to the New World by the middle of the eighteenth century. By the end of the eighteenth century, this "freedom of conscience" was taken for granted by innumerable Christians in the colonies-now-become-states, and that, combined with the Enlightenment's emphasis of reason over revelation, of equality, of autonomy, and liberty and justice for all, became the keys of the political structures the Framers articulated for the New Nation.

In analyzing this history, we saw that the Framers of the Constitution did not utilize any religious ethic to formulate the basic ethical principles of the New Nation. We saw how exclusive and grounded on specific myths both the Jewish and Christian religions and their sacred writings were, so far removed from the political ideals articulated later by the Framers of the Constitution. We also encountered what Steven Green referred to as the "intentional" myth some Christians created about the United States always being intended as a Christian nation but one which also afforded religious freedom. We saw his articulation of the different stages this myth took, and how many present-day evangelistic people are devoted to rereading the history that way, even if their picture is more aspirational than factual. More than that, it undermines democracy.

The question of where an ethical base would be derived became obvious, since religions were incapable of being inclusive enough to embrace all citizens in their differences. We saw that two geniuses of the late nineteenth century and early twentieth century, who grew up in Christian homes with a father who was a Christian pastor, eventually found an ethic that was *more inclusive* than a Christian ethic or any religious ethic. Both Nietzsche and Schweitzer discovered the real base of ethics not in some calculation of pain and pleasure or what is for the good for the many, or even some "categorical imperative" such as Kant's, but rather in *instinct* itself. Rather than leaving "altruism" or "self-denial" as the proper ethical stance, thereby challenging the natural instinct of "will-to-power" or "will-to-live," we saw Rawls's discovery, through his familiarity with Hume and especially Kant, that principles have to be *agreed to voluntarily* for an ethic to exist. However, he was convinced that for one to decide correctly on any principles which others would also agree to, all parties would have to hypothetically remove themselves from all irrational, inherited, accidental, or "happenstance" elements by which one might have some advantage over others. This enabled Rawls to formulate basic principles of an ethic that was no longer dependent upon any religion, even though he too had been raised as a Christian.

His answer was this hypothetical exercise of placing oneself beyond one's vested interests by imagining oneself in the "original position" of the social contracting, behind a "veil of ignorance." He assumed that agreement among people depended upon reasonable discussion, and here, among various places, he was able to formulate a difference between what an ethic for a nation, especially for a democratic republic, would require vis-à-vis any ethic of a specific religion or other comprehensive doctrine of ethics. The differences included different constituencies, scopes, utilization of reason or myths, and comportments, which meant that many unique associations one has may require some ethical norms, which may or may not be similar to what is required by the nation's ethical principles. But the latter is wholly inclusive of all citizens, is totally voluntary in one's acceptance, and utilizes common reason rather than requiring some special form of supra-rational faith in myths or supranatural events. These differences he articulates show *why* the "separation" of religion from government is necessary in a democratic republic. Only a democratic republic can supply the structure of unanimous agreement which includes an understanding that many different comprehensive schemas will be held among the different citizens, and this will be natural, not an aberration, which means that *only* a democratic republic can accommodate religious pluralism. But it can do so only if citizens comply with the basic principles of that "original position" which means complying with the Constitution or generally applicable laws. This is the key.

But to realize this, "majoritarianism" has to end. We saw the majoritarianism came to these shores with the European immigrants in three forms: white, male, and Christian. After more than 400 years, it still festers and erupts, sometimes making it clear that some citizens are not really committed to the national interests, but only their own very personal, limited interests. Its capacity to destroy a democracy by *undermining trust* in leaders, in elections, in the basic structures of our government, in education and actual facts is deadly. Whether it is simple fear of the unknown or different, or arrogance about one's specific absolutized religion, or comes in more virulent and violent forms of racism, xenophobia, misogyny, or other, it has to end. Both Madison and Rawls feared majoritarianism as the most likely candidate to annihilate a democracy. Rather than teaching our new generation how they can make a fortune without going to college, it probably is time to cut the favoritism to parochial and private schools in giving them taxes which belongs to public schools, and insist that the public schools educate all of our children about the meaning of democracy or a democratic republic, of true equality of opportunity, of the value of a liberal arts education which helps them appreciate various aspects of our shared culture that are not merely measured in terms of profit.

If majoritarianism can finally be transcended, there will *not* be a conflict between the ethic underlying the democratic contract we all embrace so long as the basic principles of that "original position" have *priority* if and when any religion or comprehensive schema conflicts with it. But until such time of conflict of ethical standards of government and religion, the religious and nonreligious need not change their behavior. But they also *cannot* expect to be *favored* by government over other people; as Jefferson insisted, people's status will neither be reduced nor enhanced. All citizens will be judged by the secular law, and this means not by their religion, as well as not by their race, wealth, sex, or other categories largely beyond their control. Now that our nation includes greater differences and varieties in religions, sexual identity, and racial and ethnic identity than ever before, we have seen that the Court seems to be going in the *wrong direction*. The Court simply cannot, must not, continue on its present trajectory of abolishing former "tests" so it can favor the Christian religion or of allowing anything to count as one's free exercise of religion when it has nothing to do with worship and would thereby open the barn door for *anything* anyone wanted to claim as their religious conviction. Nor can the Court continue to emphasize that government itself has *its own* religion, since that blatantly violates the letter and spirit of the First Amendment. At this stage of our country's struggle to realize its most noble ideals, we cannot afford to destroy citizens' trust in the Court which is supposed to be the "exemplar of public reason" and arbiter of equal justice for all under the law. The United States seems to be at a crossroads today as much as it was in 1789, with pressing decisions to be made about inclusion and a democracy rather than exclusion and favoritism of a select few or even fascism. The books warning us of this in racist, xenophobic, and misanthropic or even economic areas are prolific. But the danger of division, animosity, resentment, inequality, and exclusion in religious terms are just as pertinent, even more so when we realize that religion is often seen by its adherents as wholly unquestionable, as Absolute.

But we know nothing as absolute; even to think of something as absolute becomes a self-contradiction, something possible only if one never seriously thinks about what that means. This means also that life is never a choice of being absolutely certain or static or hopelessly relative in our lives. We adjust within our contingent interdependence with others in an inclusive, symbiotic relationship in our humanizing project, manifesting a sense of social solidarity, and as we take responsibility to decide how to help shape ourselves within our contingent relationships, we find that we should have no need to dictate to or coerce others to embrace a single form of identity or race or sexual preference, or any static symbol or only one specific religion, certainly not through trying to force the others by legal means to embrace symbols that are meaningful only to one group of citizens. We are all in process, so ideas and changes will continue just as time does not stop. And time, accompanied by entropy, still run only in one direction, so we are called to move *forward with change* while we live, through reason and reasonable argument rather than by coercion or futile attempts to try to stop the clock or "turn the clock back" to restore some imagined "Golden Age" that never really existed.

My hope for the future is that humanity develops an inclusive *uniting ethic* before it is too late, one which preserves humanity—all humanity—as well as *all living species*, that it develops an *inclusive view* of all forms of life that have their own interests in living, their own "will-to-live," as do humans. I hope that we can become, as paleoanthropologist, Richard Leakey, admonished, "better tenants" of this Earth,[1] so our descendants do not have to find another home elsewhere, even though Stephen Hawking thought we might need to locate such a new planet within this century because of the ways we have adversely affected this one. Above all, I hope that our values are rooted in the instinctual life-affirming "will-to-power" and "will-to-live" and as we identify with the presence and subjectivity of others, we can have the good sense to learn to value each other, to accept our differences, to work out arrangements or agreements to live together, to move beyond feelings of any forms of superiority over others, to realize that life's meaning is found *within our relationships*. We might start that process in all seriousness by simply sitting down and writing up a hypothetical agreement which we would be willing for anyone to offer to us, and if we can think of ourselves *without* our inherited or accidental privileges or advantages, we may quickly discover the same two principles as the ethical base just as John Rawls articulated. If we do learn how to live together, there may be no natural or supranatural end to this process, but if we fail to learn that, our dehumanization could put an end to humanity quite soon. Destroying the principles of our democracy would be the first big step toward this dehumanization or annihilation of the human species. But we can do better.

The great, late astrophysicist Carl Sagan emphasized the same point by contrasting the interdependence of shrimp and algae with the human failure to think in the "long term." The shrimp and algae "discovered" their *mutual dependence* on each other three million years ago, long before *Homo sapiens* came on the scene. But, Sagan insisted, even if we are late comers on the scene,

[o]ur planet is indivisible. . . . Like it or not, we humans are bound up with our fellows, and with the other plants and animals all over the world. Our lives are intertwined. . . . If we are not graced with an instinctive knowledge of how to make our technologized world a safe and balanced ecosystem, we must figure

out how to do it. We need more scientific research and more technological restraint. It is probably too much to hope that some great Ecosystem Keeper in the sky will reach down and put right our environmental abuse. It is up to us.

It should not be impossibly difficult. Birds—whose intelligence we tend to malign—know not to foul the nest. Shrimps with brains the size of lint particles know it. Algae know it. One-celled micro-organisms know it. It is time for us to know it too.[2]

As joint tenants in trusting, realistic, interdependent mutual autonomy of equal people, we can avoid the heteronomy and tyranny of any and all absolutisms, and with respect and civility make the necessary compromises as we work together to make this Earth better for the entire family that comprises it. We are not wistfully hoping to "go home again" or to something else that is fantastically utopian, but recognize more fully that we are already "home," and always have been, and "home" is a large and very diverse family of joint tenants that give meaning to our lives.

NOTES

1. Richard Leakey and Roger Lewin, *Origins Reconsidered: In Search of What Makes us Human* (New York: Doubleday, 1992), 359.

2. Carl Sagan, *Billions & Billions: Thoughts on Life and Death of the Brink of the Millennium* (New York: Random House, 1997), 67–68.

Appendix

Cited Select Supreme Court Cases

1. ALPHABETICAL ORDER

Abington Township v. Schempp, 374 U.S. 203 (1963)

Agostini v. Felton, 521 U.S. 203 (1997)

Aguilar v. Felton, 473 U.S. 402 (1985)

Alberto Gonzales, Attorney General, et al., v. O Centro Espirita Beneficente Uniao de Vegetal, et al., 546 U.S. 418 (2006)

Allegheny County v. Pittsburg A.C.L.U., 492 U.S. 573 (1989)

Armistead v. United States, 277 U.S. 438 (1928)

Arizona Christian School Tuition Organization v. Winn, 563 U.S. 125 (2011)

Arizona v. Evans, 514 U.S. 1 (1995)

Arizona v. Gant, 556 U.S. 332 (2009)

Bivens v. Six Unknown Named Agents, 403 U.S. ?? (1971)

Board of Education v .Allen, 391 U.S. 236 (1968)

Board of Education of Westside Community Schools, et al., v. Mergens, by and through her next Friend, Mergens, et al., 496 U.S. 226 (1990)

Board of Kiryas Joel Village School Dist. v. Grumet, 512 U.S. 687 (1994)

Bob Jones University v. U.S., 461 U.S. 574 (1983)

Bowen v. Kendrick, 487 U.S. 589 (1988)

Bowen v. Roy, 476 U.S. 693 (1986)

Braunfeld v. Brown, 366 U.S. 599 (1961)

Brewer v. Williams, 430 U.S. 387 (1977), reheard as *Nix v. Williams*, 467 U.S. 431 (1984)

Brown v. Board of Education, 347 U.S. 483 (1954)

Burwell, Sec. of Health & Human Services, et al., v. Hobby Lobby Stores, Inc., et al., 573 U.S.___; 134 S.Ct., 2751 (2014)

Cantwell v. Connecticut, 310 U.S. 296 (1940)

Capitol Square Review & Advisory Bd. v. Pinette, 515 U.S. 753 (1995)

Cherokee Nation, The v. The State of Georgia, 1 Peters 5, 1 (1831)

Kendra Espinoza, et al., Petitioners v. Montana Department of Revenue, et al., 591 U.S. (2020) (slip opinion, No. 18-1195)

Lamb's Chapel v. Center Moriches School Dist., 508 U.S. 384 (1993)

Larson, Commission of Securities, Minnesota Dept. of Commerce v. Valente, 456 U.S. 228 (1982)

Lee v. Wiseman, 505 U.S. 597 (1992)

Lemon v. Kurtzman, 403 U.S. 1 (1971)

Levitt v. Committee for Public Education & Religious Liberty, 413 U.S. 472 (1973)

Locke, Governor of Washington, et al., v. Davey, 540 U.S. 712 (2004)

Lynch v. Donnelly, 465 U.S. 668 (1984)

Lyng, Sec. of Agriculture v. Northwest Indian Cemetery Protective Assoc., 485 U.S. 439 (1988)

Mapp v. Ohio, 367 U.S. 643 (1960)

Marsh v. Chambers, 463 U.S. 783 (1983)

Masterpiece Cakeshop vs. Colorado Civil Rights Commission, 584 U.S. ___, 138 S.Ct. 1719 (2018)

McCollum v. Board of Education, 333 U.S. 203 (1948)

McCreary County, Kentucky v. ACLU of Kentucky, 545 U.S. 844 (2005)

McDaniel v. Paty, 435 U.S. 618 (1978)

McGowan v. Maryland, 366 U.S. 420 (1961)

Meek v. Pittenger, 421 U.S. 349 (1975)

Minersville School District v. Gobitis, 310 U.S. 586 (1940)

Mitchell v. Helms, 530 U.S. 793 (2000)

Mueller v. Allen, 468 U.S. 388 (1983)

Murdock v. Pennsylvania, 319 U.S. 105 (1943)

Norwood v. Harrison, 413 U.S. 455 (1973)

O'Lone v. Estate of Shabazz, 482 U.S. 342 (1987)

Oregon v. Mitchell, 400 U.S. 112 (1970)

Pierce v. Society of Sisters, 268 U.S. 510 (1925)

Pleasant Grove City, Utah, et al., v. Summum, 555 U.S. 460 (2009)

Prince v. Massachusetts, 321 U.S. 158 (1944)

Reed v. Town of Gilbert, 576 U.S. ___; 135 S.Ct. 2218 (2015)

Reynolds v. U.S., 98 U.S. 145 (1879)

Robbins v. California, 453 U.S. 420 (1980)

Roemer v. Board of Public Works of Maryland, 426 U.S. 736 (1976)

Ronald W. Rosenberger, et al., v. Rector & Visitors of Univ. of Virginia, et al., 515 U.S. 819 (1995)

Roberts v. United States Jaycees, 468 U.S. 609 (1984)

Roe v. Wade, 410 U.S. 113 (1973)

Salazar, Sec. of Interior, et al., v. Buono, 559 U.S. 700 (2010)

Samuel A. Worcester v. The State of Georgia, 6 Peters 515 (1832)

Santa Fe Independent School Dist. v. Doe, individually and as Friend of her Minor Children, et al., 530 U.S. 290 (2000)

Serbian Eastern Orthodox Diocese for U.S. and Canada v. Milivojevich, 426 U.S. 626 (1976)

Sherbert v. Verner, 374 U.S. 398 (1963)
Sloan v. Lemon, 413 U.S. 835 (1973)
South Carolina v. Katzenbach, 383 U.S. 301 (1966)
Stone v. Graham, 449 U.S. 39 (1980)
Terry v. Ohio, 392 U.S. 1 (1968)
Texas Monthly, Inc. v. Bullock, 489 U.S. 1 (1989)
Tilton v. Richardson, 405 U.S. 602 (1971)
Thomas v. Review Bd. of Indiana Employment Security Division, 450 U.S. 707 (1981)
Torcaso v. Watkins, 367 U.S. 488 (1961)
Town of Greece, N.Y. v. Susan Galloway, 572 U.S. ___; 124 S.Ct. 1871 (2014)
Trans World Airlines, Inc. v. Hardison, 432 U.S. 636 (1977)
Trinity Lutheran Church of Columbia, Inc., v. Comer, Dir. Missouri Dept. of Natural
    Resources, 582 U.S. ___; 137 S.Ct. 2012 (2017)
Two Guys from Harrison Allentown, Inc. v. McGinley, 366 U.S. 582 (1961)
United States v. Lee, 455 U.S. 255? (1982)
United States v. Seeger, 380 U.S. 163 (1965)
United States v. Janis, 428 U.S. 433 (1976)
Valley Forge Christian College v. Americans United, 454 U.S. 464 (1982)
Van Orden v. Perry, 545 U.S. 677 (2005)
Wallace v. Jaffree, 472 U.S. 38 (1985)
Watson v. Jones, 13 Wall 179 (1872)
Walter Lee v. International Society for Krishna Consciousness, 505 U.S. 830 (1992)
Walz v. Tax Commission of City of N.Y., 397 U.S. 664 (1970)
Weeks v. U.S., 232 U.S. 383 (1914)
Welsh v. U.S., 398 U.S. 333 (1970)
West Virginia v. Barnette, 319 U.S. 624 (1943)
Widmar v. Vincent, 454 U.S. 263 (1981)
Wisconsin v. Yoder, 406 U.S. 205 (1972)
Witters v. WA Dept of Services for the Blind, 474 U.S. 481 (1986)
Wolf v. Colorado, 338 U.S. 25 (1949)
Wolman v. Walter, 433 U.S. 229 (1977)
Zelman, Superintendent of Public Instruction of Ohio, it. al. v. Simmons-Harris,
    et al., 536 U.S. 639 (2002)
Zobrest, et al. v. Catalina Foothills School District, 509 U.S. 1 (1993)
Zorach v. Clauson, 343 U.S. 306 (1952)

2. BY YEAR

Cherokee Nation, The, v. The State of Georgia, 1 Peters 5, 1 (1831)
Samuel A. Worcester v. The State of Georgia, 6 Peters 515 (1832)
Watson v. Jones, 13 Wall 179 (1872)
Reynolds v. U.S., 98 U.S. 145 (1879)
Davis v. Beason, 133 U.S. 333 (1890)
Weeks v. U.S., 232 U.S. 383 (1914)

Frothingham v. Mellon, 262 U.S. 447 (1923)

Pierce v. Society of Sisters, 268 U.S. 510 (1925)

Armistead v. United States, 277 U.S. 438 (1928)

Cochran v. Louisiana State Board of Education, 281 U.S. 370 (1930)

Cantwell v. Connecticut, 310 U.S. 296 (1940)

Cox v. New Hampshire, 312 U.S. 569 (1941)

Jones v. Opelika, I & II, 317 U.S. 584 (1942, 1943) (overturned)

Minersville School District v. Gobitis, 310 U.S. 586 (1940)

Murdock v. Pennsylvania, 319 U.S. 105 (1943)

West Virginia v. Barnette, 319 U.S. 624 (1943)

Follett v. McCormick, 321 U.S. 573 (1944)

Prince v. Massachusetts, 321 U.S. 158 (1944)

Girouard v. United States, 328 U.S. 61 (1946)

Everson v. Board of Education of Ewing TP, 330 U.S. 1 (1947)

McCollum v. Board of Education, 333 U.S. 203 (1948)

Wolf v. Colorado, 338 U.S. 25 (1949)

Kedroff v. St. Nicholas Cathedral of Russian Orthodox Church in North America, 344 U.S. 94 (1952)

Zorach v. Clauson, 343 U.S. 306 (1952)

Brown v. Board of Education, 347 U.S. 483 (1954)

Mapp v. Ohio, 367 U.S. 643 (1960)

Braunfeld v. Brown, 366 U.S. 599 (1961)

Gallagher v. Crown Kosher Super Market of Mass., Inc., 366 U.S. 617 (1961)

McGowan v. Maryland, 366 U.S. 420 (1961)

Torcaso v. Watkins, 367 U.S. 488 (1961)

Two Guys from Harrison Allentown, Inc. v. McGinley, 366 U.S. 582 (1961)

Engle v. Vitale, 370 U.S. 421 (1962)

Abington Township v. Schempp, 374 U.S. 203 (1963)

Sherbert v. Verner, 374 U.S. 398 (1963)

United States v. Seeger, 380 U.S. 163 (1965)

Katzenbach v. Morgan, 384 U.S. 641 (1966)

South Carolina v. Katzenbach, 383 U.S. 301 (1966)

Board of Education v. Allen, 391 U.S. 236 (1968)

Epperson v. Arkansas, 393 U.S. 97 (1968)

Flast v. Cohen, 392 U.S. 831 (1968)

Terry v. Ohio, 392 U.S. 1 (1968)

Oregon v. Mitchell, 400 U.S 112 (1970)

Walz v. Tax Commission of City of N.Y., 397 U.S. 664 (1970)

Welsh v. U.S., 398 U.S. 333 (1970)

Bivens v. Six Unknown Named Agents, 403 U.S. ?? (1971)

Gillette v. U.S. and Negre v. Larsen, 401 U.S. 437 (1971)

Lemon v. Kurtzman, 403 U.S. 1 (1971)

Tilton v. Richardson, 405 U.S. 602 (1971)

Wisconsin v. Yoder, 406 U.S. 205 (1972)

Committee for Public Education & Religious Liberty v. Nyquist, 413 U.S. 756 (1973)

Hunt v. McNair, 413 U.S. 734 (1973)

Levitt v. Committee for Public Education & Religious Liberty, 413 U.S. 472 (1973)

Norwood v. Harrison, 413 U.S. 455 (1973)

Roe v. Wade, 410 U.S. 113 (1973)

Sloan v. Lemon, 413 U.S. 835 (1973)

Meek v. Pittenger, 421 U.S. 349 (1975)

Roemer v. Board of Public Works of Maryland, 426 U.S. 736 (1976)

Serbian Eastern Orthodox Diocese for U.S. and Canada v. Milivojevich, 426 U.S. 626 (1976)

United States v. Janis, 428 U.S. 433 (1976)

Brewer v. Williams, 430 U.S. 387 (1977), reheard as *Nix v. Williams*, 467 U.S. 431 (1984)

Trans World Airlines, Inc. v. Hardison, 432 U.S. 636 (1977)

Wolman v. Walter, 433 U.S. 229 (1977)

McDaniel v. Paty, 435 U.S. 618 (1978)

Committee for Public Education & Religious Liberty v. Regan, 444 U.S. 646 (1980)

Robbins v. California, 453 U.S. 420 (1980)

Stone v. Graham, 449 U.S. 39 (1980)

Heffron v. International Society for Krishna Consciousness, 452 U.S. 263 (1981)

Thomas v. Review Bd. of Indiana Employment Security Division, 450 U.S. 707 (1981)

Widmar v. Vincent, 454 U.S. 263 (1981)

Larson, Commission of Securities, Minnesota Dept. of Commerce v. Valente, 456 U.S. 228 (1982)

United States v. Lee, 455 U.S. 255? (1982)

Valley Forge Christian College v. Americans United, 454 U.S. 464 (1982)

Bob Jones University v. U.S., 461 U.S. 574 (1983)

City of Mesquite v. Aladdin's Castle, Inc., 455 U.S. 283 (1983)

Marsh v. Chambers, 463 U.S. 783 (1983)

Mueller v. Allen, 468 U.S. 388 (1983)

Lynch v. Donnelly, 465 U.S. 668 (1984)

Roberts v. United States Jaycees, 468 U.S. 609 (1984)

Aguilar v. Felton, 473 U.S. 402 (1985)

Grand Rapids School District v. Ball, 473 U.S. 373 (1985)

Wallace v. Jaffree, 472 U.S. 38 (1985)

Bowen v. Roy, 476 U.S. 693 (1986)

Goldman v. Weinberger, 495 U.S. 503 (1986)

Witters v. WA Dept of Services for the Blind, 474 U.S. 481 (1986)

Corporation of Presiding Bishop (LDS) v. Amos, 483 U.S. 327 (1987)

Edwards v. Aguillard, 482 U.S. 578 (1987)

Hobbie v. Unemployment Appeals Commission of Florida, 480 U.S. 142 (1987)

O'Lone v. Estate of Shabazz, 482 U.S. 342 (1987)

Bowen v. Kendrick, 487 U.S. 589 (1988)

Employment Div., Dept. of Human Resources of Oregon v. Smith, I, 485 U.S. 660 (1988); *II*, 494 U.S. 872 (1990)

Lyng, Sec. of Agriculture v. Northwest Indian Cemetery Protective Assoc., 485 U.S. 439 (1988)

Allegheny County v. Pittsburg A.C.L.U., 492 U.S. 573 (1989)

Frazee v. Illinois Dept. of Employment Security, 489 U.S. 829 (1989)

Hernandez v. Commissioner, 490 U.S. 680 (1989)

Texas Monthly, Inc. v. Bullock, 489 U.S. 1 (1989)

Board of Education of Westside Community Schools, et al., v. Mergens, by and through her next Friend, Mergens, et al., 496 U.S. 226 (1990)

Jimmy Swaggart Ministries v. Bd. of Equalization of California, 493 U.S. 378 (1990)

Church of Lukumi Babalu Aye, Inc. v. Hialeah, 508 U.S. 520 (1991)

Lee v. Wiseman, 505 U.S. 597 (1992)

Walter Lee v. International Society for Krishna Consciousness, 505 U.S. 830 (1992)

Lamb's Chapel v. Center Moriches School Dist., 508 U.S.384 (1993)

Zobrest, et al. v. Catalina Foothills School District, 509 U.S. 1 (1993)

Board of Kiryas Joel Village School Dist. v. Grumet, 512 U.S. 687 (1994)

Arizona v. Evans, 514 U.S. 1 (1995)

Capitol Square Review & Advisory Bd. v. Pinette, 515 U.S. 753 (1995)

Ronald W. Rosenberger, et al., v. Rector & Visitors of Univ. of Virginia, et al., 515 U.S. 819 (1995)

Agostini v. Felton, 521 U.S. 203 (1997)

City of Boerne v. Flores, 521 U.S. 507 (1997)

Mitchell v. Helms, 530 U.S. 793 (2000)

Santa Fe Independent School Dist. v. Doe, individually and as Friend of her Minor Children, et al., 530 U.S. 290 (2000)

Zelman, Superintendent of Public Instruction of Ohio, it. al. v. Simmons-Harris, et al., 536 U.S. 639 (2002)

Elk Grove Unified School Dist., et al., v. Newdow, et al., 542 U.S. 1 (2004)

Locke, Governor of Washington, et al., v. Davey, 540 U.S. 712 (2004)

Jon B. Cutter, et al. v. Reginald Wilkinson, Director, Ohio Dept. of Rehabilitation & Correction, 544 U.S. 709 (2005)

McCreary County, Kentucky v. ACLU of Kentucky, 545 U.S. 844 (2005)

Van Orden v. Perry, 545 U.S. 677 (2005)

Alberto Gonzales, Attorney General, et al., v. O Centro Espirita Beneficente Uniao de Vegetal, et al., 546 U.S. 418 (2006)

Hein, Director, White House Office of Faith-Based & Community Initiatives, et al., v. Freedom from Religion Foundation, Inc., 551 U.S. 557 (2007)

Arizona v. Gant, 556 U.S. 332 (2009)

Pleasant Grove City, Utah, et al., v. Summum, 555 U.S. 460 (2009)

Christian Legal Society Chapter of the Univ. of CA, Hastings College of Law v. Martinez, et al., 561 U.S. 661 (2010)

Salazar, Sec. of Interior, et al., v. Buono, 559 U.S. 700 (2010)

Arizona Christian School Tuition Organization v. Winn, 563 U.S. 125 (2011)

Hosanna-Tabor Evangelical Lutheran School and Church v. EEOC, et al., 565 U.S. 171 (2012)

Burwell, Sec. of Health & Human Services, et al., v. Hobby Lobby Stores, Inc., et al., 573 U.S.___; 134 S.Ct., 2751 (2014)

Town of Greece, N.Y. v. Susan Galloway, 572 U.S. ___; 124 S.Ct. 1871 (2014)

EEOC v. Abercrombie & Fitch Stores, Inc., 575 U.S. ___; 135 S .Ct 2038 (2015)

Holt v. Hobbs, 574 U.S. ___; 135 S.Ct. 853 (2015)

Reed v. Town of Gilbert, 576 U.S. ___; 135 S.Ct. 2218 (2015)

Trinity Lutheran Church of Columbia, Inc., v. Comer, Dir. Missouri Dept. of Natural Resources, 582 U.S. ___; 137 S.Ct. 2012 (2017)

Masterpiece Cakeshop vs. Colorado Civil Rights Commission, 584 U.S. ___, 138 S.Ct. 1719 (2018)

Kendra Espinoza, et al., Petitioners v. Montana Department of Revenue, et al. 591 U.S. (2020) (slip opinion, No. 18-1195)

Bibliography

Ahlstrom, Sydney E. *A Religious History of the American People*. New Haven: Yale University Press, 1972.

Andersen, Kurt. *Evil Geniuses: The Unmaking of America*. New York: Random House, 2020.

Augustine, St. *Concerning the City of God against the Pagans*. Translated by Henry Bettenson. Middlesex, England: Penguin Books, 1972.

Backus, Isaac. "A History of New England." 1774–1775, *Stokes* 1; 307–309, in Kurland, *Founders' Constitution*. Vol. 5, p. 65.

Barry, Brian, *Theories of Justice*. Berkeley, CA: University of California Press, 1989.

Barzun, Jacques. *From Dawn to Decadence—1500 to the Present: 500 Years of Western Cultural Life*. New York: Harper Collins Pub, 2000.

Berkin, Carol. *The Bill of Rights: The Fight to Secure America's Liberties*. New York: Simon & Schuster, 2015.

Bloom, Harold. *The American Religion: The Emergence of the Post-Christian Nation*. New York: Touchstone Book, 1992.

"The Body of Liberties of the Massachussets Colonie in New England" (1641), MHS Collections (3rd ser.), 8:216, 226, 231, 232, 234–236, in Kurland, *Founders' Constitution*. Vol. 5, pp. 46–48.

Clark, Hunter R. *Justice Brennan: The Great Conciliator*. New York: A Birch Lane Press Book, 1995.

Clark, W. Royce. *Ethics and the Future of Religion: Redefining the Absolute*. Lanham, MD: Lexington Books-Fortress, 2021.

———. "The Legal Status of Religious Studies Programs in Public Higher Education." In *Beyond the Classics? Essays in Religious Studies and Liberal Education*, edited by Frank E. Reynolds and Sheryl L. Burkhalter. Atlanta, GA: Scholars Press, 1990, 109–139.

———. *Will Humanity Survive Religion: Beyond Divisive Absolutes*. Lanham, MD: Lexington Books/Fortress Academic, 2020.

Coxe, Tench. "An American Citizen." I-III, In *The Debate on the Constitution, Part One*. New York: The Library of America, 1993, 20–30.

Crossan, John Dominic. *The Birth of Christianity: Discovering What Happened in the Years Immediately After the Execution of Jesus*. San Francisco: Harper, 1998.

Currie, David P. *The Constitution in the Supreme Court: The Second Century: 1886–1986*. Chicago: University of Chicago, 1990.

Curry, Thomas. *Farewell to Christendom: The Future of Church and State in America*. New York: Oxford University Press, 2004.

The Dalai Lama, His Holiness. *Ethics for the New Millennium*. New York: Riverhead Books, 1999.

Dawkins, Richard. *The God Delusion*. London: Bantam Press, 2006.

The Debate on the Constitution: Federalist and Antifederalist Speeches, Articles, and Letters During the Struggle over Ratification, Part One. New York: The Library of America, 1993.

Dippie, Brian. *The Vanishing American: America's White Attitudes and U.S. Indian Policy*. Lawrence, KS: University of Kansas Press, 1982.

Dworkin, Ronald. *Freedom's Law: The Moral Reading of the American Constitution*. Cambridge, MA: Harvard University Press, 1996.

———. *Law's Empire*. Cambridge, MA: Harvard University Press, 1986.

———. *A Matter of Principle*. Cambridge, MA: Harvard University Press, 1985.

———. *Religion Without God*. Cambridge, MA: Harvard University Press, 2013.

———. *Taking Rights Seriously*. Cambridge, MA: Harvard University Press, 1977.

Feuerbach, Ludwig. *The Essence of Christianity*. Translated by George Eliot. New York: Harper Torchbooks, 1957.

Flay, Joseph C. *Hegel's Quest for Certainty*. Albany, NY: State University of New York Press, 1984.

Foucault, Michel. *The Order of Things: An Archaeology of the Human Sciences*. New York: Vintage Books, 1994, 1970.

Freud, Sigmund. *The Future of an Illusion*. Translated by James Strachey. New York: W.W. Norton & Co., 1961.

Gordon, Thomas. "Cato's Letters." No. 38, 22 July 1721, *Jacobson 93–95, 96, 101*, in Kurland, *Founders' Constitution*. Vol. 1, pp. 46–47.

Green, Steven K. *Inventing a Christian America: The Myth of the Religious Founding*. New York: Oxford University Press, 2015.

Guha, Ramachandra. *India After Ghandi: The History of the World's Largest Democracy*. New York: HarperCollins Publishers, 2007.

Hegel, G. W. F. *The Phenomenology of Mind*. Translated by J. B. Baillie. New York: Harper Torchbooks, 1967.

———. *Philosophy of History* (Sibbee, Tr.) Robert Maynard Hutchins, Editor-in-Chief. *Great Books of the Western World, Vol. 46: Hegel*. Chicago: Encyclopedia Britannica, Inc., 1952.

———. "The Spirit of Christianity." In *Early Theological Writings*, translated by T. M. Knox. New York: Harper Torchbooks, 1961.

Heidegger, Martin. *Being and Time*. Translated by John Macquarrie and Edward Robinson. New York: Harper & Row, Pub., 1962.

Hoffer, Eric. *The True Believer*. New York: Harper & Bros, 1951.

"House of Representatives, Amendments to the Constitution." 15, 17, 20 August 1789, *Annals* 1:729–731, 755, 766 in Kurland, *Founder's Constitution*. Vol. 5, pp. 92–94.

Hughes, Richard T. *Myths America Lives By: White Supremacy and the Stories That Give Us Meaning*, 2nd ed. Urbana, IL: University of Illinois Press, 2018.

Hume, David. "Of the Original Contract." 1752, in Kurland, *Founders' Constitution*. Vol. 1. pp. 49–52.

Jacoby, Susan. *Strange Gods: A Secular History of Conversion*. New York: Pantheon, 2016.

James, William. *The Varieties of Religious Experience: A Study in Human Nature*. New York: University Books, 1963.

Jefferson, Thomas. "A Bill for Establishing Religious Freedom." 12 June 1779, *Papers* 2: facing 305, in Kurland, *Founders' Constitution*. Vol. 5, p. 77.

———. "Jefferson to Albert Gallatin." In Kurland, *Founders' Constitution*. Vol. 5, p. 105.

———. "Notes on Debates in Congress, 2–4 July 1776." *Papers I: 314–319* in Kurland, *Founders' Constitution*. Vol. I, pp. 522–524.

———. "Notes on the State of Virginia." *Query* 17, 157–161, 1784 in Kurland, *Founders' Constitution*. Vol. 5, pp. 79–80.

———. "Thomas Jefferson, Autobiography." 1821, *Works*, 1:71, in Kurland, *Founder's Constitution*. Vol. 5, p. 85.

———"Thomas Jefferson to Danbury Baptist Association." 1 January 1802, *Writings* 16:281, in Kurland, *Founders' Constitution*. Vol. 5, p. 96.

Jones, Robert P. *The End of White Christian America*. New York: Simon & Schuster, 2016.

Kamisar, Yale, Wayne R. LaFave and Jerold H. Israel. *Basic Criminal Procedure*. St. Paul, MN: West Publishing Co., 1980.

Kant, Immanuel. *Kant: Immanuel Kant's Moral and Political Writings*. New York: The Modern Library. 1949.

———. *Religion Within the Limits of Reason Alone*. Translated by Theodore M. Greene and Hoyt H. Hudson. New York: Harper Torchbooks, 1960.

———. "What is Enlightenment?" In *The Philosophy of Kant: Immanuel Kant's Moral and Political Writings*, edited by Carl Frederick. New York: The Modern Library, 1949.

Kendi, Ibram X. and Keisha N. Blain, eds. *Four Hundred Souls: A Community History of African America 1719–2019*. New York: Random House, 2020.

Ketcham, Ralph. *James Madison: A Biography*. Charlottesville, VA: University Press of Virginia, 1990.

Kierkegaard, Soren. *Fear and Trembling and The Sickness Unto Death*. Translated by Walter Lowrie. New York: Doubleday Anchor, 1954.

Küng, Hans and Karl-Josef Kuschel, eds. *A Global Ethic: The Declaration of the Parliament of the World's Religions*. New York: SCM Press, London/Continuum, 1993.

———. *On Being a Christian*. Translated by Edward Quinn. New York: Wallaby Book, Simon & Schuster, 1978.

————— and Helmut Schmidt. *A Global Ethic and Global Responsibilities: Two Declarations*. London: SCM Press, Ltd., 1998.

Kurland, Philip B. and Ralph Lerner. *The Founders' Constitution*. 5 Vols. Chicago: The University of Chicago Press, 1987.

Leakey, Richard and Roger Lewin. *Origins Reconsidered: In Search of What Makes us Human*. New York: Doubleday, 1992.

Lee, Erika. *America for Americans: A History of Xenophobia in the United States*. New York: Basic Books, 2019.

Levi, Leonard W. *The Establishment Clause: Religion and the First Amendment*. New York: Macmillan Pub. Co., 1986.

Lewin, Nathan. "William J. Brennan." In *The Justices of the United States Supreme Court 1789–1978: Their Lives and Major Opinions*, edited by Leon Friedman. Vol. V. New York: Chelsea House, 1978.

Locke, John. "A Letter Concerning Toleration 1689." *Montuori* 17–25, 31–22, 34, 45, 65–69, 89, 91, 93, in Kurland, *Founders Constitution*. Vol. 5, p. 53.

—————. *The Reasonableness of Christianity*. Stanford, CA: Stanford University Press, 1958.

—————. *Second Treatise of Government*. Indianapolis: Hackett Pub. Co., 1980.

Madison, James. "Detached Memoranda." ca. 1817, W. & M. W., 3d ser.; 3:554–560 (1946) in Kurland, *Founders' Constitution*. Vol. 5, p. 103.

—————. *The Federalist*, X and LI, in James Madison, Alexander Hamilton and John Jay, *The Federalist Papers*, edited by Isaac Krammnick. New York: Penguin Books, 1987.

—————. "James Madison to Rev. Adams." §68, in Kurland, *Founders Constitution*. Vol. 5, pp. 106–107.

—————. "James Madison to Edward Livingston." 10 July 1822, *Writings* 9:100–103 in Kurland, *Founder's Constitution*. Vol. 5, p. 105.

—————. "James Madison to William Bradford." 24 January 1774, Papers 1:106 in Kurland, *Founders Constitution*. Vol. 5, p. 60.

—————. "Memorial and Remonstrance." In *The Papers of James Madison*, edited by Rutland. Vol. 8, 10 March 1784–28 March 1786. 1973, pp. 299, 301.

—————. *The Papers of James Madison*, 10 Vols. Edited by Robert A. Rutland, et al. Chicago: The University of Chicago Press, 1973.

—————. "A 'Prolix' Comment on Mason's 'Objections'; James Madison to George Washington." New York, October 18, 1787, in *The Debate on the Constitution, Part One*, p. 350.

—————. "Proclamation." 16 November 1814. *Richardson* 1:558, in Kurland, *Founders' Constitution*. Vol. 5, p. 103.

—————. "Vices of the Political System of the United States." In *The Papers of James Madison*, edited by Rutland. Vol. 9, pp. 345–358.

Maier, Pauline. *Ratification: The People Debate the Constitution, 1787–1788*. New York: Simon and Schuster, 2010.

Malone, Dumas. *Jefferson and His Time*. 5 Vols. Boston: Little, Brown and Company, 1974.

Marty, Martin E. *When Faiths Collide*. Malden, MA: Blackwell Pub., 2005.

"Maryland Act Concerning Religion." 1649, *Maryland Archives* I: 244–247 in Kurland, *The Founders' Constitution.* Vol. 5, pp. 50–51.

McConnell, Michael W. "Free Exercise as the Framers Understood It." In *The Bill of Rights: Original Meaning and Current Understandings*, edited by Eugene W. Hickok, Jr. Charlottesville: University Press of Virginia, 1991.

Mead, Sidney E. *The Lively Experiment: The Shaping of Christianity in America.* New York: Harper & Row, 1963.

—————. *The Nation with the Soul of Church.* New York: Harper & Row, 1975.

Michael Morgan, and Edmund S. Morgan. *The Diary of Michael Wigglesworth 1653–57: The Conscience of a Puritan*, 1965.

Michaelis, David. *Eleanor.* New York: Simon & Schuster, 2020.

Monsma, Steve. *Healing for a Broken World: Christian Perspectives on Public Policy.* Wheaton, IL: Crossway Books, 2008.

Montesquieu. "Spirit of Laws." Bk. 2, ch. 2, 1748, in Kurland, *Founders' Constitution.* Vol. 1, pp. 47–49.

Morrison, Samuel Eliot. *The European Discovery of America: Vol. 1: The Southern Voyages, 1492–1616.* New York: Oxford University Press, 1974.

Niebuhr, Reinhold. *Moral Man and Immoral Society: A Study in Ethics and Politics.* New York: Charles Scribner's Son, 1960.

Nietzsche, Friedrich. "The Antichrist." In *The Portable Nietzsche*, translated by Walter Kaufmann. New York, 1954.

—————. *Basic Writings of Nietzsche.* Translated by Walter Kaufmann. New York: Modern Library, 1968.

—————. "Beyond Good and Evil." In *Basic Writings of Nietzsche*, translated by Walter Kaufmann. New York: The Modern Library, 1968.

—————. "Ecce Homo." In *Basic Writing of Nietzsche*, translated by Walter Kaufmann. New York: Modern Library, 1968.

—————. "On the Genealogy of Morals." In *Basic Writings of Nietzsche*, translated by Walter Kaufmann. New York: Modern Library, 1968.

—————. *The Portable Nietzsche.* Translated by Walter Kaufmann. New York: Viking Books, 1954.

—————. "Thus Spoke Zarathustra." In *The Portable Nietzsche*, translated by Walter Kaufmann. New York: Viking Books, 1954.

—————. *Twilight of the Idols in The Portable Nietzsche.* Translated by Walter Kaufmann. York: Viking Books, 1954.

Pannenberg, Wolfhart. *Anthropology in Theological Perspective.* Translated by Matthew J. O'Connell. Philadelphia: The Westminster Press, 1985.

—————. "Dogmatische Erwägungen zur Auferstehung Jesu." *Kerygma und Dogma* XIV (1968): 2.

—————. *Jesus—God and Man.* Translated by Lewis L. Wilkins and Duane A. Priebe. Philadelphia: The Westminster Press, 1968.

—————. *Systematic Theology* (3 vols.). Translated by Geoffrey W. Bromiley. Grand Rapids: William B. Eerdmans Pub. Co., 1991, 1994, 1998.

"Pennsylvania Charter of Liberty, Laws Agreed Upon in England." etc. 1682. *Thorpe 5:3062–63*, in Kurland, *Founders' Constitution.* Vol. 5, p. 52.

Pfeffer, Leo. *Religion, State, and the Burger Court.* Buffalo, NY: Prometheus Books, 1984.

Phillips, Derek L. *Toward a Just Social Order.* Princeton, NJ: Princeton University Press, 1986.

Pole, J. R., *The Pursuit of Equality in American History.* Berkeley: University of California Press, 1978.

Rawls, John. *Political Liberalism.* New York: Columbia University Press, 1993.

———. *A Theory of Justice.* New York: Columbia University Press, 1971.

Reimarus: Fragments. Edited by Charles H. Talbert. Translated by Ralph S. Fraser. Philadelphia: Fortress Press, 1970.

Ricks, Thomas E. *First Principles: What America's Founders Learned from the Greeks and Romans and How That Shaped Our Country.* New York: HarperCollins, 2020.

Rorty, Richard. *Contingency, Irony, & Solidarity.* Cambridge: University of Cambridge, 1989.

"Royal Commission for Regulating Plantations." 28 April 1634, *Bradford 422–425,* in Kurland, *Founders' Constitution.* Vol. 1, pp. 611–612.

Rubenstein, Richard, *After Auschwitz: History, Theology, and Contemporary Judaism,* 2nd ed. Baltimore: The Johns Hopkins University Press, 1992.

Sagan, Carl. *Billions and Billions: Thoughts on Life and Death at the Brink of the Millennium.* New York: Random House, 1997.

Scharlemann, Robert P. "The Argument from Faith to History." In *Inscriptions and Reflections: Essays in Philosophical Theology* edited by Scharlemann. Charlottesville, VA: University Press of Virginia, 1989.

———. *The Being of God: Theology and the Experience of Truth.* New York: The Seabury Press, 1981.

———. *The Reason of Following: Christology and the Ecstatic I.* Chicago: The University of Chicago Press, 1991.

Schleiermacher, Friedrich. *The Christian Faith.* Edited by H. R. Mackintosh and J. S. Stewart. Edinburgh: T. & T. Clark, 1960.

———. *The Life of Jesus.* Translated by S. Maclean Gilmore. Edited by Jack C. Verheyden. Philadelphia: Fortress Press, 1975.

Smith, H. Sheldon, Robert T. Handy and Lefferts A. Loetscher. *American Christianity: An Historical Interpretation with Representative Documents, Vol. l, 1607–1820.* New York: Charles Scribner's Sons, 1960.

Schweitzer, Albert. *The Mysticism of Paul the Apostle.* Translated by William Montgomery. London: A. & C. Black, Ltd., 1931.

———. *The Quest of the Historical Jesus: A Critical Study of its Progress from Reimarus to Wrede.* Translated by W. Montgomery. New York: The Macmillan Company, 1959.

———. *The Philosophy of Civilization.* Translated by C. T. Campion. New York: The Macmillan Company, 1960.

Soelle, Dorothee. *Choosing Life.* Translated by Margaret Kohl. Philadelphia: Fortress, 1981.

Strauss, David Friedrich. *A Life of Jesus Critically Examined.* Translated by George Eliot. Philadelphia: Fortress Press, 1972.

Tawney, R. H. *Religion and the Rise of Capitalism*. New York: Mentor, 1953.

Tillich, Paul. *Systematic Theology*. 3 vols in 1. Chicago: University of Chicago Press, 1967.

Tribe, Laurence H. *American Constitutional Law*, 2nd ed. Mineola, NY: The Foundation Press, Inc., 1988.

———. *Constitutional Choices*. Cambridge, MA: Harvard University Press, 1985.

Tushnet, Mark. *Red, White, and Blue: A Critical Analysis of Constitutional Law*. Cambridge, MA: Harvard University Press, 1988.

Twain, Mark. "The Turning Point of My Life." In *The Family Mark Twain*. New York: Dorset Press, 1988, 1129–1135.

Weinreb, Lloyd L. *Natural Law and Justice*. Cambridge, MS: Harvard University Press, 1987.

Werner, Martin. *The Formation of Christian Dogma*. New York: Harper & Row, 1957.

White, G. Edward. *The Marshall Court & Cultural Change: 1815–1835*. New York: Macmillan Co., 1988.

Williams, Roger. "The Bloody Tenent, or Persecution for Cause of Conscience." 1644, *Stokes 1:196–197*, 198, 199, in Kurland, *Founders' Constitution*. Vol. 5, pp. 48–49.

Index

Note: Page numbers followed by 'n' refer to notes.

About the Author

W. Royce Clark, PhD, JD, is professor emeritus of Pepperdine University. He began teaching religion in college in 1961 in Portland, Oregon. He received his PhD from the School of Religion of the University of Iowa in 1973, with his dissertation being directed by the late Robert P. Scharlemann. He is the author of *Will Humanity Survive Religion? Beyond Divisive Absolutes* (2020), *Ethics beyond Religion: Redefining the Absolute* (2021), and *An Ethic of Trust: Mutual Autonomy and the Common Will to Live* (2021).

During his 31 years with Pepperdine (1970–2001), Prof. Clark taught undergraduate and graduate classes in the history of religions, modern and contemporary Christian thought, and many courses in ethics as well as biblical studies courses, and organized team-taught courses in human values and introduction to religion. After receiving his JD from Pepperdine School of Law in 1985, he taught courses in the law of religion and state. Beginning in 1986, he and two colleagues organized and taught a five-semester course of study in the "Great Books." He has published in the areas of euthanasia, the legal status of religious studies in higher education, post-Holocaust theology, and on particular religious thinkers, including Wolfhart Pannenberg, Friedrich Schleiermacher, and Richard Rubenstein. He has participated in many professional societies and seminar groups, presenting papers on various topics such as the alteration of the ethics behind the criminal law "exclusionary rule," the idea of reconciliation in Dostoevsky, ultimate concern and Susan Sontag, and religious hermeneutics and Constitutional interpretation, among other topics.